Trophies of War and Empire

Trophies of War and Empire

The Archival Heritage of Ukraine,
World War II,
and the
International Politics of Restitution

Patricia Kennedy Grimsted

Distributed by Harvard University Press
for the
Harvard Ukrainian Research Institute

Publication of this volume has been made possible by the Jaroslaw M. and Olha Duzey and the Myroslav and Irene Koltuniuk endowed publication funds for Ukrainian studies at Harvard University.

Cover photos: Koch and Rosenberg (Bild 183/R70659), courtesy of the Bundesarchiv-Koblenz, Germany. Secret report with Beria's resolution courtesy of GA RF (fond 5325/10/2027). Both images reproduced with permission.
Cover design: R. De Lossa.

Library of Congress Cataloging-in-Publication Data

Grimsted, Patricia Kennedy.
  Trophies of war and empire : the archival heritage of Ukraine, World War II, and the international politics of restitution / Patricia Kennedy Grimsted.
    p. cm. -- (Harvard papers in Ukrainian studies)
Includes bibliographical references and index.
  ISBN 0-916458-76-8
  1. Archives--Ukraine--History--20th century. 2. Restitution--Ukraine. I. Title: Archival heritage of Ukraine, World War II, and the international politics of restitution. II. Title. III. Series.
  CD1739.6 .G76 2001
  026.9477--dc21
                                        2001002058

A Ukrainian-language version, edited by Dr. Hennadii Boriak, deputy chief of the State Committee on Archives of Ukraine (DKAU), will be published in Kyiv under the auspices of the DKAU and the State Service for the Control of the Transmission of Cultural Treasures Across the Borders of Ukraine, Ministry of Culture of Ukraine. For information on this edition, contact the editors at the Ukrainian Research Institute, at: HURI Publications, 1583 Massachusetts Ave., Cambridge, MA 02138 USA, *E-mail:* <huri@fas.harvard.edu>.

The Ukrainian Research Institute was established in 1973 as an integral part of Harvard University. It supports research associates and visiting scholars who are engaged in projects concerned with all aspects of Ukrainian studies. The Institute also works in close cooperation with the Committee on Ukrainian Studies, which supervises and coordinates the teaching of Ukrainian history, language, and literature at Harvard University.

Contents

   1. *top:* ERR schematic map showing routes of systematic archival and library looting throughout Europe. *bottom:* Schematic map of book restitution from the Offenbach Archival Depot.
   2. *top:* German archival officials load material for transit out of Lviv to the Abbey of Tyniec in 1944. *bottom:* The Abbey of Tyniec, site of German storage of archival treasures.
   3. *top:* Signing ceremony in Prague of the act transferring the Ukrainian Historical Cabinet (UIK) to the Soviet Union, 1945. *bottom:* Two Soviet officers and Capt. Isaac Benkowitz with first shipment of Soviet books out of the American Zone in postwar Germany, from the Offenbach Archival Depot.

Foreword

In the extremely rich Western literature on the history of the USSR, its institutions and its ideologically shaped administrative practices, the only titles dealing with the archival system and archival policy issues are signed "Patricia Kennedy Grimsted." The present book, built around the theme of the displaced archival heritage of Ukraine, sums up the results of 35 years of research in, and daily working contacts with, the archives of the USSR and of post-Soviet Ukraine and Russia. It is a synthesis of archival and historical culture. Nothing escapes Grimsted's attention—no international event, no publication in any European language connected with the reconstitution of the archival legacy of Ukraine or the other two major themes of the book, the Nazi plunder, and subsequent Soviet counter-plunder, of cultural treasures in the occupied countries. By her universal curiosity and exceptional productivity, she clearly belongs to the tradition of Renaissance erudition.

The book, conceived in part as a "technical file," is intended to make known—and thus to help address—the archival legal issues arising from the cultural plunder of the Second World War and the dissolution of the USSR. All issues analyzed herein concern Ukraine directly in its search for its past.

With regard to legal precedent for Ukraine in the past, we should not forget that at the beginning of the twentieth century, the learned public of Western Europe had precious little information on Ukraine. They could read in *The Everyman Encyclopaedia* (11 volumes), published just before World War I:

> Ukraine, a part of Poland. The term was first applied to the Tartar frontiers of Poland, and later to the district about the middle Dnieper. In the 17th century, the portion East of the Dnieper passed to Russia, and forms Little Russia. At the second partition of Poland (1793) the western portion also passed to Russia.

The definition given in the *Nouveau Larousse Illustré* (7 vols.), published some ten years earlier, contains a bit more geographical data:

> Ukraine (russe *Oukraïna,* polonais *Ukraïna,* c'est-à-dire la Région frontière), contrée de la Russie mériodionale, embrassant les gouvernements de Kiev, de Tchernigov et de Poltava. Il est arrosé par le Dniéper, grossi du Pripet, qui forme dans l'Ukraine ses fameux rapides. L'Ukraine fut le lieu, où se forma, à partir du XVIè siècle, la célèbre nation des Cosaques.

From the same encyclopedia, we find that "Ukrainian" means a person born or resident in Ukraine. There was little more for the public than this.

*   *
*

The rules coined by diplomatic practice prior to the First World War for the settlement of archival litigation between dynasties or States with a long past, proved inapplicable in Eastern Europe. If they were indeed applied, they had disastrous consequences. In contrast with the western half of the continent, where political/provincial, ethnic, and linguistic borders remained relatively stable, in Eastern Europe the borders moved constantly through the last twelve centuries. Empires expanded and collapsed, countries emerged, vanished, and reappeared, migratory movements for economic, religious, or political reasons never stopped, so that no East European region, whether stemmed from a kingdom, a principality, a duchy, a county, or any other entity, had—until the Second World War—a homogenous population. Various languages and denominations co-existed everywhere.

Between the Congress of Vienna and 1992, the territory of Central and Eastern Europe was completely reorganized. Instead of four multinational empires, as in 1815, the space is now divided, after many wars, occupations, and redrawings of borders, between 25 "nation-states," in most of which national minorities make up 10 to 40 percent of the population. Another East European phenomenon—political emigration—has accompanied the history of every nation there for the past two, and in some cases three, centuries. The archives of exile therefore also constitute part of the East European nations' memory.

The extreme complexity of reconstituting the national memory of a nation without permanent statehood, a "nation without history" in the terminology of Otto Bauer, is masterfully presented in Grimsted's "Descriptive Typology of the Ukrainian Archival Legacy Abroad." It may serve as a model to other nations for developing the typology of their own scattered archival heritage. I wonder, however, whether it is appropriate to use the term "foreign imperial power" for designating the State in which a nation lived for centuries together with other nations. The only concept that can be instrumental in solving archival conflicts between Successor States of former empires—*joint heritage,* as proposed by UNESCO and the International Council on Archives—is considered with apprehension by most countries potentially concerned. Both those who detain the disputed archives and those who request their transfer, fear the weakening of their position by implicitly admitting the rights of the other party. The overcautious reception of the joint heritage approach by professionals—and its blunt rejection by diplomats at the conference where the Vienna Convention of 1983 was prepared—discouraged further intergovernmental efforts to pursue the study of the idea, and to promote it and test its feasibility. Still, no alternate method has been devised to facilitate negotiating the devolution of archives that interest more than one Successor State of a dissolved empire.

A pathetic phenomenon can be observed in many newly independent countries. Oblivious of the archival heritage existing within the national borders, the press, public opinion, and local authorities concentrate their attention on the records relating to the nation's history that are located abroad—primarily in the custodial institutions of the former metropolitan power. In those countries where disputed archives are detained, the defense of the status quo is no less deplorable. This defense arises from a widespread belief that the possession of "foreign" archives (e.g., the archives of former colonial holdings) adds to the wealth and patriotic glory of a country.

When passion opposes passion, rational arguments advocating a negotiated agreement can hardly prevail. This is the reason why UNESCO and the ICA have not focused on the settlement of actual conflicts, but rather on the development of a "thesaurus" of concepts and terms acceptable to all States. By this means we hope to create the conditions for conducting meaningful dialog between States.

Grimsted agrees with the principles and the terminology recommended by UNESCO, but she does not acquiesce to the inertness of the international organizations in the face of the immense problems that her enquiry has unveiled. She hopes that the UN will undertake preparing, in a not too distant future, a new convention on the succession of States with respect to archives, in order to replace the aborted one produced by the Vienna Conference (1983). She also urges the establishment of an international committee to deal with displaced archives and archival restitution.

In spite of the urgency, there is little chance, for the time being, that such a body is created at the decision-making intergovernmental—or even at the consultative, non-governmental level. Governments prefer to handle sensitive issues separately, case per case, through as many bilateral negotiations as necessary. A number of countries requesting restitution, perhaps all of them, also detain archives claimed by other countries. They might not be ready to follow the same principles in both directions. The preservation of a free hand in this matter also corresponds to the wishes of diplomats, who highly appreciate the ability to integrate token restitutions into their protocols for visiting dignitaries. Good relations, then, can be showcased at no cost by a strong, symbolic gesture.

The main obstacle, however, lays in the situation of Russia, which is now like a besieged fortress. Russia must contend not only with the fourteen Successor States of the USSR and their archival pretensions to a common imperial heritage, but at the same time it must confront the numerous countries to which belong Russia's "trophy archives." These archives have been hidden during the 55 years since the end of World War II. Any initiative, whether with the UN, with UNESCO, or with the Council of Europe, for creating an international committee on the restitution and devolution of archives, would now automatically appear as a maneuver aimed at forming a "united coalition" against Russia. Any initiative, that is, unless it came from Russia itself.

The chapters on the looting of archives, libraries, and art by the Nazis and the plunder of cultural "trophies" organized in all the occupied territories by the Soviet authorities form a fantastic and tragic thriller. Patricia Grimsted's admirably thorough inquiry—in German, Russian, Ukrainian, Polish, and American archives—has meticulously shown the inner workings of the Nazi plundering and the Soviet counter-plunder. Additional details will, of course, still come to light, especially on the fate of displaced archives of which all traces have been lost. But the history of the greatest archival tragedy of modern times will not have to be rewritten. With this book we know what happened and how it happened.

That tragedy has not yet come to an end. The law adopted in 1996 by the two houses of the Russian parliament (and signed by Yeltsin only in 1998) on the nationalization of foreign cultural property made the Russian State heir and continuator of the practice of plunder both of the Third Reich and of Stalin's USSR. By its July 1999 resolution that prescribed the restitution of looted cultural property to the allies of the USSR during the War, the Constitutional Court of the Russian Federation cut at least the disastrous linkage with Nazi Germany. It confirmed, however, Russia's right to disregard international law, including the clauses on the respect and restitution of cultural property, contained in various international instruments and treaties subscribed to by the Russian Empire before 1917, the USSR, and even the Russian Federation, when joining the Council of Europe in 1995.

Historians and political scientists can probably explain why democracy and the rule of law became antagonistic concepts in post-communist Russia. Her readers will, however, agree with Grimsted that, notwithstanding this unhappy development, the Second World War must be finished.

Ukraine and Poland, the two countries which suffered most from Nazi occupation, are opting, in principle, for a settlement with Germany regarding displaced archives. The argumentation against restitution, hastily compiled in 1994–95 by Russian politicians seeking popularity, will have to be dropped. It is incompatible with the Russian raison d'état, which requires the establishment of the rule of law in the country and normal relations with all European States.

Patricia Kennedy Grimsted's *Trophies of War and Empire,* opens a new chapter in the history of archival literature. It places archives in the very heart of 20th-century politics, wars, cold wars, and power games. It offers a "good read" to professionals as well as to the non-specialized public. Let us hope that all those who are vested with responsibility in the complex field of applying international legal rules to resolve archival conflicts—archivists, lawyers, and diplomats alike—will read it.

Charles Kecskeméti
Paris, May 2000

Technical Note

Transliteration of Cyrillic throughout the text uses the standard of the Ukrainian Research Institute at Harvard University, which is modified from the Library of Congress standard. Some commonly used geographic terms, such as "oblast′" and "krai" have been anglicized, and hence do not appear in italics—and in the former case, without the final soft sign. A few personal and geographic names such as Yeltsin, Moscow, and Warsaw have been retained in the form most generally known in the West. Kyiv is being rendered in the Ukrainianized form, standard since independence, rather than the earlier Russified form "Kiev," previously better known in the West. For historical references to localities then officially part of the Reich during World War II, such as Silesia, Western Poland, and Western Bohemia, I use then official (and usually more familiar) German forms with the Polish or Czech variants in parentheses on first reference—Ratibor (*Pol.* Racibórz), etc., unless there is a common accepted English variant, such as Silesia or Cracow.

The term "archives" usually appears only in the plural in English, but the singular form in translation from the Ukrainian and Russian has been retained here, where appropriate, since the distinction between singular and plural as in Russian and Ukrainian usage is important, particularly with reference to a single repository or the records of a single agency.

The archival term "fond" (which is used in both Ukrainian and Russian) has been anglicized, rather than using an incorrect or misleading translation, such as "fund" or "collection." The term came to the Soviet Union from the French in the 1920s, but not without some change of meaning and usage. Some writers have rendered it in English as "collection," but in many instances that is incorrect from an archival standpoint, because a "fond" in French, Ukrainian, and Russian is basically an integral group of records from a single office or source, usually arranged as they were produced in their office of creation. However, in Soviet archival usage, since all archival materials within a given repository are divided into fonds, the term can also embrace "collections" (that is, archival materials brought together by an institution or individual without respect to their office of origin or order of creation). American archivists might prefer the more technical American "record group," which in British usage would normally be "archive group," but the Soviet (and now Ukrainian and Russian) usage of the term "fond" is much more extensive, as a "fond" can designate personal papers and/or collections as well as groups of institutional records.

I likewise usually retain the Ukrainian term *opys* (plural *opysy*)—Russian *opis'* (plural *opisi*). Although it could be often correctly rendered as "inventory" or "register" in English, its function is broader. In Soviet (and now Ukrainian and Russian) archival usage, *opysy* serve both an administrative and a descriptive function. *Opysy* are the numbered hierarchical subdivisions within a fond that list all of the files, or storage units (*Ukr. sprava/Rus. dela* or *edinitsa khraneniia*); sometimes they represent rational or chronological divisions within a fond (the "series" or "subgroup" in English and American usage), but often they represent *ad hoc* divisions, frequently determined by when the files were acquired. At one and the same time *opisi* provide official administrative and security control over all file units in the fond and provide a descriptive inventory as the basic finding aid for the fond.

In citations for former Soviet-area archives, numbers are given sequentially thusly: 000/000/000 fol. 000, representing the *fond,* then *opys* or *opis',* and finally, the *sprava* or *delo (ed. khr.),* followed by the folia cited.

Peculiarities also arise in bibliographic forms. It has become increasingly prevalent in Ukraine and Russia for books to be published by institutional "sponsors," while the "publisher" is listed as a printing house with no editorial input into the volume. Where possible, I have tried to indicate volume sponsors in the bibliography, while omitting this information in the footnotes. The notes generally follow the author/title, short title system, wherein full citation is given at first usage in a chapter, with a short title used thereafter. The only exception to this system is a series of high-usage citations, listed in the abbreviations section starting on p. xxxviii, that are always given with short forms in the notes. This was necessary for considerations of space. As well, I have tried to keep relevant bibliographic annotation and supporting information in the bibliography, again to avoid clogging the notes, which—I am sure the gentle reader will agree—are ample enough already.

Abbreviations used in Text, Notes, and Bibliography (Acronyms and Short Titles)

Acronyms:

ACLS	American Council of Learned Societies, New York
AGAD	Archiwum Główne Akt Dawnych (Main Archive of Early Acts), Warsaw
AMSAB	Archive-Museum of the Socialist Labor Movement, Ghent *since late 1999* Amsab, Institute of Social History
AN SSSR	Akademiia nauk SSSR (Academy of Sciences of the USSR)
AN URSR	Akademiia nauk URSR (Academy of Sciences of the UkrSSR), *now* NAN—Natsional'na Akademiia nauk Ukraïny
APKr	Archiwum Państwowe w Krakowie (State Archive in Cracow), Cracow
AP RF	Arkhiv Prezidenta Rossiiskoi Federatsii (Archive of the President of the Russian Federation), Moscow
AVPRI	Arkhiv vneshnei politiki Rossiiskoi imperii (Archive of the Foreign Policy of the Russian Empire), Moscow, *formerly* AVPR (Arkhiv vneshnei politiki Rossii [Archive of the Foreign Policy of Russia])
BAB	Bundesarchiv (Federal Archives), Berlin-Lichterfelde
BAK	Bundesarchiv (Federal Archives), Koblenz
BAN	Biblioteka Akademii nauk (Library of the [Russian] Academy of Sciences), St. Petersburg
BDIC	Bibliothèque de Documentation Internationale Contemporaine (Library of Contemporary International Documentation), Université de Paris (IXème), Nanterre
BN	Biblioteka Narodowa (National Library), Warsaw
CC	Central Committee (*Rus.* Tsentral'nyi komitet—TsK)
CDJC	Centre de Documentation Juive Contemporaine, Archive (Center of Contemporary Jewish Documentation, Archive), Paris
ChGK	Chrezvychainaia gosudarstvennaia komissiia po ustano- vleniiu zlodeianii nemetsko-fashistskikh zakhvatchikov i

ikh soobshchnikov i prichinennogo imi ushcherba grazhdanam, kolkhozam, obshchestvennym organizatsiiam,
gosudarstvennym predpriiatiiam i uchrezhdeniiam SSSR
(Extraordinary State Commission for the Establishment and
Investigation of Crimes of the German-Fascist Aggressors
and Their Accomplices and for the Appraisal of the Losses
Incurred by Citizens, Collective Farms, Social Organizations, State Enterprises and Institutions of the USSR)

CIA   *See* ICA/CIA

CITRA   Conférence internationale de la Table ronde des
                       archives/International Conference of the Round Table on
                       Archives (ICA)

CPSU   Communist Party of the Soviet Union (*Rus.* KPSS
                       [Kommunisticheskaia partiia Sovetskogo Soiuza])

CWIHP   Cold War International History Project, Washington, DC

DAKO   Derzhavnyi arkhiv Kyïvs´koï oblasti (State Archive of Kyiv
                       Oblast)

DKAU   Derzhavnyi komitet arkhiviv Ukraïny (State Committee on
                       Archives of Ukraine), *before 1991* HAU

DSP   *Rus.* Dlia sluzhebnogo pol´zovaniia ([classfied] for internal
                       use only)

ERR   Einsatzstab Reichsleiter Rosenberg

FSB   Federal´naia sluzhba bezopasnosti Rossii (Federal Security
                       Service of Russia)

GAF   Gosudarstvennyi arkhivnyi fond (State Archival Fond)

GARF   Gosudarstvennyi arkhiv Rossiiskoi Federatsii (State
                       Archive of the Russian Federation), Moscow, *formerly*
                       TsGAOR SSSR and TsGA RSFSR

GAU   Glavnoe arkhivnoe upravlenie pri Sovete Ministrov SSSR
                       (Main Archival Administration under the Council of
                       Ministers of the USSR), 1960–1991, *often* Glavarkhiv
                       See under HAU for Ukrainian counterpart

GBL   Gosudarstvennaia biblioteka im. V. I. Lenina (Lenin State
                       Library), Moscow, *now* RGB

GKO   Gosudarstvennyi komitet oborony (State Committee for
                       Defense)

Glavarkhiv   *See* GAU

GMDS   German Military Documents Section, U.S. Army

GPB	Gosudarstvennaia Publichnaia biblioteka im. M. E. Saltykova-Shchedrina (M. E. Saltykov-Shchedrin State Public Library), St. Petersburg, *now* RNB
HAG	Hauptabeitsgruppe (Main Task Force Group [of the ERR])
HAU (*Rus.* GAU, Glavarkhiv)	Holovne arkhivne upravlinnia (Main Archival Administration), *often* Holovarkhiv, *after 1999* DKAU —pry Radi Ministriv URSR (under the Council of Ministers of the UkrSSR), 1960–1991 —pry Kabineti Ministriv Ukraïny (under the Cabinet of Ministers of Ukraine), *after* 1992
HURI	Harvard Ukrainian Research Institute
IAI RGGU	Istoriko-arkhivnyi institut Rossiiskogo gosudarstvennogo gumanitarnogo universiteta (Historico-Archival Institute of the Russian State University for the Humanities), Moscow, *earlier* MGIAI
ICA/CIA	International Council on Archives, *French* Conseil International des Archives
IDC	Inter Documentation Company, Leiden
IISH/IISG	International Institute of Social History, Amsterdam, *Dutch* IISG (Internationaal Instituut voor Sociale Geschiedenis)
ILC	International Law Commission, under the United Nations
IMLI	Institut mirovoi literatury im. M. A. Gor'kogo RAN (M. A. Gor'kii Institute of World Literature RAN), Moscow
IREX	International Research & Exchanges Board
IUAD (*earlier* IUA)	Instytut Ukraïns'koï arkheohrafiï i dzhereloznavstva im. Mykhaila Hrushevs'koho NAN (Institute of Ukrainian Archeography and Source Studies NAN), Kyiv, *before April 1995* IUA (Institute of Ukrainian Archeography)
KGB	Komitet gosudarstvennoi bezopastnosti (Committee for State Security)
KP[b]U	Komunistychna partiia [bil'shovykiv] Ukraïny (Communist Party [Bolsheviks] of Ukraine)
LNB	L'vivs'ka natsional'na biblioteka im. V. Stefanyka NAN Ukraïny (V. Stefanyk National Library NAN), Lviv, *under* NAN (*earlier under* AN URSR)
LV ABM	Landesverwaltung der Archive, Bibliotheken und Museen (Provincial Authority for Archives, Libraries, and Museums), Kyiv, *under* RKU

MFA&A	Monuments, Fine Arts & Archives (officers under U.S. Army and OMGUS)
MGB	Ministerstvo gosudarstvennoi bezopasnosti (Ministry of State Security of the USSR), Moscow
MGIAI	Moskovskii gosudarstvennyi istoriko-arkhivnyi institut (Moscow State Historico-Archival Institute), *now* IAI RGGU
MGU	Moskovskii gosudarstvennyi universitet (Moscow State University)
MID	Ministerstvo inostrannykh del (Ministry of Foreign Affairs)
MVD	Ministerstvo vnutrennikh del (Ministry of Internal Affairs), *before 1946* NKVD
NAN	Natsional'na Akademiia nauk Ukraïny (National Academy of Sciences of Ukraine)
NBU (*often* NBUV)	Natsional'na Biblioteka Ukraïny im. V. I. Vernads'koho NAN (V. I. Vernads'kyi National Library of Ukraine), Kyiv, *before May 1996* TsNB
NKVD	Narodnyi komissariat vnutrennikh del (People's Commissariat of Internal Affairs), *after 1946* MVD
NTSh	Naukove tovarystvo im. Shevchenka (Shevchenko Scientific Society)
OAD	Offenbach Archival Depot (OMGUS)
OMGUS	Office of Military Government, United States
PRO	Public Record Office (National Archives), London
RAN	Rossiiskaia Akademiia nauk (Russian Academy of Sciences)
RGADA	Rossiiskii gosudarstvennyi arkhiv drevnikh aktov (Russian State Archive of Early Acts), Moscow, *formerly* TsGADA
RGAE	Rossiiskii gosudarstvennyi arkhiv èkonomiki (Russian State Archive of the Economy), *formerly* TsGANKh
RGALI	Rossiiskii gosudarstvennyi arkhiv literatury i iskusstva (Russian State Archive of Literature and Art), Moscow, *formerly* TsGALI SSSR
RGANI	Rossiiskii gosudarstvennyi arkhiv noveishei istorii (Russian State Archive of Contemporary History), Moscow, *before March 1999* TsKhSD

RGASPI
: Rossiiskii gosudarstvennyi arkhiv sotsial'no-politicheskoi istorii (Russian State Archive of Socio-Political History), Moscow, *before March 1999* RTsKhIDNI

RGAVMF
: Rossiiskii gosudarstvennyi arkhiv Voenno-Morskogo Flota (Russian State Archive of the Navy), St. Petersburg, *formerly* TsGAVMF

RGB OR
: Rossiiskaia gosudarstvennaia biblioteka, Otdel rukopisei (Russian State Library, Manuscript Division), Moscow, *formerly* GBL

RGGU
: Rossiiskii gosudarstvennyi gumanitarnyi universitet (Russian State University for the Humanities), Moscow

RGIA
: Rossiiskii gosudarstvennyi istoricheskii arkhiv (Russian State Historical Archive), St. Petersburg, *formerly* TsGIA SSSR

RGVA
: Rossiiskii gosudarstvennyi voennyi arkhiv (Russian State Military Archive), Moscow, *formerly* TsGASA *and before 1946* TsAKA, TsGAKA, *since March 1999* includes the holdings of the former TsKhIDK/TsGOA

RGVIA
: Rossiiskii gosudarstvennyi voenno-istoricheskii arkhiv (Russian State Military History Archive), Moscow, *before 1941* TsVIA, *1941–1992* TsGVIA

RKU
: Reichskommissariat Ukraine (Reich Commissariat of Ukraine), headquartered in Rivne

RL/RFE
: Radio Liberty/Radio Free Europe, Munich, *later* part of the Open Media Research Institute, Prague

RMbO
: Reichsministerium für die besetzten Ostgebiete (Reich Ministry for the Occupied Eastern Territories [USSR])

RNB
: Rossiiskaia natsional'naia biblioteka (Russian National Library), St. Petersburg, *formerly* GPB

RSHA
: Reichssicherheitshauptamt (Reich Security Main Office)

RTsKhIDNI
: Rossiiskii tsentr khraneniia i izucheniia dokumentov noveishei istorii (Russian Center for Preservation and Study of Records of Modern History), Moscow, *formerly* TsPA (Tsentral'nyi Partiinyi Arkhiv [Central Party Archive]), *since March 1999* RGASPI

RZIA

Russkii zagranichnyi istoricheskii arkhiv pri Ministerstve inostrannykh del Chekhoslovatskoi Respubliki (Russian Foreign Historical Archive under the Ministry of Foreign Affairs of the Czechoslovak Republic)

SSRC

Social Science Research Council

SMERSH

"Smert' shpionam" ("Death to Spies"; military counter-espionage units under the Chief Intelligence Directorate, GRU [Glavnoe razvedyvatel'noe upravlenie])

SNK

Sovet Narodnykh komissarov (Council of People's Deputies, 1917–1946), *also* Sovnarkom

SVAG

Sovetskaia voennaia administratsiia v Germanii (Soviet Military Administration in Germany)

SVR

Sluzhba vneshnei razvedki Rossiiskoi Federatsii (Foreign Intelligence Service of the Russian Federation)

TsAKA

Tsentral'nyi arkhiv Krasnoi Armii (Central Archive of the Red Army), *after 1941* TsGAKA (Tsentral'nyi gosudarst-vennyi arkhiv Krasnoi Armii), *after 1946* TsGASA (Tsentral'nyi gosudarstvennyi arkhiv Sovetskoi Armii), *after 1992* RGVA

TsDAHO

Tsentral'nyi derzhavnyi arkhiv hromads'kykh ob'ednan' Ukraïny (Central State Archive of Public Organizations of Ukraine), Kyiv, *formerly* PA TsK KPU (Partiinyi arkhiv Tsentral'nogo komiteta Kommunisticheskoi partii Ukrainy)

TsDKFFA

Tsentral'nyi derzhavnyi kinofotofonoarkhiv Ukraïny im. H. S. Pshenychnoho (H. S. Pshenychnyi Central State Archive of Documentary Films, Photographs, and Sound Recordings of Ukraine), Kyiv, *formerly* TsDAKFFD URSR

TsDAKFFD URSR

Tsentral'nyi derzhavnyi arkhiv kinofotofonodokumentiv URSR (Central State Archive of Documentary Films, Photographs, and Sound Recordings of the UkrSSR), Kyiv, *now* TsDKFFA

TsDAMLM

Tsentral'nyi derzhavnyi arkhiv-muzei literatury i mystetstva Ukraïny (Central State Archive-Museum of Literature and Art of Ukraine), Kyiv, *1966–1992* TsDAMLM URSR (of the Ukrainian SSR)

TsDAVO

Tsentral'nyi derzhavnyi arkhiv vyshchykh orhaniv vlady i upravlinnia Ukraïny (Central State Archive of Highest Agencies of Power and Administration of Ukraine), Kyiv, *formerly* TsDAZhR URSR

TsDAZhR URSR	Tsentral'nyi derzhavnyi arkhiv Zhovtnevoï revoliutsiï URSR (Central State Archive of the October Revolution, UkrSSR), Kyiv, *now* TsDAVO
TsDIA URSR (*Rus.* TsGIA)	Tsentral'nyi derzhavnyi istorychnyi arkhiv URSR (Central State Historical Archive UkrSSR), Kyiv, *after 1958:* —TsDIA URSR u m. Kyievi, *often* TsDIA-K, *now* TsDIAK —TsDIA URSR u m. L'vovi, *often* TsDIA-L, *now* TsDIAL
TsDIAK (*Rus.* TsGIAK)	Tsentral'nyi derzhavnyi istorychnyi arkhiv Ukraïny, Kyïv (Central State Historical Archive of Ukraine, Kyiv), *formerly* Tsentral'nyi derzhavnyi istorychnyi arkhiv UkrRSR u m. Kyievi—officially TsDIA UkrRSR u m. Kyievi; *often* TsDIA-K
TsDIAL (*Rus.* TsGIAL)	Tsentral'nyi derzhavnyi istorychnyi arkhiv Ukraïny, Lviv (Central State Historical Archive of Ukraine, Lviv) *formerly* Tsentral'nyi derzhavnyi istorychnyi arkhiv URSR u m. L'vovi—*officially* TsDIA URSR u m. L'vovi; *often* TsDIA-L
TsGAKFFD UkrSSR (*Ukr.* TsDAKFFD)	Tsentral'nyi gosudarstvennyi arkhiv kinofotofono-dokumentov UkrSSR (Central State Archive of Documentary Films, Photographs, and Sound Recordings of the UkrSSR), Kyiv, *now* TsDKFFA Ukraïny
TsGADA SSSR	Tsentral'nyi gosudarstvennyi arkhiv drevnikh aktov (Central State Archive of Early Acts of the USSR), Moscow, *now* RGADA
TsGAKA	Tsentral'nyi gosudarstvennyi arkhiv Krasnoi Armii (Central State Archive of the Red Army), *before 1941* TsAKA, *1946–1992* TsGASA, *after 1992* RGVA
TsGALI SSSR	Tsentral'nyi gosudarstvennyi arkhiv literatury i iskusstva SSSR (Central State Archive of Literature and Art of the USSR), Moscow, *now* RGALI
TsGAOR	Tsentral'nyi gosudarstvennyi arkhiv Oktiabr'skoi revoliutsii (Central State Archive of the October Revolution) —SSSR, Moscow, *now* GA RF —UkrSSR, Kyiv, *now* TsDAVO
TsGASA	Tsentral'nyi gosudarstvennyi arkhiv Sovetskoi Armii (Central State Archive of the Soviet Army), *before 1941* TsAKA, *1941–1946* TsGAKA, *after 1992* RGVA
TsGAVMF SSSR	Tsentral'nyi gosudarstvennyi arkhiv Voenno-Morskogo Flota SSSR (Central State Archive of the Navy of the USSR), Leningrad, *now* RGAVMF, St. Petersburg

TsGIA (*Ukr.* TsDIA)	Tsentral´nyi gosudarstvennyi istoricheskii arkhiv (Central State Historical Archive of the USSR) —SSSR, Leningrad, *now* RGIA, St. Petersburg —UkrSSR, Kyiv and Lviv (TsGIAK and TsGIAL)
TsGIAK (*Ukr.* TsDIAK)	Tsentral´nyi gosudarstvennyi istoricheskii arkhiv UkrSSR v g. Kieve (Central State Historical Archive of the UkrSSR in Kyiv), Kyiv
TsGIAM	Tsentral´nyi gosudarstvennyi istoricheskii arkhiv v Moskve (Central State Historical Archive in Moscow), *absorbed by* TsGAOR SSSR, 1961–1992; *now* part of GA RF
TsGOA SSSR	Tsentral´nyi gosudarstvennyi osobyi arkhiv SSSR (Central State Special Archive of the USSR), Moscow, *1992–1999* TsKhIDK, *since March 1999* part of RGVA
TsGVIA	Tsentral´nyi gosudarstvennyi voenno-istoricheskii arkhiv (Central State Military History Archive), Moscow, *before 1941* TsVIA, *after 1992* RGVIA
TsK	Tsentral´nyi komitet (Central Committee; usually used with regard to the Communist Party)
TsKhIDK	Tsentr khraneniia istoriko-dokumental´nykh kollektsii (Center for the Preservation of Historico-Documentary Collections), Moscow, *formerly* TsGOA SSSR, *since March 1999* part of RGVA
TsKhSD	Tsentr khraneniia sovremennoi dokumentatsii (Center for Preservation of Contemporary Documentation), Moscow, *formed on the basis of current records of the CC CPSU, since March 1999* RGANI
TsNB	Tsentral´na naukova biblioteka im. V. I. Vernads´koho NAN (V. I. Vernads´kyi Central Scientific Library), Kyiv, *now* NBU, *earlier* TsNB AN URSR
TsVIA	Tsentral´nyi voenno-istoricheskii arkhiv (Central Military History Archive), Moscow, *after 1941* TsGVIA, *after 1992* RGVIA
TsVMA	Tsentral´nyi voenno-morskoi arkhiv (Central Naval Archive), Gatchina
UIK	Ukraïns´kyi istorychnyi kabinet (Ukrainian Historical Cabinet—under the Ministry of Foreign Affairs of the Czechoslovak Republic), Prague
UNESCO	United Nations Educational, Scientific, and Cultural Organization

UNR	Ukraïns'ka narodna respublika (Ukrainian National Republic)
UPA	Ukraïns'ka povstans'ka [povstancha] armiia (Ukrainian Insurgent Army)
UPSR	Ukraïns'ka Partiia Sotsialistiv-Revoliutsioneriv (Ukrainian Party of Socialist Revolutionaries); *also various foreign branches referred to as* Ukraïns'ka Zahranychna Partiia Sotsialistiv-Revoliutsioneriv (Ukrainian Party of Socialist Revolutionaries Abroad)
USDRP	Ukraïns'ka sotsial-demokratychna robitnycha partiia (Ukrainian Social Democratic Workers' Party)
US NA	National Archives of the United States, Washington, DC, and College Park, MD
VGBIL	Vserossiiskaia [*formerly,* Vsesoiuznaia] gosudarstvennaia biblioteka inostrannoi literatury im. M. I. Rudomino (M. I. Rudomino All-Russian [*formerly,* All-Union] State Library of Foreign Literature), Moscow
VKP[b]	Vsesoiuznaia Kommunisticheskaia partiia [bol'shevikov] (All-Union Communist Party [Bolsheviks])
VNIIDAD	Vserossiiskii [*formerly,* Vsesoiuznyi] nauchno-issledovatel'skii institut doku-mentovedeniia i arkhivnogo dela (All-Russian [*formerly,* All-Union] Scientific-Research Institute for Documentation and Archival Affairs), Moscow
VUAN	Vseukraïns'ka Akademiia nauk (All-Ukrainian Academy of Sciences)
YIVO	Yidisher Visenshaftlikher Institut (Jewish Scientific Research Institute), *before* 1939 in Vilnius; *now* in New York City
ZAGS	Zapis' aktov grazhdanskogo sostoianiia (Registry of Vital Statistics), *Ukr.* ZAHS
ZAHS	Zapys aktiv hromadians'koho stanu (Registry of Vital Statistics), *Rus.* ZAGS
ZNiO	Zakład Narodowy im. Ossolińskich (Ossoliński National Institute), Lviv, *now,* in Wrocław, *frequently* "Ossolineum"
ZUNR	Zakhidna Ukraïns'ka narodna respublika (Western Ukrainian National Republic)

Commonly used short titles:

Actes de la 17ème CITRA
International Council on Archives/Conseil international des archives. *Actes de la dix-septième conférence de la Table ronde des archives. Cagliari 1977. La constitution et la reconstitution des patrimoines archivistiques nationaux.* Paris: ICA, 1980.

Archives of Russia, 2000
Archives of Russia: A Directory and Bibliographic Guide to Holdings in Moscow and St. Petersburg. English edition, Ed. Patricia Kennedy Grimsted. Armonk, NY: M.E. Sharpe, 2000.

Arkhivna ta rukopysna Ukraïnika
Arkhivna ta rukopysna Ukraïnika. Materialy rozshyrenoï mizhvidomchoï narady po obhovorenniu Derzhavnoï prohramy "Arkhivna ta rukopysna Ukraïnika" v Kyievi, 17 zhovtnia 1991 roku. Ed. Ol'ha Todiichuk, Vasyl' Ul'ianovs'kyi, and Hennadii Boriak. Kyiv: IUA, 1992. [=Naukovo-dovidkovi vydannia z istoriï Ukraïny, 18; Problemy edytsiinoï ta kameral'noï arkheohrafiï: Istoriia, teoriia, metodyka, 1.]

Arkhivy byvshikh KP
Sbornik materialov po mezhdunarodnoi konferentsii "Arkhivy byvshikh kommunisticheskikh partii v stranakh tsentral'noi i vostochnoi Evropy," Stara Ves', 28 sentiabria–1 oktiabria 1995 goda. Warsaw, 1996.

"Betr: Sicherstellung"
"Betr: Sicherstellung": NS-Kunstraub in der Sowjetunion. Ed. Wolfgang Eichwede and Ulrike Hartung. Bremen: Edition Temmen, 1998.

Boriak, *Natsional'na arkhivna spadshchyna Ukraïny*
Boriak, Hennadii. *Natsional'na arkhivna spadshchyna Ukraïny ta derzhavnyi reiestr "Arkheohrafichna Ukraïnika": Arkhivni dokumental'ni resursy ta naukovo-informatsiini systemy.* Kyiv, 1995.

Captured German Records
Captured German and Related Records: A National Archives Conference. Ed. Robert Wolfe. Athens, OH: Ohio University Press, 1974. [=National Archives Conferences, 3.]

CITRA 1993–1995
International Council on Archives/Conseil international des archives. *Archival Dependencies in the Information Age, CITRA 1993–1995: Proceedings of the Twenty-Ninth, Thirtieth and Thirty-First International Conferences of the Round Table on Archives. XXIX Mexico 1993, XXX Thessaloniki 1994, XXXI Washington 1995/L'interdépendance des archives: Actes des vingt-neuvième, trentième et trente et unième conférences internationales de la Table ronde des archives. XXIX.* Dortrecht, 1998.

Conventions and Recommendations of Unesco
UNESCO. *Conventions and Recommendations of Unesco Concerning the Protection of the Cultural Heritage.* Paris: Unesco, 1983.

Cultural Treasures, 1994
Cultural Treasures Moved Because of the War—A Cultural Legacy of the Second World War Documentation and Research on Losses: Documentation of the International Meeting in Bremen (30.11.–2.12.1994). Ed. Jost Hansen, Dieter Opper, and Doris Lemmermeier. Bremen: Koordinierungsstelle der Länder für die Rückführung von Kulturgütern beim Senator für Bildung, Wissenschaft, Kunst und Sport, 1995.

Displaced Books: Bücherrückgabe
Displaced Books: Bücherrückgabe aus zweierlei Sicht: Beiträge und Materialien zur Bestandsgeschichte deutscher Bibliotheken im Zusammenhang von NS-Zeit und Krieg, 2nd ed. Hannover: Laurentius Verlag, 1999. [=Laurentius Sonderheft.]

Dossier on Archival Claims
Council of Europe. *Reference Dossier on Archival Claims.* Ed. Hervé Bastien. Strasbourg: Council of Europe, 1997 (CC LIVRE [97] 1).

Grimsted, Archives: Estonia, Latvia, Lithuania, and Belorussia
Grimsted, Patricia Kennedy. *Archives and Manuscript Repositories in the USSR: Estonia, Latvia, Lithuania, and Belorussia.* Princeton: Princeton University Press, 1981.

Grimsted, Archives: Ukraine
Grimsted, Patricia Kennedy. *Archives and Manuscript Repositories in the USSR: Ukraine and Moldavia,* Book 1: *General Bibliography and Institutional Directory.* Princeton: Princeton University Press, 1988.

Kul'tura i viina
Kul'tura i viina: Pohliad cherez pivstolittia. Ed. Viktor Akulenko and Valentyna Vrublevs'ka, et al. Kyiv: Adrys, 1996. [=*Povernennia kul'turnoho nadbannia Ukraïny: Problemy, zavdannia, perspektyvy,* 7.]

Lesy Belaruskikh materyial'nykh
Materyialy Mizhnarodnaha "kruhlaha stala" "Lesy Belaruskikh materyial'nykh i dukhoŭnykh kashtoŭnastsei u chas Druhoi susvetnai vainy i paslia iae (peramiashchenne, vyiaŭlenne, viartanne)." Ed. Adam Mal'dzis. Minsk: Belaruski fond kul'tury, 1996. [=*Viartanne,* 3.]

LNB Dokumenty
Krushel'nyts'ka, Larysa, ed. *L'vivs'ka naukova biblioteka im. V. Stefanyka NAN Ukraïny: Dokumenty, fakty, komentari.* Lviv: LNB, 1996.

Materialy natsional'noho seminaru, Chernihiv, 1994
Materialy natsional'noho seminaru "Problemy povernennia natsional'no-kul'turnykh pam'iatok, vtrachenykh abo peremishchenykh pid chas Druhoï

svitovoï viiny." *Chernihiv, veresen' 1994.* Ed. Oleksandr K. Fedoruk,
Hennadii V. Boriak, Serhii I. Kot, et al. Kyiv, 1996. [=*Povernennia
kul'turnoho nadbannia Ukraïny: Problemy, zavdannia, perspektyvy*, 6.]

Matwijów, Walka o lwowskie dobra kultury
Walka o lwowskie dobra kultury w latach 1945–1948. Wrocław: Towarzystwo
Przyjaciół Ossolineum, 1996.

Mezhdunarodnaia okhrana
Mezhdunarodnaia okhrana kul'turnykh tsennostei. Ed. Mark Moiseevich
Boguslavskii. Moscow: Mezhdunarodnye otnosheniia, 1979.

Mizhnarodna okhorona
*Mizhnarodna okhorona, zakhyst i povernennia kul'turnykh tsinnostei (zbirnyk
dokumentiv).* Ed. Iu. K. Kachurenko. Kyiv: IUA, 1993.

Povernennia kul'turnoho: Dokumenty, 2
Povernennia kul'turnoho nadbannia Ukraïny: Dokumenty svidchat', 2. *Ukraïns'ki
kul'turni tsinnosti v Rosiï: Arkheolohiia kolektsiï Ukraïny.* Comp. Svitlana
Beliaieva et al. Ed. Petro Tolochko et al. Kyiv, 1997.

Povernennia kul'turnoho, 1993 [3]
Povernennia kul'turnoho nadbannia Ukraïny: Problemy, zavdannia, perspektyvy.
Kyiv, 1993.

Povernennia kul'turnoho, 4
Povernennia kul'turnoho nadbannia Ukraïny: Problemy, zavdannia, perspektyvy,
no. 4. Comp. N. O. Hudimova. Ed. Olena Aleksandrova, Hennadii V. Boriak,
V. P. Ishchenko, and Valentyna B. Vrublevs'ka. Kyiv, 1994.

Povernennia kul'turnoho, 5
Povernennia kul'turnoho nadbannia Ukraïny: Problemy, zavdannia, perspektyvy,
no. 5. Kyiv, 1994.

Povernuto v Ukraïnu
Povernuto v Ukraïnu. Ed. Oleksandr Fedoruk et al. Kyiv: Natsional'na komisiia z
pytan' povernennia v Ukraïnu kul'turnykh tsinnostei pry Kabineti Ministriv
Ukraïny. 2 issues available through 1999.
No. 1: Comp. Valentyna Vrublevs'ka and Liudmyla Lozenko. Kyiv: Tov.
"Tanant," 1997.
No. 2: Comp. Valentyna Vrublevs'ka, Iaroslava Muzychenko, and Larysa
Borodenkova. Kyiv: Tov. "Triumf," 1999.

Pravovi aspekty restytutsiï
*Materialy naukovo-praktychnoho sympoziumu "Pravovi aspekty restytutsiï
kul'turnykh tsinnostei: Teoriia i praktyka": Kyïv, hruden' 1996.* Ed.
Oleksandr K. Fedoruk, Iurii S. Shemshuchenko, et al. Kyiv, 1997.
[=*Povernennia kul'turnoho nadbannia Ukraïny: Problemy, zavdannia,
perspektyvy*, 10.]

Problemy zarubezhnoi arkhivnoi Rossiki
Problemy zarubezhnoi arkhivnoi Rossiki: Sbornik statei. Ed. Vladimir P. Kozlov.
Moscow: Informatsionno-izd. agentstvo "Russkii mir," 1997.

Restitutsiia bibliotechnykh sobranii
*Restitutsiia bibliotechnykh sobranii i sotrudnichestvo v Evrope. Rossiisko-
germanskii "kruglyi stol," 11–12 dekabria 1992 g., Moskva: Sbornik
dokladov.* Ed. S. V. Pushkova. Moscow: Rudomino, 1994.

Restytutsyia kul'turnykh kashtoŭnastsei
*Restytutsyia kul'turnykh kashtoŭnastsei: Prablemy viartannia i sumesnaha
vykarystannia (iurydychnyia, navukovyia i maral'nyia aspekty): Materyialy
Mizhnarodnai navukovai kanferentsyi, iakaia adbylasia u Minsku pad ehidai
UNESCO 19–20 chervenia 1997 h.* Ed. Adam Mal'dzis et al. Minsk:
Natsyianal'ny navukova-asvetny tsentr imia F. Skaryny, 1997. [=*Viartanne*,
4.]

Return of Looted Collections
*The Return of Looted Collections (1946–1946). An Unfinished Chapter:
Proceedings of an International Symposium to Mark the 50th Anniversary of
the Return of Dutch Book Collections from Germany.* Ed. F. J. Hoogewoud
and E. P. Kwaardgras. Amsterdam, 1997.

"Russkaia, ukrainskaia i belorusskaia èmigratsiia," 1995
*Mezhdunarodnaia konferentsiia "Russkaia, ukrainskaia i belorusskaia èmi-
gratsiia v Chekhoslovakii mezhdu dvumia mirovymi voinami. Rezul'taty i
perspektivy issledovanii. Fondy Slavianskoi biblioteki i prazhskikh
arkhivov," Praga, 14–15 avgusta 1995 g.: Sbornik dokladov/International
Conference "Russian, Ukrainian and Belorussian Emigration between the
World Wars in Czechoslovakia. Results and Perspectives of Contemporary
Research. Holdings of the Slavonic Library and Prague Archives," Prague,
August 14–15, 1995: Proceedings.* 2 vols. Prague, 1995.

The Spoils of War: WWII and Aftermath
*The Spoils of War: World War II and Its Aftermath. The Loss, Reappearance, and
Recovery of Cultural Property.* Ed. Elizabeth Simpson. New York: Henry N.
Abrams, 1997.

Die Trophäenkommissionen
Kolasa, Ingo, and Klaus-Dieter Lehmann, eds. *Die Trophäenkommissionen der
Roten Armee: Eine Dokumentensammlung zur Verschleppung von Büchern
aus deutschen Bibliotheken.* Frankfurt-am-Main: Vittorio Klostermann,
1996. [=*Zeitschrift für Bibliothekswesen und Bibliographie*, Sonderheft 64.]

Ukraïna v mizhnarodno-pravovykh vidnosynakh
Ukraïna v mizhnarodno-pravovykh vidnosynakh. 2 vols. Kyiv: Iurinkom Inter,
1996–1997.
Book 1: *Borot'ba iz zlochynnistiu ta vzaiemna pravova dopomoha.* Ed. V. L.
Chubariev and A. S. Matsko. Kyiv: Iurinkom Inter, 1996.

XXX *Trophies of War and Empire*

Book 2: *Pravova okhorona kul'turnykh tsinnostei*. Ed. V. I. Akulenko and Iu. S. Shemshuchenko. Kyiv: Iurinkom Inter, 1997.

Ukraïns'ka arkheohrafiia 1988

Ukraïns'ka arkheohrafiia: Suchasnyi stan ta perspektyvy rozvytku. Tezy dopovidei respublikans'koï narady, hruden' 1988 r. Kyiv; Arkeohrafichna komisiia AN URSR, 1988.

U.N.T.S.

United Nations Treaty Series. Treaties and international agreements registered or filed and recorded with the Secretariat of the United Nations.

Viartanne

Viartanne: Dakumenty i arkhiŭnyia materyialy pa prablemakh poshuku i viartannia natsyianal'nykh kashtoŭnastei, iakiia znakhodziatstsa za mezhami Respubliki Belarus'. 4 vols. Minsk, 1992–1997.

Washington Conference, 1998

Washington Conference on Holocaust-Era Assets, November 30–December 3, 1998: Proceedings. Ed. J. D. Bindenagel. Washington, DC: GPO, 1999. [=U.S. Department of State, Publication 10603.]

Wnioski rewindykacyjne

Wnioski rewindykacyjne księgozbioru Ossolineum oraz Dziel sztuki i zabytków ze zbiorów lwowskich. Ed. Jan Pruszyński. Warsaw: Ministerstwo Kultury i Sztuki, 1998. [=Polskie dziedzictwo kulturalne, Seria C: Materiały i Dokumenty.]

Preface and Acknowledgments

This study is a natural outgrowth of two major aspects of my research and writing over recent decades—the preparation of archival directories and the historical analysis of displaced archives. Although no specific grant funding was received for the current study, the research travel and experience that made it possible was nonetheless facilitated by grants for other projects. Since it also draws on numerous earlier publications, I am accordingly indebted to numerous editors and publishers, as well as many institutions, friends, and colleagues with whom I have worked over the years.

My Soviet-area archival directory series was funded over the two decades through 1990 by a series of grants from the National Endowment for the Humanities, while field research in the Soviet Union and several countries of Eastern Europe was supported by the International Research & Exchanges Board (IREX). Throughout the past two and a half decades, the Ukrainian Research Institute at Harvard University (HURI) has accorded me the status of Institute Associate and provided me a home base, with an office, library and computer facilities, and the intellectual advantages of a university environment. I am deeply indebted for the encouragement and support of successive HURI directors: Professors Omeljan Pritsak, George Grabowicz, and Roman Szporluk. Some of the matching grant funds for the Ukrainian phases of my work have come from the Ukrainian Studies Fund (USF) and the Canadian Institute of Ukrainian Studies (CIUS). In recent years, the USF, presently directed by Dr. Roman Procyk, has generously supported some of my travel to Ukraine, computer equipment, and related expenses, along with even more extensive support for my colleagues in Ukraine.

Several decades of gathering materials for my Soviet and post-Soviet area archival directory series and related research projects have heightened my interest in the dispersal of Ukraine's archival heritage. The Ukrainian directory volume that I compiled was the last in its series to be prepared when the Soviet Union was still intact.[1] The political situation in the mid-1980s did not permit publication of the directory in Ukraine because of the revealing information and bibliography it contained—a clear example of the reference problems for Ukrainian archives at that time.

---

[1] Patricia Kennedy Grimsted, *Archives and Manuscript Repositories in the USSR: Ukraine and Moldavia,* Book 1: *General Bibliography and Institutional Directory* (Princeton: Princeton University Press, 1988).

Soviet glasnost, followed by Ukraine's independence, changed this. First, soon after the directory's appearance, the newly revived Archeographic Commission of the Ukrainian Academy of Sciences called for my assistance in an augmented version for publication in Kyiv that was to become part of a national archival information system for Ukraine.[2] As an initial step, in the spring of 1994, thanks to a generous grant from the Eurasia Foundation, work started on a computerized repository-level archival directory with a bibliography of reference materials (with the program "ArcheoBiblioBase" based at the newly organized Institute of Manuscripts of the V. I. Vernads'kyi National Library of Ukraine (NBU).[3] Further implementation was delayed, but a preliminary website based on the updated data was launched in English in 1998. An updated directory appeared in May 2000 with a Ukrainian-language website later that year.[4] Liubov Dubrovina, who

---

[2]   The larger implications and concrete plans were discussed in a number of conferences, symposia volumes, and specialized studies. See, for example, *Arkhivna ta rukopysna Ukraïnika. Materialy rozshyrenoï mizhvidomchoï narady po obhovorenniu Derzhavnoï prohramy "Arkhivna ta rukopysna Ukraïnika" v Kyievi, 17 zhovtnia 1991 roku,* ed. Ol'ha Todiichuk, Vasyl' Ul'ianovs'kyi, and Hennadii Boriak (Kyiv: IUA, 1992) [=Naukovo-dovidkovi vydannia z istoriï Ukraïny, 18; Problemy edytsiinoï ta kameral'noï arkheohrafiï: Istoriia, teoriia, metodyka, 1]. See also the later formulation, *Natsional'na arkhivna informatsiina systema: Struktura danykh (Materialy dlia obhovorennia),* ed. L. A. Dubrovina with the participation of O. V. Sokhan' (Kyiv: HAU; NAN; TsNB; IUA, 1994).

[3]   Until May 1996, NBU was known as the Central Scientific Library (TsNB) of the National Academy of Sciences (NAN) of Ukraine. The project has benefited from the joint sponsorship of the Main Archival Administration of the Cabinet of Ministers of Ukraine (HAU), the Ministry of Culture of Ukraine, Institute of Ukrainian Archeography and Source Study (IUAD), and the Ukrainian Research Institute at Harvard University (HURI). Ukrainian data files were drawn from those used for my 1988 Ukrainian archival directory. The computer system "Archeo-BiblioBase," already operative in Russia, was adapted for Ukrainian use by Iurii Liamin with the assistance of Oleh Sokhan'. See Patricia Kennedy Grimsted, "Biblioteka–arkhiv: Shliakh do intehruvannia (Avtomatyzovanyi dostup do arkhivnoï informatsiï dlia Rosiï, Ukraïny ta inshykh nezalezhnykh derzhav kolyshn'oho Soiuzu)," *Bibliotechnyi visnyk* 1994 (5–6): 26–29.

[4]   See *Arkhivny ustanovy Ukraïny: Dovidnyk,* ed. O. S. Onytsenko, R. Ia. Pyrih, L. A. Dubrovina, H. V. Boriak, et al. (Kyiv, 2000) [=Arkhivni zibrannia Ukraïny, Spetsial'ni dovidnyky]. "Archives of Ukraine" can be accessed through HURI's website at Harvard University: <http://www.huri.harvard.edu/abbukr/index.html>. See Liubov Dubrovina's review of my 1988 directory in *Ukraïns'kyi arkheo-hrafichnyi shchorychnyk,* n.s. 2 (Kyiv, 1993): 399–401; and Boriak's report: "Proekt komp'iuternoho dovidnyk 'ArkheoBiblioBaza' iak skladova 'Arkhivnoï

directs the Institute of Manuscripts in NBU, while serving as coordinator of our directory efforts has also assisted in many phases of the present study. I am also grateful to successive TsNB/NBU directors who have encouraged our collaboration, and especially the present director, Oleksii Onyshchenko.

Exploration of many issues in this volume, and the directory and archival research involved, has been dependent on the good offices of the Main Archival Administration of Ukraine (as of December 1999, the State Committee on Archives of Ukraine, DKAU), headed first from before 1991 by Borys V. Ivannenko, together with deputy directory Volodymyr Lozyts'kyi. While it is impossible to name all who have assisted at various junctures, I am particularly grateful to Ruslan Ia. Pyrih, first as director of the former Ukrainian Communist Party Archive (now TsDAHO), and then, since 1998, as chief of the Main Archival Administration. Many thanks are due the directors and archivists of the several national archives who have facilitated my research, especially including TsDAVO director, Larysa V. Iakovlieva and her staff, since the vast majority of my Kyiv research for this volume was conducted there. Liubov Z. Histova, long-time director of TsDIAK, obligingly gave me access to the formerly secret files (*opys* 2) of the administrative records of TsDIAK, which provided the essential basis for many of the revelations in Chapter 9. In Lviv, the late Orest Matsiuk, whom I have known from many visits, was exceedingly helpful. His untimely death while this volume was in preparation was a true loss to the field.

My interests and work in the subject area of this volume developed from my close association with the Archeographic Commission, since its reestablishment in Kyiv in 1987. In 1991 it was reorganized and expanded as the Institute of Ukrainian Archeography (IUA). Since 1995 it has been known as the Mykhailo Hrushevs'kyi Institute of Ukrainian Archeography and Source Study (IUAD).[5] IUAD has been the heart and soul of historical and

---

ta rukopysnoï Ukraïniky,'" in *Natsional'na arkhivna informatsiina systema "Arkhivna ta rukopysna Ukraïnika" i komp'iuterizatsiia arkhivnoï spravy v Ukraïni*, pt. 1: *Informatizatsiia arkhivnoï spravy v Ukraïni: Suchasnyi stan ta perspektyvy: Zbirnyk naukovykh prats'* (Kyiv: IUAD, 1996): 189–92.

5   In the Russian Empire, the term "archeography" traditionally referred to the collection, description, and analysis of medieval manuscript books and other early historical documents. This was especially seen in connection with the work of the Imperial Archeographic Commission (from 1834), and in Ukraine with the Kyiv Archeographic Commission—the so-called Temporary Commission for the Collection of Early Documents (*Vremennaia komissiia dlia razbora drevnikh aktov*), which was established in 1843. In Soviet official state archival usage the term was associated more generally with the methodology of historical docu-

archival reform, and revived archeographic efforts in the context of Ukrainian independence.[6] From the outset, this study owes much to the hospitality of IUAD in Kyiv and encouragement of its director, Pavlo Sokhan', in associating me with the activities of the Institute as part of collaborative relations with HURI.

In his capacity as former IUAD deputy director, Hennadii Boriak has had a major role throughout the research and writing of this book. His intellectual energy and enthusiasm and our joint research and descriptive efforts in several countries have contributed much to the present study; he and his family also have always provided warm hospitality in Kyiv and made many of the arrangements for my research and consultations. As of April 2000 Boriak has been appointed the Deputy Chief of the National Committee on Archives of Ukraine—DKAU. He currently is editing a Ukrainian edition of the present volume that will be sponsored by DKAU. Serhii Kot, now associated with Institute of History at the Ukrainian Academy of Sciences in Kyiv, helped me clarify a number of issues involved in the present study on the basis of his own extensive recent research on Ukrainian cultural restitution issues.

I remain grateful to Iaroslav Dashkevych, who now heads the IUAD Lviv Branch. His friendship and many consultations during the preparation of my earlier archival directory helped me uncover many relevant materials. He generously provided guidance from his encyclopedic knowledge of Ukrainian

---

mentary editing for the publication of ideologically selected historical sources and official documentary publications. Although the term "archeography" is rarely used in Western literature, it merits retention as appropriate to the Russian and Ukrainian post-Soviet context.

[6]   For a recent discussion of the development and concept of archeography in a Ukrainian and Russian historical context, see the monograph by Hennadii Boriak, *Natsional'na arkhivna spadshchyna Ukraïny ta derzhavnyi reiestr "Arkheohrafichna Ukraïnika." Arkhivni dokumental'ni resursy ta naukovo-informatsiini systemy* (Kyiv, 1995). See also the introductory essay by Liubov Dubrovina, "Kodykohrafiia—Arkheohrafiia—Kodykolohiia (vzaiemozv'iazky ta rozmezhuvannia," in L. A. Dubrovina and O. M. Hal'chenko, *Kodykohrafiia ukraïns'koï ta skhidnoslov'ians'koï rukopysnoï knyhy i kodykolohichna model' struktury formalizovanoho opysu rukopysu/Kodikografiia ukrainskoi i vostochnoslavianskoi rukopisnoi knigi i kodikologicheskaia model' struktury formalizovannogo opisaniia rukopisi* (Kyiv: IUA, 1992) [=Problemy edytsiinoï ta kameral'noï arkheohrafiï: Istoriia, teoriia, metodyka, 9], esp. pp. 7–13 (Ukrainian) and pp. 76–82 (Russian). A brochure reviewing IUA activities and publications for the period 1987–1993 was issued in honor of the 150-year anniversary of the Archeographic Commission in Kyiv—*Arkheohrafichna komisiia ta Instytut ukraïns'koï arkheohrafiï Akademiï nauk Ukraïny, 1987–1993* (Kyiv, [1993]).

historical culture and archival affairs. My acquaintance with the late professor Fedor Maksymenko of Lviv State University, the veritable dean of Ukrainian bibliography, was also of tremendous importance for my research, although, Soviet authorities kept our contacts to a minimum. Also now associated with IUAD in Lviv, Iaroslav Isaievych provided important advice over many years and read several chapters—to their considerable profit. During several earlier visits, specialists in the Manuscript Division of the Stefanyk Library in Lviv assisted with my coverage of their holdings, despite numerous Soviet-period restrictions. Liliana Hentosh, from Lviv State University, also commented on several chapters and helped track down references while she was a visiting scholar at HURI.

One of the most pressing concerns—especially in the context of Ukrainian independence and the desire to solidify the cultural legacy of the new national state—has been the identification and description of archival holdings abroad relating to Ukraine.[7] The concept of "archival Ucrainica abroad" became a catch phrase for the dispersed archival legacy of Ukraine.[8] Preliminary booklets already survey Ukrainian-related archival holdings in several countries,

---

[7]   See Pavlo Sokhan' and Vasyl' Danylenko, "Perspektyvy diial'nosti viddilu vyvchennia ta publikatsiï zarubizhnykh dzherel z istoriï Ukraïny," *Ukraïns'kyi arkheohrafichnyi shchorichnyk,* n.s. 1 (1992): 42–45; and Vasyl' Ul'ianovs'kyi, "Do kontseptsiï naukovo-doslidnoï ta vydavnychoï diial'nosti naukovo-informatsiinoho viddilu," ibid., 47–53.

[8]   In traditional scholarship and library usage, the term "Ucrainica," similar to the term "Rossica," usually referred to printed books *about* Ukraine. In the pre-revolutionary Russian Empire, reference was often to specifically foreign imprints as, for example, the "Rossica" Collection in the Imperial Public Library in St. Petersburg. With reference to collections abroad, bibliophile use of the term usually implied early (pre–nineteenth-century) books printed in Russia (including Slavonic books of Russian origin) in collections outside of Russia. Since the Revolution, Russian and Ukrainian specialists use the terms more broadly, and often include archival materials from and relating to Ukraine or Russia. In the present essay, I use the concept "archival Ucrainica" to exclude printed books, but to include manuscripts and other archival materials of all types held abroad—not only medieval-type manuscript books (codices). It should be noted that in post-1991 Ukraine—in contrast to traditional international usage—Ukrainian specialists are beginning to use the term "Ucrainica" for all Ukrainian manuscript books and other archival materials as well as printed books, both within Ukraine and abroad.

and more are under way, while a bibliographic compendium of available descriptions is nearing completion.[9]

The opening of archives and publishing possibilities in the context of Ukrainian independence has made many new archival sources available, opened new historiographic perspectives, and totally recast the possibilities of archeography. My pre-independence work on a second historical book of my directory of Ukrainian archives has had to be substantially abandoned.[10] Yet the interdependence of the archival legacies of Ukraine and of those foreign powers who had ruled Ukrainian lands over the centuries were already outlined in my 1986 essay dealing with problems of tracing the documentary records of a divided nation, for which Ukraine stood out as a prime example.[11] Those problems now come together with more fundamental conceptual issues about the archival heritage of Ukraine. Those in turn mesh with others resulting from the cataclysmic developments and displacements on the cultural front during and after World War II that have recently come to the fore in public attention and international archival circles. The present volume serves as an initial conceptual and methodological clarification for some of these matters.

My work—over many years—in preparing archival directories and guides for researchers covering the entire space of the former Soviet Union has made me sensitive to the new international dimension of post-Soviet archival problems. Efforts to update directory information about archival holdings in Moscow and St. Petersburg have increased my awareness of the extent to which these former imperial capitals preserve the joint archival heritage of all

---

[9]   My comprehensive survey of reference literature describing archival Ucrainica abroad will appear eventually as a working paper on the HURI website <www.huri.harvard.edu/workpaper/index.html>. The survey is modeled on, and adapted from, my earlier coverage of archival Baltica and Belorosica abroad—"A Preliminary Bibliography of Descriptions of Archival Materials Originating in or Relating to Estonia, Latvia, Lithuania, and Belorussia Now in Collections Outside the USSR," in Grimsted, *Archives: Estonia, Latvia, Lithuania, and Belorussia,* Appendix 5, pp. 717–830.

[10]   As explained in the preface of Grimsted, *Archives and Manuscript Repositories: Ukraine,* book 2 was intended to cover the history of archives in the Ukrainian SSR.

[11]   Grimsted, "The Archival Legacy of Soviet Ukraine: Problems of Tracing the Documentary Records of a Divided Nation," *Cahiers du Monde russe et soviétique* 28 (January–March 1987): 95–108. When that article was written, such problems could not then be openly discussed in Ukraine. It grew out of seminar presentations in Cambridge, MA; Washington, DC; and Paris.

the newly independent successor States to the former Russian Empire and Soviet Union, as well as many specific components of the Ukrainian archival heritage.[12] Ukraine becomes a perfect case study for the problem of a newly independent nation trying to define, and to the extent possible reconstruct, its archival heritage.

My analysis of the post-Soviet legal basis for archives in Russia, as presented in Chapter 1, draws on my monograph on the post-1991 Russian archival scene, first published in Amsterdam in 1997.[13] I have been very gratified for the close cooperation with Russian archival colleagues over the past decade, since the ArcheoBiblioBase directory project was introduced there in 1990. Vladimir P. Kozlov, who serves as the principal Russian editor, has been associated with the project since he aided its inception. He deserves my appreciation in connection with work on a number of related publiccations, including the present one. Kozlov, as Chief Archivist of Russia, now heads the Federal Archival Service of Russia (Rosarkhiv) and teaches in the Historico-Archival Institute (now part of the Russian State University for the Humanities). The opportunity for extensive periods of residence in Moscow led to daily working relationships with many Russian archivists, and I owe particular thanks to my ArcheoBiblioBase coordinator, Lada Repulo, who now heads the International Department for Rosarkhiv, and the several assistants who have also helped with aspects of this study.

Funding for the collaborative ArcheoBiblioBase venture in Russia came largely from IREX, the Smith-Richardson Foundation, and the Soros Foundation, with further assistance from the International Institute of Social History (IISH) in Amsterdam, of which I have been an Honourary Fellow since 1997. IISH director Jaap Kloosterman has played an important role in my

---

[12] An expanded Russian-language edition was published in 1997: *Arkhivy Rossii: Moskva i Sankt-Peterburg. Spravochnik-obozrenie i bibliograficheskii ukazatel'*, comp. Patricia Kennedy Grimsted, Lada V. Repulo, and Irina V. Tunkina; ed. Mikhail D. Afanas'ev, Patricia Kennedy Grimsted, Vladimir P. Kozlov, and Vladimir S. Sobol'ev (Moscow: "Arkheograficheskii tsentr," 1997). A further expanded and updated English-language edition has just appeared: *Archives of Russia: A Directory and Bibliographic Guide to Holdings in Moscow and St. Petersburg*, English-language version ed. Patricia Kennedy Grimsted (Armonk, NY: M.E. Sharpe, 2000). See also the ArcheoBiblioBase website for "Archives of Russia," which serves as an outlet for updated information on Russian archives and related publications. The address is in note 14 below.

[13] See, for example, my *Archives of Russia Seven Years After—"Purveyors of Sensations" or "Shadows Cast to the Past"?* (Washington, DC, 1998) [=CWIHP Working Papers, 20].

Russian activities, publications, and related efforts on the international archival front.[14]

The challenges involved in reconstituting a national archival heritage are not new to me, given my work on archival Rossica and Sovietica abroad, both in the Soviet and post-Soviet Russian contexts.[15] A number of Russian colleagues, including Vladimir P. Kozlov, Tat'iana F. Pavlova, Irina V. Pozdeeva, and Evgenii V. Starostin, and Sarah V. Zhitomirskaia made important contributions to my research in this area. I am particularly grateful to Vsevolod V. Tsaplin, not only for scrutinizing my Rossica essay, but even more for making available to me a copy of his hitherto unpublished intended doctoral dissertation, presenting a fundamental, source-based study of many archival developments during World War II, which was also important for the second part of my study.

The proposed typography of archival Ucrainica abroad presented as Chapter 4 represents an adaptation, as appropriate to Ukraine, of an essay that grew out of my presentation at a Moscow conference on archival Rossica in December 1993, sponsored by Rosarkhiv.[16] I am grateful to Rosarkhiv colleagues, and particularly Vladimir Kozlov, for inviting me to take part in that conference, which gave me an opportunity to participate in significant discussions of the issues involved with him and other colleagues. An updated study of Rossica retrieval efforts is now in preparation, research for which contributed directly to my consideration of the retrieval of Ucrainica in Chapter 9.

---

[14]   The English-language ArcheoBiblioBase website is maintained now by IISH at <http://www.iisg.nl/~abb>.

[15]   See, for example, my "Foreign Collections and Soviet Archives: Russian Archaeographic Efforts in Great Britain and the Problem of Provenance," in *The Study of Russian History from British Archival Sources,* ed. Janet M. Hartley (London–New York: Mansell, 1986). See also my exploratory essay on archival Rossica and Sovietica abroad in the new post-Soviet Russian context: "Zarubezhnaia arkhivnaia Rossika i Sovetika. Proiskhozhdenie dokumentov ili ikh otnoshenie k istorii Rossii (SSSR), potrebnost' v opisanii i bibliografii," *Otechestvennye arkhivy* 1993 (1): 20–53.

[16]   A published version in Russian, "Arkhivnaia Rossika/Sovetika—K opredeleniiu i tipologii russkogo arkhivnogo nasprediia za rubezhom," appears in *Trudy Istoriko-arkhivnogo instituta* 33 (Moscow, 1996): 262–86, and is also published in the conference proceedings, *Problemy zarubezhnoi arkhivnoi Rossiki: Sbornik statei,* by V. P. Kozlov (Moscow: Inf.-izd. agentstvo "Russkii mir," 1997), pp. 7–43.

A great number of archivists in Moscow have assisted me with this study. I am grateful to many archivists in the former TsKhIDK (now part of RGVA)—the major repository for European trophy archives. These valued colleagues include former director Mansur M. Mukhamedzhinov, present director Vladimir N. Kuzelenkov, deputy director Vladimir I. Korotaev, and section head Tat'iana A. Vasil'eva. In RGASPI (earlier TsKhIDNI), I should particularly mention the assistance of director Kyril M. Anderson and deputy directors Oleg N. Naumov and Valerii N. Shepelev. The assistance of Deputy Director Vitalii Affani in RGANI (earlier TsKhSD) has also been important. Among many colleagues in GA RF who facilitated research for this volume, I particularly appreciate the assistance of director Sergei V. Mironenko, former acting director Tat'iana F. Pavlova, former deputy director Aliia I. Barkovets, and Ol'ga N. Kopylova, all of whom also shared with me their thoughts and the results of their own findings on related problems.

The new possibility of reintegrating Ukrainian culture and archives at home with those exiled components in the diaspora raise a host of novel issues. Since large parts of the Ukrainian archival heritage currently remain dispersed outside the borders of independent Ukraine, issues of restitution and retrieval to the homeland are on the minds of many, even before they know exact locations or have access to descriptive publications. This has been apparent in rhetorical discussion in the press. It also is seen in the activities of the National Commission for the Return of Cultural Treasures to Ukraine, which, when established in December 1992, appointed me to be a foreign consultant. In connection with reforms instituted by the Ukrainian government in 1999, the National Commission was reorganized under the Ministry of Culture as the State Service for the Control of Transmission of Cultural Treasures Across the Borders of Ukraine. Oleksandr Fedoruk, who headed the National Commission, and now heads the State Service, has encouraged the preparation of this volume (and particularly the forthcoming Ukrainian version), and I have appreciated his input at numerous turns. My aim here is to provide a useful context by means of a scholarly investigation, not only for scholars and archivists, but also for politicians and cultural specialists who are dealing with the issues on a national political level.

The identification and description of archival Ucrainica abroad in the post-Soviet era have become closely tied to the problem of reconstituting the national archival heritage in the context of the legal principles surrounding the succession of States. But there has not yet been adequate research and serious publication on the subject, especially from a general East European perspective. The problems of locating and defining Ukraine's displaced archival heritage should heighten appreciation of similar perplexities for other emerging nations and newly independent successor States. Discussion of such perplexities and the lack of conclusiveness in their resolution points to the urgency of formulating guidelines and establishing effective mechanisms for resolving such issues on an international level.

The international legal context discussed in Chapter 3 was first prepared in 1993, and has had several readings by members of the ICA Executive Committee. In this connection, I am particularly indebted to Charles Kecskeméti, during his tenure as Secretary General of the International Council on Archives (ICA) for numerous consultations and discussions. I also benefited from discussions with Leopold Auer, Eric Ketelaar, Erik Norberg, and other members of the ICA Executive Committee. Some of my recommendations coincided with those incorporated into the ICA Position Paper adopted in April 1995, which is accordingly added as Appendix VII of this book. Some of my recommendations and planned appendixes for this publications also served as a basis for the Council of Europe 1996 compendium on archival claims (as discussed at the end of Chapter 3). Those publications and my intervening discussion with international archival leaders have in turn been helpful in clarifying my own formulation in the present study. I appreciate the ICA's invitation to me to participate as an observer in the October 1994 Conference of the International Round Table on Archives (XXX CITRA) in Thessalonica, where issues of displaced archives were a major consideration.

Lyndel V. Prott of the UNESCO Secretariat in Paris also has lent her advice for the formulation of Chapter 3, and has been particularly helpful in supplying me with literature about the UNESCO Committee dealing with cultural restitution issues, which she earlier chaired. I also gratefully acknowledge the assistance of Axel Plathe of UNESCO and Giussepi Vitiello, who heads the Cultural Secretariat for the Council of Europe.

The second part of this book draws particularly heavily on my research and publications over the last decade on archival materials displaced in the course of World War II and its aftermath. Revelations in fall 1990 and 1991 about displaced European archives captured by Soviet authorities after World War II,[17] along with the continuing unresolved problems of their appropriate restitution, have greatly complicated international discussions of archival Ucrainica and Rossica in recent years. My first report on the fate of Ukrainian cultural treasures during World War II, in collaboration with IUA Deputy Director Hennadii Boriak, took place, at the First International Conference of Ukrainian Studies in Kyiv in August 1990. It later appeared in article form in

---

[17]   Among my efforts at the time to publicize this issue, see Evgenii Kuz'min's interview of me, "'Vyvesti...unichtozhit'...spriatat'...,' Sud'by trofeinykh arkhivov," *Literaturnaia gazeta* 39 (2 October 1991): 13.

Germany and a monograph in Ukraine.[18] Some of the materials presented here serve to update that coverage. A more focused update of that earlier monograph is also in preparation.

Most recently, Hennadii Boriak was closely involved in the spade work for our location of the Sing-Akademie Collection in Kyiv in the summer of 1999, and we owe much credit for the definitive identification to Christoph Wolff, William Powell Mason Professor of Music at Harvard, dean, until recently, of its Graduate School of Arts and Sciences, and author of a recently published, highly acclaimed biography of J. S. Bach.[19]

Participation in the series of conferences devoted to World War II subjects over the past decade has contributed to discussion in various parts of this study, including the coverage in Chapter 12. My successive studies of "Displaced Archives on the Eastern Front during World War II" were presented at several conferences, including the fall 1994 UNESCO-sponsored conference in Chernihiv, and the "Spoils of War" symposium in New York City in January 1995.[20]

My research on some of the specific Nazi looting agencies, whose holdings were later seized by Soviet authorities has served as a further basis for Chapter 8.[21] My findings on that subject were first presented at a symposium in Amsterdam in 1996. Through participation in that symposium I had an opportunity to become better acquainted with the research of Dutch and Belgian colleagues who share many of my research interests and have been exceedingly helpful in subsequent years. Most particularly I should mention

[18] See my article version, "The Fate of Ukrainian Cultural Treasures during World War II: The Plunder of Archives, Libraries, and Museums under the Third Reich," *Jahrbücher für Geschichte Osteuropas* 39(1) 1991: 53–80.

[19] *Johann Sebastian Bach: The Learned Musician* (New York: W. W. Norton and Co., 2000).

[20] See my "Captured Archives and Restitution Problems on the Eastern Front: Beyond the Bard Graduate Center Symposium," in *Spoils of War: WWII and Aftermath*, pp. 244–51, 270–71. Expanded versions of my study appeared first as a research paper in Amsterdam in 1996, Grimsted, *Displaced Archives on the Eastern Front: Restitution Problems from World War II and Its Aftermath* (Amsterdam: IISH, 1996) [=*IISG Research Papers*, 18].

[21] P. K. Grimsted, "New Clues in the Records of Archival and Library Plunder: The ERR and RSHA VII Amt Operations in Silesia," in *The Return of Looted Collections (1946–1946). An Unfinished Chapter: Proceedings of an International Symposium to Mark the 50th Anniversary of the Return of Dutch Book Collections from Germany*, ed. F. J. Hoogewoud, E. P. Kwaardgras et al. (Amsterdam: IISH, 1997), pp. 52–67.

Frits Hoogewoud and Evert Kwaadgras, the conference organizers, and Willem de Vries, whose research on the Special Music Commando (Sonderstab Musik) of the Einsatzstab Reichsleiter Rosenberg parallels my own. My Belgian colleagues Michel Vermote and Wouter Steenhaut, director of the Archive-Museum of the Socialist Labor Movement (AMSAB) in Ghent, have been exceedingly gracious in sharing with me the results of their own research involving displaced Belgium archives in Moscow and in providing travel support from AMSAB on several occasions. Seymour J. Pomrenze, the first director of the Offenbach Archival Depository (the main U.S. restitution center for books and archives after the war), and subsequently active in the Captured Records Branch of the U.S. National Archives, was the guest of honor in Amsterdam. I appreciate his help and consultation on several occasions in the U.S.

Because of my continuing research on the subject, some of my provisional findings in Chapter 8 are being expanded in my planned monograph on those same Nazi looting agencies.[22] My continuing research on U.S. postwar restitution efforts has led to documentation for five more U.S. restitution transfers to the USSR in addition to the thirteen from Germany and one from Austria mentioned in Chapter 6.[23]

Developments in connection with the passage of the Russian law to nationalize the cultural treasures brought to the Soviet Union after World War II have been covered in my recent publications; they are now updated in the present Chapter 10.[24] Regarding Russian restitution issues, I am grateful for consultations with Valerii Kulishov and Nikolai Nikandrov of the Restitution Office of the Ministry of Culture, and Minister of Culture Mikhail Shvydkoi. I also appreciate the assistance of Ekaterina Genieva, director of

---

[22]   See also my forthcoming, "Twice Plundered or 'Twice Saved'? Russia's 'Trophy' Archives and the Loot of the Reichssicherheitshauptamt," in *Holocaust and Genocide Studies* 4(2) September 2001.

[23]   These will be documented in a CD-ROM soon to be released in collaboration with the U.S. National Archives: *U.S. Restitution of Nazi-Looted Cultural Treasures to the USSR, 1945–1959: Facsimile Documents from the National Archives of the United States,* comp. and with an intro. by Patricia Kennedy Grimsted, foreword by Michael J. Kurtz (Washington, DC: GPO, 2001).

[24]   See chapter 8 in my *Archives of Russia Five Years After—"Purveyors of Sensations" or "Shadows Cast to the Past"?* (Amsterdam: IISH, 1997); and my separate article "'Trophy' Archives and Non-Restitution: Russia's Cultural 'Cold War' with the European Community, *Problems of Post Communism* 45(3) (May/June 1998): 3–16.

the All-Russian State Library of Foreign Literature (VGBIL), and Mikhail Afanas'ev, director of the State Public Historical Library of Russia (GPIB).

Considerable research was done in Poland, given the many components of Ukrainian-related records and manuscript collections that were to be found there, as well as the literature that described them. Work there was supported by a series of exchange visits sponsored by IREX, and additional IREX travel grants. I am grateful for the assistance of numerous Polish colleagues over the years, particularly archivists in the Main Archive of Early Records (AGAD—Archiwum Główne Akt Dawnych), with whom I have been associated on several collaborative projects, especially Marek Sędek, earlier AGAD division head, who now directs the Archive of the Foreign Ministry; Władysław Stępniak, former AGAD director, who is now deputy director of the State Archival Directorate (NDAP); and Irena Sułkowska-Kurasiowa, now retired from the Institute of History. Close collaboration with these and other Polish colleagues in researching the fate of the archives of the Polish-Lithuanian Commonwealth has enhanced my sensitivity to the general complexities of the archival heritage of East European successor States.[25]

I am grateful to the reference staff in the University Libraries in Warsaw, Cracow, and Wrocław, the Catholic University in Lublin, in the National Library (Biblioteka Narodowa) in Warsaw—and especially the late Krystyna Muszyńska and her colleagues in the Manuscript Department—and the Ossolineum in Wrocław. My preparation of annotated microfiche editions of the early catalogs of the Ossolineum manuscript holdings, based on research in both Lviv and Wrocław, gave me insights on the problems for researchers

---

[25] Irena Sułkowska-Kurasiowa collaborated with me in the study and reference aid, *The "Lithuanian Metrica" in Moscow and Warsaw: Reconstructing the Archives of the Grand Duchy of Lithuania.* (Cambridge, MA: Oriental Research Partners for the "Harvard Series in Ukrainian Studies," 1984). Recent collaborative research attention has focused on another key Ukrainian-related component, a large part of which still remains in Moscow—*Rus'ka (Volyns'ka) metryka. Rehesty dokumentiv koronnoï kantseliariï dlia ukraïns'kykh zemel' (Volyns'ke, Bratslavs'ke, Kyïvs'ke, Chernihivs'ke voievodstva), 1569–1673/ The Ruthenian (Volhynian) Metrica: Early Inventories of the Polish Crown Chancery Records for Ukrainian Lands 1569–1673,* comp. Hennadii Boriak, Patricia Kennedy Grimsted, Natalia Iakovenko, Irena Sułkowska-Kurasiowa, and Kyrylo Vyslobokov; with an introduction by Patricia K. Grimsted (Kyiv, forthcoming). See also my earlier article, "The Ruthenian (Volhynian) Metrica: Polish Crown Chancery Records for Ukrainian Lands, 1569–1673," *Harvard Ukrainian Studies* 14(1/2) June 1990: 7–83; "Rus'ka metryka: Knyhy pol's'koï koronnoï kantseliariï dlia ukraïns'kykh zemel', 1569–1673 rr.," *Ukraïns'kyi istorychnyi zhurnal* 1989 (5): 52–62, and numerous other articles on related groups of records.

and the archival issues involved in archival transfers in connection with the resettlement of ethnic populations; in this connection I benefited from consultations with specialists such as the late Stefan Inglot and other Polish colleagues who had been resettled from Lviv.

The late Professor Aleksander Gieysztor, a friend and colleague since his directorship of the Institute of History at the University of Warsaw, and later as director of the Royal Castle Museum and president of the Polish Academy of Sciences, was helpful in various phases of my study; it is my deepest regret that he did not live to scrutinize the present volume, which he had encouraged and several chapters of which we had discussed in earlier drafts.

My most recent IREX travel grant to Poland (fall 1999) gave me an opportunity to review a number of issues and verify details, especially for Chapter 11 on Polish-Ukrainian restitution issues. Among those of particular help with arrangements and consultations during that trip, as relevant for my present study, were Professor Wojciech Kowalski of the University of Silesia, Maciej Matwijów and his colleagues in the Manuscript Department of the Ossolineum, Hanna Laskarzewska of the Biblioteka Narodowa, and Władysław Stępniak of the State Archival Directorate. Dutch musicologist Willem de Vries, who accompanied me on most of that venture, shares many of my research interests on the lost and displaced European cultural legacy and availed me of the benefits of his parallel research on these matters.

Opportunities to survey Ukrainian-related sources in the archives of Hungary, the Czech Republic, and Romania have increased my base of information about developments there. Various IREX research grants made possible my research trips in many cases. Most particularly, research travel in Czechoslovakia and Poland in the summer of 1991 with Ukrainian colleagues opened up many more details about the fate of seized and evacuated Ukrainian archives and other cultural treasures.[26] Our archival work in Czechoslovakia owed much to the good auspices of the national archives, then headed by Oldřich Sládek, who kindly helped with arrangements for our research, as did Professor Ivan Hlaváček, who heads the chair for archival studies and auxiliary historical disciplines at Charles University. In Prague, thanks to the help of the knowledgeable archivist Raisa Machatková, we found more details about the Ukrainian Historical Cabinet and other Ukrainian collections in Prague before their transfer to Kyiv after the war. The director of the Slavonic Library (Slovanská knihovna), Milena Klimová,

---

[26]   See my report (with H. V. Boriak and N. M. Iakovenko), "Memorial'na arkheohrafichna ekspedytsiia po Chekho-Slovachchyni: Slidamy kul'turnykh tsinnostei, vyvezenykh z Ukraïny pid chas Druhoï svitovoï viiny," *Ukraïns'kyi arkheohrafichnyi shchorichnyk*, n.s. 2 (1993): 437–45.

was helpful in trying to clarify details of the transferred RZIA and UIK library materials. My participation in the recent directory of holdings relating to the Austro-Hungarian Empire added still another perspective.[27]

Research travel in Germany in 1991 was funded in part by an NEH research travel grant, and subsequent research travel in Germany during 1993 and 1994 was funded by a collaborative grant from the American Council of Learned Societies in association with the Center for Eastern Research (Ostforschungstelle) of the University of Bremen. I am grateful to Professor Wolfgang Eichwede, who directs that center, for involving me and my Ukrainian collaborators in his research program on World War II cultural displacements. Several associates in the Bremen project were helpful in facilitating our research at various stages, including Gabriele Freitag, Andreas Grenzer, Ulrike Hartung, Anja Heuss, and Marlene Hiller.

Research in the German Bundesarchiv was considerably facilitated by several archivists there, among whom Kai von Jena and Wilhelm Lenz deserve special thanks. I also appreciate numerous discussions of displaced archives and restitution problems with Bundesarchiv President Professor Friedrich Kahlenberg. When still a graduate student at the University of Hamburg, Ralf Bartoleit served as my research assistant in both the Bundesarchiv and the Archive of the German Foreign Ministry, and he also assisted me during the summer of 1990 in Kyiv, when we first had a chance to work through the records of the Einsatzstab Reichsleiter Rosenberg and the Provincial Authority for Archives, Libraries, and Museums (LV ABM) under the Reich Commissariat Ukraine (RKU). I appreciate the assistance of the late Professor Hans Torke and Klaus Goldmann with arrangements in Berlin, and Klaus Oldenhage in Potsdam. Markus Wehner served ably as my research assistant there.

In Paris, I am grateful for consultations at the National Archives about holdings and restitution issues with Chantal de Bonazzi and Paule René-Bazin. Archivists at the Centre du Documentation Juive Contemporaine (CDJC) were attentive to my research needs there, among the files of the Einsatzstab Reichsleiter Rosenberg. Helène Kaplan, now retired from the Bibliothèque de Documentation Internationale Contemporaine (BDIC), provided considerable assistance during my Paris visits, as well as the interest we share in the fate of the Turgenev Library.

Research on World War II and restitution developments in Washington, DC, was funded by a research grant from the Kennan Institute for Advanced

---

[27] See P. K. Grimsted, "Ukraine," in *A Guide to East-Central European Archives*, ed. Charles W. Ingrao (Houston, Rice University Press, 1998), pp. 171–200 [=*Austrian History Yearbook* 29(2) 1998].

Russian Studies in 1994, and I had several later opportunities for research in the U.S. National Archives, especially in the OMGUS and U.S. restitution records, both there and in Koblenz. I am grateful for the assistance of archivists Robert Wolff, Timothy Mulligan, Robin Cooksen, Richard Boylan, Rebecca Collier, and most recently Gregory Bradsher. Assistant Archivist Michael Kurtz, and former Acting Archivist Trudy Peterson, took time out of their busy schedules on many occasions to discuss issues regarding U.S. restitution policies and related arrangements. In Washington, I also benefited from discussions with specialists in the U.S. Holocaust Memorial Museum, Brewster Chamberlain and Carl Modig, and, most recently, in connection with the RSHA records, Jürgen Matthäus. Konstantin Akinsha, Lynn Nicholas, and Elizabeth Simpson have all been generous in time and sharing with me their findings in regard to displaced cultural treasures and restitution issues.

The rapid changes in the legal and political situation of archival issues in Ukraine and Russia have resulted in a corresponding need to update and expand my coverage, especially since parts of the present study were first completed in late 1993 and early 1994. The second part was added, initially as a single chapter in early 1995, but subsequently expanded to the series of chapters as now presented. It was continuously updated as the book was being prepared for publication throughout 1999; we were forced to select December 1999 as the cut-off point for new material so that the editorial process could be completed. All of the updating, serial revision, and reediting would make this an exceedingly difficult book for any editor. HURI's director of publications, Robert De Lossa, took over the editing from a junior colleague and has responded with unusual acumen, molding my oft-changing and unruly text with his skilful refinements. Dr. Lubomyr Hajda—a long-time friend and one-time research assistant—helped with the final proofing, for which I am grateful.

References are provided at several points to a number of my related studies still under way, although ultimate publication details are not yet available in all cases. With this in mind, I and my HURI publication sponsors would welcome comments and critical response to this still preliminary and ongoing presentation. The address for editorial correspondence is to be found on the copyright page.

PKG

Cambridge, MA

May 2000

POSTSCRIPT

During the final stages of the book's long editorial process, a number of significant events and developments occurred that potentially impact the text in various ways. These include the first international conference in Moscow on displaced cultural treasures (April 2000); a new Russian law amending the April 1998 law nationalizing Soviet "spoils of war" (May 2000); an international forum sponsored by the Council of Europe in Vilnius on Holocaust-era cultural assets (October 2000); two more Russian archival restitution transfers to France (March and October 2000), which included almost all of the Soviet-captured Masonic and Jewish archives of French provenance in Moscow; the first Russian transfer of books to France from the Turgenev Library in Paris (December 2000); a Ukrainian-German agreement signed for the return of the Sing-Akademie collection to Berlin (January 2001), and a premiere of one of its musical scores in Boston (March 2001); Russian restitution from the Hermitage of some of the fragmentary frescoes of St. Michael of the Golden Domes (February 2001); new Russian archival restitution agreements signed with Belgium and Greece; and major progress in archival restitution negotiations between Ukraine and Poland, to name but a few. A number of significant new publications and new websites reveal fresh data and new approaches that require appraisal in the context of this study. Given the on-going and ever-changing nature of international restitution politics, a book of this breadth would never see the light of day if it were constantly revised to reflect every last development. In order to bridge any gap that results from revision or expansion that could not be undertaken at the last minute, and to reflect the author's further studies in these areas, the website of the Ukrainian Research Institute will provide a link at its description of the present book relevant for new literature that expands on what is presented here.

—PKG March 2001

INTRODUCTION

Reconstituting the Archival Heritage of Ukraine: The Historical and Ideological Context

"Does Ukraine Have a History?"

Mark von Hagen opened a roundtable discussion of Ukrainian history in the Fall 1995 *Slavic Review* with an article bearing this controversial and provocative title.[1] The question of whether *any* nation "has a history" cannot be fully answered without turning to its archives, because it is precisely a nation's archives that are simultaneously the concrete record and the abstract reflection of its historical development. Due to the particular history of Ukraine and the lasting effects there of repeated wars and imperial domination, von Hagen's question must be broadened: *"Does Ukraine have an archival heritage?"* Historians in newly independent Ukraine thus face a double burden that is forcing them to tackle the intellectual problems of reconstituting the archival heritage of Ukraine at the very same time that they must fundamentally reassess the national history received from the Soviet period.[2]

For Ukraine, the preservation and dispersal of the archival heritage records and reflects the dispersal of the Ukrainian nation—as well as the

---

[1] Mark von Hagen, "Does Ukraine Have a History?" *Slavic Review* 54(3) Fall 1995: 658–73. That article is followed in the discussion by George G. Grabowicz, "Ukrainian Studies: Framing the Contexts," pp. 674–90, with replies by Andreas Kappeler, "Ukrainian History from a German Perspective," pp. 691–701; Iaroslav Isaievych, "Ukrainian Studies—Exceptional or Merely Exemplary?" pp. 702–708; Serhii M. Plokhy, "The History of a 'Non-Historical' Nation: Notes on the Nature and Current Problems of Ukrainian Historiography," pp. 709–16; and Yuri Slezkine, "Can We Have Our Nation-State and Eat It Too?" pp. 717–19.

[2] As witnessed by recent archeographic efforts within the historical community there. For a recent perspective on these issues see the monograph by Hennadii Boriak, *Natsional'na arkhivna spadshchyna Ukraïny ta derzhavnyi reiestr "Arkheohrafichna Ukraïnika": Arkhivni dokumental'ni resursy ta naukovo-informatsiini systemy* (Kyiv: NAN; IAUD; IR TsNB; HAU, 1995).

discontinuity and fragmentation of its history. Ukraine in its present borders was established as a result of a series of Soviet fiats, with frontiers that evolved with the implementation of Soviet political dictates and imperial pretensions. This configuration differs sharply from what "Little Russia" (*Rus.* Malorossiia) or the "Southwest Land" (Iugo-zapadnyi krai) was as part of the pre-revolutionary Russian Empire. The transformation of *Kiev,* "the Mother of Rus'" into *Kyiv,* the capital of a budding independent nation, requires sophisticated and multi-faceted historical analysis. There is a basic contradiction in the fact that Ukrainian archivists strive to identify and describe the Ukrainian archival and manuscript heritage as both distinct from and, in many instances, part of the common heritage of the previous imperial regimes that governed various parts of Ukraine's territory. The ability to delineate this distinction and commonality will create for future generations a source base with which to write and analyze a new history of Ukraine. Moreover, those in the forefront of the new historical awakening realize that balanced interpretations of Ukrainian history will come only from extensive exploration of hitherto suppressed archival sources and forbidden literature.

With the collapse of the Soviet communist-controlled system, archives in Ukraine and Russia are opening their doors, and the contents of Soviet era library "special collections" (*Rus. spetskhrany*) and archival "Secret" and "Special Secret Divisions" (*Rus. osobye spetsotdely*) are being released to public scrutiny to an extent never dreamed possible a decade ago.[3] Along with this, efforts are under way to reunite Ukrainian culture and archives at home with lost or exiled components in the Ukrainian diaspora.

Centuries of ideologically-oriented suppression and distortion of Ukrainian history, misinformation about the sources on which its history should be based, and repression of those who could have prepared it, have left few researchers and archivists adequately prepared for the task. Accordingly, major efforts in reeducation are desperately needed. During the Soviet period, fewer effective finding aids and source publications were issued in Ukraine than in Russia. This is indicative of the ways in which the intellectual impact of the Soviet era has been more disastrous for Ukraine than for Russia. Furthermore, for modern archives and libraries it is not

---

[3]   For a general appraisal of the current post-Soviet Russian archival scene, see my *Archives of Russia Seven Years After—"Purveyors of Sensations" or "Shadows Cast to the Past"?* (Washington, DC, 1998) [=*CWIHP Working Paper,* 20]. See also my earlier survey "Russian Archives in Transition: Caught between Political Crossfire and Economic Crisis," *American Archivist* 56 (Fall 1993): 614–62; and "Beyond Perestroika: Soviet-Area Archives after the August Coup," *American Archivist* 55 (Winter 1992): 94–124.

enough simply to open their doors to the outside world, but it is equally crucial to provide what Western archivists would call "intellectual access"—the reference systems that will identify and guide researchers to appropriate sources.[4] With this in mind, it is remarkable that even in the first decade after independence no new guides to Ukrainian state archives have appeared.

The reconstitution of the national archival heritage cannot occur in the abstract without a dedicated archival information system to describe it both at home and abroad. Archival claims and retrieval cannot and should not precede description. Professional description must identify provenance, migration, and the circumstances of alienation, among other elements. Preparation of information systems and related reference aids, however, must proceed as part of a more general effort to reform the archival administrative system in line with post-Soviet public needs. This means developing new professional archival cadres and reorienting historical thinking and research methodology within broader historiographic perspectives.

The Revival of Archeography and the History of Archives

Pre-revolutionary Russocentric Political Roots. One of the most essential first steps here is the revival of the pre-revolutionary tradition of archeography as the scholarly work of identifying, collecting, describing, and publishing manuscripts and other historical sources. This must include those sources outside Ukraine as well as those within.[5] In pre-revolutionary Ukrainian territories under the Russian Empire, archeographic traditions and the creation (or non-creation) of archives in Ukraine, as was the case with other phases of political and cultural life, were deeply affected by Russian imperial ideology and the politics of russification. Those effects were analyzed recently in connection with the 150th anniversary of the Kyiv Archeographic Commission. In 1843, the Russian governor-general of Kyiv Gubernia, Dmitrii Gavrilovich Bibikov, in advocating the Commission's establishment, wrote:

---

[4]   P. K. Grimsted, *Intellectual Access to Soviet-Area Archives: What Is to Be Done?* (Princeton: IREX, 1992). See especially the chapter on archival repression in the 1930s, and further discussion by Boriak, *Natsional'na arkhivna spadshchyna Ukraïny.* See also the updated discussion of reference systems in Grimsted, "Increasing Reference Access to Post-1991 Russian Archives," *Slavic Review* 56(4) Winter 1997: 718–59.

[5]   See the explanatory note in the Preface above, p. xxx, fn. 4.

> The main purpose of the Kyiv Commission for the Analysis of
> Early Acts…consists of following the path of historical research,
> to encourage the return to Russian nationality in South-West
> Russia and Lithuania, which has been weakened by Catholic
> propaganda and Polish patriotism.[6]

The Kyiv Archive of Early Record Books was founded a decade later in
1852. It had as its primary function the protection, appropriate utilization, and
the prevention of fraud using the early court record books from the Right-
Bank Ukrainian lands that had been part of the Polish-Lithuanian
Commonwealth.[7] The politics of the creation and maintenance of nineteenth-
century institutions such as this—with the government utilization of
archeography and archives to further the Russian imperial policy of "Official
Nationality"—had a direct bearing on future archival developments in the
Russian and Soviet empires. This is an area that begs for more careful
consideration and research both in Russia and Ukraine.[8]

Bureaucratic Roots under the Austro-Hungarian Empire. Archival
traditions were much stronger and much less politicized in western Ukraine.
Immediately after the Partitions of the Polish-Lithuanian Commonwealth
brought Polish and Ukrainian lands under Austrian domination, archives
were organized in Lviv to consolidate the local records of judicial and
administrative authorities from throughout the Polish lands variously called
Ruthenia or Halych (Ruś, Galicja). Established in 1784, the Galician Archive

---

[6]   See my "Archeography in the Service of Imperial Policy: The Foundation of the
Kiev Archeographic Commission and the Kiev Central Archive of Early Record
Books," *Harvard Ukrainian Studies* 17(1–2) June 1993: 34.

[7]   Ibid., pp. 27–44. Further details are revealed in the monograph by Oleh I.
Zhurba, *Kyïvs'ka Arkheohrafichna komisiia: Narys istoriï i diial'nosti* (Kyiv, 1993).
See also Zhurba, "Problemy ta perspektyvy doslidzhennia diial'nosti Kyïvs'koï
arkheohrafichnoï komisiï," in *Materialy iuvileinoï konferentsiï, prysviachenoï 150-
richchiu Kyïvs'koï arkheohrafichnoï komisiï (Kyïv, Sedniv, 18–21 zhovtnia 1993 r.),*
ed. Pavlo Sokhan' and Hennadii Boriak (Kyiv, 1997), pp. 34–50 [="Problemy
edytsiinoï ta kameral'noï arkheohrafiï: Istoriia, teoriia, metodyka," 30].

[8]   I personally confronted the difficulties that the Russian archival establishment is
having in dealing with such analysis, when a translation of my article was turned
down by the Moscow editors of *Arkheograficheskii ezhegodnik* as being "too
political." A similar situation with some present-day Ukrainian specialists occurred
when I was attacked for my "politicization" of nineteenth-century archeographic
efforts in Ukraine when I presented my paper at the 1993 conference honoring the
150th anniversary in Sedniv (see preceding note).

for Early Castle- and Land-Court Records (*Lat.*, Caesareo-regium antiquorum actorum terrestrium et castrensium galiciensium tum corroborationis documentorum officium) was commonly known as the Bernardine Archive, since it occupied the former Bernardine Monastery. It became what is now the oldest continuous archive in Ukraine. Archives for municipal records continued the strong tradition already established. Bureaucratic authority introduced preservation in controlled archival facilities and thorough description of existing records. Language use for the archives first continued in Latin, as it had been during the Polish period, but then gradually shifted to German. Polish and Ukrainian also remained official languages of administration—in contrast to the situation in eastern Ukraine, where russification was the official policy for archives or archeographic operations. When the Bernardine Archive was reorganized in 1878, it had an official Polish as well as German name. The influence of Western historical and archeographic traditions brought serious, professional descriptive practices to archives and manuscript collections alike. These were continued under Polish rule, when the Galician Crownland became part of the newly established Polish Republic. In practice, however, Polish or Polish-related records and collections were strongly favored over Ukrainian ones in what was then called Eastern Little Poland (Małopolska Wschodnia). Ukrainian archives and manuscript collections, while not repressed, largely went undescribed in western Ukraine.

Sovietization with Political and Ideological Control. After the 1917 revolutions in eastern Ukraine, archeographic traditions and archives throughout the common "Soviet Fatherland" were even more subject to ideological control, since they were part and parcel of a communist historical orthodoxy that predicated political control over the archival system.[9] Under the Soviet regime, archival and library reference systems were organized to promote the so-called "unified Soviet masses" (*narod*). When Lenin issued his 1918 decree "On the Reorganization and Centralization of Archival

---

[9]   On the corresponding development of archeography in Russia and the USSR, see two recent articles by the head of the Department of Archival Affairs and Archeography at the Historico-Archival Institute of the Russian State University for the Humanities (IAI RGGU)—Aleksandr D. Stepanskii, "Arkheografiia: Termin, ob″ekt, predmet," *Otechestvennye arkhivy* 1996 (3): 16–25; and his earlier article, "K 225-letiiu russkoi arkheografii," *Otechestvennye arkhivy* 1992 (6): 16–24. Although the author does not elaborate on the political and ideological overtones often associated with the discipline, he cites a number of other important traditional Russian and Soviet theoretical and practical writings on the subject.

Affairs" (which centralized Russian archives and established a strong centralized agency to administer them), he recognized the importance of archives to the new Bolshevik regime in terms of political and ideological information control over historical records. The decree was raised to mythic proportions in subsequent decades and became the cornerstone of Soviet archival theory and practice.[10]

As archives were brought under strict state control during the 1920s, the non-Russian republics initially saw a brief decade of national regeneration. The official "ukrainianization" policy of that period saw the exiled historian and political leader Mykhailo Hrushevs'kyi return to Ukraine and contribute to the flowering of Ukrainian historical scholarship and many important archeographic achievements. Cultured, well-educated archival leaders still knew foreign languages and were part of the world intellectual community. Archival transfers from Moscow enriched repositories in Ukraine with some important components of the Ukrainian archival heritage that had been taken to the metropolis under imperial Russian rule.

The rise of Stalin and consolidation of his totalitarian rule changed this. Archives were not exempt from Stalin's imposition of narrow Marxist-Leninist ideological restraints on historical scholarship and on all other phases of intellectual and academic life. During the 1930s, archives were increasingly forced to confine their reference functions to strict Party guidelines, predicated on Marxist-Leninist conceptions of history. The non-Russian republics were particularly hard hit by the purge of "bourgeois nationalists" in connection with forced russification and the outlawing of archival work in native languages.

Ukraine was more vulnerable than other parts of the USSR, because resistance to collectivization led to extreme national repression. During the early 1930s, the purge of Hrushevs'kyi and other leading historians was paralleled by the abolishment of the Archeographic Commission and firing of well-trained, experienced archivists. Archivists fluent in foreign languages were particularly suspect.[11] Archivists who professionally described sources—rather than showing how a given group of documents portrayed the struggle against the ruling class or revealed "enemies of the regime"—were

---

[10] See my "Lenin's Archival Decree of 1918: The Bolshevik Legacy for Soviet Archival Theory and Practice," *American Archivist* 45(4) Fall 1982: 429–43, which cites many Soviet publications on the subject.

[11] On the All-Union level, see the article by Russian archivist A. P. Pshenichnyi, "Repressii arkhivistov v 1930-kh godakh," *Sovetskie arkhivy* 1988 (6): 44–48, but the author did not begin to reveal the extent of archival purges in Ukraine and made no attempt to put them in a broader intellectual context.

purged. Many types of records not pertaining to Party themes simply were not described or their inherent nature and provenance not recorded. Hence few adequate reference tools are available from that period.

Official archival reports from the 1930s in Ukraine reflect the extent of archival purges. A prime example of the hysteria and anti-scholarly attitudes generated from within official circles is seen in a 1934 Ukrainian Archival Administration report that complained, in classical Soviet jargon, that, "[current] scholarly publications [are] completely inadequately organized for the use of documents [by those who have] the concrete aim of unmitigated assistance to the Party [and this is] due to remaining counterrevolutionary bourgeois-nationalist and Trotskyite contrabands on the historical front."[12] Denunciations of individual archivists for the sins of inappropriate description of archival documents mirror the mentality and horror stories of the Moscow show trials. A 1937 "Report on the Situation of Archival Affairs in the UkrSSR" complained about the "bourgeois-nationalist orientation" brought about by "the circle of Enemies of the People, Trotskyites, and bourgeois-nationalists."[13] Purges were followed by more purges.

A prime example of this vicious cycle is the tragic fate of the Kyiv Archive of Early Acts—the major historical archive for records of Right-Bank Ukraine prior to the nineteenth-century. During the 1920s it had grown to a prominent position in Ukrainian historical scholarship. Its purge began in January 1931 with the arrest of its director, Viktor Romanovs'kyi, and another senior archivist.[14] By the end of 1934, its entire staff of competent historian-archivists had been eliminated, including its last director to be a qualified as a historian, Oleksander Ohloblyn. He was branded as "the ring leader of the Ukrainian nationalist, counter-revolutionary club."[15] Among their crimes, one archivist "prepared card files with document-by-document descriptions without regard for revolutionary struggles"; another "permitted the use of documents in the archive by individuals who were against collectivization in agriculture"; while still another permitted an exhibit of documents portraying seventeenth-century religious struggles between Catholics and Orthodox "without adequate attention to class differentiation."[16] An inspector's report mentioned that by 1938, further

12 TsDAVO, 14/1/1733, fol. 28.
13 TsDAVO, 14/1/1754, fol. 6–6v.
14 TsDAVO, 14/1/1318.
15 "Vysnovky pro VUTsADA" (3.II.1934), TsDAVO, 14/1/1729, fols. 76, 77, 78, and 80.
16 Ibid. Subsequent reports—all in Russian—repeat many of the same points. The 1934 report (file no. 1733, fol. 7), among others, explains the reasons for Ohloblyn's dismissal. The official reason for dismissal was later quoted in an émigré publication

descriptive work was impossible on the early records in the archive, because
no one in the archive knew Latin or Polish.[17] A 1941 report (in Russian) lists
only five scientific workers remaining in the archive, all with favorable Party
credentials, but none of whom had the adequate experience, historical
training, or knowledge of the requisite languages needed to complete the
planned program of archival description.[18]

An official textbook published by Glavarkhiv in Moscow in 1940, not
surprisingly attempted to put a positive spin on the situation:

> The improved condition of state archives in the years of the
> Stalinist Constitution contributed to the stature and improved staff
> of archival workers.
>
> Under the direction of Party and Soviet organizations archival
> agencies reviewed the cadres of workers and fired from the
> archives the disguised enemies of the people, and also people who
> were not guaranteeing positive archival development. Archival
> agencies were filled with new cadres of workers from the ranks of
> the Party and Komsomol, and from among non-Party Bolshe-
> viks.[19]

Control over archives was deemed so important under Stalin that in 1938
the State Archival Administration was shifted to the People's Commissariat
for Internal Affairs (NKVD), under the direction of Stalin's security
henchman, Lavrentii Beria. As phrased in the contemporary Glavarkhiv
textbook:

> The transfer of the entire state archival fortune to the conduct of
> the most important political agency of the USSR demonstrated the
> high worth which Party and government leadership held archival
> development. In the conditions of capitalistic encirclement and
> preparations for the capitalistic offensive on the USSR...the use
> of archival documents acquired a tremendous political signifi-
> cance.

---

by Vasyl′ Omel′chenko, as "introducing bourgeois nationalism into the scientific
work of the archive." See his "Oleksander Ohloblyn (zhyttia i diial′nist′)," in *Zbirnyk
na poshanu prof. d-ra Oleksandra Ohloblyna/Collected Essays in Honor of Professor
Alexander Ohloblyn* (New York, 1977), p. 59 [=Ukraïns′ka Vil′na Akademiia Nauk u
SShA, *Naukovyi zbirnyk* 3].

[17] TsDAVO, 14/1/1842, fol. 20. See also an additional report from the late 1930s,
TsDAVO, 14/1/1930, fols. 75–83.

[18] As to their experience, one had been hired in 1935, one in 1938, and the
remaining three in 1940—TsDAVO, 14/1/1930, fol. 83.

[19] A. V. Chernov, *Istoriia i organizatsiia arkhivnogo dela v SSSR (Kratkii ocherk)*,
ed. D. S. Baburin (Moscow: GAU NKVD SSSR, 1940), p. 222.

> Under the direction of the renowned Soviet intelligence services in protecting the interests of the Soviet people, archival agencies of the USSR extracted still greater results in their daily practical work, liquidating the after effects of spoilers in the archives and exposing mortal enemies of the Party and people.[20]

Reference priorities were dramatically shifted in many archives. Professional archival description and normal reference work virtually came to a halt, as archival efforts under the NKVD were diverted to operational security activities to aid in the bitter repression and reign of terror of the Stalinist years. The extent of repressive politicization and control over archives in the Stalin period is again revealed in the introduction to the official 1940 textbook for archivists:

> Archival workers must know to whom and for what they give out archival documents or information from them, and they must meticulously verify everything that is taken out of the archive. They must be certain that documents communicated do not fall into the hands of enemies of the people and will not be used for harmful purposes.
>
> An archival worker must not be needlessly talkative and must not reveal to all and everyone what he does in the archive and what is held in the archive. That might be used by the enemy and might reveal needed information to him.
>
> Every Soviet archival worker must understand that great state importance is entrusted to him and with integrity justify the trust placed in him.[21]

The tragic consequences of the liquidation of a generation of professionally trained historians and archivists were inadequate reference work in the archives and, perhaps more importantly, that no one was left to train younger specialists. The suppression of professional archival standards thus had a multiplying effect on subsequent generations of Soviet and present-day archivists.

More immediately for our current analysis, these Soviet traditions directly affected archival developments during World War II, including evacuation and preservation priorities, and the incentives for archival retrieval and "operational" work in the aftermath of war that will come to the forefront in the second part of this study. The reflection of that politico-ideological context needs to be understood in considering the archival legacy and descriptive parameters today.

---

[20] Chernov, *Istoriia i organizatsiia arkhivnogo dela*, p. 226.
[21] Ibid., p. 14.

Archives and the Succession of States

With the fall of empires and the process of decolonization, many problems arise in the succession of States in relation to state property, including cultural property, held in the metropolis. Archives often assume a relatively minor role in the public consciousness. A report of the Director General of UNESCO attempts to right the balance by asserting their real importance:

> Archives are universally recognized as an essential part of the heritage of every national community. Since they are indispensable in the development of national awareness and identity, they constitute a basic part of the cultural property of States.[22]

An earlier statement in connection with a report on archival claims prepared for UNESCO in 1977 included the further explanation that,

> ...[archives] not only document the historical, cultural and economic development of a country and provide a basis for a national identity; they are also a basic source of evidence needed to assert the rights of individual citizens.[23]

The Special Rapporteur of the International Law Commission (ILC) of the United Nations General Assembly went a step further in a 1976 report, which was again repeated in the 1978 UNESCO report:

> ...while one can conceive of a State without a navy, for example, it is impossible to imagine one without a currency...and without archives...which constitute...those kinds of State property which are most essential and most widespread—so much so that they can be said to derive from the very existence of the State.

---

[22]   *Report of the Director General on the Study Regarding Problems involved in the Transfer of Documents from Archives in the Territory of Certain Countries to the Country of Their Origin*, UNESCO General Conference Twentieth Session (Paris, 1978) (20 C/102), §7. [Reprinted below in Appendix I.] An earlier version of the statement appeared in the text prepared by ICA Secretary-General Charles Kecskeméti, *Archival Claims: Preliminary Study on the Principles and Criteria to Be Applied in Negotiations* (Paris: UNESCO, 1977) (PGI-77/WS/1), p. 7. The quoted paragraph comes from the *Final Report* of the "Consultation group to prepare a report on the possibility of transferring documents from archives constituted within the territory of other countries, Paris, 16–18 March 1976" (Paris: UNESCO, 1976) (CC-76/WS/9), dated 1 April 1976, p. 2.

[23]   Kecskeméti, *Archival Claims*, p. 7.

...Secret or public, [archives] constitute a heritage and a public
property which the State generally makes sure is inalienable and
imprescriptible.[24]

In the context of the succession of States in the wake of the dissolution of
the Soviet Union, archives raise unique questions that need to be dealt with as
a special category of state and cultural property, subject to international legal
precedents and accepted professional norms. In the words of the UNESCO
report, "archives have an official and legal status different from that of most
types of cultural property."[25] Even the above-quoted comment regarding a
navy becomes appropriate at a time when Ukrainian archivists have
pretensions on the records of the Black Sea Fleet and other naval records that
were taken from Ukraine to Russia during imperial Russian and Soviet rule.
As the ILC Special Rapporteur further emphasizes, "archives...may prove to
be indispensable both to the successor State and to the predecessor State, and
owing to their nature they cannot be divided or split up..."[26]

The Fragmented Archival Heritage of Ukraine. Archival problems are
more complicated for successor States such as Ukraine that have long been
subject to imperial rule.[27] The process of identifying the archival heritage of
Ukraine is much more complex than for those newly independent states that
had a significant historical tradition of self-rule before they were annexed by
the Russian Empire or Soviet Union. Consider also the question of physical
space: the present territory of independent Ukraine has constituted a single
administrative entity only since 1954—never before that. It is therefore
difficult to identify the present configuration of Ukraine with a "nation"

---

[24] *Eighth report on succession of States in respect of matters other than treaties:
Draft articles with commentaries on succession to State property*, by Mohammed
Bedjaoui, Special Rapporteur (A/CN.4/292, and A/CN.4/322), as quoted by
Kecskeméti, *Archival Claims*, p. 7, and again in the *Report of the Director General*,
UNESCO (1978; 20 C/102), §10, §11. See also Bedjaoui's analysis and repeated
quotes from earlier UNESCO reports presented in a 1979 report, published in
Yearbook of the International Law Commission, 1979 (New York, 1981), II, pt. 2,
pp. 77–78. (Reprinted below as Appendix I.)

[25] As quoted by Kecskeméti, *Archival Claims*, p. 7, and again in the *Report of the
Director General*, UNESCO (1978; 20 C/102), §9.

[26] Bedjaoui as quoted in *Yearbook ILC, 1979*, II, pt. 2, pp. 77–78.

[27] See my earlier 1986 discussion of these problems in "The Archival Legacy of the
Soviet Ukraine: Problems of Tracing the Documentary Records of a Divided Nation,"
Cahiers du Monde russe et soviétique 28 (January–March 1987): 95–108.

because that configuration was created by external force, rather than by the natural historical outgrowth of a nation-state. The Baltic republics had known independence during the interwar period and made considerable strides to develop their own national archival systems. Present-day Ukraine has no such political, territorial, or archival precedents. Hence, the independent process of Ukrainian archival development is beginning on the basis of the Soviet-imposed system, together with the remnants of imperial Russian and Polish precedents, with the accretion of other precedents in different regions.

Because the present Ukrainian lands were subject over the centuries to a variety of political regimes ruling from political centers outside Ukraine itself, many of the most important groups of state archival records pertaining to—and, in some cases, of provenance in—present-day Ukraine are located outside Ukrainian borders. For Ukraine it is not just a matter of looking first and foremost to Russia and the present Russian federal archives for historical and contemporary records. Archival perspectives also need to encompass deposits in the bordering states and former imperial capitals of Poland, Austria, Hungary, the now separate Czech and Slovak republics, Romania, and Turkey—that is, in all the successor States to the major powers that earlier governed the lands that now constitute Ukraine.

From a technical archival standpoint this means a tremendous fragmentation and dispersal of records—both those produced by state and societal functions within Ukrainian lands and those pertaining to Ukrainian history. It also means that records of direct Ukrainian pertinence have been the result of, and long subject to, divergent record-keeping practices and archival traditions. Compare, for instance, the nature of the records from Muscovite and later Russian Imperial administration in eastern Ukraine, with those created under Hungarian and later Czech rule in Transcarpathia, with those created under Austrian (and later Austro-Hungarian) imperial rule in Galicia and Bukovyna, with Romanian records from Northern Bukovyna when that area was part of the interwar Romanian state, and with Turkic and Tatar records from those regions that formed part of the Crimean Khanate and the Ottoman Empire. Of course, Polish archival traditions are the strongest and most complicated to unravel, especially in western Ukraine (and for several centuries in central or right-bank Ukraine). This diversity makes it necessary for scholars and archivists dealing with the Ukrainian archival legacy to know not only the history and languages of those past-governing countries, but also to be familiar with their record-keeping and archival practices.

Sovietized Archival Description in Ukraine. To make matters even more complicated, many such records are now arranged and described as part of the central records of those external political regimes that served as the metropolis. They were subject to the archival theory and practices of their foreign rulers and to the imposition of standards that often sought to de-emphasize and at times completely suppress any specifically Ukrainian elements. Even at a most basic level, the term "Ukraine" was hardly permitted under the Russian Empire before 1905. Subsequent Soviet archival administration imposed a centralized command system and superimposed a standardized arrangement and descriptive norms on the complex, multi-faceted archival records that were retained in Ukraine. On the positive side, such developments now provide a standardized base that makes computerized information systems much easier to establish than in countries such as the United States that never practiced standardized archival description before the late 1980s. Conversely, the Soviet political and ideological standards were not sensitive to Ukraine's multinational and multilingual archival legacy. Linguistic and terminological norms instilled in the description of all archival holdings now make it difficult to identify earlier groups of multi-lingual records and their multi-ethnic creating agencies.

As part of the standardized process, earlier institutional names for creating agencies were roughly translated into sovietized Ukrainian equivalents, and then later listed only in sovietized Russian forms, thus obliterating their original German, Polish, Hungarian, Romanian, or Czech names. For example, the only available reference directory of western Ukrainian state institutions for the period before 1939, published in 1955 in Lviv *only* in Russian, gives only a few parenthetical citations to original Polish or German forms (often truncated and inaccurate) of institutional names. It completely omits their earlier official Ukrainian versions such as those used under Austrian and Polish rule. By contrast, the Austrians and Poles had adopted bilingual or even trilingual forms for official state usage in Ukrainian territory.[28]

During the 1980s, the only printed guides to Ukrainian oblast archives were issued in the Russian language alone, with no cross-references to institutional names in their original language or even to their contemporary official Ukrainian forms. The 1983 guide to the Ivano-Frankivsk (*earlier Ukr.* Stanyslaviv) Oblast State Archive is a prime example of the incongruity of introducing Russian institutional names in an area where Russian was never even a second language of government before 1939.[29] The Soviet

---

[28] *Uchrezhdeniia Zapadnoi Ukrainy do vossoedineniia ee v edinom ukrainskom sovetskom sotsialisticheskom gosudarstve: Spravochnik*, ed. I. L. Butych and V. I. Strel'skii (Lviv: Izd-vo LGU, 1955).

[29] *Gosudarstvennyi arkhiv Ivano-Frankovskoi oblasti: Putevoditel'*, 2nd ed., compiled by V. I. Gritsenko et al. (Kyiv: GAU pri SM UkrSSR, 1983). Before 1939

Russian variants of the names for record groups, or *fonds* as they are designated in Soviet usage,[30] are virtually unrecognizable in terms of the official names of the creating agencies found in original documents. The process of sovietization and russification accordingly made it more difficult to find and identify records in those regions and to relate local records with contiguous files created or remaining outside the borders of Ukraine.

Cold War Isolation. The imposition of Party and NKVD cadres to replace well-educated historians and professional archivists, together with Soviet arrangement and descriptive standards, were only two aspects of the problem. Even more serious for scholarship, the "iron curtain" that separated Ukraine from the West had deep historiographic and archival repercussions by tightening Ukrainian dependence on intellectual standards established in Moscow and propagated through the dominant Soviet system. Normal research visits to Poland, Czechoslovakia, Turkey, or other relevant archives were virtually impossible for all but a chosen few Ukrainian researchers and archivists. Participation in international archival conferences was rare for Ukrainian representatives. Hence, published scholarship within Ukraine remained isolated from many crucial sources and many important components of Ukrainian culture and political life in emigration. By the same token, during the Cold War decades, Western scholars—including Ukrainian émigrés—were limited in their knowledge of, and access to, archives in Soviet Ukraine. As a result, considerable scholarship published abroad regarding Ukraine, and the Soviet Union more generally, was based only on limited holdings in foreign archives.

Archival control and restrictions on access directly affected public knowledge about many extant parts of the Ukrainian archival legacy. Even more tragically, both domestic and diaspora Ukrainian scholarship—and hence the writing of the history of Ukraine—has been isolated from the foreign and émigré archival Ucrainica that been held in top secret archives in Kyiv. During the Soviet regime public availability of information about émigré archival Ucrainica abroad was minimal; nonetheless, intelligence,

---

the city was called Stanisławów in Polish, Stanyslaviv (later Stanyslav) in Ukrainian, and Stanislau in German. During the Austrian period (1790–1918), official records were kept in all three languages.

[30]   For the term and concept of the *fond* see the Technical Note above, pp. xv–xvi. For more details regarding Soviet archival arrangement and the terms involved, see my *A Handbook for Archival Research in the USSR* (Washington, DC: IREX, Kennan Institute, 1989), especially pp. 60–71.

counterintelligence, and other security organs had extensive data about such materials. This was the case because during and immediately after World War II. Security authorities secretly seized some of the most important collections of archival Ucrainica for their own "operational" purposes or to keep them out of the hands of "bourgeois nationalists" and potential "anti-Soviet" enemies of the regime. Contrary to popular belief, as shown in Chapter 9, most of the Ukrainian-language material "retrieved" by Soviet forces was taken to Kyiv rather than to Moscow.

As a result of those postwar efforts, some of the most revealing and politically sensitive archival Ucrainica that was taken out of Ukraine or created abroad by Ukrainian émigrés during the interwar period now resides in Kyiv. Because those collections were used only for "operational purposes" and closed to public research, they have never been professionally (from an archival standpoint) arranged and described, nor properly analyzed in an archeographic context. Today, not even a rudimentary list is publicly available of the original collections that were brought to Kyiv and their provenance. Neither is their a list of the several hundred Soviet-style fonds (record groups) into which these materials were artificially divided and assigned once they arrived in Kyiv.

New Opportunities and Imperatives with Independence

Years of isolation from archival Ucrainica created or based in the diaspora have now ended. With their demise, we have new opportunities to utilize "lost" or exiled sources for Ukrainian history and culture that reside in hitherto top secret collections at home and to explore those parts of the Ukrainian archival heritage that are found in neighboring countries and in the diaspora. As well, there are new incentives and imperatives to professionally describe and utilize the now expanded resources open to researchers in Ukraine. The historiographic context of Ukrainian scholarship is being re-defined on the basis of foreign published literature and newly opened documentation. At the same time, Western scholars—including émigrés—who had interpreted history and life in Soviet Ukraine from afar now have unprecedented opportunities for archival research in Ukraine and Russia. There is even hope for the return of some fugitive Ukrainian archival materials now dispersed abroad (or at least microform copies), including all official public records of Ukrainian provenance that are still located in other countries.

The outset of this work, however, must be a determination of what constitutes "archival Ucrainica." The reconstitution of the archival heritage of Ukraine must begin with the location and professional description of this material. Archival reference work has higher priority than ever before as an essential component of the developments and opportunities that have arisen since 1991. Along with this, as Ukraine implements its own domestic archival reform, it must now construct a new international archival profile, which necessarily involves the international legal context for archival claims and restitution.

The first part of this study presents a preliminary analysis of several major aspects of the problem from an international perspective:

(1)   We must identify the national archival heritage of Ukraine vis-à-vis Russia and other Soviet successor States. The legal definition of the Ukrainian archival legacy involves its relationship to the parallel "Archival Fond of the Russian Federation," as the successor to the Russian and Soviet empires. But it also involves practical definitions that go beyond new laws—with the precise distinction between the archival principles of "provenance" and "pertinence," and with sensitivity to groups of records that should be considered the "joint heritage" of Ukraine and one or more of the successor States.

(2)   On a more practical level, this analysis further involves implementing the search for archival Ukrainica abroad, including the identification of those records in the imperial metropolis that may potentially be subject to claim by one or more other successor States. We must examine some examples of potential archival pretensions, as they have or are being set forth in recent years and at the same time consider the search for international norms.

(3)   We must undertake a survey of international legal precedents for archival devolution and claims in the connection with the break-up of empires and the succession of States, boundary transfers, and wars. In addition to this, we must survey recent legal developments (conventions, agreements, resolutions, and recommendations) under the auspices of the United Nations, UNESCO, and the International Council on Archives.

(4)   We must elaborate a typology for different categories of archival materials that may be subject to different legal consideration as an essential component of identifying and defining archival Ucrainica abroad (and within the widely scattered archival Rossica and Polonica). This must necessarily involve institutional and territorial provenance, circumstances of alienation and migration, the present location and archival arrangement of the materials, and legal factors affecting ownership.

In the immediate post-1991 context, potential archival devolution growing out of the succession of States was forgotten in Russia. This occurred in the face of new revelations about the extensive West European archival materials in Russia that had been displaced during and after World War II and European demands for restitution. In Ukraine, issues of potential restitution on the basis of the succession of States became enmeshed in issues of restitution of records that were lost or that had not returned home from the wars. At the same time, new revelations show the extent to which the archival heritage of Ukraine has been affected by wartime destruction and displacements. Hence, in the second part of this study we turn to an examination of more substantive developments affecting archives as part of the larger problem of displaced cultural treasures during World War II and its aftermath:

(5)   First, we explore the destruction and displacement of archives during World War II, raising new problems of evaluating Soviet evacuation and destruction statistics, as well as examining examples of Nazi plunder and Soviet postwar archival retrieval.

(6)   Western Allied cultural restitution policies have been little studied until recently, and Western Allied restitution to the USSR was never publicized during the Soviet period. Such issues provide an important backdrop to subsequent restitution and reparation policies on the Eastern Front. These matters are complicated by frequent allegations that many cultural treasures plundered by the Nazis still remain in the West and that cultural treasures restituted to the USSR by the Western Allies were not all returned to Ukraine.

(7)   The Soviet cultural reparations policy involving the "Spoils of War" also has not been exposed until recently. Many problems are still unresolved about the extent and provenance of cultural treasures that came to the USSR after the war as "compensatory cultural reparations," and the extent of the Ukrainian component of these treasures. New revelations about cultural "trophies" continue to come to light, highlighted in 1999 by the revelation of the long-lost Sing-Akademie collection from Berlin that surfaced in Kyiv.

(8)   More data is coming to light about Soviet archival plunder—seizures of Nazi records, as well as archival materials from many European nations that had earlier been plundered by Nazi agencies. The Ukrainian component was small, but nonetheless remains important, particularly in terms of captured Nazi records in Ukraine.

(9)   As a case study of the issues involved and an important component of
       the archival heritage of Ukraine, we discuss the "retrieval" and transfer
       to Kyiv and Moscow of Ukrainian and related Russian émigré archives
       from Czechoslovakia and other countries as they were "liberated" by
       the Red Army following World War II. The extensive émigré archival
       Ucrainica that was transferred to Kyiv after the war for "operational"
       purposes remains virtually unknown to researchers, because those
       materials still have not been professionally arranged and described.

(10)   As we turn to post-Soviet restitution policies in Ukraine and Russia in a
       European context, we first need to consider the background and
       reaction to Russia's law nationalizing cultural treasures brought to the
       USSR after the war.

(11)   Ukrainian-Polish restitution raises issues of the appropriateness of
       archival transfers that result from redrawn boundaries and the forced
       resettlement of ethnic populations. The division of the symbolic
       Ossolineum from Lviv stands out as a case study of the problems
       involved. Other archival Ucrainica in Poland and Polonica in Ukraine
       need to be considered within the new international climate and
       negotiations under way between the two countries.

(12)   The goodwill engendered by recent Ukrainian restitution to Germany
       and German restitution to Ukraine contrast remarkably in policy with
       the impasse over cultural restitution between Russia and Germany.
       Several recent international conferences devoted to the Spoils of War,
       restitution, and the identification of "Holocaust-Era Assets" have
       provided an international forum and focus international attention on
       displaced cultural treasures, including archives, and restitution issues.

Many of these developments affect both potential archival claims as a
result of the succession of States and restitution issues for archives displaced
during and after the war. Analysis in this context may help clarify the
problems of defining the archival heritage of Ukraine, and issues involved in
the reconstitution of that heritage. In such analysis, Ukraine may serve as a
case study of the interaction on the Eastern Front of archival problems arising
as a result of the succession of States and those lost or displaced as a result of
World War II.

Part I

The International Legal Context

CHAPTER 1

Defining the Archival Heritage of Ukraine:
Russia and Pretensions of Soviet Successor States

The establishment of independent nations in the former Soviet republics raises a host of problems in respect to the archival heritage of successor States. The Russian Federation's difficulty in accepting "the end of empire" and in dealing with Ukraine in a role other than as "Big Brother" complicates matters in all areas of their relations. The current use by Russians of the term "near abroad" for the successor States of the former Soviet Union is symbolic of the fact they still are considered by Russia to be a close, dependent sphere of influence.

Archives, as the legal record of past governmental and other institutional functions in society and the body politic, at once reflect more general processes and require special consideration in terms of their uniqueness. Because the archives of the Russian Federation now hold the vast majority of the most important records of the former communist empire as well as the predecessor Russian Empire, Russian archives remain the central focus for all of the newly independent successor States.

As the central successor State to the vast former Russian and Soviet empires, the Russian Federation bears an especially heavy burden to recognize, identify, and to provide appropriately for the legitimate archival heritages of other successor States. In an ideal world, provisions would be made and definitions established for the identification of government records and manuscript collections created locally in imperial outposts and subsequently transferred to Moscow or St. Petersburg as components of political or cultural imperialism. These "outposts" include the core territories of what are now newly independent States. Thus far, however, the Russian government has shown little sensitivity to this issue.

Conversely, Russian interest is growing in archival materials relating to Russian history and culture now held in other successor States, especially given the extent of resettlement of ethnic Russians within various parts of the former Soviet Union. Such issues will involve a host of claims and counterclaims. But on what grounds are such claims to be presented and resolved? I have investigated a few of the issues involved in an earlier discussion of

Rossica abroad[1]—I first elaborated a prospective "typology of archival Rossica" at the conference "Archival Rossica Abroad" held in Moscow in December 1993.[2] That conference did not deal with the "near abroad," as was apparent in a critical comment from the floor by a Russian who wanted to retrieve his own family papers and other "Rossica" from Kyiv. "We are not ready to deal with that issue yet," was the official concluding reply of one of the conference's key organizers, Rosarkhiv Deputy Chairman (now Chairman and Chief Archivist of the Russian Federation) Vladimir Petrovich Kozlov. The lack of Russian preparedness to face the issue was apparent from the fact that no participants from any newly independent states were on the program.

Ukraine and other successor States, however, *are* ready to deal with archival "Ucrainica" in the "near abroad," as well as in further reaches of the Ukrainian diaspora. Political relations between Ukraine and the Russian Federation by 1999, however, had not reached a point where constructive negotiations could take place. It also will not be easy to coordinate efforts and resolve conflicting claims for Ukraine and other successor States that are politically in a much weaker position vis-à-vis their former imperial master. Ukraine's need for natural gas and other resources from Russia, as well as its growing multi-billion dollar debt to Moscow, relegate any potential archival claims to a low priority in diplomatic negotiations. Nonetheless, recognition of international precedents and an international perspective on the matter is crucial as Ukrainian archival leaders try to develop their own priorities from a Ukrainian perspective.

[1]   See an earlier version of this section, "Archival Rossica/Sovietca Abroad: Provenance or Pertinence, Bibliographic and Descriptive Needs," *Cahiers du Monde russe et soviétique* 34(3) 1993: 431–37. See also my earlier discussion in "Beyond Perestroika: Soviet-Area Archives after the August Coup," *American Archivist* 55(1) Winter 1992, especially pp. 102–106.

[2]   A revised version of my conference presentation, "A Prospective Typology of Archival Rossica," is published in Russian as "Arkhivnaia Rossika/Sovetika. K opredeleniiu i topologii russkogo arkhivnogo naslediia za rubezhom," in *Trudy IAI* 33 (Moscow, 1996): 262–86. Compare the abridged typology presented by Vladimir P. Kozlov, "Vyiavlenie i vozvrashchenie zarubezhnoi arkhivnoi Rossiki: Opyt i perspektivy," *Novaia i noveishaia istoriia* 1994 (3[16]): 13–21.

International and Soviet Archival Principles

International archival principles recognize the primacy of national laws governing the inalienable status of records of state and other public agencies. They accordingly affirm that the definition of state property and the potential transfer of ownership of public archives are dependent on legislative acts of the State that created them. The Russian Federation today considers itself the principal successor State to the Russian Empire and the Soviet Union—as well as to the RSFSR. Because of this, the potential transfer of records in connection with the succession of States becomes more complicated for other successor States of the USSR, all of which are anxious to define and retrieve the archival heritage of their own nations.

Provenance and Pertinence. The appropriate definition of the national archival legacy of Ukraine and other successor States must start with the internationally recognized distinction between the principles of "provenance" and "pertinence." In the Ukrainian case this means the difference between archival materials "created in" what is now the territory of Ukraine by Ukrainian authorities and then alienated from Ukrainian lands, and those materials that were created outside of present-day Ukrainian lands but that could be defined as "relating to" Ukraine or Ukrainian lands (regardless of those materials' place or agency of creation). Of importance here is the distinction between records of the imperial central government that were created as a result of central state and Communist Party of the Soviet Union (CPSU) functions—and for which there should be no republic-level pretensions for the original files themselves—and records of local agencies of Ukrainian republic-level state and Communist Party (CP) rule that are of provenance in the territory of Ukraine itself but were later taken to the center. Official state and related CP records are the easiest to identify in this connection and the most straightforward in terms of claims or pretensions.

The Integrity of Fonds. The international archival principle of provenance respects the integrity of fonds (*Ukr.* and *Rus., fondy*) from a given public agency and prescribes their maintenance intact in the natural order of their creation.[3] Since "archives" according to international definition are a body of records created as a natural outgrowth of the operation of their creating agency, rather than documents collected at the whim of collectors, they must be preserved intact as the records are accumulated and transferred to archival

---

[3]   Regarding the use of the archival term "fond," see the Technical Note above, pp. xv–xvi.

repositories as integral archival fonds. Yet, in Russian archives many files, or groups of documents within files, have not always been retained in their order of creation. Many present fonds from earlier centuries, in fact, constitute miscellaneous collections of files and documents torn from the context of their creation, and often even bound, with no respect for their original order in their creating agency. For example, the specialized subject-oriented *razriady* (collections) of the State Archive of the Russian Empire (Gosu-darstvennyi arkhiv Rossiiskoi Imperii), established in St. Petersburg in 1834 as a collecting point for top-level state papers and those of the imperial family, created *razriady* of files from different groups of records. In the process of their utilization by imperial offices, they nonetheless became *archives*, or integral groups of records in their own right, as apparent in the legal name of the repository where they were housed. The principle of the "integrity of archival fonds" becomes difficult to apply in such cases.

Likewise, the establishment in 1920 of the Archive of the October Revolution (Arkhiv Oktiabr'skoi revoliutsii—AOR) as a historical collecting agency caused many judicial and police files associated with the revolution-ary movement to be displaced from their original record groups and assem-bled as collections for special analysis and utilization. The fact that AOR collections became one of the founding components of the Central State Archive of the October Revolution of the USSR (TsGAOR SSSR, now part of GA RF) gave it the status of an *archive,* although those archives holding the contiguous bodies of records from which the AOR collections were drawn (such as the Russian State Historical Archive—RGIA) may argue today that AOR files should be restored to the integral groups of records, or fonds, from whence they were taken. The unfolding drama of declassified "Special Files" (*Rus. Osobye papki*) in the Archive of the President of the Russian Federation (AP RF) and other high-security establishments, drawn from top-level Politburo, MVD, or other agency records, is one of the contemporary examples of files preserved apart from the contiguous records of their creating agencies that have become archives, or integral groups of records in their own right.

Such archival practices may be perfectly normal for governmental functions but, like the historical practice of assembling subject-related documentary collections, they complicate the identification of provenance and the maintenance of the integrity of fonds. From archival and scholarly standpoints, it is still important to recognize that misplaced archival frag-ments, stray volumes, or individual charters that have for centuries been displaced—either from the office of their origin or destination, or from the order of their creation—were subsequently arranged, described, and put into scholarly citations as an integral part of the receiving central archive or other manuscript collection. Over the years, such artificial collections gain an integrity of their own that must also be respected. Hence, if an ad hoc decision is now made for the return of some or all of the original documents to their appropriate archival home outside of Russia, it is nonetheless essential to keep archival-quality xerox or microform copies, appropriately annotated copies of related finding aids, and transfer documentation available to researchers with the collection where they have long resided.[4]

Joint Heritage and Ongoing Records of Functional Pertinence. There are many integral groups of records in the imperial metropolis that may potentially be subject to claim by one or more successor States. Such records in international archival parlance should be considered of "joint heritage" to the extent that access and, ideally, appropriate official copies will need to be furnished to Ukraine and/or other successor States. Land-survey, census, and central taxation records will be important in establishing land or property claims once privatization procedures are in place. In the area of ongoing government records, legitimate claims are being aired by Ukraine and other successor States for the right of access to, and copies of, records held in Russia involving their own citizens, as well as related reference aids for such files. Especially important is the identification of records that should be considered of immediate functional pertinence, such as Soviet army and foreign passport files, employment personnel records, and records of vital statistics (*Ukr.* ZAHS/*Rus.* ZAGS),[5] all of which are needed for administrative continuity and ongoing state functions in respect to citizens of successor States. In most cases, however, it would not be administratively or archivally sound, or even technically possible, to separate Ukraine-pertinent files out for physical transfer of the originals from central offices.

The National Heritage and the Soviet Concept of the "State Archival Fond." Following the breakup of the Soviet Union, Ukraine and other newly independent successor States are trying to define their own legitimate archival heritage. Efforts to put archival affairs on a legal basis, as part of broader goals to put government on a constitutional footing, necessarily involve the definition of the national archival heritage in a more national and publicly responsive formula than existed under Soviet rule. However, both newly independent Ukraine and the Russian Federation have inherited the

---

4   The obligatory *delo fonda* (administrative file for the record group) usually serves this purpose in Russian archival practice. The secrecy still attached to these files—which under Soviet archival regulations could not be communicated to researchers (especially foreigners)—reduces their open availability.

5   Here and elsewhere, see the Abbreviations list, pp. xvii and following.

strong Soviet legal conception of the "State Archival Fond" (Gosudarstven-nyi arkhivnyi fond—GAF), which under Soviet rule provided an institutional and conceptual basis for the nationalization and legal control over all archival materials of state and society.[6] During the Soviet period, there was a separate "State Archival Fond of the Ukrainian SSR," but it was limited to holdings within the republic, and that did not prevent the alienation of local military records or, for example, unique geological survey data and feature film productions created in Ukrainian lands, as the central government in Moscow saw fit.

By virtue of the totalitarian nature of Soviet government and its impera-tive to control all records of society, as well as its lack of respect for individual or private rights vis-à-vis state power, the "State Archival Fond" in its Soviet conceptualization embraced all types of archival records from economic, social, and cultural spheres that would not be considered state records in non-communist countries. Thus, the obliteration of the line between state and private property arose in connection with the many previously non-state records and other archival materials that were national-ized after the revolution according to official Soviet archival decrees (and hence legally according to Soviet definition). Many Church manuscript collections had actually come under state control long before 1917. Although initially limited to accumulated records in state institutions and nationalized private institutional archives and manuscript collections, the "State Archival Fond" was later extended to include the records of all cultural, religious, and private agencies, commercial institutions and cooperatives, and those of trade and professional unions. It embraced not only paper records, but also films and photographs, architectural and engineering plans, medical and scientific records, as well as all types of manuscript collections and personal papers of important figures.[7]

---

[6]   The term "fond" in the present context of the entire documentary legacy of the nation is a different legal concept than the one for "fond" that was developed in Soviet archival practice for individual record groups. It is appropriate to use the Soviet russified term in this instance as well, because the same word is used in Ukrainian and Russian for both meanings.

[7]   Regarding the Soviet conception of the "State Archival Fond," see the earlier discussion and bibliography in my *A Handbook for Archival Research in the USSR* (Washington, DC: IREX, Kennan Institute for Advanced Russian Studies, 1989), pp. 3–10; and idem, "Lenin's Archival Decree of 1918: The Bolshevik Legacy for Soviet Archival Theory and Practice," *American Archivist* 45(4) Fall 1982: 429–43. An English translation of the decree issued by Lenin in 1918, "O reorganizatsii i tsentralizatsii arkhivnogo dela" (1 April 1918) is appended to that article. The article also references subsequent decrees that extend the scope of state archival control,

Such a legal concept of a "state archival fond"—or "state archival heritage"—does not exist in the United States and most Western countries. Quite by contrast in the United States, for example, the National Archives and Records Administration is limited by law to the control and custody over records of the Federal Government. There is no concept of state proprietorship over the records involved. These records are in fact considered in the public domain, open for free use by all and not subject to copyright or sale of their "information value." Going to the other extreme in the U.S., there is no state regulation of records of the private sector—and there are rarely federal resources to help preserve even manuscripts of cultural luminaries.

The CPSU Example. Of particular relevance in this connection, and as one of the anachronistic "legalities" of the Soviet system, the official Soviet State Archival Fond in its pre-August 1991 formulation did not legally include Communist Party records, thereby arbitrarily excluding the most important records of the ruling apparatus of "state" power and the control of society. Although technically non-"state," CPSU, Komsomol, and subsidiary CP republic-level records were created under the totalitarian system of Party control which would necessarily mean that such records should be considered part of the records of state and functions of government on all levels. The same would apply to records of the Comintern, the Cominform, and other agencies involved in CP international activities that affected many foreign countries. This principle would also extend to the records of other Party societal and economic functions that would normally not be considered part of "government" in the non-communist world. Post-Soviet archival laws in both Russia and Ukraine, in defining their respective national "Archival Fonds" accordingly extend state archival agency control not only to the comprehensive nationalized legacy of Soviet state archival practices, but to CP archives as well.[8]

---

many of which are printed in *Sbornik rukovodiashchikh materialov po arkhivnomu delu (1917–iiun´ 1941 gg.)* (Moscow, 1961).

[8] Of particular importance in this regard is the collection of papers from the conference in Poland in 1995 that was devoted to former CP archives, with reports by Vladimir P. Kozlov from Russia and Ruslan Ia. Pyrih from Ukraine—*Sbornik materialov po mezhdunarodnoi konferentsii "Arkhivy byvshikh kommunisticheskikh partii v stranakh tsentral´noi i vostochnoi Evropy," Stara Ves´, 28 sentiabria–1 oktiabria 1995 goda* (Warsaw, 1996). See especially the report by Ruslan Pirog [Ruslan Pyrih], "Arkhivy Kompartii Ukrainy: Problemy intergratsii v sistemu gosudarstvennoi arkhivnoi sluzhby," pp. 64–66.

The fact that most central records of CPSU rule are now held in Moscow, as is appropriate according to their provenance, undoubtedly means that they will be preserved there for posterity. They are a prime example of the "Joint Archival Heritage" of the former Soviet Union and successor States. The importance—and functional pertinence—of these records to the government, economy, and culture of all successor States and those of the former Soviet bloc raises the need for furnishing copies of finding aids and authenticated copies of relevant fonds or files (or both) to the affected States themselves, according to the terms of international archival practice.

State versus Private Records. International archival principles, as practiced in other countries outside the Socialist bloc, would normally distinguish at the outset between public archives, i.e., records of state and other public agencies and records of the private sector, including religious and business records, manuscript collections of private and academic institutions, and personal papers. Such distinctions are still virtually impossible in Ukraine and other parts of the formerly Soviet countries, due to the obliteration of private property under Soviet communist rule, the nationalization of all types of private records, the slowness of reintroducing privatization in the post-Soviet world, and the current legal restraints to the restitution of nationalized property, including archival materials. Until the issue of privatization is resolved on the level of new laws and constitutions for Ukraine and other successor States, archival claims in the private or "non-state" realm cannot be handled appropriately. Presidential decrees or court actions on the basis of previous communist-inspired constitutions may momentarily dismiss or temporarily resolve retrospective claims. However, the issue of papers or collections created by ethnic Ukrainians that happened to be resident in, or that are now held in nationalized repositories in what is now the Russian Federation, cannot be easily resolved without further general legislation and equitable agreements on such issues. International archival principles have not been adequately formulated in this area.

Professional Description. Another principle well recognized in international archival circles is that no archival claim can be appropriately discussed without professional description of the records involved in the context of, and with reference to, the original point and office of creation of the documentation in question. Such description, as will be seen below, must also take into account migratory data—that is, precise notation of original institutional origin or previous archival arrangement (or both), the transfer or seizure of such files, and the present location and archival context of the files in question. Thus, an initial prime requirement in the definition of the national archival legacy and in formulation of potential claims is appropriate physical and intellectual access to locator files for the institution currently holding the records, including, where necessary, reference to existing and earlier (if possible, original) chancery registers, *opysy/opisi*, internal accession registers, and the control file (or administrative record) for individual fonds (*spravy fonda/dela fonda*), and other descriptions of the documentation under consideration.[9] Under Soviet archival practice, many such finding aids were restricted from researchers, and even in post-Soviet Russia, many of them are still not openly available to the public.

New Archival Laws and CIS Agreements

Those concerned with archival matters in successor States need to pay particular attention to archival legislative developments in Russia. They need to understand Russian claims and pretensions to the entire archival legacy of the Russian Empire and the Soviet Union. At the same time, as they define their own national archival legacy, it may be helpful to take into account international archival precedents and the various agreements, conventions, and resolutions that have been sought in the past to resolve such problems for successor States in an international framework.

New Russian Archival Law and Regulations. With the adoption of a new "Basic Legislation of the Russian Federation on the Archival Fond of the Russian Federation and Archives," passed by the Russian parliament on 7 July 1993, there was hope that Russia was on its way to a full constitutional, normative basis for the regulation of archival affairs.[10] The initial law soon required more detailed elaboration, but further explication came not as a

---

[9]   Further discussion in terms of description of type and migratory details will be considered in Chapter 4.

[10]   "Osnovy zakonodatel'stva Rossiiskoi Federatsii ob Arkhivnom fonde Rossiiskoi Federatsii i arkhivakh" (Moscow, 1993), 7 July 1993 (no. 5341–I), *Vedomosti S"ezda Narodnykh deputatov RSFSR i Verkhovnogo Soveta RSFSR,* 1993, no. 33, statute 1311. The law also was published in *Novaia i noveishaia istoriia* 1993 (6): 3–11, followed by an analysis by Vladimir P. Kozlov, "Printsipy 'Osnovy zakonodatel'stva Rossiiskoi Federatsii ob Arkhivnom fonde Rossiiskoi Federatsii i arkhivakh,'" pp. 12–15. An additional August 1993 government regulation, "O realizatsii gosudarstvennoi politiki v arkhivnom dele," Sovet Ministrov—Pravitel'stvo Rossiiskoi Federatsii, Postanovlenie, 23 August 1993, no. 838 (*Sobranie aktov Prezidenta i Pravitel'stva RF,* 1993, no. 35, statute 3342), should also be noted, although it contains no additional texts or clarifications that directly relate to the present discussion.

normative act or legislation but, given the new Russian political milieu by that time, as a regulation (*polozhenie*), confirmed by presidential decree (*ukaz*), on 17 March 1994.[11]

The "Basic Legislation" of July 1993 defines and provides for public access and protection of the Russian archival heritage to an extent previously unknown in the Russian Empire or the Soviet Union. It continues the tradition known under Soviet rule of strong state control over the archival heritage of the nation, although it provides for some modification of that legal entity in both concept and formulation. In keeping with the legacy of Soviet nationalization, the 1993 law defines the Archival Fond of the Russian Federation to include all previously nationalized holdings. As defined there, the Archival Fond of the Russian Federation is even more comprehensive than its Soviet predecessor, although it is divided into "state" and "non-state" parts. Even then, according to the new Russian law, all archival materials are ultimately subject to state norms and regulations, and export is prohibited without state permission.[12]

Current Russian law dismisses the possibility of retrospective claims for nationalized, formerly private archives and other cultural property from individuals and institutions, such as churches and other religious groups. Religious institutions, businesses, and individual émigrés or their families are especially strongly affected by the more explicit statement that all previously nationalized private and organizational records now constitute an integral component of the "state" part of the Archival Fond of the Russian Federation.

Copyright provisions are dealt with by two other 1993 laws in Russia, and, in accordance with Russian adherence to the Berne International Copyright Convention, there is a strong assertion of copyright for an individual or his heirs, even for materials on deposit in state repositories. Archives that now acquire copyrighted materials, especially materials of personal origin, draw up appropriate agreements, because unlike the situation during the Soviet period, state proprietorship in Russia now extends to the repository holding the manuscripts, even in cases where copyright is applicable. Nevertheless, ultimate jurisdiction over the private manuscript legacy still rests with the state in terms of retrospective claims.

---

[11] "Ob utverzhdenii polozheniia ob Arkhivnom fonde Rossiiskoi Federatsii i polozheniia o Gosudarstvennoi arkhivnoi sluzhbe Rossii": Decree of the President of the Russian Federation, 17 March 1994, no. 552, *Sobranie aktov Prezidenta i Pravitel'stva RF*, 1994, no. 12 (21 March), statute 878. See more detailed analysis of crucial sections of the text below.

[12] "Ob Arkhivnom fonde Rossiiskoi Federatsii," 17 March 1994, §5 and §6.

Although due provisions for public use of archival documents are assured in the July 1993 "Basic Legislation" and its later extensions, strong state proprietary rights to the archival heritage of the nation also still leave no room for a more Western concept of the "public domain." Indeed, the right of Rosarkhiv or individual federal archives to sell licenses for commercial use or publication was provided for in a temporary Rosarkhiv regulation of February 1993, but is no longer in effect.[13] A more formal regulation is still in preparation.

Since the enactment of the "Basic Legislation" in 1993, some legal problems have arisen in the Russian archival realm that were not sufficiently clarified in the law; others require further attention. By the end of 1998 a new draft law had been prepared and circulated for consideration among archivists. But since this law has not been adopted, it is not appropriate to comment on it here.[14]

The Archival Fond of the Russian Federation and the Heritage of Other Successor States. In a convention signed by archivists of the CIS and ratified by President Yeltsin in July 1992, Russia already claimed possession of the entire central archival legacy of the USSR as the rightful legal successor State to the Soviet Union. Nevertheless, as defined in the original 1993 "Basic Legislation," there were no obvious pretensions that would threaten the archival heritages of successor States of the Russian Empire and Soviet Union, because the "state part" of the Archival Fond of the Russian Federation was defined to include "all archival fonds and archival documents created and to be created by all federal agencies of state power and government...as well as archival fonds and archival documents received in established order from societal and religious associations and organizations, juridical and physical individuals" (§6). In addition, however, it clearly

---

[13] "Vremennye polozheniia o poriadke zakliucheniia litsenzionnykh dogovorov na ispol'zovanie dokumentov gosarkhivov i tsentrov dokumentatsii RF v kommercheskikh tseliakh," adopted by the Rosarkhiv Collegium 10 February 1993, and published in *Otechestvennye arkhivy* 1993 (2): 112. See also the federal regulation, "O litsenzirovanii deiatel'nosti po obsledovaniiu sostoianiia arkhivnykh fondov, ekspertize, opisaniiu, konservatsii i restavratsii arkhivnykh dokumentov": Postanovlenie Pravitel'stva RF, 14 July 1995, no. 747, *Sobranie zakonodatel'stva RF,* 1995, no. 31 (31 July), statute 3134; also published in *Otechestvennye arkhivy* 1995 (5): 3–6.

[14] See "O vnesenii izmenenii i dopolnenii v Osnovy zakonodatel'stva Rossiiskoi Federatsii ob Arkhivnom fonde Rossiiskoi Federatsii i arkhivakh," draft federal law, *Otechestvennye arkhivy* 1998 (6): 22–33.

embraced all of those holdings already deposited in federal-level state archives within the Russian Federation, and it was noticeably silent on devolution to or potential claims from successor States.

The State Archival Fond of the Russian Federation was defined in much more detail in the archival Regulation of 17 March 1994. For example, while the text of the July 1993 Russian law made no specific mention of CPSU records as being part of the Archival Fond RF, both CPSU and Komsomol records were specifically included in the "state part" of the Archival Fond RF; this duly confirmed the nationalization of CPSU archives decreed by Yeltsin in August 1991.[15]

The March 1994 regulation also appears much more defensive in terms of potential claims from former Soviet republics, and even from countries that at one point lay wholly or in part within the Russian Empire, such as Finland or Poland. Three clauses of clarification in the first introductory paragraph deserve note in this regard:

(1) The Archival Fond RF is therein defined to constitute "archival fonds and archival records of state institutions, organizations, firms, and government institutions existing on the territory of Russia in the entire extent of her history, and also institutions of religious confessions until the moment of the separation of the Church from the State." (§I.1) The use of "Russia" in this clause, it should be noted, is in contrast to the second paragraph of the regulation, which limits its claims to archives and records of agencies "existing on the territory of the Russian Federation." There is no time limit specified, and "Russia" is not distinguished from the more extensive territory of the pre-revolutionary Russian Empire, or from the regions known as "Rus'" (now predominantly Ukraine and Belarus). The fact that the Russian language in the clause fails to distinguish between "Russia" and "Rus'" with reference to the medieval Kyivan state and appanage principalities would potentially rule out Ukrainian and Belarusian pretensions on early manuscripts and other archival materials of provenance in their own present territories. As presently worded, there could be potential conflict with the July 1992 CIS Archival Agreement, which establishes the principle that successor

---

[15] "Ob Arkhivnom fonde RF," 17 March 1994. See the earlier RSFSR presidential decrees "O partiinykh arkhivakh" (24 August 1991), no. 83, printed in *Otechestvennye arkhivy* 1992 (1): 3, together with the decree founding the new archival centers based on the former CPSU archives (21 October 1991), no. 532 (p. 4).

States "have the right to the return of those fonds created within their territory and which at various times were separated from them."[16]

(2) The third clause adds another claim to the effect that the Archival Fond RF also comprises "archival fonds and archival records of Fatherland state institutions and military units existing and/or having existed abroad." If "abroad" in this clause were construed to include the "near abroad," as the term is now used for former Soviet republics (such an interpretation is not excluded), this could suggest the retroactive inclusion of records of local Russian imperial or Soviet agencies of state or military administration. As distinguished from other paragraphs mentioning specifically records of agencies of "state" and limiting themselves to "the territory of the Russian Federation," there is here a clearly worded sense of "Fatherland," implying the whole former Soviet Union and Russian Empire, with no exclusion for records of local state and military authorities in former non-Russian areas that are no longer a territorial part of the Russian Federation. Should this paragraph be extended to successor States, it would also potentially conflict with the July 1992 CIS Archival Agreement.

(3) The seventh clause adds still another claim to "archival fonds and archival documents of juridical and physical entities (persons), which have been received through legal means into state proprietorship, including those from abroad."[17] In its current wording, this conceptualization of Russian claims to all archival materials held in public or private archives within the Russian Federation today (including those of foreign provenance) offers no exclusion for materials of provenance in the territory of successor States.

In terms of potential claims for restitution, much will hinge on the interpretation of the phrase "through legal means." Under a Russian imperial or Soviet regime, which essentially did not recognize Western concepts of "law," the state was accustomed to consider an imperial or Soviet "decree," or even an order by state authorities as a *de facto* legal instrument. This would leave earlier state seizures open to interpretation as "legal" under the juridical usage of the regime that seized them, in the same way that Russia now affirms the "legality" of the nationalization of all previously private manuscript collections held in state repositories, including those of academic

---

[16]   "Soglashenie o pravopreemstve v otnoshenii gosudarstvennykh arkhivov byv-shevo Soiuza SSR," Moscow, 6 July 1992, article 3. Reprinted with English translation below as Appendix V.

[17]   "Ob Arkhivnom fonde RF," 17 March 1994, §1.

and religious bodies. Such a formulation shows Russian insensitivity to what might otherwise be legitimate pretensions on the part of successor States of the Russian and Soviet empires, including Ukraine, to reconstitute their own national archival heritage in accordance with the principle of provenance and international precedents.

Independent Russian Agency Archives of All-Union Importance. Another reformulation, or clarification, included in the March 1994 Regulation is also relevant in the present context in regard to the interests of successor States. Namely, continuing in the Soviet tradition, many of the most highly significant state agencies of an all-union character that earlier had the right to retain their own records independently of the all-union archival agency Glavarkhiv are now quite explicitly and by name given the right to the long-term retention of, "archival fonds and archival records retained in their agency archives...along with those of their subordinate institutions, organizations, firms, and military units...according to special arrangements with Rosarkhiv" (§7). The list includes such key agencies as the Ministries of Defense, Foreign Affairs, Internal Affairs, and Atomic Energy, along with the Federal Counterintelligence Service (since renamed the Federal Security Service— FSB) and the Foreign Intelligence Service (SVR).[18]

An August 1991 presidential decree called for the transfer of the former KGB archives to Rosarkhiv (then Roskomarkhiv) control, and a blue-ribbon presidential Commission to Organize the Transfer and Accession of Archives of the CPSU and KGB SSSR to State Repositories and their Utilization, appointed in October 1991, called for the establishment of a special archival center in Moscow under Roskomarkhiv for KGB documentation.[19] But the projected center was never established, and a new April 1992 federal law "On Operational-Investigatory Activities" formally established information

---

[18] Ob Arkhivnom fonde RF," 17 March 1994, §7.

[19] The RSFSR presidential decree "Ob arkhivakh Komiteta gosudarstvennoi bezopasnosti SSSR" (24 August 1991), no. 82, is printed in *Otechestvennye arkhivy* 1992 (1): 3. See E. Maksimova, "Arkhivy KPSS i KGB perekhodiat v sobstvennost' naroda," *Izvestiia* 28/29 August 1991.

Regarding the commission and its recommendations, see the revealing article on the KGB archives by Nikita Petrov, "Politika rukovodstva KGB v otnoshenii arkhivnogo dela byla prestupnoi... ," *Karta: Nezavisimyi istoricheskii zhurnal* (Riazan) 1 (1993): 4–5. The internal report by the presidential commission, which was presented to the Supreme Council of the Russian Federation over Dmitrii Volkogonov's signature in February 1992, was published as an appendix—"Reshenie ob arkhivakh KGB" (pp. 6–7).

regarding KGB operational methods, agents, and their informants in the category of state secrets.[20] The March 1994 archival regulation lists the major two KGB successor organizations, the Federal Security Service (FSB) and the Foreign Intelligence Service (SVR), among those now accorded special consideration in terms of the long-term retention of their own records in their own separate archives, and two other KGB successor agencies were added to the list in a March 1996 amendment.[21] These regulations were revised in the 1995 federal law "On Operational-Investigatory Activities," but the same archival provisions are repeated, while in the latest formulation the information elements mentioned earlier remain "confidential."[22] The fact that all of these agency records are not transferred to permanent federal archives continues to limit open public research access, but for successor States such as Ukraine, it also means that official access or copies require negotiation with the controlling agencies outside of Rosarkhiv channels. A subsequent presidential decree in the spring of 1995 gave the Ministry of Foreign Affairs the right to permanent retention of its own archives.[23]

---

[20] "Ob operativno-rozysknoi deiatel'nosti": Law of the Russian Federation, 29 April 1992, no. 2506–1, *Vedomosti S"ezda Narodnykh deputatov RF i Verkhovnogo Soveta RF*, 1992, no. 17 (23 April), statute 892; amendments to the law are recorded in *Vedomosti S"ezda*, 1992, no. 33, statute 1912.

[21] The 1996 amendment to the 1994 archival regulation provides for the long-term retention of archives by the Federal Border Service (*Federal'naia pogranichnaia sluzhba RF*) and the Federal Agency for Government Communications and Information (*Federal'noe agentstvo pravitel'stvennoi sviazi i informatsii pri Prezidente Rossiiskoi Federatsii*) under the President of the Russian Federation—"O vnesenii izmenenii v Polozhenii ob Arkhivnom fonde RF, utverzhdennom Ukazom Prezidenta RF ot 17 marta 1994 g., no. 552"—"Ob utverzhdenii—": Decree of the President of the Russian Federation, 1 April 1996, no. 460, *Sobranie aktov i postanovlenii Prezidenta i Pravitel'stva RF*, 1996, no. 15 (8 April), statute 1575.

[22] "Ob operativno-rozysknoi deiatel'nosti": Federal Law, 12 August 1995, no. 144–FZ, *Sobranie zakonodatel'stva RF*, 1995, no. 33 (14 August), statute 3349. See also the 1999 modification: "O vnesenii izmenenii i dopolnenii v Federal'nyi zakon 'Ob operativno-rozysknoi deiatel'nosti'": Federal Law, 5 January 1999, no. 6–FZ, *Sobranie zakonodatel'stva RF*, 1999, no. 2 (11 January), statute 233. This 1995 law replaces the 1992 law (above, fn. 20). A paragraph in the new law places all information about current agents and their informants of the FSB and its predecessors in the category of "confidential," and requires written permission for access.

[23] "O Ministerstve inostrannykh del Rossiiskoi Federatsii": Decree of the President of the Russian Federation, 14 March 1995, no. 271, *Sobranie zakonodatel'stva RF*, 1995, no. 12 (21 April), statute 1033. Article 5 gives MID the right to retain its archives permanently.

Another group of key specialized archives—listed in the same privileged category in the same paragraph that are also of crucial importance to successor States—include the Russian Geological Fond, the Russian State Fond of Data on Environmental Conditions, the Central Cartographic-Geodesic Fond, the Central State Fond of Standards and Technical Conditions, and the State Fond of Motion Pictures (Gosfil'mofond). These centralized repositories developed under Soviet rule retain crucial unique records of provenance from throughout the former Soviet Union—from geological, hydrometric, and cartographic survey data to the archival copies and editing outtakes of all feature and many documentary films produced in all republic-level film studios.[24]

According to this latest regulation, the length of time and nature of their temporary and depository storage and usage is unspecified by law, and remains "to be established in agreement between the State Archival Service of Russia and the named federal agencies of executive power, organizations, and firms" (§7). Since there is little likelihood that any of these repositories are about to turn over their well-established archival repositories to Rosarkhiv or to the newly independent successor States, such a statement is tantamount to a prolongation of the status quo in terms of separate agency archives that are independent of Rosarkhiv administration. Since the collapse of the Soviet Union, there has been no general provision for dividing the holdings of any of these archives on a territorial basis, nor have funds been available to make extensive copies available to the newly independent States. The situation with respect to negotiated arrangements between these independent archives and Rosarkhiv as of late 1994 was analyzed in print, but there is no mention of arrangements made with successor States.[25]

Considerable interest has also focused on the all-important top-level Politburo and Central Committee records in the Archive of the President of the Russian Federation (AP RF), which still remains independent of Rosarkhiv control. A September 1994 Russian Presidential directive clarified declassification procedures for CPSU records, appointed a new commission on declassification, and called for further transfers of historical materials from the Presidential Archive to more open public repositories.[26] Subse-

---

[24]   "Ob Arkhivnom fonde RF," 17 March 1994, §7. Details about all of these repositories and others are also included in *Archives of Russia 2000*.

[25]   Igor' N. Tarasov and Tat'iana N. Viktorova, "Novye aspekty sotrudnichestva Rosarkhiva s ministerstvami i vedomstvami," *Otechestvennye arkhivy* 1995 (2): 15–19.

[26]   "Razporiazhenie Prezidenta Rossiiskoi Federatsii ot 22 sentiabria 1994, no. 489-RP [O poriadke rassekrechivaniia dokumentov]," published in *Rossiiskaia gazeta* 27

quently, there have been considerable transfers to what are now the two Russian federal-level public archives that retain CPSU records—namely the Russian State Archive of Socio-Political History (RGASPI; predominantly for pre-1953 records, which now also includes Komsomol records) and the Russian State Archive of Contemporary History (RGANI; which embraces more contemporary materials of the post-Stalin era). Most significantly in April 1999, most of the remaining personal papers of Stalin himself and his secretariat have been transferred to RGASPI, but it is uncertain how soon they will be declassified and open to the public.[27]

The Ukrainian Archival Law. The 1993 Ukrainian law, "On the National Archival Fond and Archival Institutions," defines a "National Archival Fond" in a much broader juridical conception than had been the case with the Soviet-period "State Archival Fond":

> The National Archival Fond consists of documents of whatever form, place of creation, and form of ownership, which are located in the territory of Ukraine, reflecting the history of the spiritual and material life of its people and other nations, which represent historical and cultural value and which have been appraised on

---

September 1994: 4, and republished in *Otechestvennye arkhivy* 1995 (1): 3, followed by a commentary by Vladimir P. Kozlov (pp. 4–5). An English translation and analysis by Mark Kramer appears in *Cold War International History Project Bulletin* 4 (Fall 1994): 89.

27   RGASPI (Rossiiskii gosudarstvennyi arkhiv sotsial'no-politicheskoi istorii) is the successor to the Central Party Archive (TsPA); from November 1991–March 1999 it was known as the Russian Center for Preservation and Study of Records of Modern History—RTsKhIDNI); its holdings now also embrace the former Central Archive of the Komsomol, which from 1992 through March 1999 was known as the Center for the Preservation of Records of Youth Organizations (TsKhDMO). RGANI is the successor to the Central Committee archive, which also embraces other current CP records; from 1991 through March 1999 it was known as the Center for the Preservation of Contemporary Documentation (TsKhSD). Those archives are described and published descriptions of them listed in *Archives of Russia, 2000.* Some of the materials transferred from AP RF are also reported there. The personal papers of top-level CPSU leaders transferred to RGASPI through 1995 are listed in *Putevoditel' po fondam i kollektsiiam lichnogo proiskhozhdeniia,* comp. Iu. N. Amiantov and Z. N. Tikhonova; ed. Iu. N. Amiantov, O. V. Naumov, Z. N. Tikhonova, and K. M. Anderson (Moscow, 1996) [=Spravochno-informatsionnye materialy k dokumental'nym fondam RTsKhIDNI, 2].

> these grounds and registered in order, according to the terms of
> this Law.[28]

The law includes components of the Ukrainian archival legacy that may
be located abroad in terms disposed to conform with international law and
archival practice:

> The National Archival Fond also includes archival documents that
> are located outside the borders of Ukraine and which, according to
> international agreements, should be returned to Ukraine.[29]

Ukraine accordingly is avoiding the more pretentious definitions earlier
pronounced by Lithuania and several other successor States, and is defining a
concept in keeping with the July 1992 Agreement for the Confederation of
Independent States (CIS) mentioned below. It has, however, expressed
interest in the revindication of displaced fragments of the national archival
heritage, while judiciously leaving the resolution of the matter to "international agreements." Nonetheless, the only international agreement in place for
Soviet successor States that currently covers the matter fails to define
appropriate components of the national archival legacy and leaves such issues
to *bilateral* negotiation rather than *international* mechanisms or designated
terms of agreement.

CIS Agreements. Complex and disputed archival claims such as these
throughout Eastern Europe will need to be resolved fairly according to
professional standards and established international archival practice, as
archivists and politicians try to unravel and resolve the archival legacy of the
Newly Independent States. Archival leaders of the Newly Independent States
met in Minsk under the auspices of the CIS in April 1992 to try to resolve the
matter of archival claims, but the resulting declaration did not conform to
international archival legal precedents and left many matters unresolved.
Paragraph 3 resolved that:

> ...all participating governments have the right to the return of
> those fonds created within their territories, relating to their his-
> tory, and which in various times were taken from within their bor-
> ders.[30]

---

[28]   "Zakon Ukraïny 'Pro Natsional'nyi arkhivnyi fond i arkhivni ustanovy,'" Kyiv,
24 December 1993, no. 3814–XII, §1.1, published in *Arkhivy Ukraïny* 1994
(4–6): 4–15, and in *Vidomosti Verkhovnoï Rady Ukraïny* 1994 (15): 86.

[29]   See "Zakon Ukraïny," §1.1.

[30]   "Predlozheniia gruppy ekspertov gosudarstv-uchastnikov SNG dlia resheniia
voprosov, sviazannykh s pravopreemstvom v otnoshenii gosudarstvennykh arkhivov,"

Such imprecise and ambiguous wording makes its interpretation and application impossible in judicial terms, as was noted by Moscow State Historico-Archival Institute (MGIAI) director, Evgenii V. Starostin.[31] The legal problems raised by the initial Minsk statement were thus similar to those involved in some far-reaching Lithuanian claims and could have led to wide-scale demands for revindication of archival records held by central authorities of the former USSR. Significantly, the revised archival agreement signed in Moscow in July 1992 by representatives of ten countries had changed wording in that article—dropping the clause "relating to their history"—to avoid the ambiguities involved and rested purely on the principle of *provenance* rather than *pertinence:*

> The Sides have the right to the return of those fonds created within their territory and which at various times were separated from them.[32]

That archival agreement was reinforced by a subsequent agreement on the restitution of cultural and historical treasures, signed by heads of state in Minsk on 14 July 1992.[33]

The archival agreement as it stands still remains much too vague for ready implementation, and the only mechanism suggested by another paragraph posits *bilateral* agreement between Russia and individual successor States. Without professional guidelines, the prospects for satisfaction rest entirely on good faith and cooperative aims on both sides of the bargaining table. A Ukrainian commentary aptly noted:

> Given the fact that every country has pretensions to the former metropolis, the Treaty lacks mechanisms which could realistically

---

Minsk, 23 April 1992. See the published version in *Vestnik arkhivista* 1993 (3[9]): 10–11.

[31] E. V. Starostin, "Professor Starostin o zatronutoi probleme," *Otechestvennye arkhivy* 1992 (4): 26–27. Starostin has since been retired as director.

[32] "Soglashenie o pravopreemstve v otnoshenii gosudarstvennykh arkhivov byvshevo Soiuza SSR," Moscow, 6 July 1992, article 3.

[33] See the official Ukrainian translation, "Uhoda pro povernennia kul'turnykh i istorychnykh tsinnostei derzhavam ïkh pokhodzhennia," in *Mizhnarodna okhorona, zakhyst i povernennia kul'turnykh tsinnostei (zbirnyk dokumentiv)* (Kyiv, 1993), pp. 66–67.

implement this work. But it foresees that in each concrete case, a
mutual agreement should be reached by the two sides.[34]

On subsequent occasions, Russian archival leaders have indicated their
willingness to undertake bilateral discussions in terms of the July 1992
agreement, but problems of implementation remain. The need for elaborating
a mechanism for implementation was noted in the protocol of a meeting of
archival directors of Soviet successor States in Moscow in October 1993.[35]
Successful implementation necessarily will involve the preparation of
appropriate guidelines and then more specific lists of fonds that individual
successor States may seek for transfer with precise and sufficiently detailed
identification and analysis of the materials involved. Without guidelines and
knowledge of international archival norms and precedents, the preparation of
such lists and the conduct of bilateral discussions will remain difficult.

The collapse of the Soviet Union is not the first instance in history of
problems of the succession of States with respect to archives. Russian and
Ukrainian archivists, together with those of other newly independent States,
have been examining international norms and precedents, while in a more
immediate context trying to formulate their own pretensions. What is most
needed is an attempt at more precise definition and typology of archival
materials in the former metropolis that constitute integral parts of the archival
heritage of successor States and the identification of those that might be
subject to claim in original or copy. The broad and inclusive definition of the
"State Archival Fond of the Russian Federation" noted above in its March
1994 formulation may leave little bargaining room for the pretensions of
successor States.

The signing of a Russo-Ukrainian agreement on archival cooperation in
December 1998 may open the grounds for improved archival relations, but it
was signed only by the respective archival administrations. (It therefore
remains only a bilateral agreement.[36]) The practical effects may ultimately
depend on broader economic and political realities. This makes a more

---

[34]   Pavlo Sokhan´ and Liudmyla Lozenko, "Vtrachene z arkhiviv. Chy nazavzhdy,"
Literaturna Ukraïna 3 (21 January 1993): 6.

[35]   "Protokol po itogam Moskovskoi vstrechi rukovoditelei gosudarstvennykh
arkhivnykh sluzhb i obshchestv arkhivistov suverennykh gosudarstv," 15 October
1993, and "Protokol zasedaniia predstavitelei obshchestv arkhivistov nezavisimykh
gosudarstv," 14 October 1993, *Otechestvennye arkhivy* 1993 (6): 92–94.

[36]   The assertion here regarding the December 1998 archival agreement between
Russia and Ukraine comes second hand, since the text has not been published and was
not otherwise available to me.

dispassionate use by Ukraine and Russia of international norms regarding restitution issues and the archival legacy of successor States more urgent than ever. Otherwise, "bilateral negotiation" or "mutual agreement" will ultimately be a matter of bargains and barter, and restitution will come about only when the receiving side has something exceptional to offer in exchange. The main problem is a lack of adequate international "laws," "conventions," or even "guidelines" while conflicting pretensions and political interests go well beyond the "laws" and precedents that do exist. This will be explored in subsequent chapters.

Beyond New Laws—Efforts to Define Archival Ucrainica

The Common Imperial Heritage. From an archival perspective, it makes no sense for archivists of newly independent States to immediately and unequivocally demand their entire share of the archival legacy remaining in Moscow and St. Petersburg archives from the seventy years of Bolshevik-Soviet rule and the centuries of imperial Russian rule that preceded the USSR. There is every reason to keep central imperial records intact and accessible to all in the place of their creation and in the context of their long-term archival arrangement. However, according to international archival norms, any integral fonds—especially parts of fonds held elsewhere—that are wholly of Soviet republic-level provenance (that is, that were created by functions of local government and administration) and that were previously misappropriated due to the lack of an adequate archival law (including seizures by the KGB, MVD, or other security agencies), should be restored to successor States. Ukrainian historians and archivists recognize the problems involved, and are particularly sensitive to the position of Russia as the Moscow/Petersburg center that is heir to the centralized archival system developed under imperial Russian and Soviet rule. In the case of files of republic-level provenance that have been incorporated into records of the central apparatus, it is essential that authenticated copies be furnished in most cases, so that the originals can remain within the record group where they have been incorporated.

The potential for conflict is particularly strong with the archival legacies of Belarus and Ukraine, especially in the context of the often-stated claim of Kyiv as "the Mother of Rus'" and the long-standing Russian view of Ukraine and Belarus as "younger Slavic brothers." Ukraine may quite legitimately claim primacy to the manuscript legacy of (Kyivan) Rus', but Russia and Belarus would make counterclaims to such treasures as part of their common cultural heritage. Despite the alleged injustice of the status quo, many manuscripts and archival documents of provenance in what is now territory of independent Ukraine are integrated into long-existing imperial collections and have gained an identity in that context. It is unlikely that Russian cultural leaders would agree to their wide-scale dislodgment, although a few symbolic manuscripts may be appropriate for return to the land of their provenance.

Belarusian Initiatives. Belarusian and Ukrainian archivists have already been trying to define their own archival legacies and are naturally concerned to locate legitimate components of their national archival heritage now held in Russia, especially since vast parts of present-day Ukraine and Belarus have been subject so long to imperial Russian rule.[37] A conference in Minsk in April 1992 (under the auspices of the Belarusian Cultural Fund and the Main Archival Administration of the Council of Ministers of the Republic of Belarus) brought together many reports on the problem of restitution and included in the published version a number of lists and other documents regarding Belarusian cultural treasures.[38] Another volume with additional collected reports regarding a wide variety of cultural treasures (including archival materials) appeared under the auspices of the Belarusian Cultural Fond in 1994.[39] Continuing the series with an additional volume in 1996, Belarus started a comprehensive compendium of documents relating to archives and other manuscript materials removed from Belarus from the eighteenth through the early twentieth century as well as more detailed inventories of specific groups of records (fonds) in Moscow and St. Petersburg.[40]

The fourth volume in the series presents the proceedings of the conference on displaced cultural treasures held in Minsk in June 1997 under UNESCO auspices. The volume includes reports on various Belarusian archival materials held abroad, along with several published documents,

---

[37] A new law on archives was issued in Belarus, 6 October 1994—"Ab Natsyianal'nym arkhiŭnym fondze i arkhivakh u Respublitsy Belarus'."

[38] This included descriptions of archives taken out of Belarus in various periods. See, *Viartanne: Dakumenty i arkhiŭnyia materyialy pa prablemakh poshuku i viartannia natsyianal'nykh kashtoŭnastei, iakiia znakhodziatstsa za mezhami Respubliki Belarus'* (Minsk: Belaruski fond kul'tury, 1992).

[39] *Viartanne—2: Zbornik artykulaŭ i dakumentaŭ* (Minsk: Belaruski fond kul'tury, 1994).

[40] *Viartanne—3: Zbornik artykulaŭ i dakumentaŭ*, ed. Adam Mal'dzis (Minsk: Belaruski fond kul'tury, 1996). See the separate sections devoted to treasures in Moscow (pp. 29–67), details of two fonds in St. Petersburg (pp. 68–180), and documents relating to archival removals from Belarus from the late eighteenth century through 1917 (pp. 205–217).

although the emphasis of the conference was more on museum exhibits.[41] Of particular note are reports on holdings from the Belarusian Archive from Prague now in Moscow and Paris (see Chapter 9, below), and the first significant survey published in Belarus of the holdings of the Francis Skaryna Belorusian Library and Museum in North London.[42] Several important presentations addressed international legal issues of cultural restitution, emphasizing the still pressing need for legal norms and guidelines and the potential role of UNESCO.

By 1990 Belarusian archivists had already published a list of Belarusian-related records in 1,834 fonds held in the former Soviet central state archives in Moscow and St. Petersburg on the basis of data available in computerized portions of the Central Catalog of Fonds compiled by the Main Archival Administration of the USSR Council of Ministers.[43] A similar publication was planned for Ukraine, but the cost of acquiring the data that the Russian archival institute VNIIDAD charged was not within Ukrainian budgetary constraints.[44]

The Common Archival Legacy of the Grand Duchy of Lithuania and the Polish-Lithuanian Commonwealth. When the principle of provenance and the integrity of existing fonds and collections is applied, conflicts regarding the disposition of the originals are sure to arise. Indeed, many components of the historical Ukrainian archival heritage, at least in terms of many state records, could be termed "functionally" and "administratively pertinent" to Ukraine and Belarus, and in some cases, representing the "common archival heritage" of other nations of Eastern Europe as well. Countries such as Ukraine and Belarus, whose present territories were long ruled by outside

---

[41] *Restytutsyia kul'turnykh kashtoŭnastsei.*

[42] Nataliia Kryvadubskaia, "Materyialy pa historyi ŭ Belaruskai bibliiatetsy i muzei imia Frantsishka Skaryny ŭ Londane," in *Restytutsyia kul'turnykh kashtoŭnastsei,* pp. 169–75.

[43] *Dakumenty pa historyi Belarusi, iakiia zberahaiutstsa u tsentral'nykh dziarzhaŭnykh arkhivakh SSSR,* ed. and comp. by A. M. Mikhal'chanka and T. A. Varab'iova (Minsk: Belaruskaia savetskaia èntsyklapedyia imia Petrusia Brouki, 1990).

[44] According to IUA sources in Kyiv, VNIIDAD was charging a fee of $1,000 for copies of files from the database, covering both holdings in the Russian Federation and in Ukraine, but IUA was unable to secure funds for the purchase. The commercialization of data of such importance to all of the newly independent states is a sad commentary on the post-1991 archival situation in Russia. See further discussion in Chapter 8.

powers and that never constituted a single political entity in their present configuration, will bear the brunt of particularly complex problems in the definition of their legitimate national archival heritage.[45]

For example, pretensions could arise from Ukraine and Belarus, and especially Lithuania itself, regarding the central royal chancery records of the Grand Duchy of Lithuania (until 1569) and, subsequently, of the Polish-Lithuanian Commonwealth (until 1795), which at its height stretched from the Baltic almost to the Black Sea. The so-called Lithuanian Metrica, in strict archival definition, represents the official register books for copies of outgoing royal chancery documents, archival copies of which were kept in Vilnius until the early eighteenth century. Moved to Warsaw in the 1740s, the books were inventoried and kept in the Royal Castle together with the Crown Metrica, the parallel records of outgoing documents for the chancery of the Kingdom of Poland and, later, the Polish-Lithuanian Commonwealth. After the Third Partition of Poland in 1795, the Lithuanian Metrica, together with other high-level archives of the Commonwealth, was confiscated by Russian Empress Catherine II from Warsaw and taken to St. Petersburg. It was subsequently moved to Moscow in 1888.

Should all of these records be transferred from Moscow to Vilnius as the independent Republic of Lithuania now demands? Or, as claimed by Polish authorities, should they be returned to Warsaw, which was their last official point of creation and archival home before seizure by Catherine II? Reflecting Russian imperial anti-Polish policies, the various archival materials were intermingled, so that the inventory published in 1888 under the title of the "Lithuanian Metrica" covered a vast collection of high-level records of the former Commonwealth with as many Polish as Lithuanian components.[46]

---

[45]   Regarding problems of the Ukrainian archival heritage, see my earlier discussion in "The Archival Legacy of Soviet Ukraine: Problems of Tracing the Documentary Records of a Divided Nation," *Cahiers du Monde russe et soviétique* 28 (January-March 1987): 95–108. Regarding Belarus, see my article "Historical Survey of Archives in the Belorussian SSR," and the bibliography in my *Archives: Estonia, Latvia, Lithuania, and Belorussia*, pp. 445–509; as well as my "Archives and Manuscript Collections in the Belorusian SSR: Soviet Standards and the Documentary Legacy of the Belorussian Nation," *Zapisy Belaruskaha instytutu navuki i mastatstva* 17 (New York, 1983): 85–102.

[46]   See *The "Lithuanian Metrica" in Moscow and Warsaw: Reconstructing the Archives of the Grand Duchy of Lithuania, including An Annotated Facsimile Edition of the 1887 Ptaszycki Inventory*, edited with an introduction by P. K. Grimsted with the collaboration of Irena Sułkowska-Kurasiowa (Cambridge, MA: Oriental Research Partners, 1984); see also my "Czym jest i czym była Metryka Litewska? (Stan obecny i perspektywy odtworzenia zawartości archiwum kancelaryjnego Wielkiego Księstwa

The Soviet Union restituted many of the Polish parts of that collection to Warsaw following the Treaty of Riga of 1921, but some remained behind. At present, all the independent nations involved would have a claim to those parts remaining in Moscow (almost none of which are directly pertinent to current Russian territories) based on "joint heritage." During the Soviet period, free microfilm copies of these records were furnished to the Soviet republics requesting them, although the quality often was poor.

Of most specific interest to Ukraine are the series of registers known as the "Volhynian," or "Ruthenian Metrica," which contain official copies of outgoing royal chancery documents addressed to Right Bank Ukrainian lands from 1569 to 1673. These records are not of Ukrainian provenance per se and were never held in Ukrainian lands. Although they were listed in one of the Ukrainian archival "restitution" lists in 1918, from the point of view of their provenance and the principle of integrity of archival fonds, they belong in Warsaw, rather than Moscow or Kyiv.[47] They are technically part of the Polish Crown Metrica, representing the official registers of outgoing documents issued by the Crown Chancery, which was seized from Warsaw by Catherine II in 1795. When the rest of the Crown Metrica was returned to Warsaw after World War I, they were torn from their contiguous body of records and retained in Moscow under the dubious principle of territorial pertinence, since Volhynian lands remained part of the USSR. Between the wars, the records were held in secret in Moscow, and it was not until the late 1980s that foreign (including Polish) scholars were given access to them.[48]

Litewskiego)," *Kwartalnik Historyczny* 92(1) 1985: 55–85; and "Układ i zawartość Metryki Litewskiej," *Archeion* 80 (1986): 121–82. The Republic of Lithuania reports a formal, but still disputed archival claim for the Lithuanian Metrica with the Russian Federation.

[47] See "Protokol zasidannia arkhivnoï sektsiï Komisiï dlia pidhotovky materialu do Myrnoho dohovoru z Rosiieiu Ministerstva narodnoï osvity UNR (Kyïv, 12.IV.1918)," in Serhii Kot and Oleksii Nestulia, *Ukraïns'ki kul'turni tsinnosti v Rosiï. Persha sproba povernennia, 1917–1918* (Kyiv: Soborna Ukraïna, 1996) [*=Povernennia kul'turnoho nadbannia Ukraïny. Dokumenty svidchat'*, 1].

[48] See my "Rus'ka metryka: Knyhy pol's'koï koronnoï kantseliariï dlia ukraïns'kykh zemel', 1569–1673 rr.," *Ukraïns'kyi istorychnyi zhurnal* 1989 (5): 52–62; and "The Ruthenian (Volhynian) Metrica: Polish Crown Chancery Records for Ukrainian Lands, 1569–1673," *Harvard Ukrainian Studies* 14(1/2) June 1990: 7–83. See also my introduction in *Rus'ka (Volyns'ka) metryka: Rehestry dokumentiv koronnoï kantseliariï dlia ukraïns'kykh zemel' (Volyns'ke, Bratslavs'ke, Kyïvs'ke, Chernihivs'ke voievodstva), 1569–1673/The Ruthenian (Volhynian) Metrica: Early Inventories of the Polish Crown Chancery Records for Ukrainian Lands (1569–1673)*, comp. Patricia

In the late 1970s and 1980s, the Ukrainian scholar Mykola Koval's'kyi gained access but incorrectly identified them as part of the Lithuanian Metrica (the collection in which it is still located in RGADA), paying lip service to traditional imperial Russian and Soviet anti-Polish pretensions.[49] At that time, microfilm copies were furnished to Ukraine, but copies were never furnished to Poland, despite long-standing official requests and the fact that the registers involved are actually of Polish provenance. Early inventories of the documents recorded in these registers are currently being prepared for publication in Kyiv as part of a collaborative project with Ukrainian, Polish, and Russian scholars. Most important in this case is the fact that the detailed early document-by-document registers should help make these records more accessible to scholars throughout the world.[50] At the same time the publication serves to highlight one of the prime early examples of the dislocation of high-level state archives and the extent to which their continued displacement has hampered historical research.

Ukraine has a more direct claim on the remaining records of the eighteenth-century Hetmanate, which were seized and brought to St. Petersburg after the Hetmanate was suppressed by Catherine II. There also will be differing claims for the surviving records of the Crimean Khanate, seized and sequestered by Catherine II after she brought the Black Sea littoral under Russian imperial domination. Problems arise here due to the extent to which the archival materials involved have been "incorporated" into imperial Russian archives, and do not remain as a separate fond or collection.

Problems in Defining "Ukraine." As mentioned at the outset, for Ukraine, a country that has never known independence in its present territorial configuration, the process of identifying and providing for the national archival heritage is much more complex than for Russia. Under the Russian Empire, even the term "Ucrainica" was hardly permitted before the beginning of the twentieth century. Because of this, few abroad would understand "Ucrainica"

Kennedy Grimsted, Hennadii V. Boriak, Kyrylo Vyslobokov, Irena Sułkowska-Kurasiowa, and Natalia Iakovenko (Kyiv, forthcoming).

[49]   See Nikolai Pavlovich Koval'skii [Mykola Koval's'kyi], *Istochniki po istorii Ukrainy XVI–XVII vv. v Litovskoi metrike i fondakh prikazov TsGADA: Uchebnoe posobie* (Dnipropetrovsk: DGU, 1979), and especially *Metodicheskie rekomendatsii po ispol'zovaniiu dokumentov Litovskoi metriki XVI g. v kurse istochnikovedeniia otechestvennoi istorii (regesty dokumentov aktovykh knig Litovskoi metriki 191–195)*, comp. N. P. Koval'skii, V. V. Strashko, and G. V. Boriak (Dnipropetrovsk, 1987).

[50]   These will be provided in *Rus'ka (Volyns'ka) metryka,* as noted above.

as anything other than a subcategory of, or even distinct from, "Rossica." Before the revolution, or at least before 1905, the Ukrainian language and the name Ukraine (hence the concept of "Ucrainica") essentially were banned in the Russian Empire. Central parts of Ukraine were euphemistically referred to as "Little Russia (*Malorossiia*)," while the Black Sea littoral and neighboring steppe was termed "Southern Russia." Today, in many collections and descriptions of archival holdings of provenance in or relating to Ukraine within the bounds of the Russian Empire, it is difficult technically to distinguish Ucrainica from Rossica. Under the Austro-Hungarian Empire in the province of Galicia after 1867, Ukrainian was one of the three official languages of government, but because western Ukrainian lands subsequently became part of a reestablished Polish Republic after World War I, "Ucrainica" in or from that area frequently became a subcategory of "Polonica."

Ethnic or Linguistic Identity. Major problems will arise if archival claims are presented on the basis of ethnic, national, or linguistic identity. A mechanism must be created to deal with such problems, especially in the realm of personal papers. Precision in what constitutes "Ukrainian" or the degree of "Ukrainian" national consciousness on the part of a given person, is difficult to define in juridical terms, given the extent of intermarriage, imperial career patterns, and population transfers of such individuals. In practice, it is even more difficult to apply these terms to specific groups of archival materials. Many individuals of Ukrainian origin—from Ruthenian gentry of the sixteenth and seventeenth century to the Khrushchevs of the Soviet period—spent a major part of their life and careers in Warsaw, St. Petersburg, or Moscow, and were thoroughly polonized, russified, or sovietized in the process. Claims for their papers based on birth or ethnic identity would be hard to substantiate.

Indeed, in the world outside of Ukraine, and among those who had not retained a strong sense of Ukrainian linguistic identity or Ukrainian national consciousness, the ethnic-based distinction between "Ukrainian" and "Russian" or "Ukrainian" and "Polish" too often lacks sufficient clarity to be used as a determinant for archival claims. The large emigrant Jewish population from the Pale of Settlement (*Rus. cherta osedlosti*) in Southern Russia (as it was then called) would almost never identify themselves as of Ukrainian origin. By the same token, forcibly resettled Poles from western Ukraine would most likely consider their origin to be Polish. Because the principle of provenance would go against claims in connection with Ukrainian émigré materials created outside of Ukrainian lands, ethnic or linguistic identity in and of itself can never be sufficient grounds for claim.

Post-revolutionary Descriptions and Transfers. Ukrainian scholars and archival specialists have long put a high priority on the identification of significant bodies of records of Ukrainian provenance that remain in the metropolis. A commission was formed immediately after the revolutions of 1917 and numerous claims were put forward in its wake. A recent publication of documents reveals the extent of these activities.[51] During the period of official "Ukrainianization" in the 1920s an initial extensive survey of Ukrainian-related holdings in Moscow repositories was published.[52] There was also a detailed survey published of pre–nineteenth-century materials of Ukrainian provenance in the predecessor of what is now the Russian State Archive of Early Acts (RGADA).[53] A significant number of Ukraine-pertinent records and records of provenance in Ukraine that had been seized by central authorities before 1917 were returned to Ukraine.[54] Some additional Ukrainian materials held by state archives under the Main Archival Administration of the USSR were restituted during the 1940s and 1950s, but full details have not been published.

Recently opened CPSU Central Committee files show that the matter reached that highest level of the Soviet political pyramid. For example, in June of 1955, as Khrushchev was consolidating power in Moscow, his successor as Secretary of the Central Committee of the Communist Party of Ukraine, Ivan D. Nazarenko, addressed an appeal to the Central Committee in the name of Comrade Mikhail A. Suslov regarding:

> ...manuscripts, historical documents, artistic productions, and archeological collections that have a direct relationship to the history and culture of the Ukrainian SSR, [which] were located in various institutions, museums, picture galleries, libraries, and archives, especially in Moscow and Leningrad...[and which] in

---

[51] Serhii Kot and Oleksii Nestulia, *Ukraïns'ki kul'turni tsinnosti v Rosiï: Persha sproba povernennia, 1917–1918* (Kyiv: Soborna Ukraïna, 1996) [=*Povernennia kul'turnoho nadbannia Ukraïny: Dokumenty svidchat'*, 1].

[52] Dmytro Bahalii and Viktor Barvins'kyi, "Ukraïns'ki arkhivni fondy v mezhakh RSFSR," *Arkhivna sprava* 1 (1925): 34–44.

[53] See A. O. Malynovs'kyi, "Ohliad arkhivnykh materiialiv z istoriï zakhidno-rus'koho prava, shcho perekhovuiut'sia u Drevlekhranylyshchi Moskovs'koho Tsentral'noho arkhivu (po 1-she liutoho roku 1926)," *Pratsi Komisiï dlia vyuchuvannia istoriï zakhidno-rus'koho ta ukraïns'koho prava* (Kyiv) 2 (1926): 1–49 (microfiche=IDC-R-11,119).

[54] See, for example, [Hnat Pavlovych] Zh[ytets'kyi], "Peredacha arkhivnykh materialov Ukrainy," *Arkhivnoe delo* 8–9 (1926): 117–23, and Ievhen Mykhailovych Ivanov, "Ukraïns'ki fondy, perevezeni z Moskvy," *Arkhivna sprava* 4 (1927): 44–65.

their time had been taken from Ukraine to Moscow and Leningrad.

He noted that "according to a decree of the Presidium of the Central Executive Council of the USSR in 1927–1928, part of them were returned to Ukraine," but he pointed out that the continued "dispersal of archival and historico-literary materials significantly encumbers scientific research work in the sphere of history and culture of the Ukrainian people."[55] An accompanying list specified predominantly literary manuscripts and autographs in eight different libraries, museums, and institutes in Moscow and Leningrad, along with pre–nineteenth-century archival materials in the Central State Archive of Early Acts (TsGADA SSSR), and a portrait by Taras Shevchenko in the Uralsk Oblast Museum.[56]

A secret answer from the Ministry of Culture in Moscow proposed the transfer from the Lenin Library of:

1) a collection of manuscripts of the Ukrainian philosopher H. S. Skovoroda and materials for his biography (ca. 1,000 folios);
2) autographs and letters of the Ukrainian social leader P. A. Kulish (up to 600 folios); and
3) autographs and letters of Kvitka-Osnov'ianenko (40 folios),

but none of the materials listed in the original Ukrainian request were to be included. From the Saltykov-Shchedrin State Public Library, transfer was recommended of "archival materials of the Ukrainian writer Holovats′kyi (464 units)," who was in fact one of the nine named writers on the Ukrainian list.

Transfer of further Shevchenko materials was denied on the grounds that:

...only five drawings and one painting by Shevchenko remain in the State Russian Museum, since 115 artistic works of Shevchenko were given to Ukraine during the period 1929 to 1948.

Nevertheless, in one case from the Tret′iakov Gallery, they agreed to have a copy prepared. The concluding explanation is revealing in terms of the rationale then involved:

The inclusion of a few works of T. G. Shevchenko in the exhibits

---

55 I. Nazarenko to CC CPSU Secretary M. A. Suslov (16 June 1955), RGANI, 5/17/544 (film roll 5732), fols. 75–76.

56 "Spisok arkhivnykh materialov, rukopisei, proizvedenii iskusstva, otnosiashchikhsia k istorii i kul′ture Ukrainskoi SSR i khraniashchikhsia v arkhivakh, bibliotekakh, muzeiakh i kartinnykh galereiakh Moskvy i Leningrada," RGANI, 5/17/544 (film roll 5732), fols. 77–79.

of the Tret'iakov Gallery and the Russian Museum serves as a
clear testimony to the unbroken friendship and collaboration of
the two brotherly nations in the cultural sphere...[57]

No answer to the request from TsGADA (now RGADA) has been found, but
the archival materials listed in the 1955 desiderata all remain there and were
obviously not transferred to Kyiv.

In the 1970s and 1980s, some of the most specifically Ukrainian-related
materials in TsGADA were surveyed by the Ukrainian historian Mykola
Koval's'kyi and his students at Dnipropetrovsk University, along with the
"Lithuanian Metrica" mentioned above. Microfilms of many files were
prepared for transfer to Ukraine, but there were no pretensions involving
transfer of original records.[58] Regrettably, Koval's'kyi's surveys were neither
comprehensive nor systematic. For the purposes of present efforts to establish
the Ukrainian archival legacy, they did not identify the provenance of the
records described. Nor did they pay adequate attention to the archival
distinction between provenance and pertinence, the arrangement of the
materials in terms of their creating agencies, nor the circumstances through
which the materials were transferred to Moscow.

Since its reestablishment in Kyiv in 1987, the Archeographic
Commission/Institute of Ukrainian Archeography has undertaken extensive
surveys of archival Ucrainica in Moscow and St. Petersburg, as well as
several foreign countries. Well intentioned plans to the contrary, a centralized
database or publicly accessible reference facility still has not been established
to encompass the data collected. Several descriptive publications have
appeared about Ucrainica archival holdings in Canada, Great Britain, and the
Czech Republic. The aim of these efforts, for the most part, has been to
facilitate research, rather than to legally define the archival heritage of
Ukraine. Most of the materials described involve no pretensions for claims.
And as such, like the Koval's'kyi-led efforts, they have not involved determination of provenance or migratory data. Since independence, however, as will
be seen in the following chapter, more attention has been devoted to locating
displaced parts of the Ukrainian archival heritage, in many cases with as least
implied pretensions for copies or transfer of the original records.

---

[57]   Deputy Minister of Culture V. Kemenov to M. A. Suslov (17 August 1955),
RGANI, 5/17/544 (film roll 5732), fols. 80–81. In a subsequent document the transfer
was approved by the CC Division on Science and Culture and authorized by the
Central Committee (folio 82).

[58]   See, for example, Nikolai Koval'skii [Mykola Koval's'kyi], *Istochniki po istorii
Ukrainy* and *Istochnikovedenie istorii ukrainsko-russkikh sviazei (XVI–pervaia
polovina XVII v.): Uchebnoe posobie* (Dnipropetrovsk: DGU, 1979).

CHAPTER 2

Retrieving the Cultural Heritage and Displaced Ukrainian Archives

The lack of adequate guidelines and norms for reconstituting the archival heritage of successor States has not prevented professional attention—and in some cases even heated discussion—regarding archival pretensions. Since Ukrainian independence, there have been many appeals in the popular press, in parliament, and in other public forums for the return or revindication of Ukrainian cultural treasures.

International Appeals and a National Commission

1991 UN Appeal. Serious Ukrainian pretensions for the return of the national archival legacy located abroad, together with other Ukrainian cultural treasures, were expressed immediately after independence by Ukrainian Ambassador Viktor Batiouk in the United Nations General Assembly, in support of the 1991 resolution on cultural restitution:

> Pursuant to the declaration on State sovereignty adopted on 16 July last year, Ukraine has the right to return to the ownership of the people of Ukraine the national cultural and historical property which is outside the frontiers of the republic. This flows from the natural right of every people to the historical and cultural property of its country created on its own territory.

Archival and manuscript materials were also intended, as Batiouk mentioned "literature" and "the literary heritage of many writers, which have, because of the unfortunate past, been scattered throughout the world...They can and must be returned."[1] As is evident in such a statement, an effort has been made to involve the principle of "provenance"—material "created on its own territory"—rather than merely property "pertinent" to Ukraine in the sense that it was created by ethnic Ukrainians worldwide.

---

[1] Viktor Batiouk speaking on 22 October 1991 (interpretation from Russian), *UN General Assembly Official Records: Forty-Sixth Session* (A/46/PV.35), pp. 11, 13. See the resolution UN adopted in 1991, "Return or restitution of cultural property to the countries of origin," 22 October 1991 (46/10), *UN General Assembly Official Records: Forty-Sixth Session*, Supplement No. 49 (A/46/49): 14–15.

The National Commission for the Return of Cultural Treasures to Ukraine: Conferences and Publications. Since its formation in December 1992, the National Commission for the Return of Cultural Treasures to Ukraine, headed by Professor Oleksandr Fedoruk, has actively pursued issues regarding the return of cultural treasures to Ukraine and seeking advice from many experts.[2] The Commission has instituted a key publications series, which has served as an outlet for the proceedings of a series of round tables, symposia, and conferences the Commission has conducted on related issues. By and large, however, the conferences have focused on problems resulting from World War II displacements (see the second part of this volume). Their efforts have frequently involved archival affairs, and as such are further directly related to our inquiry.

In July 1993, a three-day regional meeting in Lviv addressed restitution questions of particular relevance to western Ukraine. A report of those meetings published by the Commission included a running bibliography of related publications to date, including those in the popular press.[3] Library losses during World War II were the prime focus for a round table meeting in Donetsk in May 1994, although many of the presentations and discussions went well beyond specific library matters.[4] A separate report was issued on the archival records of the Rosenberg Special Command (Einsatzstab Reichsleiter Rosenberg—ERR) held in Kyiv, which, as will be discussed further in Chapter 5 below, are one of the richest sources available on ERR looting activities in the USSR.[5]

A larger international conference, or "National Seminar," as it was called, under UNESCO sponsorship was held in Chernihiv at the end of September 1994, specifically devoted to "Problems of Restitution of National Cultural Treasures Which Were Lost or Displaced during the Second World War." In addition to general presentations from the presidium on the opening day—attended by an audience of over 300—subsequent separate, and usually

---

[2]   "Postanova Kabinetu Ministriv Ukraïny No. 732—'Pro utvorennia Natsional'noï komisiï z pytan' povernennia v Ukraïnu kul'turnykh tsinnostei'" (28 December 1992) and "Polozhennia pro Natsional'nu komisiiu z pytan' povernennia v Ukraïnu kul'turnykh tsinnostei" (18 October 1996) in *Ukraïna v mizhnarodno-pravovykh vidnosynakh,* book 2, pp. 687–92.

[3]   *Povernennia kul'turnoho nadbannia Ukraïny: Problemy, zavdannia, perspektyvy* (Kyiv, 1993).

[4]   Ibid., no. 4 (Kyiv, 1994).

[5]   Ibid., no. 5 (Kyiv, 1994). The short summary report on the ERR records was unfortunately incomplete and in parts inaccurate in its assessment of these materials.

simultaneous sections were devoted to issues of museums, libraries, and archives. Again, many of the presentations went well beyond the wartime period and included various popular appeals for the return of Ukrainian cultural treasures, and, in terms of archives, more specific discussions of displaced archival Ucrainica abroad.[6] Attention again focused on World War II six months later, in the spring of 1995, when the National Commission hosted a Ukrainian-German round table in Odesa devoted to displaced cultural treasures during the war. There was further amplification of several subjects that had already been presented the previous year in Chernihiv.[7]

A broadly based survey of problems involving the displaced Ukrainian cultural legacy was presented in a lengthy essay by Serhii I. Kot, published by the Commission as a separate issue of the series. An introductory chapter deals with international legal aspects, and subsequent chapters provide details on Ukrainian cultural treasures taken to Russia in different historical periods.[8]

An important 1996 symposium in Kyiv sponsored by the Commission devoted to legal aspects of displaced cultural treasures and restitution brought together many leading international specialists who have been grappling with these problems in recent years. Short presentations by the participants appeared in the 1997 volume of the Commission series.[9] Many aspects of the

---

[6]   A part of the proceedings of the Chernihiv conference appeared in the series issued by the National Commission—*Materiialy natsional'noho seminaru "Problemy povernennia natsional'no-kul'turnykh pam'iatok, vtrachenykh abo peremishchenykh pid chas Druhoï svitovoï viiny." Chernihiv, veresen' 1994* (Kyiv, 1996) [*=Povernennia kul'turnoho nadbannia Ukraïny: Problemy, zavdannia, perspektyvy*, 6].

[7]   See the published proceedings of the roundtable—*Kul'tura i viina: Pohliad cherez pivstolittia*, ed. Viktor Akulenko, Valentyna Vrublevs'ka, et al. (Kyiv: Adrys, 1996) [*=Povernennia kul'turnoho nadbannia Ukraïny: Problemy, zavdannia, perspektyvy*, 7]. Wolfgang Eichwede references specific examples of recent restitution between Germany and Ukraine in his paper, "Ukraina idet svoim putem," pp. 9–11. See below, Chapter 12.

[8]   See Serhii I. Kot, *Ukraïns'ki kul'turni tsinnosti v Rosiï: Problema povernennia v konteksti istoriï ta prava* (Kyiv, 1996) [*=Povernennia kul'turnoho nadbannia Ukraïny: Problemy, zavdannia, perspektyvy*, 8]. Unfortunately, like a number of the other materials published by the Commission, the survey was published without any citations to the extensive documentation involved and hence cannot serve as an adequate basis for discussion, evaluation, or possible claims.

[9]   *Materiialy naukovo-praktychnoho sympoziumu "Pravovi aspekty restytutsiï kul'turnykh tsinnostei: Teoriia i praktyka": Kyïv, hruden' 1996*, ed. Oleksandr K. Fedoruk, Iu. S. Shemshuchenko, et al. (Kyiv, 1997) [*=Povernennia kul'turnoho nadbannia Ukraïny: Problemy, zavdannia, perspektyvy*, 10].

discussion are dealt with below in this chapter, while the recommendations of the Symposium appear below, pp. 574–77, as Appendix X.

For Ukrainian archives in an international context, the most important presentation was made by Volodymyr S. Lozyts′kyi, deputy chief of the Ukrainian Archival Administration. It appeared as well as an article in *Arkhivy Ukraïny*.[10] For the first time in a Ukrainian publication, Lozyts′kyi sketches the international historical background starting with Swedish archival transfers in the seventeenth century. He also mentions the significant archival transfers to successor states that coincided with the the dissolution of the Austro-Hungarian Empire.[11] Since that time, Lozyts′kyi has prepared a study of international archival relations, particularly in the context of Ukrainian participation in the International Council on Archives.[12]

In addition to its sponsored series of conferences and publications in Ukraine, members of the Commission have also been active in coordinating restitution issues abroad with neighboring countries. Representing the National Commission at the 1997 UNESCO-sponsored conference on restitution issues in Minsk, Fedoruk emphasized "the return to Ukraine of cultural treasures lost in different times and under different historical situations" as "one of the most important directions of state cultural policy." And Fedoruk again emphasized the success of the official policy of joint restitution with Germany "in a construction spirit" as indicating and enabling

---

[10]   Volodymyr S. Lozyts′kyi, "Pravovi zasady mizhnarodnoho spivrobitnytstva v haluzi restytutsiï arkhivnykh fondiv i dokumentiv: Istoriia, problemy, perspektyvy," in *Materiialy naukovo-praktychnoho sympoziumu "Pravovi aspekty restytutsiï kul′turnykh tsinnostei: Teoriia i praktyka,"* pp. 54–62.

[11]   In the article Lozyts′kyi also discusses other relevant developments for Ukraine following World War I (although in that latter period he does not discuss some of the problems and complexities involved and the criticism of the results by the international archival community). He omits mention of the archival transfers resulting from the Treaty of Riga of 1921 between Poland, Russia, and Ukraine, and makes no analysis or commentary on its effects. He refers, sometimes imprecisely, to some of the post-World War II developments under UNESCO and the International Council on Archives (ICA), including microfilming. Regrettably, in the version of the presentation that was later published in *Arkhivy Ukraïny,* Lozyts′kyi's essay also lacks any documentation to appropriate treaties and to the extensive international literature involved. As an initial sketch, however, the article sets forth many of the crucial problems in connection both with issues of the succession of States and of wartime displacements.

[12]   This book includes a number of related documents and was produced in connection with lectures in the archival program at Kyiv University for Culture and Art. See Volodymyr S. Lozyts′kyi, *Istoriia mizhnarodnoho arkhivnoho spivrobit-nytstva (1898–1998 rr.)* (Kyiv, 1999).

"new directions of cooperation." Citing the 1996 conference in Kyiv, he also emphasized the need for new and more effective international legal norms as a basis for international cooperation in the field.[13] Despite a high point in 1997—when the Commission celebrated its fifth anniversary with a series of publications and presentations—by the spring of 1999, the Commission had been reduced in status from its authoritative position directly under the Council of Ministers to being a de facto arm of the Ministry of Culture, with the new name of the State Service for Control of the Transmission of Cultural Treasures Across the Borders of Ukraine.[14]

National Commission Foreign Retrieval Efforts. Efforts by the National Commission have brought about the retrieval of considerable Ukrainian cultural treasures from the Ukrainian diaspora. Those associated with the Commission have been actively traveling and establishing ties with Ukrainian artistic and cultural leaders abroad in an effort to encourage the transfer of cultural treasures created or collected by émigrés of Ukrainian descent to the Ukrainian homeland. Unlike the 1991 Ukrainian diplomatic pronouncement in the United Nations, however, the Commission appears not to observe the distinction between cultural treasures created in Ukraine and then alienated, and those cultural treasures that were created abroad. As can be seen in their declarations and publications, they frequently use the term "return" even for material produced by Ukrainian émigrés outside Ukraine. It certainly may be desirable today to reunite the Ukrainian homeland with the diaspora, and to bring to Ukraine important products of the Ukrainian diaspora (for instance, of governments and cultural leaders in exile), but it is nonetheless important to observe the legal distinctions involved. And for archival claims, the distinction is crucial, in cases where formal claims may arise.

The Commission is now publishing brochures listing its receipts from abroad, starting with a 1997 issue that covered acquisitions received from 1993 to 1997. A second issue appeared in 1999, covering receipts during 1998. Inappropriately entitled "Returned to Ukraine," very few of the contents were created in Ukrainian lands, and most had not been held before in Ukraine, although there are a few materials mentioned that are restitutions

---

[13]   Oleksandr Fedoruk, "Restitutsiia i vozvrashchenie kul'turnykh tsennostei— vazhnyi faktor mezhdunarodnogo sotrudnichestva," in *Restytutsyia kul'turnykh kash-toŭnastsei*, pp. 15–20; quotations are from pp. 15 and 16.

[14]   Oleksandr Fedoruk, "Zberezhennia natsional'nykh kul'turnykh tsinnostei—na koryst' suchasnoï tsyvilizatsiï," *Halyts'ka brama* 1997 (12[36]): 3.

of materials seized by the Nazis during World War II.[15] Both brochures have appended lists of cultural treasures including archival materials received, but the precise sources and names of donors are not indicated in individual cases, nor are there references to more detailed descriptions of the materials that have been published elsewhere in some cases.

These "Returned to Ukraine" lists have a generous showing of Ukrainian library and archival materials, predominantly from émigré sources. Among the largest and most significant examples, transfers include personal papers, memorabilia and library books of the Ukrainian author and political activist Ivan Bahrianyi (1906–1963), received from Germany. The library and personal papers of the Ukrainian historian at the Sorbonne, Professor Arkady Joukovsky, who was honored as a Foreign Member of the National Academy of Sciences of Ukraine, were presented to the recently established Ol'zhych Library in Kyiv. A large part of the Ol'zhych Library, which honors the Ukrainian poet and political activist Oleh Ol'zhych (1907–1944), included other receipts from Paris. The personal papers of Ol'zhych, transferred to Ukraine from the Czech Republic, however, went to the Institute of Literature under NAN. Some additional Ol'zhych archival materials came from Slovakia as well as the Czech Republic and included papers of Oleksandr Oles' (1878–1944). Personal papers of the Ukrainian poetess from Brazil, Vira Vovk (Wira Wowk; Selians'ka) were presented to the Central Archive-Museum of Literature and Art (TsDAMLM); her personal library was divided among several libraries in Kyiv. Personal papers totaling 96,000 units of the theatrical personality Ulas Samchuk (1905–1978), received from Canada, also went to TsDAMLM, although some of the memorabilia went to the Samchuk Museum in Ternopil Oblast. Papers, photographs, and memorabilia of the poetess Lesia Ukraïnka (1871–1913) and the Kosach family, received from the United States, went to an institution entitled the Museum of Luminaries of Ukrainian Culture—Lesia Ukraïnka, Mykola Lysenko, Panas Saksahans'kyi, and Mykhailo Staryts'kyi.

In April 1999, remaining records of the UNR Mission in Switzerland were presented to Ukraine and deposited in TsDAVO in Kyiv. There they joined other exiled UNR records received earlier from the National Archives in Canada and files from the UNR government in exile in the USA (1984–1992).

---

15 *Povernuto v Ukraïny*, ed. Oleksandr Fedoruk et al., no. 1 (Kyiv: Natsional'na komisiia, 1997); and no. 2 (Kyiv, 1999). Regrettably, the lists indicate only the originating country and do not indicate the specific source of the acquisitions.

The Dovzhenko Legacy. Of particular significance because they were transferred from Russia are several sets of materials relating to the well-known Ukrainian film director, Oleksandr Dovzhenko (1894–1956). These include personal papers with over 2,000 units, over 310,000 frames of film, memorabilia, and books from Dovzhenko's personal library.[16] As it turns out, however, the transfers involved cannot be considered an official act of restitution from Russia to Ukraine, but were rather purchased from a private source in Russia. Indeed, the Dovzhenko case is a good example of the problems involved in both definition and potential restitution of the archival heritage of Ukraine, because despite this transfer, the major and most important part of Dovzhenko's archival and cinematographic legacy nevertheless remains in Russia.

Dovzhenko's second wife, the Russian actress and film director Iuliia Sol′ntseva, agreed, at the end of the 1960s, to the permanent transfer of Dovzhenko's most important personal papers to what is now the Russian State Archive of Literature and Art (RGALI, then TsGALI) in Moscow, where a separate fond was established. The archival materials, memorabilia, and library books transferred to Kyiv in 1993–1994 accordingly represent only materials that TsGALI choose not to accession for permanent preservation. The transferred materials have now all been deposited in the Central State Archive-Museum of Literature and Art (TsDAMLM) in Kyiv, which intends to establish a special museum honoring Dovzhenko (currently there is a special exhibit there, not a full-fledged museum). Recently, in connection with the centenary of the birth of Dovzhenko, a publication of his complete diary was proposed, since earlier only fragmentary ones were issued. However, RGALI quite legally refused official Ukrainian requests for a xerox copy of Dovzhenko's diary, because the diary was among that part of his papers that are closed until 2009, according to the official RGALI accession agreement with Iuliia Sol′ntseva.[17]

Meanwhile, Dovzhenko's most important cinematographic legacy—archival copies of his films and editing outtakes—remains on permanent deposit in Gosfil′mofond, the former all-union, now Russian, feature film archive in suburban Moscow. The Dovzhenko Film Studio in Kyiv has its own museum honoring the film director, which has long been collecting archival materials relating to Dovzhenko, but the film studio has not been

---

16 *Povernuto na Ukraïny*, no. 1, appendix 1, nos. 2, 15, 76, and 81.

17 I am grateful to Serhii Kot for advising me about the Dovzhenko legacy, including the negotiations with RGALI and the transfer of additional materials to Kyiv. Kot is currently preparing a documented account of this transfer with which he has been directly involved in the negotiations.

able to afford the high prices demanded for copies of Dovzhenko's films, the archival copies of which remain in Gosfil'mofond, along with other related materials. Distribution rights likewise remain in the hands of Gosfil'mofond and its licensed distributors.

Identifying Cultural Treasures in Russia. Although there is still no general agreement for cultural restitution or devolution with the Russian Federation, in recent years, Ukrainian specialists under Commission sponsorship have started an active program of identifying specific cultural treasures known to be located in Russia. An initial list of objects from Ukrainian museums located in Russia was published in the popular cultural magazine *Pam'iatky Ukraïny* in 1994, including a few charters and important manuscript treasures. The preface enumerates several required transfers of cultural treasures to Moscow and Leningrad from Ukrainian museums during the Soviet period.[18] Similar in plan to the Belarusian series mentioned earlier, a collection of relevant documents regarding the identification and revindication of cultural treasures appeared in 1996, covering a wide range of initiatives taken immediately after the 1917 revolutions, with 107 documents from the years 1917 and 1918.[19] A year later, a register of over 800 Ukrainian archeological and anthropological collections in Russia appeared, as another concrete step in the attempt to establish a comprehensive survey of the extent and nature of cultural treasures that were taken to the imperial capitals from Ukrainian lands over the centuries.[20]

In introducing the latter register, Fedoruk spoke of the significance of identifying the national cultural heritage. He mentioned the series of conferences that have taken place on the subject, their resolutions and appeals for cultural restitution as of fundamental importance to the nation, and the related context of international law.[21]

---

[18]   Adriana V'ialets', "Svit maie pochuty," with the appended "Spysok predmetiv iz muzeïv Ukraïny: U zbirkakh muzeïv ta inshykh skhovyshch Rosiï," *Pam'iatky Ukraïny* 1994 (1–2[25]): 84–91.

[19]   Serhii Kot and Oleksii Nestulia, *Ukraïns′ki kul′turni tsinnosti v Rosiï: Persha sproba povernennia, 1917–1918* (Kyiv: Soborna Ukraïna, 1996) [=*Povernennia kul′turnoho nadbannia Ukraïny: Dokumenty svidchat′*, 1].

[20]   *Ukraïns′ki kul′turni tsinnosti v Rosiï: Arkheolohiia kolektsiï Ukraïny*, comp. S. Beliaeva et al.; ed. P. Tolochko et al. (Kyiv, 1997) [=*Povernennia kul′turnoho nadbannia Ukraïny: Dokumenty svidchat′*, 2].

[21]   Oleksandr Fedoruk, "Natsional′na kul′turnaspadshchyna—skarbnytsia narodu," in *Ukraïns′ki kul′turni tsinnosti v Rosiï: Arkheolohiia kolektsiï Ukraïny*, pp. 6–11.

Cataloguing World War II Losses. Given the comparatively high extent of cultural devastation and loss in Ukraine during the Second World War, Ukrainian pretensions are particularly strong about cultural treasures taken from Ukraine during the war but that are now held in Russia. As will be seen in more detail in Chapter 4, there are three important categories of treasures involved:

1) those that were evacuated by Soviet authorities at the beginning of the Nazi invasion but were not returned to Ukraine;
2) those that were seized by Nazi authorities, restituted by the United States from Germany to Soviet authorities, but then subsequently retained in Moscow; and,
3) the many cultural treasures that disappeared during the war whose fate has not been identified.

It is equally possible that the items in this third category may now be held in Russia or they may still be somewhere in the West—or they may have been destroyed.

An initial catalog of losses from the Museum of Russian Art in Kyiv, including many icons known to have been evacuated by the Nazis in the fall of 1943, was issued in 1994.[22] Although reliable Nazi inventories and shipping lists exist in Kyiv for some of the plundered art, individual items have not been matched against extant Nazi lists. Nor has it been possible in most cases to match up individual items with the copies of restitution property cards from the American occupation zone in Germany that are now available in Kyiv (see Chapter 6). Issued in Russian, the catalog may help Russian museums verify the listings, especially since Ukrainian specialists suspect that some of the icons returned from the West now remain in Moscow. However, the fragmentary descriptions can only be termed a preliminary list, since the publication includes no pictures of the lost works of art nor sufficient documentation for identification purposes or for entry into international databases.

Addressing the need for further identification, especially in this third "fate unknown" category, the National Commission for the Return of Cultural Treasures to Ukraine issued an English-language catalog in 1998 listing 474 paintings from the fourteenth through the nineteenth centuries that

---

[22] *Katalog proizvedenii Kievskogo muzeia russkogo iskusstva, utrachennogo v gody Velikoi Otechestvennoi voiny 1941–1945 gg. (zhivopis', grafika),* comp. Mikhail D. Faktorovich, Ekaterina I. Ladyzhenskaia, and Lidiia A. Pel'kina; ed. Mikhail D. Faktorovich (Kyiv, 1994).

were lost, as a result of the war, from the Museum of Western and Oriental Art in Kyiv.[23] This initial issue by the museum of a series of planned catalogs of its losses apparently also has not been compared against American property-card listings. Neither has there been any attempt to match the entries with Nazi inventories and shipping lists in Kyiv archives. Unlike the catalog of losses from the former Museum of Russian Art, however, there are black-and-white pictures of selected paintings.[24]

The Case of the St. Michael Cathedral.   Although negotiations are under way in a few specific cases, there appears to be no general willingness on the part of Russian authorities to resolve restitution issues with newly independent States any more than with Western Europe. Today, the national-patriotic mood in Russia reflects a nostalgia for union with Russia's "Slavic brothers" and regret at the loss of empire. Such sentiments are reinforced by the strong belief that among the new nations in the "Near Abroad" Ukraine cannot be culturally independent, because it shares the common Slavic heritage of Rus'. In the Russian-language historical usage, "Rus'" is still rarely differentiated from "Russia."

One of the most famous, and for Ukraine most symbolic, cases is the fate of the twelfth-century mosaics from the St. Michael Cathedral of the Golden Domes. Just before the church itself was blown up in 1934–1936 under the guise of "urban renewal" (although obviously as part of Stalin's anti-religious campaign) most of the mosaics were removed in a last-minute effort. Specialists from Leningrad were brought in to assist in "the delicate operation," but not all of them could be saved in time. The mosaics subsequently were retained in a storage area closed to the public in the St. Sophia Cathedral museum complex in Kyiv. The most famous mosaic of Saint Demetrius of Thessalonica (known as Dmytrii Soluns'kyi in Ukrainian), two frescoes, and a fragment of a bas-relief from the cathedral were sent for an exhibition to the State Tret'iakov Galley in Moscow in 1938, but were not returned before the war.[25] Other mosaics and frescoes, which were looted by the

---

[23]   *Catalogue of Works of Western European Painters Lost during Second World War*, comp. Olena Roslavets; ed. Oleksandr Fedoruk et al. (Kyiv, 1998).

[24]   And, indeed, if catalogs of art losses are going to be effective for international databases, it is essential that pictures of all lost items be provided where possible and that entries are correlated with available documentation regarding migration from existing Nazi reports and other sources.

[25]   The destruction of that cathedral and other architectural monuments in Kyiv is documented by Titus D. Hewryk, *The Lost Architecture of Kiev* (New York: Ukrainian Museum, 1982), pp. 12–16. At the time of publication, Hewryk did not

Nazis and then returned to the USSR, are now held by the Hermitage and the Russian Museum in St. Petersburg as well as the Novgorod Architectural Museum-Preserve.

In October 1943 the retreating Nazis carefully packed most of the mosaics and frescoes remaining in Kyiv and shipped them as spoils of war, first to Cracow, accompanied by the Ukrainian museum specialist, Petro Kurinnyi (Petr Kurinnoi), and then to the Castle of Höchstädt in Bavaria. Remaining Nazi shipping reports in Kyiv document the seizure in precise detail.[26] Since Ukrainian independence and the revival of the Orthodox Church in Ukraine, the Kyiv landmark cathedral is being rebuilt, but many of its most important surviving frescoes are now in Russia. Recently, Kyiv specialists led by Serhii Kot have been tracing the fate of these irreplaceable cultural treasures based on Nazi reports, American restitution documentation, and other sources available in Kyiv and Moscow. A well-documented article on the subject appeared in early 1999 in the popular cultural magazine *Pam'iatky Ukraïny,* an entire issue of which was devoted to the fate of the monastery and its cathedral.[27]

The Ukrainian claim for the mosaic of Saint Demetrius, which adorns many Russian publications on the art and culture of "Kyivan Rus'," is complicated. In a 1998 Moscow newspaper piece, the Tret'iakov Gallery deputy director commented that Ukraine has no case for restitution, because, according to their records, that mosaic came to Moscow on exhibit before the war, and then was traded for several Ukrainian paintings that went to the

---

have all of the documentation now available in Kyiv. Remaining mosaics and frescoes in Kyiv are now displayed in an exhibition in St. Sophia Cathedral.

[26] Precise Nazi reports found in Kyiv even identify the railroad wagon numbers used for their initial transport to Cracow (TsDAVO, 3676/1/225, fols. 271–274).

[27] Serhii Kot and Iurii Koreniuk, "Mykhailivs'ki pam'iatky v rosiis'kykh muzeiakh," in *Pam'iatky Ukraïny* 1999 (1[122]): 63–82, XXVI–XXVIII. The issue also contains detailed analysis and newly published documents on the destruction and rebuilding of the cathedral. See also an article covering the materials in the Tret'iakov Gallery by Kot and Koreniuk, "Rosiia povynna povernut' Ukraïni tsinnosti z Mykhailivs'koho Zolotoverkhoho soboru v Kyievi," *Stolytsia* 1997 (11[36]): 6, 9; a documented report by Kot on the wartime migration of these treasures appears in *Spoils of War: International Newsletter* 5 (June 1998): 37–41. Since that article was published, Kot reports that he has been able to identify the materials as having been in the U.S. Munich Collecting Point. (See also Chapter 6, p. 218.) Kot also discusses the principles and facts involved in the issue in his article "Restytutsiia chy konfiskatsiia?: Rosiis'kyi zakon pro peremishcheni pid chas Druhoï svitovoï viiny kul'turni tsinnosti ta Ukraïna," *Polityka i chas* 1998 (8), especially pp. 29–34.

Museum of Russian and Ukrainian Art in Kyiv. (Kyiv specialists note that the only document to have surfaced certifying the "trade"—a "copy" that was not fully signed—may not be authentic.) The Hermitage director is adopting a more flexible position, but the Kyiv mosaics now held in that museum came in 1953, having first been transferred to Novgorod after their return from the West. Meanwhile, the director of the Novgorod Museum, which still has five frescoes and a fragmentary mosaic, claims that they came to Novgorod before the war, from whence they were seized by the Nazis. But he defers to higher authorities for a solution: "If the Government decides they should be given back, we will pack them up and send them off."[28]

Restitution negotiations move slowly and not without rancor, as was obvious in Moscow meetings and official diplomatic notes in the summer of 1998 and postponed meetings in 1999. A favorable outcome was suggested in press comments by the Russian minister of culture in September 1999, but, in fact, as of that date there was little hope that St. Demetrius would return to Kyiv.[29] Given the symbolic importance of these negotiations, and the further complexity that they represent the adornment of a church destroyed by the Soviet regime, the outcome will undoubtedly affect other cases. Indeed this was one of the first restitution cases with the former union republics to be aired in the Russian press, compared to the furor over non-restitution of wartime trophy cultural treasures from the West and especially with Germany (see Chapter 10). In at least one of a July 1998 series of articles in the Moscow newspaper *Kommersant Daily,* the frescoes from the Golden Domes Cathedral were mentioned as examples of the many cultural treasures removed during the war from Ukraine and now retained in Russia following their postwar restitution (that was one of the parts of the Moscow text that was reprinted in Kyiv).[30] Several of the other comments from Russian

[28]   A series of comments appeared with the full-page article by Tat'iana Markina, "Mozaiki Mikhailovskogo sobora mogut vernut'sia na Ukrainu," *Kommersant Daily* 119 (4 July 1998): 7—among those quoted are Lidiia Iovleva, Deputy Director for Science, State Tret'iakov Gallery, "Togda schitali, chto...obmen ravnotsennyi"; Mikhail Piotrovskii, Director, State Hermitage, "Eksponaty mogut byt' vozvrashcheny"; and Nikolai Grinev, of the Novgorod State Consolidated Museum-Preserve, "Takie voprosy dolzhny reshat'sia na urovne pravitel'stva."

[29]   The press comment was widely reported abroad by the Associated Press, but officials in the Ministry of Culture in Moscow clarified the issue to me in an October 1999 meeting, ruling out any possible transfers from the Tret'iakov Gallery.

[30]   "Ukrainskie tsennosti ostalis' v Rossii," first appeared in *Kommersant Daily* 119 (4 July 1998): 7, as part of the larger series of comments with the article by Tat'iana Markina; that segment was reprinted in *Kievskie vedomosti* 1 August 1998: 10.

cultural leaders favored restitution, including those of a spokesman for the Moscow Patriarchate who asserted that the frescoes "should certainly be returned to the Church." However, he used the occasion to advance yet another criticism of the independent Orthodox Church in Ukraine, which the Moscow Patriarchate refuses to recognize.[31] Although not mentioned in his presentation, the Golden Domes Cathedral had been under the Kyiv Metropolitanate for most of its existence, and was in fact built centuries before the Moscow Patriarchate was established in 1589. The present bitter split in the Orthodox Church in Ukraine further complicates retrospective claims for nationalized Church property that ended up in imperial capitals.

Indicative of avid Russian rejection of cultural restitution to Ukraine, one unsigned Russian argument in the newspaper presentation went so far as to suggest that these treasures should not be considered "Ukrainian." Three reasons were given: first, Ukraine did not exist when the monastery was built in the twelfth century; second, Ukraine should not have a monopoly on the cultural legacy of "Kyivan Rus'"; and, third, the monastery, built by Prince Sviatopolk, represented the political policy of uniting the dispersed appanage principalities, which in turn symbolized the creation of a general Rus' spiritual sphere.[32] The articles in this collection of press treatments do not suggest easy or speedy resolution. They also illustrate the broader political context that will further complicate resolution of archival restitution issues.

Potential Archival Pretensions

Archival Pretensions. The most detailed statement to date of Ukrainian pretensions for archival materials in Russia has not been presented formally to Moscow, but has rather been described in a series of popular articles in a 1994 issue of *Pam'iatky Ukraïny* (no. 3–6). Similarly, more general claims were spelled out earlier in a January 1993 appeal in *Kyïvs'ka starovyna* by Liudmyla Lozenko, representing the Main Archival Administration of Ukraine, and Pavlo Sokhan', director of the Institute of Ukrainian Archeogra-

---

[31] Protoierei Viktor Petliuchenko, Deputy Head of the Division of Foreign Church Relations, Moscow Patriarchate, "Freski i mozaiki dolzhny byt' vozvrashcheny tserkvi," in *Kommersant Daily* 119 (4 July 1998).

[32] "Delezh kul'tury i razdel istorii." The comments appeared in *Kommersant Daily*, 4 July 1998, as part of the larger complex of comments with the article by Tat'iana Markina; that segment was reprinted in *Kievskie vedomosti* 1 August 1998: 10.

phy of the National Academy of Sciences of Ukraine.[33] With considerable rhetoric, Lozenko and Sokhan´ list examples of a long series of alienated archival materials taken to Russia from Ukrainian lands from the twelfth through the twentieth centuries, including manuscript collections from Church sources, and others collected by archeographic expeditions under the auspices of the imperial and later Soviet Academies of Sciences. They underscore the importance of "the location and return to the homeland of all written sources of the historical cultural heritage of Ukraine," and call upon the government to support this "matter of great national-cultural significance for the state."

A better documented version of that presentation, with a similar lengthy recounting of specific Ukrainian archival materials that were seized by central imperial authorities and transferred to archives in Moscow and St. Petersburg, appeared in the issue of *Pam'iatky Ukraïny* mentioned above.[34] But none of the published versions clarify the distinction between official records of state and records of other organizations such as the church or those collected by archeographic expeditions under the auspices of the Academy of Sciences, nor do they adequately document the seizures or present locations in terms of archival signatures.[35] A few examples of the types of problems that arise are worth consideration here, several of which have now been examined in the Ukrainian popular press.

Records of Central Imperial Agencies. Russian and Ukrainian archival specialists are now generally in agreement that Ukraine should not have any

---

[33]   Liudmyla Lozenko and Pavlo Sokhan´, "Povernuty pysemni skarby," *Kyïvs´ka starovyna* 1993 (2): 2–9.

[34]   Liudmyla Lozenko, "Arkhivni vtraty Ukraïny: Vyvezene do Rosiï," *Pam'iatky Ukraïny* 1994 (3–6[26]): 87–91.

[35]   Further efforts are still needed in the professional identification of the materials involved, the precise circumstances of their migration, and the current location and archival context of the files or manuscript books. Lozenko and Sokhan´ assured me that a more extensive and scholarly version of their presentation was in preparation in the form of a precise list of fonds, indicating their date of removal from Ukraine and their present location. Although a preliminary version has been in circulation in archival circles in Kyiv, it has not yet appeared in print. The subject is discussed in a broader theoretical perspective and with more scholarly detail, with citations to available literature, in the monograph by Hennadii Boriak, *Natsional'na arkhivna spadshchyna Ukraïny ta derzhavnyi reiestr "Arkheohrafichna Ukraïnika" : Arkhivni dokumental'ni resursy ta naukovo-informatsiini systemy* (Kyiv, 1995), especially pp. 196–99.

pretensions to the records of central state authorities created and remaining in the metropolis. Some present fonds comprising integral groups of wholly Ukrainian-pertinent documentation might potentially be subject to claim as having direct administrative or territorial pertinence to Ukraine. But the principle of "administrative" or "territorial pertinence," as noted above, is too elusive for concrete application, and most of the records involved were clearly created predominantly in the imperial capitals and constitute records of central Muscovite or Russian governing authorities.

For example, in the Russian State Archive of Early Acts (RGADA, formerly TsGADA), there are several fonds with documentation from the College of Foreign Affairs and the so-called Malorossiiskii prikaz, such as the fonds known as "Malorossiiskie dela" within the early records of the Posol'skii prikaz (fond 124; 1522–1781), the Malorossiiskii prikaz (fond 229; 1649–1722), the Malorossiiskaia èkspeditsiia Senata (fond 262; 1685–1761), and the so-called Razriad XIII—Malorossiiskie dela (fond 13; 1606–1790) collected from various sources in the nineteenth-century State Archive of the Russian Empire. Most of these fonds are not presently arranged in the natural order of their original creation—as chronological, integral records of their creating agencies. Rather, they have become more technically "collections." Some of these fonds may well contain scattered documents that were seized, at one time or another, by the central authorities. As such, some of them may be subject to legitimate claims on behalf of successor States.

The archival future of these records may nonetheless be subject to question or counterclaim by Russian authorities, because they remain part of integral collections that were established as such in central Muscovite or Russian imperial offices ("incorporated" files in Western parlance). These records were not deemed appropriate for restitution in the 1920s or in the 1950s, although some of them were mentioned in both periods as desiderata. Although the explanations from archival authorities in Moscow at the time have not been located, they were undoubtedly deemed to have achieved a permanent archival status of their own. A similar situation applies to early collected documentation in RGADA and AVPRI relating to Crimea and the eastern steppe frontier. Given their basic constitution within the records of central Russian imperial government, as part of those central archives over the centuries, it would be difficult to argue conclusively today for transfer of the originals to Ukraine. Certainly, however, the transfer of official copies, and copies of all related finding aids, would indeed be within normal bounds of archival traditions in connection with the succession of States. As previously mentioned, microfilms were often transferred under Soviet rule at minimal or no cost, but in most cases not all of the relevant finding aids were included, and the films were not always of satisfactory quality.

Pre-revolutionary Records of Local Administration in Ukraine. Like the situation in RGADA for the early period, there are many important records of Ukrainian pertinence within the gubernia [provincial] records in the Russian State Historical Archive (RGIA, formerly TsGIA SSSR) in St. Petersburg. Gubernia reports to central authorities, however, naturally belong to the records of the imperial government to which they were addressed. Copies usually were retained in the records of local gubernia chancelleries together with incoming instructions and correspondence from central imperial offices. Those, should remain as a matter of course in their local place of creation in the case of gubernia now part of Ukrainian lands. Ukraine would have no pretension to the outgoing originals of gubernia reports forwarded to the imperial capital (which are now held in RGIA). By the same token, there should be no question that the chancellery copies retained locally, together with other supporting local gubernia administrative records created within present Ukrainian territories, now all constitute part of the national archival heritage of Ukraine.

Church Records. Among pre-revolutionary archives, the records of the Russian Orthodox Church and those portions that constitute records of the Kyiv Metropolitanate also are subject to controversy. With the current bitter split of the Orthodox Church in Ukraine, it is unlikely that an immediate solution will be found for an appropriate division of church records. Furthermore, in Russia there has been a general reluctance to permit the return to the Orthodox Church of manuscript books and archival materials that were originally taken from monasteries and other Orthodox institutions. The case for those from Ukrainian lands that have ended up in the imperial capitals will not be easy to pursue. Church property is still at the heart of the controversy over the split in the Orthodox Church in Ukraine, and the manuscript legacy and church records should naturally constitute part of any settlement. The Russian argument against the return of the mosaics from the St. Michael's Cathedral mentioned above is indicative of the type of rationale that may be involved. Church archives and manuscript collections will undoubtedly be subject to even longer dispute, because all of these were nationalized during the Soviet regime, and current Russian law does not provide for the return to non-state proprietorship of any nationalized records.

The records of other religious denominations are also involved. The Russian State Historical Archive (RGIA) in St. Petersburg holds the records of the Greek Catholic (Uniate) Metropolitanate, including parts of the Church archives seized from Kyiv after the suppression of the Greek Catholic Church by Nicholas I in 1839.[36] Pretensions for the return of such materials to one or another successor republic would be difficult to justify without the resultant irreparable damage to the integrity of fonds for several reasons: they are—and have long remained—part of the archives of central government; they are *pertinent* to Belarus and Lithuania as well as Ukraine; and, they are not easily divisible along clear-cut present-day national boundaries. Nevertheless, Ukraine has a more legitimate case for their return because the seat of the Greek Catholic Metropolitanate was based in Ukraine until the Church was abolished in 1839 under Nicholas I and the records were created in and seized from Kyiv. Of course, requests for copies of finding aids and authenticated copies of appropriate groups of records or individual files, or documents by other successor States to whom the records are pertinent, especially Belarus and Lithuania, should certainly be honored.

Military Records. Military records raise difficult problems today for Russian authorities, particularly because of the strong Soviet tradition of centralizing all military records in Moscow and Leningrad. Most significantly, Moscow archival authorities systematically required the transfer of all military-oriented files from throughout Ukraine to the Central State Archive of Military History (TsGVIA, now RGVIA), the Central State Archive of the Red Army (TsAKA) and later the Soviet Army (TsGASA, now RGVA) in Moscow, and the Central State Archive of the Navy (TsGAVMF, now RGAVMF) in Leningrad. In some cases, much earlier than the war, other Ukrainian military records from the period of civil war and the struggle to establish an independent Ukrainian state were seized by Moscow authorities. For example, instructions for the transfer were issued in 1934, and a list of those transferred to TsGVIA has been found in Glavarkhiv records in Kyiv.[37]

A revealing survey of the fate of military records, which were created in Ukrainian lands and alienated to Moscow, has recently been published in Kyiv by Liudmyla Lozenko of the staff of the Main Archival Administration of Ukraine. An earlier version was prepared together with the retired archivist Ivan L. Butych. Emphasis is on the existence of local military archives in the 1920s and 1930s in Ukraine, and the extent to which many of their holdings

---

[36] *Opisanie dokumentov arkhiva zapadno-russkikh uniatskikh mitropolitov,* 2 vols. (St. Petersburg, 1897–1907). The first volume covers charters and other documents 1470–1700, the second 1701–1839.

[37] See the 1934 instructions for transfers to TsGVIA (before 1941, TsVIA) and TsAKA (after 1941, TsGAKA, and after 1946, TsGASA), copies of which remain in TsDAVO, 14/1/1740, fol. 27. See the letter of transmittal and list of fonds transferred to TsGVIA (15 April 1938), TsDAVO, 14/1/1754, fols. 112–120.

were transferred to the centralized military archives in Moscow and Leningrad. In addition to materials relating to military affairs that were removed in the 1930s, they cite some 3,000 military-related fonds—with over 80,000 files—that were transferred during the years 1951–1972.[38] The relatively popular-level articles do not discuss all of the examples of such transfers, nor were the authors apparently aware of the extent of Nazi surveys and seizures of local Ukrainian military records from Ukraine during World War II. But the well-documented exposure of the problem, particularly the documentation regarding related discussions during the struggle for Ukrainian independence after the 1917 revolutions and subsequent specific transfers to Moscow and St. Petersburg, is an important contribution to a broader understanding of the issues involved.

As Lozenko notes, some post-revolutionary records were initially housed in local military archives in Ukraine, but following the significant seizure of local military records by Nazi authorities during the war, Soviet authorities established more rigid requirements for transfer to Moscow afterwards. Military records from the interwar period (through 1941) went to what is now the Russian State Military Archive—RGVA. A comprehensive 1990–1991 two-volume guide shows the extent of Ukrainian holdings there, starting with records from 1917 and the period of civil war through holdings that pertain to 1941.[39] More details about the RGVA holdings of records of White Army units during the Civil War and the struggle to establish an independent Ukrainian state, many of which had been seized both in Ukraine and in Prague after World War II, are now described in a 1998 guide, which provides comprehensive coverage of those long-secret fonds that are now open for research in RGVA.[40]

---

[38]   Liudmyla Lozenko starts her survey with the seventeenth century; see "Ukraïns'ki viis'kovi arkhivy—vidibrana spadshchyna," *Pam'iatky Ukraïny* 1994 (3–6[26]): 109–115. See also Ivan Butych and Liudmyla Lozenko, "Povernuty viis'kovi arkhivy," *Uriadovyi kur'ier* 1992 (59); and Boriak, *Natsional'na arkhivna spadshchyna Ukraïny*, especially p. 197.

[39]   *Tsentral'nyi gosudarstvennyi arkhiv Sovetskoi Armii: Putevoditel'*, comp. T. F. Kariaeva, N. D. Egorov, O. V. Brizitskaia, et al.; ed. M. V. Stegantsev and L. V. Dvoinykh, 2 vols. (Minneapolis: East View Publications, 1991–1993). A supplement covering fonds that were subsequently declassified is in preparation.

[40]   *Putevoditel' po fondam Beloi Armii*, comp. N. V. Pul'chenko, N. D. Egorov, and L. M. Chizhova; ed. N. D. Egorov and L. V. Dvoinykh (Moscow: Russkoe bibliograficheskoe obshchestvo; Izd. firma "Vostochnaia literatura" RAN, 1998; Rosarkhiv; RGVA) [=Academia ROSSICA, vol. 4]. Other pre-1941 published guides to Civil

Many of the military records that remained in Ukraine in 1941 were seized by Nazi authorities during the Second World War, when military archivists from the Heeresarchiv immediately followed the 1941 invading armies. Records from Ukrainian lands, including Western Ukraine, were shipped either to the Heeresarchiv branch in Vienna or the branch in Danzig-Oliva and subsequently were not returned to Ukraine.[41] It has not yet been possible to verify which of those military records seized by Nazi authorities were retrieved after the war. There are undocumented reports that some of them were retrieved by Soviet authorities and retained in Moscow.

One example of the pre-revolutionary documentation from Ukraine held in Moscow is presented in a 1992 article which surveys materials in RGVIA relating to cities in Right-Bank Ukraine, predominantly cartographic and other graphic materials from the pre-revolutionary Military Science Archive of the General Staff (Voenno-uchenyi arkhiv Glavnogo shtaba—VUA). Such a study presents a vivid example of the extent to which the archival legacy of Ukraine is intricately tied to that of Russia. While Ukraine quite appropriately may want copies of all such materials, clearly most of those covered would not be subject to claim in the original, since they are part of central record groups or incorporated into files or an established larger collection assembled by Russian imperial military authorities.[42]

Another important example of the Ukrainian military archival legacy is the fate of the Central Naval Archive of the Black Sea Fleet, dating from the late eighteenth through the early twentieth century, which, until 1928, had been held in the port city of Mykolaïv in Ukraine. The issue of the Black Sea Fleet—a thorny one in recent years between Russia and Ukraine—also has an archival aspect, as is revealed in another recent article by Lozenko in *Pam'iatky Ukraïny*. In this case, Lozenko published a memorandum on the issue prepared by the Ukrainian historian Oleksandr Ohloblyn in 1929 at the

---

War records are listed in Grimsted, *Archives of Russia, 2000* and are also available in microfiche editions from IDC.

[41] See more details about Nazi-looted military records from western Ukraine in Chapter 5. See Chapter 8 regarding the fate of the Heeresarchiv records.

[42] P. A. Rychkov, "Dzherela Rosiis'koho derzhavnoho voienno-istorychnoho arkhivu do istoriï mistobuduvannia u Pravoberezhnii Ukraïni," *Arkhivy Ukraïny* 1992 (5–6): 52–61. A catalog of the VUA holdings was completed before 1917, but now a complete new electronic guide to the VUA collections in RGVIA is in preparation by Primary Source Microfilms, which should reveal more details about those holdings. The work is part of the Russian Archives project.

time that the records were removed to Leningrad.[43] Ohloblyn articulated Ukrainian claims and concerns about the fate of the national archival heritage. Prepared during the period of Ukrainianization in the 1920s, on the eve of the bitter repression of the Ukrainian national historical and intellectual traditions that followed in the 1930s, Ohloblyn's appeal again raises the issue of the legitimate claims of a successor State to archival materials created on its territories by an imperial regime—issues that deserve consideration today in a broader international context.

Despite the fact that many local military fonds of Ukrainian provenance have since been arranged and described as part of central military records, they nonetheless should be candidates for return to Ukraine. They do, in fact, constitute records of local military authorities in Ukrainian lands that normally should have been retained in the place of their creation as part of gubernia-level or republic-level records, before they were appropriated by Moscow. But even pending restitution discussions, most important for Ukraine is the acquisition of copies of the new guides to military records in Moscow—which were not even mentioned by Lozenko and in other recent articles. Ukrainians may have reason to question why so few copies of those guides, like those of the RGVA guides, are now available in Ukrainian libraries. But since such publications have been produced with Western sponsorship on a commercial basis in Russia, Ukraine can no longer expect Soviet-style handouts; even in Russia few copies are to be found in libraries.

Records of Soviet Security Agencies. KGB and MVD records raise more complicated issues, but those created within Ukraine would be expected to remain under Ukrainian jurisdiction. As recently as 1991, however, a significant quantity of MVD records of Ukrainian provenance—including, for example, 425 files pertaining to the Ukrainian Insurgent Army (UPA) during and immediately after World War II—were transferred to Moscow. Following considerable negotiations, microfilms totaling some 152,000 frames from the MVD files were prepared, but the Ukrainian side was

---

[43] Liudmyla Lozenko, "O. Ohloblyn pro arkhiv Chornomors´koho flotu," *Pam'iatky Ukraïny* 1994 (3–6[26]): 116–19. Pre-revolutionary records of the Black Sea Fleet are listed in the newly published *Rossiiskii gosudarstvennyi arkhiv Voenno-Morskogo Flota: Annotirovannyi reestr opisei fondov (1696–1917)*, comp. T. P. Mazur (St. Petersburg: "Blits," 1996); post-revolutionary records are listed in *Rossiiskii gosudar-stvennyi arkhiv VMF: Spravochnik po fondam (1917–1940)*, comp. M. E. Malevin-skaia; ed. T. P. Mazur, 2 vols. (St. Petersburg: "Blits," 1995).

required to pay an exceedingly high price in hard currency to obtain copies.[44] Despite numerous high-level demands, the originals have not been returned to Kyiv. This is in contrast to the case of the highly publicized demands of Lithuania for the return of local KGB files alienated from the republic, many of which were finally returned from Moscow. Such a situation in regard to MVD/KGB records removed from Ukraine (and still held in Moscow) does not accord with normal international respect for records of local agencies created within the territory of a subject nation. However, established grounds for appeal about such procedures are lacking in international law, which complicates claims from the former Soviet republics.

Central security files, copies, or both, that were forwarded to CPSU offices regarding repressed individuals from successor States raise other issues. To be sure, appropriate files are needed for the rehabilitation of politically repressed individuals, and, likewise, personal papers and documentary materials seized by central security agencies from local citizens will require further identification and appropriate restitution. New Russian laws require the declassification of files pertaining to politically repressed individuals, but the law does not provide for the return of the originals, let alone to successor States of which the individual or his heirs are citizens.[45]

Communist Party Files from Ukraine—The Khrushchev Example. Even more serious in terms of reconstituting the Ukrainian archival legacy and rewriting Ukrainian history during the Soviet period is the problem of displaced documentation at the highest level of Ukrainian political life. This is seen in the case of a political leader who started his career in Ukraine and then ascended to the Kremlin—Nikita Khrushchev (Mykyta Khrushchov). It has recently come to public attention that when Khrushchev moved from his post as Secretary of the Communist Party of Ukraine to the All-Union level in Moscow, he ordered that all of his pronouncements, speeches, and many other documents be torn from Ukrainian CP files and delivered to Moscow. As a result, no copies remain in Kyiv today of many of the most essential documents from the period of Khrushchev's tenure as Ukrainian CP Secretary. To make matters more difficult, despite the 1991 Russian presidential

---

[44] This matter is documented by Boriak, *Natsional'na arkhivna spadshchyna Ukraïny*, p. 197 and fn. 52 (pp. 335–36). The originals are now held in the Central Archive of Internal Troops (*Tsentral'nyi arkhiv vnutrennikh voisk*) under the MVD in Moscow.

[45] A documented list of Russian laws and regulations relating to human rights, rehabilitation, and the politically repressed is included in the compilation of laws relating to archival affairs in *Archives of Russia, 2000*, Appendix 1.

decree that all Party records were to be turned over to state archival authorities, such documents from the Khrushchev period remain locked away in the top secret Presidential Archive (AP RF) in Moscow.[46] This is certainly not the only case of similarly displaced official records and the disruption of the integrity of fonds, but it serves as a glaring example of the problem of locating and reconstituting the legitimate national archival heritage of Ukraine. Since the Khrushchev files were deliberately removed from their Ukrainian archival context, there is solid justification for their return to Ukraine. However, given that the act of removal was accomplished while Khrushchev was All-Union CPSU First Secretary, it is likely that these files will be permanently retained in Moscow.

The Khrushchev example follows the earlier removal from Ukraine of almost all original Lenin and Stalin documents, in addition to the established procedure for the regular transfer to Moscow of copies of all high-level Ukrainian CP documentation. Other high Ukrainian CP leaders who continued their careers in Moscow also tended to leave many of their papers there. Many of the personal papers of Petro Shelest, as another example, were turned over to RTsKhIDNI (now RGASPI), the successor to the former Central Party Archive (TsPA), in Moscow in the early 1990s.[47] Ukrainian pretensions for most other major groups of central CPSU records in Moscow, which would be considered records of central imperial authorities and the joint heritage of all former Soviet republics, would necessarily be limited to complete sets of microform copies together with relevant finding aids.

Personal Papers. Personal papers of individual Ukrainian political or cultural figures who wrote in the Ukrainian language and considered themselves "Ukrainian" throughout their lives may be clear enough to

---

[46]   I am grateful to former TsDAHO director Ruslan Ia. Pyrih for calling my attention to this problem on which he was preparing a detailed report. A short version appeared together with several illustrative documents—Ruslan Pyrih, "Vylucheni dokumenty Mykyty Khrushchova," *Pam'iatky Ukraïny* 1994 (3–6[26]): 129–31. Pyrih's paper, although not delivered at the 1994 Chernihiv conference, appeared in the proceedings, "'Ukraïns'kyi arkhiv' Mykyty Khrushchova: Problemy vidnovlennia ta vykorystannia," in *Materialy natsional'noho seminaru, Chernihiv, 1994*, pp. 182–87.

[47]   See *Putevoditel' po fondam i kollektsiiam lichnogo proiskhozhdeniia*, comp. Iu. N. Amiantov and Z. N. Tikhonova (Moscow, 1996), pp. 321–22 [=Spravochno-informatsionnye materialy k dokumental'nym fondam RTsKhIDNI, 2]. The Shelest papers, received from Shelest himself before his death in 1996, constitute fond 666, but have not yet been arranged and described.

recognize—wherever they may be found. However, as noted above, precise geographic, ethnic, and national interrelationships are not always easy to distinguish or apply unilaterally, given past political realities in Ukrainian lands. The importance of keeping integral groups of records or personal papers of a family or an individual intact is fundamental. Questions arise, though, about the extent to which such principles should be applied to materials that, based on their place of creation, are not legally of provenance in present-day Ukraine. In the case of institutions or individuals that migrated—voluntarily or forcibly—in the course of their lives, further difficulties arise in appropriate assignation of provenance to the entire fond, or, in the case of migration, its division. Career patterns in imperial Russia and the Soviet Union inevitably involved considerable migration to and from the imperial capitals, and so, understandably, the disposition of related archives is divided. The case of the now divided Dovzhenko archival legacy discussed above is a prime example; because Dovzhenko's second wife was Russian and quite legally donated his papers to RGALI, there is little chance of their transfer to Ukraine.

As another example of the problems faced here, how is one to classify the papers of the Ukrainian-born writer "Mykola Hohol'," son of Cossack gentry and educated in Nizhyn, whom most of the world knows as the "Russian" literary giant "Nikolai Gogol"? And what of the descendants of the well-known "Polish" writer Aleksander Fredro, some of whose heirs considered themselves Polish, while other family members consciously took a Ukrainian identity, including the eminent Ukrainian Greek Catholic Metropolitan Andrei Sheptyts'kyi? And what of the archival remains of the Barvins'kyi/Barwiński family? Some members, who at one point or another in their career, considered themselves Polish, later identified themselves as Ukrainian, and insisted on spelling their names accordingly.

Political fate and changing national frontiers, linguistic requirements, imperial career patterns, intermarriage, and other factors all could mean that many individuals wrote and published in different languages during different periods of their lives. The polonization of the Ruthenian gentry in the seventeenth century had its counterpart in the russification of Polish-Ukrainian gentry in the nineteenth century and the further forced russification under Soviet rule, even within the Ukrainian SSR. There is little question about the name "Shevchenko" in the nineteenth century, but what of the Soviet Russian ambassador to the United Nations with the same family name who spent most of his adult life in Soviet Russian service and often refused to identify himself as Ukrainian? In large part because Ukraine did not exist as a state, Ukrainian émigrés or exiles have become citizens of other countries, which means that their lives and careers cannot be considered linked purely to Ukraine. Conversely, distinctions purely along lines of citizenship can overlook important differences among ethnic Ukrainians, Poles, Russians, Jews, or Armenians, or those of other foreign background who have lived most of their lives and became prominent in what is now Ukraine.

Manuscript Collections. Further discussion will be needed regarding matters of non-state institutional manuscript collections, such as those of the Church and other religious bodies, and the collections made by state-sponsored archeographic commissions and other academic bodies, such as universities and the Academy of Science. In these cases, the distinction between "state" and "private" becomes more blurred in both pre-revolutionary Russian and Soviet contexts. In Russian archival and archeographic practice, as in other countries, the distinction between public records and the private papers of a public official was often vague, as public officials tended to keep documents of state or copies thereof in their own private or family papers.

Over the centuries, many well-known private or institutional manuscript collections often contained their fair share of archival materials that could technically be termed official documents of state, although they became separated from the body of records in which they were created. This was particularly true of pre–nineteenth-century documents, even more so of records of provincial administration created further from the center, where few adequate facilities for record or archival storage were developed before the late nineteenth century. As a result, it is often difficult to identify precisely state documents and record books that happened to have become part of personal papers or family collections, or manuscript collections held under Church, academic, or other library auspices. Difficulties are compounded because such documents may have been prepared in multiple copies, or specific copies may have been prepared at the time or later for a state official yet considered part of his or her own private papers.

A specific case in point for Ukraine is the collection amassed in St. Petersburg before 1917 by the Imperial Archeographic Commission, an officially sponsored, but mainly privately endowed, academic enterprise. Given the lack of adequate local archives in many areas and of a well-established central historical archive in the imperial capitals, the Archeographic Commission served a tremendously important role in locating, describing, and ensuring the preservation of historical archival materials and manuscript books from throughout the Russian Empire. From present-day Ukrainian lands, they amassed many local institutional records from the seventeenth and eighteenth centuries and earlier, including those from military fiefs and patrimonial estates, local monasteries, bishoprics, and churches, together with an impressive number of early charters and manuscript books that were found in different local areas. The Archeographic Commission provided a tremendously valuable archival service in assuring the preservation of important historical documentation, and, in some cases, major groups of government records that otherwise were not being preserved locally.

The collections were brought together and described in St. Petersburg, and now most of them remain in the Archive of the St. Petersburg Branch of the Institute of Russian History, which in fact was established on the basis of the Archeographic Commission collections.[48] It is unlikely that Russian cultural, academic, and archival authorities would willingly agree to the breakup of these long-established and well-described collections in the former imperial capital, although by right, and according to the 1992 CIS Agreement, Ukraine would have good reason for claim.

Nevertheless, Ukrainian complaints about the seizures—and pretensions to the return—of many local materials is understandable in the present context of international concern about the heritage of nations newly independent in the post-colonial era. A recent article in *Pam'iatky Ukraïny* outlined the archeographic activities of the Library of the Academy of Sciences (BAN) and the Library of Moscow State University (MGU) in Ukraine during the Soviet period and listed precise examples of recent seizures of 18 sixteenth- and seventeenth-century manuscripts and 64 early printed books from Ukrainian lands by archeographic expeditions of the library of Moscow State University during the period 1971–1981.[49]

---

[48] For a current description of these collections as they are now organized in St. Petersburg, see the published guide with extensive bibliographic citations to earlier, more detailed descriptions and inventories—*Putevoditel' po arkhivu Leningradskogo otdeleniia Instituta istorii*, comp. I. V. Valkina, et al.; ed. A. I. Andreev et al. (Moscow–Leningrad: Akademiia nauk SSSR, 1958). See also the recent more complete list of fonds, *Fondy i kollektsii arkhiva: Kratkii spravochnik*, comp. G. A. Pobedimova and N. B. Sredinskaia (St. Petersburg: "Blits," 1995).

[49] Osyp Danko, "Vkradena Bibliia: Rosiis'ki arkheohrafichni ekspedytsiï v Ukraïni i naslidky ïkhn'oï dial'nosti," *Pam'iatky Ukraïny* 1994 (3–6[26]): 74–79. The list appears as an appendix—"Pam'iatky vyvezeni pol'ovymy arkheohrafichnymy ekspedytsiiamy Moskovs'koho derzhavnoho universytetu v 1971–1981 rokakh," 78–79. Professional descriptions of many of these manuscripts have been prepared at MGU as part of the catalog series issued by the library (see full bibliographic data in *Archives of Russia*, entry G–2).

Microform Copies

The exchange of quality microform copies of major groups of records and their finding aids will undoubtedly be the most satisfactory means of resolving many disputed claims, as has become the norm in international archival practice. As the United Nations International Law Commission (UN ILC) Special Rapporteur noted in a 1979 report dealing with problems arising in the succession to State property in the context of the succession of States:

> Of all State property, archives alone are capable of being dupli-
> cated, which means that both the right of the successor State to re-
> cover the archives and the interest of the predecessor State in their
> use can be satisfied.[50]

With the demise of the Soviet empire, it makes ultimate archival sense to provide successor States with extensive, comprehensive runs of microform copies of those state and CPSU records they deem most important and relevant for current administrative use by republic-level government, economic, social, and cultural agencies, and authenticated copies of specific documents needed by individual citizens for pension or other legal purposes. Microform copies, however, are no panacea for the immediate settlement of archival claims and can never fully replace the originals or the archival context in which they were held. Copies cannot resolve all disputes because of the difficulty of photographing bound volumes without destroying essential evidence preserved in their bindings, or of reproducing faded or bleeding ink. Moreover, modern reproductive equipment is sadly lacking in former Soviet lands, and in many cases, existing finding aids are inadequate for filming purposes. A legally and archivally well-informed inter-republic commission will be needed to deal with disputed archival claims and facilitate the flow of reference information and needed copies.

It must further be recognized that for appropriate analysis in a historical context, historians and cultural and political analysts may need access to, and copies of, complete groups of records from imperial agencies, and not just the few files or individual documents that most directly involve the specific successor State. For example, it is not enough to receive copies only of those Politburo resolutions specifically dealing with Ukraine; access is also needed to the records of the entire meetings where those resolutions were formulated and to appropriate supporting documentation from other sources. In this way

---

[50] Mohammed Bedjaoui, Special Rapporteur, as quoted in his 1979 report (A/CN.4/322), *Yearbook ILC, 1979*, II, pt. 2: 77–78.

the sense of the resolution can be understood in its broader political and intellectual or ideological context.

The need for context in analyzing archival materials makes it clear that successor States will have reasonable demands for comprehensive copies of entire runs of Politburo and other central CPSU records. The fact that many of these files and their finding aids are now being filmed with extensive foreign sponsorship should be a particularly appropriate occasion to satisfy the needs of newly independent Soviet successor States. Indeed, thanks to the large-scale collaborative program between Rosarkhiv and the Hoover Institution on War, Revolution, and Peace in Palo Alto, California, almost all *opisi* of post-revolutionary fonds in the former Central Party Archive (now RGASPI), a few declassified files in the former Central Committee archive (now RGANI), and post-revolutionary fonds in the State Archive of the Russian Federation (GA RF) are now commercially available on microfilm. Copies of the *opisi* and documentary series filmed are distributed abroad by the British publisher Chadwyck-Healey, with significant royalties to the Russian archives.[51] Subsequent stages of the project were supposed to provide microform copies of more complete files of original documents within specific series deemed of the highest political importance. Unfortunately, however, following bitter public criticism and alleged Rosarkhiv mismanagement, the project was curtailed in the winter of 1995–1996, thus limiting future possibilities of significantly expanded offerings.[52]

Rosarkhiv retains the right to distribute copies of the microfilms within the territories of the former Soviet Union, according to the terms of the Rosarkhiv–Hoover–Chadwyck-Healey Agreement, which would make it appropriate to propose low-cost copies to successor States. Given the extent of the project, and high cost of the microfilms abroad, royalties are certainly insufficient to cover the costs of microform distribution even within Russia, particularly when Russian archives themselves do not even have adequate funds from government budgets to pay full salaries to their staff. Accordingly, outside subsidies would still be needed to distribute free or low-cost copies of these and other available microforms to Ukraine and other Soviet successor States. After all, involved are the central archives of the regime that

[51]   A full updated catalog is available on the Chadwyck-Healey website— <http://www.chadwyck.com>; or (outside USA)—<http://www.chadwyck.co.uk>.

[52]   See more details regarding the curtailment of the Hoover project in my *Archives of Russia Seven Years After: "Purveyors of Sensations" or "Shadows Cast to the Past"* (Washington, DC, 1998) [=CWIHP Working Paper, 20]: ch. 11, with regard to other commentaries, and an analysis there of reference problems involved with the finding aids produced (ch. 12).

governed Ukrainian lands for over seventy years in some parts and over forty in others; it is fitting that the microform copies of *opisi* and, to the extent possible, of the records themselves, of that government (including the Communist Party) should be available locally in Ukraine.

The Rosarkhiv–Hoover–Chadwyck-Healey project could play a decisive role in the ongoing tradition of the ICA and UNESCO program that aims to supply archival microforms to former colonial regimes elsewhere in the world (see Chapter 3). Microform copies have proved to be a viable solution in many cases of disputed claims and issues of the joint archival heritage of one or more countries, and funding to extend the program to the newly independent States of the former Soviet Union should be a high priority. There have been international precedents whereby former imperial powers have made low-cost, and even sometimes cost-free, copies to their former colonies that are now successor States to the empire. However, Ukrainians have little hope that Russia will be willing or able to furnish copies free of charge. "Of course, it would be marvelous for our specialists to have copies, even of the inventories already filmed, here in Kyiv," remarked Ukrainian archival director Ruslan Pyrih, who now heads the State Committee on Archives of Ukraine. "But when the present Ukrainian government does not even give the archives enough money for staff and militia guards, let alone paper clips, how can we possibly think of buying microfilms?"[53]

Searching for International Norms

The terms of the July 1992 agreement among Soviet successor States on archival transfers, as indicated above (pp. 39–40), contain no mechanism for implementation. There are still no detailed guidelines, nor is there a statement of principles regarding what types of materials under what circumstances might be subject to restitution. Unfortunately, the situation further reflects traditional Soviet preference for bilateral agreements. These will eventually be needed in most instances, but, in a post-Soviet context, may all too often be left to barter and current political interests rather than long-term established professional norms.

Various commentaries, including the Ukrainian newspaper discussion by Lozenko and Sokhan´ mentioned above, have noted the importance of conforming to United Nations and UNESCO norms for the restitution of cultural treasures. Following the Minsk agreement in April 1992, the Russian historian and retired archival director Vsevolod V. Tsaplin presented an illuminating, documented analysis of some of the judicial precedents for

[53]   Ruslan Ia. Pyrih, in a conversation with the author in July 1996.

archival transfers in earlier treaties involving pre-revolutionary and Soviet Russia. The presentation had immediate implications for the possible restitution of archival materials involving present successor States of the USSR.[54] Evgenii V. Starostin's commentary was critical of some points advanced by Tsaplin, but appropriately emphasized the need for significant microfilm exchange and for reference to earlier considerations of these issues by UNESCO and the International Council on Archives (ICA).[55] Unfortunately, however, neither the Ukrainian authors, Tsaplin or Starostin, nor most of the specialists involved in the CIS negotiations were then significantly aware of many of the important international legal precedents and United Nations activities and the vast international literature relating to archival transfers and other problems of cultural restitution. While the above-mentioned 1996 study by Lozyts'kyi presented important Ukrainian-relevant examples, it was insufficient in its historical perspective and lack of attention to significant literature on the subject.

Under Rosarkhiv auspices in Moscow, the All-Russian Scientific-Research Institute on Documentation and Archival Affairs (VNIIDAD) deputy director, Viacheslav D. Banasiukevich, headed a group study on international law and archival practice with regard to displaced archives, but, again, much of the Western published literature on the subject was not available for their analysis. The people involved were not aware of many of the international precedents and they had little international experience outside of the Soviet bloc with problems in the field.[56] A number of issues of crucial importance in defining the national archival heritage and resolving archival claims in the post-Soviet area consequently have not been given sufficient attention. Nevertheless, most important in the Banasiukevich study is the recommendation that the International Council on Archives should be called upon to further the analysis of such questions and formulation of appropriate guidelines based on international law and archival precedents.

---

[54] V. V. Tsaplin, "O prave sobstvennosti na arkhivnye dokumenty v diplomaticheskikh aktakh dorevoliutsionnoi i sovetskoi Rossii," *Otechestvennye arkhivy* 1992 (4): 20–25.

[55] E. V. Starostin, "Professor Starostin o zatronutoi probleme," *Otechestvennye arkhivy* 1992 (4): 26–27.

[56] V. D. Banasiukevich et al., "Mezhdunarodnoe arkhivnoe pravo i zarubezhnaia praktika peremeshcheniia arkhivnykh dokumentov (Nauchnyi doklad)" (typescript; Moscow, 1993). See also the author's published article, representing the text of his report at the Rosarkhiv conference on Rossica in Moscow, December 1993: V. D. Banasiukevich, "O pravovykh aspektakh mezhdunarodnogo peremeshcheniia arkhivnykh dokumentov," *Otechestvennye arkhivy* 1994 (2): 6–10.

For Ukraine, Lozyts'kyi, who was then an official representative on the ICA Executive Committee, likewise has recommended more direct ICA involvement in this area.

Banasiukevich repeated this recommendation during the symposium on archives at the UNESCO-sponsored conference on displaced cultural treasures during World War II in Chernihiv in September 1994.[57] A resolution from the Chernihiv conference was addressed to UNESCO requesting further analysis of the issues, although the request more broadly related to cultural treasures and did not distinguish any specific problems for archives.[58] Also appropriate would have been an additional communication of such a resolution with specific attention to archives to the International Council on Archives. Two weeks later in Thessalonica, the ICA devoted a major part of its annual International Round Table Conference to the issue of displaced records and problems of restitution; unfortunately, there was no Ukrainian representative present. The UNESCO representative who was present learned of the Ukrainian resolution only afterwards, and hence was not able to report it.[59]

Banasiukevich did not participate in the 1996 conference on legal issues of restitution in Kyiv. Instead, Russia was represented by the former Soviet-era archival director, Emina Kuz'mina, who serves as an advisor to the Russian Duma Committee on Culture and had strongly supported the campaign for the Russian law nationalizing Russia's cultural trophies. In the case of the 1996 conference, UNESCO was represented by Lyndel Prott, who long chaired the Intergovernmental Committee for Promoting the Return of Cultural Property to its Country of Origin or its Restitution in Case of Illicit Appropriation. The recommendations of that conference again look to UNESCO for support and assistance in resolving these issues:

> …to continue efforts for further updating international legal norms in the sphere of protection, repatriation, restitution of cultural treasures and creation of effective mechanisms of international co-operation in this sphere;
>
> …to bring national laws in the sphere of protection, repatriation and restitution of cultural treasures in line with the norms of inter-

[57] V. D. Banasiukevich, "Pro metodychne zabezpechennia peremishchennia arkhiviv," *Materialy natsional'noho seminaru, Chernihiv, 1994*, pp. 182–87.

[58] See the published recommendations, "Rekomendatsiï Natsional'noho seminaru z problem povernennia natsional'no-kul'turnykh pam'iatok, vtrachenykh abo peremishchenykh pid chas druhoï svitovoï viiny," *Materialy natsional'noho seminaru, Chernihiv, 1994*, pp. 321–29.

[59] Personal conversation with the principals.

national law, to emphasize Member States' liability for the non-fulfillment of their obligations in the sphere of protection, repatriation and restitution of cultural treasures as parties to international conventions and agreements;

...to promote international exchange of information on the lost or illegally transferred cultural treasures which are subject to repatriation.[60]

In fact, ICA (with UNESCO support) has long been monitoring the issue of archival claims and potential restitution, especially in light of decolonization in the post–World War II period. As will be seen in the following chapter, there have been many ICA, UN, and UNESCO discussions and resolutions on the subject of promoting the reconstitution of the dispersed archival heritage of various nations. But despite the significant progress in this regard in different parts of the world, adequately detailed working international norms and guidelines have never been agreed upon. Although many basic archival principles have become common modus vivendi in international archival circles, even basic internationally accepted recommendations for transfers of displaced archives and for resolving issues of archives and manuscript collections in connection with the fall of empires and the succession of States have never been adequately compiled.

What is needed on the international front today is not more resolutions or another agreement that provides for more bilateral discussions and bilateral agreements. Realistic guidelines and mechanisms should involve more precise attempts to define in principle, and with concrete examples, the nature and types of archival materials that might be legitimately subject to claim in terms of their provenance, and additional data regarding the circumstances of migration (and/or alienation from the homeland) that might substantiate claims. Ideally, such norms and guidelines should be worked out in consultation with ICA and UNESCO specialists in cultural restitution and claims. Both sets of specialists have been considering such matters quite independently from different perspectives in recent decades. Hence, the VNIIDAD recommendation and the Ukrainian appeal to UNESCO following the 1994 conference in Chernihiv and the 1996 conference in Kyiv are particularly appropriate in the present context.

The lack of appropriate guidelines had the most disastrous consequences in May and June 1994, when the Russian parliament used the deficiency of international law and regulations for archival restitution and the lack of basis

---

[60] "Recommendations of scientific and practical symposium 'Legal aspects of restitution of cultural treasures: Theory and practice,'" in *"Pravovi aspekty restytutsiï,"* pp. 194–95. Reproduced below in Appendix X.

in Russian law as an excuse to put a stop to an archival restitution to France that was then already well under way under a duly signed bilateral diplomatic agreement. That led to a Russian moratorium on all cultural restitution resulting from World War II displacements until April 1998, when a Russian law that nationalized those cultural treasures was enacted (see Chapter 10).

Russian archival leaders were well prepared for the appropriate restitution in the case of many of the World War II trophy archives in Russia, conforming to professional international standards, even without new international guidelines. However, in Russia, political forces led by emotional national issues were stronger than professional, and even diplomatic, agreements. If the Russian parliament puts so many impediments on restitution of cultural treasures plundered by Soviet authorities at the end of the war from West European countries, what hope is there to expect appropriate restitution of archival materials to former Soviet republics? The many international issues involved will be discussed further in the next two chapters, before turning to problems of displaced archives and restitution resulting from World War II itself.

CHAPTER 3

Provenance, Pertinence, and Patrimony: International Historical and Legal Precedents

When "Records Follow the Flag"

Many of the complex problems relating to the archival legacy of Ukraine, like those of other parts of the Russian Empire and former union republics of the USSR, at home and in the diaspora, have historical precedents in other parts of the world that should provide a context for adjudication and resolution. Such issues have always arisen with the demise of empires, although their resolution has not been without disputed claims. A considerable body of literature has appeared on the subject that would be important to review in the present context. Of particular note is the essay by the German-American archivist Ernst Posner, "The Effect of Changes of Sovereignty on Archives," first presented 28 September 1939 as an address to an archival gathering in Washington, DC.[1] At the outbreak of war on the Eastern Front, Posner recognized that "the treatment of archives in connection with the cession and annexation of territory has been, and is still, in the first place a matter of international law." As Posner pointed out, "archives everywhere have come to be considered public property, sharing this character with public grounds, buildings, fortifications, and so on...as such as consequences of a change of sovereignty...the records follow the flag."[2]

Nevertheless, Posner argues convincingly that the integrity of archives must also reign supreme. The principle of provenance must be respected, as meaning that a body of records "must be preserved in its original form and at the place of its origin." As he clearly recognizes, "records that are torn from the body of which they are an organic part lose in value and meaning. Hence 'archival amputations' must be avoided, even where a political structure is

---

[1] Posner's article was first published in the *American Archivist* 5(3) July 1942: 141–55.

[2] Posner, "The Effect of Changes of Sovereignty on Archives," p. 169.

entirely destroyed."[3] Posner asks rhetorically, "Does it follow that all the records relating to the ceded territory must be delivered up, including those of a purely historical character and those preserved with the central administrative bodies and in the national depositories of the ceding state?"[4] In the course of his analysis, Posner points to many historical precedents where this has happened to the detriment of archives and scholarship.

Posner had one significant predecessor in addressing the subject on a general level: a French jurist, Louis Jacob, in a doctoral thesis defended in 1915, analyzed a number of historical examples of archival transfer problems in the context of Europe's changing frontiers and the rise and fall of empires over the centuries.[5] Although Jacob approached the problems as a lawyer rather than an archivist, he emphasized the basic archival principles of the integrity of records and that "while annexations may require changes of sovereignty in public archives as well, it should not force their displacement, where displacement could be avoided."[6]

The Polish archival director Józef Paczkowski in 1923 provided important insights regarding problems in archival transfers in connection with changes of boundaries. But, in recognizing "the established custom of rendering of records relating to territories was a corollary to changes of sovereignty," he also noted the extent that such transfers could result "in leaving the keys to one's house in the hands of a neighbor." But he came down most strongly against the practice in which historical records had been literally "cut apart with knife or scissors to retain or destroy documents of interest to the other party." Among his concluding points was that "archives should never be considered spoils of war," and that the practice of "destroying the integrity of fonds" or of "cutting out pages...should be absolutely contemned as being totally contrary to the elementary precepts of civilization as well as those of science." As an urgent recommendation, he proposed a collaborative analysis of past treaties in connection with archival transfers.[7] Although the project was never undertaken at that time, as we shall see, it has

---

3   Ibid., p. 177, p. 180.

4   Ibid., p. 169.

5   Louis Jacob, *La Clause de livraison des archives publiques dans les traités d'annexation* (Paris: M. Giard & E. Brière, 1915).

6   Jacob, *La Clause de livraison des archives*, p. 105.

7   Józef (Joseph) Paczkowski, "La remise des actes en connexion avec les changements de frontières entre les États," in *La Pologne au V-e Congrès International des Sciences Historiques, Bruxelles 1923* (Warsaw, 1924), pp. 199–211; see especially Paczkowski's conclusions, pp. 210–11.

since been implemented in a number of international drafts. At that point, however, archivists were more concerned with the transfers that were taking place in connections with the break-up of the Russian and Austro-Hungarian Empires in accordance with the postwar treaties.

A year before the Nazi invasion, another Polish archivist, Jadwiga Karwasińska, took up the matter again in addressing the International Congress of Historical Sciences in 1938, pointing out the long-established principle for the revindication of archives in connection with changes of sovereignty: "Occupying first place" became the principle "that administrations must have at their disposition the archives of their predecessors. This involves the remission to the administrations of the new regime the archives of the old regime that concerns the ceded territories."[8] At the same time, another well-respected Polish archivist, Józef Siemieński emphasized the importance of "respect for fonds (*respect des fonds*)" as the basic principle for archival arrangement, which should extend to the "reconstruction" or "reintegration" of fragmented fonds as integral bodies of records when in the past they have been split within a single archival repository, among several repositories, and even on the international level among the archives of different countries.[9] Although Siemieński's analysis might place a higher value on the principle of "territorial pertinence" than would archivists in countries that had not been subjected to so much brutal historical partitioning, the principles he sets forth and the recognition of the need of nations for the records and the integrity of records of previous governing powers is particularly applicable for contemporary Ukraine.

In retrospect, Posner and many other archivists have been extremely critical of the unfavorable effects of the archival settlements following World War I, both the Treaty of St. Germain (with Austria) and the Treaty of Trianon (with Hungary), whereby the records of the Austro-Hungarian Empire were broken up and fragmented. Archivists have had no quarrel with those treaties whereby both Austria and Hungary were required to return all records (including communal and private) seized in the course of invasion. More complicated and damaging to the integrity of archives, those countries were required to "give up...all the records, documents and historical material possessed by public institutions which *may have a direct bearing* on the

---

8   Jadwiga (Hedvige) Karwasińska, "La remise des archives dans les traités de l'Est européen," in *VIIIè Congrès International des Sciences Historiques, Zurich 1938; Communications Présentées*, vol. 1 (Paris, n.d.), pp. 52–53.

9   Józef (Joseph) Siemieński, "Respect des fonds. Application internationale," in *VIIIè Congrès International des Sciences Historiques, Zurich 1938; Communications Présentées*, vol. 1 (Paris, n.d.), pp. 63–65.

history of the ceded territories and which have been removed since 1868." By the same token, the new States and the States receiving part of the territory of the Austro-Hungarian Empire also were required to hand over to Austria and Hungary "the records, documents and materials dating from a period not exceeding twenty years *which have a direct bearing on the history or administration of the territory of"* Austria and Hungary.[10] In Posner's view the hard-to-define principle of pertinence was given too strong a role rather than the principle of provenance. As a result of this the integrity of many Austrian and Hungarian record groups was compromised. Writing in 1939, he said that as a result of earlier archival transfers, "the modern holdings of the Vienna archives have been torn apart in a most undesirable way."[11] Many of the principles advanced by Posner with their emphasis on the importance of the preservation of the integrity of record groups (fonds) have subsequently been recognized as international norms.

As Posner noted, somewhat more complicated wording for archival adjustments, at the insistence of Poland, is found in the Treaty of Riga (1921) between Poland, Russia, and Ukraine. This treaty resulted in the restitution of archives, manuscript collections, and other enumerated materials to the reconstituted Republic of Poland.[12] Actual deliveries to Poland, despite lengthy work by Polish commissions, were not viewed as satisfactory in many cases. A number of reports and analyses of the transfers were published in the 1920s, particularly on the Polish side.[13] There has been continuing criticism about the incomplete transfers to Poland according to the Treaty of Riga, including archives and manuscript collections that had been seized by Catherine II when Poland was partitioned at the end of the eighteenth

---

[10]   The full texts of those treaties are conveniently reprinted as appendices to *The Spoils of War: World War II and Its Aftermath. The Loss, Reappearance, and Reco- very of Cultural Property*, ed. Elizabeth Simpson (New York: Harry N. Abrams, 1997), pp. 282–84 (emphasis added).

[11]   Posner, *Archives and the Public Interest*, p. 179.

[12]   The full text of the Treaty of Riga (1921), is also reprinted in *The Spoils of War: WWII and Aftermath*, pp. 284–85.

[13]   See, for example, Edward Kuntze, "Sprawy rewindykacyjne. Prace Delegacji Polskiej w Moskwie i ich metoda," in *Pamiętnik IV Powszechnego Zjazdu Historyków Polskich w Poznaniu, 6–8 grudnia 1925*, vol. 1, section VIB (Lviv, 1925); Kazimierz Tyszkowski, "Rewindykowane rękopisy Biblioteki Publicznej w Petersburgu," ibid., vol. 2: *Protokoły*, pt. 2, *Dodatki*, pp. 230–36; Józef Siemieński, "Rewindykacja Archiwów Koronnych," *Archeion* 1 (1927): 33–60; Witold Suchodolski, "Wykonanie art. XI traktatu ryskiego w zakresie archiwów państwowych," *Archeion* 1 (1927): 66–78.

century. But some of the materials held back by the Russian side from central Polish records were on the basis of changes of frontiers and again on the principle of territorial pertinence. Other local nineteenth-century Polish records were retained in Moscow for various political reasons. These precedents are of particular importance for Ukraine, but still require full scholarly analysis. A recent Polish analysis by Wojciech Kowalski from the standpoint of restitution of cultural treasures supplements earlier ones that concentrated on archives.[14]

Since WWII a large international literature has grown on the effects of the decolonization process and wartime looted and captured records on archival claims and transfers. For example, a lengthy analysis of historical precedents going back to the sixteenth century by Joachim Meyer-Landrut, published in Germany in 1953, brought together extensive scholarship on the international legal problems involved.[15] A 1964 study by Ludwig Engstler examined the broader problem of cultural restitution in general in the context of international law from medieval times through the postwar efforts of UNESCO, and in the process paid considerable attention to archives.[16] A number of such past studies have brought together an extensive bibliography of earlier literature on the subject, but a full international bibliography is still needed. And many of those studies dealing with the broader issue of cultural restitution pay inadequate attention to specific problems of displaced archives and archival restitution—or non-restitution—as they have been practiced in Eastern Europe involving independent countries of the former Soviet and other neighboring countries in the former Soviet bloc.

---

[14] Wojciech W. Kowalski, *Art Treasures and War* (London: Institute of Art and Law), esp. pp. 29–33, which covers comparatively the post-World War I treaties on the issue. See also the earlier analysis of Kowalski, concentrating on problems involved with the legacy of World War II: Wojciech Kowalski, *Liquidation of the Effects of World War II in the Area of Culture* (Warsaw: Institute issue of Culture, 1994), and the Polish version which includes appended texts of many related documents: *Likwidacja skutków II Wojny Światowej w dziedzinie kultury* (Warsaw: Institute of Culture, 1994).

[15] Joachim Meyer-Landrut, "Die Behandlung von staatlichen Archiven und Registraturen nach Völkerrecht," *Archivalische Zeitschrift* 48 (1953): 45–120. The study was based on a dissertation defended in Göttingen in 1951.

[16] Ludwig Engstler, *Die territoriale Bindung von Kulturgütern im Rahmen des Völkerrechts* (Cologne and Berlin: C. Heymann, 1964) [=Annales Universitatis Saraviensis, Schriftenreihe der Rechts- und Wirtschaftswissenschaftlichen Fakultät der Universität des Saarlandes, vol. 8].

ICA Resolutions, Cagliari, and the 1978 UNESCO Report

In the decades since its formation after World War II, the United Nations in general, and UNESCO and the International Council on Archives (ICA) in particular, have made considerable efforts to collect and analyze legal norms and historical precedents from diplomatic treaties and archival practice over the centuries. A number of the annual meetings of the International Round Table on Archives (CITRA), which brings together the heads of national archives throughout the world under ICA auspices, have addressed the issue of the appropriate arrangements for archives in the light of decolonization and restitution problems for archives displaced by war or other factors.[17] Many of the international precedents and jurisdictional problems involved that could put the Soviet-area problems in historical and international legal perspectives and assist adjudication have been considered in the framework of the United Nations.

Warsaw CITRA, 1961. Already in 1961, despite the height of the Cold War, the Sixth Conference of the ICA Round Table (CITRA) in Warsaw concluded two important resolutions involving matters of restitution and transfers of archives. First, in terms of procedures aimed at avoiding problems of purely political decisions regarding archives, the Round Table resolved:

> (2) The VIth International Conference of the Round Table on Archives deems necessary that, in any discussion leading to clauses of international treaties relating to archives, the advice of the concerned archivists be required.[18]

And second, addressing the specific issue of mutual restitution of displaced archives during World War II:

> Considering that archives are for every nation part of the most valuable cultural property and that each nation has the right to hold its own archives;
>
> On the base of international law and in order to promote peace and friendship among peoples;

---

[17]   See the first Ukrainian-language history of international archival cooperation, with particular focus on the ICA, by Volodymyr S. Lozyts′kyi, *Istoriia mizhnarodnoho arkhivnoho spivrobitnytstva (1898–1998 rr.)* (Kyiv, 1999).

[18]   First published in *Actes de la Sixième conférence internationale de la Table ronde des archives. Les archives dans la vie internationale* (Paris, 1963). Reprinted in *Dossier on Archival Claims*, p. 33.

> The VIth International Conference of the Round Table on
> Archives deems desirable to call on archival institutions and
> archivists all around the world, asking them to take the suitable
> measures for returning to their rightful owners archives groups
> and documents which have been displaced during World War
> II.[19]

In a major substantive report to the 1961 CITRA meetings, the French
archivist Robert-Henri Bautier raised the issue of the origins and evolution of
international law on archives and presented specific examples of archival
components in various treaties dating from the thirteenth century to the
present.[20] Further references were added in the 1976 report of the International Law Commission (ILC) by Mohammed Bedjaoui in connection with
draft articles for a convention on problems of the succession of States with
respect to state property.[21]

In 1976, UNESCO had already taken an important stand regarding
archives seized in wartime as well as those resulting from colonial rule. As
clearly affirmed in a report of the Director General:

> Every national community has the right to its identity such as has
> been developed in the course of its history. Human harmony re-
> quires that national communities should help each other in this
> search for truth and historical continuity. Military and colonial
> occupation do not confer any special right to retain archives
> acquired by virtue of that occupation.[22]

Although not explicitly stated, the implication is clear that such seized
archives should be returned.

Cagliari CITRA, 1977. The sixteenth session of the ICA annual International Round Table Conference (CITRA) assembled in Cagliari in 1977 was

---

[19]   Ibid.

[20]   Robert-Henri Bautier, "Les archives et le droit international," in *Actes de la
Sixième CITRA,* pp. 11–56.

[21]   *Eighth report on succession of States in respect of matters other than treaties,* by
Mohammed Bedjaoui (A/CN.4/292), with bibliographic references to earlier reports
on p. 7. (See also above, Introduction, p. 11n24.)

[22]   "Report by the Director General on the Study of the Possibility of Transferring
Documents from Archives Constituted within the Territory of Other Countries or
Relating to their Territory, within the Framework of Bilateral Agreements" (19C/94,
§3.1.1 August 1976, from the 19th General Conference in Nairobi). As quoted by
Charles Kecskeméti in his 1994 CITRA report, "The Action by Unesco and ICA since
1976, Part 2," in *CITRA 1993–1995,* p. 84.

specifically devoted to the issues of archival claims in light of decolonization, boundary changes, the succession of States, wars, and other instances where part of the legitimate national archival legacy is located abroad. As part of the resolutions of the conference:

> [T]he Round Table reaffirms the right of each State to recover archives which are part of its heritage of archives and which are currently kept outside its territory, as well as the right of each national community to have access, under agreed conditions, to records belonging to other countries and relevant to its own history, and to copy them...[23]

Of particular importance, three basic international archival principles, discussed in Chapter 1, were recognized in the resolutions—namely:

> The Round Table underlines that the *principle of the respect of the integrity of archive groups* should be used as a controlling principle in the settlement of disputed archival claims.

> The Round Table nevertheless recognizes that the concept of *functional pertinence* may be relevant in particular circumstances.

> The Round Table underlines the advantage of referring to all of the criteria deriving from *the principle of provenance* for determining the patrimonial ownership of disputed archives, and also emphasizes the value of the *concept of common patrimony* as a regulator in establishing the right of access to archives for the authorities and the citizens of countries participating in the patrimony.[24]

The full resolutions, published papers, and reports of that conference deserve study by archival specialists and other authorities resolving the archival legacies of the successor States of the Soviet Union.

Of special importance in this regard was a preliminary study by ICA Secretary General Charles Kecskeméti prepared for the Cagliari Round Table.[25] In his conference report, Kecskeméti included a chart of historical precedents regarding archival transfers in international treaties going back to

---

[23]   See the official version of the Cagliari proceedings: *Actes de la 17-ème CITRA*, p. 100. I quote the English translation of the resolution included as an appendix to *CITRA 1993–1995*, p. 245.

[24]   Ibid.

[25]   Kecskeméti, *Archival Claims*.

the seventeenth century which, drawing on the earlier studies of the subject mentioned above, was later expanded by Bernard Mahieu.[26]

Kecskeméti's general report later served as the basis for an official UNESCO report, which has still not been superseded as the best orientation on the subject.[27] As late as October 1994, American archivist Frank B. Evans pointed out that Kecskeméti's report demonstrated that "there was very little agreement on either principles or procedures for making transfers following the creation of new states, whether they resulted from the dissolution of former empires, reestablishment of formerly sovereign States, or from decolonization."[28]

ICA Model Agreements. Among the later results of the 1978 UNESCO report was a study by Kecskeméti and the Dutch legal specialist Evert Van Haar on model agreements and conventions relating to the transfer of archives, issued under UNESCO sponsorship in 1981.[29] Further analysis of this document and its amplification with additional elements attuned to post-communist regimes would be helpful today.

ICA Guides to Sources for the History of Nations. UNESCO also provided continued support for the ambitious ICA compilation and publication of an impressive series of "Guides to the Sources of the History of Nations," covering sources relating to Latin America, Africa, and Asia, that are held in

---

[26]   See Bernard Mahieu, "Tableau historique des accords portant sur des transferts d'archives," *Actes de la 17-ème CITRA*, pp. 39–69. See also reference to the expanded form of this report mentioned in fn. 40 below and reproduced in Appendix V. That chart did not, however, appear in the 1978 published version of the UNESCO report.

[27]   The revised Kecskeméti text was published by UNESCO as "Report of the Director-General on the Study of Problems Involved in the Transfer of Documents from Archives in the Territory of Certain Countries to the Country of Their Origin," 24 August 1978 (20C/102). This is included as Appendix I below.

[28]   Frank B. Evans, "The Action by Unesco and ICA since 1976," a paper presented at the first working session, "Disputed Archival Claims: the Legal Framework," *CITRA 1993–1995*, p. 72. See "Report of the Director General" 1978 (20C/102), §16 and §17 (in Appendix I).

[29]   Charles Kecskeméti and Evert Van Haar, *Model Bilateral and Multilateral Agreements and Conventions Concerning Transfer of Archives* (Paris, 1981) (PGI-81/WS/3).

various other countries outside those areas.[30] Initially envisaged by Robert-Henri Bautier, the project had started in 1959. The tradition and methodology further developed out of the 1978 report of the Director-General of UNESCO mentioned above. Particularly attentive to sources relating to former colonial areas, the aims of the project for the reconstitution of national archival heritage have potential implications for newly independent successor States to the Soviet Union.[31]

Despite the general success of the UNESCO/ICA "Guides" series, it is not clear that the descriptive format, type, and extent of archival repositories covered would adequately serve as a prospective model for description of archival Ucrainica and/or Rossica abroad. In that connection, it is important to review the 1981 methodological pamphlet by Belgian archivist Jean Pieyns, which served as a feasibility study on database development for the project.[32] The UNESCO/ICA plan was understandably principally aimed at coverage of major state archives. However, for adequate description of archival Ucrainica abroad (and for Rossica and Polonica) coverage is needed of important holdings in more private, ethnically oriented collections. Many of these have not been well described in published or computer-accessible sources. The cost of such a project increases as more detail and deeper coverage are added; without such inclusions, however, the results will have only limited information value for research.

ICA Microfilm Assistance Initiative. A third major initiative to assist the preservation and/or reconstitution of national archival heritages, recommended in 1978 by the ICA and UNESCO, was in the area of microform copies. This likewise deserves examination today in terms of Ukrainian

---

[30]   A bibliography of those volumes already published and addresses for orders of specific volumes is included in the *List of ICA Publications/Liste des publications du CIA. 1992* (Paris: ICA/CIA Secretariat, 1992), pp. 12–17.

[31]   A thorough survey review of the ICA "Guides" series prepared by the German specialist Karl J. Bauer appeared in Germany with comments about the strengths and weakness of the holdings in, and resulting descriptive contributions from, different European countries, which vary in their level and thoroughness of coverage. See his "Ein Quellenführer zu Geschichte der Nationen," *Historische Zeitschrift* 255 (1992): 667–706.

[32]   Jean Pieyns, *Feasibility Study of a Data Base on National Historical Sources in Foreign Repositories* (Paris: UNESCO, 1981) (PGI-81/WS/25). At the time of publication, the series title indicated was being used rather than the current one. The study included appended sample questions, and actual standardized, recommended questionnaires to be used in canvassing archives in connection with the UNESCO/ICA series.

efforts in reconstituting the national archival heritage. Plans were realized through a 1981 UNESCO-funded proposal for "the creation of an internationally financed and managed microfilm assistance fund to facilitate the solution of problems involved in the international transfer of archives and in obtaining access to sources of national history located in foreign archives."[33] In 1985, the 23rd General Conference of UNESCO agreed on "the development, in cooperation with the International Council on Archives, of a general plan for the reconstitution of the archival heritages through the transfer of microforms."[34] Attention at that time was principally directed towards the reconstruction of the archival heritages of countries in Africa and Asia that, although they had achieved independence from European colonial powers, were without major segments of their own national archival heritage. Problems of implementation always hinged on costs and the need for subsidies, since the former imperial powers who held most of the records in question were hardly willing to subsidize—let alone undertake on their own—the massive preparation of microforms required.

A number of international meetings held over the next few years under ICA sponsorship culminated in a special international conference on microfilming programs in Trier, West Germany, in March 1987, effectively launching the ICA program. Priorities were drawn up of records deemed of "joint heritage," those of general regional interest, or records with disputed claims. However, the microfilming assistance program, as reported most recently at the 1994 ICA Round Table Conference (CITRA) in Thessalonica, has had only marginal results because of inadequate funding. During the entire 1988–1992 period, despite the ICA recommendation for an initial minimum of $150,000 per year, there was a total budget of only $93,280. Only a handful of projects in French or United Kingdom repositories have been undertaken to date, and since 1993 no funding at all has been available through ICA.

The program essentially ended in early 1994, when its principle supporter, Amadou A. Bousso, retired from the UNESCO Secretariat. In his 1994 CITRA report, Anthony Farrington, who has directed the ICA project since 1992, recommended that the project should continue, but he suggested

---

[33] Ivan Borsa, *Feasibility Study on the Creation of an Internationally Financed and Managed Microfilm Assistance Fund to Facilitate the Solution of Problems Involved in the International Transfer of Archives and in Obtaining Access to Sources of National History Located in Foreign Archives* (Paris: UNESCO, 1981) (PGI-81/WS/10).

[34] As cited by Kecskeméti, "Activities of Unesco and ICA since 1976, Part 2," in *CITRA 1993–1995*, p. 83.

that financing should be "at least $1 million per year for ten years," to be divided among member states of the European Community.[35] He appeared unaware, however, of the potential needs in Eastern Europe and Eurasia following the collapse of the Soviet Union. Recognizing the general interest in continuing the microfilm program, the 1994 Round Table resolution was specifically directed to a review of the past developments and "calls on the Executive Committee of ICA, in cooperation with UNESCO, to reactivate and review the International Microfilming Programme, and in particular to investigate fully existing and new sources of funding," along with other more technical matters.[36]

In light of more recent developments in Eastern Europe and Eurasia in the wake of the collapse of the Soviet Union, it would be appropriate to revitalize and extend such a proposal within the East European archival context, which had not been included in earlier ICA initiatives. As one key example, a consortium under the aegis of the Council of Europe has contributed to an electronic information and reproduction project for the Comintern Archive held in Moscow, whose fate have important political and historical implications for many countries. Using a state-of-the art computerized technology specially adapted for the Comintern Archive, the project under sponsorship of the ICA and the Council of Europe will take a number of years to complete, but if technical problems can be overcome, it will result in the most advanced archival information retrieval system yet to be introduced in Russia.[37] In the meanwhile, microfiche production of Comintern congress files is well under way under commercial auspices.[38]

---

[35] "The ICA's International Microfilming Project—Is There a Future?" in *CITRA 1993–1995*, pp. 120–24. Farrington quoted a rounded figure of $90,000, but the more precise figure is documented in the Kecskeméti report noted below.

[36] XXX CITRA, Thessalonica 12–15 October 1994, RESOLUTION 2. See Appendix V.

[37] See the report by RTsKhIDNI (now RGASPI) director Kyrill M. Anderson, "Novyi oblik Arkhiva Kominterna," *Otechestvennye arkhivy* 1998 (1): 17–20. A more detailed report "O mezhdunarodnom proekte komp'iuterizatsii Arkhiva Kominterna," by project coordinator, Oleg Naumov appears in *Nauchno-informatsionnyi biulleten' RTsKhIDNI* 1998 (10): 5–27. An initial brochure announcing the project has been released by the ICA, "Les Archives du Komintern: Une Histoire qui intéresse le monde" (Paris, 1997). As of the end of 1999, serious technical problems still impede work on the project.

[38] Complete files of congresses and plenums have been filmed in RGASPI (formerly RTsKhIDNI) in Moscow, together with the related finding aids, and by 1997, six segments were available for purchase from Inter Documentation Company–IDC,

Although Comintern archives are of less direct significance to Ukraine and other newly independent former Soviet republics, the Rosarkhiv-Hoover project covering CPSU and other archives (see Chapter 2, pp. 77–78), which has also found a commercial basis in the West, is of much more direct potential relevance. Soviet successor States, however, will be unable to pay the high prices for these commercially available material in the foreseeable future. They will continue to need subsidies in this area.

Archives and the Unratified 1983 Vienna Convention on the Succession of States

Preparatory Literature and Reports. During the years following the Cagliari conference, discussion of the archival problems involved with the displaced national heritages continued under the auspices of the United Nations General Assembly in the context of drafting a convention on the "Succession of States in Respect of Matters Other than Treaties." In addition to codifying provisions for the transfer of state property and state debts, this convention includes a separate section on state archives. Preparation of draft articles dealing with state property and state debts had already been taken up by the UN International Law Commission (ILC) in a series of meetings starting in 1976 and continuing through 1978 and 1979. During 1979, a number of special meetings of the ILC were devoted specifically to archival matters. In preparing draft articles, the ILC brought together significant legal opinions, analyzed international treaty precedents, and informed international legal opinion regarding historical archival practice. A summary introductory discussion was published covering the definition and role of state archives, claims to archives and the protection of the national cultural heritage with note of relevant actions by UNESCO and the United Nations, and principles and disputes concerning archives in the context of the succession of States.[39]

Leiden, the Netherlands. An electronic searchable diskette reproduces the relevant *opisi* in Russian, German, and English.

[39]   Bedjaoui, Mohammed, Special Rapporteur, "Eleventh report on succession of States in respect of matters other than treaties," *Yearbook ILC, 1979* (New York, 1981), II, pt. 1: 67–124. See also the summary of 1979 ILC meetings in *Yearbook ILC, 1979*, I: 138–68 and 189–95; and the draft articles on archives and commentary in ibid., II, pt. 2: 77–86. See also subsequent ILC discussion of the problems in preparation for the convention in *Yearbook ILC 1980* (1982), I: 99–118; II, pt. 1, 1–12 (report); *Yearbook ILC 1981* (1983), I: 236–44, 247–50, 281–86 (summary of

The ILC benefited from the preliminary studies of Kecskeméti and other submissions to the ICA Round Table conferences, although a representative of the ICA was not included in its deliberations. Significantly, the ILC report included an expanded version of the above-mentioned chart of provisions for archival transfers in international treaties since the seventeenth century— "Non-Exhaustive Table of Treaties Containing Provisions Relating to the Transfer of Archives in Cases of Succession of States" (to include 183 positions), with an accompanying analysis of various examples of past practice and disputes.[40]

The 1983 Convention Adopted but Unratified. The 1983 "Vienna Convention on Succession of States in Respect of State Property, Archives and Debts," was adopted at the conclusion of a lengthy United Nations conference in Vienna (1 March–8 April 1983) by experts from ninety nations.[41] The fact that the Convention itself devoted a separate section to archives as requiring special consideration from other issues of general state property demonstrates international recognition of the specificity of the issues involved. The lengthy preparatory discussion by the ILC and the conference sessions devoted specifically to archival problems brought together experienced international legal opinion and amplified many of the different issues involving the transfer of archival records.[42] In light of extensive considera-

---

meetings); II, pt. 1: 5–42. See also the summary discussion in the *Yearbook of the United Nations* 35 (1981): 1227–1230; 36 (1982): 1383; and 37 (1983): 1119.

[40]   This more complete, revised version was published in *Yearbook ILC, 1979*, II, pt. 1: 82–93. Supporting general principles, analysis, and bibliography follow, pp. 93–124. This is reproduced below as Appendix II. Of course, with the more recent breakup of the Soviet Union and other countries such as Yugoslavia, there are now more examples of treaties to be analyzed, but the chart as then formulated still serves as a starting point. Noticeably, too, many of the WWII and post-WWII archival agreements involving the USSR, its constituent republics, and other countries in the communist bloc are not included.

[41]   "Vienna Convention on Succession of States in Respect to State Property, Archives and Debts," United Nations Conference on Succession of States in Respect to State Property, Archives and Debts, Vienna, 1 March–8 April 1983 (A/Conf. 117/14); pt. III, art. 19–31, is devoted specifically to archives. See also the "Final Act of the United Nations Conference on Succession of States in Respect to State Property, Archives and Debts" (A/Conf. 117/15). The text of Pt. III is reproduced in Appendix IIIa.

[42]   See, most particularly, the archival section (pt. 3) of the ILC report on the draft convention in *Report of the International Law Commission on Work of its Thirty-*

tion of archival transfers in earlier treaties, the convention sought to codify and confirm existing norms from previous treaties and international archival practice. Because the international archival community (e.g., the ICA) was not directly involved in the ILC deliberations, the proposed text of a UN convention dealing with archival transfers in light of the succession of States that was drafted by the ILC failed to take into account some of the specific archival issues and to clarify adequate terminology as set forward in earlier ICA reports.

Indeed, the Convention itself was never ratified and, hence, as of late-1999, has never taken effect. Since many member states abstained or voted against the adoption of the text, the conference failed to produce a legal document that could be accepted as an international norm. Only five countries signed on soon afterwards—Algeria, Argentina, Egypt, Niger, and Peru. (Fifteen ratifications were required for the treaty to come into force.) During the eleven years following its adoption, the Convention was signed by a total of only eleven countries, but ratified by only five.

Apparently unaware of the serious problems of the convention and the recommendations against accession by the ICA, five more newly independent States signed on later, following the breakup of Yugoslavia and the USSR. Estonia was the first country to submit an official accession to the Convention in October 1991. Following independence, Ukraine also ratified the convention on 8 January 1993, as did Georgia soon afterwards. Most recently, Macedonia signed in accession in September 1997.[43] Undoubtedly, their leaders were unaware of the severe criticism raised of the archival

---

Third Session, May 4–June 24, 1981, published as *Offical Records of the General Assembly, Thirty-Sixth Session*, Supplement 10 (A/36/10). The Soviet Union was represented on the ILC by Nikolai A. Ushakov. See also the preparatory "Analytic Compilation of Comments of Governments on the Final Draft Articles on Succession of States in Respect to State Property, Archives and Debts," 24 January 1983 (A/Conf. 117/5), especially 108–121. Various reports of individual meetings of the 1983 conference and related conference materials were published separately in mimeographed format and on microfiche. Most bear the series identification A/Conf. 117.

[43] As of April 1999, the Vienna Convention was signed by Algeria, Argentina, Croatia, Egypt, Estonia, Georgia, Macedonia, Niger, Peru, Ukraine, and Yugoslavia—according to data in the Office of Treaties at the United Nations, New York (see the UN website <http://www.un.org/Depts/Treaty>). Only Croatia, Estonia, Georgia, Macedonia, and Ukraine have ratified the treaty.

section by the ICA report, but to its negligence, the ICA had never published or widely circulated its "Professional Advice."[44]

ICA Critique and Recommendations. After the 1983 conference, an ICA Working Group of international archival leaders from seven countries was commissioned to study the Vienna Convention and to evaluate whether it "might contribute effectively to the settlement of existing or potential archival claims resulting from succession of States and whether the clauses of the Convention were compatible with internationally recognized principles and practices of archive administration." The archivists involved, although all from European countries, were nonetheless sensitive to the point of view of newly independent states as well as that of former colonial powers.[45] Their categorical conclusion that the Vienna Convention "does not provide an adequate basis for dealing with succession of States in respect of archives" was set forth in an ICA advisory paper, together with analysis and suggestions for improvement in the wording of various paragraphs.[46]

They recognized that the wording of the archival section suffered from attempts to harmonize it with broader issues of the disposition of state

---

[44] Presumably the new signatory nations wanted to be able to quote the convention in support of their own claims, but little did they realize that their adherence to that convention might make it almost impossible for the United Nations to produce an improved variant with respect to archives. Those nations, including Ukraine, that signed may have been more concerned with the more politically explosive provisions of the convention with respect to state property and debts. Archives should never have been included in the same convention, nor should such a convention have been pushed through without more prior consultations with the international archival community, particularly as represented by the ICA.

[45] The working group consisted of Dr. Leopold Auer (Austria), ICA representative at the UN Centre, Vienna; Dr. Eckhart G. Franz (Germany), Secretary of the International Round Table Conference (CITRA): Dr. Oscar Gauye (Switzerland), former ICA President; Dr. Charles Kecskeméti, then ICA Executive Secretary, and Rapporteur of the Working Group; Dr. Eric Ketelaar (the Netherlands), ICA Secretary for Standardization; Dr. Evert van Laar (the Netherlands), ICA Secretary for Development; and Peter Walne (Great Britain), ICA Secretary for Publications.

[46] "Professional Advice on the Vienna Convention on Succession of States in Respect of State Property, Archives and Debts, Part III, State Archives (art. 19 to 31)" (Paris: ICA, 1983) (document CE/83/12). My discussion of the text appears in an earlier form in my "Archival Rossica," pp. 938–40. "Professional Advice" was appended to Kecskeméti's presentation at the 1994 CITRA in Thessalonica. The ICA first published it as an appendix in *CITRA 1993–1995*, pp. 250–55. It is included below as Appendix IIIb.

property and the even thornier issue of the assumption of state debts by successor States. Among the important considerations raised by the ICA "Professional Advice" was the requirement for detailed and accurate description of archival fonds or their component parts that are to be transferred, a provision that was not included in the Vienna Convention. As they noted:

> Transfer of the Property of State archives cannot take place... without a special legal instrument duly approved by the competent authorities of the States concerned and *listing specifically and precisely the record/archive groups and/or sub-groups (and, if necessary, records) which shall pass from one State to the other* (§2.1.1).

They further noted that:

> ...the major current disputed archival claims, with the exception of those originating from the removal of archives as a result of warfare, are due to the absence of archival agreements (§2.1.4).

Equally important, in the definition of those categories of archives to be transferred, the Vienna Convention includes as one category those archives that "relate exclusively or principally to the territory to which the succession of States relate" (article 28). But as the ICA specialists concluded, this:

> ...definition merely rewords the 'principle of territorial pertinence' which has been rejected by the studies conducted under the auspices of UNESCO as incompatible with the principle of provenance and inapplicable because of its ambiguity (§2.2.ad ii).

The ICA Working Group notes the need in that paragraph for possible exceptions in the case of major migration or the resettlement of population and "archives of military occupation authorities." Both such categories of records still require further international legal attention and the formulation of at least provisional recommendations, particularly in light of boundary changes and population resettlement wrought by World War II, and the extent of Nazi wartime occupation records and postwar records of Allied military government in Germany and Austria. In further emphasizing the principle of "provenance" rather than "pertinence," the ICA group suggested correcting the phrases "archives belonging to a territory" or "having belonged to a territory" to "archives constituted within the territory." Thus, the text should read: "...archives constituted within the territory before it became dependent from [*sic*] the predecessor State and subsequently integrated in the State archives of the predecessor State whether preserved *in situ* or removed from the territory..." (§2.2.ad iii).

In connection with the important "principle of respect for the integrity of archive group fonds," the Working Group also noted that "the odd wording of the title of article 25 in the English version is certainly due to a wrong translation from the French 'Sauvegarde de l'intégrité des fonds d'archives d'État'" (§2.4). They also sought the addition of an article (as had been proposed by Switzerland but rejected) recognizing "the concept of 'joint heritage,' already approved by the General Conference of UNESCO" (§2.5). They concluded—with regrets—that many such problems "could have been avoided had the International Law Commission and the Vienna Conference called for archival expertise in wording the text" (§3.2). As it is, the Working Group concluded, the 1978 UNESCO Report mentioned above remains the best orientation on the subject.[47]

Despite the failure of ratification of the Vienna Convention and its inadequacy for dealing with archives, the ICA Working Group recognized that the "extensive historical compilation and analysis will be of invaluable help to any State in negotiating the settlement of disputed archival claims" (§1.1). In sum, it would be highly beneficial to the post-communist successor States to revisit the proceedings of the Vienna conference as well as the preparatory work of the International Law Commission (in light of the ICA "Professional Advice" and related published archival discussion at the time), together with the earlier 1978 UNESCO Report.

A Polish Analysis. Poland has not ratified the 1983 Vienna Convention. Nevertheless, Polish archivists have taken a more favorable view of it than many other European archivists, particularly since they have tended to support the principle of "territorial pertinence" more than archivists of other countries.[48] Poland, like Ukraine, is a country whose territorial integrity has been altered many times over the centuries and whose national archival heritage has been scattered and displaced among previously ruling States. It thus is duly sensitive to the complexities of reconstituting a national archival heritage.

The 1989 monograph by Polish historian and archive director Władysław Stępniak, *Sukcesja państw dotycząca archiwaliów* (Succession of States in Respect to Archives), is the most detailed analysis of the background and

---

[47]   Reference is to the "Report of the Director-General" 1978 (20 C/102) (see above fn. 27 and Appendix I).

[48]   See, for example, the often criticized 1977 pamphlet of Tadeusz Walichnowski, *Przynależność terytorialna archiwaliów w stosunkach międzynarodowych* (Warsaw: PWN, 1977). Professor Walichnowski was the director of the Polish State Archival Administration, a post he held until the end of 1992.

implications of the 1983 Convention to date.[49] Although it appeared several years before the collapse of the Soviet Union and was most specifically oriented towards a Polish perspective, it also deserves consideration today. Stępniak summarizes the preparatory legal analyses and working meetings preceding the 1983 Vienna Convention with copious citations of the published discussions and documentation prepared by the UN International Law Commission. He provides a detailed analysis of the Vienna Conference and the resulting Convention itself.

Although Poland was not one of the few nations that acceded to the treaty, Stępniak on the whole is positive regarding the Vienna Convention and its potential applicability. Unfortunately, however, his discussion does not appear to be aware of the unpublished ICA "Professional Advice," which evaluates the shortcomings of the 1983 Convention. Neither does he recommend the 1978 UNESCO Report, which the ICA still recognizes as authoritative. While his study draws especially on Polish experience and some of the specific Polish revindication problems, Stępniak places more credence in the doctrine of territorial or functional pertinence than the ICA advisory group would. Stępniak's helpful multi-national bibliography, although it emphasizes Polish literature, is still important because many of the studies cited in it have not been widely known abroad.

Austrian Discussion. In the wake of the abortive Vienna Convention, other European archivists have recalled the 1941 essay by Ernst Posner and his criticism of what he considered to have been ill-fated archival adjustments following the breakup of the Austro-Hungarian Empire. The Austrian state archivists Leopold Auer and Christiane Thomas, for example, presented a case study of the Austro-Yugoslav Convention of 1923 that well demonstrates the extent to which complexities involved in archival negotiations, as a result of the succession of States, are still unresolved.[50] The authors

[49] Władysław Stępniak, *Sukcesja państw dotycząca archiwaliów* (Warsaw: PWN, 1989). Stępniak includes a Polish translation from the English-language version of the 1983 Vienna Convention (A/Conf. 117/14). See also Stępniak's earlier report on the Vienna Convention, "Klauzule archiwalne Konwencji Wiedeńskiej z 8 IV 1983 roku," *Archeion* 79 (1985): 5–38.

[50] Leopold Auer and Christiane Thomas, "The Execution of the Austro-Yugoslavian Convention on Archives: A Case Study in State Succession," *Information Development* 1(3) 1985: 169–75. With specific reference to the Austro-Yugoslav Convention, that paper drew on a longer study by Gerhard Rill, Elisabeth Springer, and Christiane Thomas, "60 Jahre österreichisch-jugoslawisches Archivüberein-kommen. Eine Zwischenbilanz," *Mitteilungen des Österreichischen Staatsarchivs* 35 (1982): 288–331, with the appended text of the agreement (pp. 332–47), and a

demonstrate that many of the problems arose because of the "absence of archival agreements," or the lack of clarity in "guiding legal principles, which are acceptable from a professional point of view to all parties concerned." Thus, they call for "the utmost necessity...to have a set of approved, clear and non-controversial criteria, worked out in cooperation with experts in international law and archivists, who must be involved in this work from the very beginning." They further insist, following the ICA "Professional Advice," that:

> ...it should be made a binding rule that, in cases of succession of
> states, a special legal instrument will be drawn up, duly approved
> by the competent authorities of the states concerned and listing
> specifically and precisely the archives, archive/record groups and,
> if necessary, records which shall pass from one state to another.[51]

Auer himself prepared a helpful survey of the general problems involved, concluding with an analysis of the 1983 Vienna Convention and supporting the criticisms presented in the ICA "Professional Advice."[52]

Post-Soviet Discussion Continues

Overcoming Iron Curtain Isolation. Revelations of the extent of displaced archives in the USSR and the problems of potential archival claims for Soviet successor States ushers in a new phase of development in issues of archival claims. Both Vsevolod Tsaplin's commendable 1992 study of provisions for jurisdiction over archival documents in diplomatic treaties of pre-revolutionary and Soviet Russia, and Evgenii Starostin's commentary on it (see above, p. 78) were prepared without knowledge of a number of important sources, including: the 1983 Vienna Convention; the ICA "Professional Advice"; the chart of international treaty provisions published first in 1977 (and in expanded form in 1979 by the UN ILC); the 1989 Stępniak monograph from neighboring Poland; or, for that matter, most other published European

---

description by Thomas of the 51 charters (1262–1338) that were transferred from the Vienna archives.

[51]   Leopold Auer and Christiane Thomas, "The Execution of the Austro-Yugoslavian Convention on Archives," p. 173.

[52]   Leopold Auer, "Staatennachfolge bei Archiven," in *Archives et bibliothèques de Belgique/Archief-en Bibliotheekwezen in Belgie* 57 (1986) 1–2: 51–68 [=*Miscellanea Carlos Wyffels*].

literature on the subject.[53] Given the standing and erudition of these men, this is a grave indication of the isolation within which Russian and other former Soviet archivists have been operating.

Even in 1996, before his presentation at the Kyiv symposium on "Legal Aspects of Restitution of Cultural Treasures," Deputy Ukrainian Archival Administration Chief Volodymyr Lozyts'kyi had been earlier unaware of the ICA "Professional Advice" and the extensive chart of international treaty provisions related to archives first published in 1977. Yet the isolation involved stems not only from what had been the intellectual and archival Iron Curtain during the Soviet period. A Moscow delegation took part in the 1961 Warsaw CITRA as well as the 1977 CITRA in Cagliari. (Ukrainian representatives were not then included.) Further worsening the matter, Ukraine did not send a representative to the all-important 1994 Thessalonica CITRA, where the matter of displaced archives was in focus.

Part of the problem derives from a very practical problem: language. Few archival leaders from Russia, Ukraine, or other newly independent states know English or French, which have become the linguae francae of CITRA and other ICA meetings. Thus, in this important transitional period, they are hampered in their effective participation in international meetings because they are dependent on interpreters who do not always know the appropriate terminology or who report only a part of what is said. They thus miss many of the innuendoes in international debates and the all-important informal conversations and professional discussions in the corridors. Even more crucially, they do not receive, and are not able to keep up with, professional Western literature. Their struggling new governments lack the funds to buy this Western literature or to send their representatives to international meetings (with the added funds necessary to send an interpreter as well). These archival specialists have therefore become dependent on limited grant funding from Western sources.

At the same time, few Western archival leaders, with the notable exception of emeritus ICA Secretary General Charles Kecskeméti, know Russian or Ukrainian. ICA has not had the funds or technical possibilities to conduct all meetings (including the all-important CITRA meetings) with qualified simultaneous interpretation in all UN languages; and much of the pertinent UNESCO, ICA, and other relevant literature has not been translated into Russian (much less Ukrainian). Hence, even basic texts are not widely

---

[53] For example, Ukrainian archival leaders assured me that they were unaware of the ICA "Position Paper." See also V. V. Tsaplin, "O prave sobstvennosti na arkhivnye dokumenty v diplomaticheskikh aktakh dorevoliutsionnoi i sovetskoi Rossii," *Otechestvennye arkhivy* 1992 (4): 20–25.

circulated (even in abstract) in international archival circles, particularly in Eastern Europe. Frustrations are further increased for archivists from non-Russian newly independent states, where today Russian-language publications are not always welcome.

International archival leaders also are often isolated from East European developments themselves. For example, in 1991, Kecskeméti contributed an article to a special issue of *American Archivist* entitled "Displaced European Archives—Is it Time for a Post-War Settlement?"[54] Kecskeméti's essay was prepared before the collapse of the USSR brought renewed urgency to the issue of archival matters that result from the succession of States, yet the problems he raised regarding captured records and displaced archives are closely related. His essay was also prepared before the West came to know about the extent of displaced European archives—still held in Moscow—that had been captured by the Nazis and in turn captured by the Soviet Union after World War II.

Kecskeméti included a few notes and some bibliographic references to previous literature on the subject. Regrettably, he made no mention of the abortive 1983 Vienna Convention, the ICA "Professional Advice" (at the time still not available in print), nor the 1989 Stępniak monograph.[55] A postwar settlement of European archival claims, as Kecskeméti proposed, or the resolution of archival claims of successor States to the Soviet Union cannot come before there is better mutual understanding of the differences between Western archival institutions and practices, and those in the former Soviet Union; a more comprehensive awareness of the international legal precedents involved; and better distribution of earlier UN documents and other professional literature on the subject.

Thessalonica CITRA, 1994. Issues of displaced archives and problems of restitution again came to the forefront in the 1994 ICA Round Table in Thessalonica, where there were updated reviews of previous developments in the field, presentations of the legal issues, and illuminating analyses of examples of lost and displaced specific groups of records. Unfortunately,

---

[54]   Charles Kecskeméti, "Displaced European Archives—Is it Time for a Post-War Settlement?" *American Archivist* 55 (Winter 1992): 132–40. See also Kecskeméti's earlier brief discussion, "Contested Records: The Legal Status of National Archives," *The Unesco Courier* (February 1985): 9–11.

[55]   In referring to his 1977 preliminary study for the Cagliari Round Table, for example, Kecskeméti told me that he had been unaware that his own helpful chart on previous treaty provisions relating to archives had been republished in expanded form in the 1979 *ILC Yearbook* (see above, fn. 40).

aside from Russia, Lithuania was the only other former Soviet republic present. Less than a month after the Chernihiv conference advocated an appeal to UNESCO (see Chapter 2, pp. 79–80), Ukraine sent no representative to what proved to be one of the most important recent international discussions of archival restitution.

The first Working Session, devoted to "Disputed Archival Claims: The Legal Framework," heard reports directly covering the subject matter of this chapter. Senior American archivist Frank B. Evans reviewed international developments from 1976 through 1983, based on his own first-hand experience as the archives program officer at UNESCO, in which capacity he also served as a UNESCO observer at the 1983 Vienna conference.[56]

Charles Kecskeméti continued the discussion with a further review of the ICA "Professional Advice."[57] He noted that, "as early as March–April 1984, it became obvious that the Vienna Convention was dead (as evidenced by the correspondence exchanged between the United Nations and ICA on this subject)." Nevertheless, Kecskeméti explained further, "its most damaging effect is the fact that the Vienna Convention exists on paper," which means that "the UN Secretariat cannot, therefore, take any initiative to reopen the question." But, as Kecskeméti was now proposing, there was good reason to separate out the archival issue, which "would allow the field of action of the new convention to be extended to include the whole body of international law relating to the transfer and restitution of archives."[58]

The necessity of further ICA action and broad consensus on matters of the reconstitution of the national archival heritage has been significantly affected by new international archival problems arising from the succession of States in Eastern Europe following the collapse of the Soviet Union and the breakup of Yugoslavia and Czechoslovakia. It has been affected even more strongly by revelations about the extent of displaced "trophy archives" from all over the European continent that have been hidden in Russia for the

---

[56] Evans, "The Action by Unesco and ICA since 1976," pp. 69–78.

[57] He stated that the only negative appraisal regarding the "Professional Advice" of which he was aware was by Professor Marco Mozzati in the context of a study of the history of Franco-Algerian archival disputes. (Algeria was one of the few countries, it should be remembered, that officially acceded to the Vienna Convention.) See Kecskeméti, "The Action by Unesco and ICA since 1976, Part 2," in *CITRA 1993–1995*, p. 82. See also Marco Mozzati, "La battaglia degli archivi," in *La modernizzazione in Asia e Africa: Problemi di storia e problemi di metodo. Studi offerti a Giorgio Borsa* (Pavia, 1989), pp. 213–44.

[58] Kecskeméti, "The Action by Unesco and ICA since 1976, Part 2," in *CITRA 1993–1995*, p. 83.

past half century and the ongoing failure of full restitution efforts within Western archival traditions. On this matter, Kecskeméti recommended a new "convention on the transfer and restitution of archives," which would "banish the term 'trophy archives' from the vocabulary," and at that same time would confirm the principle that "public archives remain inalienable other than by an enactment of a legislative body, or by decision of equal legal value, of the state which had created them." Indeed, "any decision to appropriate archives, seized during military campaigns or times of occupation, taken by the state holding them, has, in fact, no legal value." And he concluded:

> In any case, the legal haze which surrounds the transfer and resti-
> tution of archives and subordinates them to makeshift measures,
> sometimes at the whim of politicians should not last indefinitely.
> It is now up to the States concerned to take initiatives which
> would allow rethinking and codifying the rules of international
> law applying to archives.[59]

The introductory report in that session by two Greek specialists provided some further clarification on definitions on the matter of the "Succession of States" and further criticism of the Vienna Convention and comments on the "Professional Advice." They also pointed out the need to consider the importance of displaced private archives and the records of military occupation, neither of which had been dealt with in the 1983 Vienna Convention. Finally, in drafting agreements, they raised the difficulty of reconciling "the interests and concerns of the parties with the principle of the integrity of archives, long established in archival learning and now formally recognized in the 1983 Convention." Complementary to that point should be the need to "include rules on the establishment of special machinery and procedures for the settlement of disputes concerning archives."[60]

A report by a French international lawyer on the legal framework set forth a more precise typology of different cases involving potential archival claims and investigated other international juridical conventions of relevance for archival claims, especially those relating to cultural property. He also tried to clarify or redefine some of the international archival principles involved.[61] Many of the principles discussed have already been developed

---

[59]   Ibid. Kecskeméti included the text of the "Professional Advice" as an appendix to his paper (see above, fn. 46).

[60]   A. A. Fatouros and George Karipsiadis, "Displaced archives in international law," *CITRA 1993–1995*, pp. 60–61.

[61]   Hervé Bastien, "About Archival Claims," XXX CITRA, Thessalonica, *CITRA 1993–1995*, pp. 62–68.

here, and the most important international conventions mentioned are also covered below. Nevertheless, that paper merits attention for references to other international instruments and relevant literature.

Several points raised in discussion are also worth noting. The Director-General of the Swedish National Archives, Erik Norberg, said, "now that this subject has been widely discussed it might be possible for ICA to publish an official policy document which would supply guidelines and advice on negotiations. ICA should not be directly involved with particular negotiations, but its advice would be very valuable." And several archivists suggested, "the reasonable and practical ways in which the Czech Republic and Slovakia had managed the division of their archives as a model." Unlike the situation in Russia, where there have been no transfers to any of the former Soviet republics, "the archives of the former Czechoslovakia had been divided between Prague and Bratislava." That had been done, the Slovak archivist responded, in a very friendly atmosphere, and between professionals," and, "where interest was joint, there would be arrangements for microfilming."[62]

Other conference sessions were also directly or indirectly pertinent to problems of archival reconstitution for Ukraine and other newly independent States of the former Soviet empire. Reports were heard from two major collecting institutions, the Hoover Institution of War, Revolution, and Peace in Palo Alto, California, and the International Institute of Social History in Amsterdam, both of which have had a major role in the rescue and preservation of displaced and frequently fugitive records relating to the communist movement in Eastern Europe that otherwise might have been destroyed. Other reports dealt with more specific dispersed records of regional interest in Africa and Asia, and two specific case studies focusing on the Eastern Mediterranean: the archives of the Patriarchate of Constantinople and the Communist Party of Greece.

The resolutions of the conference highlighted the intense international concern "that solutions be found to disputed claims arising from the displacement of archives as a result of the Second World War and of the process of decolonization." Among other points, the first CITRA resolution:

> ...recalls the accepted archival principles that archives are inalienable and imprescriptible, and should not be regarded as "trophies" or as objects of exchange, [and]

---

[62] "Plenary Discussion—Session 2," *CITRA 1993–1995*, p. 103. Quoted comments by Mr. Biljan (Honorary Member of ICA), Mr. Norberg (Sweden), and Mr. Kartous (Slovakia).

> ...confirms the support of the archival community for the princi-
> ples embodied in the [1978] report of the Director General to the
> 20th session of the General Conference of UNESCO (20C/102).

Although no new specific initiatives were underwritten, nor principles expressed that differed markedly from those of the past, it was recommended that the ICA Executive Committee "lend its support to bilateral and multilateral professional efforts aimed at ending disputed claims inherited from the period 1923–1989 and at resolving new problems confronting States formerly part of federations which have dissolved." There was also a reaffirmation of support for initiatives "by relevant intergovernmental organizations...with their member States...intended to settle disputed claims and reconstitute the historical heritage of each nation."[63] While, as already noted, Ukraine was not represented in Thessalonica, at that period, there was no representative for Eastern Europe and the Commonwealth of Independent States on the ICA Executive Committee, despite the direct concerns raised at the conference regarding that area. Beginning with the ICA International Congress in Beijing in September 1996, however, a Ukrainian representative was appointed to the ICA Executive Committee, as a participant in alternate status. Despite this fact, Ukrainian attendance at ICA/CITRA meetings has not been consistent.

Washington, DC, CITRA, 1995. The 1995 CITRA meeting in Washington, DC, where issues of "War, Archives, and the Comity of Nations" also centered attention on the issue of displaced archives, but again, a Ukrainian representative did not attend.[64] Of particular interest to our discussion, the Archivist of the Netherlands (since retired), Eric Ketelaar, analyzed the efforts at protection and accountability of archives during World War II by professional archivists. He illustrated their incompatibility with the aims of exploitation and looting by the Nazi agencies with which they often competed.[65] An American report on the problems of microfilming captured

---

[63]   XXX CITRA, Thessalonica, 12–15 October 1994, RESOLUTION 1. See Appendix V. Of significant note in the present context, the Russian delegation was among three abstentions in the otherwise unanimous CITRA vote on the resolution.

[64]   The proceedings of the Washington, DC, CITRA (1995) are included in the same volume with the Thessalonica proceedings, *CITRA 1993–1995*, which is currently available as a ".pdf" download on the ICA website.

[65]   Eric Ketelaar, "Archivists in War," XXXI CITRA, Washington, DC, in *CITRA 1993–1995*, pp. 159–63.

records before return is also of relevance to those considering restitution policies.[66]

Most directly relevant to our discussion was the presentation by Austrian Archivist Leopold Auer, who dealt more directly with problems of restitution following what was "probably the largest mass movement of archives in history" as "was accomplished during World War II for reasons of politics, ideology, military strategy, and state intelligence." Auer dealt respectively with legal, political, and professional aspects, before turning to a balance sheet of restitution and non-restitution after 1945. Auer advanced four major recommendations of note: (1) "the compilation of a list of displaced archives/records"; (2) "[the compilation of] guidelines for the promotion of bilateral or multilateral agreements to overcome the regrettable lack of agreement on generally accepted and recognized principles for the solution of archival claims;" (3) "the availability of microform copies of displaced records;" and (4) the "creation of an international committee on displaced archives similar to that of UNESCO for the restitution of cultural property."[67]

Non-State Archives and the Post-Soviet Context

Non-State Archives and the CPSU Example. In considering a projected new international convention that will facilitate the resolution of complicated and confused claims, recognition in a post-Soviet context also should be given to additional problems that were not adequately and specifically clarified in the earlier UNESCO and UN archival reports mentioned above, especially those leading up to the abortive 1983 convention. The 1983 Vienna Convention, dealing as it does with the succession of States, is concerned specifically with the legacy of state records in the context of international law. This grows out of the clear distinction in international law and practice—outside of the Socialist bloc—between public archives, archives of societal organizations and political parties, and private archives created by organizations and individuals outside state agencies. Yet, such distinctions are not always clear cut, and do not apply in the communist world, as is apparent in the earlier discussion of archival principles from the Soviet period. Since Communist Party records have been nationalized and

[66] Geraldine N. Phillips, "Duplication before Restitution: Costs and Benefits—the US Experience," XXXI CITRA, Washington, DC, in *CITRA 1993–1995*, pp. 167–71.

[67] Leopold Auer, "Restitution of Removed Records Following War," XXXI CITRA, Washington, DC, in *CITRA 1993–1995*, pp. 172–78.

considered as state records after 1991 in most former communist countries, the issue will undoubtedly also affect the status of certain types of archival Rossica and Ucrainica abroad and prospective claims of other States. Although this provision was aptly mentioned in the 1978 UNESCO report (20C/102, II §13), the fact that it was not provided for in the 1983 Vienna Convention is one more reason for its inadequacy with respect to archives.

Communist Party and Comintern Records. The lack of a government based on Western concepts of law in the former Soviet Union, together with the fact that the USSR frequently isolated itself from international norms and did not always conform to Western archival practice, makes it harder to apply traditional Western juridical criteria retroactively. Most important in this connection are the archives and agency records of Communist Party agencies, which remained outside of state archival administration and did not even constitute a legal part of the so-called "State Archival Fond of the USSR" before August 1991. Clearly, the Russian presidential seizure of Party records throughout the former Soviet Union and provisions for their transfer to state archival control following the attempted coup in August 1991 were predicated on this realization.

The March 1994 definition of the "Archival Fond of the Russian Federation" explicitly recognizes CPSU and Komsomol records under state proprietorship as the records of the controlling political, administrative, and economic power for all aspects of life in the area. But another presidential decree the same month asserted the right of presidential control over the historical records in the Archive of the President (AP RF). Following subsequent public outcry and criticism in the press, a September 1994 presidential decree established provisions for declassification of CPSU records and encouraged their more rapid transfer to public repositories under Rosarkhiv control.[68] Such transfers, however, have not been completed in Russia, and even many of the high-level files subsequently transferred to public archives have not yet been opened to public scrutiny. In fact, since the 1993 Russian law "On State Secrets," there has been a noticeable backswing in the form of reclosing specific fonds and in slowing the declassification process for records of the Comintern, the Cominform, the CPSU International Department, and related files involving CPSU international activities, which were previously open for research in 1992 and early 1993. These records are obviously of direct pertinence to Ukraine and all other former communist-bloc countries as well as to the communist movements in other countries throughout the world.

---

[68] Relevant decrees and archival regulations are discussed in Chapter 1.

State versus Private Property. The ICA has traditionally limited its attention predominantly to official state archives. In dealing with post-communist regimes in Eastern Europe, however, the issue of non-state records and previously nationalized records must also be considered. Many archival materials, including important manuscript collections, need to be treated in terms other than those for state archives. Yet there are inadequate legal grounds for dealing with them as personal or institutional private property in the current Ukrainian and Russian contexts.

The lack of distinction between public and private archives has become more important in the case of Soviet successor States today, including Ukraine and other communist-dominated countries of Eastern Europe. This is apparent in the extent to which both the July 1993 and March 1994 definitions of the Archival Fond of the Russian Federation include previously nationalized records in the "State Part" of the Archival Fond, regardless of their original status. The extent to which even "non-State" records are considered part of the Archival Fond RF also points up the problem.

There are—and undoubtedly will be more—questions in court about the "legality" of Soviet nationalization and the legal status of archives and manuscript collections from the private sector that were nationalized according to Soviet-style decrees. The question has already been raised, for example, in several countries whether the re-establishment of religious agencies free from state control should require the return of Church archival records to Church control, and if the reversion of monasteries to Church authorities should require the return of their culturally unique manuscript collections gathered over many centuries that were nationalized under pre-revolutionary Russian or Soviet rule. So far, the return of nationalized archives and manuscript collections to any religious authorities is not provided for by law, and has not occurred in practice, in either post-1991 Russia or Ukraine.

Many manuscript collections and personal papers also contain documents (or copies thereof) of provenance in state or other institutional records and manuscript books or literary manuscripts that can be considered national cultural treasures. Many such important collections are already held in Russian archives or other manuscript repositories and thereby automatically come under the new Russian archival law defining them as part of the "Archival Fond of the Russian Federation." Some of these archival materials or manuscript books are also subject to claim as part of the national archival and cultural heritage of more than one successor State.

The question has also been raised as to whether the restitution of citizenship to Ukrainian émigrés and exiles should involve restitution of the property of their forebears, including personal or family archives and manuscript collections that were nationalized under Soviet rule. Does Ukraine have the right to demand the return of archives seized during WWII by the Nazis that had been nationalized on the eve of the war in western Ukraine, but that are now claimed as the property of the resettled Polish population in Poland or of Polish émigré organizations abroad? And what about Jewish collections that were seized by the Nazis and not restituted to their country of provenance by American authorities because of the annihilation of Jewish communities there? Indeed, many such Jewish archives from Soviet-held areas of Eastern Europe were transferred to successor institutions in the West or to Israel after the war. The related legal status of archival materials alienated abroad by émigrés and exiles as well as records created by Ukrainian institutions in exile or the diaspora, some of which were seized by Soviet authorities after the Second World War, will also require clarification.

Restitution of nationalized archives, manuscript collections, and personal papers, as mentioned earlier, has been ruled out by President Boris Yeltsin of the Russian Federation and by the new Russian archival law. But the further international legal resolution of these highly contested problems will be inconclusive until there is implementation of adequate legal codes in Russia and Ukraine with clarification of the legal status of private property and the rights of inheritance, and subsequent adjudication in the courts. Earlier UN and UNESCO deliberations have not adequately addressed such issues. Nevertheless, there are many historical precedents of nationalization and secularization in various countries, even those whose constitutions guarantee the right of private property. International efforts are necessary to seek clarification and codified precedents in national and international law, which may assist resolution of claims in Ukraine and other formerly communist countries.

The 1983 Vienna Convention did not deal with non-state archival materials because it was more narrowly concentrated on official state records as part of a convention dealing with state property and state debts. At the ICA Round Table in Thessalonica, Frank Evans recalled his memorandum dated 26 March 1983 regarding the Vienna Convention—noting the extent to which the proposed convention "ignored the fact that legal definitions of archives varied significantly between socialist and market economy countries, especially with regard to the scope and status of private property."[69] This legal situation has become even more confused today, as many post–Soviet-bloc States move towards the legalization of private property.

---

[69]   Evans also recently noted this problem in his 1994 CITRA report, "The Action by Unesco and ICA since 1976," *CITRA 1993–1995*, pp. 69–78.

United Nations and UNESCO Conventions and
Resolutions Relating to Cultural Property

With the more extensive content of archives in the post-Soviet rule, as apparent in the definitions of both the Archival Fond of the Russian Federation and the National Archival Fond of Ukraine, many displaced materials that might be considered "cultural property" rather than strictly state archives need to be considered in terms of archival claims. Hence, we should examine other UN and UNESCO conventions and resolutions that relate to cultural property and the national cultural heritage. Their relevance was pointed out by the ILC report in preparation of the archival section of the 1983 Vienna Convention, although the problem was ignored by that convention.[70] Reports at the 1994 CITRA meetings in Thessalonica and the 1996 CITRA meetings in Washington likewise referenced many of these developments, and the ICA now appears prepared to deal with these broader issues as well, which makes it more important to review them here.

The 1954 Hague Convention. The frequently cited 1954 "Hague Convention on the Protection of Cultural Property in the Event of Armed Conflict" makes specific provision for the protection of manuscripts, books, and archives in times of war. The protocol issued separately, but signed on the same day, addresses the question of restitution, which was not included as a paragraph in the convention itself. It requires the restitution or return of any cultural goods that may have been displaced and that are located by the signatory powers at the end of hostilities, thus reinforcing the earlier Hague Convention of 1907.[71] It can be argued, however, that neither this convention nor its protocol is worded so as to operate *retroactively* in terms of restitution of earlier displaced cultural property, that there is no specific requirement for restitution or return of archives or other cultural property that are still displaced from previous wars. Nevertheless, since the 1954 Convention's preamble states that it is "guided by the principles established by the Hague conventions of 1899 and 1907 and the Washington Pact of 15 April 1935," where cultural pillage was specifically forbidden, those countries that signed

---

[70] See the section devoted to previous UNESCO and UN actions in the ILC report mentioned above, *Yearbook ILC, 1979* (New York, 1981), II, pt. 1: 78–82.

[71] "Convention for the Protection of Cultural Property in the Event of Armed Conflict," adopted at the Hague, 14 May 1954, as published in *Conventions and Recommendations of Unesco Concerning the Protection of the Cultural Heritage* (Paris, 1983), pp. 13–49, together with the "Protocol to the Convention and the Conference Resolutions," and "State of Ratifications and Accessions as at 31 July 1982."

the earlier conventions should be bound by those principles. The lack of specific retroactive reference and provisions for restitution, and the fact that not all countries signed all of those instruments may, however, leave room for legal maneuvering.

The importance of the 1954 Hague Convention to the issue of cultural property and archives in wartime made it the subject of special analysis at the 1996 Washington, DC, CITRA meetings. The Finnish archivist Markkü Jarvinen, then serving as archivist of UNESCO, presented a succinct analysis of the background of the convention, its main clauses, including specific references to manuscripts and archives, applications of the convention, conclusions about some problems in its applicability to archives, and regrets over the lack of governmental diligence in reporting on its basis. These matters have been complicated by the fact that by the end of 1994 there had only been 84 signatory countries (88 by June 1996).[72]

Restitution components in the 1954 Hague Convention were strengthened by a Second Protocol in March 1999, particularly by putting more responsibility on art market professionals. It termed wartime attacks on cultural property as "criminal."[73] The UNESCO website should be consulted for accession information regarding the protocol. At present, however, it appears unlikely that the protocol will have much direct bearing on displaced archives resulting from World War II.

The 1970 UNESCO Convention on Illicit Transfer. The 1970 UNESCO "Convention on the Means of Prohibiting and Preventing the Illicit Import, Export and Transfer of Ownership of Cultural Property" is also pertinent to manuscripts and archival materials.[74] It is not applicable retroactively, however, and applies only in cases where the countries involved have ratified the convention. Hence, it will not be helpful in resolving many of the current

---

[72] See the analysis by Markkü Jarvinen, "Convention of The Hague of 1954: Convention for the Protection of Cultural Property in the Event of Armed Conflict," *CITRA 1993–1995,* pp. 147–55. Jarvinen provides a bibliography, noting several important commentaries that provide further analysis, although none directly dealing with archival aspects.

[73] "Second Protocol to the Hague Convention of 1954 for the Protection of Cultural Property in the Event of Armed Conflict," The Hague, 26 March 1999. See the analysis by Jean-Marie Schmitt, "UNESCO: Attacks on Cultural Property Criminalised. A New Protocol Allows for Prosecution of Organisations and Individuals, Putting Pressure on Art Market Professionals," *The Art Newspaper* 93 (June 1999): 6.

[74] UNESCO, *Records of the General Conference, 16th Session,* vol. 1: *Resolutions,* pp. 135–41.

problems for Ukraine, almost all of which involve cultural treasures transferred before 1970.

An important commentary on the 1970 convention prepared for UNESCO by the Swiss legal specialist Ridha Fraoua helps clarify a large number of the issues and problems of implementation.[75] Many of the author's conclusions regarding the inadequacy of the convention, related analysis as well as programmatic recommendations, are developed more fully in his earlier doctoral dissertation devoted to the problem of restitution.[76] As Fraoua and others have pointed out, the issue of restitution has not been brought under normative acts in international law and is not adequately covered in other existing UN or UNESCO conventions in the cultural realm. Most particularly, neither the 1954 Hague convention nor the 1970 convention deal with issues of retroactive restitution or with transfers in connection with decolonization and the succession of States, such as are relevant in connection with current issues of archival Ucrainica and other cultural treasures abroad.

The 1995 Unidroit Convention. Similarly, the Unidroit Convention (enacted 4 June 1995) on stolen or illegally exported cultural objects, which is also applicable to archives, presumably will not provide much help for long-pending issues of archival restitution.[77] The various provisions of the convention are well analyzed with examples in a commentary by the international lawyer specializing in cultural issues Lyndel Prott.[78] The ICA

---

[75] Ridha Fraoua, *Convention concernant les mesures à prendre pour interdire et empêcher l'importation, l'exportation et le transfert de propriété illicites des biens culturels (Paris, 1970). Commentaire et aperçu de quelques mesures nationales d'exécution* (Paris, 1986) (CC–86/WS/40).

[76] Ridha Fraoua, *Le trafic illicite des biens culturels et leur restitution. Analyse des réglementations nationales et internationales. Critiques et propositions* (Fribourg, 1985) [=Travaux de la Faculté de droit de l'Université de Fribourg Suisse, 68].

[77] The English text is reprinted in *The Spoils of War: World War II and Aftermath*, Appendix 12, pp. 308–311, with signatures through 29 June 1996. See also Kurt Siehr, Assistant Editor of the *International Journal of Cultural Property*, "Restitution of Stolen Cultural Objects and Statute of Limitations," *Spoils of War: International Newsletter* 2 (15 July 1996): 9–10.

[78] Lyndel V. Prott, *Commentary on the UNIDROIT Convention on Stolen and Illegally Exported Cultural Objects, 1995* (Leicester: Institute of Art and Law, 1997). That publication includes the full text of the convention and also the earlier 1954 Hague Convention, the 1970 Convention, and the European Directive of 15 March

took an active part in analyzing and commenting on technical problems in drafting appropriate references in relevance to archives, before the final draft had been decided upon.[79] However, it was obvious that the ICA recognized the need to consider "cultural property" differently than archives or to clarify wording in the Convention, if archives were to be included.

The Unidroit Convention is applicable only among signatory nations and does not adequately apply to archival issues. Neither does it provide for retroactive restitution. Its most serious deficiency is that it normally covers instances of theft or illegal export only within three years of their apprehension. Although the "absolute time limit" can be extended to a longer period, claims are not possible fifty years after the theft, unless exceptions are elaborated by national legislation. It thus will be difficult to invoke this convention in the case of displaced archives and other cultural treasures from the Second World War. The convention also was not intended to resolve disputed issues of archives removed by former imperial powers, or related archival matters in connection with the succession of States.

Given the legal vacuum covering the archival problems under discussion, new initiatives are needed on the international level.

UN and UNESCO Resolutions. Resolutions and recommendations of international bodies and conferences cannot officially fill the vacuum of law, as important as they may be for international public opinion and legal pressure. There have, nevertheless, been a long series of UN resolutions and UNESCO recommendations treating broader aspects of the problem of cultural restitution in different contexts, many of which by extension explicitly mention archival materials and manuscripts. Most of them cite and reaffirm the provisions of earlier ones. Although many UNESCO resolutions mention "archives, manuscripts, books, and documents," many of them do not deal technically with the issues of archives as distinct from other cultural property. Nevertheless, in dealing with issues of restitution in connection with displaced archival materials, and especially to the extent that they may include non-State materials, it is also important to follow carefully UN and UNESCO discussions and recommendations in the broader area of cultural

---

1993 on the Return of Cultural Objects Unlawfully Removed from the Territory of a Member State (93/7/EEC).

[79] "Opinion of the International Council on Archives Relating to the Unidroit Draft convention, 20 April 1995," published as an appendix in *CITRA 1993–1995*, pp. 206–207.

restitution as well as ICA materials dealing more specifically with State archives.

For example, reference has been made in an archival context to the resolution adopted in 1976 by the Fifth Conference of Heads of State or Government of Non-Aligned Countries, whereby that Conference reaffirmed earlier resolutions of the UN General Assembly "concerning the restitution of works of art and manuscripts to the countries from which they have been looted"; as the text of the resolution continues,

> [The Conference] requests urgently all States in Possession of works of art and manuscripts to restore them promptly to their countries of origin, [and]
>
> Requests the Panel of Experts earlier appointed by UNESCO which is entrusted with the task of restoring those works of art and manuscripts to their original owners, to take the necessary measures to that effect.[80]

The fact that the United Nations General Assembly has adopted a long series of resolutions on the subject, repeated every year or two since 1972, is indicative that the problem persists, and that the resolutions have been ineffective in promoting solutions.[81]

Further UN Resolutions 1991–1999. Ukraine first took an active interest in this issue as an independent country in the United Nations when the 1991 UN resolution on cultural restitution was being considered. Soon after the August 1991 declaration of Ukrainian independence, the Ukrainian Ambassador to the United Nations General Assembly, Viktor Batiouk, in the course of discussion of the proposed resolution noted that "Ukraine itself cannot be indifferent to its own cultural heritage, which, at various times, has been either illegally or forcibly removed beyond the bounds of its own territory."

---

[80]   As quoted from *Documents of the Fifth Conference of Heads of State or Government of Non-Aligned Countries*, annex IV, Resolution 17 (A/31/197: 136), in *Yearbook ILC 1979*, II, pt. 1: 82.

[81]   See, for example, "Return or restitution of cultural property to the countries of origin," resolution 3026 A (XXVII), 18 December 1972; no. 3148 (XXVIII), 14 December 1973; 3187 (XXVIII), 18 December 1973; 3391 (XXX), 19 November 1975; (31/40), 30 December 1976; (32/18), 11 November 1977; (33/50), 14 December 1978; (34/64). 29 November 1979; (35/127 and 35/128), 11 December 1980; (36/64), 27 November 1981; (38/34), 25 November 1983; (40/19), 21 November 1985; (42/7), 22 October 1987; and (44/18), 6 November 1989. The preamble of each successive resolution lists preceeding resolutions on the subject adopted by the General Assembly; all are printed in the *UN General Assembly Official Records*.

He recognized that "Ukraine has the right to return to the ownership of the people of Ukraine the national, cultural, and historical property which is outside the frontiers of the republic." At the same time, he applauded the work of the United Nations in this realm:

> We welcome the active role of the United Nations and its special-ized agencies in the return or restitution of cultural property to their countries of origin. The efforts of the United Nations and UNESCO in promoting bilateral and multilateral negotiations for the return or restitution of cultural, artistic or archival property and in compiling descriptions of them, limiting the illegal trade in them in publicizing them warrant all our support and approval.[82]

The General Assembly approved the 1991 resolution reaffirming that:

> ...the restitution to a country of its objets d'art, monuments, museum pieces, archives, manuscripts, documents and any other cultural or artistic treasures contributes to the strengthening of international cooperation and to the preservation and flowering of universal cultural values through fruitful cooperation between developed and developing countries...[83]

It added a call for UNESCO to prepare a report on its implementation.

Since all of these resolutions directly or implicitly also refer to archives and manuscript collections, in dealing with issues of return or restitution in connection with displaced Ukrainian archives and archival Ucrainica abroad, it is important to consider these and other UN and UNESCO discussions and recommendations in the broader area of cultural restitution. A similar resolution was adopted by the UN in November 1993 on "Return or Restitu-tion of Cultural Property to the Countries of Origin," which again recalls earlier resolutions and urges member States that have not done so to sign and ratify the 1970 Convention.[84] Further indicative of the continuing unresolved international issues involved in the area of displaced cultural treasures and restitution, and the ineffectiveness of previous resolutions, additional

---

[82]   Viktor Batiouk speaking on 22 October 1991 (interpretation from Russian), *UN General Assembly Official Records: Forty-Sixth Session* (A/46/PV.35), pp. 11, 13.

[83]   "Return or restitution of cultural property to the countries of origin," 22 October 1991 (46/10), *UN General Assembly Official Records: Forty-Sixth Session*, Supple-ment No. 49 (A/46/49): 14–15.

[84]   "Return or restitution of cultural property to the countries of origin," 2 November 1993 (A/RES/48/15), *UN General Assembly Official Records: Forty-Seventh Plenary Meeting* (2 November 1993), Supplement No. 49 (A/50/49). The preamble includes a complete list of preceding resolutions on the subject adopted by the General Assembly.

resolutions were adopted by the General Assembly in December 1995 and in November 1997.[85] Similar to regular earlier reports on related developments, a report prepared by UNESCO was adopted in 1997 by the United Nations Secretary General.[86] The 1997 resolution carried the instruction that a similar report on the implementation of the resolution be submitted to the 1999 (54th) session of the General Assembly, and that an agenda item on the subject also be scheduled there.

The UNESCO Committee on Restitution. Various resolutions may provide general guidelines for interpretation in light of broader UNESCO principles, but often individual cases require special *ad hoc* examination. Hence, in 1978, UNESCO established "an intergovernmental committee for dealing with negotiations for the restitution or return of cultural property to the countries having lost such property as a result of colonial or foreign occupation."[87] The statutes of the advisory committee clarified the intended scope of its activities and defined "cultural property" as including "historical and ethnographic objects and documents including manuscripts," as well as other types of non-written objects.[88] As explained in the Committee "Guidelines,"

---

[85] "Return or restitution of cultural property to the countries of origin," 11 December 1995 (A/RES/50/56), *UN General Assembly Official Records: Fiftieth Session*, Supplement No. 49 (A/50/49); and 25 November 1997 (A/RES/52/24), *UN General Assembly Official Records: Fifty-Second Session,* Supplement No. 49 (A/52/49). In each case, the preamble again includes a complete list of preceeding resolutions on the subject adopted by the General Assembly.

[86] "Report of the Director-General of UNESCO on the Action Taken by the Organization On the Return of Cultural Property to the Countries of Origin or its Restitution in case of Illicit Appropriation," 25 June 1997 (A/52/211).

[87] "Proposals of the Director-General with a view to the establishment of an intergovernmental committee entrusted with the task of seeking ways and means of facilitating bilateral negotiations for the restitution or return of cultural property to the countries having lost such property as a result of colonial or foreign occupation," UNESCO General Conference Twentieth Session, Paris 1978 (20C/86, Annex II), dated 29 September 1978. The proposals include the Final Report by the UNESCO committee of experts meeting in Dakar, 20–23 March 1978. A special issue of the UNESCO journal *Museum* (31[1] 1979) is devoted to the establishment of the Committee and issues of return and restitution of cultural property.

[88] "Statutes of the Intergovernmental Committee for Promoting the Return of Cultural Property to its Countries of Origin or its Restitution in Case of Illicit Appropriation," Resolution of the 20th Session of the General Conference (October-November 1978) (20 C/Res 4/7.6/5). The reference is to Article 3 §1. A copy is

archives are not mentioned specifically because they were covered by the previous separate UNESCO 1978 report mentioned above and since international mechanisms for cooperation in the domain of national archives already existed. Also, the focus for the UNESCO Committee is normally on museum objects, not state archives. They recognized, nevertheless, that:

> ...particular components of certain archive materials can be considered as museum objects in their own right, because of their historical and cultural significance, and therefore may fall within the purview of the Intergovernmental Committee.[89]

The Committee adopted a "Standard Form concerning Requests for Return or Restitution" in 1985 as the basic instrument for negotiations and, with the participation of the International Council of Museums (ICOM), has drawn up detailed "Guidelines" for its use.[90] The form and guidelines are intended to promote bilateral negotiations before requests are formally submitted to the UNESCO committee. The insistence on presentation of precise details of the seizure of the property in question from the country of its origin and other data from both the requesting and holding State, which would be important to the Committee in assessing the significance of the object to both parties and its present condition, is also particularly relevant to prospective archival negotiations, as are many of the definitions and the legal clarification presented. The published "Guidelines," as most recently revised, include a number of important studies of principles and related advisory documents, including a draft code of practice since adopted by major art and rare book dealers in the United Kingdom.

---

included in *Conventions and Recommendations of Unesco Concerning the Protection of the Cultural Heritage.* See also the latest (1989) "Rules of Procedure" (CC-89/CONF-213/COL-3).

[89]   UNESCO, Intergovernmental Committee for Promoting the Return of Cultural Property to its Countries of Origin or its Restitution in Case of Illicit Appropriation/Comité intergouvernemental pour la promotion du retour de biens culturels à leur pays d'origine ou de leur restitution en cas d'appropriation illégale, "Guidelines for the Use of the 'Standard Form Concerning Requests for Return or Restitution'" (CC-86/WS/3; reprinted 1992), p. 5.

[90]   UNESCO, "Standard Form Concerning Requests for Return or Restitution/ Formulaire type pour les demandes de retour ou de restitution" (CLT-86/WS/1) and "Guidelines" (CC-86/WS/3; reprinted 1992). The printed "Guidelines" also include a copy of the "Standard Form," the "Statutes" of the Committee, and the 1970 UN convention mentioned above.

As of 1997, the Committee itself has had only nine sessions and has heard only seven cases dealing principally with works of art and museum exhibits, such as Greece's claim for the return of the Parthenon marbles. The Committee has had only one recent petition concerning stolen manuscripts—from the Czech National Library, but since their current location had not been determined, it was unable to act. It is worth noting that the Soviet Union was a member of the Committee since its establishment.[91] The request for the return from Russia of the Kyiv mosaics from the Golden Domes Cathedral was raised by one Committee member during the ninth session, but the matter was not considered as a formal claim.[92]

The definition and clarification of many principles and issues involved for cultural property has perhaps been more important in the work of the Committee than the actual resolution of claims. Many crucial issues that also affect archival materials have been discussed and analyzed by UNESCO in its deliberations, even though definitive principles and procedures have not been formulated that would be applicable to the current issues of archival Ucrainica abroad. Hence, the literature produced by the Committee and other related studies need to be considered carefully by those authorities now dealing with issues of displaced Ukrainian cultural treasures abroad, especially those involving museum quality manuscripts, in addition to other more technical archival recommendations involving state archives produced by the ICA.

For example, the UNESCO principles dealing with "the reassembly of dispersed heritages" recognize several points that are particularly pertinent to

[91] The series of limited-distribution published Committee reports (issued in all six languages of UNESCO), submitted in each case to the General Conference of UNESCO are all listed in the bibliography. See also the summary overview of UNESCO actions in the area during the period 1973–1987: "Retour et restitution de biens culturels: Aperçu succinct" (Paris, 1987) (CLT-85/WS/41), with a list of cases handled by courts outside of the committee as well as resolutions of the UN and UNESCO on the subject. See also the "Statement by outgoing Chairman, Lyndel V. Prott," 31 August 1991 (CLT-91/WS/6), which summarized the achievements and weaknesses of the Committee to that date. My presentation here regarding the work of the Committee owes much to Prott, currently Chief of the International Standards Section, Division of Physical Heritage of the UNESCO Secretariat, which also supervises the work of the Committee in Paris. She both discussed the work of the Committee with me and provided me with copies of its relevant publications.

[92] As a "proposal for improved collaboration," and noted that "Ukraine was currently searching for several thousand items of cultural property." See the 5 August 1997 Committee report on its Ninth Session, Paris, 16–19 September 1996, p. 5—available on the UNESCO website (29C/REP.12).

issues of early historical documents and unique manuscripts—such as would be applicable in the Ukrainian case. For instance, as is well stated in the important 1978 deliberations establishing the UNESCO Committee:

> The question whether an object belongs to one culture or another poses difficult problems to which even historians do not always have solutions. Such is the case of cultural property used by several cultures in succession, or which has become part of another national culture (§15).

They further recognize that:

> ...the notion of country of origin itself is often ambiguous. It can indicate the country in which the work was created, the country of which its author is a national, or the last country to hold the object before its removal. As a result of the changing of national boundaries and State succession in the course of history, the three elements do not always coincide, and contemporary events show that these processes still continue (§16).

Such a statement is particularly applicable to many examples of archival Ucrainica and problems of its identification on the basis of language, national origins, changing borders, and resettlement of national population groups.

Furthermore, the same UNESCO report also recognizes special principles affecting *collections*, as opposed to integral groups of records (whether of state or non-state provenance), in affirming that:

> ...unique collections, especially those systematic and comprehensive collections made by competent scholars, require special consideration on account of their inestimable scientific value. Such collections should not be permanently divided by restitution or return. Special negotiations with the countries of origin will be necessary in such cases (§19).

In this UNESCO text there is no specific reference to manuscript collections, but the wording is certainly applicable to those as well.[93] There

---

[93]   "Principles and Conditions of the Restitution or Return of Cultural Property to its Country of Origin," pp. 3–6, or the "Final Report of the UNESCO Committee of Experts on the Establishment of an Intergovernmental Committee Concerning the Restitution or Return of Cultural Property," Dakar, 20–23 March 1978, printed as "Proposals of the Director-General with a view to the establishment of an intergovernmental committee entrusted with the task of seeking ways and means of facilitating bilateral negotiations for the restitution or return of cultural property to the countries having lost such property as a result of colonial or foreign occupation," UNESCO General Conference Twentieth Session, Paris 1978 (20C/86, Annex II), dated 29 September 1978.

is also no clarification of the issue of important, and sometimes unique, state documents that have fallen into private hands. In Western practice, these would qualify as private property. There is no law that requires that they be turned over to the state, or that provides for the restitution of those documents or stray files that earlier would normally be considered as constituting official state records. Similar issues often apply to "collections" of state documents in the course of government operations, such as the sections (*razriady*) of the nineteenth-century State Archive of the Russian Empire or the top secret "Special Files" (*Osobye papki*) of the Archive of the President of the Russian Federation mentioned above. But the text should not be seen extending to integral groups of agency records, whether from state, communal, or religious institutions.

The UNESCO Committee "Guidelines" also appropriately recognize the distinction between "ownership" and "legal status." Discussion has further sought to clarify the legal status of objects in private ownership as opposed to public possession, which in turn might prove useful as privatization returns to Ukraine and other areas of the former Soviet Union. Unlike the situation in the Soviet Union and as codified in the new Russian archival law, "in most West European and American countries the state does not have legal power to force private owners to return an object or a collection of objects unless it can be proved that their own national laws have been violated." The UNESCO discussion recognizes the need for compensation when seeking restitution or return of objects that have been subject to bona fide purchase.[94] But there are few instances where official state archival materials have been sold on the art market, except for early trophy charters or unique political or literary autographs.

Further, the UNESCO Committee "Guidelines" establish and explain the "distinction between the notions of 'return' and 'restitution.'" In short,

> ...the term "restitution" should be used "in case of illicit appropriation," i.e., when objects have left their countries of origin illegally, according to the relevant national legislation and with particular reference to Unesco's 1970 Convention on the subject.
>
> The term "return" should apply to cases where objects left their countries of origin prior to the crystallization of national and international law on the protection of cultural property.[95]

---

94 UNESCO, International Committee for Promoting the Return of Cultural Property, "Guidelines," pp. 7–8.

95 Ibid., p. 11.

Such distinctions in definition, however, are *not* appropriate in the case of current archival issues in Eastern Europe. The term "restitution" indeed carries a more legal claim, but appropriate archival restitution hardly started in 1970, and there should be no time limit in the case of displaced state records. The 1970 UNESCO convention, as noted above, did not adequately address such issues for archives. The term "restitution" was, and still is, in current use with reference to records captured during World War II, and, in many instances, to earlier cases of seized or otherwise displaced records. Nonetheless, the experience of the UNESCO Committee dealing with cultural restitution and return, and particularly the attempt to define principles and practices and to adopt functional guidelines could well prove helpful to those dealing with similar current issues of archival "restitution."

The potential Ukrainian role in cultural restitution on the international level, and the importance of the Committee as a forum for Ukrainian restitution interests, has increased since 1995, when Ukraine became a formal member of the Committee. Ukraine would now like to see the Committee take a larger role in East European restitution issues, as was apparent in the recommendations of the 1996 Kyiv conference on legal aspects of restitution problems, which called for a special session of the UNESCO Committee with dealing with problems for Ukraine and Belarus. The 1997 Minsk conference on "The Restitution of Cultural Treasures: Problems of Repatriation and Common Usages (Legal, Scientific, and Ethical Aspects)" added a similar point to its resolutions.[96]

As we have seen, many aspects and problems of displaced archives and archival restitution could profit from the experience of that UNESCO Committee, and the broad experience of its former Chair, Dr. Lyndel V. Prott. Prott herself answered the appeal for such a meeting, noting the Committee's potential authority in such cases if "bilateral negotiations fail." She pointed out, as seen above, that for the unsettled issues of restitution of cultural property growing out of World War II neither the Protocol to the 1954 Hague Convention nor the 1970 UNESCO Convention discussed above "are directly applicable...because their provisions are not retroactive, although the principles of the Hague Convention represent customary international law." She further noted the ways in which "mediation through the Committee may have some advantages," especially so that the states

---

[96]   The "Final Document" (which is published in Belarusian, Russian, and English) is published in *Restytutsyia kul'turnykh kashtoŭnastsei*. See the additional report by Oleksandr (Aleksandr) Fedoruk, *Spoils of War: International Newsletter* 5 (June 1998): 58–59.

could "exchange their views in a neutral forum" and "avail themselves of the experience of the UNESCO Secretariat in this field."[97]

In the meantime, during the meeting of the Committee of Paris in early 1999, the Committee adopted a draft of the "Principles for the Resolutions of Disputes Concerning Cultural Heritage Displaced during the Second World War," which Prott had first enunciated in the 1995 conference presentation in New York (see Chapter 12 below). In a draft resolution, the Committee agreed to consider the "Principles" and, if approved, present them to the General Conference of UNESCO for consideration.[98] Although, mediation of the UNESCO Commission might prove most productive in instances where cultural property other than archives were involved, clearly, some cases involving archives might also profit from such mediation. Nevertheless, the recommendation of the Austrian archivist, Leopold Auer, in the 1996 Washington, DC, CITRA meetings for the "creation of an international committee on displaced archives similar to that of UNESCO for the restitution of cultural property," may in the long run prove to be a much sounder proposal for dealing with archival problems.[99]

Recent ICA Initiatives

Proposed ICA Committee. The idea of an international commission or committee under the ICA specifically prepared to deal with issues of displaced archives and archival restitution has become even more important within the context of current developments in Eastern Europe and the vast quantities of displaced archives still awaiting "return" or "restitution" on the Eastern Front. As we have seen, there are problems specific to archives that need to be dealt with differently than collections of libraries and museums. Professional archivists who have been active over the past fifty years in dealing with such issues, and who have seen the nature of the problems

[97] Lyndel V. Prott, "The Role of UNESCO 'International Committee for Promoting the Return of Cultural Property' in the Resolution of Disputes Concerning Cultural Property Removed in Consequence of the Second World War," *Spoils of War: International Newsletter* 5 (June 1998): 59–61.

[98] "Principles for the Resolutions of Disputes Concerning Cultural Heritage Displaced during the Second World War" (Paris: UNESCO, January 1999) (CLT-99/CONF.203/2). The draft of a report of with the text of the "Principles" and a reprint of Prott's article from the *Spoils of War: International Newsletter* was issued by UNESCO for limited distribution.

[99] Leopold Auer, "Restitution of Removed Records Following War," pp. 172–78.

develop and change in focus, undoubtedly should be called upon to help draft guidelines in the archival field and, where necessary, assist in the adjudication of disputed claims. International professional experience, rather than bilateral negotiations alone, may prove essential, given the many specific problems for previously suppressed nations and newly independent successor States in Eastern Europe. Displaced archives as a result of war and resettlement of ethnic populations need to be taken into account as part of the broader problems of reconstituting the national archival heritage and in recognizing the "joint common heritage" of integral bodies of records created by previous imperial regimes.

In the first instance, such a committee could be called upon to study the issues from an international perspective, taking into account previous ICA deliberations on the subject, the parallel work of the UNESCO Committee and the experience of its Secretariat, and the research and deliberations of the International Law Commission leading up to the abortive 1983 Vienna Convention. In addition, such a committee could serve in an advisory role in trying to formulate claims or resolve specific issues. Finally, or possibly in conjunction with the officially appointed UNESCO Committee, it could serve a role in arbitration. In terms of the latter function, its services ultimately could only be successful where the parties to a dispute would be willing to submit to arbitration in order to resolve claims.

The extent of pending and unresolved claims, the complexity of the problems involved, the international (as opposed to bilateral) dimensions of many of the cases, and failure to reach solution make it clear that the issues often cannot be resolved in a simple or purely bilateral framework. The need for the proposed international committee is urgent. This is particularly true in the case of archives displaced during and immediately after World War II, which often involve materials representing the archival heritage of several nations that have become intermingled in transit.

This also is true of issues involving Soviet successor States. The status of inalienable records of state may be easy enough to define. However, given the still murky legal context and inadequate legal traditions and precedents of the post-Soviet world in which Ukraine must live and operate, the definition of documents and manuscripts in terms of "their countries of origin" and "original owners" is not always clear-cut in terms of many archival materials. As newly independent States such as Ukraine shed the legacy of Soviet rule and try to formulate appropriate new legal codes, it would be helpful to have international normative guidelines specifically dealing with archives and an international forum for consultation and legal advice. Ukraine and other successor States to the USSR could profit from broader international experience and better familiarity with archival traditions, in addition to the Russian or Soviet examples that are still too often taken as the norm.

Problems of the right of access to documents in connection with the "rehabilitation of the politically repressed" may still conflict with the rights of "privacy," "state secrets," and the revelation of ciphers, methods, or agents used by security services. Issues of "ownership," "public domain," "private property," "copyright," and the right of government intervention or control, as such legal concepts involve archives, personal papers, and manuscript collections, need to be examined and where possible clarified in terms of varying international traditions, usage, and legal contexts, given the frequent distinctions and discrepancies between Soviet and Western practice in these regards. Whereas some such issues may find common ground with librarians and museum curators, as could be dealt with by the UNESCO Committee, legal records of state and public agencies, like the private papers of individuals—when considered in terms of their importance for the national archival heritage—need to be handled by archival professionals rather than those who deal principally with museum exhibits.

ICA 1995 Guangzhou Position Paper. A Position Paper entitled "The View of the Archival Community on the Settling of Disputed Claims," adopted by the ICA Executive Committee at its meeting in Guangzhou in April 1995, is based on the realization of "an unprecedented accumulation of unresolved problems concerning the restitution and devolution of archives." Most notably, in the post-1945 period:

> ...the repatriation of archives seized during hostilities has not been systematically dealt with and, at the global level, the emergence of a hundred or so sovereign states through the process of decolonisation has occurred without there being specific instruments for the devolution of archives.

The ICA recognizes the uselessness of the 1983 Vienna Convention because it was "established without a consensus among States" and "without regard to how applicable the proposed measures are"(§2). Accordingly:

> ...the ICA believes the time has come to put an end to the exceptional conditions which have lasted fifty years and to begin getting rid of disputed archival claims arising from the Second World War, decolonisation and the breakup of federations following the events of 1989.[100]

---

[100] "The View of the Archival Community on the Settling of Disputed Claims," Position Paper adopted by the ICA Executive Committee ICA at its meeting in Guangzhou, 10–13 April 1995, *CITRA 1993–1995*, pp. 256–58. The full text is presented below as Appendix VII.

The Position Paper recognizes the value of bilateral "negotiations between the interested parties," but given the extent and complexity of the current problems, recommends that "an international consultation seems essential if the situation is to get back to normal" (§3). Among the aims of the consultation would be:

> ...to establish a typology of cases, to devise a conceptual framework acceptable to all and to draw up principles to be observed during the preparation of bilateral agreements.

In terms of "Concepts and Principles," the Paper suggests that:

> ...the body of documents relating to the settling of disputed archival claims which UNESCO and ICA produced between 1974 and 1994 provides a sufficient basis to open up the desired consultation (§3).

The international principles summarized are basically those that were dealt with earlier in this chapter, although the position paper does not include all of the issues dealt with here, since it still limits itself to "public records." It does not mention an international committee or commission, as suggested earlier, although presumably such a "consultation" would ideally involve a more formal institutional entity under the ICA. On an optimistic note, the Position Paper concludes with the conviction:

> ...that a shared willingness to co-operate can, within a reasonable time, set right the abnormal situation which has resulted from political constraints in the post-war decades (§4).

Despite such initiatives, however, the 1996 ICA International Congress on Archives in Beijing heard no discussion on this issue, and many archivists were still adopting a "wait and see" attitude regarding the possibilities of further negotiation with the Russian Federation in light of legal developments there on restitution issues, to be discussed in more detail in later chapters of this study.

ICA-RAMP 1998 Study on Archival Claims. Following up in a practical vein on the ICA 1995 Guangzhou Position Paper, the ICA, with UNESCO agreement in the summer of 1996, conducted a survey of member states through the administration of a questionnaire to the national archival administrations of 83 countries. The results of the survey have been analyzed and reported by the Austrian archivist Leopold Auer in a UNESCO pamphlet in the Records and Archives Management (RAMP) series.[101] Auer's introductory remarks reinforce the conclusions of this chapter:

> Despite all UN, UNESCO and ICA resolutions and recommendations on the subject, there has been no agreement on guidelines for dealing with disputed archival claims and the potential restitution of the archives. Neither the issue of restitution nor of state succession with relation to archives has been brought under normative acts in international law.[102]

Auer's perceptive analysis of the results of the questionnaire are indicative of the pending, unresolved problems involved. Forty-five (over half) of the archival administrations did not respond at all; six countries (most of which are known to have pending claims) gave no reason for their desire not to participate; two more (France and the United Kingdom, both of which have pending claims) considered participation inopportune at the moment; while Finland also preferred bilateral negotiations with the Russian Federation. Five countries (Botswana, Cape Verde, Japan, Luxembourg, and Portugal) "reported no disputed claims," although potential claims are known for at least two of those countries. The 24 archival administrations responding positively to the initial questionnaire—with data regarding a total of 61 disputed claims—were administered a second questionnaire, but detailed replies were received from only 17 countries. Auer lists all of the cases reported and carefully analyses the responses, while noting a number of errors and inconsistencies and significant gaps in reporting almost all categories of claims of which the ICA was aware from other sources.

Notably, Ukraine did not participate in the survey—neither did any other country considered part of the Commonwealth of Independent States (CIS), except for the Russian Federation.[103] The three Baltic republics provided the lone non-Russian replies from the NIS; while all of their claims involved state succession, for the most part, the claims were broadly based rather than specifying any specific record groups or collections.[104] The lack of CIS response, including from Ukraine, would explain the fact that only 25 claims reported involved state succession. As Auer remarked, "State succession after

---

[101] Leopold Auer, *Disputed Archival Claims. Analysis of an International Survey: A RAMP Study* (Paris: UNESCO, 1998).

[102] Auer, *Disputed Archival Claims*, p. 1.

[103] Perhaps CIS participation would have been higher had the literature and questionnaires been circulated in Russian as well as English and French.

[104] Interestingly enough, the Lithuanian claim involved the records of the Lithuanian Metrica, as discussed in Chapter 1 above, pp. 43–46.

the dissolution of the Soviet Union is, of course, of much more importance than is discernible in the present survey," and as he added in conclusion, "we do know from other sources that such issues exist and are of major importance."[105]

All of the "simple restitution cases" reported result from World War II, and almost all claims in that category "are made on the Russian Federation."[106] Noticeably, the Russian Federation participated in the survey, although it did not report or comment on any of the pending claims against itself. In fact, the only disputed claim Russia named was its own claim against the United States for that small part of the Smolensk Party Archive held in the U.S. National Archives (see Chapter 6).

Since the full text of Auer's analysis and evaluation is available on the Internet, there is no need for more detailed analysis here, nor for further comment on his analysis of the type of claims, nature of the fonds involved, the possibility of microfilm solutions, and legal basis and access. Worthy of note, however, is Auer's observation of the extent to which responses revealed "that information on disputed claims…seems to be very fragmentary," the total lack of reference "to any of the existing literature on the issue," and the extent to which "every party was focusing on its special claim without taking advantage of the experience of others."[107] He accordingly concludes with the need for "dissemination of relevant information"—and I would add in more relevant languages—and for "the raising of awareness." Auer's conclusion is essentially correct—"the issue is not only a professional one," but also, and even more importantly, "a problem involving political interest and national pride." As he aptly puts it, "Where the political will is lacking, a solution of disputed archival claims will not be possible."[108] This will become clear in the chapters that follow.

The April 1995 ICA Position Paper discussed earlier also recommends international consultation and an eventual new convention to rectify the matter of displaced archives. As seen above, in early 1999 the principles enunciated by Lyndel Prott in 1995 are being further considered by UNESCO as more official "Principles for the Resolutions of Disputes Concerning Cultural Heritage Displaced during the Second World War."[109]

---

[105] Auer, *Disputed Archival Claims*, pp. 20, 24.

[106] Ibid., p. 20.

[107] Ibid., p. 23.

[108] Ibid., p. 24.

[109] UNESCO, International Committee for Promoting the Return of Cultural Property, "Principles for the Resolutions of Disputes Concerning Cultural Heritage

Two of Auer's final points in connection with potential solutions are also worth noting: namely the extent to which "most respondents are in favour—although with some significant distinctions—of consultations of archival experts, of intergovernmental consultations and of the joint preparation of data bases and finding aids." Undoubtedly, the realization that ultimately political decisions will be required for resolution may lessen the willingness of some countries—including Russia—to place any reliance on outside means and "to adhere strictly to bi-lateral contacts," thus avoiding open international discussion.[110] Representatives of seven countries advocated a legal instrument on the level of UNESCO as a possible solution; five put more reliance on the Council of Europe. Although twelve countries suggested the potential value in preparation of a legal instrument on the level of the United Nations, this was rejected in the case of Croatia, Slovenia, Germany, and the Russian Federation, suggesting again their preference for bilateral solutions. Nevertheless, Auer views the problem in a broader perspective and realizes "the necessity" on the international front for "a set of approved, clear and uncontroversial criteria, worked out from the very beginning in co-operation with experts in international law and archives." And, in a similar vein to his presentation at the Washington, DC, CITRA, he closes in recommending that "the creation of an international committee, similar to that of UNESCO for the restitution of cultural property, including the restitution of displaced archives, might be useful."[111]

European-Wide Focus on Restitution at the Official Level

Since the revelation in 1990 and 1991 of West European archives and other cultural treasures in Russia resulting from displacements during World War II and its aftermath, the European Community has been exceedingly active in demanding their return or restitution to the country of origin.

1991 European Community Resolution on the Return of National Archives. Archives specifically were the target of a EEC resolution drafted in 1990 and adopted 24 January 1991, although there the specific target were archives of developing nations that had been former colonies of European

---

Displaced during the Second World War" (Paris: UNESCO, January 1999) (CLT-29/CONF.203.2). See also fns. 97 and 98 above.

[110] Auer, *Disputed Archival Claims*, p. 22.

[111] Ibid., p. 24.

States. The resolution cited many past UN and other international agreements and resolutions on the subject, and expressed, among other basic principles, that:

> A.   whereas the right to culture and to information concerning history is a fundamental right of individuals and of nations,
>
> B.   whereas the wish of certain countries to reconstruct their cultural inheritance is a legitimate cultural aspiration, on the understanding that archives created and built up outside these countries should rather be regarded as part of a common cultural heritage,
>
> C.   whereas archives represent a major contributory factor in the preservation of a people's or a group's cultural identity, testifying as they do to its historical, cultural or economic development...

Among the many points worth noting, the resolution

> 8.   Demands that the Member States, acting in a spirit of mutual understanding and solidarity, should grant all requests from the ACP [Africa, Caribbean, Pacific] countries for the return of cultural artifacts and archives, where these are, within the criteria established by UNESCO, of fundamental spiritual and cultural value;
>
> 9.   Believes that in principle the developing countries have a legitimate right to the return of their archives, but considers there is a need for appropriate guarantees of the conservation of archives and cultural artifacts, including those of minority groups...

Whereas this resolution was not at all basically directed towards Russia, its example is nonetheless pertinent here. Neither Ukraine nor Russia today are members of the EEC, although they may still aspire to eventual membership. Hence it is important to emphasize some of the basic principles and demands of the European Community directed specifically to parallel archival restitution questions.[112]

1993 Directive on Restitution by the European Economic Community. Restitution proceedings within Europe were facilitated in 1993 by the adoption of a European directive on the restitution of cultural property illegally transferred within the European Union. Accordingly, it is not immediately applicable for Ukraine or the Russian Federation. The Directive is principally oriented to facilitate the recovery of stolen national treasures, but in its list of categories of objects to be covered specifically includes

---

[112] "Resolution on the Right of Nations to Information Concerning their History and the Return of National Archives," 24 January 1991 (A3-0258/90), in *Dossier on Archival Claims*, pp. 4–6.

"archives and any elements thereof, of any kind, on any medium, comprising elements more than 50 years old," and also "photographs, films and negatives thereof," along with "incunabula and manuscripts, including maps and musical scores, single or in collections."

The Directive is in many ways similar to the intent of the Unidroit Convention, and intended to deal with the illegal traffic in cultural objects. As well it is intended to "apply only to cultural objects unlawfully removed from the territory of a Member State on or after 1 January 1993." However, a subsequent article states that "each Member State may apply the arrangements provided for by this Directive to requests for the return of cultural objects unlawfully removed from the territory of other Member States prior to 1 January 1993." Given its main focus, the Directive is not applicable to the issues covered here involving archival devolution in connection with the succession of States or displaced archives as a result of World War II and its aftermath. Nevertheless, the enactment of this Directive by the EU and its very existence adds more authority to cultural restitution imperatives.[113]

ICA-Council of Europe Dossier. Discussion of the issues of displaced archives and restitution claims in Europe shifted to the hearing rooms of the Council of Europe in the fall of 1995. Particularly, when the issue of membership for the Russian Federation came up for hearings, there were a number of objections, among them that Russia's performance with respect to the restitution of archives and other cultural property to European countries. Some West European leaders considered that resolution of restitution issues should have been a condition for Russian membership, although that requirement was not imposed. Nonetheless, conditions attached to Russian accession required the signature of an "intent" to resolve restitution issues for archives and cultural treasures of European States that are still held captive in Russia (see Chapter 10). That issue was not raised with the Ukrainian bid for membership, and Ukraine was admitted to the Council several months before Russia in September 1995 (see Chapter 12).

In the process of hearings in Strasbourg, the Council of Europe was working closely with the ICA, and together they brought together many of the documents that were earlier prepared for appendices to this volume. A special Council of Europe *Dossier on Archival Claims* was issued in January,

---

[113] "Council Directive 93/7/EEC of 15 March 1993 on the Return of Cultural Objects Unlawfully Removed from the Territory of a Member State." *Official Journal* L 074, 27/03/1993: 0074–0079.

1997, prepared in close consultation with the ICA.[114] In fact, an earlier draft of some chapters of this study were requested by the ICA for background briefings, and the research paper that served as the basis for the second part of this volume was published by the ICA later in 1996.[115]

Mention of the resulting ICA/Council of Europe dossier on archival claims is accordingly a fitting conclusion for this chapter. The fact of the appearance of these important, and unfortunately little-known documents in the Strasbourg dossier confirms their appropriateness and strengthens the need for the present commentary. As Auer concluded in the RAMP study on archival claims discussed above, information regarding international issues of disputed claims appears to be scant, and the extent to which the Iron Curtain kept Ukrainian archivists and political leaders isolated from direct participation in international archival experience and the circulation of literature on the subject is still strongly felt today.

Conclusions

Now that the Iron Curtain no longer isolates former Soviet lands from the rest of the world, there is significant interest for Russia, Ukraine, and other successor States to seek rapprochement with the other countries of Europe. Ukraine and the Russian Federation have both now been seated by the Council of Europe, but common European archival issues, and particularly those involving restitution, remain unresolved. They continue to be discussed in numerous international symposia and working sessions, some of them under ICA auspices. Many thorny problems in the definition and reconstitution of the archival heritage of formerly dispossessed nations such as Ukraine, need to be further pursued in an international context.

Provision for claims on behalf of successor States for the restitution of displaced archives resulting from imperial rule was provided in the July 1992 CIS Agreement discussed in the previous chapter and reaffirmed in subsequent annual meetings of archival leaders from the former Soviet area. At the same time, the principle was affirmed that the "Archival Fond of the Russian Federation" was the successor to all holdings in the central archives of the Soviet Union and those of the CPSU as well, leaving little room for serious negotiation with successor States. Only bilateral negotiation was suggested,

---

[114] *Dossier on Archival Claims.*

[115] Patricia Kennedy Grimsted, "Displaced Archives on the Eastern Front during World War II: Restitution Problems from World War II and Its Aftermath," *Janus: Revue internationale des archives/International Archival Journal*, 1996 (2): 42–77.

and the Russian Federation still prefers to deal only bilaterally with other nations on restitution as well. In December 1998 the chief archivists of the Russian Federation and Ukraine signed a bilateral agreement on archival cooperation, but the text of the agreement has not yet appeared in print. It will obviously be several years before its practical effectiveness can be appraised.

As later chapters in the second part of this study will show, the only bilateral solutions to problems of displaced archives involving Russia recently effected to date involve large payments or "barter" as a principle ingredient for restitution. Bilateral solutions alone thus far are not proving satisfactory for many nations that consider they have legitimate claims. The ICA April 1995 Position Paper recognizes the need for a better legal framework and more adequate international guidelines and norms for agreements for the restitution of displaced archives as a result of war and those to be transferred in connection with the succession of States. These still remain to be formulated, but too often international resolutions and guidelines are shunned by politicians. Hope has been placed in the UNESCO Committee for Promoting the Return of Cultural Property. But we see that for archival claims, a parallel committee under the ICA would be advisable. There is much common ground among all issues of displaced cultural treasures and many types of displaced archives. Yet many current archival claims are not even being considered, let alone resolved, precisely *because* there are no accepted international agreements or guidelines that distinguish archives from other cultural property.

The recognition of the general international legal context and precedents for archival devolution, together with the resolution of post-Soviet area-specific problems, however, will not resolve the problem of archival claims. It is becoming increasingly clear that legal clarification alone is not producing solutions. Often we are faced with different conceptions of law and legality, growing out of divergent historical traditions and present national political and economic interests. Regardless of what guidelines may be adopted in the future, most fundamental is the international goodwill and the professional recognition that archives are an integral and inalienable part of state and societal functions, and that, with few exceptions, they belong in the place of their creation and deserve to be kept intact in the order of their creation. These principles have been expressed in CITRA resolutions going back to 1961. They were affirmed in the 1978 UNESCO report and a subsequent series of UNESCO and UN resolutions. The 1995 ICA Position Paper is only one of the more recent affirmations.

Unfortunately, those principles have not been unilaterally recognized, nor are they alone resolving the issues of displaced archives. Even when the advice of professional archivists is brought to bear in domestic or international arenas, too often their advice is either not heard or overlooked by politicians. Since the specific issues of World War II displacements are now grossly complicating the broader problem of the reconstitution of the national archival heritage for Soviet successor States, a review of those developments is in order for the second part of our study. But first it is worthwhile to consider the types of archival materials involved among those that are displaced from their homelands.

CHAPTER 4

Towards a Descriptive Typology of the Ukrainian Archival Heritage Abroad

As we have seen, both the principle of provenance and the distinction between provenance and pertinence may not be sufficient in identifying what might be considered the legitimate archival heritage of Ukraine. The distinction between the provenance and pertinence of records may be particularly difficult to apply for archival Ucrainica within the former Russian Empire and Soviet Union. A more specific typology is needed in attempting to define legally the archival heritage of Ukraine in general and the components of the "National Archival Fond" of Ukraine now located in the diaspora in particular. Given a national history that is chronologically broken and often territorially dispersed, it is frequently important to identify archival components of Ucrainica abroad that, while pertinent to Ukrainian history and culture, cannot legally be defined as part of the "National Archival Fond." Usually, it is not enough simply to apply a label "archival Ucrainica" without further designation of the types or nature of the records or fragmented archival materials involved.

The problems of appropriate identification of archival "Ucrainica" are further increased with materials now held abroad because—before the recent emergence of an independent Ukraine—the distinction between "Ukrainian" and "Russian," "Polish" and "Ukrainian," or "Austro-Hungarian (or "Austrian" or "Hungarian)" and "Ukrainian" tended to decrease proportionately with the distance from the homeland, the precision of ethnic identity, or the degree of "Ukrainian" national consciousness. Indeed, in most parts of the world outside Ukraine (even in Russia proper), and especially among those that had not retained any sense of Ukrainian identity or Ukrainian national consciousness, the distinction between "Ukrainian" and the "parent" Russian, Polish, Austrian, Hungarian, or Romanian seat of government was often obliterated.

Even more misleadingly, until this decade the term "Russia" was often used synonymously with, or instead of, the more correct designation "Soviet Union" in many countries, including both England and the United States. Many people failed to recognize that Ukrainian is not a dialect of the Russian language or that Ukrainians had pretensions to independent statehood.[1] Many second- or third-generation families whose ancestors emigrated to the United States or Canada from western Ukraine in the late nineteenth century (then part of the Austro-Hungarian Empire) are not even aware that they are of Ukrainian ancestry. Most of the more recent émigrés from Odesa will identify themselves as "Russian" or "Jewish," for example, and have not learned the Ukrainian language. The Russian language has been dominant in eastern Ukraine for so long that many well-educated, otherwise liberally oriented ethnic Russians often deny that Ukrainian should be treated as a separate language. Numerous other examples can be adduced to show that the concept of Ukrainian distinctiveness, both linguistically and nationally, has long been discounted not only abroad, but also by Ukraine's neighbors, especially Russia.

Archival "Ucrainica" abroad may thus be found with a number of potentially different national or ethnic labels and may be subject to counter-claims by other national or ethnic groups, depending on their perceptions of the concept of "Ukrainian." This leads to the further complication that relatively few documents of present Ukrainian territorial provenance or pertinence among official foreign government records will surface with an appropriate "Ukrainian" label, although the lack of such labels may not lessen the relevance or "pertinence" of the contents to the present-day history of Ukraine. Such complex issues were not raised by earlier UN/ICA discussion, particularly during the decades when the term "Soviet" or "Fatherland" replaced national identities and suppressed conflicting ethnic claims or pretensions. Now that the "common Soviet Fatherland" no longer exists, such issues deserve appropriate consideration if there is to be a realistic juridical attempt to define and identify the "Ukrainian" archival legacy abroad. While it is appropriate to distinguish "Ukrainian" from "Russian" or "Belarusian," it may also be necessary to recognize a common heritage in terms of legitimate pretensions of other successor States that may simultaneously claim the same materials as part of their own national heritage.

---

[1]   For example, at the height of the movement for independence in 1990, as was widely reported on television, visiting British Prime Minister Margaret Thatcher, when asked if her country would consider establishing an embassy in Kyiv, replied that the British government does not have a consulate in Texas. See the helpful discussion on this point in the brochure by Frank Sysyn, "Russia or the Soviet Union? There Is a Difference" (Cambridge, MA: Ukrainian Studies Fund, [1986?]).

*   *
*

Archival materials abroad that are of provenance in Ukraine or pertain to Ukraine while it was within the Russian Empire or the Soviet Union take many forms. They are part of many foreign record groups or documentary collections in both state and private repositories. Significant quantities of archival Ucrainica abroad have, unfortunately, not found their way to public repositories and have not been appraised or described at all. Many significant deposits risk disintegration in damp basements or unprotected attics, while many unique and valuable materials are consigned to the trash bin by later generations or subsequent tenants who have no appreciation for the potential value of such resources. Journalistic materials are especially problematic, given the difficulty of storing the various media used, the need for reusing recording media (especially in economically depressed areas), and the uncertainty of what topics of the moment will have lasting historical value.

Aggressive outreach efforts are under way today by numerous Ukrainian organizations to encourage the return of archival Ucrainica to its homeland. Similar efforts are under way in Russia, and, in some cases, there may be considerable overlap. To be sure, most of the materials brought out of the home-country by émigrés or brought home by foreigners in Ukraine are too fragmentary or ephemeral to merit archival processing costs. To date, however, even those that have found their way to local university libraries, historical societies, or ethnic archives as tidbits of foreign exotica have not been adequately described nor open to research. There also is a need for Western institutions to expand the facilities available for collecting and processing those treasures that do deserve permanent preservation and whose legal owners are not prepared to transfer them to Ukraine.

Once preservation is assured in the West or in Ukraine, it is critical to follow through with professional, dispassionate description in accordance with international archival reference standards. An important component in such description is the inclusion of facts regarding provenance and subsequent migration of the archival documents in question. Many archival institutions and library manuscript divisions in Ukraine and Russia would not normally add such data to public catalog entries, but most such institutions retain accession registers that, at least, could reveal their own source of acquisition. Even if, in specific cases, there would be no reason for claims or pretensions, notations of provenance and migratory details are crucial for the full identification and utilization of the documents involved, and for the establishment of possible relationships to contiguous materials elsewhere abroad or in Ukraine itself.

In describing the varied complex of Ucrainica abroad—especially if there are any pretensions to return or restitution in original or copy—it is helpful to distinguish basic categories of documentation or types of materials involved. Such distinctions will be helpful for the purposes of identification and discussion of potential legal claims. The legal status of the documents involved (and hence the application of international agreements, historical precedents, and professional archival practice), may vary depending on the category of documents. Most survey descriptions of Ucrainica abroad, including official discussions of Ucrainica within the context of other displaced archival materials, have not adequately identified typological distinctions. Nor have the authors of the descriptions been adequately concerned with provenance and the facts of migration. Since most have not been concerned with potential restitution (or the right to copies), they have failed to adequately delineate many complex legal problems of their present disposition.

Despite tremendous interest in various parts of the world, there has yet to be an adequate definition of what constitutes archival Ucrainica or the Ukrainian component in archival Rossica or Polonica abroad. A viable typology has not been established either of categories or types of documentation based on provenance and the circumstances of its alienation.[2] This lack reflects a more general deficiency in international archival literature and legal practice of attempts to define the types of potentially displaced fragments of the archival heritage of any nation and the principles, procedures, and guidelines that might be appropriate in different cases for restitution or return in original or copy. Similar limitations are apparent in international archival literature promulgated by the International Council on Archives (ICA), and broader cultural restitution problems posited by UNESCO, as discussed above.

The typology presented here has grown and been revised several times, but still remains a preliminary formulation. It will require further revision in

---

[2]   The present chapter is revised from my conference presentation in Moscow in December 1993 regarding the parallel problem of defining the Russian archival legacy abroad. The typology that follows is adapted for Ukraine from the preliminary typology for Rossica published as "Arkhivnaia Rossika/Sovetika: K opredeleniiu i topologii russkogo arkhivnogo naslediia za rubezhom," in *Trudy IAI* 33 (Moscow, 1996): 262–86, and in *Problemy zarubezhnoi arkhivnoi Rossiki*, pp. 7–43. For an initial and less detailed categorization of archival Rossica abroad, see the presentation by Vladimir Kozlov at the same Moscow conference: "Vyiavlenie i vozvrashchenie zarubezhnoi arkhivnoi Rossiki: Opyt i perspektivy,"*Novaia i noveishaia istorii* 1994 (3): 13–23.

the course of discussion with professional archivists, international lawyers, and others who have tried to resolve such matters in different countries. As set forth here, categories have been defined specifically with regard to Ukrainian-pertinent documentation, growing out of analysis of Ukrainian archival history and descriptive efforts of documentation relating to Ukrainian history and culture. Some of the categories have already been mentioned above in the discussion of Ukrainian pretensions for materials held in the Russian metropolis and in reference to international precedents. In some cases, potential distinctions may not always be apparent, and in other cases, there may be overlap between categories. Still, it is helpful to try to establish appropriate categories with examples and to explain how a different legal status may often be involved.

Most archivists would undoubtedly agree that professional description with typological classification needs to be directed to two major components, namely,

1. the institutional and territorial provenance of the materials in question, and
2. the circumstances of their alienation from the homeland.

In terms of possible pretensions for return or restitution, subsequent descriptive attention needs to be directed to two other important components, namely,

3. the present location and arrangement of the materials within their current archival context, and
4. any existing agreements or legal factors (where appropriate and if data is available) that could affect their present proprietary status.

1. Institutional and Territorial Provenance

Ideally, descriptive components and typological distinctions within archival Ucrainica abroad should reflect:

*   the creating agency (or author, or copyist for a manuscript book);
*   the territorial provenance at the point of creation;
*   the functional purpose, sponsor, or circumstances of its creation;
*   the group of records with which it would have first been retained;

- the archive, library, or other repository where it was first stored apart from its creating agency, as well as subsequent ones, in the case of migrated documentation.

On the basis of international respect for the principles of territorial origin and provenance, a distinction must initially be made between archival materials created in Ukrainian lands—even when those lands were a part of the Russian Empire, the Soviet Union, or another State—and then alienated abroad, and those records or personal papers created abroad, including documentation created by émigré communities in the diaspora, or those legitimately acquired in the course of business by institutions, organizations, or individuals abroad. In the case of records of official or private institutions that have moved their legal base of institutional operation from one country to another, it will be important to identify the operational base during specific dates in the institutional charter or act of incorporation. In some cases of combined or migratory records, it may be necessary to consider dividing or subdividing the records according to dates and their country of creation.

Within this first component—the provenance and circumstances of creation—it might be appropriate in terms of defining archival Ucrainica to distinguish two main complexes of materials:

The first—or Ukrainian—complex of categories (see section 1.A, "Documentation Created by the Ukrainian Government, Ukrainian Institutions, or Individuals," below) includes documentary materials created by:

- the government of Ukraine;
- local agencies of imperial foreign governments operating in Ukrainian lands;
- other institutions registered with foreign imperial regimes, based in what are now Ukrainian lands;
- individuals (regardless of nationality) who are subjects of Ukraine or ethnic Ukrainians who were subjects of the Russian Empire and, later, the Soviet Union.

These materials would be of prime interest to Ukraine today in terms of the "Ukrainian" archival heritage in the broadest sense. It should be noted, however, that with the resurgence of Ukrainian nationalism (and chauvinism) in some quarters, "Ucrainica" may also be used in the narrower sense of Ukrainian ethnicity or language.

A second—foreign—complex of materials (see section 1.B, "Documentation Created by Foreigners," below) would be those created by:

- foreign governments;

- other institutions;
- individuals.

To be sure, there will be cases where it may not be appropriate to distinguish sharply between "Ukrainian" and "foreign," or between the "near abroad" and the "farther abroad." Furthermore, as noted above, in terms of personal papers, major problems arise in distinguishing precisely along purely linguistic or ethnic lines.

It could be argued that these simple categories are sufficient and further typological distinctions are not necessary, but given different operative legal and cultural situations, it is appropriate to establish somewhat narrower categories that reference the place, as well as type, of institutional or individual creator.

1.A. *Documentation Created by the Ukrainian Government, Ukrainian Institutions, or Individuals* (13 categories):

1.A.1. Official records of earlier Ukrainian government agencies operating within present Ukrainian lands or in exile. This category would involve any possible fragments of official state records created by Ukrainian government agencies that might have been seized by other imperial regimes or taken abroad by émigrés. These would include the records of the Zaporozhian Sich and the eighteenth-century Cossack Hetmanate based in Hlukhiv and Chernihiv and its local branch administrative bodies. This category would also include all of the records of the Central Rada and Ukrainian National Republic (UNR) during the struggle for Ukrainian independence after the revolutions of 1917 and the West Ukrainian National Republic. Any such parts of state archival records extant abroad, many of which were seized by later imperial powers, would now legitimately constitute part of the national archival heritage of Ukraine.

Of particular interest now is the fate of records of the UNR. It is understandable that after the collapse of the independent Ukrainian state in 1920 and the failure of the West Ukrainian National Republic, many of the leaders involved were forced to flee, taking with them some of the records of that government into exile. Additional records were created by that government in exile, for example, during the period the UNR was based in Tarnów, Poland. In the next two decades those records were widely scattered in Paris, Berlin, Vienna, and Prague. During the Second World War, many were confiscated by the Nazis and further displaced. After the war, some were taken to the United States or Canada and, as mentioned in the introduction, many more were captured by Soviet authorities and brought to Kyiv and Moscow. Pending definitive arrangement and more thorough description, it is difficult to determine which parts of the original records are preserved in Kyiv and Moscow.[3] Obviously, records of those governments in exile are also of prime interest for Ukraine, although their legal status may involve further complications. Of a special positive note in this connection was the transfer to the Main Archival Administration in Kyiv in an official ceremony in March 1996 of documentation of the Ukrainian government (UNR) in exile from the National Archives of Canada.

1.A.2. Diplomatic or other official records and miscellaneous archival materials created abroad by Ukrainian missions or representatives of official Ukrainian institutions and organizations. There are a few important examples of official Ukrainian diplomatic representatives abroad or other institutions that were representing Ukraine and that were directly subservient to, or that were operating as branches of, official government institutions based in Ukraine itself. These would include the records of the Permanent Representative of the Ukrainian Socialist Republic in Moscow as well as various trade missions, all of which remain in Moscow.

Since Ukraine was considered an official founding member of the United Nations, Ukraine now also has a legitimate claim for the records (almost all of which remain in Moscow) of the Ukrainian missions to the United Nations (New York), UNESCO (Paris), and other official international bodies. This remains the case, despite the fact that Ukrainian representation was effectively subservient to Soviet Union representatives in most instances.

It is unlikely that Ukraine would have any legitimate pretensions for Ukrainian-pertinent files within state records of official Russian/Soviet diplomatic, consular, or intelligence units that were operating abroad under an earlier regime. For example, there may well be a few Ukrainian-related files among the records of the pre-revolutionary Russian Embassies in Paris and Washington, DC, that are now held in the Hoover Institution in California, but today these should legitimately be returned to Russia, not Ukraine.[4]

---

[3]   Details about the wartime and postwar fate of the Petliura Library and widely scattered UNR records are documented in my article, "The Odyssey of the Petliura Library and the Records of the Ukrainian National Republic during World War II," *Harvard Ukrainian Studies* 22: 181–208. A companion piece "The Postwar Fate of the Petliura Library and the Records of the Ukrainian National Republic" is published in *Harvard Ukrainian Studies* 21(3–4): 395–462.

[4]   Concerning the fate of the records of the pre-revolutionary Russian Embassy in the United States, see John H. Brown, "The Disappearing Russian Embassy Archives, 1922–1939," *Prologue* 14 (Spring 1982) 1: 5–13. The fact that they were legally transferred for deposit in a private archive during a hiatus in diplomatic relations with

The related pre-revolutionary Russian consular records from the United States and Canada that had been held in the U.S. National Archives were returned to Moscow in 1989.[5]

There is particular Ukrainian interest now in retrieving the foreign diplomatic records of the UNR created during the struggle for Ukrainian independence during the Civil War; most of these records remained abroad for political reasons after the failure of that government. Some of them were transferred to the USSR after World War II from various sources. For example, a few files from the UNR Embassy in Berlin that were brought from Prague with the RZIA collections are now held in Moscow.[6]

1.A.3. Official records of central agencies charged with administration of Ukrainian lands on the part of previously governing imperial regimes. Official records would involve those of Russia, Poland, Austria, Hungary, Austria-Hungary, Romania, and Turkey. For purposes of analysis, these fall into two subcategories. The first subcategory covers records of imperial governing agencies that form separate, distinguishable groups of records that are uniquely pertinent to territories now comprising the Ukrainian successor State. As an example of central agencies under the Russian Empire, mention was made earlier of the records of the Malorossiiskii prikaz ("Little Russian" [Ukrainian] bureau) and the Malorossiiskaia èkspeditsiia Senata ("Little Russian" [Ukrainian] Department of the Senate) now held in Moscow. These form isolated groups of records specifically involved with the administration of Ukrainian lands. There are some international archival precedents for claims to transfer the originals of such records to the successor State, but given current preferences to keep the central records of an imperial govern-

---

the USSR complicates legal claims. Nevertheless, transfer documents quoted by Brown affirm the proviso that the records would be returned to Russia when a legitimate government was established there. Microfilms of these records have recently been given to Russia as part of the Rosarkhiv project with the Hoover Institution.

[5]   The formal restitution ceremony took place in Moscow in May 1989 during the meetings and under the auspices of the U.S.-USSR Commission on Archival Cooperation. Microfilm copies remain in the U.S. National Archives, and microfilmed copies of files from Russian consulates in Canada remain in the National Archives of Canada.

[6]   These are now held in GA RF, fond 5889, 36 units, 1918–1926. See more details in Chapter 9.

ment intact in the place of creation, the transfer of copies would be in order here.

The second subcategory covers remaining cases, especially under the post-revolutionary Soviet system, when government and/or CPSU agencies of central control and command did not keep separate records for highest-level decisions that affected individual union republics. This includes, for example, various files (including *osobye papki)* of specific interest to Ukraine during the entire Soviet period that are interspersed throughout the massive records of the Central Committee and Politburo of the CPSU and its subsidiary departments. It also includes records of various central state agencies, such as the Council of Ministers of the USSR, Gosplan, and others. Given the fact that Ukrainian-relevant files do not constitute a separate group—or even a separate sub-group (in Ukrainian or Russian archival terms a separate *opys/opis´*)—of these records, Ukraine has appropriate pretensions to an authenticated copy of and the right of access to relevant blocks of the complete record group in order to understand and interpret individual files in an appropriate context. In this case, there could certainly be no claim for the originals, although Ukraine would have every reason to seek copies of the complete records of the governing body as needed, including all Ukrainian-specific files not already available on microfilm in Kyiv.

1.A.4. Official state records of provincial, regional, or local agencies based within Ukrainian lands created by authorities of previously governing imperial regimes (including the Communist Party of Ukraine under Soviet rule). Under the Russian Empire, for example, there is no question that local gubernia or court records, created by the Russian governor-general or gubernia administrations within the lands of successor States, would be considered of provenance within those States and hence legally part of their own archival legacies. Thus, records of the Kyiv, Volhynian, and Podolian Governorships-General are of provenance in Kyiv and, hence, part of the Ukrainian national archival heritage. Original outgoing gubernia reports to central authorities in St. Petersburg or Moscow, by contrast, would be part of the records of the central government. If there are gaps in the copies of the outgoing records that were kept locally, however, it would be fitting to request copies from the records of the central authorities.

Likewise, under Soviet rule, there would be no question about jurisdiction over local Ukrainian Communist Party, MVD, and KGB records that were created in present Ukrainian lands. However, many of these have been removed from Kyiv and remain in central Russian archives.

1.A.5. Records of official Ukrainian military units or distinctive Ukrainian components of Russian/Soviet armed forces. There have been relatively few official Ukrainian military units abroad over the centuries. Most of the scattered files of UNR military units that came to Moscow after World War II with the RZIA collections were turned over to Ukraine in 1962.

As mentioned above, the central records of the Black Sea Fleet were created, and for a long time held, in the Ukrainian port of Mykolaïv, but there are understandably dual claims to those records. Ukraine claims the records on the basis of the provenance of their creation and long-time storage; alternately, Russia claims the records on the grounds that the fleet was part of the Imperial (and later Soviet) Navy. Nevertheless, Ukraine does have pretensions on at least a part of the records of the Black Sea Fleet, according to the terms of resolution of the dispute over the fleet itself. The provision of copies of such records that would be of dual claim is in order.

Other military records for which there could be pretensions include those of Ukrainian fronts, armies, or units within imperial Austrian, Polish, Russian and Soviet armies, including local induction and operational records of local military commands. Many such local military records were removed from Ukraine by Nazi military archival authorities during World War II and have not been returned. Many other local military records were removed to Moscow either in the 1930s or after the war and deposited in central all-union military archives. These, too, would merit restitution on the basis of their provenance and initial archival location within the Ukrainian SSR.

In the case of the records of "Ukrainian Fronts" during World War II, however, it would be harder to establish definitive claim to the originals. Such high-level military units were an integral and subordinate part of the Red Army, and it would not be fitting to destroy the integrity of their records. Complete microform copies, along with complete copies of the relevant finding aids to the records of "fronts" operating in Ukraine—or of those of predominantly Ukrainian composition operating abroad—and complete records of their commanding units would be appropriate to claim.

1.A.6. Specialized Documentation from Ukrainian Lands Taken to Imperial Centers, including Ukrainian Film Productions, Audiovisual, and Other Scientific Documentation. During the Soviet period, various types of specialized documentation of Ukrainian provenance other than official state records were centralized in all-union archives in the imperial capital. These include data in numerous scientific areas such as the Central Cartographic-Geodesic Fond, the State Geological Fond, the State Fond of Data on Environmental Conditions and Hydro-Meteorology, and the Central State Fond of Standards and Technical Specifications, to name the most significant permanent depositories. These would have been considered legal deposits under Soviet law and have been declared legally part of the Archival Fond of the Russian Federation. These archives were reorganized under administration of the successor agencies of the Russian Federation but, as noted above, they are administered independently of Rosarkhiv.

The Commission on Cinematography of the USSR required the deposit of the archival copy of all feature films, editing outtakes, scenarios, and related archival materials produced in all republic-level film studios throughout the Soviet Union in its centralized film archive, Gosfil′mofond, in Belye Stolby outside Moscow. Ukrainian productions for all-union television and radio were also centralized in the corresponding State Television and Radio Archive, Gosteleradiofond in Moscow. The situation with regard to documentary films and sound recordings was less centralized because, although copies of many republic-level productions were transferred for deposit in centralized audiovisual archives in Moscow, parallel audiovisual archives were also maintained on the republic level, which was not the case for feature films and television productions.

The question now is: do Ukraine and other newly independent successor States have a claim to the master films and related archival materials produced in their studios over the past fifty years? If they remain exempt from claim under current Russian archival law, does that mean that adequate copies of the data and their information systems have been granted to newly independent successor States? The current disposition of such important republic-level archival materials and original film masters of Ukrainian provenance will obviously require further negotiation, along with appropriate provisions for their preservation and copyright administration in Ukraine.

1.A.7. Records created abroad (outside the former Russian/Soviet Empire) by representatives of other non-diplomatic official Ukrainian/Soviet state institutions. Many more such "official" records exist from the Soviet period than from pre-revolutionary years because the state had such a wide function in all aspects of economic and social life, and hence records of representation abroad in many non-diplomatic spheres would also be considered official state records. In this category we would include official Ukrainian trade missions, press representatives, and Ukrainian representatives to international organizations (other than those with diplomatic status). If, in fact, the agencies were purely Ukrainian, Ukraine naturally would have pretensions for their records, while pretensions for files created by or relating to Ukrainian participants in general all-union missions would be harder to substantiate.

1.A.8. Documentation of Ukrainian non-state, private institutions such as businesses, churches, or cultural agencies not under official state control. This category would include representatives abroad of Ukrainian institutions or organizations officially licensed to conduct business within Ukraine. In most countries such records would be subject to laws of private or corporate property, although under the Soviet regime they would have most likely been nationalized.

1.A.9. Documentation of illegal or exiled organizations and individuals, including clandestine and dissident groups operating within Ukrainian lands during the Russian imperial or Soviet regimes. This category consists of much high-interest documentation of Ukrainian political parties, military and para-military organizations (such as the Ukrainian Sich Riflemen [Ukraïns'ki sichovi stril'tsi] and the Ukrainian Insurgent Army [Ukraïns'ka Povstans'ka Armiia—UPA]), suppressed Church groups, community groups, underground and dissident groups or individuals. However, because of their illegal and/or clandestine status under prevailing imperial regimes, legal claims or the right of recovery may be more difficult than would be the case of official, licensed, legal institutions.

During the Soviet period, large quantities of illegal (or, as it was sometimes called, "unofficial") documentation was seized by the central all-union KGB and its foreign intelligence service operating abroad, and subsequently became incorporated in all-union-level KGB records. Such documentation was also seized by local NKVD, MVD, or KGB authorities and became incorporated in Ukrainian KGB or MVD records. As mentioned earlier, major groups of Ukrainian MVD and KGB records (including significant quantities of UPA documentation) were removed to Moscow in 1991. Since these were clearly alienated records of local Ukrainian prove-nance, it would be out of place for imperial all-union authorities to establish definitive claim to the originals or to charge exorbitant fees for copies. Under normal international archival arrangements, such local records should be subject to claims in the same category as other local records mentioned above (see 1.A.4. "Official state records of provincial, regional, or local agen-cies..."), but Western concepts in this regard obviously have not yet been accepted in the transitional post-Soviet Russian body politic and archival world; in Moscow these files remain in agency custody rather than in public archives.[7] It is not known how many files relating to or manuscript materials created by Ukrainian dissidents, or surveillance records of foreign Ukrainian émigrés, are still maintained among former KGB records in Moscow.

In many cases, copies of some Ukrainian dissident literature and under-ground samizdat (Ukr. *samvydav*), as well as semi-published periodicals,

---

[7]   These transfers were subject to official protest and petition for return, but as noted above, the files themselves remain in Moscow, and Ukraine has been obliged to pay a high price for microfilm copies.

were sent abroad for publication or broadcast by Radio Liberty and others. They are preserved in RL/RFE archives or by Ukrainian groups in the West.[8] Many papers of exiled Ukrainian "bourgeois nationalists" also remained abroad, although some were seized by the Nazis in various European countries and subsequently brought back to Ukraine by Soviet authorities after the war. During World War II, Nazi authorities also collected many files of Ukrainian émigré organizations abroad; a few of those files of groups operating in Poland, for example, were seized by Soviet authorities at the end of the war and are now held in the former Special Archive (TsGOA; now part of RGVA) or in GA RF, while others were transferred to the former Central Party Archive (now RGASPI).[9] Others are held with the Prague materials in TsDAVO and TsDAHO in Kyiv. Although records of those organizations operating abroad would be considered of foreign provenance and not subject to claim by Ukraine, there are no grounds for their remaining in Moscow.

1.A.10. Personal papers of individual Ukrainians, including Ukrainian émigrés. There are many important groups of personal papers of prominent Ukrainians created in Ukrainian lands that were legitimately taken abroad by, or for, individual exiles or political or intellectual émigrés. Copies or originals of important government documents have often become incorporated into private personal files of government leaders. Normally, once they have become lodged there, they would not be subject to claim or removal in most countries.

Many of these are now intricately related to subsequent personal papers created in emigration or exile. Personal papers in most countries outside the Socialist bloc would constitute "personal property" and would be subject to the laws of the creator's present country of citizenship. They would be

---

[8] See the published series, *Arkhiv Samizdat*, issued by Radio Liberty (RL) and the microfiche collections prepared by IDC. The bibliographies published while the materials were still in Munich cover independent imprints and local periodicals retained in RL facilities in Munich. Under the auspices of the Open Media Research Institute (OMRI), supported by the Soros Foundation, the RL/RFE archives have been transferred from Munich and are now organized in the Open Society Archive in Budapest, which opened in March 1996 as a public research archival center under the newly established Central European University.

[9] Further discussion of these materials follows in Chapter 9. See, for example, the files of Ukrainian nationalist political organizations in Poland during the 1930s held among the records of the Heeresarchiv, Zweigstelle Danzig, RGVA, fond 1387K/2, nos. 7 and 8.

subject to jurisdiction, according to the dispositional wishes of their creator, heir, or current owner, as well as copyright laws.

1.A.11. Manuscript books, autographs, and collections of historical documentation. Many important collections of manuscript books and other historical documentation of Ukrainian provenance have been taken at various times to the imperial capitals of Moscow and St. Petersburg. Different principles need to be resolved in terms of pretensions for their restitution. In terms of materials held in Russia from the "near abroad," many manuscript books and historical documents were collected in Ukrainian lands by various "archeographic expeditions," starting in the early nineteenth century with the work of the Imperial Archeographic Commission. Similar examples arise in the many archeographic expeditions sent out, for example, by the Library of the Academy of Sciences (BAN) and the Institute of Russian Literature (Pushkinskii Dom) in Leningrad, and the Library of Moscow State University during more recent Soviet decades. Also of considerable importance are ethnographic collections gathered from Ukrainian lands on expeditions by various museums and ethnographic research institutes, both before 1917 and during the Soviet period.

Local churches and remaining private holdings were stripped of their earliest manuscript treasures, which were brought to central repositories in Moscow and St. Petersburg, where they remain today. The extent to which the manuscript divisions of major libraries, museums, and other institutes in Moscow and St. Petersburg have taken in manuscript riches and folklore treasures from throughout the empire is receiving more attention in successor States following the collapse of the USSR, but few Russian cultural or scientific officials would want to consider restitution of imperial treasures. New Russian laws and presidential decrees have ruled out restitution of previously nationalized archival materials and cultural treasures, and, undoubtedly, Russian authorities will still claim that all of these seizures were legal at the time, and that institutions in Russia were responsible for their "rescue," preservation, and, in many cases, restoration. In addition, Russians are quick to point out the extent to which works of Russian and foreign art and other cultural treasures previously held in Russian lands were distributed to the former Soviet republics, especially after World War II.[10]

---

[10]   As an example of the most blatant right-wing Russian statements and claims, see the article in *Pravda* (which has been adopting an extreme nationalist position in this regard): Vladimir Teteriatnikov, "Ograbiat li vnov' russkii narod? Tragicheskaia sud'ba tsennostei, peremeshchennykh v rezul'tate Vtoroi mirovoi voiny," *Pravda* 73 (22 May 1996): 4. In his list of "offenses" in terms of transfers from Russia and

In terms of the traditional or "farther" abroad, émigrés account for the alienation of vast quantities of archival materials from, and relating to, Ukraine. Along with personal papers, many émigrés took with them important collections of historical documentation, manuscript books, and audiovisual materials. During the 1920s and 1930s, noted Ukrainian political figures and intellectuals who fled to the West and settled in Czechoslovakia, Germany, or other countries were able to bring with them archival materials from many important Ukrainian institutions or individuals, as well as their own personal papers. Like personal papers, in most countries outside the Socialist bloc manuscript collections would constitute "personal property" of their creator or collector. Problems now arise in how to categorize more specifically official Ukrainian state archival materials that were taken abroad by émigrés. Most such materials are already subject to the laws of the countries in which their legal owners (either individual or institutional) reside. The Soviet seizure of the Russian Foreign Historical Archive (RZIA) and the associated Ukrainian Historical Cabinet (UIK) in Prague in 1945, negotiated officially as "gifts," is a special case.[11]

The fate of Polish manuscript collections from Lviv is discussed below. In the schema used here, they would now be considered "foreign"-created collections; their migration is most relevant to the post-World War II resettlement of Polish population from western Ukraine. Somewhat different problems arise in connection with the fate of the manuscript collection of the Armenian Metropolitanate of Galicia and other Armenian manuscripts from the Lviv University Library, most of which were taken from Lviv in Nazi shipments in the spring of 1944 and are now mostly in Poland. Some manuscripts from this collection have been integrated into the collections of the Ossolineum in Wrocław, although some parts of the collection taken earlier from Lviv are now held in Vienna. The disposition of this former collection is complicated by the fact that the collection itself has been dispersed and by the fact that its pre-1939 legal owner, the Armenian Metropolitanate, had not been reestablished in Lviv. An additional complexity arises from the fact that the Matenadaran, the official Armenian State manuscript repository, in agreement with civic and church authorities in

---

restitution of cultural treasures, the author (now an American citizen) includes a number of transfers to former Soviet republics, including Ukraine.

[11]   See further discussion of these materials in Chapter 9. See also my earlier discussion in "Archival Rossica/Sovietica Abroad—Provenance or Pertinence, Bibliographic and Descriptive Needs," *Cahiers du Monde russe et soviétique* 34(3) 1993: 463–65.

Yerevan, has established itself as caretaker for the Armenian manuscript legacy from all over the world. Other complications regarding provenance and previous ownership arise in the case of the other Oriental and Church Slavonic manuscripts removed from Lviv at the same time.[12]

Manuscript collections, individual rare manuscript books, famous autographs, and films and other audiovisual materials cannot always be handled according to the same principles as state archives and personal papers. The analysis of UNESCO regarding respect for assembled collections and other general principles for dealing with cultural property mentioned in Chapter 3 is relevant in this case. What is most important today for the many highly prized early Slavic manuscripts and Ukrainian autographs held abroad is the professional description of the texts and the open admission of the details of their migration and of their present location, so that scholars may know if and where the texts have been preserved. Once such description has been accomplished, an international commission of experts to evaluate claims may ultimately be the just solution in complicated cases. Whatever the outcome, as ICA and UNESCO resolutions set forth, there should be no compromise or limitation put on the right to receive complete, high-quality copies.

1.A.12. Records created abroad by private Ukrainian émigré organizations or community groups. Considerable interest will now be found in many records of émigré groups, such as cultural, church, and fraternal organizations created abroad that continued to preserve Ukrainian traditions in emigration. Many of them were in close contact with the homeland and followed developments there, both on official and underground levels. Like the papers of prominent individual émigrés, they contain significant incoming correspondence or other materials of Ukrainian origin.

In the West, all such groups of records would be protected by laws respecting private or cultural property in the country where they were created or where they now reside. Thus, institutional records of Ukrainian community organizations created in Prague, Munich, Paris, or New York, however "pertinent" to Ukraine and important in terms of Ukrainian history and culture, must be considered of foreign provenance and subject to the laws of the country of their creation. Pretensions might arise, however, regarding the

---

[12] See also my specific references to the Armenian manuscripts in Grimsted, *Archives: Ukraine*, pp. 574–77 (especially nos. NL-390–NL-396). As explained in scholarly literature cited there, some of the manuscripts held before 1939 by the Lviv Armenian Uniate Archbishopric are dispersed in different collections in Lviv, Vienna, and Wrocław, as well as in Warsaw. See further discussion in Chapter 11.

records of successor organizations to parent institutions in Ukraine, or those of institutions or organizations that have been reestablished in Ukraine since the collapse of Soviet rule.

During World War II, Nazi authorities appropriated many archives and scattered files of Ukrainian émigré organizations abroad. Many of those seized by the Nazis were in turn seized by Soviet authorities at the end of the war or in the immediate postwar years. The largest volume of Ukrainian émigré archival material seized abroad and transferred to the USSR are now held in TsDAVO in Kyiv, although some were requisitions by central Soviet authorities in Moscow. These materials, together with the transfers to Kyiv and Moscow in connection with the "gifts" of RZIA and UIK and extensive documentation from other émigré sources in Czechoslovakia, Poland, Germany, and other countries will be discussed in Chapter 9.

1.A.13. Collections of Ukrainian archival materials created abroad and/or Ukrainian components of other collections. Many archives or libraries of Ukrainian émigré groups abroad contain collected documentary sources or literary manuscripts and other miscellaneous archival materials of Ukrainian origin. Like the personal papers of émigrés, they would be considered private property and are normally protected by laws respecting private cultural property in the country where they now reside. In most countries, documents legally purchased at auction or from literary dealers are considered, by virtue of purchase, the legal property of their new owners, even if their prior origins may be suspect. Where there are provisions for claims for materials with prior illegal transfers, statutes of limitation often apply. This would also be the case with Ukrainian components of other established Western archives or manuscript repositories throughout the world.

1.B. *Documentation Created by Foreigners* (5 categories):

A second major complex of documentation would be records created by foreign sources (governments, semi-private or private institutions and organizations, or individuals). To be sure, under international law and accepted archival practice in many Western countries, most such documentary materials created by foreigners in, or *pertaining to*, Ukraine, including personal papers, records of private organizations, and especially documentation created abroad, would never be subject to claim as an official part of the national archival heritage. Some might even suggest that this broad complex of material is not really "archival Ucrainica" *per se*.

It should be noted, however, that in traditional scholarship and library usage, the term "Rossica" or "Ucrainica" usually referred to *foreign* imprints *about* Russia or Ukraine such as the "Rossica" collection in the pre-revolutionary Imperial Public Library in St. Petersburg (see Preface, p. xxxv, fn. 8). In bibliophile usage abroad, the terms "Rossica" and "Ucrainica" usually implied early (pre-nineteenth century) books printed in Russia or Ukraine (including Slavonic books of Russian imperial origin) in collections outside Russia or Ukraine. More recently, the term "Ucrainica" is being prefaced with the word "archival" to extend its scope to unpublished materials. As well, it is being used both in the sense of foreign-created materials and those created in Ukraine.

Many such materials are of legitimate interest for their revelations and pertinence to Ukrainian history and culture. Many of them, as will be noted below, even contain important original "Ukrainian" documentation. Hence, these categories also require description in the context of a program for archival Ucrainica.

1.B.1. Diplomatic or consular records of official missions of a foreign state residing in Ukrainian lands, and/or Ukrainian-pertinent materials within diplomatic records of foreign missions resident in the Russian Empire and the Soviet Union, Poland, or other countries once exercising dominion over present-day Ukrainian territory. A wealth of Ukrainian-pertinent sources remain among diplomatic and consular records of foreign states, but there can be no question that such archival records, and the miscellaneous documentation incorporated in those records, were legitimately taken abroad. According to diplomatic precedents, even consular records of a foreign state created in Kyiv, Lviv, or Odesa should remain under the jurisdiction of the country that created them. Given diplomatic practices during recent centuries, there are no grounds for demanding the return even of high-interest, intercepted, or decoded Russian/Ukrainian documents to be found among such records. To be sure, requests would be justified for copies of documents from years already declassified and open for research in foreign archives.

The extensive Ukrainian-pertinent documentation is often difficult to locate within existing records of foreign embassies in Russia, Poland, or Austria. Rarely do they have Ukrainian-pertinent labels. Even on the highest diplomatic level, foreign governments had one embassy in the Russian Empire (and later, the Soviet Union), in the Austro-Hungarian Empire and its successor States, in Poland, and in the Ottoman Empire. Hence, for example, British Foreign Office records with diplomatic correspondence bearing the archival/record group designation "Russia," "Poland," "Austria," and so forth, contain reports and documentation from present-day Ukrainian lands that were, in different periods, part of the larger body politic. Reports from western Ukraine before 1918 would be filed with embassy records from Vienna, and hence would be part of the archival/record group "Austria," rather than "Russia," whereas the reports from the same areas during the sixteenth through eighteenth centuries, and again from 1919 to 1940, would have come from embassies in Cracow or Warsaw and would be filed within the archive/record group "Poland." In British records, for example, most file designations bearing the term "South Russia" require further analysis as to whether the documentation included should be considered of Russian or Ukrainian "provenance," "pertinence," or of joint Russian/Ukrainian relevance. Archivists or established subject-authority files may differ in the labels they applied, based on the extent of their geographic knowledge and ethnic sensitivity. Even if a qualified, ethnically perceptive archivist correctly assigned an official file designator to one historical period, changing boundaries may now make that designation obsolete. A subsequent archivist or indexer most probably would not have time to reexamine the contents of the files themselves before entering the label into a new index listing.

1.B.2. Records of wartime foreign military and occupation authorities in Ukrainian lands. In most instances, foreign military records have been legitimately claimed by nations that created them, and are usually viewed as the property of the invading army or navy, as is stated in the 1995 ICA Position Paper (see Appendix VII, §1.v, p. 558). Thus, the original documents of invading armies are most often found in the archives of the invading country (France during the Napoleonic wars and Germany during the two World Wars). In the course of many wars, invaders managed to evacuate their records or subsequently recover them in later military encounters or treaty negotiations. There are many examples over the centuries of military archives that were seized by invading armies and then seized again in subsequent wars. Nazi authorities during World War II were particularly diligent in this respect, and they managed to locate and seize many earlier military records in Ukraine, especially those relating to military operations against Germany during World War I—from both sides of the battle line.

According to international archival practice, as pointed out by the April 1995 ICA Position Paper, records of military occupation have traditionally been treated differently than local peacetime or civilian occupational records of an imperial regime. Clearly, occupational records involving civilian institutions and civilian populations in occupied lands should be considered as a sub-category because they are of joint heritage (interest); they are important to the occupiers as well as the countries being occupied—the aggressors as well as the vanquished. Hence, it is essential that copies be made available to both countries involved. A good example of bilateral cooperation in connection with occupation records was the German-American joint project for describing and microfilming the records of the American occupation government in Germany after World War II (OMGUS).

During World War II, Nazi forces retreating from Soviet lands attempted to destroy or evacuate with them their occupation records, and in many cases they succeeded. In some cases, however, Soviet authorities later found and seized Nazi occupation records in the West. For example, some of the records of the Reich Ministry for Occupied Eastern Territories (Reichsministerium für die besetzten Ostgebiete—RMbO) are now held in Moscow (former TsKhIDK), although a much larger part was captured after the war by U.S. authorities and subsequently returned to Germany as the nation that created them.[13] Similarly, a major part of the related records of the Rosenberg Special Command (Einsatzstab Reichsleiter Rosenberg—ERR), which the Nazis managed to evacuate to the West, was also captured by U.S. forces and later returned to Germany.[14] Another major group of ERR records was seized by Soviet authorities after the war; the largest group is now held in Kyiv (TsDAVO), while a few miscellaneous files are now held in Moscow (RGVA) and Vilnius.[15] While German archives have a legitimate right to claim the Rosenberg records and those of other Nazi occupation agencies in Kyiv, Ukrainian archives will undoubtedly want copies of other Ukrainian-relevant parts of the same fonds and others from the occupation period

---

[13] The RMbO records captured by American authorities were microfilmed together with the records of the Einsatzstab Reichsleiter Rosenberg (ERR); thus, the microfilm publication series (EAP 99) includes both record groups intermingled. See *Guides to German Records Microfilmed at Alexandria, VA,* no. 28: *Records of the Reich Ministry for the Occupied Eastern Territories, 1941–1943*. All of those records were subsequently returned to Germany and rearranged.

[14] The records of the Einsatzstab Reichsleiter Rosenberg (ERR) captured by the American Army were eventually filmed as part of the same microfilm publication series (EAP 99) intermingled with the records of the RMbO (see previous note). After their return to Germany they were processed and described as a separate record group (Bestand NS 30). They are now held in the new archival facility in Berlin-Lichterfelde.

[15] See Chapter 8 for further discussion of ERR. Other highly important Rosenberg documents, however, were "incorporated" into Nuremberg trial records, copies of which were made available to all of the Allies. A few additional original Rosenberg files remain in the Center for Contemporary Jewish Documentation (CDJC) in Paris, and a few remain in the Netherlands Institute for War Documentation (NIOD, earlier RIOD) in Amsterdam, and in YIVO in New York City. Other ERR files were incorporated into OMGUS restitution records in US NA and BAK.

pertaining to Ukraine that are now held in Berlin, Koblenz, Paris, and Moscow.

1.B.3. Records of foreign non-governmental business firms, cultural, church, press, or other organizations with branch operations in Ukraine (or Ukrainian lands of the Russian Empire/Soviet Union). Many pertinent records of private institutions (including churches and religious groups, charity organizations and relief missions, business firms, the journalistic media, and political groups) that had offices or branch operations in the Russian Empire or the Soviet Union are still preserved abroad. We would also include in this category (or perhaps as a sub-category) records of international organizations, such as the Red Cross, Amnesty International, Greenpeace, and others that have had missions or contacts with Ukraine. In most international practice, such records would have been legitimately taken abroad as private or corporate property. Under the Communist regime, however, foreign business and other institutional records created in the Russian Empire and remaining there were nationalized. The status of many such records may be subject to claim from the foreign institutions involved, but, at the same time, there will undoubtedly be considerable Ukrainian interest in receiving copies of records held abroad of firms that were operating in Ukraine.

In a few cases, there are specific firms or organizations that were operating only in Ukrainian lands and, thus, as a whole may be considered archival Ucrainica. In other cases, records of large firms or organizations that operated throughout the Russian Empire or the Soviet Union may contain Ukrainian-specific documentation, although, as mentioned above, it may rarely be described as such. For example, the Rosarkhiv-Hoover exhibit, "Making Things Work: Russian-American Economic Relations, 1900–1930," that opened in Moscow (November 1992) and subsequently in Palo Alto, California (March/April 1993), included many samples of important business records of American companies operating in Russia in the late nineteenth and early twentieth centuries, with even a few documents of Ukrainian origin and/or pertinence.[16]

---

[16]   See the bilingual catalog of the exhibit, *Chtoby dela shli: Rossiisko-amerikanskie èkonomicheskie otnosheniia, 1900–1930 gg./Making Things Work: Russian-American Economic Relations, 1900–1930. An Exhibition Catalog for a Joint Historical Exhibit of Documents and Photographs Organized by the Hoover Institution of War, Revolution, and Peace and the Committee on Archival Affairs of the Russian Federation (Roskomarkhiv)* (Stanford, CA: Hoover Institution Press, 1992).

1.B.4. Personal papers of foreigners resident in Ukraine. Personal papers of foreign visitors or those resident in Ukraine from all walks of life also have to be considered, including their writings (or the documentary materials assembled for such writings) about visits to Ukrainian lands such as Kyiv, Volhynia, or "South Russia." Although such personal papers would clearly be considered private property of their owners, they may be of considerable interest for their Ukrainian relevance. Among the many foreigners resident in Russia (or, specifically, Ukraine) over the past centuries, scholars, journalists, and diplomats have gathered extensive first-hand reports of Ukrainian and, more broadly, Russian/Soviet developments, hand copies of documentary materials, and audiovisual materials. Many have kept diaries or journals, and have written about their experiences in letters, reports, or subsequent essays.

1.B.5. Manuscript and documentary collections of foreigners resident in Ukraine. Visiting foreigners, and even officially accredited diplomats, have been known to take with them many manuscripts and historical documents that were not licensed for export under existing laws. The difficulty of proving that the materials were not purchased or exported under diplomatic immunity may make prosecution impossible. In some instances, the statute of limitations would complicate claims or pretensions.

Foreigners resident in Ukraine have also gathered official or reproduced copies of important state or underground documents and audiovisual materials. More recently, scholars are returning with microfilms and photocopies of archival documents, interviews with public or literary figures, and academics of note; they are bringing surveys and questionnaires, and sometimes even hastily constructed databases compiled during lengthy research visits and joint projects. Graphic materials, engravings, prints, drawings, maps, and photographs require special attention in the description of personal papers and manuscript collections. Film footage, sound, and more recently video recordings are of prime significance.

2. Circumstances of Alienation and Subsequent Migration

In our typology of archival Ucrainica abroad, as a second main complex of categories, it is essential to distinguish the date and circumstances under which documentation was removed from Ukraine. For example, were the materials in question alienated from Ukraine legally, or were they exported without regard to law? Even if the statute of limitations may now make formal legal action impossible, the knowledge of such details may serve to exert moral influence in connection with requests for copies that might otherwise be difficult to obtain. Eight categories are worth considering in this context:

2.A. Outgoing official or private correspondence with organizations and individuals abroad, together with documents or other manuscripts legitimately alienated by gifts or official presentations.

An original charter addressed and sealed by Bohdan Khmel´nyts´kyi or Petro Doroshenko in the seventeenth century, for example, and a document signed by Petliura or any other twentieth-century Ukrainian government or Party leader addressed to a foreign office or individual, wherever it may now be located, would normally be considered to be part of (and hence belonging to) the records of the institutional or personal addressee, not the creator. Although such documents would indeed be relevant—or "pertinent"—to Ukrainian history, there could be no legal claim for restitution of the original. By the same token, original letters of a Ukrainian writer addressed to a foreign friend or colleague could not be subject to claim. It is nevertheless crucially important to identify them as "pertinent" to the Ukrainian cultural heritage, and it would often be highly desirable to add *copies* to the writer's personal papers held in Ukraine.

2.B. Records or collections transferred abroad in connection with, or existing in, neighboring States or former colonies as a result of changing international borders or ecclesiastical administrative districts and/or the forced migration of ethnic populations.

Records of local government of former imperial authorities obviously belong in the territory that was governed, although it is understandable that the governing power may also require copies. Hence, state records *created within* present Ukrainian lands by *local authorities* of former imperial governing agencies based within present Ukrainian lands would legitimately be subject to claim, although the former imperial regime undoubtedly would have considerable interest in the retention of microform copies.

The issue of forced migration of ethnic populations complicates claims. The redrawing of Western Soviet boundaries, especially Polish-Soviet boundaries with the annexation of Western Ukraine, and the forced resettlement of Polish and Ukrainian populations after World War II brought major claims for the repatriation of Polish cultural objects from territories relinquished to the USSR. However, the agreements drafted by the Polish side were never signed, and what repatriation occurred was handled on an ad hoc basis through a bilateral commission with the Ukrainian SSR without any carefully defined principles or signed agreement.[17] Although there were major archival adjustments and revindications in the postwar decades, many cases of displaced and seriously fragmented archives were never resolved.[18]

This is complicated by the necessity of respecting the provenance of official state or semi-state records and their patrimony within the territory of their creation, and, conversely, by the necessity of respecting the cultural heritage of resettled populations. The issue is further complicated by the necessity of preserving the integrity of existing groups of state records and library manuscript collections. Thus, various compromises may be required and many problems remain unresolved. On both sides of the frontier, the immediate resolution of such problems of disposition becomes more difficult because of the frequent prior lack of adequate agreements and precise descriptions compiled for files within the series (*opysy/opisi*) of affected fonds (or parts of fonds involved).

In terms of non-governmental institutional bodies, church records are particularly important in this respect. For example, most of the records of the Greek Catholic diocese of Przemyśl (*Ukr.* Peremyshl) are now held in Poland, although part of the territory of that diocese is now in Ukraine (Przemyśl itself was part of Ukraine according to the 1939–1941 bounda-

---

[17] The original Polish claims are explained from a legal standpoint by Wojciech Kowalski, *Likwidacja skutków wojny w dziedzinie kultury,* 2nd ed. (Warsaw: Instytut Kultury, 1994), esp. pp. 86–90 (the text of documents is found on pp. 177–87); also see the English-language version, *Liquidation of the Effects of World War II in the Area of Culture* (Warsaw: Institute of Culture, 1994), pp. 84–88. For the fate of Polish cultural treasures from Lviv, see the impressive study by Maciej Matwijów, *Walka o lwowskie dobra kultury w latach 1945–1948* (Wrocław: Towarzystwo Przyjaciół Ossolineum, 1996).

[18] See the habilitation dissertation by Krystyna Wróbel-Lipowa, *Rewindykacja archiwaliów polskich z ZSSR w latach 1945–1964* (Lublin: Uniwersytet Marii Curie-Skłodowskiej, 1982).

ries).[19] Clearly, records involving the Ukrainian population of the diocese are involved. Some files are of provenance, and of direct pertinence, to western Ukraine, and some related diocesan files are actually held in Lviv.

Most of the remaining records of the Roman-Catholic archdiocese of Lviv were revindicated to Poland in 1946.[20] Significant parts of the archive were reportedly destroyed after the Soviet annexation of the area in 1939, and some documentation was removed from Lviv at the end of the war under Nazi aegis. Most of the remaining records are now held in Lubaczów, Poland, the seat of the Ecclesiastical Administrator of the archdiocese, although some of the parchments survive in Lviv. That body of records, dating back to the fourteenth century, is of obvious Lviv provenance. However, given the forced migration of the majority of the Polish population and the Soviet suppression of the Roman Catholic Church in western Ukraine, its revindication to Poland was most appropriate.[21] There is no question, however, that on the basis of provenance Ukraine would be entitled to complete microform copies of the documents and all relevant finding aids, although such arrangements were not suggested at the time of the transfer.

Similar problems arise in the case of records of various Roman Catholic monastic orders, such as those of the Dominican Order that were revindicated from Lviv after the war and that are now held in Cracow. In the latter case, however, some early manuscripts from the Pochaïv Monastery that were taken with the Dominican archive from Lviv could probably be subject to restitution, although the history of the religious affiliations of the monastery are complicated. Some of the manuscripts themselves could hardly be considered Dominican or of Dominican provenance, although they had become Dominican property on the grounds that the Dominican friars were responsible for rescuing the materials that might otherwise have been destroyed during the Soviet reconquest of the area.[22]

---

[19]   The older part of the Przemyśl diocesan records are held in the local state archive in Rzeszów. See the brief coverage of this and other Church archives in Poland in the directory by Hieronim Eugeniusz Wyczawski, OFM, *Przygotowanie do studiów w archiwach kościelnych* (n.p.: Wyd-wo "Calvarianum," 1989[1990]).

[20]   Matwijów, *Walka o lwowskie dobra kultury*, pp. 123–24.

[21]   See the annotations to the finding aids prepared in the interwar period for the Roman Catholic Church archives, when they were still in Lviv, as listed in Grimsted, *Archives: Ukraine*, pp. 480–81. More details are given in Chapter 11.

[22]   Although there is no published description of these materials, I had an opportunity in the 1980s to examine some of the finding aids in Cracow, thanks for the Dominican archivist there, Father Mazur. It was my understanding that at least some of them were removed under German auspices at the end of the war, but according to

Library manuscript collections can likewise succumb to political disruption. One of the most blatant examples of an inappropriately executed transfer of the cultural heritage of the resettled Polish population resulted in the ruthless division of the library and manuscript holdings of the Ossoliński National Cultural Institute (Zakład Narodowy im. Ossolińskich)—the most important Polish library in Eastern Europe. The Ossolineum (as it is usually known in English) was abolished after Soviet annexation of Western Ukraine in 1939, and its library holdings absorbed along with others into the Lviv Branch of the Library of the Academy of Sciences of the UkrSSR. Part of the library holdings, along with archival materials of the former Ossolineum and a few other Polish cultural treasures from Lviv, were officially transferred in 1946 and 1947 from Lviv to Wrocław (the newly polonized, formerly German city of Breslau). The transfer of the Polish cultural center was decreed as a "gift to the Polish people," in the wake of the resettlement of the Polish population, following the redrawing of Polish national boundaries following WWII.

Ukrainian national and territorially pertinent claims were put forward locally in Lviv requiring that manuscripts "relating to Western Ukraine and the history of all Ukraine" and also "productions of Ukrainian writers" were to remain in Lviv. While those vague principles based on "territorial" and "ethnic cultural" pertinence were never set forth with professional guidelines, nor agreed upon by the two sides, the division took place hastily without respect for the integrity of collections or integral groups of personal or family papers. Almost half of the manuscript holdings from the former Ossolineum and related institutions remained in Lviv, but with a blatant disregard for the integrity of fonds and collections. In some cases, even numbered volumes of the same manuscript were split between Lviv and Wrocław, to the expected detriment to subsequent scholarship.[23]

The Ossolineum case serves as a prime example of the types of problems that can occur in the realm of library manuscript collections rather than state archives, when political expediency and vague ethnic and territorial principles dictates disrespect of professional cultural and archival traditions. The

---

Matwijów, *Walka o lwowskie dobra kultury,* pp. 123–24, they were transferred in May 1946.

[23] See the thorough account by Matwijów, *Walka o lwowskie dobra kultury*, pp. 71–114, and Matwijów′s survey listing of the Ossolineum manuscripts remaining in Lviv—"Wniosek rewindykacyjny zbiorów Zakładu Narodowego im. Ossolińskich—Rękopisy," in *Wniosek rewindykacyjny*, pp. 36–47. See further details in Chapter 11.

principle of provenance understandably may not always be foremost when library manuscript collections and personal and family collections are involved. However, the attempt to superimpose and apply the elusive principle of "territorial pertinence" or "ethnic national interest" to the extent of splitting up integral volumes of a single manuscript as well as the large collection of which it forms part goes against viable archival and scholarly standards.

A joint Polish-Ukrainian commission is now studying the matter, but passions currently run so high over the issue that the claims and counterclaims will be difficult to resolve within the foreseeable future. If the original manuscript collections themselves are not eventually reintegrated in the manner in which they were created, it will be most important in this and similar cases to exchange quality microforms of the manuscripts and all relevant finding aids (including historical descriptions and card files), together with a dispassionate preparation of professional manuscript descriptions and the identification of the present location of the holdings. Also to be included would be a correlation between present and previous catalog numbers of those holdings located elsewhere. The preliminary microfiche editions of the Ossolineum catalog series in 1989 could provide a starting point, and new digital techniques provide an opportunity to facilitate the task and simplify electronic searching.

In terms of manuscript collections, many Latin and Polish manuscript books, incunabula, and early printed books from the University of Lviv Library were also evacuated to Poland in April 1944. Evacuated under the supervision of Polish specialists from Lviv who themselves were being forcibly encouraged to resettle in Poland, the shipment included medieval Latin illuminated manuscripts from the Abbey of Tyniec (near Cracow) and many important Polish manuscripts. Given the postwar fate and depolonization of Lviv University under Soviet rule and the suppression of the Roman Catholic Church, it is hard to argue today that these manuscripts are a legitimate part of the *Ukrainian* national archival heritage. After the war, the evacuated manuscripts and early imprints were officially claimed by Soviet authorities as having been seized by the Nazis from Lviv during the war, but without knowledge of their evacuation or actual fate.[24] Later, when it was discovered they had been found in Poland, an official claim was filed by Soviet authorities. In the course of diplomatic negotiations, however, the

---

[24]   For example, a claim addressed to American authorities from Soviet occupation authorities in Germany has been found for a long list of early printed books and incunabula that had been seized from Lviv—US NA, RG 260 (OMGUS), Ardelia Hall Collection.

claim was amended to cover only the "non-Polish" materials. Reportedly, some of the manuscripts and early printed books were prepared for return to Lviv, but the Roman Catholic, Polish, and Oriental manuscripts remain in Poland, and Soviet authorities never insisted on restitution, given the Polish, Latin, and Roman Catholic orientation of the texts.[25]

2.C. Official Ukrainian archival materials created in Ukraine and removed from Ukrainian lands by imperial governing authorities.

Over the centuries, many archival materials of Ukrainian provenance have been removed from the country by imperial authorities and are still held in the former imperial capitals. For example, parts of the records of the Zaporozhian Sich, the Crimean Khanate, and the Cossack Hetmanate, which at one time or another were removed to imperial capitals, remain in archives there. Extradition is more difficult in cases when the files have been re-arranged and incorporated into central records of imperial authorities. These and many other archival seizures during the Soviet period have been mentioned earlier.

2.D. Non-official archival materials created in Ukraine and removed by imperial governing authorities.

With the collapse of the Soviet Union, successor States have begun to claim various cultural treasures alienated to the imperial capitals. Attention is also focused on the Soviet tendency for centralized collecting points for various specialized types of archival materials, from geodesic and geological data to archival copies of feature films, which would not normally be considered records of state or public archives in most countries of the world. A similar but less straightforward case is that of academic and scholarly collections brought together in imperial capitals. The example of manuscript books, folklore, and ethnographic materials collected from Ukrainian lands by academic and museum archeographic expeditions from Moscow and Leningrad has already been discussed above.

---

[25]   Regarding the Soviet claims and negotiations over the transfer from Poland, see Matwijów, *Walka o lwowskie dobra kultury*, pp. 156–57. Matwijów has been unable fully to document this matter. See also Matwijów's article, "Ewakuacja zbiorów polskich ze Lwowa w 1944 r.," *Rocznik Lwowski* 1995/1996: 31–46. See citations of earlier descriptions with correlation to present call numbers for those now in Warsaw (Biblioteka Narodowa) in my *Archives: Ukraine*, pp. 574–77.

2.E. Archival materials seized in wartime by enemy authorities or looting by individual soldiers.

Many of the points mentioned above would also be applicable to archival materials and other cultural treasures looted in time of war. Yet, historically, archival materials and other cultural property looted in wartime have often been handled differently. As detailed above, the 1954 UNESCO international convention dealing with the protection of cultural property—including archives—in time of armed conflict, updated the earlier conventions signed at the Hague in 1899 and 1907. The convention itself makes specific mention of manuscripts, books, and archives, but it is limited to provisions for "protection." A protocol signed on the same day has a paragraph ensuring restitution or return after the cessation of hostilities. Since the convention itself is not retroactive and does not require restitution of cultural treasures looted in previous wars, it can be circumvented by countries not bound by the previous 1907 Hague convention; the latter has an unambiguous prohibition against seizing cultural treasures and archives as spoils of war. Generally, in the late twentieth century there has been a reaffirmation by UNESCO and ICA of international agreements outlawing wartime booty in cultural property and, particularly in the realm of archives, affirming the principles that archives, even when subject to past seizures, should be returned or restituted to the country of their creation.

Throughout the centuries, wars on Ukrainian soil have been the occasion for the loss, destruction, and seizure of archives, but the details have yet to be set forth with sufficient documentation. The Second World War and its aftermath was more costly in archival displacements than any previous war in history, as I will show in Part II of this book. Documentation of the displacements is still under way. There is also a new awareness in Ukraine of the extent to which displaced cultural treasures from Ukraine that were restituted by the Western Allies have not necessarily been returned to Ukraine. As far as can be determined in the archival sphere, however, almost all of the archival materials that were evacuated by the Nazis were recovered and returned to Ukraine.[26]

---

[26]   See more details in Chapters 5 and 6. See also my article, "The Fate of Ukrainian Cultural Treasures during World War II: The Plunder of Archives, Libraries, and Museums under the Third Reich," *Jahrbücher für Geschichte Osteuropas* 39(1) 1991: 53–80. See also the Ukrainian booklet version (which has appended documents), written with the collaboration of Hennadii Boriak, *Dolia skarbiv ukraïns'koï kul'tury pid chas Druhoï svitovoï viiny: Vynyshchennia arkhiviv, bibliotek, muzeïv* (Kyiv: Arkheohrafichna komisiia AN URSR, 1991; 2nd ed., Lviv, 1992).

2.F. Materials legitimately removed as personal or corporate property, such as business records or personal papers of Ukrainian émigrés or their families.

Laws in different countries at different times may govern the right of removal, and the nationalization of archives under the Soviet regime complicates claims. Records of officially registered "joint ventures" may be more complicated in terms of export possibilities. Normally, records of private firms and individuals under the laws of most Western countries are not subject to state control. In Russia and Ukraine, however, the long period of Soviet rule has left a tradition of strong state control over the cultural heritage of both nations.

The new Russian archival law extends state archival control and prohibition of export to private papers of cultural or political leaders deemed belonging to the "non-State part" of the Archival Fond of the Russian Federation. Ukrainian law, on the other hand, is not yet clear in regard to the right to pretensions or claims on the papers of important Ukrainian émigré political leaders or cultural figures that were taken abroad in political or cultural emigration. Law in most foreign countries would consider such alienated materials protected as private property, especially if the émigré or his heirs were already citizens of a foreign country. The extent of the legal "gray area" of such claims, increased by time (and the legally defined statute of limitations in many countries) will mean that claims for repatriation in original and copy will largely rest on goodwill and ad hoc arrangements in individual cases.

2.G. Archives or other manuscript cultural treasures deliberately alienated by commercial sale abroad by the state, undercover agents, or private individuals.

Another complicating factor in establishing and arbitrating claims for cultural treasures is that some of the items sought in the West or claimed by Soviet authorities in the postwar restitution process were actually sold abroad during the interwar period. Information has long been available in the West about the extensive sale of cultural treasures in the 1920s and 1930s—including rare manuscript books—by the Soviet regime or its undercover agents to help support industrialization and the creation of a war machine. Documentation of sales from Russian holdings has been impressive, particularly with regard to imperial collections from Moscow and St. Petersburg.[27]

In some cases, Ukrainian materials were involved; they were rarely described as such, however. It is well known, for example, that ancient gold artifacts from Ukrainian lands were seized in the 1920s and taken to Moscow and Leningrad; some were sold abroad by Soviet authorities. Other treasures were melted down for gold or silver, including elaborate silver bindings from religious manuscripts. More research and precise retrospective descriptive efforts are necessary to identify the Ukrainian component, and the extent to which Ukrainian archival materials or manuscript books were involved.

With democratization and abandonment of Communist Party myths, archives are being opened. This will aid the location of such alienated manuscripts and follow the paths of other archival treasures abroad. The most sensational recent revelations published in Russia to date have been based largely on Western publications.[28] But some new Russian research is getting under way on this important subject, including the issue of sales from the Hermitage.[29]

---

[27]   See the extensive study on the sale of art by Robert C. Williams, *Russian Art and American Money, 1900–1940* (Cambridge, MA: Harvard University Press, 1980); and P. N. Savitskii, *Razrushaiushchie svoiu rodinu (snos pamiatnikov iskusstva i rasprodazha muzeev SSSR)* (Berlin: Izd. Evraziitsev, 1936). Extensive documentation and a recent bibliography about the sale of books as well as art is provided in the introduction by Robert H. Davis, Jr. and Edward Kasinec, in *Dark Mirror: Romanov and Imperial Palace Library Materials in the Holdings of the New York Public Library: A Checklist and Agenda for Research*, comp. Robert H. Davis, Jr. (New York: Norman Ross Publishing, 1999). See also the earlier articles by Germaine [Zhermena] Pavlova, "The Fate of the Russian Imperial Libraries," *Bulletin of Research in the Humanities* 87(4) 1986–1987: 358–403, esp. 370–403, and Robert H. Davis, Jr. and Edward Kasinec, "Witness to the Crime: Two Little-Known Photographic Sources Relating to the Sale and Destruction of Antiquities in Soviet Russia during the 1920s," *Journal of the History of Collections* 3(1) 1991: 53–59.

[28]   For example, A. Mosiakin, "Prodazha," *Ogonek* 6 (4–11 February 1989): 18–22; 7 (11–18 February 1989): 16–21; 8 (4–11 March 1989): 26–29. The Mosiakin series draws heavily on the Williams study cited above.

[29]   The short, popular book by Iurii N. Zhukov, *Operatsiia Ėrmitazh: Opyt istoriko-arkhivnogo rassledovaniia* (Moscow: Moskvitianin, 1993), is also significantly based on the Williams study; although the author has done some additional archival research predominantly in foreign trade records in RGAE (earlier TsGANKh) and GA RF (previously TsGA RSFSR), he has not used the archives of the Hermitage itself. A scholarly analysis by Elena P. Borisova, "Vlast' i istoriko-kul'turnoe nasledie natsii: Organizatsionno-pravovoe oformlenie èksporta muzeinykh tsennostei v kontse

Research on the subject has been starting in Ukrainian archives. For example, lists were recently uncovered in Kyiv of 2,669 silver and other valuable religious artifacts appropriated from Ukrainian churches during the famine of 1922, most of which were sold as precious metal.[30] Documentation has also come to light regarding the sale of cultural valuables from the Museum of Art of the Ukrainian Academy of Sciences (Muzei mystets'tva VUAN). These treasures, sold over the protest of museum specialists in Kyiv, included twenty Western masterworks in 1928, such as a 1512 Gobelin tapestry sold for 150,000 rubles that was featured in the *Illustrated London News* in 1930 as "one of the finest Gothic tapestries at present in England,"[31] followed by forty works of Western art in 1930 and eight in 1931.[32] Thus far, however, no information has appeared regarding manuscript materials of Ukrainian provenance among the materials sold abroad.

More recently, in the context of the current economic crisis, there have been alarming tales of a new wave of black-market sales of Ukrainian library and museum treasures abroad, but full documentation of such transactions is not available. Obviously, it is tremendously important for the sake of preserving the Ukrainian archival heritage to stop further outflow and profiteering at the expense of culture. Should that deny an artist the right to sell his works abroad? Some still argue that the artist would not have such a right if his productions were financed by state subsidy. But what about

---

1920–30-x godakh," in *Rossiiskaia gosudarstvennost': Opyt i perspektivy izucheniia: Materialy mezhvuzovskoi nauchnoi konferentsii, 1–3 iiunia 1995 g. Chteniia pamiati professora T. P. Korzhikhinoi* (Moscow: IAI RGGU, 1995), pp. 95–99, details the institutional context created for the export of cultural treasures at the end of the 1920s and early 1930s.

[30]   See, for example, DAKO, R-2412/2/268 (*sprava* 269 is a carbon copy), "Opis' muzeinykh predmetov, vydelennykh iz chisla tserkovnykh tsennostei Ukrainy," lists church artifacts collected from throughout Eastern Ukraine.

[31]   DAKO, R-2412/2/195, including a certified copy of secret documents from the VUAN Museum of Art (fols. 12–13). See the *Illustrated London News* 19 August 1930: 4. Copies of documents regarding paintings sold for export from the same museum, despite numerous staff objections, are to be found in the same file and the adjacent file no. 194. These sales of Western art abroad from the Museum of Art (VUAN) are the same ones that were revealed in an undocumented article by Konstantin Akinsha, "Bol' otechestva—Pechal'naia istoriia 'Adama i Evy,'" *Ogonek* 51 (17–24 December 1988): 32–33. Although Akinsha did not identify his sources, he explained to me that his article was based on documents found in Kyiv museum files; he did not find other documents revealing the sale of art of Ukrainian provenance.

[32]   DAKO, R-2412/2/194.

struggling dissident artists, without work or subsidy, or those today no longer financed by the cultural subsidies that existed under Soviet rule?

In most countries and in most cases, there would be no legal grounds for seeking the return of cultural treasures that were legally sold and repurchased without compensation to present owners. More questions will arise, however, if there is proof that the sales were made illegally for personal profit or gain. Whatever the circumstances of the sale, it is important to identify and document the alienated objects as well as the facts of their migration and sale.

2.H. Manuscripts and archival materials illegally alienated from Ukraine by theft or unauthorized export.

The problem of prosecuting theft and illegal traffic in cultural property is exceedingly difficult on an international level. As mentioned above, the extensive traffic in stolen and illegally exported cultural property led UNESCO to enact a convention in 1970 dealing with the problem, which is now supplemented by the UNIDROIT convention. However, those conventions are not applicable retroactively and are effective only in cases where the countries involved have ratified them. Hence, they cannot be directly applied to cases involving archival Ucrainica abroad, most of which was alienated before 1970. The problem of illegal export was mentioned above in regard to manuscripts collected by visiting foreigners and diplomats and is also pertinent below in the consideration of émigré collections abroad.

Auction galleries in many countries are usually required to exhibit items offered for sale in advance, to provide an opportunity for legitimate claims regarding potentially stolen property. Subsequently, the law in many countries assures legal ownership to those who purchase such items in good faith, despite the fact that they may have at one time been contraband. Furthermore, relevant statutes of limitations would apply in cases of acquisition long ago. Since many such alienated treasures were subsequently legally purchased abroad and, with new legal owners, have since risen tremendously in value, it is doubtful that the funds required for their repurchase and return to their homeland could be a high priority in many cases. Most important today is their precise identification in terms of origin, which might encourage present private owners to make testamentary bequests or tax-deductible donations to their original home.

3. *Present Location and Arrangement of Archival Ucrainica Abroad*

The present location of archival Ucrainica and its arrangement within its current archival context are important factors in determining the possibilities for return or copies of the materials involved. Additional notation is needed of all prior locations, legal owners, and dates of transfer. The actual repository where the materials are presently located, however, is often much less important than the physical arrangement of the materials involved.

The most important considerations in connection with the present arrangement are as follows: the extent to which the documents can still be identified as an integral group of records; the extent to which the documents have been removed from the context of their creating body of records; and, in the case of documents that have been removed from their original body of records, the extent and time of which they may have been incorporated into other fonds or into individual private papers, or that they have become part of artificially assembled collections.

A major issue bearing on prospective restitution efforts is the case of what Western archivists would call "incorporated records," whereby such documents may be considered differently than they would be if they still constituted an integral fond or group of institutional records. Here, the internationally recognized archival principle of respect for the integrity of fonds may sometimes be at odds with displaced fragments that have become incorporated into integral groups of foreign archival records. Given the strong need for respect for the integrity of fonds as noted above in the ICA "Professional Advice" and "Position Paper," documents or files abroad from, or pertaining to, Ukraine that have become incorporated into integral groups of foreign archival records would normally not be subject to claim except in copy. Such was the case with the Rosenberg documents that had been incorporated into Nuremberg Trial records mentioned above (p. 157n15), or other documents that have been presented as official exhibits in court cases and therefore, by law, must remain part of the court records. Similarly, state documents, or copies of state documents, that have been incorporated into private papers would not normally be subject to retroactive claim by state archives as part of state records. In cases of incorporated records or manuscripts, more thorough documentation of their provenance, significance, and the circumstances of their alienation abroad will be required in order to justify any pretensions for their transfer or restitution.

Similar problems apply to documents that have been incorporated into or now form part of a famous and long-established manuscript collection. Because international norms usually also respect the long-established collections, it is also important to note the earlier physical location and past arrangement of the materials in question, and the circumstances under which they have been "incorporated" into other fonds or collections.

An intermediary situation, but still with the potential for conflict, may be relevant in many instances, whereby individual manuscripts, autographs, earlier charters, or groups of documents may have been integrated into larger institutional holdings in a library, institute, or historical society without regard to their provenance. Such documents may have been rescued or purchased in good faith from those who conveyed them abroad or from intermediary dealers. These documents might thereby be considered part of the collection of that repository and given a permanent archival home. Yet when their displaced location has been discovered, the original repository may still want to submit a claim. Their status as part of a new artificial collection may not have the same moral or legal weight as documents that have been newly incorporated into official state records. Yet given the UNESCO respect for collections, the fact of their legal purchase, and the lapse of time usually involved, it would be difficult to substantiate claims in most countries, despite the fact of what may have been their illegal or inappropriate removal from their original group of records or their illegal or quasi-legal transfer at some point of their migration. The more valuable the document in question, the more difficult equitable resolution of claims becomes. In many such cases, it will only be goodwill and arbitration, rather than legal standards or principles, that can find a satisfactory solution.

4. *Agreements or Other Legal Factors Affecting Ownership*

In considering pretensions for return, restitution, or copies, it is also crucial to examine carefully any specific agreements or other relevant legal factors that could affect the present status and ownership of the documents in question, such as pretensions from previous owners. In the case of gift or bequest, there may be letters of deposition or transfer. In the case of purchase, there may be a certificate of origin or a bill or contract of sale. There may have been a prior purchase from an auction house or dealer by the collector who later bequeathed the collection. In some cases, specific groups of documents may be subject to prior bilateral or international agreements. More important than the character of the repository or institution (state, semi-official, or private) where archival Ucrainica may reside today is the reference to their current archival arrangement (as discussed above) and their status of "legal proprietorship." The legal status of the documents involved and the application of international agreements and historical precedents may vary with such distinctions.

Many of the problems in this discussion arise from the fact that at present there are no adequate internationally agreed-upon conventions, agreements, or detailed accepted procedures or formulae for archival restitution (or return, if we recognize the UNESCO distinctions in the use of these two terms). Although there have been general ICA recommendations, there also are no commonly recognized rights to copies of archival materials from, or relating to, different countries now located abroad. As shown in Chapter 3, such matters have not been adequately covered by earlier UNESCO and ICA discussions, resolutions, or agreements.

Two other major problems involve the lack of recognition of private property and the extent of nationalization under the Soviet Union, both of which carry over into the post-Soviet Ukrainian republic. Even today, many Ukrainian archivists lack sensitivity to the status of private archives abroad, and to the fact that, in many countries, national archives are legally founded to deal only with records created by official government bodies. The many decades of the Soviet system of centralized state command administration and disrespect for private rights may, in some cases, lead to a lack of respect for private property abroad: few Western countries provide for such a broad government-sponsored archival program as was known in the Soviet Union and continues with the new Russian—and Ukrainian—archival laws today. Many Ukrainian-related materials still remain in private hands and legally constitute private property in the countries where they are held, not being subject to any type of governmental archival control.

*   *

*

Ukrainian archivists and other intellectuals today understandably place a high priority on the identification, location, and, if possible, retrieval of displaced or "lost" Ukrainian culture abroad. Nevertheless, the long-standing mutual secrecy and conspiratorial suspicion between Soviet authorities and Ukrainian and other émigré communities abroad have grossly impeded the flow of information in both directions. During the Cold War decades, the insular, chauvinist possessiveness with which many Soviet archival authorities tended to view all Ukrainian/Soviet-related archival materials abroad as their just patrimony—regardless of the circumstances of their creation, alienation from the homeland, or the wishes of their legal owners—aroused suspicions and negative reactions on the part of Ukrainian émigré communities abroad. In turn, this impeded the possibility of equitable arrangements for access and photocopies for a long time. In some instances, Ukrainian émigré groups even feared publishing descriptions of the materials they held or making information about them known in public catalogs for fear that Soviet authorities would find and attempt to hijack (i.e., seize or "recapture") the materials. They had been known to do so in the post-World War II decade. The Soviet seizures of the Russian Historical Archive (RZIA) and the Ukrainian Historical Cabinet (UIK) in Prague in 1945, the Petliura materials in Cracow and Vienna, and other émigré collections have established a Cold War context in the archival world that will be hard to overcome in the minds of older émigrés abroad.

The categories set forth above require further clarification and refinement, but they should serve as a basis for subsequent discussion. It has been clear from the above discussion that "provenance" and the "integrity of fonds" usually weigh heavier than "functional pertinence" and/or "territorial pertinence"; nonetheless, clarification is required with typological distinctions in individual cases. Such terms require precise definition and amplification in regard to the circumstances of migration and understanding the current and prior archival arrangement. Greater detail is also needed for descriptive components that denote national, ethnic, linguistic, or religious affiliation.

As we have seen, in some cases, neither previous ownership nor the place of preservation can be the sole determining factor in the resolution of dispositional claims. Special factors often have to be examined on a *de facto* basis in individual cases. Such issues deserve clarification, and, where possible, codification and incorporation into detailed working recommendations such as in the international legal framework suggested above as a potential role for ICA. Guidelines already established by the UNESCO committee may help, but archival materials, as should be clear from the analysis above cannot simply be handled as "cultural property." What is most important today is a new post-Soviet willingness to analyze and resolve such issues from a multi-national perspective, with a new international sensitivity to the problems involved in disputed claims, and a willingness to see appropriate resolution on a professional archival level in the context of international law and international archival practice.

Now that we have tried to examine the international legal context of displaced archives and possible typological distinctions regarding the nature and disposition of the materials involved that might lead to claims or restitution, we turn to the ruthless world of war and its Cold War aftermath, where "civilized nations" paid little heed to law or to recognized international principles in the archival realm.

Part II

Displaced Archives During World War II
and Its Aftermath

CHAPTER 5

Measuring Losses in the World War II Context: Evacuation, Destruction, Plunder, and Retrieval

While the Second World War was at its height in November 1942, the Embassy of the USSR in Washington, DC, issued an *Information Bulletin* condemning the Nazi cultural atrocities and looting that were taking place on the Eastern Front. In conclusion, it reminded the world:

> Article 56 of the Hague Convention, on the Laws and Usage of Land Warfare, of October 18, 1907, to which Germany is a party, forbids the seizure, damaging and destruction of property of educational and art institutions, as well as of historic monuments, and articles of scientific and artistic value belonging to individuals and societies as well as to the State. But the Hitlerite clique in criminal manner tramples upon the rules and laws of warfare universally accepted by all civilized nations.[1]

There is no question but that the Nazi regime wrought the most horrific cultural devastation to the European Continent in history. Lynn Nicholas' prize-winning book, *The Rape of Europa* provides a vivid picture of Nazi brutality in the sphere of art sales and seizures, suggesting many of the problems involved, although it inadequately covers the Eastern Front.[2] The scholarly analysis by Jonathan Petropolous, *Art as Politics in the Third Reich: The Collecting Policies of the Nazi Elite*, focuses attention on the underlying Nazi cultural policies, but again does not drawn on newly opened sources in the East.[3] While both these notable studies reveal the brutal policies practiced by the Nazi invaders and help put Eastern developments in a European perspective, neither of them deal with the problems of calculating cultural losses, reparations, postwar Soviet cultural seizures, and cultural restitution in the Soviet Union and its successor States.

[1]   Embassy of the USSR, *Information Bulletin* 138 (19 November 1942): 6.

[2]   Lynn H. Nicholas, *The Rape of Europa: The Fate of Europe's Treasures in the Third Reich and the Second World War* (New York: Alfred A. Knopf, 1994).

[3]   Jonathan Petropolous, *Art as Politics in the Third Reich: The Collecting Policies of the Nazi Elite* (Chapel Hill: University of North Carolina Press, 1996).

The fiftieth anniversary of the end of World War II and the defeat of Nazi Germany has come and passed, and a new century is upon us, but civilized nations are still agonizing over the cultural treasures ravaged and looted in the course of that war and its aftermath, many of which still remain displaced. At the beginning of the anniversary year, Chairman of the National Commission for the Return of Cultural Treasures to Ukraine Professor Oleksandr Fedoruk, addressing an international forum on the "Spoils of War" at the Bard College Center for the Visual Arts in New York City, noted that "World War II is not over because plundered cultural treasures have not yet been returned to their legitimate owners."[4] Professor Wolfgang Eichwede, Director of the Center for East European Research at the University of Bremen, speaking at the same conference, highlighted the fact that "Two-thirds of all cultural losses suffered by the former Soviet Union are losses of Ukraine." But today, in contrast to the bitter Russian-German controversies over the spoils of war, he noted, "the Ukrainians are anxious to research their losses, not in a spirit of confrontation, but in one of cooperation with the Germans."[5] Four years later, Professor Fedoruk is repeating those same statistics and that same attitude in Kyiv, realizing that "the problems of restitution are among the most difficult [facing Ukraine], from legal, political and diplomatic relations." While at the same time he emphasizes that there should be "No Statute of Limitations for the Return of the National Legacy."[6]

The reconstitution of the national archival heritage of Ukraine immediately involves consideration of the losses and displacements during World War II. International legal precedents relating to the succession of States and those relating to wartime restitution, as we have already seen, are often intertwined. And on the more immediate practical level, international restitution issues for Russia and Ukraine growing out of archival displacements during World War II and its aftermath greatly complicate the resolution of archival problems relating to the succession of States in a post-Soviet environment.

---

[4]   Oleksandr (Alexander) Fedoruk, "Ukraine: The Lost Cultural Treasures and the Problem of their Return," in the proceedings of the Bard symposium, *The Spoils of War: WWII and Aftermath*, p. 72.

[5]   Wolfgang Eichwede, "Models of Restitution (Germany, Russia, Ukraine)," in *The Spoils of War: WWII and Aftermath*, p. 219.

[6]   Oleksandr [Alexander] Fedoruk, "Net sroka davnosti vozvrashcheniiu natsional'nogo naslediia," *Moskovskii komsomolets v Ukraine* 1–8 July 1999: 14.

Reinterpreting Destruction and Displacements:
The Historiographic Context

Issues of archival losses, displacements, plunder, and restitution in connection with World War II have been inadequately studied in an East European context until recently, and those studies that have appeared remain incomplete. For example, the most thorough study to date of Soviet archives during the war, prepared in the 1960s by the Russian historian-archivist Vsevolod V. Tsaplin, could never be published during the Soviet regime.[7] Two chapters of that earlier study relating to archival retrieval after the war appeared in print recently, but none of Tsaplin's findings regarding archival evacuation and intentional Soviet destruction has yet been published.[8]

The Author's Analysis and Russian Criticism. When archives started to open in Ukraine and Russia during the period of glasnost in the late 1980s, more extensive research could be started on issues of cultural plunder during and after the war. An initial report on the subject that I presented at the First International Conference on Ukrainian Studies in Kyiv in August 1990 aroused tremendous interest.[9] That was the first revelation of the wealth of documentation available about wartime cultural plunder in major groups of Nazi records long held secret in Kyiv that could supplement those long available in the West. At the same time it was possible to utilize the recently opened records of the Soviet Archival Administration (Glavarkhiv/GAU) and the Extraordinary Commission on Occupation Atrocities (ChGK) in both Moscow and Kyiv (see more below). Research continued, while my preliminary findings with emphasis on Ukraine, presented in a major article in Germany in 1991 and a Ukrainian-language monograph with documents

---

[7]   Vsevolod V. Tsaplin, "Arkhivy, voina i okkupatsiia (1941–1945 gody)" (Moscow, 1968; typescript with hand corrections by the author, signed and dated 20 January 1969). Tsaplin kindly provided me with a copy of his typescript in 1991; it has since been deposited with his personal papers in RGAE, 777/1/11. At the time his study was prepared, Tsaplin did not have access to archives outside the USSR, nor could he use many important Nazi records in Moscow and Kyiv, which are now open for research.

[8]   See Vsevolod V. Tsaplin, "O rozyske dokumentov, pokhishchennykh v gody voiny iz arkhivokhranilishch SSSR," *Otechestvennye arkhivy* 1997 (5): 7–25; and (6): 12–28.

[9]   An initial report on this subject was presented to an overflowing conference session of the First Congress of the International Association of Ukrainian Studies by the present author in association with Hennadii Boriak (Kyiv, 30 August 1990).

appended in Lviv, have already revealed many new data and interpretations, as well as sample newly available documents.[10]

While many Ukrainian scholars sought to follow our lead in further analysis of the newly opened sources, some of the data presented were severely criticized in the Russian press, most especially by Aleksandr M. Mazuritskii who now is Vice-Rector of the University for Cultural Studies in the Moscow suburb of Khimki and principal library representative on the Commission for Restitution of the Russian Federation.[11] Mazuritskii's criticism was not based on additional data or contrary archival revelations, but grew out of disagreements with the point of view and new approaches presented, especially regarding intentional Soviet archival and library destruction, that took issue with many traditional Soviet conceptions. Obviously, it is very difficult for Russians trained in the Soviet period and Soviet historiographic views about what many continue to call the "Great Patriotic War" to understand Western viewpoints on the issue of postwar restitution and other policies during the war.

Now that many more—although, regrettably, still not all—of the relevant archives are open, including the records of Nazi occupation authorities in the USSR and other Soviet-captured Nazi records held in Russia and Ukraine, more detailed study is under way of the seizure of archives on the Eastern Front by various Nazi agencies and the postwar seizure of archives abroad by

---

[10]   See my "The Fate of Ukrainian Cultural Treasures during World War II: The Plunder of Archives, Libraries, and Museums under the Third Reich," *Jahrbücher für Geschichte Osteuropas* 39(1) 1991: 53–80; Ukrainian version (with Hennadii Boriak): *Dolia skarbiv ukraïns'koï kul'tury pid chas Druhoï svitovoï viiny: Vynyshchennia arkhiviv, bibliotek, muzeïv* (Kyiv: Arkheohrafichna komisiia AN URSR), 1991; 2nd ed. Lviv, 1992), which cites much of the earlier literature on the subject. The Ukrainian monograph version includes a series of important facsimile documents.

[11]   Aleksandr M. Mazuritskii, "Restitutsiia knizhnykh sobranii," *Knizhnoe obozrenie* 1993 (3): 54–56; the entire article is a critique of a partial Russian résumé of my article, "The Fate of Ukrainian Cultural Treasures." At a conference in Chernihiv in 1994, Mazuritskii indicated that he was not aware of the Ukrainian version, prepared in collaboration with Hennadii Boriak, that included many supporting documents. He also admitted that he reads neither English nor German. While some of his comments simply represent points taken out of context, he had not seen my supporting documentation for other points—or claims that it was not available to him. As a result of this type of criticism, some of which Mazuritskii repeated during my presentation at a conference at the Russian National Library in St. Petersburg in October 1998, I have made efforts below to more clearly document the findings and conclusions with which Mazuritskii took issue.

the victorious Red Army.[12] A survey of Soviet-wide displaced archives and postwar restitution developments appeared in 1995 and has subsequently been revised several times.[13] Some additional findings can be presented here.

The Bremen Project. In the meantime, during the 1990s, a team of researchers from the Center for East European Research (Forschungsstelle Osteuropa) of the University of Bremen, directed by Wolfgang Eichwede, has been gathering documentation on Nazi cultural plunder from Soviet lands and postwar restitution by the Western Allies, largely to counter some of falsified claims that have dominated the historical and political "Cold War" presentation of these subjects during the Soviet period. Copies of documentation from European (including former Soviet) and U.S. archives were assembled and made available to researchers in Bremen. For a number of years the project was generously supported by the Bremen Senate as a compensatory goodwill gesture towards Russia in the hope of retrieval and restitution of the Bremen Kunsthalle treasures that had been removed from the castle where they were stored for safety and taken to the USSR after the war as part of the Soviet Army's trophy loot.

Several reports on the archival research undertaken by the German specialists in the United States, Germany, Russia, and Ukraine were presented at a symposium in Bremen in late 1994. Although most of the emphasis at the Bremen symposium was on art, some papers also touched on other archival sources for the cultural displacements, and clues regarding other displaced cultural treasures, some of which ended up in the Soviet Union. Of importance in this respect were contributions by representatives of Belgium, France, Hungary, Germany, Luxembourg, Poland, and Ukraine.[14]

---

[12] Regarding archives, see Grimsted, "Archival Rossica/Sovietica Abroad: Provenance or Pertinence, Bibliographic and Descriptive Needs," *Cahiers du Monde russe et soviétique* 34(3) 1993, esp. pp. 449–52, and 463–65.

[13] These surveys update the 1991 article. See my "Displaced Archives and Restitution Problems on the Eastern Front in the Aftermath of the Second World War," *Contemporary European History* 6(1) 1997: 27–74.

[14] See the published symposium proceedings: *Cultural Treasures Moved Because of the War—A Cultural Legacy of the Second World War. Documentation and Research on Losses: Documentation of the International Meeting in Bremen (30.11.–2.12.1994)*, ed. Dieter Opper and Doris Lemmermeier (Bremen, 1995; Koordinierungsstelle der Länder für die Rückführung von Kulturgütern beim Senator für Bildung, Wissenschaft, Kunst und Sport). See especially the reports prepared by Andreas Grenzer, "Research Project 'Fate of the Treasures of Art Removed from the Soviet Union during World War II'" (pp. 124–32), and "Report on the Archive

In 1996, the project produced a CD-ROM reconstruction of the property cards describing half a million plundered cultural treasures from Soviet territories that were returned to the USSR from American restitution centers in Germany after the war. (See further details in Chapter 6.)

A 1997 monograph on the plunder by the Nazi Foreign Ministry's so-called Künsberg Commandos (Sonderkommando Künsberg) by one of the Bremen group, Ulrike Hartung, provides considerable documentation on some of the most brutal Nazi trophy hunters in the early years of the war on the Eastern Front.[15] At the same time, Anja Heuss prepared a separate article with some additional details on the Künsberg Commandos.[16] Among their many exploits, they were the group0 responsible for the removal of the Amber Chamber and other treasures, including 27,200 library books from the imperial palaces in suburban Leningrad. Both authors, as we will see below, document the plunder of libraries and archives in Ukraine by the Künsberg Commandos.

An article that same year by two other members of the Bremen group describes and documents cultural plunder by other Nazi agencies, many of whom were active in Ukraine.[17] More recently, an impressive volume of collected articles resulting from the work of the Bremen group includes

---

Situation in Russia as It Relates to Researching the Losses of Cultural Property" (pp. 142–45), and Anja Heuss, "Archives in the Federal Republic of Germany on Art Theft—An Overall View" (pp. 135–41). French reports were presented by Marie Hamon (pp. 43–63—regarding the French archives on the subject that are still closed, see especially pp. 60–62) and Philippe Sprang (pp. 150–51).

[15] Ulrike Hartung, *Raubzüge in der Sowjetunion: Das Sonderkommando Künsberg 1941–1943* (Bremen: Edition Temmen, 1997). Hartung cites many of the same folders from the Künsberg records of which I have copies that were gathered by my research assistant.

[16] Anja Heuss, "Die 'Beuteorganisation' des Auswärtigen Amtes: Das Sonderkommando Künsberg und der Kulturgutraub in der Sowjetunion," *Vierteljahrshefte für Zeitgeschichte* 45(4) October 1997: 535–56. Heuss also cites many of the same folders from the Künsberg records noted by Hartung and which I have used. Heuss is presently also preparing a dissertation on the subject.

[17] Gabriele Freitag and Andreas Grenzer, "Der deutsche Umgang mit sowjetischem Kulturgut während des Zweiten Weltkrieges: Ein Aspekt nationalsozialistischer Besatzungspolitik," *Jahrbücher für Geschichte Osteuropas* 45(2) 1997: 223–72. See also the Freitag and Grenzer article included in *"Betr: Sicherstellung,"* pp. 20–66. The same authors provide an overview of some of the evacuation efforts in their article "Die Evakuierung von sowjetischen Kulturgütern im Zweiten Weltkrieg," *Osteuropa* 47(1) 1996: 922–31.

overviews of the Nazi looting operations from the USSR, the U.S. restitution program, including returns to the USSR, and some limited information about the fate of cultural treasures returned to the USSR.[18] The emphasis again is on art, but the extensive bibliographies and survey articles included bring together extensive research on the plunder and restitution of cultural treasures on the Eastern Front. One of the editors, Ulrike Hartung, has provided a brief survey of Nazi library plunder on the Eastern front as part of a new German anthology on displaced books.[19]

Thanks to the tremendous body of new documentation available, we now realize the extent to which many of the Soviet claims regarding massive losses and transfers of archival materials from Soviet lands as a result of the war were exaggerated and must be reinterpreted. Much more research is still needed in the area. The legacy of incomplete or inaccurate Soviet-style reports, propaganda excesses regarding the war, and otherwise closed sources still strongly affect present-day attitudes towards the patterns of wartime cultural plunder and restitution politics.

Soviet Losses and Destruction Reconsidered

One important component in the "revisionist" interpretation of wartime archival losses that needs to be taken into account is the Soviet evacuation program and the related extensive and intentional Soviet destruction of sensitive files from the secret divisions of many archives that they could not evacuate to the East during the summer of 1941 in order to prevent them from falling into enemy hands. This matter is related to the larger issue of postwar Soviet statistics and reports on wartime losses and destruction. In general, it is a very painful and sensitive subject for those who grew up within the shackles of Soviet historiography of the war, even in the post-Soviet era, but it is one that has received too little attention. This issue is of crucial importance for historians today, because it explains major gaps in records for many Soviet-period records.

---

[18] *"Betr: Sicherstellung."* The bibliography there shows the extent of research in archives in Russia and Ukraine as well as Germany and the United States.

[19] Ulrike Hartung, "Der deutsche Umgang mit sowjetischen Archiven und Bibliotheken im Zweiten Weltkrieg," in *Displaced Books: Bücherrückgabe,* pp. 42–51. The 1999 edition of this compendium includes several other articles on library and book plunder.

ChGK Wartime Loss and Destruction Statistics. In November 1942, an official commission was established for reporting war crimes, damage, and losses—the Extraordinary State Commission for the Establishment and Investigation of Crimes of the German-Fascist Aggressors and Their Accomplices and Appraisal of the Losses Incurred by Citizens, Collective Farms, Social Organizations, State Enterprises and Institutions of the USSR (ChGK). The creation of the commission was typical of the centralized command system under which the Stalinist regime operated. Its very name reveals something of the Soviet propagandistic framework within which its official reports were made. The reams of ChGK records are now open for research in Moscow, as are the earlier top secret reports about Soviet intentional archival destruction in 1941. More preliminary ChGK files are also open for research in Kyiv. Although these latter files provide considerable documentation, many of their conclusions and statistics cannot be taken at face value.

Moscow specialists from the Russian Ministry of Culture, who are trying to establish a database of wartime cultural loses, have reported some of the difficulties they have encountered with the ChGK records. Among other problems, the ChGK made the methodological mistake of "grouping information about losses under one title 'Destroyed, Damaged, Lost, and Removed'," which does not make it possible to distinguish between those categories. This serious deficiency in the ChGK statistics has now been openly admitted by Russian specialists in the Ministry of Culture who are working on restitution problems.[20] That systematic error in reporting now makes it impossible to compile discrete lists of items documented as missing and to distinguish within those labeled "removed," items not yet returned, as is still necessary for searching half a century later. Nor is it possible to adjust the totals when specific treasures earlier reported as "lost" or "removed" have later been found.

In Ukraine, for example, according to the official ChGK report about Nazi destruction and confiscation in Kyiv that appeared in *Pravda* on 1 April 1944:

> The German Fascist invaders…destroyed museums and took to
> Germany all of the exhibition materials they contained. German
> occupying forces stole over four million books from book depos-

---

[20]   While I have earlier discussed various problems of these records with specialists in Ministry of Culture, now a published complaint to this effect appears in the report by Nikolai Nikandrov, "Russia," in *Spoils of War: International Newsletter* 6 (February 1999): 50–52 (the quote is from p. 51). Also involved in my discussions was Valerii D. Kulishov, who formerly headed the restitution office in the Ministry.

its in Kyiv libraries. From only a single library of the Library of
the Academy of Sciences the Hitlerites took to Germany more
than 320,000 various valuable and unique books, periodicals, and
manuscripts...[21]

The report blames the "Fascist barbarians" for "the destruction and plunder of
the Kyiv Monastery of the Caves [Kyievo-Pechers'ka Lavra] between
October and December of 1941, including the dynamiting of the Assumption
[Uspens'kyi] Cathedral on 3 November and the plunder of that and adjacent
buildings after the destruction." Furthermore, "the Germans took away the
most valuable exhibits from the Historical Museum in the Lavra, including
the entire armory collection of approximately 4,000 items."[22]

The reliability of the *Pravda* article is cast in serious doubt, not only by
its propagandistic tone, but by the many counter reports circulating in Kyiv to
the effect that it was Soviet rather than German agents who were responsible
for many acts of destruction, particularly in 1941. Not surprisingly, among
the records of the Nazi Rosenberg Command (ERR), then headquartered in
Ratibor (*Pol.* Racibórz; in Silesia), we find a top secret German commentary
on the *Pravda* article:

> The statement by the Bolshevik investigative commission which
> is supposed to establish German "crimes" contains both lies and
> truth. Generally speaking, the Bolsheviks attribute all destruction
> in the city to the Germans, not even excepting objects which, as
> the whole world knows, have been destroyed by the Bolsheviks
> themselves. Thus, all buildings on the main street of Kyiv,
> Khreshchatyk, and in addition numerous other buildings in the
> city were blown up with the aid of time fuses and destroyed
> shortly after the occupation of Kyiv by German troops. This is

---

[21]   "Soobshchenie Chrezvychainoi Gosudarstvennoi Komissii po ustanovleniiu i
rassledovaniiu zlodeianii nemetsko-fashistskikh zakhvatchikov i ikh soobshchnikov i
prichinennogo imi ushcherba grazhdanam, kolkhozam, obshchestvennym
organizatsiiam, gosudarstvennym predpriiatiiam i uchrezhdeniiam SSSR. O
razrushenniiakh i zverstvakh, sovershennykh nemetsko-fashistskimi zakhvatchikami v
gorode KIEVE," *Pravda* 1 March 1944. The ChGK report was also published
separately in a somewhat more detailed version, with a pressrun of 100,000 copies
(Moscow, 1944); see the quoted portions, p. 4. A copy was submitted as one of the
Soviet depositions at the Nuremberg Trials in 1945—see GA RF, 7445/2/94,
fols. 194–197.

[22]   "Soobshchenie ChGK o razrushenniiakh v gorode KIEVE," p. 4.

true also with regard to the Assumption [Uspens′kyi] Cathedral of
the Lavra.[23]

The fact that this was a secret report for internal circulation and that it fully
admits that some of the damage was in fact wrought by the Nazi invaders
increases its credibility. Soviet accounts during and after the war, in contrast,
all followed the official ChGK version, attributing the destruction of
structures along the Khreshchatyk and other buildings in Kyiv in September
1941 to the Nazis. In the 1960s, however, Soviet partisans were credited for
the demolitions. Streets were renamed in their honor and several, such as
Ivan D. Kudria (*pseud.* Mazym), were awarded for their "heroic deeds." [24]

Western accounts of the destruction of Kyiv during the war, including
the Khreshchatyk and the Assumption Cathedral, have long attributed that
brutal devastation to the scorched-earth policy of time-bombing the center of
Kyiv by the retreating Soviet forces including partisan units, although the
destruction orders or other definitive documentation have never surfaced.[25]
Since there are undoubtedly many still-classified documents relating to
different underground and partisan Soviet operations and other possibly
revealing sources that have not been declassified, we cannot come to
definitive answers in many cases.

The issue of the destruction of the Assumption Cathedral, which is now
being rebuilt after Ukrainian independence, remains a prime example of the
controversial interpretations of wartime guilt. Soviet authorities continued to
attribute its destruction to the Nazis, refused to rebuild it, and left the rubble
prominently displayed in the Lavra. The German side is more prepared today

---

[23] "Bolschewistische Greuelpropaganda über 'Zerstörungen und Grausamkeiten der
deutsch-faschistischen Eroberer in der Stadt Kiew,'" signed by Reichardt, appended to
a secret memorandum dated Berlin, 13 June 1944. A Ratibor German translation of
the *Pravda* article remains filed with an ERR report—Stabsführung IV/3 (Ratibor,
15 April 1944), BAK, R 6/170, fols. 47ff; a photocopy is held in US NA, EAP
99/1085.

[24] See Titus D. Hewryk, *The Lost Architecture of Kiev* (New York: Ukrainian
Museum, 1982), especially pp. 37–39 (the Khreshchatyk). Hewryk documents the
Soviet renaming of streets and other heroic awards.

[25] Hewryk describes the destruction of the Khreshchatyk with reference to many
émigré-published accounts and memoirs in *The Lost Architecture of Kiev*, pp. 37–39
(Khreshchatyk) and pp. 51–53 (Assumption [Uspens′kyi] Cathedral). Hewryk's
account cites Radio Liberty files and memoirs of Ukrainians who found refuge in the
West. Several of the Künsberg reports from Kyiv (see below, fns. 59 and 60) also
mention the dynamiting by the retreating Soviet forces and partisan agents.

to take at least some of the blame for the catastrophe and was even considering assisting the reconstruction effort, although by late 1999 that assistance had not yet materialized. Nevertheless, the Soviet version can be further brought to question with the recent discovery of an original postwar report from a local Soviet citizen explaining its destruction when German ordinance specialists were unable to remove the dynamite laid by Soviet commandos.[26] Alternatively, some see the recently revealed pictures taken from across the Dnipro by a German photographer as proof that the Nazis intentionally planned the destruction.[27] Current Ukrainian public opinion on the matter remains sharply divided.[28]

Soviet authorities quite rightfully blamed the Nazis for the plunder of the armory collection from the Lavra; however, to their credit, German ordinance squads successfully removed the dynamite laid by Soviet commandos in the foundations of the Historical Museum in the Lavra which housed that famous armory collection, and hence ensured its preservation.[29] The fact that the de-

---

[26] That document, found among recently opened Kyiv Communist Party files, edited by Serhii Kot, appears as "Malovidomyi dokument z istoriï ruinuvannia pam'iatok Kyievo-Pechers′koï Lavry pid chas Druhoï svitovoï viiny," in *Ukraïns′kyi arkheohrafichnyi shchorichnyk*, n.s. 3–4 (1999): 575–92. The fact that this documentary testimony was purged from the official ChGK report on the incident forwarded to Moscow suggests the extent to which ChGK often tampered with the evidence. See the earlier discussion of this matter in Grimsted, "The Fate of Ukrainian Cultural Treasures," pp. 57–59, 63.

[27] The pictures of the explosion received recently from Bremen, Germany, are published with commentary by Hryhorii Poloiushko in *Khronika 2000* 17–18 (1997): 365–67. In fact, however, since the Nazis certainly must have realized the risks involved in attempting to remove the dynamite, the fact that they accordingly completely evacuated the premises and planted a photographer to witness the possible explosion does not contradict the explanation that they were actually trying to remove the mines already laid by Soviet agents.

[28] See the 1997 analysis of the various alternative accounts of the destruction of the cathedral by Serhii Kot, "Zahybel′ Uspens′koho soboru: Versiï…," *Khronika 2000* 17–18 (1997): 348–64. As Kot shows, recent research appears to point more and more fingers at Soviet rather than Nazi responsibility for initially laying the charges.

[29] See the retrospective report of Dr. Dieter Roskamp, HAG-Kiev (15 July 1942), to ERR Berlin, T-454, roll 21, frame 001090 (EAP 99/54). The German specialist reported that "several kilos of uncharged dynamite were found bored in the basement foundations of the Historical Museum in the Lavra," where "retreating Soviet forces had been foiled in their attempt to blow up that building by the timely communication of a worker to the German military."

mining operation was successful gives further credence to the argument that
the Nazis were also attempting to remove the mines from the Assumption
Cathedral. By contrast, the earlier falsified ChGK report of the total Nazi
responsibility for destruction in Kyiv that was submitted by Soviet authorities
to the Nuremberg Tribunal has not been corrected in the public mind-set
about the war, nor in world opinion.[30]

It is clear that Nazi authorities in Kyiv in November 1941 were planning
to stay in the Ukrainian capital indefinitely, belying the idea that they would
undertake the destruction of its monuments, and similar Soviet mining
operations occurred in Kharkiv. "Scorched earth" and mining tactics,
following Stalin's orders, were likewise planned by Soviet authorities for
other cities, although documentation is still fragmentary.

Soviet Archival Evacuation. Although Soviet orders for the extensive time-
bombing of Kyiv, and similar alleged destruction in other areas, have not yet
been found, Soviet orders for the destruction of archives in the summer of
1941 have come to light and the execution of those orders in many areas can
now be convincingly documented. For example, a Soviet evacuation instruction, dated 18 July 1941, which the Nazis found and translated in Dnipropea-
trovsk, gave the ominous order: "If it is impossible to bring out the materials
designated for evacuation, they are to be burned unconditionally."[31] As
evident in newly opened files, such orders were widely issued and carried out
in many war areas, especially in Ukraine.[32]

---

[30] One of the actual Commission depositions (GA RF, 7021/65/10, fols. 19–22)
regarding the Nazi destruction of the Assumption Cathedral was submitted as USSR
exhibit 247 (GA RF, 7445/2/107, fols. 162–166, with a German translation,
fols. 167–172).

[31] Pechurov, director of the Archival Administration NKVD-Dnipropetrovsk to
Solotuchin, director of Dnipropetrovsk State City Archive (TOP SECRET—VERY
URGENT) (18 July 1941), copy in German translation, TsDAVO, 3206/5/21, fol. 27.
That document that I found in German records in Kyiv in the summer of 1989 was my
first indication of the Soviet scorched-earth policy of archival destruction. See also the
corresponding recently declassified instructions of Ukrainian Glavarkhiv chief
Gudzenko to Pechuro (5 July 1941 and 25 July 1941), TsDAVO, 14/1/2314/19.
Regarding Stalin's appeal for destruction of property, see below, fn. 43.

[32] Gudzenko to Chibriakov (Kharkiv, 8 August 1941), GA RF, 5325/10/856,
fols. 1–2, detailing especially heavy intentional destruction in Volhynia, Zhytomyr
(later blamed on German bombing), Rivne, Stanyslaviv, Kharkiv, and Odesa, to name
only a few Ukrainian examples. Deputy Chief NKVD UkrSSR Riasnoi and Chief AU
NKVD UkrSSR Shkliarov to Chief GAU NKVD SSSR Nikitinskii (Kyiv, 16 August

The first study to reveal and discuss seriously the problems of archival evacuation and destruction is the still-unpublished chapter in the Tsaplin monograph mentioned above. Tsaplin's account now needs to be augmented with additional documentation that has since become publicly available, particularly from Communist Party and Nazi sources.[33] Immediately after the Nazi invasion was under way during the summer of 1941, Soviet authorities organized massive evacuation efforts, which can be documented in considerable detail in the now declassified records of the Main Archival Administrations (Glavarkhiv) of the USSR in Moscow, and of the UkrSSR in Kyiv, and in files remaining in many individual archives.[34] Recently published documents from the July 1941 Central Committee *osobaia papka* (special file) on wartime evacuation demonstrate that certain secret and top secret categories of archives were indeed among the high state priorities for evacuation, together with NKVD archival personnel, high-level personnel of the Academy of Sciences, and state treasures.[35]

Soviet authors have traditionally praised the evacuation efforts, as the author of a 1990 account marvels that, despite the adverse war conditions, Ukrainian archivists succeeded in evacuating over a million files to the

---

1941), GA RF, 5325/10/856, fols. 3–8. See also the later summary report of Nikitinski and Gorlenko to Deputy Commissar NKVD S. N. Kruglov (Moscow, 10 April 1942), GA RF, 5325/10/836, fols. 53–70. The corresponding Ukrainian files with outgoing copies were finally available for consultation in Kyiv in June 1994—TsDAVO, 14/1, especially files 2314 and 2315; they contain copies of the above-cited reports and additional correspondence with individual oblast archives regarding evacuation and destruction. For example, see the instructions by Gudzenko to different oblasts (25 July 1941), TsDAVO, 14/1/2314, fols. 19–26.

33   Tsaplin, "Arkhivy, voina i okkupatsiia (1941–1945 gody)." Many of the details and conflicting reports about evacuation and destruction at the beginning of the war, including in Ukraine, are analyzed in his ch. 3, pp. 164–307. Tsaplin did not have access to many important sources now available, especially from CPSU sources. Understandably—for that period in Moscow—he did not use Nazi documentation.

34   Considerable documentation about the Soviet evacuation efforts remains among the records of the Main Archival Administration of the USSR in Moscow—GA RF, fond 5325, *opis´* 10 and the formerly top secret *opis´* 2; many of the reports on Ukrainian evacuations and destruction are collected in *opis´* 10, files 856 and 857. Comparable files are now available to researchers among the records of the Main Archival Administration of the Ukrainian SSR in TsDAVO (fond 14).

35   "Pervye dni voiny: èvakuatsiia (po materialam 'osobykh papok' Politbiuro TsK VKP[b])," ed. Zh. G. Adibekova, *Otechestvennye arkhivy* 1995 (2): 28–37. See the more detailed archival instructions cited above in fns. 31–32.

Ukrainian evacuation centers such as Zlatoust (Cheliabinsk Oblast, RSFSR).[36] A problem with this laudatory analysis arises, though, from several facts. First is the kinds of "cultural treasures" Soviet authorities chose for evacuation: it was chiefly fonds relating to the revolutionary movement (such as pre-revolutionary police records) and high-level—and especially secret—files from the immediate post-revolutionary period that were shipped east. Second, because of the speed of the Nazi invasion and the lack of rolling stock available for the evacuation of archives, they left behind many of the earliest and historically most valuable records. Third is the extent to which they ordered the destruction of archival materials they were unable to evacuate. The results of the efforts, in terms of archival legacy of Ukraine and the future possibility of writing about Ukrainian history, were disastrous. Thus, one of the prime reasons for the earlier secrecy coupled with the self-righteous Soviet propagandistic line may well be the fact, now well documented, that a great deal of the wartime damage, including the destruction of archives and cultural monuments, was carried out intentionally by Soviet authorities, rather than by the Nazi invaders.

The first published study critical of the Soviet archival evacuation effort appeared in Moscow in 1990. In it, author Ol'ga N. Kopylova cites the figure of only five to six percent for materials evacuated from republic- and oblast-level archives in front line areas, laments the lack of attention to pre-revolutionary fonds, and exposes frightening statistics about the extent of deliberate destruction of historically valuable materials in "overburdened" agency archives.[37] The Moscow archivist, while emphasizing central all-union archives, did not cover the extent of destruction in Ukraine of records that had already been assigned for permanent archival preservation, nor did she explain the underlying priorities of the evacuation efforts. The importance of

---

[36]   Lidiia V. Maksakova, *Spasenie kul'turnykh tsennostei v gody Velikoi Otechestvennoi voiny* (Moscow, 1990), p. 53. Maksakova cites many of the earlier published Soviet sources and secondary accounts, but continues the traditional simplistic Soviet polemical tone about the war and the cultural atrocities wrought by the "fascist invaders" alone, without critical review of many newly opened Soviet sources on the subject and without reference to German documentation.

[37]   Ol'ga N. Kopylova, "K probleme sokhrannosti GAF SSSR v gody Velikoi Otechestvennoi voiny," *Sovetskie arkhivy* 1990 (5): 37–44. More details are presented in Kopylova's candidate disseration, "Tsentral'nye gosudarstvennye arkhivy SSSR v gody Velikoi Otechestvennoi voiny, 1941–1945 gg." (Moscow: RGGU, 1991), which the author kindly made available to me. I appreciate her helpful advice about the location of further documentation relating to Ukraine.

her research and her publications, opening the subject to public discussion, however, deserves special emphasis.

Ukrainian Evacuation Priorities and Wartime Imperatives. The evacuation priorities mentioned above can be better understood when we read the work plan for the Ukrainian state archival service during 1942 in the evacuated center of Zlatoust. Even in the midst of World War II, the archival reference service had as its top priorities "the operational and scientific aims" of the secret police in their continuing search for enemies of the regime:

> Proceeding from the wartime situation and according to the orders of NKVD SSSR General Commissar of Security Comrade Beria No. 001345, the State Archival Administration NKVD UkrSSR plans the following basic tasks for 1942:
>
> 1) Complete investigation of documentary materials for operational security-police (*operativno-chekistskikh*) aims, i.e., the elucidation and reporting of counterrevolutionary elements by going through the documentary materials of the state archives—in the first order registering personnel of punitive organs of tsarist times, of the bourgeois provisional government, security (*okhrana*) divisions, gendarme administration, police, prisons, intelligence sections, counter intelligence, national guards (*derzhvarty*), members of the bourgeois-nationalist parties and organizations, Trotskyites, Rightist spies, diversionists, etc.
>
> 2) Establish reference handbooks for the organs of state security and NKVD—
> a) of bourgeois-nationalist parties in Ukraine, and
> b) of the system of punitive organs of tsarist and bourgeois nationalist governments in Ukraine including existing intelligence and punitive organs in Western Ukraine.[38]

Accordingly, evacuation priorities were given to records from the secret divisions of state archives that were needed for such investigatory work.

Politically oriented, Communist inspired documentary publication projects also drained resources from normal reference work in the archives under the NKVD, even during those tragic wartime years. For example, third in order of tasks assigned to the evacuated Ukrainian archives in Zlatoust in the 1942 work plan was to "plan and prepare a documentary collection for the 25th anniversary of the October Revolution"; and this even ranked above the

---

[38] The work plan bears the signature of Shkliarov as Director of the Administration of State Archives NKVD UkrSSR (Zlatoust, 4 December 1941), GA RF, 5325/10/856, fols. 39–40, with the appended lists of fonds that had been evacuated for the purpose (fols. 41–51).

more understandable wartime task: "4) To prepare and publish documents and articles on defense themes."[39] Regrettably, the narrow political and ideological focus of such publications in Soviet archives during the Stalin years grossly lowered the scholarly level of archival work and archeographic productions.

Soviet authorities had little time for archival evacuation after the swift German invasion, and there were inadequate facilities to transport and house the archival heritage of the vast western areas of the USSR. In hindsight, we may regret the priorities of the regime, and regret that more of the Ukrainian archival heritage was not evacuated, but it is important to recognize the political and operational motives for those priorities. Since 1991, there have been new revelations that a number of cultural treasures from Ukrainian museums that were evacuated eastward did not return to Ukraine.[40] In the archival sphere, however, the secret fonds and high-priority police and security service records that were evacuated survived the war, so far as is known. There is no evidence that the archival records evacuated by Soviet authorities were not returned to Ukraine, except in a few instances where appraisal authorities decided on the destruction of specific groups of records. One such example for Poltava has recently been documented by Serhii Kot involving the destruction of over 12,500 files from five fonds of revolutionary courts and military materials in 1919.[41]

Ukrainian Archival Destruction: the Bonfires of 1941. Interestingly enough, the recently published documents from the Central Committee *osobaia papka* in Moscow mentioned above do not include the orders for destruction of archives. Archival specialists suggest that such high-level orders might well have only been delivered orally or in coded telegrams that

---

[39]   GA RF, 5325/10/856, fol. 40.

[40]   See, for example, "Ukrainskie tsennosti ostalis′ v Rossii," *Kommersant Daily* 119 (4 July 1998): 7, reprinted in *Kievskie vedomosti* 1 August 1998: 10. The Moscow version of that article appeared as part of the larger complex of comments with the article by Tat′iana Markina on the fate of the frescoes from the St. Michael Cathedral (see above, Chapter 2, p. 62n28).

[41]   "Vypiska iz protokola Ekspertnyi poverechnyi kommissii GAU NKVD SSSR" (1943), signed by Balashova found in the records of the Poltava Oblast State Archive—GA Poltavskoi oblasti, R-1505/1/118, fols. 1–5. Kot is preparing a report on evidence of destruction he has found, and I appreciate his sharing this example with me prior to publication.

were not retained with other files.[42] Nevertheless, multiple copies of the orders going out to individual archives for destruction of records that were not (or could not be) evacuated have been found among Archival Administration records both in Moscow and in Kyiv. The implementation of those orders has been well documented, as Tsaplin earlier also reported.

The official 1999 Rosarkhiv publication on wartime archival losses in Russia also discusses archival evacuation and notes, but does not document, extensive archival destruction in numerous Russian regions in July 1941. The authors quote Stalin's "scorched earth" policy announced in his 3 July 1941 "Appeal to the Soviet People" to the effect that "valuable property...which cannot be removed should be destroyed unquestionably."[43] However, in their presentation of losses for individual Russian archives, the compilers do not distinguish among records intentionally destroyed in the summer of 1941, plundered by the Nazis, or later destroyed in bombing or by other causes.

The extent to which Ukrainian authorities were ordered to destroy archives they were unable to evacuate in line with this policy has now been documented in shocking detail. Deliberate destruction of archives on the eve of Nazi invasion was understandable for a Soviet regime that had much to hide, and particularly in Ukraine by authorities anxious to prevent secret files with potentially compromising documentation—dangerous to Soviet citizens and useful to the Nazi propaganda machine—from falling into enemy hands.

The intentional destruction of virtually the entire Communist Party archives in Kyiv and several other cities, large parts of many local state archives, and even more agency archives that had not been transferred to permanent repositories, while quite understandable from a Soviet wartime perspective, now means that these tragic losses can only indirectly be blamed on the "fascist invader."[44] Two examples from Ukrainian oblast archives

---

[42] "Pervye dni voiny: èvakuatsiia," *Otechestvennye arkhivy* 1995 (2): 28–37. The editor reconfirmed to me in 1999 that he still has not found those orders in the files themselves. Ciphered documents have still not been declassified.

[43] See the introduction to the volume compiled by Rosarkhiv specialists, *State Archives of the Russian Federation: Lost Archives Funds*, book 1, comp. Elena E. Novikova and V. I. Zvavich; ed. Pavel V. Khoroshilov, Nikolai I. Nikandrov, and Anatolii I. Vilkov (Moscow–St. Petersburg, 1999; Ministry of Culture), pp. 15–16; Although no archival documentation on the matter is provided, the compilers quote Stalin's appeal (pp. 15, 26) and reference the earlier Grimsted discussion.

[44] The losses were enumerated in a report from Kyiv to Moscow—Minaeva to Karavaev, "Spravka o sostoianii i rabote oblastnykh partiinykh arkhivov obkomov KP(b)U na 1.III.45 r.," RGASPI, 71/6/253, fols. 34–53. More detailed reports of the destruction in Kyiv are preserved in Kyiv, for example, I. M. Mironova, "Dokladnaia

suggest the extent of destruction of the Ukrainian archival legacy. In Odesa, after archivists protested the destruction orders and refused to destroy pre-revolutionary records, the archivist left in charge received oral orders from the local NKVD superiors "to use his own discretion as to burning possibilities" after it became clear "they would receive no more transport" for evacuation. He later reported that:

> I fulfilled that order, destroying a significant part of the materials from the Soviet period (5 July 1941), and with one secret packet and some accounting records, together with a group of workers from the archive, fled from Odesa to Uralsk.[45]

According to a more detailed account, in Mykolaïv in the early days of August they had

> five trucks going day and night taking materials from the storage areas to the electric power station, a bread factory, the public baths, and other buildings with full security provisions. They were burned by day. The entire archive was burned with the exception of the library with the law codes of the Russian Empire.[46]

Arriving Nazi archivists were frank about destruction from German bombing. For example, in Chernihiv, they were distressed to find that "the largest Oblast Archive depository in the Catherine Church had been destroyed by bombs and that the building of the oblast archival administration burned down after bombing."[47] But the Nazis were also forthcoming in their assessment of the destruction by departing Soviet authorities. In Poltava, for example, they found the building that housed the Party Archive had been destroyed by an explosion with no records remaining, and "the archive in the church by the market had been burnt out by the Bolsheviks," and "even the

---

zapiska (26–30.VI.45)" (11 August 1945), TsDAHO, 39/3/468, and a secret stenogram of a meeting devoted to reports on the subject (21 March 1945), TsDAHO, 39/3/467, fols. 41–42 (Kyiv).

[45] "Dokladnaia zapiska," V. A. Bassak to Shkliarov (Uralsk, 31 December 1941), GA RF, 5325/10/857, fol. 18. See the Odesa protest by Politkin to Shkliarov (9 July 1941), TsDAVO, 14/1/2314, fol. 21, and related correspondence about the Odesa protests in the same file.

[46] "Dokladnaia zapiska," head of the Archival Division of the UNKVD Mykolaïv (Nikolaev) Oblast D. P. Ryl'skii to Shkliarov (Uralsk, 12 February 1942), GA RF, 5325/10/857, fol. 26v.

[47] Report on the Winter and Grazin visit (30–31 July 1942) (Kyiv, 3 August 1942), TsDAVO, 3206/5/2, fols. 12–16 (2nd copy, fols. 17–19).

records in the City State Archive had been burned before the Soviets left."[48] In Kyiv, the major repository for records from the 1920s and early 1930s was totally consumed by fire set by retreating Soviet forces in September 1941 in the Feodosii Church, adjacent to the Lavra, and those parts of the Party Archive that were not evacuated were likewise totally destroyed.[49]

In Kharkiv, the Nazis reported that the Party Archive had been taken to a factory and burned. With regard to the Central State Historical Archive in Kharkiv, they were informed that the Soviets had intentionally started a fire in the adjoining building, and that local citizens who had tried to extinguish the fire and save the archive were shot on the spot.[50] A 1944 Ukrainian CP report confirms the burning of a substantial part of the Kharkiv Party Archive, and notes that "testimonials (*akty*) were not prepared for the burned materials."[51]

Party archival authorities in Kharkiv subsequently bemoaned that "Destruction of materials was carried out in a highly disorganized manner and that many materials were destroyed which should not have been."[52] But such comments came too late, after the tragic damage had been done. The extent of losses to the archival legacy of Ukraine will be difficult to calculate, because also destroyed were many current records, part of which would normally have been slated for permanent archival retention. The effect of the lacunae from the 1920s and 30s in many Ukrainian archives for historical scholarship is incalculable, and we have even less of a sense of what pre-revolutionary materials went up in smoke. Equally important, in terms of its

---

[48] Winter, report on visit to Poltava (29 October–5 November 1941), TsDAVO, 3206/5/1, fols. 436–437.

[49] "Kratkii spisok materialov, pogibshikh pri pozhare v Fedosiiskoi tserkvi" (September 1941), TsDAVO, 3206/5/1, fols. 314–315; a German translation of the list is appended to the Winter report for 16–27 November 1941, fols. 327ff.; the fire is also mentioned in the report itself, fol. 319. The Germans were not sure what parts of the Party Archives had been evacuated or destroyed by Soviet authorities, but we know from official Party reports cited below that all the the Kyiv Oblast Party Archive and most of the central Party Archive was intentionally destroyed.

[50] Winter report (Kharkiv, 2–4 November 1941), TsDAVO, 3206/5/1, fols. 437–437v.

[51] S. G. Shtanagei to Minaeva "Otchet o rabote khar'kovskogo oblastnogo partiinogo arkhiva za 1944 god" (2 February 1945), TsDAHO, 39/3/92, fol. 22.

[52] Shtanagei, head of the Kharkiv Oblast Party Archive, as quoted in "Soveshchanie arkhivnykh rabotnikov obkomov KP(b)U" (21 March 1945), RGASPI, 71/6/253, fol. 78.

effect on the archival heritage of Ukraine, archivists were under orders to destroy or damage the archival reference system and finding aids, even if they did not have the possibility of evacuating or destroying all of the records themselves. The full documented story of this destruction in Ukraine remains to be compiled, despite the persistence of the Soviet propagandistic dogma about the Great Patriotic War that attributes all wartime destruction to the Nazi invader, as certified in earlier official ChGK attestations.

Nazi Museum on Soviet Destruction in Kyiv. The Nazis themselves tried to use the Soviet destruction during the summer of 1941 for their own propaganda ends during their occupation of Kyiv. "The destruction by the Bolsheviks of cultural monuments in the city of Kyiv," including those specifically "ruined by the Soviets in the period 22.VI–19.IX.1941," were among the well-illustrated exhibits in the Nazi-organized Kyiv Museum-Archive of the Transitional Period (*Muzei-Arkhiv Perekhodovoï doby m. Kyieva*), which operated from April through the fall of 1942.[53] The museum was directed by the Ukrainian historian Oleksandr Ohloblyn in association with a number of Ukrainian intellectuals.[54] During its short existence the museum managed to collect significant documentation about Soviet destruction of many cultural monuments and archives in Ukraine in October and November of 1941.

Other exhibits (that were mounted or at least planned) dealt with Soviet cultural destruction, especially of religious monuments during the interwar period, including the Soviet 1936 demolition of the St. Michael Cathedral of the Golden Domes in Kyiv. The Nazis managed to evacuate the records of the museum and the archival and photographic materials they had collected for it, when they left Ukraine. But many of those records were found by Soviet authorities and returned to Kyiv, where most of them are now held in

---

[53] "Zvit pro robotu Muzeiu-arkhivu perekhodovoï doby za cherven' 1942 r.," DAKO, R-2412/1/2, fol. 21.

[54] Ohloblyn directed the Kyiv Archive of Early Acts in 1933–1934 after many of the earlier more established Ukrainian historical specialists had been purged. He briefly served the Nazis as head of the Kyiv city council in the early period of occupation. Regarding Ohloblyn, see the appreciative article by Vasyl' Omel'chenko, "Oleksander Ohloblyn (zhyttia i diial'nist')," in *Zbirnyk na poshanu prof. d-ra Oleksandra Ohloblyna/Collected Essays in Honor of Professor Alexander Ohloblyn,* Ukraïns'ka Vil'na Akademiia Nauk u SShA, *Naukovyi zbirnyk* 3 (New York, 1977), pp. 57–63. Professor Ohloblyn died in Massachusetts in 1992. Omel'chenko refers to Ohloblyn's directorship of the museum without explanation of its nature or function, "Oleksander Ohloblyn," p. 60.

the State Archive of Kyiv Oblast—DAKO; while the photographic materials were deposited in the Central State Archive of Documentary Films, Photographs, and Sound Recordings of the UkrSSR (TsDAKFFD). The materials were held in secret during the Soviet period, but were finally opened for research after independence.[55]

Reported Library Destruction. So little has been published in Russia and Ukraine about Soviet intentional destruction of cultural treasures that my own earlier revelations were among the issues most bitterly criticized by the Russian library specialist Aleksandr M. Mazuritskii.[56] Not having worked directly with Nazi materials, Mazuritskii specifically took issue with my reference to a Nazi report to the effect that 100,000 volumes from the restricted Special Collections (*spetskhran*) of the Central Scientific Library of the Academy of Sciences (TsNB) that could not be evacuated by the retreating Soviets were burned by them as the Nazis were advancing towards Kyiv. That destruction (albeit still without corroboration from other sources), together with statistics about evacuations, was reported by the head of ERR library operations in Ukraine, Dr. Josef Bentzing. He also mentioned library destruction at the Kyiv Pedagogical Institute.[57] Indications of library destruction are rare compared to evidence regarding the destruction of archives. Orders from Moscow for the destruction of special library collections as well as later Soviet reports detailing such actions have not been

---

[55] As arranged in DAKO, fond R-2412 consists of two inventories—*opys* 1 (nos. 1–33) consists of the museum office records, while *opys* 2 (nos. 1–270) comprises documentation collected for exhibits. In September 1990, I was refused access to half of the items requested from the second *opys* and a third of those requested from the first, but the fond was later opened for research. See the newspaper article by Ihor Hyrych, "Arkhiv-Muzei Perekhodovoï doby pro ruinatsiiu Kyïvs′kykh pam′iatok u 1918–1942 rokakh," *Starozhytnosti* 1992 (1): 5. Photographic materials from the museum deposited in TsDAKFFD URSR were integrated into the general archival holdings, and hence, present archivists have not been able to locate the materials or an inventory of the photographs received.

[56] Mazuritskii, "Restitutsiia knizhnykh sobranii," *Knizhnoe obozrenie* 1993 (3): 54–56. Mazuritskii repeated this criticism in his talk at the 1994 Chernihiv conference, "Koordynatsiia diial′nosti bibliotek Rosiï ta Ukraïny z pytan′ kul′turnykh tsinnostei, peremishchenykh pid chas Druhoï svitovoï viiny," in *Materialy natsional′noho seminaru, Chernihiv, 1994*, p. 302.

[57] Bentzing's report (6 June 1942) is found among the records of the RKU Administration of Libraries, Archives, and Museums, TsDAVO, 3206/5/4, fol. 73. Bentzig was simultaneously working with the ERR.

found (though we have evidence of such for archives). However, the same incident involving destruction of books in TsNB has been relayed by a Ukrainian library specialist in a recent survey of library developments in Ukraine during the war.[58]

Nazi Archival Plunder

Unquestionably, Ukrainian archives were left in greater devastation by World War II than had ever been experienced during previous wars. However, in terms of overall archival losses in Ukraine, much more can be attributed to intentional Soviet destruction in the summer of 1941 than to wartime Nazi plunder. As noted above, Nazi bombing also accounted for losses in some localities, and in other cases, later wartime destruction in the fighting also must be considered.

Nazi archival plunder was carried out during the war and occupation by a number of different and often competing agencies. In the case of archives, rarely were the plundered materials taken simply for "loot," but rather different groups of records were taken by different Nazi agencies for quite specific military, intelligence or counterintelligence, politico-ideological, racial-genealogical, or other purposes. The rationale involved has been analyzed in some previous publications, and further analyses are being prepared.

Actual Nazi plunder of archives in Ukraine was comparatively much less extensive than was the case for Ukrainian libraries, museums, and other cultural institutions. With the exception of archival materials taken for specialized purposes by specific agencies during the occupation, it was a general Nazi policy to retain archives in situ. When it came time for retreat, the Nazis had very limited rolling stock, and hence were very selective about what they took with them.

Remarkably, many Nazi records can still be adduced that give precise details of plundered archives and other cultural property. The level of meticulous detail with which Nazi authorities described archival shipments, even down to box labels and the numbers and destinations of the railroad wagons involved, is, at times, astounding. Comprehensive data files on Nazi archival shipments still need to be compiled in Ukraine, although considerable fragmentary information about various archival plunder has been

---

[58] Iuliia Lazorenko, "Dolia bibliotek pid chas Druhoï svitovoï viiny," *Bibliotechnyi visnyk* 1995 (6): 8–10. The reference to intentional destruction in TsNB is found on p. 8, but there is no further documentation of the incident.

published in studies mentioned earlier. Only a few examples are cited here.

Künsberg Commandos. The first significant archival plunder in Ukraine was carried out at the start of the war by the Künsberg Commandos under the Nazi Foreign Office. Their activities have been well documented in several studies by the Bremen group. From Kyiv, the Künsberg squads did not raid archives per se. Their loot included the Armor Collection from the Historical Museum in the Kyiv Caves Monastery complex and some other museum exhibits, but they otherwise concentrated on library holdings, taking a total of 370 crates containing approximately 60,000 volumes in their main shipment from Kyiv. They took a significant collection of 4,200 volumes of manuscript and early printed books removed from the Volodymyr Cathedral and the Central Library of the Academy of Sciences in Kyiv (TsNB), and 5,000 volumes from the so-called Bibikov Collection (predominantly the Polish Royal Library) and from TsNB. They likewise removed books from the collection of Metropolitan Flavian. After their receipt in Berlin, most of the library materials from Kyiv were turned over to the Einsatzstab Reichsleiter Rosenberg (ERR) and transported to their Central Library facility in the Austrian Tyrol. Approximately 50,000 volumes of Judaica were included in the Künsberg shipments from Kyiv, which were eventually transferred to the Institute for the Study of the Jewish Question in Frankfurt.[59]

The Künsberg mission in Odesa, however, involved one of the few examples of their archival plunder in Ukraine. In that connection they were following special orders from one of Alfred Rosenberg's deputies, Georg Leibbrandt, who headed one of the main divisions of the Ministry for the Occupied Eastern Territories—RMbO under Rosenberg. Leibbrandt, himself born in the Odesa district and a recognized scholar of German settlers in the Russian Empire, had visited Odesa archives several times in the early 1920s and 30s, when he was still working for the Deutsches Ausland Institut. In

---

[59] Several Künsberg documents found in the archive of the Nazi Foreign Office (Auswärtiges Amt) in Bonn note that 4,211 volumes were taken from Kyiv from the "Volodymyr Cathedral and the Staatsbibliothek," as TsNB was then known by the Germans—for example, that statistic appears in several lists in the file, PA AA, Sonderkommando v. Künsberg, R 27558/35 (1941–1943); other lists include 5,000 volumes from the "Bibikov Collection." The figure of 350 crates from Kyiv appears in several reports, but the available inventories in those files include many museum materials, including the armory collection—e.g., PA AA, R 27575/52. See also the references as documented by Heuss, "Das Sonderkommando Künsberg," pp. 547–48. I have documented the eventual disposition of these library materials from other sources; an account of this is in preparation.

connection with his research program on the area, which later came under the RMbO in 1941, he developed a specialized collection of research materials, the so-called *Sammlung Leibbrandt*. When the opportunity arose for plunder with the Nazi invasion, Leibbrandt ordered the removal of a number of important Odesa record groups relating to foreign settlers and German churches in the area. The Künsberg Commandos also found the records of the German Consulate in Odesa.[60] At the end of the war, Leibbrandt's special collection was evacuated to one of the saltmines in Saxony before Berlin was bombed, where it survived the war. Located by Soviet authorities, it was eventually returned to Odesa.[61]

The ERR, the Reichsarchiv, and Local Looting. The most serious archival plunder later during occupation and at the end of the war was handled by two principal Nazi agencies. Archival plunder by the Special Commandos under Alfred Rosenberg, the so-called Einsatzstab Reichsleiter Rosenberg (ERR) particularly involved Ukrainian Communist Party archives from Dnipropetrovsk and Kirovohrad. Nazi professional archival director for Ukraine Georg Winter first visited Dnipropetrovsk in May and June 1942 and was so impressed with "the only Party archive they had discovered so far" that he "personally spent some time putting it in order." In July, one of his assistants, the Orientalist Erich Lüddeckens, found 120 bundles from the secret division

---

[60] Archival plunder in Odesa is mentioned in several files, some providing details of the fonds involved. A figure of 3,000 volumes of German-related records from the Odesa archive are noted in one report (12 November 1941), PA AA, R 27575/52 (1941–1943); another appended summary report (10 November 1941) gives more details about the archival materials from Odesa and specifically mentions them for the Leibbrandt Collection. Leibbrandt's orders are also mentioned in the "secret" printed account of the Künsberg expeditions in Ukraine (p. 12), preserved in PA AA, Inland, IIg, 441. Hartung, *Das Sonderkommando Künsberg*, p. 41–42 (esp. fn. 190); Heuss, "Das Sonderkommando Künsberg," p. 548, document the Künsberg archival plunder in Odesa from most of the same documents I consulted. However, neither of them mention the tie with Georg Leibbrandt (1899–1902), which I have substantiated from other sources, including Künsberg reports. Regarding the Sammlung Leibbrandt research unit, see Gabriele Camphausen, *Die wissenschaftliche historische Russlandforschung im Dritten Reich 1933–1945* (Frankfurt-am-Main: Peter Lang, 1990), pp. 213–24 [=Europäische Hochschulschriften, Series III: Geschichte und ihre Hilfswissenschaften, 418], but that study does detail the archival plunder from Odesa.

[61] Chechkov to Nikitinskii, GA RF, 5325/2/1620, fols. 158–159. Another report (13 November 1945) notes that 230 crates from Odesa were recovered in the Stassfurt mine, TsDAVO, 14/7/56.

of the archive that "the Bolsheviks had not evacuated or burned," and by February 1943, he completed an inventory of the oblast Party Committee records. They were shipped in a single freight car to Cracow in October 1943, and then on to the ERR "anti-Bolshevik" research center in Ratibor, where they arrived 2 November. ERR archival specialists also found Party records from Zaporizhzhia and Uman, which were prepared for shipment. At least twenty crates from Party and Komsomol committees in six different *raions* of Kirovohrad Oblast were turned over to the Nazi Reich Security Main Office (Reichssicherheitshauptamt VII—RSHA) further west in Silesia.[62]

Plunder by Nazi professional archivists from the Reichsarchiv involved major shipments from the Kyiv Archive of Early Acts and the evacuation of historical archives from Lviv. Troppau (*Czech* Opava) with its various surrounding castles was the major Nazi archival center for archival records shipped from the USSR, including for the Kyiv archive and a few other record groups from Ukraine. While almost all of the Lviv historical archives were evacuated—more for the purpose of preservation against anticipated bombing than actual plunder—went to the closer haven of the Abbey of Tyniec near Cracow. These and other examples will be documented below, because many, if not most, of the archival materials evacuated to those sites were later retrieved by Soviet authorities.

Nazi wartime occupation reports also attest to considerable local looting or attempted looting in Ukraine. For example, a June 1943 Nazi report from Kyiv reports the theft of 80 packages (one-half ton) from one of the churches in the Kyiv Caves Monastery complex that was being used for archival storage during the war. Some of the materials were recovered.[63] Later during the final evacuation from Kyiv in October 1943, one entire freight train wagon of archival materials from the Kyiv Archive of Early Acts, which had

---

[62] The seizure of Ukrainian Party archives and their transport to Silesia are fully documented in Grimsted, *The Odyssey of the Smolensk Archive: Captured Communist Records for the Service of Anti-Communism* (Pittsburgh, 1995) [=Carl Beck Occasional Papers in Russian and East European Studies," 1201], esp. pp. 20–23. See, especially Winter's report (3–4 June 1942), TsDAVO, 3206/5/2, fol. 631, and his monthly report to the ERR (June 1942), TsDAVO, 3676/1/26, fols. 37–39; Lüddeckens report (1 July 1942), TsDAVO, 3206/5/21, fols 23–26, 43–48, and his typescript inventory (2 February 1943), TsDAVO, 3206/5/21, fols 373–582 (2nd copy, fols. 586–784), and 3206/5/14, fols. 1–150. Shipping details have not been found for the Zaporizhzhia and Uman records.

[63] See, for example, LV ABM reports (5 June 1943), TsDAVO, 3206/5/1, fols. 164–169.

not had a Nazi escort, was offloaded and looted in Voronezh en route to Kamianets-Podilskyi.[64]

Plundered Ukrainian Archives Still Missing? Some other archival materials, along with other cultural treasures, to be sure, did fall victim to outright Nazi plunder, albeit for specific agency purposes, and insofar as is known were not retrieved after the war. Comprehensive, authoritative compilations comparing the out-shipments reported by the Nazis and those we know to have been retrieved by Soviet authorities still need to be compiled, based on Nazi records as well as Soviet sources.

Many of the earlier Soviet-period reports, and particularly those prepared immediately after the war for the ChGK, tended to attribute Nazi plunder or destruction even to materials destroyed in situ by Soviet authorities in the summer of 1941 or during the bitter fighting and Soviet bombing in 1943/1944. They also blame the Nazis for looting materials that were in fact evacuated with the agreement of local specialists in 1943/1944 to protect them from destruction with the approaching war front.

More details are now available from Nazi documentation regarding the precise archival materials from Ukraine that were plundered by the Nazis, in addition to those destroyed or evacuated for wartime protection. While their fate has been accounted for in a large number of cases, there are some notable exceptions—namely military records and many of the genealogical materials.

Military Records: the Heeresarchiv. Many military records that were seized by Nazi military archival authorities from the Heeresarchiv have not, so far as is known, come back to Ukraine. In the case of western Ukraine, precise records of these German seizures are preserved among the records of the Nazi archival administration in Galicia, and others among surviving files from the Danzig-Oliva (*Pol.* Gdańsk-Oliwa) branch of the Heeresarchiv, which are now preserved in Moscow.[65]

The records that were seized include, for example, records of military-related institutions during the Polish interwar period, Polish mobilization records with detailed inventories, including files relating to Polish reserve

---

[64]   See the detailed account in the report of 29 November 1943, TsDAVO, 3206/5/1, fols. 396–397; also Winter to SA Potsdam (1 December 1943), TsDAVO, 3206/5/9, fol. 207.

[65]   Records of the Nazi archival administration in Galicia are preserved in Lviv, TsDIAL, fond 755. Those of the Heeresarchiv are preserved in Moscow, RGVA, fond 1256K, and the Danzig-Oliva branch as fond 1387K.

officers, records of the military court in Lviv and the military railway administration in Lviv, Ukrainian military records from 1918–1919, and records of the Ukrainian nationalist paramilitary Sich Riflemen (*Ukraïns′ki sichovi stril′tsi*), among others. One major initial shipment from Lviv totaled some 20 tons, filling two railway freight cars. Another 10 tons, filling a single freight car, were dispatched from Stanyslaviv (*now* Ivano-Frankivsk), and included records of the 11th Carpathian Division. Some 11 tons, filling another freight car, were dispatched from Ternopil; and another half ton was shipped from Sambir. Also included in these shipments were 6 to 7 tons of Austrian and Polish military records that were found in Lviv archives, including some from military institutions in Poznań, Katowice, and Łódź that had earlier been evacuated to Lviv. All of these materials were transferred to the German Military Archives (*Heeresarchiv* and *Vereinigte Wehr-Evidenzstellen*) in Vienna or to the Branch Military Archive in Danzig-Oliva (*Heeresarchiv Zweigstelle Danzig-Oliva*). Further information about shipments from Galicia and eastern Ukraine as well are found among the records of the Heeresarchiv in Moscow.[66] If any of the plundered military records were recovered by Soviet authorities, they were most likely retained in Moscow, because after the war the centralization of military records from throughout the USSR in Moscow and Leningrad was accelerated. Thus far, however, the location of those records known to have been evacuated from western Ukraine has not been documented.

German Genealogical Records. Another important Nazi target for archival plunder were the records of German communities in Ukraine.[67] One example of the seizures noted above was the Odesa archival materials plundered under order of Georg Leibbrandt. Special instructions went out to German archivists and other agencies involved in archives, such as the ERR, that all such

---

[66] TsDIAL, 755/1/218, fols. 7–8. Included there are lists of materials sent from Lviv and Ternopil, as well as a few files from Stanyslaviv in 1941. The records of the Sich Riflemen are specifically mentioned as being dispatched to Vienna. Shipments to Danzig in 1942 are noted in a report dated 16 September 1942 (fol. 15). Additional correspondence and reports relating to these shipments are found in subsequent papers in this file. See also the reports in file numbered 118, and the detailed summary of the military-related archival shipments in an undated 1943 report in file no. 32, fol. 46. See also the additional shipping reports from Ukraine in the Heeresarchiv records in Moscow (e.g., below, Chapter 8, p. 285n13 and n. 14).

[67] A separate, thorough study is needed of this subject, because of the extent of documentation available from many sources. For obvious political reasons, these seizures were neglected during the Soviet regime.

records were to be evacuated, especially during the closing year of the war, when the Nazis were in retreat. For example, in Dnipropetrovsk Dr. Karl Stumpp, a German genealogical expert, headed a special office (Sonderkomando Stumpp) under the RMbO/RKU for locating and dealing with persons of German ethnic background in Ukraine, the so-called *Volksdeutsch*. He and his agents seized a large group of records, particularly those from German communities. A portion of the archival materials the Nazis had looted from Dnipropetrovsk was later found in Germany and returned. Some of these German genealogy-related materials that had been incorporated into the records of the Deutsches Ausland Institut, with which both Stumpp and Leibbrandt were long associated, ended up with the Nazi records captured by the U.S. Army. Those files found their way to the Library of Congress after the war, although they were eventually returned to Germany. It is possible that some of the plundered Dnipropetrovsk files remain with that record group in Germany.[68]

Another group of records from German communities had been taken from Mykolaïv, part of which was sent to Berlin and another part to Königsberg.[69] There were other seizures in Volhynia, including for example, German church and school records from Lutsk.[70]

Remaining records of German communities in Galicia were also targeted for inventory and removal early in the war. Of particular note in this regard was the German Evangelical Church in Lviv, of which a history was immediately commissioned, together with registers of the extant records. Extant parish registers from Lutheran Evangelical churches were carefully recorded and prepared for shipment, along with records from German colonies in Dornfeld, Einsiedel, and Falkenstein, among others.[71] These and other

---

[68] See Meshkov, *Dnipropetrovs'ki arkhivy, muzeï ta biblioteky*, pp. 11–14, and the earlier brief report by Meshkov, "Dnipropetrovs'ki arkhivy pid chas druhoï svitovoï viiny," *Materialy natsional'noho seminaru. Chernihiv, 1994*, pp. 188–91. See the Nazi description and inventory of the German settlement records included, TsDAVO, 3206/5/3, fols. 119–123. Full microfilms, together with inventories of the records of the Deutsches Ausland Institut (DAI) remain in the Manuscript Division of the Library of Congress. Other microfilmed German community records remain in the U.S. National Archives. Original DAI records now are in Stuttgart.

[69] Regarding the Mykolaïv records, for example, see TsDAVO, 3206/5/3, fols. 148–150.

[70] Regarding the Lutsk records, see, for example, the 28 January 1944 report, TsDAVO, 3206/5/2, fols. 396–397.

[71] See the history of the Lviv community and related papers in TsDIAL, 755/1/171; regarding other records seized, see for example, files 91, 126, 127, and 248.

German metricular registers from the church archives were sent to Posen (*Pol*. Poznań), where the Nazis had organized a special genealogical research center for German communities in Eastern Europe, the so-called *Landesippenstelle*. Later, that center was relocated in the Filipinów Monastery in Gostyń, further south in Silesia.[72]

Jewish Community Records. In some areas of Ukraine, the Nazis also seized many other genealogical records, and especially those of Jewish communities.[73] A centralized Jewish genealogical research center was established in Berlin, the so-called *Zentralstelle für jüdische Personenstandsregister,* under the Reichssippenamt, and instructions called for all records located to be forwarded there.[74] These plans were only partially carried out, however, due to the poor state of organization of local Jewish records and the difficulties authorities had in getting them organized for shipment.

Nazi lists of extensive runs of Jewish registers looted from various cities and villages in Galicia are available, including those from Lviv,[75] Ternopil,[76] Stanyslaviv,[77] and Sambir,[78] among others. Local communities were

---

[72] The specific German records mentioned are not now held in TsDIAL. Some of them are reportedly now held in Poland, but further research on this subject is needed.

[73] Records of these shipments with precise details about the extent of parish registers or other genealogical materials from which communities are to be found in a number of folders among the records of the Nazi archival administration in Galicia, TsDIAL, fond 755, among the ERR and Nazi Archival Administration files in TsDAVO in Kyiv, and among the records of the Nazi Sippenstellen records in Germany—BAK, NS 39.

[74] The address of this bureau was given as Oranienbürgerstr. 48, Berlin N 4, which was a former synagogue. See, for example, the instructions dated 29 June and 2 July 1942 and related correspondence in TsDIAL, 755/1/123.

[75] See, for example, the report by Polish archivist Michał Wąsowicz, "Verzeichnis der im Staatsarchiv Lemberg (Dominikanerkloster) befindlichen jüdischen Personalstandregister," 22 July 1942, TsDIAL, fond 755/1, d. 129. The original is in the Bundesarchiv, R 146/67. This report lists extant metricular registers held in the Dominican Monastery depot of State Archive in Lviv from Jewish communities in Bilyi Kamin (Biały Kamień), Brody, Busk, Novyi Iarychiv (Jaryczów Nowy), Krakovets (Krakowiec), Shchyrets (Szczerzec), Lviv-Znesinnia (Lwów-Zniesienie), Velyki Mosty (Mosty Wielkie), Nemyriv (Niemirów), Oleshytsi (Oleszyce), Peremyshliany (Przemyślany), Radekhiv (Radziechów), Sokal, Svyrzh (Swirz), Vynnyky (Winniki), and Zolochiv (Złoczów), some of which dated back to the nineteenth century.

[76] Metricular registers from Jewish communities in Husiatyn (1815–1909), Melnytsia (1829–1852), and Ternopil (1816–1863) were reported in the State Archive

apparently doing all they could to delay these shipments, suspecting their sinister intent. Stryi reported in September 1943 that they could not get all the metricular registers together, and a report came in from Stanyslaviv that in one village in their district, the Jewish community had destroyed their metricular books.[79]

The possible survival and present whereabouts of all those that were shipped has also not been established, so far as is known, although recent Israeli efforts have been extensive in this area. After the war, the type of genealogical materials and church records the Nazis had looted were not a high priority for Soviet archival authorities. While the Nazi shipping lists were kept in secret in Lviv among the Soviet-captured occupation records, no one there has paid any attention to them in compiling reports on Nazi looting, and appropriate claims were never filed. At least now the actual records seized can be better documented and further research undertaken to determine their fate after they were shipped to Berlin or Poland during the war.

Nazi Library and Other Cultural Plunder. As noted earlier, Nazi archival plunder from Ukrainian lands was much less extensive than was the case for plunder from libraries and museums. The general lines of library plunder have already been suggested by earlier published studies, but a comprehensive documented account of library shipments and their destinations is still needed. Catalogs or databases of individual libraries and museums or individual regions need to take into account Nazi as well as Soviet documentation. For indeed, wartime Nazi reports that were captured by Soviet authorities after the war provide much more precise detail than the hastily compiled ChGK reports prepared with minimal documentation by returning Soviet authorities immediately following the conflict.

Oleksandr Fedoruk, who heads the Ukrainian Restitution Commission,

---

in Ternopil—BAK, R 146/67. See also "Verzeichnis jüdischen Matrikenbucher," MS, Ternopil (29 February 1944), TsDIAL, 755/1/05, fols. 19–20.

[77] "Verzeichnis der im Staatsarchiv Stanislau befindlichen jüdischen Matrikenzweitschriften," compiled by Kuchta (25 September 1942), included records from Zolotvyna (1916–1931), Iezupil (1923–1931), Mariiupil (1922–1931, 1936), Halych (1923–1931, 1936), Bohorodchany (1919–1931, 1936), and Lysiets (1919–1931)—BAK, R 146/67.

[78] Sambir lists compiled by Johann Baranecky (8 August 1942) include holdings from Drohobych (scattered), Skole (1916–1937), Sokołow (1869–1875), Stryi (1869–1937), and Turka (1931 and 1937)—BAK, R 146/67.

[79] Reports of 8 July and 17 September 1943, TsDIAL, 755/1/405, passim.

quotes the figure of 51 million books that disappeared from Ukrainian libraries during the war.[80] Another specialist cites the figure of over 50 million books "plundered, looted, and taken to Germany."[81] The significance of those statistics is not clear, nor can we assume that all of those lost were actually plundered, or that all of the plundered books were taken to Germany. Local looting and destruction also have to be taken into account. As we have seen, ChGK statistics do not differentiate among figures for items destroyed, plundered, or lost, and they were never counter-checked against available German documentation. Nazi shipments were alternately measured in crates, railway wagons, or tons, and often individual numbers of volumes were not counted in the haste. Hence, only rough estimates can be given for plundered books.

Nazi plunder from Ukrainian libraries vastly surpassed archival plunder, but only a few of the shipments went to Germany itself. The largest shipments from Ukraine—especially at the end of the war in the summer and fall of 1943—went to the ERR center in Ratibor (*Pol.* Racibórz) in Silesia, where an estimated two million or more volumes from all over the USSR and Western Europe were concentrated by 1944. Extensive shipments went especially from Kyiv and Kharkiv libraries, but it is doubtful that the total plundered from Ukraine sent to Ratibor reached more than one million volumes.

Other shipments from Ukraine went to the Central Library of the Hohe Schule under the ERR, which at the end of the war was concentrated in the Monastery of Tanzenberg in the Austrian Tyrol; but Ukrainian holdings there were limited to about 10,000 volumes, principally those taken initially by the Künsberg Commandos, according to postwar British findings.

Probably not more than half a million books from Ukraine (including Judaica and Hebraica) ended up in western Germany at the end of the war, according to U.S. restitution statistics to be discussed in the next chapter. A comprehensive account, based on reliable documentation, still needs compilation. While the 50-million figure may represent total losses, it remains exceedingly doubtful that the Nazis managed to plunder and ship west more than a couple of million at the most. Similar problems remain in establishing statistics for losses and Nazi plunder from Ukrainian museums; much research lies ahead.

[80] Fedoruk, "Ukraine: The Lost Cultural Treasures" in *The Spoils of War: WWII and Aftermath*, p. 73.

[81] Lazorenko, "Dolia bibliotek pid chas Druhoï svitovoï viiny," *Bibliotechnyi visnyk* 1995 (6): 8.

Soviet Search and Retrieval Operations

Soviet Archival Retrievals. The official Soviet inflated statistics about the totality of Nazi destruction and plunder also led to minimal reporting—and few publicly available data—about the extensive and largely successful Soviet archival recovery operations after the war. Recently opened files in Moscow and Kyiv and other capitals are revealing considerable new details regarding postwar retrieval by Soviet authorities. Some of the successful retrieval operations were first documented in the 1968 dissertation by Tsaplin, the relevant chapters of which were recently published. However, no effort was made to update the references or supplement them with additional recently declassified documentation.[82]

For Ukraine, these include the highly successful missions sent to Romania, Czechoslovakia, and Poland to retrieve the Ukrainian archival treasures that the Nazis and their Romanian allies had earlier evacuated. During 1945 alone, according to a year-end Glavarkhiv secret report, fifteen wagons were sent from Czechoslovakia to Ukraine and Latvia, and six wagons from Poland to Lviv.[83] Others followed in 1946. Three freight-car loads taken by the Künsberg brigade from the Odesa archives for Nazi leader Georg Leibbrandt early in the war were found in a salt mine in Saxony and returned in 1946.[84]

Some of the Nazi-looted Communist Party archival materials from Dnipropetrovsk and Kirovohrad shipped to Silesia by the Einsatzstab Reichsleiter Rosenberg (ERR) were likewise returned.[85] Twenty crates of the

---

[82] See Tsaplin, "Arkhivy, voina i okkupatsiia (1941–1945 gody)" and the two-part article "O rozyske dokumentov, pokhishchennykh v gody voiny iz arkhivokhranilishch SSSR," *Otechestvennye arkhivy* 1997 (5): 7–25; and (6): 12–28. Many of the files he did cite have been subsequently rearranged with new *opis'* and item numbers, which unfortunately are not reflected in the published articles.

[83] "Spravka o rezul'tatakh raboty GAU NKVD SSSR po vozvrashcheniiu v Sov. Soiuz dokumental'nykh materialov GAF SSSR i o vyvoze v SSSR arkhivov inostrannogo proiskhozhdeniia," signed by Golubtsov and Kuz'min (15 December 1945), GA RF, 5325/10/2148, fols. 1–4.

[84] Chechkov to Nikitinskii, GA RF, 5325/2/1620, fols. 158–159. Another report (13 November 1945) notes that 230 crates from Odesa were recovered in the Stassfurt mine, TsDAVO, 14/7/56. Regarding the plundering by the Künsberg Commandos, see above, esp. fns. 59 and 60.

[85] The return of Ukrainian Party archives is documented in Grimsted, *The Odyssey of the Smolensk Archive*, esp. pp. 20–23.

Kirovohrad records were found intact by Soviet authorities in the summer of 1945.[86] Many of the Dnipropetrovsk records came back by way of Minsk the following year, but archivists have shown that what was returned was only a part of what the Nazis had shipped to Ratibor in Silesia. Soviet authorities had requested a search of the Ratibor area in postwar years, but without success. A recent, well-documented study by Dnipropetrovsk archivist Dmytro Meshkov documents wartime developments and losses in that oblast, including those records that were not returned from Ratibor.[87]

Although Soviet reports initially claimed that the Nazis destroyed or looted the entire Central State Archive of Documentary Films, Photographs, and Sound Recordings (TsDAKFFD) in Kyiv, some 500 crates with 50,000 negatives were recovered by Soviet authorities in the Dresden area after the war and returned to Kyiv in 1946–1947, and another 17,190 were retrieved from Vienna.[88] There were serious complaints at the time of their return that they came without any finding aids or reference materials, but that is quite understandable, given Soviet destruction policies mentioned above. Quite probably, Kyiv archivists, who were unable to evacuate the archive, followed Soviet orders for the destruction or at least displacement of finding aids in the summer of 1941. More recently in 1992, additional photographs looted by the ERR from Kyiv, together with many that they took themselves, were found in the Bundesarchiv in Koblenz with a larger Nazi photograph collection. Most of that collection had earlier been restituted to the Bundesarchiv by the Library of Congress.[89] In 1997, a collection of over 4,000 pictures was

---

[86] The recovery of the Kirovohrad materials in Silesia is documented in a telegram from the Ukrainian CP historian Shevchenko to Litvinov, TsDAHO, 1/23/1484, fol. 15.

[87] Dmytro Meshkov, *Dnipropetrovs'ki arkhivy, muzeï ta biblioteky v roky Druhoï svitovoï viiny: Anotovanyi perelik dokumentiv i materialiv* (Kyiv, 2000), p. 11 [=Dolia kul'turnykh skarbiv Ukraïny pid chas Druhoï svitovoï viiny: Arkhivy, biblioteky, muzeï, 3; Problemy edytsiinoï ta kameral'noï arkheohrafiï: Istoriia, teoriia, metodyka, 24]. See also his earlier brief report by Meshkov, "Dnipropetrovs'ki arkhivy pid chas Druhoï svitovoï viiny," in *Materialy natsional'noho seminaru. Chernihiv, 1994*, p. 190.

[88] According to a July 1946 report, Pshenichnyi, "Dokladnaia zapiska o prodelannoi rabote TsGAFFKD MVD UkrSSR za 1-e polugodie 1946 g." (13 December 1946), GA RF, 5325/2/1620/113.

[89] See the report by Hennadii V. Boriak, "U ramkakh proektu 'Dolia kul'turnykh tsinnostei vyvezenykh z Ukraïny pid chas Druhoï svitovoï viiny,'" *Arkhivy Ukraïny* 1993 (1–3): 83–84.

returned to Kyiv from Koblenz.[90]

Unlike the situation with art and other museum exhibits, there is no evidence that Ukrainian archival materials that were looted by the Nazis and later retrieved by Soviet authorities did not go back to Ukraine. Although some archival materials surely were lost or destroyed en route, the loss and destruction subsequently documented frequently do not add up to the initial ChGK figures. Once those figures had been filed, however, they were rarely revised.

Lviv Archives from Poland. Another bitter irony of archival preservation due to Nazi evacuation can be seen in western Ukraine. During the winter and spring of 1944, as the Red Army was pushing west and bombs started to fall on Lviv, the Nazis succeeded in evacuating a large percentage of the historical archives from Lviv to the Benedictine Abbey of Tyniec high above the Vistula, near Cracow. This was done with the approval of Polish archival directors in Lviv, who negotiated an agreement with the Nazis not to take the materials further west, as they had first planned. Between 25 January and 26 May, at least eight or nine shipments, most by rail but some of the later ones by truck, went from Lviv to Cracow, and most of the materials were transferred further to Tyniec.[91] These evacuations clearly should not be considered plunder, as there is no question about the intent to preserve the archive in the face of anticipated bombing and violent warfare in the city of Lviv. A year later, all of the evacuated treasures from the Lviv historical archives were retrieved intact by Soviet authorities and returned to Lviv in April 1945.[92] In the meantime, the—fortunately—almost empty building that had housed them in Lviv was devastated by Soviet bombs on Easter Sunday

---

[90]   Elena Mashchenko, "Ukrainskie arkhivy vozvrashchaiutsia na rodinu," *Zerkalo nedeli* 48(165) 29 November 1997: 15; Ihor Petrov, "Nimets'ki foto vykryvaiut' zlochyny NKVS," *Chas* 27 February–5 March 1997: 71; Olena Grinchenko, "Chy potribne nam zoloto skifiv?" *Den'* 119 (25 June 1997): 7.

[91]   Detailed inventories of the contents of the 1944 Lviv shipments are found among the Nazi archival records in Lviv, TsDIAL, 755/1/285. Some of these details are documented by Grimsted, "The Fate of Ukrainian Cultural Treasures," pp. 71–72; and the Ukrainian version, *Dolia skarbiv ukraïns'koï kul'tury*. None of the previous publications mentioning Lviv evacuations fully document the shipments and their return, but such a report is in preparation.

[92]   One recently declassified report on some of the six freight cars returned from Tyniec (via Cracow), 18 May 1945, is found in TsDAVO, 14/7/55, fols. 19–20. They are also described in several other Glavarkhiv reports available both in Kyiv and Moscow.

(New Style) in April 1944.[93] There were, however, a number of Polish manuscript treasures, mainly from Lviv libraries, that were also evacuated at the same time and never returned.[94] More controversy remains regarding their fate. This will be discussed in Chapter 11.

There were a number of subsequent Soviet scholarly claims that some valuable charters from the Lviv archives were not returned.[95] A serious study of the parchment charters lost from the Lviv archive was prepared by the Lviv historian Oleh Kupchyns'kyi and published in 1982. It lists only part of the archival materials evacuated on the basis of Soviet postwar official reports. The author was unaware of, or not given access to, the careful German reports of the evacuations that provide precise detail about each shipment, with inventories of the contents of each crate.[96] One important group of charters (and possibly a few early register books) was removed from Cracow and taken to the Nazi archival center in Troppau, from whence they were later retrieved by Soviet archival scouts.

Some charters from Lviv Roman Catholic sources were transferred with other Catholic Church archives to Poland, although most of them still remained in Lviv. The latter group, to be sure, did not return to Lviv, because the Polish Catholic Church subsequently claimed them, along with additional Roman Catholic Church records that were officially transferred to Poland in 1946.[97] The need to modify further the Soviet account of lost charters arises

---

[93] Pictures of the destroyed archival building in Lviv and an account of the bombing are among the personal papers of the Polish archivist Karl Badecki, who directed the Lviv archive at the time, now held in the Jagellonian Library in Cracow.

[94] See Maciej Matwijów, "Ewakuacja zbiorów polskich ze Lwowa w 1944 r.," *Rocznik Lwowski* 1995/1996: 31–46. See also the Matwijów monograph, *Walka o lwowskie dobra kultury w latach 1945–1948* (Wrocław: Towarzystwo Przyjaciół Ossolineum, 1996).

[95] Most of the charters were taken first to Skawina, the railroad junction close to Tyniec, with the third shipment on 1 February 1944, which contained 28 numbered crates; 814 parchment charters (1234–1796) were packed in crates nos. 1–4. TsDIAL, 755/1/285, fols. 66, 74–83.

[96] See Oleh Antonovych Kupchyns'kyi, "Vtracheni perhamentni hramoty mist i sil Halychyny XIV–pershoï polovyny XIX st.," in *Bibliotekoznavstvo ta bibliohrafiia: Mizhvidomchyi respublikans'kyi zbirnyk statei* (Kyiv, 1982), pp. 72–95. Soviet scholars were not permitted to cite Nazi reports; even today, many are loathe to do so.

[97] One report signed by the Polish archivist Karl Badecki mentions plans to pack 320 parchment charters, together with 354 record books and an additional 115 fascicles from the archive of the Roman Catholic Cathedral in Lviv, but these were not specified in the shipping lists in that file—TsDIAL, 755/1/285, fol. 93; it is not

from the recently revealed top secret report that at least 128, or perhaps as many as 227, charters from the Polish period, including some dating back to the fourteenth century, were maliciously destroyed in 1946 after their return to Lviv in a curiously unexplained incident of sabotage within the archive building itself.[98]

Retrieval of Romanian-Looted Archives. While considerable data has been presented about looting by the Nazis and retrieval from Germany, often overlooked for Ukraine is the even more extensive archival looting by Romanian authorities during the war. After Romania had been overrun by the Nazis and had become allied with the Axis, Romanian authorities were given responsibility for occupation in adjacent areas in Ukraine. Romanian archival seizures—from Odesa and the Black Sea Coast, from Moldova, and from Bukovyna—greatly outnumbered those removed by the Germans themselves from all of Ukraine. One aggregate Glavarkhiv report suggested a total of 9,297 fonds with 94,249,438 file units were removed by the Romanians, and another 872,973 volumes of library books and 32,000 newspapers.[99]

In 1945 Soviet authorities already had a mission in Romania retrieving plundered Ukrainian archives. Fifty-four wagons were retrieved from Romania to Ukraine and Moldova by the end of the year.[100] But that statistic was only for retrieved files and did not take into account the extensive

---

clear if these were sent with a separate shipment in February or a later one in March. See Matwijów, *Walka o lwowskie dobra kultury*, pp. 123–24. Matwijów does not document any wartime evacuations from Roman Catholic sources, but he did not have access to the Nazi records in Lviv; I was earlier given oral reports by Catholic specialists in Poland regarding those developments.

[98]   Reports about this incident, first directed to the Ukrainian Party secretary, were forwarded to Moscow archival authorities at the time and are now found in recently opened Glavarkhiv files there. See T. Strokai to N. S. Khrushchev (5 June 1946), GA RF, 5325/2/1620/127, and the subsequent report of Gudzenko to Nikitinskii (26 July 1946), fol. 145, and (17 July 1947), fol. 147. One report raises the destroyed figure to 227.

[99]   Loburenko to Nikitinskii (27 September 1944), fol. 3–3v (cc fol. 4–4v). A more detailed breakdown follows explaining statistics and Romanian destinations for materails from Akkerman, Odesa, and other cities.

[100]   "Spravka o rezul'tatakh raboty GAU NKVD SSSR po vozvrashcheniiu v Sov. Soiuz dokumental'nykh materialov GAF SSSR i o vyvoze v SSSR arkhivov inostrannogo proiskhozhdeniia," signed by Golubtsov and Kuz'min (15 December 1945), GA RF, 5325/10/2148, fols. 1–4. See also Tsaplin, "O rozyske dokumentov," pp. 12–14.

Romanian records, especially police files and wartime occupation records, that were seized by Soviet authorities for intelligence analysis. Many other Romanian records of provenance in and relating to recently annexed areas of Northern Bukovyna and Transcarpathia were also transferred from Romania after the war.[101]

Considerably more research needs to be done by specialists who are prepared to question the ChGK statistics and weigh simplistic ChGK conclusions against the numerous other reports that are becoming available. We also now have access to many precise reports by Nazi archivists with their findings immediately after arrival, to say nothing of many long-suppressed files with Nazi archival surveys and appraisals on the Eastern Front, including detailed shipping lists for many evacuations.[102] Those, too, cannot always be taken at face value, but they, and other CPSU and Glavarkhiv declassified files, help to create a more precise account. The truth about what was destroyed by both sides and how, and about what was evacuated by both sides and why, is not easy to establish. But we must try. Certainly, as we have seen, in the case of Kyiv we need to look beyond and behind the 1944 ChGK report in *Pravda* for that truth. It will take years of painstaking research to arrive at an authoritative history of archival and library developments during and immediately after the war, and given all the variables, reliable statistics are becoming more difficult to substantiate. Nevertheless, some of the "blank spots" in Soviet histories of the war already are coming into focus, and new details about wartime destruction, plunder, and postwar retrieval make it possible to present a far more complex—but also more realistic—picture.

---

[101] In recently declassified files of HAU URSR records, there are numerous other reports about materials returned to Ukraine from Romania—TsDAVO, 14/7/55, 55–57, and 90, among others. Additional reports are found in GA RF, 5325/10/1883 and 1884, and 5325/2/992994, 1352, and 1704, among others. See also Chapter 8, p. 302n68.

[102] A recent dissertation defended in Kyiv, based on extant Nazi documentation and other sources, provides an essential starting point for study of the Nazi archival administration in Ukraine during the war—Maryna H. Dubyk, *Arkhivna sprava v okupovanii Ukraïni (1941–1944 rr.)*, Avtoreferat dysertatsiï na zdobuttia naukovoho stupenia kandydata istorychnykh nauk (Kyiv, 1997).

CHAPTER 6

Western Allied Restitution in the Postwar Context

War Losses and Western Archival Restitution

The popular Soviet mind-set about the war and postwar developments had an enormous blind spot regarding the extent of Western restitution of Nazi-looted archives and other cultural treasures to the USSR, including Ukraine. The past suppression of information led to an almost total lack of public knowledge regarding the restitutions made from various American collection centers in occupied Germany during the years 1945 through 1949.

After the triumph over Nazi Germany, growing disagreements between the USSR and the Western Allies about the fate of Germany and with respect to reparation policies prevented a quadripartite agreement for cultural restitution. As a result, restitution (or non-restitution) programs were handled differently in each zone of occupation of Germany and Austria. After the Potsdam Conference in the fall of 1945, the unilateral American program of restitution to the country of origin started in full force from the over 1,800 salt mines, castles, and other depositories where the Nazis had hidden their loot.

There have been several studies of the Western Allied restitution program, but the most thorough general study with a detailed survey of international legal and procedural matters among the Western occupying powers in Germany does not even mention restitution to the USSR.[1] Most recently, the Polish international legal scholar Wojciech Kowalski has analyzed the varying concepts of restitution, "restitution in kind," and their

---

[1]   Regarding the U.S. restitution program, see especially the doctoral dissertation by Michael J. Kurtz (now Assistant Archivist of the U. S. for the National Archives), *Nazi Contraband: American Policy on the Return of European Cultural Treasures, 1945–1955* (New York: Garland Press, 1985). See also Kurtz's contribution, "The End of the War and the Occupation of Germany, 1944–52. Laws and Conventions Enacted to Counter German Appropriations: The Allied Control Council," in *The Spoils of War: WWII and Aftermath*, pp. 112–16, which summarizes some of the legal developments affecting restitution by the Allied Control Council.

practical developments from a legal standpoint that emphasizes the restitution of cultural treasures and, particularly, art.[2]

Part of Lynn Nicholas' *Rape of Europa* follows the efforts—within the Western invading armies—of specially appointed Allied "Monuments, Fine Arts, and Archives Officers" to monitor the protection of cultural treasures. The book contains excellent sections that survey postwar restitution by the Western Allies. Because her book was written before the revelation of the Russian spoils of war, she does not deal with postwar developments on the Soviet front or the issue of restitution to the USSR.[3] This area was so little known in the West that, when queried on the matter at a 1995 Bard Symposium in New York, the participating directors of the postwar U.S. restitution centers had no recollection of shipments to the USSR.[4]

[2]   Wojciech W. Kowalski, *Art Treasures and War: A Study on the Restitution of Looted Cultural Property, Pursuant to Public International Law* (London: Institute of Art and Law, 1998), especially chapters 2 and 3. See also Kowalski's earlier study, *Liquidation of the Effects of World War II in the Area of Culture* (Warsaw: Institute of Culture, 1994); and his *Likwidacja skutków II Wojny Światowej w dziedzinie kultury*, 2nd ed. (Warsaw: Institute of Culture, 1994).

[3]   Lynn H. Nicholas, *The Rape of Europa: The Fate of Europe's Treasures in the Third Reich and the Second World War* (New York: Alfred A. Knopf, 1994), see especially chapters 8–10 regarding the invasions and chapters 11–13 on American postwar restitution.

[4]   The Bard Symposium devoted separate sessions to the legal and practical implementation of the Western policy of cultural restitution and the Soviet policy of cultural appropriation "for compensatory cultural reparations." My intervention—a question raised on the matter in the discussion period of the session on the American restitution program—was the only reminder during the symposium of U.S. restitution to the Soviet Union at the start of the Cold War. When none of the participating restitution center directors recalled such shipments, I pointed out a relevant U.S. Army document that I had reprinted several years earlier in the Ukrainian edition of my study of displaced cultural treasures during and after the war (see fns. 5, 15, and 30, below). See also my "Captured Archives and Restitution Problems on the Eastern Front: Beyond the Bard Graduate Center Symposium," in *The Spoils of War: WWII and Aftermath*, p. 246.

The Record of American Restitution

Restitution to the USSR. Complete records of the American transfers have long been open to the public in the West, including property cards for individual items and detailed inventories of restitution shipments. In answer to inquiries by Soviet authorities in the fall of 1948, the Restitution Division of the Property Branch of OMGUS prepared a list of 13 restitution shipments with over half a million items that were turned over to Soviet authorities between September 1945 and September 1948 from U.S. restitution centers in Germany. Materials returned included many types of cultural treasures, from eight freight cars in October 1947 with components of the Neptune Fountain from Peterhof (found in underground storage vaults in Nuremberg) to over 168,000 treasures from Ukraine (found in the castle of Höchstädt and the Abbey of Buxheim in Bavaria), as well as archival materials and library books. An accompanying memorandum noted that the number of items returned to the USSR "amounted to a far greater number of items than the number of items officially claimed [by Soviet authorities]." The text of the list of shipments and accompanying memorandum was first published in Ukraine in 1991 as an appendix to a study by Boriak and Grimsted of the fate of cultural treasures from Ukraine during and after the war.[5]

Restitution to Ukraine itself is more difficult to document because American authorities officially handed over materials to Soviet representatives in Germany and had no knowledge about their subsequent

---

[5]   See the official U.S. Army list and explanatory text first published in facsimile as an appendix to Grimsted and Boriak, *Dolia skarbiv ukraïns'koï kul'tury pid chas Druhoï svitovoï viiny: Vynyshchennia arkhiviv, bibliotek, muzeïv* (Kyiv: Arkheohrafichna komisiia AN URSR, 1991), pp. 117–19. (It appears here as Appendix IX.) The original list and covering memorandum (20 September 1948) are from US NA, RG 260 (OMGUS), Property Division–Restitution Branch, box 723. The list, "Restituted Russian Property," was enclosed with a report from Richard F. Howard, Deputy Chief for Cultural Restitution (MFA&A), dated Karlsruhe, Germany (20 September 1948). Regarding the inventories and property cards, see fn. 15, below. Another copy of the list of shipments to Russia is found in the Ardelia Hall Collection, box 38, but that copy lacks the accompanying memoranda and does not indicate the Kyiv components. In the case of the return of the Neptune Fountain, a four-page German-language inventory of its components is attached to the official receipt for the eight freightcars, found in RG 260, Property Division, Restitution Branch, box 40, Soviet Munich receipt no. 5. See also the article by Karin Jeltsch, "Der Raub des Neptunbrunnens aus Schloss Peterhof," in *"Betr: Sicherstellung,"* pp. 67–74.

fate. American Army personnel used the term "Russian" with reference to all parts of the Soviet Union, and sometimes made no distinction as to the "Ukrainian" component. Ukrainian authorities were denied direct access to U.S. restitution centers. However, apparently in response to some official inquiry, one surviving copy of the U.S. Army list of restitution shipments to "RUSSIA" through fall 1948 mentioned above, specifically notes that at least "167,717 of the 534,120 items of Restituted Russian Property" were from Kyiv.[6] Other analyses, and specifically those undertaken by Bremen specialists, suggest that no less than 350,000 Ukrainian cultural treasures were among those restituted to Soviet authorities, although most probably American restitution specialists had not identified all of them as Ukrainian.[7]

Restitution to Ukraine. Based on increasing documentation, there are now strong Ukrainian pretensions about the cultural treasures (including icons) turned over to Soviet authorities from the West that were not subsequently returned to Kyiv. Because the Soviet Union did not participate in the Western allied restitution process after the war, and maintained secrecy about its own trophy seizure operations, there was little sharing of data with the public. Even today, many of the comparable files regarding the Soviet receiving side of the restitution process, such as the records of the Property Division of the Soviet Military Administration in Germany (SVAG), the Soviet collection centers in Germany, and distribution centers in the USSR from the State Fond for Literature (Gosfond) and the Central Repository of the Museum Fond, located in suburban Leningrad palaces, have either not been located in their entirety or remain closed to the public. A report about the operation of the latter agency at the Chernihiv 1994 conference suggests some of the problems involved and the fact that only part of its records survive.[8] Ukrainian specialists recently have been trying to document the fate of some of the cultural treasures that did not come back to Kyiv, but the task is exceedingly difficult, given the inadequacy of open records.

---

[6]   The Kyiv totals are specified in the official U.S. Army list and explanatory text cited in fn. 5, above.

[7]   See, for example, "Ukrainskie tsennosti ostalis' v Rossii," *Kommersant Daily* 119 (4 July 1998): 7. Full documentation for the higher figure has not appeared in print, although reportedly it has been established by Bremen researchers.

[8]   Irina Matveeva, "Diial'nist' Tsentral'noho skhovyshcha muzeinykh fondiv po rozshuku vtrachenykh kul'turnykh tsinnostei u pershi povoienni roky," *Materialy natsional'noho seminaru, Chernihiv, 1994*, pp. 243–46.

One prime example is the fate of the now dispersed mosaics from the St. Michael Cathedral of the Golden Domes in Kyiv about which Ukrainian specialists have been conducting special investigations. As noted earlier in Chapter 2, many of those frescoes have been identified in Moscow, Petersburg, and Novgorod museums. It is clear that at least the ones in Moscow were sent there before the war, and as yet full documentation has not been found regarding the migration of those in St. Petersburg and Novgorod. Subsequent to their October 1943 shipment to Cracow and thence to the Bavarian castle of Höchstädt, they passed through the U.S. Army Collecting Point in Munich, along with many other museum treasures from Ukraine. Some of the mosaics did return to Kyiv, but no documents have been found nor explanation of their transfer, nor of the transfer of others to the Russian museums where they are now housed. According to Ukrainian historian Serhii Kot, who has been analyzing the various available sources, of the 27 frescoes and 1 mosaic seized by the Nazis and taken to Germany, only 14 items (fragments of 1 mosaic, 10 frescoes, and 3 crates of fragments) were returned to Kyiv after the war.[9] Now that the St. Michael Cathedral has been rebuilt in Kyiv, there is a greater urgency for their return to Ukraine.

Although incomplete postwar records may plague the documentation of many cases of wartime losses of cultural treasures, a few recently opened files among the records of the Committee on Cultural and Educational Institutions of the RSFSR in Moscow do, nevertheless, contain some important documents involving both shipments from Germany and distribution of retrieved cultural treasures. Although remaining documentation there is exceedingly fragmentary, but transfer documents have been preserved that bear signatures from Ukrainian museums for at least some of the receipts from the West.[10] Documents there, however, match up with only a few of the

[9]   See especially the latest publication by Serhii Kot and Iurii Koreniuk, "Mykhailivs'ki pam'iatky v rosiis'kykh muzeiakh," in *Pam'iatky Ukraïny* 1999 (1[122]): 63–82; the German shipping list and the official list of restituted items are published as documentary appendices (pp. XXVI–XXVIII).

[10]   In 1997 I was granted special permission to examine files within the partially declassified series (*opis'* 2) of the records of the RSFSR Committee on Cultural and Educational Institutions (Komitet po delam kul'turno-prosvetilel'skikh uchrezhdenii) (predecessor of the Ministry of Culture), GA RF, A-534/2, which still are not open to all researchers. For example, among shipments to the USSR in one list from June 1946 were 26 crates from the UkrSSR, including materials from an herbarium, an entomological collection, and negatives and books from the Institutes of Biology and Zoology—T. Zuev to A. A. Zhdanov (6 June 1946), GA RF, A-534/2/10, fol. 218.

U.S.-Soviet signed receipts, and some of the Soviet documents bear no indication whence or when the materials were received. The Bremen group also surveyed this problem to a limited extent and cites some of the same documents regarding the materials returned. But their researchers have also found inadequate documentation, and not all files were available to them.[11] None of this Moscow documentation deals with archives.

More documentation for museum exhibits is nonetheless available from American sources, even though it may not always be sufficient for identification purposes. As one of the most impressive achievements of the Bremen project (Forschungsstelle Osteuropa) mentioned above, a computerized German-language version of these "Property Card—Art" files, was released on CD-ROM in 1996, presenting a German-language version of data from the half-million property cards and claims for cultural objects returned from the U.S. Zone of Occupation to the USSR.[12] In addition to a copy presented to the Ukrainian Commission for Cultural Restitution, a copy was presented by German Chancellor Helmut Kohl to Russian President Boris Yeltsin. It also is under study by restitution specialists in the Ministry of Culture in Moscow. The 1998 Bremen volume includes a good overview of the U.S. restitution program, and some limited information about the

---

One signed receipt (with notation of corresponding U.S. property card numbers), dated 6 November 1947, specifies 1,127 museum items from Kyiv among 2,391 items received from the American Zone, GA RF, A-534/2/14, fols. 10–19, fol. 34, fols. 39–40. Another file (GA RF, A-534/2/13), includes receipts for 40 crates for the Kerch Museum (fol. 3), 268 items for the Historical Museum in Kyiv (fols. 9–15), and others being transferred to Feodosiia in Crimea in 1948 (although Crimea was not administratively part of the UkrSSR until 1954).

[11] By and large the Bremen team received copies of documents from the same set of files that I examined for this study, but it is not clear that all of those files were open to them. See Ulrike Hartung, "Die Weg zurück: Russische Akten bestätigen die Rückführung eigener Kulturgüter aus Deutschland nach dem Zweiten Weltkrieg. Probleme ihrer Erfassung," in *"Betr: Sicherstellung,"* pp. 170–208. The documents cited are the same that I examined in GA RF, fond A-534, *opis'* 2. The German researchers themselves had not examined these files *de visu*, but copies apparently had been obtained for them.

[12] Wolfgang Eichwede and Ulrike Hartung, "Property Cards Art, Claims and Shipments. Amerikanische Rückführungen sowjetischer Kulturgüter an die UdSSR nach dem Zweiten Weltkrieg"—Die CD der Arbeitsstelle "Verbleib der im Zweiten Weltkrieg aus der Sowjetunion verlagerten Kulturgüter" (Bremen: Forschungsstelle Osteuropa, 1996).

return of various cultural treasures to the USSR.[13] A shorter summary was presented by one of the Bremen participants in the 1995 Odesa Roundtable.[14]

Copies of the original U.S. Army "Property Cards—Art" that were prepared at U.S. restitution centers in Germany for over half a million items returned to the USSR (most particularly from the Munich Collecting Point) were located and identified in the Bundesarchiv in Koblenz in 1993. They were soon thereafter photocopied and a set of the copies of the archival originals was presented to Ukraine in 1994. The presentation of the copies made a sensation among Ukrainian museum specialists at a special archival-museum section of the UNESCO-sponsored conference on World War II cultural displacements held in Chernihiv in September 1994.[15] Previously, Ukrainian cultural specialists had no idea that such records even existed. A number of Ukrainian museums have since undertaken a careful examination of these files, but they have been having difficulty matching up the property card descriptions with the missing cultural property and, especially, with Nazi inventories and shipping records.

---

[13]   Gabriele Freitag, "Die Restitution von NS-Beutegut nach dem zweiten Welt-krieg," in *"Betr: Sicherstellung,"* pp. 170–208.

[14]   Gabriele Freitag, "Okhrana pamiatnikov iskusstva v amerikanskoi zone i politicheskaia restitutsiia," in *Kul'tura i viina: Pohliad cherez pivstolittia*, ed. Viktor Akulenko, Valentyna Vrublevs'ka, et al. (Kyiv: Adrys, 1996), pp. 27–32.

[15]   The copies of the "Property Cards–Art" made available to Kyiv came from the records of the Collection Center in Munich, in BAK, B 323, which I first examined in Koblenz in 1993 together with then IUA Deputy Director Hennadii Boriak. We appreciate the assistance of Anja Heuss, who had earlier been working with these records on behalf of the Bremen project. The entire file was subsequently copied for presentation at the Chernihiv conference. See Boriak, "Bremens'kyi proekt 'Dolia kul'turnykh tsinnostei, vyvezenykh z SRSR v roky Druhoï svitovoï viiny' (FRN): Kameral'ni metodyky i problemy doslidzhennia istoriï arkhivnykh dokumentiv," in *Materialy natsional'noho seminaru. Chernihiv, 1994*, pp. 251–60.

Also found in that same record group is a summary inventory prepared from the property cards (organized by Soviet repository of origin), "Verzeichnis der Treuhandverwaltung von Kulturgut München bekanntgewordenen Restitutionen von 1945 bis 1962 USSR A–Z," BAK, B 323/578. Additional copies of the property cards and photographs of the materials restituted to the Soviet Union are available in the files of the various Collection Points in the U.S. Zone of Occupation that are held as part of the records of the U.S. Office of Military Government in Germany, US NA, RG 260 (OMGUS).

The Problem of Missing or Non-Existent Inventories. The difficulty of documenting postwar transfers is at the heart of current restitution controversies both in Russia and Ukraine. Russian Ministry of Culture specialists now claim that no inventories were presented with the U.S. restitution transfers. In fact, the Soviet copies of the American transfer documents and inventories of the cultural restitution transfers have not been located in Russia. To be sure only summary inventories were prepared for the official transfer documents by American restitution authorities, but more detailed documentation on these transfers has long been open in the U.S. National Archives and the Bundesarchiv in Germany. In the past, these were fully open to Soviet specialists if they chose to investigate; they continue to be open to Russian specialists. In some cases, admittedly, the sketchy descriptions on U.S. art property cards makes precise identification difficult, if not impossible.

The situation of several years ago has changed and Russian specialists from the Ministry of Culture now fully admit that the transfers took place. (Though politicians in the Duma still tend to claim that they did not.) Recently, Nikolai Nikandrov, a specialist in the Restitution Office of the Russian Ministry of Culture, complained about the lack of inventories received from the American side:

> Between 1945–47, the Americans handed over 13 loads of museum exhibits, books, archives, etc. to the Soviet Government. As we understand now, detailed lists of contents were not submitted together with the loads, at least we are still unable to find any trace of them. We also have witnesses that cultural items, which arrived to Berlin, terminal Derutra, did not have item lists attached.[16]

Nikandrov spoke openly about these problems at the 1997 conference on restitution in Minsk, in the most detailed Russian presentation to date on the subject. He cites, for example, the figure of 2,391 crates in the Derutra warehouse in Berlin on October 1947, "but not a single inventory...or other reference lists of contents." Given the lack of inventories, "correlation of information on restituted cultural treasures from the American Zone with

---

[16] A complaint to this effect has been published in the report by Nikolai Nikandrov, "Russia," in *Spoils of War: International Newsletter* 6 (February 1999): 50–52 (the quote is from p. 52). The same complaint has been made to me on numerous occasions by Nikandrov and other specialists in the cultural restitution office in the Ministry of Culture.

documentation we have from Russian archives is virtually impossible. And even the card files... given to the USSR (from the Federal Archives in Koblenz and the National Archives in Washington) have insufficiently concrete data."[17] Given the American copies of the transfer papers that are preserved in the U.S. National Archives, there is no question that at least summary inventories had been prepared for most shipments and undoubtedly accompanied the receipts signed by Soviet restitution officials—at least the U.S. copies are preserved.

Archival materials were usually minimally described, if at all, in the American lists, since property cards were not usually prepared for books and archival materials in the same way as they were for art and other museum exhibits. Hence, it is not surprising that the property cards presented to Ukraine yielded no archival materials that had not been accounted for earlier. Nevertheless, and interestingly enough, archives were front runners in the American restitution process after the war. The first U.S. Army restitution transfer to Soviet authorities, dated 20 September 1945, comprised four freight wagons with some 1,000 packages of "archival material removed by the Germans in 1943 from Novgorod," which was "currently stored at the Preußisches Geheimes Staatsarchiv" in Berlin-Dahlem.[18] Russian archival authorities, however, as late as 1998 reported no knowledge or documentation about this American restitution shipment.[19] In the case of the

---

[17] Nikolai Nikandrov, "Problemy vyiavleniia kul'turnykh tsennostei prinadlezhashchikh odnoi strane i peremeshchennykh na territoriiu drugoi strany v gody Vtoroi mirovoi voiny," in *Restytutsyia kul'turnykh kashtoŭnastsei,* pp. 58–67; the quotation is from pp. 60–61.

[18] A receipt for this shipment, from the U.S. Headquarters, Berlin District, signed by Lt. Col. Constantin Piartzany [*sic*] in Berlin (20 September 1945), together with a four-page list of box numbers for the 333 crates in the four numbered railway wagons, is found in US NA, 260, Ardelia Hall Collection, box 40, but no further description of the contents has been located in American restitution records.

[19] Soviet receipts for this shipment have not been found, and a Rosarkhiv inquiry to Novgorod in 1996 reported no documentation available there. Other specialists from Novgorod, as late as the fall of 1998, have been unable to find any local documentation regarding the return of such a shipment to Novgorod, although obviously further research is necessary. See the comment to this effect in response to my mention of this transfer in the introduction to *Summary Catalogue of the Cultural Valuables Stolen and Lost during the Second World War,* vol. 4: *State Archives of the Russian Federation: Lost Archives Funds,* comp. Elena E. Novikova et al.; ed. Pavel V. Khoroshilov et al., book 1 (Moscow: "IKAR," 1999), p. 19.

Novgorod archival materials (and presumably also some from Pskov) returned directly from Berlin before the opening of the U.S. restitution centers, even survey fond-level inventories of the contents of the 333 numbered crates have not been found among remaining U.S. records; the official transfer inventories listed only the numbers of the crates as they were loaded in the four numbered railroad freight wagons in Berlin. No indication of their contents has been found so far.[20]

The lack of adequate inventories in the Novgorod case contrasts to those in the other twelve shipments of cultural treasures listed in the U.S. Army document cited above. The fact that even official Russian Ministry of Culture specialists have not been able to locate the official Soviet copies of those documents with the accompanying U.S. inventories may suggest that they were not forwarded by SVAG restitution officials to the Soviet distribution center in Berlin, or to the subsequent distribution center in suburban Leningrad. Since Russian officials have not yet found this important documentation, copies are being provided from the U.S. National Archives, which may help resolve some of the remaining controversies about materials not returned to Ukraine and elsewhere.[21]

Although matching and tracing transfers may not still be possible in all cases, additional information about the contents and migration of specific shipments may help identify their movements, even if data on individual items may not always be available. In any case, more open international sharing of what limited documentation is available might assist both Russian and Ukrainian specialists to trace more exactly which of the materials identified by U.S. specialists in Germany as being of Ukrainian origin were or were not appropriately forwarded to Ukraine after their arrival in the USSR. The extant American inventories will then need to be compared against what records do remain of incoming shipments in Russian archives. This also might help to counter the criticism that many cultural treasures

---

[20]   This is most likely the same group of materials mentioned in ERR reports and inventories, which reference four wagons from Novgorod, Pskov, and Gatchina, that were first shipped to Riga and then Berlin: TsDAVO, 3676/1/136, fols. 53–78. The inventory is accompanied by a report by German archivist Wolfgang Mommsen (8 September 1942), fols. 74–76. Further research on this matter is under way.

[21]   See my forthcoming publication *U.S. Restitution of Nazi-Looted Cultural Treasures to the USSR, 1945–1959: Facsimile Documents from the National Archives of the United States,* comp., with an intro., by Patricia Kennedy Grimsted; forward by Michael J. Kurtz (Washington, DC: GPO, 2001). Russian and Ukrainian editions are also under way.

from Soviet lands found by the Americans after the war were not returned to the USSR and are now found in the United States.

The misinformation and incomplete information hitherto available about wartime pillage and restitution transfers has had disastrous effects in the political arena. Indeed, the extent to which information about Western Allied restitution was suppressed in the Soviet Union was apparent in the parliamentary debates in July 1996 over the law to nationalize the cultural booty seized by Soviet authorities. Russian Duma leaders kept repeating that none of the Nazi-looted cultural treasures were returned from Germany. "Now we are asked to return...what we received from the aggressor. We ourselves, we received nothing that had been taken away."[22] There was often the implication that, if they were not kept in Germany, then they must have all been taken to America. The same point of view is still heard today in both Ukraine and Russia. Available documentation, including documents from Soviet sources, however, do not support such statements.

Library and Archival Restitution Reconsidered

Book Restitution—Offenbach. Some archival materials, including manuscript books, were included in the three major restitution shipments that went to the USSR from the Offenbach Archival Depository (OAD) near Frankfurt, which was the centralized collection point and restitution center for books and archives in the U.S. zone of occupation. Characterized as "the American antithesis to the ERR" and "the biggest book restitution operation in library history," OAD processed over three million displaced books and manuscripts (and related ritual treasures) for restitution between its opening in the winter of 1946 through its closure in April 1949.[23]

---

[22]   Aleksandr A. Surikov, addressing the Council of the Federation, quoted in *Sovet Federatsii Federal'nogo Sobraniia, Zasedanie deviatoe, Biulleten'*, no. 1(107), 17 July 1996, p. 59. The same argument was also presented by Nikolai Gubenko, p. 60.

[23]   Leslie I. Poste, *The Development of U.S. Protection of Libraries and Archives in Europe during World War II* (Fort Gordon, GA: U.S. Army Civil Affairs School, 1964; revised from a doctoral dissertation prepared at the University of Chicago, 1958), devotes a chapter to OAD, 258–301, with a chart of out-shipments by country, 299–300. Poste's concluding statement about OAD is repeated on p. 310. See also Poste's earlier article, "Books Go Home from the Wars," *Library Journal* 73 (1 December 1948): 1699–1704. See also the recent article by F. J. Hoogewoud, "The Nazi Looting of Books and Its American 'Antithesis': Selected Pictures from the

Offenbach records show that a total of 273,645 books were restituted to the USSR between 2 March 1946 and 30 April 1949, on the basis of confirmed library stamps, ex libris, or other markings.[24] The first of two Soviet transfers on 10 June 1946 contained at least 242 cases for Ukraine out of 760 cases (with ca. 59,000 books out of 160,000) and the second on 31 July 1946, involved at least 23 out of 295 cases (with ca. 5,000 books out of 65,000); an October 1947 shipment involved additional Kyiv designated "books and documents" out of a total of 40,395 units. Another estimated 11,000 Kyiv books were included in an April 1947 shipment from the Munich Collecting Point. In addition, many other cases of books from Ukraine found in the American zone were turned over to Soviet authorities outside of the actual collection centers.[25]

Yet to this day, Russian specialists appear to have no knowledge or appreciation of the Offenbach efforts or the spirit of cultural restitution behind it. This may be partly due to inaccurate or incomplete reporting of receipts by Soviet authorities. Now, however, only fragmentary documents about Western restitution are open to researchers in Russia, although possibly there are more files among the still-closed records of the Soviet Military Administration in Germany (SVAG). And—to add to the confusion—in Soviet trans-shipments from Germany, true trophy books became indiscriminately intermixed with retrieved books that had been looted by the Nazis from Soviet libraries.

Recently, the Russian library specialist Aleksandr Mazuritskii acknowledged the Soviet "receipt from Offenbach of 100,000 books that had

---

Offenbach Archival Depot's Photographic History and Its Supplement," *Studia Rosenthaliana* 26(1–2) 1992: 158–92, which reproduces selected photographs from the albums illustrating OAD operations. Further reports on the Offenbach operations, together with the reminiscences of the first director, Col. Seymour J. Pomrenze, were presented at a conference in Amsterdam honoring the fiftieth anniversary of restitution from OAD and appeared as "Offenbach Reminiscences and the Restitutions to the Netherlands," in *Return of Looted Collections*, pp. 10–18.

24   This figure for outshipments to the USSR is cited by Poste, *U.S. Protection of Libraries and Archives* (pp. 298–300), which corresponds to the figures found in the OAD records I have examined myself in US NA, RG 260.

25   These figures are compiled from the official U.S. Army list indicating the Kyiv component of "Restituted Russian Property," cited in fn. 5, above, and other restitution receipts, inventories, and Offenbach records found in US NA, RG 260. I have found indications of scattered other direct returns to Soviet authorities from other OMGUS sources.

been taken by the Nazis from Ukraine and Belarus," but he does not document the dates of transfer or his source.[26] A St. Petersburg librarian, Irina Matveeva, who has been investigating book displacements and restitution during the war, quotes archival sources indicating that the Soviet Center for the Storage of Museum Fonds in suburban Leningrad received one shipment of eight freight cars (1,055 crates) from Offenbach via Berlin in August 1946 with 115,000 to 116,000 books, but there is no indication of the specific destinations to which those particular books were sent.[27] This is undoubtedly the same shipment indicated on a Soviet receipt from Berlin (found among Soviet trophy brigade records) dated 19/20 August 1946 acknowledging "8 wagons of books that had been transported by the Germans from the Soviet Union. The given books were sent by the Soviet Restitution Mission from Offenbach, located in the American Occupation Zone" and it was indicated that they were "owned by scientific organizations in Belarus and Ukraine," with a total of 1,055 crates.[28] The Berlin receipt was signed by Margarita Rudomino, who headed the Trophy Library Brigade in Berlin, and there is further documentation to indicate that those books were being joined to one of the trophy shipments to Gosfond.[29] Given the

[26] Aleksandr M. Mazuritskii, *Ocherki istorii bibliotechnogo dela perioda Velikoi Otechestvennoi voiny, 1941–1945 gg.* (Moscow, 1995), p. 153. I questioned Mazuritskii about these figures and pointed out references to him on several occasions, but he is unconvinced and claims to have been unable to confirm the figures cited.

[27] Irina Matveeva, "Problemy vozvrashcheniia knizhnykh fondov," in *Lesy belaruskikh materyial'nykh*, pp. 21–22. Matveeva describes the remaining records (30 folders) of that agency (Tsentral'naia khranilishcha muzeinykh fondov Leningradskikh prigorodnykh dvortsov), with which she has been working. The same figures are given in Matveeva's chart "Deiatel'nost' Tsentral'nogo khranilishcha muzeinykh fondov i primernye svedeniia o postupleniiakh knizhnykh fondov iz chisla vozvrashehennykhy v Rossiiu," in, *Informatsionnyi biulleten' Rossiiskoi bibliotechnoi assotsiatsii* 11 (St. Petersburg, 1998): 183. For the "return" from Offenbach (19 August 1946), she lists 8 wagons, 1,055 crates, but only 115 (instead of 115,000) books from "scientific organizations of Ukraine and Belarus."

[28] Guliaev to M. I. Rudomino (20 August 1946), GA RF, A-534/2/12, fol. 247; the second reference is dated 19 August 1946 (fol. 248), and there is a receipt signed by Rudomino (20 August 1946), fol. 250.

[29] Copies of the Soviet receipts also remain in the Rudomino papers now in the possession of her son Adrian Vasil'evich, including the document signed by Guliaev

documentation from the Center for Museum Fonds in suburban Leningrad, we can assume that the books were further forwarded there. Subsequent reports of distribution of those books within the USSR have not been found with any breakdown as to how many were actually forwarded to Ukraine.

The figures cited undoubtedly cover the first two Offenbach transfers to the USSR of 10 June and 31 July 1946, since the total of 1,055 crates indicated in the Soviet Berlin receipts coincide with the total of 760 and 295 crates in the American transfer documents. However, the total number of books received by Soviet authorities is only approximately half those reported as sent by U.S. sources. Whereas U.S. documents indicate a total of approximately 225,000 books transferred, Soviet figures of 115,000 books received suggest that either the American figures were wrong, or that there were about twice as many books in each crate than the Soviet estimates; otherwise we would be left with the unlikely hypothesis that approximately 110,000 books disappeared from the 1,055 crates between Offenbach and the Leningrad Center. Soviet Berlin documents do not indicate the number of books, but it is doubtful the crates would have been opened and counted before shipment onto the USSR. As it is now, the Soviet statistics of books received represent only approximately one-third of the 273,645 books for which Soviet restitution officers signed receipts in Offenbach. Since Rudomino left Berlin in November 1946, later receipts would be found in SVAG records rather than those of the Soviet Trophy Library Brigade. Among the thorough documentation available of the operation of her Commission in Berlin, no records have surfaced of book restitution shipments directly to Kyiv from Germany.

According to U.S. records, there was at least one more major shipment from Offenbach in October 1947, of 40,395 items, which also included Ukrainian "library and archival material."[30] No Soviet documentation has surfaced indicating additional books restituted to Soviet authorities from Offenbach or those received from other American and British sources, including those from Austria. The Matveeva report on the suburban

---

(19 August 1946), entitled "Kharakteristika imushchestva, prinadlezhavshego Sovetskomu Soiuzu," which is quoted above.

[30] The U.S. copy of the act of transfer (receipt no. 281) for the 24 October 1947 shipment with a total of 40,395 units, lists the institutions and numbers of cases for each, many of them Ukrainian: US NA, RG 260, Restitution Shipments Receipts, box 40. However, the U.S. aggregate list of 13 shipments (see fn. 5, above) does not indicate Ukrainian books among them. There also were several later, smaller transfers.

Leningrad center cites receipts from SVAG in April 1948 of another eight freight car loads (ca. 130,000 volumes) and in June, 254 crates (ca. 40,000 volumes), but the sources are not indicated. In a report at the 1994 conference in Chernihiv, Matveeva did not indicate that any of the Ukrainian books referenced came from Offenbach, and apparently she was not aware that other Ukrainian cultural treasures mentioned had come from American restitution centers.[31] With the growing Cold War and the extent of Soviet trophy shipments, Soviet authorities at the time obviously were not interested in advertising the American restitution program. While the book shipments referenced above came to the suburban Leningrad center, other receipts were being handled by the Moscow-based Gosfond, which was also distributing trophy books from Germany. But again, distribution records appear to be incomplete for that agency. Mazuritskii claims he has "been unable to find the records of Gosfond," and suggests their "possible disappearance during purges of that agency in the 1950s."[32]

The Offenbach totals, to be sure, are very small in comparison to the losses of Ukrainian libraries at the hands of the Nazi invader. It should be pointed out, however, that only a small proportion of the books plundered by the Nazis from Ukraine reached Germany itself and many more thousands were retrieved by Soviet authorities in Silesia and other areas, including those parts of Germany that were liberated by the Red Army. We know, for example, of the large shipment from the Ratibor (*Pol.* Racibórz) area in April 1945 and the shipment of approximately one million books to Minsk in the fall of 1945. One of the Rudomino reports on the Library Group of the Trophy Brigade emphasizes the difficulties involved, noting another major shipment in September 1945 of Soviet books retrieved on Polish territories sent from Słubice (near Frankfurt-am-Oder) to Moscow.[33]

---

[31] Matveeva, "Diial'nist' Tsentral'noho skhovyshcha," pp. 243–46.

[32] Mazuritskii, *Ocherki istorii bibliotechnogo dela*, p. 147. Mazuritskii's remarks, also published in a separate article in a Russian library journal, are quoted and reaffirmed by Ingo Kolasa in his preface to *Die Trophäenkommissionen*, pp. 16–17.

[33] The difficulties involved in searching for Nazi-looted books, with specific mention of that shipment from the Polish side of the Oder is mentioned by Rudomino in her secret report "Itogi raboty Bibliotechnoi gruppy Komitet po kul'tury pri Osobom kommissii Soveta Ministrov SSSR po Germani, mai 1945 g.–avgust 1946," a copy of which remains in her papers now in the possession of her son Adrian Vasil'evich.

An example of an unfulfilled Soviet claim among the Offenbach records is a list of predominantly Polish and Roman Catholic rare and manuscript books taken from the Lviv University Library during the war. Soviet authorities complained that this was an example of cultural treasures that surely must have been sold in the West or taken to the United States. In fact, however, the early imprints and manuscripts listed had all been catalogued before the war by Polish specialists; all have since been accounted for in the Biblioteka Narodowa in Warsaw. Potential claims for their return were later dismissed by Soviet authorities, since the books and manuscripts involved were mostly of Polish provenance.[34]

Given the inadequacy of records, it is no wonder that Ukrainian specialists have had difficulty tracking down library losses and returns. This point was well made by Olena Aleksandrova, the Deputy Director of the Parliamentary Library in Kyiv, speaking to the 1997 Minsk conference on restitution. She spoke about the need for more open cooperation among librarians of Russia, Belarus, and Ukraine, among others, in sharing information about losses and transfers. She also proposed an international group of librarians to deal with the problems, discuss possible solutions, and share available archival information.[35]

Judaica and Hebraica from Kyiv. Almost all of the Jewish materials gathered for the ERR Frankfurt Institute for the Study of the Jewish Question and its nearby Hungen depository (ca. 1,500,000 units), which also housed West European Masonic collections, were processed for restitution at OAD for return to their former homes in Paris, Amsterdam, and Rome. Most of the Nazi shipments of Judaica and Hebraica from Soviet lands also ended up in the West, most of them having been sent to the Frankfurt Institute or Hungen, in Hesse. At least 100,000 volumes of Judaica and Hebraica from Kyiv had been shipped to Frankfurt and Hungen during the war, indeed, almost all that the Nazis found there.[36] Those that survived the war were likewise processed

---

[34]   The Lviv inventory for the missing manuscripts, early printed books, and incunabula is appended to the Soviet claim, now found among the Offenbach records in US NA, RG 260. See below, Chapter 11, p. 442n43 for the identification of these manuscripts in the Biblioteka Narodowa.

[35]   Olena [Elena] Aleksandrova, "Poteri bibliotek Ukrainy: Problemy vyiavleniia i poiska," in *Restytutsyia kul'turnykh kashtoŭnastsei*, pp. 92–98.

[36]   See, for example, "Bericht über die vorläufige Sichtung der Judaica und Hebraica in Kiew," TsDAVO, 3676/1/50, fols. 10-13; Zölffel to Benzig (17 September 1942), TsDAVO, 3206/5/16, fol. 417, with mention of Dettmann and Fuchs as being in

through OAD. Today, there are still inadequate specific records about what percentage of the Judaica and Hebraica seized from Kyiv by the Nazis was returned to the USSR. And it is also now difficult, if not impossible, to determine how many volumes in the large Hebraica collections in Kyiv originally were confiscated from Kyiv to Germany and later returned to Kyiv, or how many may have come from other places.[37]

Because of the lack of successor Jewish institutions in Kyiv and the fact that many Western Jewish leaders at the time feared suppression of Jewish culture and Hebraic studies by the Stalinist regime, many manuscripts and books that were identified in OAD as coming from the USSR were instead turned over to the Jewish Cultural Reconstruction (JCR) organization, as noted below. Many of them then ended up in Israel. In terms of archival materials, at least ten files from the records of the former Institute of Jewish Proletarian Culture in Kyiv are found among the Smolensk Communist Party files that were taken from OAD to the United States.

British and American Book Restitution from Austria. The U.S. Army list of restitution shipments mentioned above does not exhaust the restitution transfers, since it does not include the many transfers, especially of books, that did not pass through the official U.S. collection points. Nor does it include those from the British Zone, nor from U.S. and British Zones of Occupation in Austria. For example, one major restitution book shipments from Austria came from the British Zone, namely books that had been collected for the Central Library of the ERR Hohe Schule, which in the course of the war had been first housed in the Grand Hotel Annenheim (near St. Andrä bei Villach) and later in the nearby Monastery of Tanzenberg in the

---

charge of the operation; Anton to Institut zur Erforschung der Judenfrage (25 September 1942), TsDAVO, 3676/1/39, fol. 2, with acknowledgement of receipt of one freight-train wagon in Frankfurt (5 October 1942), fol. 4; and further references to collections sent "one wagon of Judaica and Hebraica from Podol and 6,000 volumes from the Jewish conservatory in Kyiv (Pavlovs'ka 2)" (29 May 1943), fol. 1. There is no evidence in available Nazi documents of Kyiv Hebraica being shipped elsewhere. Bookplates and other markings from many Kyiv Hebraic collections are contained in the Offenbach records.

[37]   The head of the Hebraica Division of the National Library of Ukraine has not found documentation about the returns, although from book markings examined, at least some books seized by the Nazis were returned. Further research is needed about the history and fate of Hebraica collections in Ukraine during and after the war.

Austrian Tyrol.[38] Extensive library holdings in many shipments were directed there from Soviet lands, including the exceptionally valuable library holdings from the imperial palaces outside of Leningrad and approximately 5,000 volumes from the (so-called by the Germans) "Bibikov Collection" from the Central Library of the Academy of Sciences (TsNB) in Kyiv that had earlier been pillaged by the Künsberg Commandos.[39] According to records found in Tanzenberg after the war, a total of 469 crates had arrived in Tanzenberg from the Foreign Office (Auswärtiges Amt) in Berlin in 1942 and 1943, marked as coming from the imperial palaces (ZAB). The British MFA&A officers who inspected the Tanzenberg facility found these crates still intact, only a few of which had been opened at all. One German report among the British records mentions books from Kyiv among the "ZAB" shipment, including some with book markings from St. Vladimir University (Kyiv), the library of General Bibikov, and the National Library of the Ukrainian Academy of Sciences.[40]

[38] See the British MFA&A "Preliminary Report on Zentralbibliothek der Hohen Schule (NSDAP)" (1 August 1945), a copy of which is found among the records of the American Commission for the Protection and Salvage of Artistic and Historic Monuments in War Areas (Roberts Commission), US NA, 239/11. In terms of Nazi records see, for example, the lengthy historical report on the library of the Hohe Schule by Cruse, "Übersicht über die Buchenteilung des ERR für die Zentralbibliothek der Hohen Schule" (1 January 1944), CDJC, CXLV-159 (2 copies); Rosenberg to Schwarz (18 January 1944), CDJC, CXLII-199. See also the "Jahresberichte für das Jahr 1942," HAG-O, Sonderstab Bibliothek der Hohen Schule (Riga, 5 January 1943), TsDAVO, 3676/1/136, fols. 237–241. Weekly reports follow, for example, fols. 222–231, 235–236, 242–251, 280–282, 283–321. See the working instructions (Berlin, 12 March 1942), fols. 433–444, the shipping plans and more detailed subject profiles, fols. 218–219, and the "Aktennotiz" (Riga, 10 November 1942), fols. 222–231, and 234. A copy of the library annual report for 1943 is found in BAK, NS 8/267. A picture of the Tanzenberg facility was found in TsDAVO, 3674/1/3, fol. 300.

[39] See the details regarding the transfer of books among the Künsberg Berlin holdings to the ERR in September 1942: Nazi reports refer specifically to what they call the Bibikov Collection from TsNB in Kyiv, and over 27,000 volumes from the palaces of Pavlovsk and Gatchina (TsDAVO, 3676/2/1, fols. 4–5, and fols. 42–57). See also the Künsberg reports cited in Chapter 5, pp. 199n59 and 200n60.

[40] MFA&A "Preliminary Report on Zentralbibliothek," p. 9, 20. The MFA&A report indentifies ZAB as "Zarenbibliothek, Gatchina," the Nazi coded case markings for the collection from the imperial libraries seized by the Künsberg group. In "Dr. Ney's report on Russian books" (11 August 1945), FO 1020/2878, ZAB-II (crates

The same records report that an additional 125 crates (marked HS) had arrived in Tanzenberg from the ERR in Kyiv on 17 March 1943, but while some were actually from Kyiv itself, a major part of those books had come from the University Library in Voronezh. Among the books from Kyiv already shelved, MFA&A inspectors found some with markings from the Kyiv Caves Monastery and some from the house of the Kyiv Metropolitan Flavian, all of which were probably held in TsNB by the time of the Nazi invasion.[41] Published British reports document the identification and return of over half a million books from the Monastery of Tanzenberg and neighboring depots, including many from the USSR. British authorities kept the German staff they found under house arrest in Tanzenberg and forced them to resort the books for return to their owners. Kyiv was specifically mentioned among the library books restituted, and descriptions have been found of the books involved in the British restitution.[42]

More documentation has surfaced recently showing that 557 crates with a total of 55,000 volumes were sent to Soviet authorities in May 1946, and another 12 crates later, bringing the total to 569 crates by mid-October 1948.[43] One of the 1946 inventories for the Russian transport specifies 46 crates with books from Kyiv, with the above-mentioned Kyiv Caves Monastery and Metropolitan Flavian books. No documentation has surfaced

---

61–175) are identified as having those Kyiv book markings, among others. A separate German report, "The Kyiv Libraries," gives more details about the Kyiv component of the books received in October 1943.

[41]   MFA&A "Preliminary Report on Zentralbibliothek," pp. 8–9, 20.

[42]   See the official British report by Leonard Wooley, *A Record of the Work Done by the Military Authorities for the Protection of the Treasures of Art & History in War Areas* (London: HMSO, 1946), pp. 39–40; and the report of the British Committee on the Preservation and Restitution of Works of Art, Archives, and Other Material in Enemy Hands, *Works of Art in Austria (British Zone of Occupation): Losses and Survivals in the War* (London: HMSO, 1946), p. 4. See the reports on the books from Kyiv in PRO, FO 1020/2878 and 2879.

[43]   The May 1946 totals were mentioned in a yearly report for 1946—FO 1020/1793. A note dated 14 October 1948 gives the total of 569 crates returned to the USSR out of 4,583 crates to all countries—PRO FO 1020/2549. In addition to the earlier 1945 identifications in the report mentioned above, a 17 February 1947 memorandum notes an additional 10 cases for Russia, which include 6 from Kyiv and then 2 more found later. I am grateful to Dr. Louise Atherton at the PRO for locating the relevant documents.

about the fate of these books. Hence, it remains unclear if all of the books received from the British by the Soviets were actually returned to Kyiv.[44]

Books collected for the library for Hitler's planned cultural center in Linz were deposited in a separate ERR cache in Villa Castiglione, Grundlsee. A large shipment from Smolensk University Library was among those found there by American authorities after the war; additional books were found in the House of Nature (Haus der Natur) in Salzburg. All were returned to Soviet authorities by the U.S. Army in 1945.[45] No record has been found of Soviet receipts. However, twenty years later a few books found by Soviet authorities in Austria were returned to Smolensk with no indication of their wartime migration.[46] Mazuritskii recently has suggested that the 1,162 books returned from Salzburg are an exception to the general lack of restitution of "those unique imprints that we lost during the war years." But he further uses that figure as proof "that in Western countries there are still books that were lost in the war years."[47]

---

[44] Other Kyiv books are mentioned in FO 1020/2879, "Russland-Transport/Russia Transport, May 1946–E." While these British files document the transfers to Soviet authorities, no Soviet documents found mention receipt. British book restitution from Austria has not been mentioned in Russian or Ukrainian sources that I have examined.

[45] See the "Weekly Report, 25 November to 1 December 1945," of Charles Sattgast, Education, Religion, Fine Arts, and Monuments Office of the U.S. Military Government, Land Salzburg, US NA RG 260, USFA, Reparations and Restitution Branch, General Records, 1945, Box 160. See also, U.S. Military Government Austria, *Report of the U.S. Commissioner* 2 (December 1945): 130. Information about the return of the Smolensk materials was also mentioned in a letter of Chief, RD&R Division OMGUS, James Garrish to Chief RD&R Division SVAG, Col. Borisov (19 September 1947), BAK, B323/497.

[46] During a visit to the library of the Smolensk Pedogogical Institute in July 1997, the head of the Rare Book Department did not believe me when I told her that books from her library had been gathered in Austria for Hitler's planned cultural center and that they were returned by the U.S. Army to Soviet authorities in 1945. She said only a few books came back to her library in the 1960s with indication that they had been found by Soviet authorities in Austria. Matveeva, "Problemy vozvrasheniia knizhnykh fondov," p. 22, and "Dial´nist´ Tsentral´noho skhovyshcha," p. 246, notes that the last books received from above in 1967 went to Smolensk from Salzburg, Austria (no figures are given). It is possible, though, that those were some that were found later. Since those were the first received by the Smolensk library, we therefore do not know the fate of the rest of the 1945 American restitution shipment from Austria.

[47] Mazuritskii, *Ocherki istorii bibliotechnogo dela*, p. 155. He does not provide documentation for that figure.

The Case of the Kyiv Archive of Early Acts. Ironically, almost all the archival materials that the Nazis found, "protected," and evacuated westward during their retreat from Kyiv in 1943 survived the war and were retrieved afterwards, although this observation runs against the Soviet party line and widespread public opinion in the former Soviet Union. By contrast, it was sometimes the very archival materials that the Nazis left behind in Kyiv in 1943 that were destroyed when the Red Army liberated the city. (And these, of course, were the same materials that the Soviets were unable to evacuate from Kyiv in 1941.)

A case in point is the record books and other materials from the Kyiv Archive of Early Acts, which were the most important Nazi archival removals from Kyiv in September and October 1943. Nazi archivists from the beginning placed a high priority on protecting this archive, because it held significant documentation on Magdeburg Law. This was important to the Nazis, because the early record books proved that the Magdeburg system of medieval municipal self rule had been granted to many cities in Ukrainian lands in the fifteenth and sixteenth centuries. The Nazis in turn took that as substantiation of long-standing German legal rights in Ukraine, which justified the Nazi *Drang nach Osten*. Nazi archivists accordingly had intended to take more of the archive than their insufficient rolling stock allowed. The Soviet ChGK report for Kyiv claims that "on 5 September 1943, the Germans mined and demolished" the University building housing the archive, and with it were "lost the materials of the historical Archive of Early Acts of incalculable value."[48] However, in point of fact, the German archivist in charge, Georg Winter, was back in Kyiv to evacuate more materials from the archive in mid-October, at which time the building was intact. A surviving Nazi report shows his order that the building be given special protection by the military after he left, given its importance to the German Reich.[49] Regrettably, the building was totally destroyed and that portion of the archive that the Nazis had not succeeded in evacuating (approximately half) was blown up, not by the departing Germans, but when the Red Army retook Kyiv in early November 1943. Fortunately, most of the

---

[48] *Pravda* 1 March 1944. See the Commission files, "Soobshchenie," GA RF 7021/65, d. 8, fol. 1–4, and "Akt" (2 December1943), fol. 6. See more regarding this report above, Chapter 5, p. 185n21.

[49] A copy of the instructions left by Winter and Mansfeld to the commandant of the German 75th Division (21 October 1943) is found in TsDAVO, 3206/5/8, fols. 200–201.

Nazi-evacuated holdings from that archive survived, half of them close to home in Kamianets-Podilskyi. Other Nazi-evacuated parts of the archive were recovered by Ukrainian archivists after the war in Czechoslovakia, some in Opava, and another part further west.[50]

Many of the oldest register books from the archive were found by the U.S. Third Army in the Bohemian castle of Trpísty northwest of Pilsen (*Czech* Plzeň), Czechoslovakia, and were restituted to the USSR on 25 October 1945. That shipment to the USSR, totaling approximately 25 freight wagons, also included extensive archives and museum exhibits from Riga, and rare books and manuscripts from the Library of the Academy of Sciences (TsNB) in Kyiv, which had ended up in the same castle and the nearby monastery of Kladruby. A copy of the official act of transfer with a twelve-page inventory signed by U.S. and Soviet authorities west of Pilsen in October 1945 is available in the U.S. National Archives.[51] Although the corresponding Soviet copy has not yet been located, documentation regarding the receipts and transfer to Kyiv and Latvia is now openly available in both Ukraine and Moscow.[52]

Despite the American restitution and the Soviet retrieval of significant portions of the archive, the official Soviet attestation submitted to the Nuremberg War Crimes Trials (as part of the ChGK report for Kyiv) claimed the Kyiv archive was completely looted and dynamited by the Nazis.[53] That official Soviet version of its loss and destruction, prepared before the discovery and return of the archive, was never corrected and has become

---

[50] Some of these details are documented by Grimsted, "The Fate of Ukrainian Cultural Treasures," pp. 58–59. A fully documented study of the "Odyssey of the former Kyiv Archive of Early Acts" is in preparation by Grimsted and Boriak. The recoveries in Kamianets-Podilskyi are noted by A. P. Pshenichnyi, "Arkhivy na okkupirovannoi territorii v gody Velikoi Otechestvennoi voiny," *Otechestvennye arkhivy* 1992 (4): 91.

[51] A ten-page inventory of the transfer, involving many Latvian archives and museum exhibits, totaling 1,160 crates (22 freight cars), was signed on 25 October 1945. US NA, RG 260, Property Division, AHC, Restitution and Custody Receipts, Box 40. A facsimile is included in my forthcoming publication (see fn. 21).

[52] Full documentation will be provided in my "Odyssey of the Former Kyiv Archive of Early Acts" (in preparation).

[53] A copy of the ChGK report, first published in *Pravda* 1 March 1944 (cf. fn. 48 above, and p. 185n21) was submitted as one of the Soviet depositions at the Nuremberg Trials in 1945—see GA RF, 7445/2/94, fols. 194–197.

deeply engraved in the popular mind, even within high Russian archival circles. As late as May 1993, the then director of the Special Archive in Moscow (then TsKhIDK, now part of RGVA) used the argument that the Nazis looted and totally destroyed this Kyiv archive to recommend against the restitution of Soviet-seized German archives held in Moscow.[54]

Even the scholarly archivist V. V. Tsaplin, whose very careful chapters on Soviet archival retrieval operations were finally published in 1997, was still not well informed on the matter. His 1997 article still alleges that Soviet authorities were unable to arrange the transfer of all the record books found in Trpísty and Kladruby, claiming that part of the materials "may well have been taken to Bavaria and is now found in West Germany, or Sweden, or even in the USA." In his own account of Glavarkhiv retrievals from Czechoslovakia, he cites many reports of materials brought back from the Kyiv Archive of Early Acts, but again, the figures do not all add up, and Tsaplin had not seen the rough inventory attached to the official U.S.-Soviet transfer document. In the case of predominantly sixteenth- and early seventeenth-century court record books that inventory attests to the return of only 717 books, although an earlier estimate suggested there were over 1,100 volumes in the Castle of Trpísty; for the eighteenth-century Rumiantsev General Description of Malorossia, the U.S. inventory noted 437 volumes.[55] The confusion appears in part to be based on erroneous, conflicting, or incomplete reports on the subject submitted to Moscow by Ukrainian archival officials, but also on the fact that neither Kyiv specialists nor Tsaplin had thoroughly researched the German wartime reports held in secret in Kyiv or the reports of the Kyiv Slavist, Nikolai Geppener, whom the Nazis took with them. These documents provide many more details about how much the Nazi archivists took from the archive and how much they had to leave behind at various points en route.[56]

---

[54] See Mariia Dement'eva (interview with V. N. Bondarev), "Osobaia sud'ba osobogo arkhiva," *Obshchaia gazeta* 13 (4 May 1993): 8.

[55] Tsaplin cites various reports that include materials returned from the Kyiv archive—"O rozyske dokumentov, pokhishchennykh v gody voiny iz arkhivo-khranilishch SSSR," *Otechestvennye arkhivy* 1997 (6): 18–20. The U.S. inventory itself appears to be incomplete in terms of court record books returned from the Kyiv archive, as Ukrainian colleagues and I have established from other documentation in Kyiv and elsewhere. While it notes only 717 volumes from the 16th and early 17th centuries, it says nothing about later ones that were in fact returned.

[56] For example, a letter from the Chief of TsDIA URSR Sheludchenko to Ukrainian Archival Adminstration Pil'kevich in 1957, in answer to an official inquiry, provides

Western Non-Restitution

War Booty. Although it is fair to say that almost all Soviet-area archives that reached the West were restituted after the war, there were some major exceptions that remained a point of friction between American and Soviet authorities in the context of the growing Cold War. There certainly was some "booty" taken by individual officers and soldiers, which went back to the States in their free Army shipments (which were not subject to customs). The most notorious case of the Quedlinburg Church treasures, looted by an American soldier from Texas and sold back to Germany by his heirs in 1991 for a "finder's fee" of nearly three million dollars, caused public outrage and legal proceedings in the United States. A special session was devoted to the case during the 1995 Bard Conference on the "Spoils of War" in New York.[57] An independent American researcher, Kenneth D. Alford has documented many other scandalous cases of looting by the American military, although some of his examples have been called into question by reviewers.[58]

Jewish Collections. Jewish collections from Eastern Europe were a major exception to the generally successful policy of "restitution to the country of provenance" from OAD. Because of the Nazi annihilation of Jewish communities in Eastern Europe and the lack of openly acknowledged successor Jewish institutions, many Jewish collections were not returned to the USSR, including large collections of Judaica and Hebraica from Kyiv that had been shipped to Frankfurt and Hungen by the ERR. Although a few

---

what appear to be incomplete statistics about materials returned and the losses from the Kyiv Archive of Early Acts as a result of the war. TsDAVO, 4703/2/35, fol. 7. Tsaplin had not seen the official transfer inventory, nor available German evacuation and shipping reports, nor the Geppener reports (published in 1991—see Grimsted and Boriak, *Dolia skarbiv*, pp. 75–96). A more detailed study of this matter is in preparation in Kyiv by Grimsted and Boriak.

[57] See the published contributions in *The Spoils of War: WWII and Aftermath*, pp. 148–58.

[58] Kenneth D. Alford, *The Spoils of World War II: The American Military's Role in the Stealing of Europe's Treasures* (New York: Birch Lane Press, 1994). The book is not well regarded by specialists.

Jewish materials were returned to Kyiv, many more valuable books and manuscripts of Ukrainian Jewish provenance were turned over to the Commission on Jewish Cultural Reconstruction (JCR) and have ended up in Yad Vashem and the National and University Library in Jerusalem.[59] Others were distributed to Jewish cultural institutions in the Diaspora.

The Baltic Exception. Archival and other cultural materials from the Baltic countries were another major exception. Because the Western Allies did not recognize the Soviet annexation of the Baltic republics, they refused to return looted Baltic materials to Soviet authorities. The above-mentioned Riga archival materials found by the U.S. Army in western Bohemia—as an exception to that policy—had already been returned in October 1945. The large holdings from the Tallinn City Archive discovered by the British-American archival team in the Grasleben salt mine near Helmstedt (British zone), on the other hand, were held back by British authorities as they tried unsuccessfully to negotiate the restitution of the Hanseatic records from Bremen, Hamburg, and Lübeck that Soviet authorities seized from the salt mines near Magdeburg and shipped to Moscow.[60] The Königsberg archive (and with it the medieval archive of the Teutonic Order, parts of which had been transferred from Poland to Königsberg by the Nazis and which had likewise been found in Grasleben) was also held back owing to the forced resettlement of the ethnic German population and the unresolved legal status of those parts of East Prussia that had been annexed to the USSR as Kaliningrad Oblast.[61]

---

[59] A list of some manuscripts that were turned over to Jewish agencies from Offenbach was found among the OAD records, US NA, RG 260, but a full analysis is now needed, given the availability of more detailed Nazi lists of the materials that were actually sent from Kyiv. Recently some of the prewar Kyiv Hebraica has been identified by Kyiv specialists in Israel.

[60] The fate and holdings of the Tallinn archive were well documented in the West. See my *Archives: Estonia, Latvia, Lithuania, and Belorussia*, pp. 743–46, 748–52. The Tallinn Archive was returned to Estonia in 1990.

[61] The Königsberg archive, first removed from Grasleben to Goslar and thence to Göttingen, it is now held in the Prussian Privy State Archive (Geheimes Staatsarchiv Preußischer Kulturbesitz), Berlin-Dahlem. See Kurt Forstreuter, *Das Preußische Staatsarchiv in Königsberg. Ein geschichtlicher Rückblick mit einer Übersicht über seine Bestände* (Göttingen: Vandenhoeck & Ruprecht, 1955) [=*Veröffentlichungen der Niedersächsischen Archivverwaltung*, 3]; and also Kurt Forstreuter, "Das Staatsarchiv Königsberg als Quelle für Allgemeine Geschichte," *Hamburger Mittel-*

Private Claims and the Lubomirski Example. Another element of non-restitution of cultural treasures evacuated by the Nazis involved those claimed by private émigrés in the West. No examples immediately come to mind in the archival realm, except for the Baltic Ritterschaft archives that remained in Marburg, Germany, where a number of manuscript books fell into this category.

In the art realm, however, continued furor has been aroused over the non-restitution and postwar fate of the Dürer drawings from the Lubomirski collection in Lviv that had been seized by Hitler's personal emissary in 1941. American restitution authorities turned the collection over to Prince Georg Lubomirski, who, having fled to the West, claimed that the terms of the family donation had been abrogated when Soviet authorities abolished the Lubomirski Museum and nationalized the Polish collections after the annexation of western Ukraine to the USSR in 1939. Lubomirski later quite legally sold the Dürer drawings at auction, which explains their dispersal in various museums in Great Britain and the United States. The disposition of the drawings remains bitterly contested with potential rival claims today from: (1) Ukraine, on the grounds that the drawings should have been returned to Lviv, from whence they had been seized by the Nazis; (2) the various U.S. and British museums that purchased the drawings in good faith when they were sold at auction by one of the Lubomirski family heirs, to whom they had been returned by American restitution authorities; and, potentially, (3) Poland, on behalf of the Ossolineum in Wrocław, as the current site of the reestablished Polish cultural center, which was transferred there after the war in connection with the resettlement of the Polish population from Lviv. Several recent journalistic accounts of the case have

---

und Ostdeutsche Forschungen 6 (1967): 9–35. See Grimsted, *Archives: Estonia, Latvia, Lithuania, and Belorussia*, pp. 748–52.

A separate issue remains in the case of the archive of the medieval Teutonic Order, because this collection had been officially ceded to Poland centuries ago, and was removed from Warsaw by the Nazis, before it was evacuated with the Königsberg archive in 1944. See the scholarly catalog of the charters, prepared after the archive was lodged in West Germany, *Regesta historico diplomatica Ordinis S. Mariae Theutonicorum 1198–1525*, ed. Erich Joachim and Walter Hubatsch, 5 vols. (Göttingen, Vandenhoeck & Ruprecht, 1948–1973). See also Emil Schieche, "Tyska Ordens arkiv, dess nuvarande ode och dess oppnande for vetenskaplig forskning," *Historisk tidskrift* 13(3) 1950: 185–97.

tapped many sources and raised conflicting issues. A well-documented case study is still needed.[62]

Intelligence Seizures and the Smolensk Example. A final category of materials that was not returned to the USSR involved documents of interest to American intelligence forces. In the context of the burgeoning Cold War and the de facto political division between Eastern and Western Europe, Russian archival materials and technical publications that might have security potential were immediately exempted from the American military commitment to restitution. In many cases, the relevant documentation had earlier been seized by Nazi forces for the same purpose. A 1946 assessment of the German Military Document Section Collection, then located at Camp Ritchie, MD, noting the inadequacy of "our existing intelligence on the USSR," explained that

> exploitation to date has revealed the fact that these documents are at present our richest source of factual intelligence on the USSR. Much of this information can never be secured from any other source.[63]

In addition to military intelligence, American intelligence units were also looking for "information the Germans had on the Communist set-up in Russia," and "information on the organization, personnel, activities, and

---

[62]   The most detailed and balanced coverage to date is that of Michael Dobbs, "Stolen Beauty," *Washington Post Magazine* 21 March 1999: 12–18, 29. Dobbs concludes in line with the opinion of the director of the National Gallery of Art in Washington, DC, that the recent Ukrainian claim probably would not stand up in court. Another well-researched account by Martin Bailey, "Hitler, the Prince and the Dürers," *The Art Newspaper* (London) 6(47) April 1995: 1–2, suggests that the drawings rightfully belong to Lviv, and that American restitution authorities probably had no right to return them to Prince Georg Lubomirski. That is also the opinion of a recent piece in the Lviv newspaper, *Vysokii zamok* 1999 (1). An earlier account of the matter by Andrew Decker, "A Worldwide Treasure Hunt," *ARTNews* Summer 1991: 136–38, raises some of the problems but lacked some of the sources uncovered by Bailey and Dobbs.

[63]   "Evaluation of GMDS Collection," summary sheet, Col. R. L. Hopkins to Chief of Staff, n.d. (April 1946?), copy US NA, RG 242, AGAR-S, no. 1377. The referenced document is a copy collected from "GMDS Background Papers, History, file 5:1 folder 1," but the original has not been located in US NA.

tactics of the Soviet system...the NKVD (or NKWD)."[64] This explains why a total of at least 5,957 items of Russian archival and other printed materials from the OAD were turned over to the U.S. Army Intelligence Division (G-2).[65]

Most famous among these Russian materials was a miscellaneous collection from the Smolensk Oblast Communist Party Archive, slightly over 500 files of which are still held by the U.S. National Archives.[66] The entire archive had been seized from Smolensk for the ERR by the German archivist Wolfgang Mommsen in 1943, shipped to Vilnius and again shipped in June 1944 to the Ratibor (*Pol*. Racibórz) area of Silesia. But the Nazis only succeeded in evacuating a small portion further west. The much more voluminous part of the archive (over four wagon-loads) was retrieved by Soviet forces near Ratibor in March 1945 and returned to Smolensk, although that information was not published in Moscow until 1991.[67] Many Russians today still repeat the Soviet falsified version that the whole archive from

---

[64] "Matters of Interest to Liaison Agent," GMDS, Camp Ritchie, MD, unsigned [n.d.] (since the memo was datelined Camp Ritchie, it would have necessarily been prepared between July 1945 and April 1946, when GMDS moved to the Pentagon), copy US NA, RG 242, AGAR-S, no. 1393 (GMDS 5:1 folder 1).

[65] Poste cites the total figure in the table of transfers to G-2 from Offenbach, Poste, *U.S. Protection of Libraries and Archives*, p. 299, but references to additional transfers are found in OAD records in US NA (RG 260).

[66] Soon after the Smolensk files were reported to U.S. intelligence authorities in October 1946, they were transferred from Offenbach to the Documents Control Section of the Intelligence Division (G-2) of OMGUS at Oberusel (near Frankfurt) and flown back to the German Military Documents Section (GMDS) at Camp Ritchie in November.

[67] Regarding the Soviet retrieval in 1945, see Valerii N. Shepelev, "Sud'ba 'Smolenskogo arkhiva,'" *Izvestiia TsK KPSS* 1991 (5): 135–38. Shepelev includes edited reports from Soviet forces in the field that found the Smolensk archive, along with library collections from Pskov, Belarus, and the Baltic republics, abandoned by the Nazis in a railroad station in Silesia. The original documents come from RGASPI (then TsPA), 17/125/308, fols. 11–12. The Soviet retrieval and return to Smolensk is further documented in my *The Odyssey of the Smolensk Archive: Captured Communist Party Archives for the Service of Anti-Communism* (Pittsburgh: REES, University of Pittsburgh, 1995). See also Valerii N. Shepelev, "Novye fakty o sud'be dokumentov 'Smolenskogo arkhiva' (po materialam RTsKhIDNI)," *Problemy zarubezhnoi arkhivnoi Rossiki: Sbornik statei* (Moscow: "Russkii mir," 1997), pp. 124–33.

Smolensk is in the United States.[68] In the case of the Smolensk files taken by U.S. intelligence agents to Washington, by 1963 both the U.S. Army and the U.S. Department of State were prepared to return them to the Soviet Union.[69] At that point, however, the CPSU Central Committee accepted the recommendation of Glavarkhiv Chief, Gennadii A. Belov, against filing an official request for restitution when it was requested by the U.S. Archivist in 1965, fearing further U.S. Cold War propaganda exploitation.[70]

In March 1992, the Archivist of the United States agreed to the return the Smolensk files now held in the U.S. National Archives.[71] Unfortunately, restitution was halted in the U.S. Congress as a result of political linkage of the Smolensk Archive to the unresolved claim for the Schneersohn Collection of Hebrew and Yiddish books held in the Russian State Library (formerly Lenin Library) in Moscow from the Schneersohn heirs in Brooklyn.[72] The Schneersohn claim had already been dismissed by Russian courts, given the background that the collection had been abandoned in a Moscow warehouse when the Hassidic forebears had fled abroad. Furthermore, as noted above, Russian law does not provide for the return of any nationalized cultural property, nor its alienation abroad.

Curiously, the controversy also involves a small Ukrainian interest. As evidence of the complexities in the wartime displacements, approximately ten files in the Smolensk collection in Washington are actually of Kyiv provenance—from the records of the Institute of Jewish Proletarian Culture of the All-Ukrainian Academy of Sciences (VUAN), dating from the 1930s, which had been seized by the ERR in Kyiv and inadvertently intermixed in the

---

[68]   See, for example, the reference by the respected Russian archivist A. P. Pshenichnyi, "Arkhivy na okkupirovannoi territorii v gody Velikoi Otechestvennoi voiny," *Otechestvennye arkhivy* 1992 (4): 94.

[69]   William M. Franklin, Director Historical Office, Bureau of Public Affairs, U.S. Department of State, to Robert H. Bahmer, Deputy Archivist of the U.S. (5 May 1963), US NA, RG 64. These and other details are documented fully in Grimsted, *Odyssey of the Smolensk Archive*.

[70]   Glavarkhiv chief G. A. Belov to the CPSU Central Committee, RGANI, 5/35/212, fols. 158–159.

[71]   Don Wilson, Archivist of the U.S., to Rudolf G. Pikhoia, Chairman of Roskomarkhiv (Washington, DC, 18 March 1992). Professor Pikhoia kindly made a copy of that letter available to me.

[72]   *U.S. Congressional Record–Senate* (31 March 1992): S 4537–40.

Smolensk materials in Germany. Some other files from that institute that were found in OAD are now held in Jerusalem.[73]

Captured Nazi Records and
Anglo-American Restitution to Germany

Allied Control Commission Law no. 2 (10 October 1945), "Providing for the Termination and Liquidation of Nazi Organizations," ordered confiscation by Military Commands "of all records [archives], documents, and other property" of Nazi agencies and organizations.[74] Although the seizure of Nazi records by all of the Allies was justified, the anticipated Allied cooperation in this venture never materialized. Even before the end of the war, Nazi archives were a top priority for Anglo-American intelligence teams as their armies swept through Germany. Anglo-American authorities worked closely together from the outset, as was evident in the "GOLDCUP" operation in the spring of 1945, which was specifically searching for ministerial personnel and archival records of the Third Reich. The Bissell-Sinclair agreement of May 1945 provided a firm basis for cooperation between Anglo-American intelligence authorities "concerning the handling and exploitation of all archives and other documents of military interest belonging to the European enemies."[75] In the summer of 1945 a Ministerial Collecting Center for

---

[73] See, for example, the Smolensk files US NA, nos. WKP 179, WKP 358, WKP 482, WKP 484, WKP 485, WKP 486, WKP 488, and WKP 490. Original folders and/or fragments remain for those files, in most cases in Ukrainian, with Kyiv archival signatures and indication that the folders themselves were printed in Kyiv. It has not yet been possible to examine all of the original Smolensk files in US NA, so possibly more files may be identified as being of Kyiv origin. Regarding the fate of the archive of the Kyiv institute, I am grateful to L. A. Dubrovina, Director of the Institute of Manuscripts in NBU (before May 1996, TsNB) and I. A. Sergeeva, head of the Judaica Division, who in May 1994 identified contingent materials from the Kyiv institute in Jerusalem.

[74] Law no. 2, as published in German, Russian, French, and English in *Official Gazette of the Control Council for Germany*, no. 1 (2nd ed., corrected) (Berlin, 29 October 1945). The English version uses the term "records" rather than "archives" and omits the word "acts [documents]" which appears in the German and Russian texts.

[75] The agreement was signed for the British by Maj. Gen. J. A. Sinclair, Director of Military Intelligence, and for the American side by Major General Clayton Bissell, Assistant Chief of Staff, G-2. A published copy has not been located, but typed copies

former ministerial personnel and archives of a non-military nature was established at Fürstenhagen (southeast of Kassel) in addition to special centers for various types of records analysis.[76] The anticipated Soviet cooperation with the Western Allies was never forthcoming.

Soviet authorities went their own route with respect to captured Nazi records. None of their findings were shared with the Western Allies, except a few selected as exhibits for the Nuremberg War Crimes Trials and publication in Ukraine as proof of Nazi barbarism.[77] But none of the Nazi records captured by Soviet authorities or left behind by the Nazis were publicly available before 1992.[78] Those in Ukraine were open for limited research as early as 1989. There is evidence in some areas, with Dnipropetrovsk as an example, that some of the Nazi occupation records

---

are found in several files in US NA, for example, 242, AGAR-S, 1, and 2006 (with related correspondence).

[76]   See the published report by the major American archival representative, Lester Born, "The Ministerial Collection Center," *American Archivist* 13 (July 1950): 237–58. Work of the Ministerial Center was coordinated, for example, with the Foreign Office archival deposits in Marburg, the Industrial Card Index at Markt Schwaben, and the Berlin Document Center, established for Nazi Party personnel and related records, in addition to other military and intelligence document centers.

[77]   There were several collections of highly selected Nazi documents published in Ukraine, many of which quite correctly identified the record group of provenance in archives in Kyiv and elsewhere. For example, the collection *Istoriia predosteregaet* (Kyiv, 1986), prepared by the Institute of the History of the Party (under the CC CPU), the Institute of History of the Academy of Sciences UkrSSR, and the Main Archival Administration (GAU UkrSSR), was also issued in German and English translation—*History Teaches a Lesson: Captured War Documents Expose the Atrocities of the German-Fascist Invaders and Their Henchmen in Ukraine's Temporarily Occupied Territory During the Great Patriotic War (1941–1945)* (Kyiv: Politvydav Ukraïny, 1986).

[78]   The most complete survey of Nazi records in Ukraine published to date appears in the recent pamphlet prepared for the Washington Conference on Holocaust-Era Assets: Hennadii Boriak, Maryna Dubyk, and Natalia Makovs'ka, *"Natsysts'ke zoloto" z Ukraïny: U poshukakh arkhivnykh svidchen'*, pt. 1 (Kyiv, 1998). A rough English translation of the list of archival sources with a brief introduction was prepared for distribution by the Ukrainian delegation: "Accumulation of 'Nazi Gold' on the Occupied Territory of Ukraine during World War II" (Washington, DC, 1998).

were destroyed during postwar decades.[79]

By contrast in the West, most of the documents selected out for the Nuremberg Trials were later published with the complete records of those trials, and Nazi personnel files were retained and organized with a microfiche indexing system in the Berlin Document Center. Most of the extensive Nazi and other German records captured by the Western Allies were transferred to various archival centers in England and America for further intelligence analysis.[80] Most of the records themselves were microfilmed with funding raised by the American Historical Association and turned over to the U.S. National Archives in 1958.[81] On the basis of U.S. Congressional approval in 1953, by 1968 almost all of the captured German records brought to the United States had been returned to Germany with the provision for open access.[82] The Western Allies all agreed that the confiscation of Nazi records

[79] Destruction of Nazi documentation in Dnipropetrovsk was related to me by archivists from the Dnipropetrovsk State Oblast Archive.

[80] The number and extent of American agencies, both civilian and military, that were involved in the collection and analysis of captured records were staggering. Full lists of the agencies, and most of the captured records held by U.S. and British agencies are available in print and have now been declassified. See, for example, U.S. Adjutant General's Office, Administrative Services Division, Departmental Records Branch, *Guide to Captured German Records in the Custody of the Department of the Army Agencies in the United States, Washington, D.C.* (Washington, DC, April, 1950); and *The Collections and Indexes of the German Military Documents Section (AG0)* (Washington, DC: CIA, May 1953; CIA/CD Research Aid, 5). Copies of these guides, among others, are found in US NA, RG 242 (GMDS reference collection).

[81] See the comprehensive published list of captured records filmed by the Western allies in Berlin, England, and the United States, "Captured German and Related Records in the National Archives (as of 1974)," in *Captured German and Related Records: A National Archives Conference*, ed. Robert Wolfe (Athens, OH: Ohio University Press, 1974) [=National Archives Conferences, 3], pp. 267–76. See also the series of finding aids produced for the films, *Guides to German Records Microfilmed at Alexandria, VA*. See also George O. Kent, "The German Foreign Ministry's Archives at Whaddon Hall, 1948–58," *American Archivist* 24 (January 1961): 43–54, and *A Catalogue of Files and Microfilms of the German Foreign Ministry Archives, 1867–1920*, comp. and ed. George A. Kent (Oxford, 1959).

[82] Congressional approval of the return came 1 August 1953—83 Congress, 1st Session, HR Report No. 1077: Disposition of Sundry Papers, as quoted and explained by Robert Wolfe, "Sharing Records of Mutual Archival Concern to the Federal Republic of Germany and the United States of America," in *Proceedings of the Xth Congress of the International Council of Archives (Bonn, 1984)*, pp. 296–97

had served its immediate purpose, and that the archives themselves belonged by right and international precedents in the country of their provenance. Policies and procedures with regard to captured German and related records, together with a discussion of their use and return, were aired at a U.S. National Archives conference in 1968.[83] Given the extent of the Cold War, however, Soviet authorities refused to cooperate with the Western Allies and, apart from the publications mentioned above, there was little knowledge of what Nazi and other German records had been captured by the USSR.

German archivists today laud "the bilateral cooperation between the U.S. National Archives and the Bundesarchiv," which "not only led to the return of almost all captured German records to Germany, but also to the joint venture of describing, appraising, and reproducing the occupation records originating from the U.S. military administration over Germany from 1944/45 to 1949."[84] These examples remain important for present negotiations between Germany and Ukraine, and potentially with Russia for two major reasons: first, none of the Nazi records seized by Soviet authorities that remain in Ukraine or Russia after 1991 have as yet been returned to Germany, or even adequately described and microfilmed.[85] And second, now that at least some of the counterpart Soviet occupation records for Germany (SVAG) are at last starting to be declassified in Moscow, thanks to a special order by President Yeltsin towards the end of 1995, parallel cooperative projects with German specialists could lead to their better description and public research utilization.[86] Traditionally, records of military occupation are

---

[=*Archivum* 32 (1986)]. Wolfe's report includes extensive references to other relevant agreements and literature regarding the restitution.

[83]   See the published conference proceedings, and especially the opening paper by Seymour J. Pomrenze, "Policies and Procedures for the Protection, Use, and Return of Captured German Records," in *Captured German Records,* pp. 5–30.

[84]   See the recent report of Klaus Oldenhage, "Bilateral and Multilateral Cooperation for the Reconstitution of the Archival Heritage," in *CITRA 1993–1995,* pp. 129–33. For more details see, for example, Josef Henke, "Das amerikanisch-deutsche OMGUS-Project: Erschliessungund Verfilmung der Akten der amerikanischen Militärregierung in Deutschland 1945–1949," *Der Archivar* 35(2) 1982: 149–57. See also Wolfe, "Sharing Records of Mutual Archival Concern."

[85]   See the lists of Nazi records in Ukraine mentioned above, fn. 39. A few highly selected portions of files have been filmed by the U.S. Holocaust Museum and are available to researchers in Washington, DC.

considered to be the property of the occupying authority, although "joint availability and use" by the occupied power should be respected. However, the fact that the Russian presidential declassification order excluded "materials relating to property matters," could technically keep all files relating to cultural treasures and restitution issues classified indefinitely.[87]

Today there is more hope that the good political relations between Ukraine and Germany and the encouraging archival relations could result in a more satisfactory arrangement covering World War II occupation records in Ukraine. In Moscow, however, given the standoff over cultural restitution, and the failure to move forward with earlier-agreed restitution, as provided for by the 1990 treaty and 1992 agreement, prospects to resolve such issues in Russia remain dimmer. The complexities and roadblocks for restitution issues, however, do not lessen the importance of a better understanding of what captured records are involved and how and where they were acquired.

---

[86] Some of the SVAG records and the related card catalogs held in GA RF had been open for limited research in the early 1990s, but were closed again by a secret presidential decree in August 1992, pending the removal of Russian troops from Germany. Another secret presidential decree at the end of August or early September 1995 called for the declassification of SVAG records.

[87] The 1995 presidential decree was security classified and hence not published, but it was explained to me by archivists in GA RF. Since there have as yet been inadequate attempts to test the measure, and subsequent declassification in GA RF was frozen because of the government failure to appoint a new declassification commission and/or revise declassification procedures, presently, few of these materials are not available for research. A cooperative Russo-German project to describe the declassified portion of the records is at present under way.

CHAPTER 7

Soviet Cultural Trophies: The Ukrainian Component

Soviet Spoils of War

Stalin's Special Committee on Reparations. In January 1943, seventeen governments, including the USSR and the Western Allies, recalled the 1907 Hague Convention and signed the "Inter-Allied Declaration Against Acts of Dispossession Committed in Territories under Enemy Occupation or Control" (5 January 1943). The declaration opposed actual cultural looting and plunder, and invalidated wartime "sales" and other "transactions apparently legal in form."[1] By the time the triumphal march of the Red Army was reaching Berlin in 1945, however, Stalin had long forgotten such "rules and laws of warfare universally accepted by all civilized nations," which Soviet authorities had cited in 1942. When victory came, he and other Soviet leaders seized what "spoils of war" they could, not unlike the earlier denounced practices of their vanquished Nazi foes. Hitler's agents had seized art and archives for the military, political, and cultural profit of the Nazi regime, including those designated among the elaborate plans for his own "Führer Museum" in Linz.

Stalin had his own plans for a Super Museum in Moscow as early as 1943, as recently revealed by Konstantin Akinsha and Grigorii Kozlov.[2] He, together with many in his entourage, viewed seizures from Germany in the

---

[1] See the text in *The Spoils of War: WWII and Aftermath,* p. 287. Regarding the legal background, see also Leslie I. Poste, *The Development of U.S. Protection of Libraries and Archives in Europe during World War II* (Fort Gordon, GA: U.S. Army Civil Affairs School, 1964), pp. 5–68 (esp. pp. 20–21ff.).

[2] Plans, including an architectural drawing, for Stalin's Super Museum were first displayed publicly at the January 1995 Bard conference in New York by Konstantin Akinsha. These developments are documented by Grigorii Kozlov, Akinsha, and Sylvia Hochfield, *Beautiful Loot: The Soviet Plunder of Europe's Art Treasures* (New York: Random House, 1995). An additional German publication by the same authors presents more details and reproduces a number of relevant documents—Konstantin Akinsha, Grigorii Kozlov, and Clemens Toussaint, *Operation Beutekunst: Die Verlagerung deutscher Kulturgüter in die Sowjetunion nach 1945* (Nuremberg: Germanisches Nationalmuseum, 1995).

cultural realm as well as in a broad economic sphere, as just reparations, retribution for the brutal devastation wrought by the German invader in Soviet lands. Besides, in European cultural tradition, hadn't Napoleon Bonaparte before him adorned his Paris capital with his spoils of war? Why shouldn't the capital of Stalin's empire have a museum to rival the Louvre?

Two weeks after Yalta, at the end of February 1945, Stalin signed a still top secret order in the State Committee on Defense—GKO (Gosudarstvennyi komitet oborony) for the establishment of a Special Committee on Reparations, headed by Marshal Georgii Zhukov in the field and by Grigorii M. Malenkov on the home front. According to statistics of the Main Trophy Administration that remain top secret, GKO and associated agencies arranged shipments totaling over 400,000 railroad wagons in 1945 alone. They ranged in content from entire factories and construction materials to furniture, pianos, and wine.[3] While the sensational 1994 publication by the military historian Pavel Knyshevskii is hardly definitive, the GKO and other documents presented for the first time are indicative of the immediate postwar mentality and demonstrate Stalin's firm commitment to "reparations in kind" in the cultural as well as the economic sphere. Many of the documents cited, however, are still classified and not publicly available.[4]

An understanding among the Allies in Yalta had essentially accepted Stalin's bid for limited economic reparations for the USSR, but Stalin extended the principle much further—to libraries and archives, as well as art, openly disrespectful of the Western Allied principle of cultural restitution. The growing wave of revelations, starting in 1990, document the broader political and ideological context of Soviet cultural and, more specifically, archival plunder at the end of the war. The plunder took place, ironically, simultaneously with Western Allied restitution of Nazi-plundered Soviet

---

[3] As revealed by Pavel Knyshevskii, *Dobycha: Tainy germanskikh reparatsii* (Moscow: "Soratnik," 1994). A few of the choice details from the Knyshevskii study, such as the text of the Stalin order mentioned, were first revealed in a sensational press account by Radio Liberty correspondent Mark Deich, "Podpisano Stalinym: 'Dobycha—tainy germanskikh reparatsii,'" *Stolitsa* 1994 (29[191]): 18.

[4] Knyshevskii's account only minimally describes the GKO and other military documents he presents with relatively little commentary. The reference to the 25 February 1945 document is given only in the text (pp. 10–11) as GKO, No. 7590ss (the "ss" meaning "top secret"); the subsequent GKO document presented is identified as RTsKhIDNI, 644/1/382, fols. 211, 212, which is in fact from the GKO fond now in RGASPI (earlier RTsKhIDNI). Archivists there informed me that the files for 1945 are still classified when I unsuccessfully attempted to verify the references. Knyshevskii also cites documents from military archives that likewise are still classified.

cultural treasures, which many Russians still claim were never returned. The only difference from Napoleon's cultural exploits was the scale of transports and the fact that the Soviet spoils of war were, for the most part, kept in top secret repositories for fifty years and never open to the Soviet citizens who had borne the brunt of the war. Only a small percentage of the Soviet spoils of war went to Ukraine. Today Ukrainians might lament that they were left out of the bounty, but even those treasures that did go to Ukraine were also hidden from the public for half a century. It is important now to consider Ukrainian aspects of the problem in relation to other parts of the former Soviet Union in order to gain proper perspective on the issues.

Ukrainian Trophy Brigades. Few revelations have appeared about the extent of direct Soviet Ukrainian involvement in postwar cultural plunder. The subject has been little studied in Ukraine and even today many prefer either to remain silent on the topic or to claim that all the cultural treasures seized from Germany were returned. This is hardly the case, as was already apparent when an initial article on trophy art looted by the Ukrainian trophy brigades first appeared in a German art magazine in 1993.[5] However, the authors have been unable to adequately document the extent of those operations. A 1996 essay by the Ukrainian historian Serhii Kot mentions trophy shipments of cultural treasures, including art and books to the USSR. However, he, too, has had difficulty locating reliable documentation. Since open sources are scant about the Ukrainian trophy brigades or Ukrainian representatives who participated in the trophy transports, we still have few precise details about what cultural trophies actually ended up in Ukraine.[6]

Extensive files have recently come to light among Communist Party records in Kyiv that report on the work of Ukrainian trophy brigades in Germany and Romania. These brigades were busily arranging massive

---

[5]   A summary account of art shipments to Ukraine by Konstantin Akinsha and Grigorii Kozlov (Grigorij Koslow), "Die Beute lag auf dem Flugplatz im Schnee," *Art* (Hamburg) May 1993: 60–64; Akinsha, who is Ukrainian, told me that the article is based on documents in the internal archive of the Kyiv Museum of Western and Oriental Art (where he worked in the 1980s) and reports of the Ukrainian brigades he found in Moscow, but the article itself is undocumented and lacks specific details. Akinsha and Kozlov also briefly mention the Ukrainian brigade in *Beautiful Loot,* pp. 131–32, and *Operation Beutekunst*, p. 33.

[6]   See Serhii Kot, "Povernuty kul′turni nadbannia mozhna, bula b dobra volia," *Viche*, n.s. 5(50) May 1996, esp. pp. 131–37.

transports to Ukraine for postwar reparations.[7] By March 1945, for example, the vice-president of the Academy of Sciences of the UkrSSR had prepared a list of 72 German scientific institutes, laboratories, and museums from which equipment should be transferred to Ukraine and an 18-page list of the specific equipment to be brought for each of 19 institutes under the Ukrainian Academy of Sciences.[8] Although most of the extant reports examined attest to the demolition and transport of factories and equipment in the transportation, communications, and scientific spheres, cultural assets were also involved.

According to a report dated 26 November 1945, the special group in Germany from the Council of People's Commissars of Ukraine had proposed the transfer of "226 enterprises with 15,832 pieces of equipment," but by November 1945, "the All-Union Special Commission (GOKO) had approved 41 enterprises for Ukraine with 4,329 pieces of equipment and 150 wagons of highway-building mechanisms." As of 15 November 1945, the report lists in the "disassembled and unloaded" category "(a) 17 enterprises..., (b) 11 wagons of Academy laboratory equipment, c) 75 paintings from the Dresden Gallery, (d) 123 cars and trucks, and 2.5 tons of books for the Library of the Academy of Sciences." Among six other items on that list were "12 tons of dishes from an exhibit at the August Welner Porcelain Factory." In the category of "disassembled, packed, and loaded in freight cars" were "(a) 2 printing plants—with 51 pieces of equipment—46 wagons [and] (b) a photographic paper factory and its readied production with 87 pieces of equipment—27 wagons."[9]

A third category "disassembled, packed, and transported to the railroad," included among eight entries "(a) 13 enterprises, (b) 150 wagons of highway-building equipment," and in terms of cultural treasures, "(d) 225 paintings from the Dresden Gallery, e) 800 albums of engravings, [and]...(g) 2 tons of technical papers (from the Architectural Administration)." The Ukrainian group was "awaiting approval by the Special Committee and the Council of

---

[7] For example, among 1945 records of the CPU Central Committee, TsDAHO, 1/23/1481 and 1/23/1482 are large files with reports on Ukrainian trophy brigade activities in Germany and Romania. A thorough study of these and later files is needed in connection with other sources.

[8] A. V. Palladin to TsK KPbU Secretary D. S. Korotchenko (14 March 1945), TsDAHO, 1/23/1481, fols. 2–17, a copy of which was forwarded to Molotov in Moscow (fols. 28–29).

[9] "Spravka o prodelannoi rabote gruppoi SNK UkrSSR v Germanii" (26 November 1945), signed by Tabulevich, TsDAHO, 1/28/1482, fols. 185–186.

People's Commissars of the USSR of two projected decrees that would transfer another 143 enterprises to Ukraine." By 26 November they had been informed by telephone that Comrade Malenkov had sent the projected decree to Marshal Zhukov with the resolution "to be decided locally." They requested "300,000 marks to be transferred to the Dresden Bank" to cover their expenses and "the allocation of 636 freight-train wagons for December to transport the 2,626 units of equipment already disassembled, packed, and transported to the railroad."[10] Now that such files are open to scholars in Kyiv, more research is needed in conjunction with Soviet all-union sources in Moscow to document the extent to which "cultural reparations" were transferred directly to Soviet Ukraine along with other "spoils of war," in addition to those transferred via Moscow.

Trophy Art. Revelations about looted art in the Soviet Union held in secret for half a century were first published in the West in a series of *ARTnews* exposés by Konstantin Akinsha and Grigorii Kozlov (December 1990–December 1991) that made headlines in Moscow and throughout Western Europe.[11] After half a century, the Trojan gold came out of hiding, and at last some of the "Hidden Treasures" could go on display in the Hermitage. Four years later, the figure of over 1,208,000 museum exhibits from Germany received by the Committee on Cultural and Educational Institutions of the Council of Ministers of the RSFSR, was quoted by *Moskovskie novosti* in October 1994. But that figure did not include those transported under the auspices of the People's Commissariat of Defense and other agencies, nor the private loot of the high command such as was found in a later raid on Marshal Zhukov's dacha.[12] Russians quote the official

---

[10]   Ibid., fols. 186–187, fol. 190.

[11]   Konstantin Akinsha and Grigorii Kozlov, "Spoils of War: The Soviet Union's Hidden Art Treasures," *ARTnews* April 1991: 130–41. As an example of Western press reaction, see the front-page banner headline in the *Observer* with a story by Martin Bailey (24 March 1991) and his follow-up account (31 March 1991): 15. Follow-up stories include articles by Andrew Decker, "A Worldwide Treasure Hunt," *ARTNews*, Summer 1991: 130–38; Akinsha and Kozlov, "The Soviets' War Treasures: A Growing Controversy," *ARTnews* September 1991: 112–19; and Akinsha, "The Turmoil over Soviet War Treasures," *ARTnews* December 1991: 110–15. See more details in Kozlov and Akinsha, *Beautiful Loot.*

[12]   These figures were quoted as a postscript to an interview by correspondent Tat'iana Andriasova with Pavel Knyshevskii regarding his 1994 book, "Dobycha—V adres komiteta po delam iskusstv postupilo iz pobezhdennoi Germanii svyshe 1 milliona 208 tysiach muzeinykh tsennostei," *Moskovskie novosti* 50 (23–30 October

figure of 1,571,995 cultural objects returned to East Germany by 1960, higher than the *Moscow News* figure for those transported to the USSR after the war.[13] Some have tried to present statistics for cultural objects remaining in Russia, but reliable statistics are still impossible. This is true particularly given the facts that: 1) many institutions have not publicly revealed details of their tophy holdings; 2) extensive holdings remain unaccounted for in private hands; and 3) many related archival sources, including Ministry of Culture surveys, continue to be classified.

In April 1998, ten days after Yeltsin signed the Russian law nationalizing all of the trophy cultural treasures brought back to the USSR after the war, an article by Mark Deich in a Moscow newspaper cited the same figures and repeated many of the revelations from the 1994 Knyshevskii book. In contrast to the "Twice Saved" exhibition of plundered canvases at the Pushkin Museum of Fine Arts in Moscow, Deich closed with the reminder that many of the trophies brought back to Moscow were already "twice stolen." Many of the Soviet trophies had initially been plundered from private individuals and occupied countries by the Nazi regime itself.[14] None of those Moscow publications mentioned the trophy art that went directly to Ukraine from Germany or that was transferred to Ukraine via Moscow, and so far there have been no trophy exhibitions in Kyiv.

One of the most important components of trophy art from Germany was the extensive holdings from the Dresden Gallery, along with other important German collections (including the Koenigs Collection from the Netherlands) that were removed from the Gross Cotta mine near Pirna and the Weesenstein Castle in Saxony, which had been their wartime shelters. The Soviet trophy brigades used Pillnitz Castle near Dresden as one of their collection points.

1994): 18. Deich's article ("Podpisano Stalinym"), the Knyshevskii book (*Dobycha: Tainy germanskikh reparatsii*), and Akinsha and Kozlov's *Beautiful Loot*, all detail the raid on Zhukov's dacha.

[13] See the figure quoted from the official protocol in the presentation by Irina Antonova, "Instances of Repatriation by the USSR," in *The Spoils of War: WWII and Aftermath*, pp. 145–46. Also quoted at that time were "121 crates of books, sound archives and musical scores, and more than 3 million archival files." Somewhat variant figures and more details are given by Petra Kuhn, "Comment on the Soviet Returns of Cultural Treasures Moved because of the War to the GDR," *Spoils of War: International Newsletter* 2 (July 1996): 45–47. Kuhn claims that 1.9 million cultural objects were returned to the GDR by the late 1980s.

[14] Mark Deich, "Dobycha—Restitutsiia po-sovetski, ili 'Sploshnaia Chemodaniia,'" *Moskovskii komsomolets* 25 April 1998: 5.

After the paintings from the Dresden Gallery arrived in Moscow in 1945, the Committee for Cultural and Educational Institutions realized that the exhibit space within the Pushkin Museum was inadequate. In symbolic tribute to the importance the Communist regime attached to the expanded museum enterprise, they recommended turning over the neighboring building that currently housed the Marx-Engels-Lenin Institute to the Pushkin Museum. That "would permit a museum of world art appropriate to the capital of the Soviet Union to be created in Moscow within a short time."[15] Stalin's museum was never created, however, and the treasures seized for it were relegated to top secret special depositories. Although some of the Dresden paintings were first exhibited in Moscow under the Khrushchev regime in 1957, before 1,240 of them were returned to Dresden, the rest of the plundered art was not seen again for half a century.[16]

Trophy Art Specifically in Ukraine. As noted above, in 1945 and early 1946, Ukrainian trophy brigades had worked independently of those from Moscow. Whereas the 1945 report quoted above noted 300 paintings from the Dresden Gallery that were shipped directly to Kyiv, the independent art specialists Akinsha and Kozlov, cite the figure of 501 paintings and two pastels from Dresden that went to Kyiv, based on a March 1955 report from the Ministry of Culture. Akinsha and Kozlov found considerable details about their transfers and subsequent fate, although they have published only a few highlights. They relate how one important Dresden shipment was delivered to Kyiv by plane with the exceptional contents of the Albrecht Dürer Triptych from the Dresden Altar, the "Birth of Jesus" by Lucas Cranach, and paintings by Paolo Veronese and Peter Paul Rubens, among others. After they landed in Kyiv, the crates were left out on the air field for a considerable time in the snow, causing considerable water damage. According to their investigations, the paintings from the Dresden Gallery itself were all forwarded to Moscow and returned to Dresden. However, not all of the paintings that had come to

---

[15] M. Khrapchenko, Chairman of the Committee, to V. M. Molotov, Deputy Chairman of the Council of People's Commissars (22 August 1945), RGASPI, 71/125/308, fols. 20–21. Molotov endorsed the proposal to be passed on to Voznesenskii and Aleksandrov in the Central Committee (7 September 1945).

[16] Akinsha and Kozlov, *Beautiful Loot*, and *Operation Beutekunst* document other details about the fate of the Dresden collection (pp. 112–32) and its eventual return (pp. 192–202). According to that account in December 1945, the Museum of Western and Oriental Art in Kyiv had received 456 Dresden paintings and 41 went to the Historical Museum. Regarding the Soviet returns to the GDR, see the brief article by Petra Kuhn in *Spoils of War: International Newsletter* 2 (July 1996): 45–47.

Kyiv from Dresden were from the Gallery itself.[17]

Left behind in Kyiv after the returns to Dresden were some paintings from private collections that had been on deposit with those of the Dresden Gallery, most of the drawings and other graphic art from the Dresden Gallery, and many of the paintings that had been received from Berlin and other German collections. A recently published 1957 chart with a report from the Ministry of Culture of the USSR enumerates raw statistics for trophy cultural goods from the GDR that were distributed to different institutions, including several in Kyiv. The Kyiv Museum of Western and Oriental Art is listed with 300 paintings, 102,200 drawings, graphics, and decorative arts (from the Dresden Museum) and 665 paintings, graphics, sculpture, and decorative arts from Berlin private collections. A small group of Dresden porcelain is listed in the Museum of Ukrainian Art. The Kyiv Historical Museum is listed as holding 173 paintings and 158 items of decorative arts.[18] Although some of those figures coincide with those cited by Akinsha and Kozlov, the discrepancies still require clarification. The latter authors also refer to Egyptian textiles and papyrus manuscripts received by the Historical Museum.[19] Although the 1957 Ministry of Culture report on which those figures are based was published in 1996 in German translation, the original Russian document is now classified in RGANI (earlier TsKhSD).[20]

---

[17] Akinsha and Kozlov, "Die Beute lag auf dem Flugplatz im Schnee," pp. 61–62. Akinsha recently elaborated his findings in a personal conversation with me in April 1999.

[18] The report lists 102,000 items from the Dresden museum and 665 from Berlin private collections: the chart lists 102,361 drawings, prints, engravings, and miniatures; 83 items of decorative arts; and 102 archeological and other materials—*Die Trophäenkommissionen*, no. 46 and 47, pp. 243–45, 248–49 (specific sources for nos. 46 and 47 are not given, but documents nos. 44–48 are reported from TsKhSD [now RGANI], 4/16/245, 430, and 465; 4/24/1790; and 4/29/ 129). Officials in the Museum of Western and Oriental Art have refused to discuss the matter with my Ukrainian colleague, and were not prepared to meet with me in Kyiv in 1999. Engravings (14) and numismatics (634) are also listed for the Historical Museum.

[19] Akinsha and Kozlov ("Die Beute lag auf dem Flugplatz im Schnee," pp. 61–63) cite receipts from Germany by the Museum of Western and Oriental Art of 1,344 portfolios and albums and 22 rolls with drawings and prints. Possibly the discrepancy may be explained if the 1957 document references individual folios, but in any case further more detailed investigation is needed.

[20] The deputy director of RGANI (earlier TsKhSD) explained to me that almost the entire Fond 4 (CPSU Central Committee Secretariat), briefly open to researchers during 1992 and early 1993, was closed after the August 1993 law "On State Secrets,"

Of particular note is the fact that many important prints, drawings, and other art treasures that had come to Kyiv from Germany after the war were not returned in the 1958 shipment to the GDR from Moscow. Ukrainian President Kuchma's return of three albums of eighteenth-and nineteenth-century prints and drawings from the Museum of Western and Oriental Art to German Chancellor Helmut Kohl in 1996 was an important gesture of reconciliation, although German museum specialists were disappointed, because they had been shown five albums earlier that year.[21] How many more such German treasures remain in Kyiv is still not known, because museum officials in Kyiv are apparently not yet prepared for total openness on the subject. While the Museum of Western and Oriental Art has prepared a list of 474 paintings that went missing from their prewar collections during the war, a comprehensive catalog of the displaced trophy art now or previously held by the museum has not yet been started.[22]

For Ukraine to pursue a true policy of openness that would allow it to profit from the international goodwill and economic advantages of restitution, it will need to enhance cooperation in revealing documentation about trophy receipts—as well as the trophy treasures themselves—according to international agreements already executed. In the Dresden case, for example, a documented report on the Ukrainian receipts (those returned to Dresden, and those remaining in Kyiv) would help specialists confirm the fate and location of many of the displaced works of art involved in the wartime destruction, displacements, seizures, and postwar transfers. This will not be easy, however, because records remain fragmentary and frequently contradictory. Often only statistics were cited in the records without full description or explanation of the actual items involved. Museums and archives are reluctant to open up these records. As mentioned earlier, many of the records, albeit incomplete, are located in Moscow. Even the secret files of the Committee on Cultural and Educational Institutions under the Council of Ministers of the Ukrainian SSR (which dealt with many trophy receipts during the postwar years) are not publicly available. They are currently

---

as not having been properly declassified. Ukrainian Archival Administration colleagues also tried to get a copy of the documents, but likewise were refused.

21   See below, Chapter 12, pp. 460–61, and the report of the transfer in *Rabochaia gazeta Ukraïna* 5 September 1996: 1.

22   *Catalogue of Works of Western European Painters Lost during Second World War*, comp. Olena Roslavets; ed. Oleksandr Fedoruk et al. (Kyiv, 1998). I use here the translation "Western" rather than "Occidental" for the museum name, since it is more common in the West. Regarding the catalog, see Chapter 2, pp. 59–60.

missing, or have been destroyed, or they are still secretly classified somewhere in the city.[23] We simply do not know.

Trophy Books and Manuscript Collections

Trophy Books from Germany. Revelations in *Literaturnaia gazeta* in October 1990 described the two-and-a-half million trophy library books received from Germany by the Academy of Sciences of the USSR that were rotting under pigeon droppings in the church of Uzkoe outside Moscow, along with many more additional millions distributed to libraries throughout Soviet lands. That first, publicly acknowledged exposé of the Soviet library seizures from Germany caused a sensation in library and cultural circles throughout the former Soviet Union and abroad, especially in Germany.[24] The most striking tragedy is that so many of the plundered library books torn from their originating collections, like almost all of the artistic masterpieces, were thereafter neglected and hidden from the public for half a century. Some of the trophy books were integrated into existing collections and well used by Soviet readers, especially in the realm of science.[25] But several librarians first reporting the hitherto top secret story of trophy books in the period of glasnost revealed that there had been extensive "cleansing" operations involving book destruction in addition to relegation to special restricted collections (*spetskhrany*) during the Soviet period. Many of the books brought from Germany represented "degenerate bourgeois ideology" and were not considered suitable for raising the "socialist consciousness" ordered by postwar Communist Party guidelines.[26]

---

[23] Ukrainian colleagues and I have examined the existing publicly available fond of this agency in TsDAVO (fond 4762), but the secret section of the fond, which presumably would retain at least some files on postwar cultural transfers, is not available. According to the TsDAVO director, those files are not to be found; because of many official inquiries, she has been trying to find them herself, she assured me on several recent occasions, but has as yet been unable to trace their fate.

[24] Evgenii Kuz'min, "Taina tserkvi v Uzkom," *Literaturnaia gazeta* 38 (8 September 1990): 10. Kuz'min now heads the Library Division of the Ministry of Culture.

[25] See, for example, the data brought together and analyzed by Pamela Spence Richards, "Scientific Communication in the Cold War: Margarita Rudomino and the Library of Foreign Literatures during the Last Years of Stalin," *Libraries and Culture* 31(1) Winter 1996: 235–46.

[26] See, for example, N. V. Kotrelev, "Plach o pogibeli russkoi biblioteki," in *Redkie knigi i rukopisi: Izuchenie i opisanie (Materialy Vsesoiuznogo nauchno-metodi-*

The 1990 exposé was only the beginning of more open discussion of the issue of trophy books in the context of World War II reparations and restitution policies. An early highlight of the "re-cleansing" process was a historic roundtable of Russian and German librarians in December 1992 devoted to the German trophy books and appropriate restitution processes. Among the active Moscow host libraries was the All-Russian State Library of Foreign Literature (VGBIL), which still bears the honorific name of Margarita Rudomino, who had directed the Soviet trophy book operation in Germany after the war. Exemplifying a spirit of openness on the part of one of the libraries that had benefited most from the German cultural trophies, VGBIL issued a catalog of sixteenth-century German imprints held by the library with exhaustive information about their historical affiliations, ex libris, and other markings.[27] Some provincial Russian libraries initially refused to participate in the conference out of protest; the directors of major libraries who were known to have received many of the trophy books claimed they had none and refused to discuss the matter. Yet in the end, despite the uproar, participants considered the roundtable a tremendous success, resulting in the establishment of a Russian-German Commission on Library Restitution. Optimism was on the rise that restitution matters could be resolved and that new aid from Germany was in store for libraries in Russia.[28]

Before the roundtable, in addition to publishing a catalog of its German rarities, VGBIL had taken the initiative in exhibiting and returning 604 books to the University of Amsterdam that Nazi looting brigades had seized from the Netherlands and that had subsequently been transferred to the USSR in

---

cheskogo soveshchaniia zaveduiushchikh otdelami redkikh knig i rukopisei bibliotek vuzov. Leningrad, 24–26 ianvaria 1989 g.) (Leningrad: Izd-vo Leningradskogo universiteta, 1991), pp. 107–109. See also the later article by two Leningrad University librarians, Aleksandr Gorfunkel' and Nikolai Nikolaev, "Kak vozvrashchat' 'trofeinye knigi': Eshche raz o zakhvachennykh vo vremia voiny kul'turnykh tsennostiakh," *Nevskoe vremia* 8(163) 14 January 1992.

27   See the published catalog of the Moscow library exhibit, *Katalog vystavki "Nemetskie trofeinye knigi v fondakh VGBIL,"* comp. and ed. E. E. Eikhman et al. (Moscow: "Rudomino," 1992).

28   Proceedings of the Roundtable were first published in German, *Restitution von Bibliotheksgut. Runder Tisch deutscher und russischer Bibliothekare in Moskau am 11. und 12. Dezember 1992,* ed. Klaus-Dieter Lehmann and Ingo Kolasa (Frankfurt-am-Main: Vittorio Klostermann, 1993) [=*Zeitschrift für Bibliothekswesen und Bibliographie,* Sonderheft 56]. A Russian edition appeared the following year: *Restitutsiia bibliotechnykh sobranii.*

1946.[29] Since the conference, however, optimism has waned as Russian politicians have refused to permit the restitution of a single volume—this despite the professional agreement among Russian librarians, the goodwill from other European countries that could be engendered, and the tremendous benefits that German libraries had promised in exchange. German librarians have been especially interested to see the return of the unique German collections and rare early imprints that are of value to Germans, but that are of much less interest in Russia than the contemporary publications that Russian libraries could acquire in exchange for the older materials.

One important document revealed at the roundtable, prepared by Margarita Rudomino herself in 1948, "based on data from SVAG," put the trophy figures received in 1945–1946 at an estimated ten million volumes or more. The document, quoted at the roundtable by Evgenii Kuz′min, was published in German translation in 1995 by the German librarian Ingo Kolasa.[30] Out of that total, five million were sent to Moscow and Leningrad—700,000 to the Lenin Library (now the Russian State Library), 500,000 to the Public Library in Leningrad (now the Russian National Library), 300,000 to the Library of the Academy of Sciences, and 50,000 to VGBIL. At least one million went to the State Literary Fond (Gosfond), for distribution to other libraries through the USSR, another million to various ministries, and half a million to the Red Army. Major problems with the trophy book system had developed by 1948, which is why Rudomino was reviewing the receipts and recommending possible solutions. "Much of the trophy literature received...had still not been processed," and many "did not even know what they had." Receiving libraries were unable to cope with the new acquisitions. Many recipients were unable to deal with the "large quantify of rare and valuable artistic editions." Gosfond still had over one million books that had not been distributed, and many "ministries did not even know what to do with the books received."[31]

---

[29] See more details below, Chapter 10, p. 394, and the reference there in fn. 15.

[30] See Evgenii I. Kuz′min, "Neizvestnye stranitsy istorii nemetskikh bibliotechnykh kollektsii v gody Vtoroi mirovoi voiny," in *Restitutsiia bibliotechnykh sobranii*, pp. 17–24.

[31] I quote from the original document, a copy of which is available in the VGBIL Archive—"Spravka o trofeinykh fondakh, privezennykh v SSSR v 1945–1946 gg." (December 1948 [date pencilled in later]), Arkhiv VGBIL, 1/29–37/20, fols. 29–31 (unsigned carbon copy). The intended receipient of the document is not indicated. I am grateful to VGBIL archivist Igor′ A. Bordachenkov for assistance in locating this document and furnishing me a xerox copy.

Problems with the trophy book program and inadequacies in selection
and distribution were rampant union-wide, as further confirmed with many
examples in a 1948 eighteen-page report prepared by the Glavlit, censorship
authority for Preservation of Military and State Secrets in Print under the
Council of Ministers of the USSR. A copy of the report delivered to the
Agitation and Propaganda Division (Agitprop) of the CPSU Central Committee, by K. Omel'chenko, who then headed Glavlit is found in the former
Central Party Archive.[32] Earlier in the year that censorship office with CP
blessing had issued a crucial instruction "On the Retention and Use of
Trophy Literature." Although the text of the regulation is still classified, other
reports in the same file make it clear that orders had gone out for the destruction of Nazi publications, "politically degenerate" literature, and "literature of
no scientific value." On the basis of that order, thorough inspections were
under way in late 1948 in all libraries known to have received trophy literature. Omel'chenko's later composite report on the inspections includes many
examples of inappropriate selection of the publications chosen for transport
and the chaotic distribution system. For example, one factory received crates
of equipment with portraits of Hitler and his top advisors enclosed. A
chemical plant received copies of classical Greek and Latin literature, while
another unsuspecting recipient got copies of the "degenerate American
magazine *Fortune* and the *Saturday Evening Post*," while still another
technical factory received French fashion magazines.[33]

After the roundtable, German specialists have been trying to document
more precisely the transfers from Germany and the fate of the trophy books.
Distressed with the lack of progress towards restitution and the growing
Russian public support for the law nationalizing all postwar trophy cultural
treasures transferred to the USSR, two leading German librarians, Klaus-
Dieter Lehmann and Ingo Kolasa, in 1996 issued a remarkable collection of
secret Soviet documents about the trophy book operations from several
different Russian sources in German translation.[34] It includes, for example,

---

[32] The composite report found in a file of the Agitation and Propaganda Division of
the CPSU Central Committee was sent with a cover note by K. Omel'chenko (7/8
September 1948), RGASPI, 17/132/97, fol. 92; the report itself on the inspection program (fols. 93–110) provides abundant examples from different parts of the USSR. It
was earlier quoted by Knyshevskii, *Dobycha*, pp. 110–11, which led me to the original text.

[33] Ibid.

[34] *Die Trophäenkommissionen der Roten Armee: Eine Dokumentensammlung zur
Verschleppung von Büchern aus deutschen Bibliotheken*, comp. and ed. Klaus-Dieter
Lehmann and Ingo Kolasa (Frankfurt-am-Main, 1996) [=*Zeitschrift für*

the library portion of a secret "Report on the Work of the Plenipotentiary of the Committee for Cultural and Educational Institutions under the Council of People's Commissars of the RSFSR in the Soviet Zone of Occupation in Germany from 6 May through 31 December 1946 [*sic*]." The full 69-page report provides annotated listings of 202 public and private German museums and libraries surveyed by the Soviet trophy brigades, under the direction of A. D. Manevskii and Margarita Rudomino, with indication of how many volumes or crates were taken from each for shipment to the USSR.[35]

Also of great interest is the earlier unpublished portion of that report (the original text is available in GA RF in Moscow) covering museums; one of its entries testifies to the shipment by plane to Moscow of all 19 crates from the Museum of the Book in Leipzig (Deutsches Buch- und Schriftmuseum), with specific mention of the Gutenberg Bible, long imprisoned in a secret safe in the Lenin Library (now the Russian State Library).[36] It was not until 1994 that a survey of that Leipzig collection appeared in print with details about the Gutenberg Bible and other German incunabula, early printed books, and manuscript treasures from the Leipzig museum, all of which are still held in Moscow.[37] According to the authors, a full scholarly catalog is now in

---

Bibliothekswesen und Bibliographie, Sonderheft 64]. GA RF directors, who were very angry about the unauthorized German publication of documents from the archive, told me that no German was shown the files or given permission to receive or publish copies; this is confirmed by the "use sheets" in the files themselves which users are required to sign when they have seen a file in the archive. See also Kolasa, "Sag mir wo die Bücher sin...: Ein Beitrag zu 'Beutekulturgütern' und 'Trophäenkommission- en,'" *Zeitschrift für Bibliothekswesen und Bibliographie* 42(4) (1995): 357–60.

[35] "Otchet o rabote Upolnomochennogo komiteta po delam kul'tprosvetuchrezh- denii pri Sovnarkome RSFSR po Sovetskoi zone okkupatsii Germanii s 6 maia po 31 dekabria 1946 [1945] g.," signed by A. D. Manevskii (Berlin, 31 March 1946), GA RF, A-534/2/10, fols. 1–69. The German translation published as "document no. 17" (*Die Trophäenkommissionen*, pp. 76–119) lacks a title and starts with p. 23 of the report (no. 56), fols. 12–13. The published version apparently is from another source, since no signature was indicated. The document I examined in GA RF, however, was signed by Manevskii. In that case and others, the German editors had not personally seen the original document in GA RF, and its full archival designation is not cited.

[36] "Otchet o rabote" (Berlin, 31 March 1946), GA RF, A-534/2/10, fols. 1–69. Another document published in the German collection (no. 31), however, does docu- ment the shipment from the Museum of the Book in Leipzig that had been found by Soviet authorities in Schloss Rauenstein, near Chemnitz (no. 37), *Die Trophäenkom- missionen*, p. 193. The Gutenberg Bible was among the special treasures sent by plane to Moscow on 3 October 1945.

[37] See the first descriptive publication in Russia by Adrian Rudomino, "Polveka v

preparation. Information about other famous trophy collections gradually is coming to light. For example, in 1999, another article describes some of the over 450 unique early book bindings in the Jakob Krausse Collection from the Saxon State Library in Dresden, also now held in the Russian State Library.[38]

At the same time, more information has been appearing in Russia about the trophy book operations in Germany after the war that were directed by Margarita Rudomino. The new materials include an article by her son, Adrian, that includes many revealing details and the publication of a series of letters and reports from her family papers. Appended is a partial, annotated list of some of the German libraries from which two million trophy books were sent to the USSR by the fall of 1946.[39] More information is also surfacing in Russia about trophy collections from other countries. Most recently, for example, VGBIL specialists issued a scholarly catalog of 1,300 early printed books, incunabula, and 8 manuscripts from the Sárospatak Calvinist College Library in northwest Hungary that surfaced in the Nizhnyi Novgorod State Oblast Universal Research Library.[40]

The allegation by Ingo Kolasa, one of the German editors of the Soviet documents, that the distribution program by Gosfond ended in "complete chaos" reflects many of the reports prepared at the time. Kolasa cites the example of a shipment of "100,000 rain-soaked trophy German books to the Central Library of the Academy of Sciences in Tblisi in the 1950s," about which the library had neither been consulted nor had space to house. As a

---

plenu," *Nashe nasledie* 32 (1994): 92–96; and Oleg Borodin and Tat'iana Dolgodrova, "Kollektsiia Nemetskogo muzeia knigi i shrifta v sobranii Rossiiskoi gosudarstvennoi biblioteki," ibid., 97–106. The Gutenberg Bible was first publicly displayed at a 1995 exhibition at the Moscow library. A Russian television film of 1995, "By the Right of the Victors" ("Po pravde pobeditelei") portrayed Adrian Rudomino, who served in the Red Army in Germany, as personally involved in its transport to Moscow.

[38] See Tat'iana Dolgodrova, "Sobranie perepletov Iakoba Krauze v Rossiiskoi gosudarstvennoi biblioteke," *Nashe nasledie* 49 (1999): 97–102.

[39] Adrian Rudomino, "Knigi voiny," *Nashe nasledie* 49 (1999): 77–93. The appended chart (pp. 94–96) represents a variant of the 69-page document cited above in fn. 34; the library portion, in a somewhat variant edition was earlier published in German *Die Trophäenkommissionen*, pp. 76–119.

[40] *Trofeinye knigi iz biblioteki Sharoshpatakskogo reformatskogo kolledzha (Vengriia) v fondakh Nizhegorodskoi gosudarstvennoi oblastnoi universal'noi nauchnoi biblioteki: Katalog*, comp. E. V. Zhuravleva, N. N. Zubrov, and E. A. Korkmazova (Moscow: "Rudomino," 1997).

result they were relegated to the basement and never even unpacked. He queries if shipments to other union republics might have met a similar fate.[41]

Trophy Books to Ukraine

Measuring Shipments to Ukraine. Speaking at the New York conference on the "Spoils of War" in January 1995, VGBIL Director Ekaterina Genieva put the trophy book figure for the entire Soviet Union at eleven million volumes from Germany, and reported that of the estimated total, three million volumes had been transferred to Ukraine.[42] Although not documented in her published presentation, the three-million figure comes from the 1948 report by Margarita Rudomino in the VGBIL archive mentioned above, and as published in German translation.[43] Examination of the unsigned report in the VGBIL archive, however, reveals the figure of two rather than three million for books sent from Germany to Ukraine.[44] That figure, as indicated in the report, was distinct from the books shipped to Moscow and Leningrad, including those turned over to Gosfond.

The same figure of two million was also given for Minsk. In the case of the Belorussian SSR, we have confirmation of major shipments from Germany and Silesia. For example, a large cache of ERR library collections, with over 1,000,000 volumes (54 freight-car loads) was recovered in the Katowice/Ratibor area and transferred to Minsk in the fall of 1945. Although some of the books were trophy collections, including some seized by the Nazis from Western Europe (Amsterdam and Paris holdings have been identified), they also contained many of the books from Belarusian libraries that had been seized by the Nazis and shipped to Ratibor for the Ostbücherei. Many of the books received after the war were transferred to various libraries

---

[41] *Die Trophäenkommissionen*, preface by Ingo Kolasa, p. 18. Kolasa had examined some of the books in question and found 16th-century imprints among them. Fifty percent of the books shipped to Tblisi, according to Kolasa, came from Bremen and were predominantly of local interest. The incident is highlighted by Pamela Spence Richards in her review of the Kolasa-edited collection, *Library Quarterly* 68(4) October 1998: 493–96.

[42] Ekaterina Genieva, "German Book Collections in Russian Libraries," in *The Spoils of War: WWII and Aftermath*, p. 222.

[43] Regarding the report, see Kuz′min, "Neizvestnye stranitsy istorii."

[44] "Spravka o trofeinykh fondakh," Arkhiv VGBIL, 1/29–37/20, fol. 29. The carbon typescript is somewhat blurred, but for Ukraine the figure clearly is a "2" rather than a "3" million.

in the Belorussian SSR, while a large number of them were later transferred to Moscow.[45] Nevertheless, many foreign books that had been seized by the Nazis from Western Europe remain in Minsk, as has been shown by a recent report.[46] This was undoubtedly also the source of the books from the Petliura Library in Paris later transferred to Kyiv. We have confirmation, as well, of extensive "cleansing" campaigns in the Belorussian SSR, which unfortunately resulted in the loss of many volumes from the Turgenev Library in Paris.[47] Quite possibly, some of the treasures from the Petliura Library also perished there.

Rudomino mentions in several personal letters from Germany that a representative from the Academy of Sciences of the UkrSSR in Kyiv was in Germany working with the Trophy Library Brigade. His reports have not surfaced in Kyiv, nor do we even know his name. As yet, no confirming documentation of the dispatch or receipt of two million books from Germany has been found in Ukraine—we have only the figure of the two-and-a-half tons of books for the Academy of Sciences, mentioned above, that were shipped to Kyiv in November 1945.

All-Union Ministry of Culture statistics cite the figure of 2,400,000 volumes transferred to 888 libraries in Ukraine during 1944 and 1945 from the State Literature Fond (Gosfond), which was charged with redistribution of books to libraries throughout the USSR after the war. Those shipments, however, went out before the big receipts from Germany. Reportedly only a small part of those transfers were trophy books.[48] The statistics for trophy

---

[45]   A report on the Minsk developments was kindly furnished to me by Frits Hoogewoud on the basis of a letter he received from G. N. Oleinik, Director of the National Library of Belarus (*Natsyianal'naia Bibliiateka Belarusi*) (25 June 1993). In that letter Oleinik dated the transfers to Moscow in the late 1970s and early 1980s, but we have other indications of earlier transfers.

[46]   See Vladimir Makarov, "Involuntary Journey of Books from Paris to Minsk," *Spoils of War: International Newsletter* 6 (February 1999): 25–27.

[47]   See Nikolai V. Kotrelev, "Plach o pogibeli russkoi biblioteki," pp. 107–109. In a footnote on the fate of trophy books (that deserves expansion as a separate study), Kotrelev documents the destruction of many volumes of books from the Turgenev Library in Paris "in an outlying Soviet library." In more recent conversation with me, Kotrelev reported that library as being in Minsk, where subsequently a large part of the library was destroyed during an "ideological purification" campaign.

[48]   Quoted by Aleksandr M. Mazuritskii, *Ocherki istorii bibliotechnogo dela perioda Velikoi Otechestvennoi voiny, 1941–1945 gg.* (Moscow, 1995; RGB, Moskovskii gosudarstvennyi universitet kul'tury), p. 146. The exact source of the figure is not provided.

books transferred to Ukraine obviously requires further investigation both from Russian sources and on the Ukrainian side, since much of the crucial documentation is either missing or still classified.

The above-mentioned 1948 Agitprop report noted that, "in Ukraine, trophy literature was received in 14 oblasts by 102 organizations, for a total of 213,581 volumes," but Omel'chenko's Glavlit agency had at that point only completed the verification of 84 organizations in 5 oblasts, totaling 187,372 volumes.[49] Those figures are obviously only a fraction of the two million volumes quoted in the 1948 Rudomino report, but as yet a full explanation for the discrepancy has not been found, nor do we know the source of the Glavlit figures. We must assume that those were among the books sent to Ukraine from Gosfond. The Glavlit report also revealed significant mismanagement in shipments to Ukraine, with one example in which the library of the Academy of Architecture of the UkrSSR received 11 tons of trophy literature in December 1947. Unfortunately, most of the shipment involved "up to 300 copies of the same titles," which they obviously could not use and had no place to store; they needed instructions as to how to dispose of the waste paper. "One must ask," states the report, "for what purpose was such 'literature' brought to the Soviet Union?"[50]

Documenting the trophy transfers to Ukraine today is exceedingly difficult, because of the lack of adequate records, but also because of the remaining reluctance of many people to face up to the issue after the long years of required silence and the recent furor over trophy books in Russia. The chaotic immediate postwar situation in Kyiv, with much of the city in ruins, also makes the trophy transfers hard to trace. The buildings of several major Ukrainian libraries that suffered most severely from Nazi plunder, such as the Korolenko Library in Kharkiv and the Library Named in Honor of the Communist Party (which Nazi reports refer to as the Kirov Library; now the National Parliamentary Library of Ukraine) in Kyiv, were completely destroyed—hence they were unable to receive any books in 1945 and 1946. The National Parliamentary Library of Ukraine, which did not even have a building after the war, today counts between 50,000 and 70,000 books seized in 1943 by retreating Nazi ERR commandos, according to Nazi reports. Recently librarians have found allegations of 50,000 books seized by various local partisan groups. They also now report having received 50,000 books after the war, including approximately 20,000 from Gosfond, 10,000 via

---

[49]   As quoted in the report cited in fn. 32, RGASPI, 17/132/97, fol. 105.

[50]   Director Grydina of the Library of the Academy of Architecture in Kyiv, as quoted in the same report, RGASPI, 17/132/97, fol. 98.

TsNB, and some restitution shipments of their own books that had been taken by the Nazis and returned from abroad. These librarians now claim that perhaps only 200 of the 50,000 books received in the postwar decade were trophy books or those bearing markings from other libraries.[51]

Many of the books transferred to the USSR from German libraries to compensate for wartime losses were integrated into existing collections without indication of whence they came, so that they may now be difficult to find. We do know that major shipments of trophy books to Ukraine went to the Central Library of the Academy of Sciences (TsNB) in Kyiv, and then many were later distributed to other libraries. However, we do not know if the 2.5 tons noted in the November 1945 shipment directly from Dresden to Kyiv for the Academy of Sciences mentioned earlier was included in the two million figure from Germany sent to Ukraine, as per the Rudomino report, or if they should be counted in addition. At least in the case of TsNB, we now know that many of those kept by that library were stored apart and only recently are they being analyzed in terms of collection or library of provenance.[52] Others received in Ukraine were undoubtedly not the types of books needed, or for which there was no shelf space, and they may have met the fate of those mentioned above in Uzkoe and Tblisi. Reportedly, book markings were removed and some trophy receipts were later destroyed in other ideological "cleansing" campaigns, as transpired in Belarus. So far, however, there has been no serious attempt to appraise the situation in Ukraine.

A recent visit to what is now the National Parliamentary Library of Ukraine brought confirmation of at least one rather special trophy collection received from Minsk in the 1980s. Of particular interest because it represents a twice-plundered Ukrainian émigré collection seized by the Nazis from Paris in 1941, rather than from Germany itself, approximately 240 books from the Petliura Library in Paris are now held in the Parliamentary Library. They were identified in what is now the National Library of Belarus in Minsk (earlier the Lenin Library) and transferred to Kyiv in 1989, although the

---

[51] As reported to me in a July 1999 interview by Olena Aleksandrova, Deputy Director of the Parliamentary Library in Kyiv on the basis of one of her own reports in preparation.

[52] One colleague in TsNB (now the National Library of Ukraine—NBU), Liubov A. Dubrovina, who heads the Institute of Manuscripts and has been researching a major anniversary history of the library, reported in 1999 that she has found no data about trophy books in the library archives. Reportedly, concerted efforts are currently under way to identify books with German book stamps that had been housed in earlier TsNB Special Collections, although the library is not yet ready to publicize its findings.

transfer was never openly reported in Kyiv.[53] Out of the 17,000 or 18,000 books seized by the Nazis from the Petliura Library in Paris, the transfer from Minsk to Kyiv involved approximately 180 books of predominantly Ukrainian provenance and another 60 books with foreign imprints (mostly French and a few German). The Parliamentary Library reports having purchased another 10 books bearing stamps of the Petliura Library at auction in Kyiv in the early 1980s, and another volume came with a collection they received from Prague.[54] Apparently, however, the Petliura Library in Paris was never informed about the discovery and transfer of the books to Kyiv.[55]

Some archival materials from the Petliura Library in Paris have also recently surfaced in Kyiv (see further below, in Chapter 9). Meanwhile, according to recent reports from Minsk, quite possibly more Petliura Library books remain there. A much larger collection of archival materials from the Petliura Library, including its own records, are now held in Moscow in the State Archive of the Russian Federation (GA RF), and even more archival materials and some books have been identified among the collections from the former top secret Special Archive in Moscow (see below).[56] Soon after 1991, as reported from the Petliura Library in Paris, a Ukrainian émigré from Paris heard about a "large carton" of books recently found in the basement of the former Lenin Library (now the Russian State Library) transported by the Red Army to Moscow marked as being from a "Ukrainian Library—Paris."

---

[53] The receipt was kindly verified for me by Olena Aleksandrova. I initially received confirmation of the transfer in a letter from Adam Mal'dzis, who heads the National Commission on Restitution in Belarus; Mal'dzis dated the transfer as having taken place in 1993–1994, but Aleksandrova established that the books were received in 1989, although the exact date was not immediately available. Mal'dzis cites the "return to Kyiv" (with no details) in his 1995 New York conference presentation, "The Tragic Fate of Belarusan Museum and Library Collections during the Second World War," in *The Spoils of War: WWII and Aftermath*, p. 80. It is also appreciatively mentioned by Aleksandrova, in her report at the 1997 conference in Minsk—"Poteri bibliotek Ukrainy: Probvlemy vyiavleniia i poiska," in *Restytutsyia kul'turnykh kashtoŭnastsei*, p. 95.

[54] That purchase was also reported by Olena Aleksandrova, Deputy Director of the Parliamentary Library in Kyiv.

[55] In a May 1999 letter, Professor Arkady Joukovsky, who has long been closely involved with the Petliura Library in Paris, wrote me that he had not heard about the transfer.

[56] See more details in my "The Odyssey of the Petliura Library and UNR Records during World War II," *HUS* 22: 181–208; and my "The Postwar Fate of the Petliura Library and the Records of the Ukrainian National Republic," *HUS* 21(3–4): 393–461.

Librarians there deny such a possibility.[57]

Plundered Ukrainian Library Books Retrieved. Undoubtedly, some of the books forwarded to Ukraine from Berlin or from Moscow and Leningrad with the trophy books were those that the Nazis had looted from Ukrainian libraries and that had been restituted by the Western Allies or retrieved by Soviet authorities. Soviet distribution authorities did not always make a breakdown between trophy books and those looted from Soviet libraries that had been retrieved, or between those restituted by the Western Allies and those retrieved by Soviet authorities themselves. They all were shipped from Germany together. Among the 100,000 trophy books that were shipped to Tbilisi were some that reportedly had been looted by the Nazis from Russian (and possibly Ukrainian?) libraries. We already saw earlier the lack of complete and accurate information in Russia about restitution receipts, and lack of appreciation for the careful sorting by book markings that had been done in Offenbach.

Over half the books identified in the American library restitution center in Offenbach were from Ukraine, but from Offenbach statistics, that would only be somewhere in the vicinity of, at most, 150,000 volumes. But we do not know if all the books identified in Offenbach with Ukrainian library stamps actually were returned to Ukraine. The Soviet receipts, transfer, or shipping documents that do exist for transfers within the USSR have yet to be compared to the Allied restitution documents receipted by Soviet restitution officers. Again, allegations that the Gosfond distribution program ended in "total chaos" and that the Gosfond records have disappeared may suggest the difficulties involved.[58]

Some books recovered by the Soviet Trophy Library Brigade that had been looted by the Nazis from Ukraine have also been mentioned in one of the reports in the collection of German-translated documents edited by Lehmann and Kolasa. For example, the Commission found materials from the Herbarium in Kharkiv listed as having been sent to the Botanical Museum in Berlin along with other scientific materials from Kyiv (among them an entomological collection and negatives from the Institute of Biology and

---

[57]   As mentioned regarding the visit of "Labynets'" with no further explanation or documentation by Vasyl' Mykhal'chuk, *Ukraïns'ka biblioteka im. Symona Petliury v Paryzhi: Zasnuvannia, rozvytok, diial'nist' (1926–1998)* (Kyiv: Vyd-vo im. Oleny Telihy, 1999), p. 103. Librarians in RGB have assured me that all trophy books were processed in the immediate postwar period.

[58]   See above, p. 263n41, and Chapter 6, pp. 224–29 (esp. fns. 23–27).

Zoology).[59] Those collections may well have been among the two million books sent from Berlin to Kyiv. Of specific Ukrainian interest, although of negative result, the Commission reported having tried to locate the House of the Ukrainian People's Rada in Berlin, where they had heard about an exhibit on "The History and Life of the Ukrainian People" during the war. But they discovered the holdings had been "liquidated by the Gestapo in 1943 and all of the materials reportedly destroyed."[60] Perhaps the "dispatched to Kyiv" figure also includes some of the books looted by the Rosenberg Commandos (ERR) that were found by U.S. Army MFA&A units and returned directly to Soviet authorities in Germany rather than passing through Offenbach. Unfortunately, no Soviet documentation on those transfers or shipments is available.

Post-1991 Research on Displaced Libraries. Although the fate of German trophy books in Ukraine has still not been adequately researched, since Ukrainian independence fresh research and the publication of revealing documentation has been progressing about the fate of Ukrainian libraries during the war in specific areas. For example, in 1997, an extensive publication of documents appeared relating to Kharkiv libraries during the war, with emphasis on the fate of the Korolenko Library. In their introduction, the compilers concentrate on establishing reliable statistics about the Kharkhiv library losses, which indeed were staggering.[61] Unfortunately, however, in that essay they do not follow the shipments from Kharkiv to Nazi collecting points, such as the ERR library center in Ratibor in Silesia (where large portions of the Korolenko Library, including its catalogs were sent by the ERR), the Central Library of the Hohe Schule in the Austrian Tyrol, and even a few specific shipments to Germany for which documents survive. Since, again, the Kharkiv compilers have not had access to any documentation about Soviet library retrievals, they were not yet able to match up any specific out shipments with those that were later returned (even in part). Given the incomplete Soviet documentation, it may not be possible to make definitive determinations in many cases, but it might be a helpful future path to try to

---

[59] Inventory dated 7 February 1946, in *Die Trophäenkommissionen*, p. 63 (document no. 12, nos. 69–72). Original in GA RF, 534/2/7, fols. 44–47.

[60] "Otchet o rabote Upolnomochennogo komiteta," (31 May 1946), GA RF, A-534/2/10, fol. 12 (the Ukrainian center was no. 20 on the list).

[61] *Bibliotechni fondy Kharkova v roky Druhoï svitovoï viiny*, comp. I. Ia. Losiievs′kyi et al.; ed. I. O. Blokhina et al. (Kyiv, 1997) [= *Dolia kul′turnykh skarbiv Ukraïny pid chas Druhoï svitovoï viiny: Arkhivy, biblioteky, muzeï*, 2].

pinpoint specific migrations, losses, and recoveries, as well as any trophy German books that may have come to specific libraries in Ukraine.

Virtually all of the recent conference reports on the wartime fate of libraries in Ukraine have completely ignored the issue of postwar trophy receipts. Notably, the displacement of library books in Ukraine during and after the war was the focus for a round table meeting in Donetsk in May 1994.[62] While much attention was directed to the looting of Ukrainian libraries during the war, no concrete data was reported on the correlated transfer of German library books to the Ukrainian SSR thereafter. The published proceedings of the library-oriented sections of the larger UNESCO-sponsored conference on World War II losses in Chernihiv in September 1994 present many reports on the appalling looting operations and losses by Ukrainian libraries. But again, nothing was said about any of the two (rather than three) million books that were reportedly shipped from Germany in compensatory reparations.[63] The issue of German books transferred to Ukraine was also not raised in a subsequent 1995 Round Table in Odesa with three German participants.[64] Obviously, more research in this area is needed, and by necessity cooperative research with specialists in Russia and Belarus as well, as was emphasized in one of the reports at the 1997 Minsk conference on restitution mentioned above.[65]

The Berlin Sing-Akademie Collection in Kyiv:
A Case Study

The most significant trophy archival and library collection to have surfaced in Ukraine to date is the long-lost music score archive from the Sing-Akademie in Berlin, now held in the Central State Archive-Museum of Literature and Art in Kyiv (TsDAMLM). The priceless Sing-Akademie collection with over 5,100 predominantly manuscript music scores embraces a major surviving

---

[62]   A brief summary digest of the proceedings is published as *Povernennia kul'turnoho, 4.*

[63]   See the many reports library sessions at the conference in *Materialy natsional'noho seminaru, Chernihiv, 1994,* esp. pp. 66–73; 228–42; 272–320.

[64]   See the published proceedings of the round table—*Kultura i viina.* See the report by Ol'ha Botushans'ka dealing with the Odesa State Scientific Library during the war and a proposal by Erna Zhytolostnova for a database on losses suffered by libraries in Ukraine (pp. 57–59).

[65]   Aleksandrova, "Poteri bibliotek Ukrainy," p. 98.

part of the musical estate of the Bach family together with manuscripts of many other eighteenth- and early nineteenth-century German composers, including compositions of many musicians associated with the Prussian court. The discovery in Kyiv resulted from my collaboration with Hennadii Boriak, then deputy director of the Hrushevs'kyi Institute of Ukrainian Archeography and Source Study in Kyiv. The collection was identified at the end of June 1999 by Christoph Wolff, professor of music and dean of the Graduate School of Arts and Sciences at Harvard University, who had been searching for the lost Bach music scores for over two decades.[66]

The Sing-Akademie, since its establishment in Berlin in 1791, although mainly a performing institution, also became a major repository for original German music scores. The musical legacy of Johann Sebastian Bach's second son, Carl Philipp Emanuel Bach (1714–1788) forms the central part of the archive, much of which has never been published or available for study and performance. Along with scores of his father's ancestors (many in autograph copies in J. S. Bach's hand) and brothers, there are over 500 scores of various members of the Bach family. Although most of the original scores of Johann Sebastian Bach were sold to the Prussian Royal Library in 1854 (later the Prussian State Library), the rest of the Bach family legacy remained in the Sing-Akademie. Also represented is a major part of the music legacy of Georg Philipp Telemann, Carl Heinrich and Johann Gottlieb Graun, Johann Adolf Hasse, Franz and Georg Benda, among many others. There are also some scores of Franz Josef Haydn, Georg Friedrich Händel, and other well-known composers. Approximately eighty per cent of the collection consists of original manuscript scores, the rest, predominantly limited-edition original lithographs or authorized performing copies. Only a provisional card catalog of the library and its rich archival holdings had been prepared before World War II, and they had never been publicly available for performance and study.[67]

---

[66] The present account draws on material originally prepared for the Harvard News Office by Christoph Wolff and myself. I am grateful to Professor Wolff for the musicological elements involved. The story of the migration and rediscovery of the collection emerged in conjunction with the final editing of the present volume. See my more detailed account, "Bach Scores in Kyiv" at <http://www.huri.harvard.edu/workpaper/grimsted/grimsted.html> and *Spoils of War: International Newsletter* 7 (August 2000): 23–35.

[67] The only published survey of the library holdings appeared in Berlin in 1966, based on recollections of Friedrich Welter, "Die Musikbibliothek der Sing-Akademie zu Berlin," in *Sing-Akademie zu Berlin: Festschrift zum 175 jährigen Bestehen*, ed. Werner Bollert (Berlin: Rembrandt Verlag, 1966), pp. 33–47.

When Allied bombing of Berlin started in 1943, Nazi authorities started wide-scale evacuation of cultural treasures to mines, monasteries, and castles in the countryside. While many German cultural treasures were systematically transported to salt mines in Saxony and other sites that remained part of postwar Germany, others were sent east to remote areas of Silesia, Bohemia, and the Sudetenland. Ninety packets of the Sing-Akademie archive were secured in 15 large crates and shipped off to the Ullersdorf Castle in Silesia, south of Breslau (*Pol.* Wrocław).[68] Silesia was an important evacuation area for Berlin cultural treasures, including major parts of the Prussian State Library, whose Musicalia and Orientalia collections, for example, went first to the elegant Castle of Fürstenstein (*Pol.* Książ), somewhat closer to Breslau, but then were later transferred to the Benedictine Abbey of Grüssau (*Pol.* Krzeszów).[69]

The postwar fate of the evacuated treasures varied widely. For example, one of the most famous displaced collections in Poland are the Berlin musicalia and other manuscript treasures from Grüssau. It was 1977 before they surfaced in the Jagellonian Library in Cracow, where most of them remain today.[70] The fate of other treasures found by the Red Army in Silesia

---

[68]   The village of Ullersdorf (*Pol.* Ołdrzychowice-Kłodzkie) is about seven kilometers southeast of Glatz (*Pol.* Kłozko) on a tributary of the Neisse River (*Pol.* Nysa), some eighty kilometers south of Breslau (*Pol.* Wrocław). Confirmation of the shipment there comes from a report—"Eigentum der Berliner-Sing-Akademie" (15 March 1945), signed by Georg Schumann, then director of the Sing-Akademie in Berlin. A copy was recently faxed from Berlin to Christoph Wolff at Harvard University, who kindly furnished me a copy.

[69]   See the survey of the evacuation operations for the Prussian State Library in *Verlagert—Verschollen—Vernichtet: Das Schicksal der im 2. Weltkrieg ausgelagerten Bestände der Preußischen Staatsbibliothek* (Berlin: Staatsbibliotheek zu Berlin-Preußischer Kulturbesitz, 1995). Gudrun Voigt provides capsule reports with pictures of all of the known evacuation sites for the Staatsbibliothek, *Die kriegsbedingte Auslagerung von Beständen der Preußischen Staatsbibliothek und ihre Rückführung* (Hannover: Laurentius Verlag Raimund Dehmlow, 1995) [=Kleine historische Reihe, vol. 8].

[70]   See the latest report on the status of the musicalia holdings of the Prussian State Library, a large part of which is now held in the Jagellonian Library in Cracow, in *Verlagert—Verschollen—Vernichtet*, especially pp. 9, 19–26. Regarding the thirty-five-year search for the German music collections in Poland, see the intriguing account by Nigel Lewis, *Paperchase: Mozart, Beethoven, Bach: The Search for Their Lost Music* (London: Hamish Hamilton, 1981). See also "Bestände aus der früheren Preußischen Staatsbibliothek in Polen," *Jahrbuch für Preußischer Kulturbesitz*

is still largely unknown, although information about them is gradually coming to light. Most of them were taken to Moscow, while only a few went to Belarus or Ukraine. Since the Sing-Akademie archive lay hidden for half a century, many feared it had been destroyed. In the mid-1970s Wolff first heard German suspicions that the collection might be located in Kyiv, but inquiries in the 1970s and 80s met only denials. The Kyiv Conservatory reported no manuscript holdings.[71]

When the matter of suspected lost Bach manuscripts in Kyiv was again raised by Wolff in the spring of 1998, in connection with what was hoped to be a definitive edition of the C.P.E. Bach legacy, their existence in Kyiv was firmly denied.[72] Suspicions were substantiated, however, by the 1996 German-language publication of the 1957 Soviet Ministry of Culture report on trophy cultural treasures cited above. That report precisely notes that the State Conservatory in Kyiv then held "5,170 items from a Berlin Music Library (Berliner Noten-Bibliothek), including works of early West European composers with first editions and manuscripts. Inventories have been prepared in the Conservatory."[73]

Officials in Kyiv initially answered that the Moscow Ministry of Culture report was probably fabricated in Germany in connection with unsuccessful restitution negotiations. In the meantime, a librarian from the Conservatory admitted, during a chance meeting with Boriak, having seen a report about a large collection of foreign music that, taking up much needed space in the small Conservatory Library, had been transferred in 1973 to the newly established Central State Archive-Museum of Literature and Art (TsDAMLM)—together with five inventory registers. Armed with that

---

29 (1995): 339–64; P. J. P. Whitehead, "The Lost Berlin Manuscripts," *Notes* 33(1) September 1976: 7–15.

[71] That report was corroborated from other sources in preparation of my directory of archival holdings in Ukraine. See Grimsted, *Archives: Ukraine*, pp. 400–401. Since one of Christoph Wolff's graduate students had contacted me regarding possible Bach manuscripts in Kyiv, I made numerous inquiries during several visits to Kyiv in the late 1970s and 1980s, but the results were all negative. The Kyiv Conservatory itself refused my request to visit, with the explanation that they had no archival materials.

[72] This was in response to inquiries by Boriak and the present author in 1998 on behalf of Christoph Wolff and the Harvard University Music Department. The Kyiv Conservatory and other Kyiv music libraries reported no trophy music holdings.

[73] Lehmann and Kolasa, ed., *Die Trophäenkommissionen*, doc. no. 46, p. 245. A large part of that document is also published in Kolasa's earlier article, "Sag mir wo die Bücher sind…," pp. 357–60.

librarian's testimony and the German-published document, and with a keen understanding of the delicate diplomatic issues involved, Boriak was able to convince authorities at the Main Archival Administration of Ukraine to pursue the matter. Archival officials became more open to the possibility that the report was genuine, when they learned that the original document—and presumably supporting documentation—was still officially classified "secret" in Moscow.[74]

Not long afterwards, confirmation came back from Kyiv that a collection of over 5,000 units of foreign manuscripts earlier held by the Conservatory was now held in TsDAMLM. They also affirmed that it possibly contained some German music, maybe even Bach scores. No one in TsDAMLM knew its provenance, or how it happened to have arrived in Kyiv. Given the long-standing association of the Harvard Ukrainian Research Institute (my home institution) with Ukrainian archives, the Main Archival Administration of Ukraine agreed to provide access for Professor Wolff and me in order to make an official appraisal of the collection.[75]

TsDAMLM is currently preparing a comprehensive guide to its holdings, including those that were previously classified. However, difficulties and hesitations to reveal the treasure continued even after our arrival in Kyiv, stemming from many factors, including the fact that the collection had never been fully "processed" for researchers.[76] The collection was being kept in optimal storage conditions—in proper acid-free archival boxes in a humidity-controlled storage area.

Since our revelation, archival authorities in Kyiv are now insisting the existence of the collection was never a secret, but nobody ever knew about its

---

[74] The German published version identifies the documents as having come from the CP Central Committee Secretariat (fond 4) in TsKhSD (now RGANI). Kyiv archival officials were refused a copy when they requested it from Moscow. I also was refused access in June/July 1999. Reportedly, the copies from which the German translations were prepared had been acquired in TsKhSD, although neither the copies themselves nor their publication had been authorized.

[75] A formal invitation was provided by the Institute of Ukrainian Archeography. The Main Archival Administration of Ukraine provided hotel and archival arrangements for Wolff, his wife Barbara (a music cataloguer at Harvard's Houghton Library), and myself. We acknowledge their kindness in so doing.

[76] This meant that, according to the Soviet-period rules still in effect, for every file we wanted to see, an archivist had to laboriously add folio numbers in pencil and prepare the necessary accompanying papers, before it could be sent to the reading room.

hiding place or what it was.[77] Certainly, the labels on the boxes—and the official listing in the register of archival fonds—would never have led anyone to its contents: "Fond 441—'Collection of Materials of Representatives of West European Literature and Art from the 17th through 19th Centuries.'" The first box randomly pulled out as a demonstration for us contained several thin bound volumes of individual music scores. The title page of the top one bore a blue library stamp with a lyre in the center, surrounded by the inscription "Sing Akademie zu Berlin." The collection contains 5,186 storage units, with five inventory registers (*opysy*). Thanks to overtime efforts by TsDAMLM archivists in processing the materials requested, during our few remaining days in Kyiv we were able to peruse a number of manuscript scores, chosen on the basis of what turned out to be the relatively thorough inventories.

Ironically, after we had viewed the materials, during a conversation with the Rector of the National Academy of Music of Ukraine (previously, the Kyiv Conservatory), we were assured that the Academy had no trophy collections, and if they had indeed had any, they were long since returned to Germany.[78] A few documents about the collection found in the Conservatory archive included the official transfer order from TsDAMLM for a "collection of manuscript and published music scores (XVII–XIXth cc.) in foreign languages with approximately 5,000 documents, together with the card catalogs and inventory registers describing the collection."[79] In the official act of transfer, however, the collection had been renamed as noted above.[80] No documents have been found relating to the arrival of the collection in

[77] See, for example, the statement at a press conference in Kyiv (10 August 1999) by Chief of the Main Archival Administration of Ukraine, Ruslan Pyrih, as quoted by Olena Nikolayenko, "Enigma of Bach's Musical Archive Solved by Harvard Professor in Kyiv," *Kyiv Post* 32 (12 August 1999). The outgoing TsDAMLM director also made such a statement when he received us in the archive.

[78] This is indicative of the continuing reluctance of many to admit to trophy collections. This assurance was given in a formal meeting with Christoph Wolff, Hennadii Boriak, and myself in Kyiv, 1 July 1999. He was obviously unaware that we had already been shown the collection in TsDAMLM.

[79] "Doruchennia" (27 July 1973), and TsDAMLM Director V. P. Koba to Conservatory Rector I. F. Liashenko (31 July 1973). Both documents were the official copies held by the Conservatory Library, copies of which were kindly furnished me by the librarian in charge.

[80] "Akt No. 2 o peredache dokumental'nykh materialov" (14 March 1973), indicating transfer from the Conservatory to TsDAMLM. By the time of its transfer, the collection was missing thirteen units.

Kyiv—only the "legend" that the collection had been found by a tank driver in a village beyond Ukrainian borders in 1945, triumphantly brought back to Kyiv, and delivered to the steps of the Conservatory (the building itself was then in ruins).[81] After their arrival, the manuscripts were stamped and complete inventories were compiled in the original language of the manuscripts. We are now relatively sure that the inventories were prepared on the basis of the original German card catalog that had come to the Conservatory in the same crates with the collection itself.[82] That card catalog still has not been found in TsDAMLM.[83]

Christoph Wolff is currently preparing a scholarly report with a musicological analysis and a preliminary description of the holdings, based on the Kyiv inventories and the manuscripts that archivists were able to prepare for us to consult. The State Committee on Archives of Ukraine, Harvard University, the Bach Archive in Leipzig, and the Packard Humanities Institute of Los Altos, California are now starting a collaborative program to make these unique materials available for research and performance. The project will be closely coordinated with the Sing-Akademie of Berlin, which still exists as a performing organization and hopes that the priceless musical sources will eventually be returned to their original home.

We still do not know about the fate of the epistolary collection from the Sing-Akademie—only one folder of Goethe letters are held with the music scores in TsDAMLM.[84] All of the early printed books from the library, many with dedicatory autographs and marginal notes, are still missing.[85] Several

---

[81]   Further efforts are under way to locate additional documentation in Kyiv. It is clear that there must also have been a truck or two involved, or maybe a whole convoy, since such a large collection would have hardly fit in one tank!

[82]   The inventories were prepared after the war by Liubov′ Favndovna Fainshtein, one of the only Jewish musicologists to have survived the anti-Semitic purges of the late 1940s and early 1950s, but who is now no longer living. Fainshtein's signature appears on the final page of each of the five bound inventory volumes, all of which are now held in TsDAMLM and are used as the *opysy* for the collection.

[83]   The official act of transfer furnished clearly includes that the card catalog had been turned over to the archive with the collection in 1973, although by then one-fifth of its cards were missing.

[84]   The Goethe letters in TsDAMLM, 441/5 are addressed to Carl Friedrich Zelter, who directed the Sing-Akademie from 1800 to 1832.

[85]   As of yet, there is no trace of them in any major Kyiv library with music holdings. There is no evidence that they were delivered to the Kyiv Conservatory after

books from the Sing-Akademie library had been returned to Berlin from Moscow in 1957, at the time of the return of the Dresden Gallery collections to East Germany. As yet, we have been unable to determine where those books were found.[86]

Today, most important for culture and scholarship, the preservation of the long-lost Berlin Sing-Akademie music archive can at last be made known to the world and openly described, studied, performed, and appreciated—within their rightful place as a major component of the common European cultural heritage. Despite the otherwise inadequate knowledge of the fate of trophy cultural treasures that came to Ukraine after the war, the identification of this collection raises new optimism about locating lost and displaced cultural treasures that have survived their wartime displacements.

---

the war, as librarians in the Academy of Music showed us the postwar accession registers for printed books. The only copy of the registers they had prepared covering the manuscripts had been transferred to the archive with the music score collection.

[86] In July 1999, Christoph Wolff was shown three books returned to Berlin in the late 1950s (now on deposit in the German State Library), but they had no Soviet book stamps that might give a clue as to what library may hold additional books from the Sing-Akademie library. All of the Moscow music libraries queried in 1999 report no trophy German music holdings.

CHAPTER 8

Soviet Archival Plunder: Nazi Records and Nazi Archival Loot between Moscow and Kyiv

Soviet Archival Plunder

Trophy Archives—Quantity and Types. Archives constituted a very small, but nonetheless very important, percentage of the overall Soviet WWII cultural plunder. Unlike art, library books, or music scores, most of the archival seizures were carried out for purposes of intelligence utilization and political control. Instructions for the seizure of archives were prepared in February 1945; early in April 1945, Deputy NKVD Commissar Sergei Kruglov recommended to Lavrentii Beria, and Beria thereupon to Viacheslav Molotov, a special mission "to search thoroughly through all German archives and libraries to effect means of preservation and bring to the Soviet Union materials, including printed editions, that have scientific-historical and operational significance for our country."[1] Many archival seizures were made by military counterintelligence agents (SMERSH). Very few archives were seized by the more general Trophy Brigade. Only in recent years has it been possible to piece together the extensive Soviet archival retrieval and plunder operations, but many potential sources are still not open.

Estimates about the quantity of archives involved are still virtually impossible to make. Various shipments were measured alternately in freight cars, crates, or tons; we don't know how tightly the freight cars were packed, and in many instances they had to be reloaded when they hit the Soviet frontier with its wider-gauged tracks. The size of crates varied tremendously; many of them included printed books and art, or, in one case, nine freight cars of steel shelving along with archival records themselves. One top secret year-end Glavarkhiv report for 1945 notes 55 wagon-loads of German and Romanian materials and 44 wagon-loads of foreign materials (predominantly French and Polish) brought to Moscow during the year, but the specific

---

[1] Kruglov to Beria (5 April 1945), GA RF, 5325/10/2025, fol. 4; a copy of the same list was addressed from Beria to Molotov (6 April 1945), fol. 5. See also the unregistered draft with a variant ending, fol. 3.

figures listed are not in accord with reports on individual shipments found elsewhere.[2] Many shipments were made by other agencies as well, even those eventually destined for state archives.

As more documentation becomes available, general patterns regarding Soviet archival plunder emerge. Soviet captured records can, for the purpose of analysis, be classified into eight principal categories (although sometimes there is overlap):

(1) records of the Nazi regime itself—with two subcategories:
    (a) central state agencies, and
    (b) local occupation authorities;

(2) records, manuscript collections, and personal papers of German Jewish, Masonic, and other private institutions and individuals seized by Nazi agencies;

(3) trophy German military and other records of predominantly historical interest;

(4) displaced official government records of other European nations, most of which had previously been seized by Nazi authorities;

(5) records, manuscript collections, and personal papers of non-German Jewish, Masonic, and other private institutions and individuals, most of which had been previously seized by Nazi authorities from occupied territories;

(6) records, manuscript collections, and personal papers from East European neighboring states and private organizations, with two subcategories:
    (a) other Axis nations, such as Romania, Hungary, and Austria, that had been allied with the Nazi regime; some records from which were considered vital because of

---

2 "Spravka o rezul'tatakh raboty GAU NKVD SSSR po vozvrashcheniiu v Sov. Soiuz dokumental'nykh materialov GAF SSSR i o vyvoze v SSSR arkhivov inostrannogo proiskhozhdeniia," signed by Golubtsov and Kuz'min (15 August 1945), GA RF, 5325/10/2148, fols. 1–4, and the accompanying top secret memorandum signed by Golubtsov, "Svedeniia o dokumental'nykh materialakh inostrannogo proiskhozhdeniia vyvezennykh v Sovetskii Soiuz v 1945 godu," fol. 5, with indication of the archives in Moscow to which they were directed. The referenced accompanying list of German materials has not been found, nor have similar reports for 1946, presumably because they are still classified within SVAG records.

their historical links with areas newly annexed to the Soviet Union, such as Galicia, Bukovyna, Transcarpathia, and parts of Moldova, and

(b) Polish records, because of their relevance to the newly annexed western Ukraine, Belarus, and Lithuania, many of which had been seized in 1939–1940;

(7) files relating to the international socialist, and especially communist, movement, many of which had been previously seized by Nazi authorities; and

(8) records, manuscript collections, and personal papers of Russian and Ukrainian émigré groups and organizations, or other files directly related to Russian or Soviet issues, some of which had also been seized by Nazi agencies.

The twin concepts of "scientific-historical" and "operational" value mentioned above became the official euphemistic passwords of archival retrieval efforts in the postwar years and were intricately involved in archival plunder in all categories. Not all of these categories require equal treatment here, because they only tangentially involve Ukraine.

Trophy Archives from Germany and Other Countries. So far as is known, none of the seizures by the Glavarkhiv NKVD special archival trophy brigades involved Ukraine, and they were all destined for Moscow. These included both German historical records, some relating directly to Russia, and files relating to the international socialist movement, seized from many different places in Germany and Eastern Europe. Representatives of the trophy brigades were understandably much more selective about archives than they were about library books. For example, a Glavarkhiv team reported at the end of October that they had "examined documentary materials in the mines of Saxony, totaling over 300 wagons from the period of the 11th to the 20th centuries," from which they chose "only seven wagons of the most topical fonds presenting interest for Soviet historical sciences and activities of operational agencies that should be brought to the USSR." In terms of "archival Rossica/Sovietica," these included the official Prussian copies of early treaties with Russia from the Prussian archives and the Ferdinand Lassalle papers, important for the Marxist correspondence they contained.[3]

---

[3] Golubtsov to I. A. Serov, "Dokladnaia zapiska o rezul'tatakh obsledovaniia dokumental'nykh materialov germanskikh arkhivov, èvakuirovannykh i ukrytykh v shakhtakh Saksonii" (Berlin, 24 October 1945), GA RF, 5325/2/1353, fol. 216; an

More extensive plunder, pure and simple—or in the Soviet view, "reparations" for Nazi devastation in Soviet lands—nevertheless served as a rationale for a number of other archival seizures among the cultural treasures assembled for shipment by the Trophy Brigade itself. For example, by November, the Commission completed its own analysis of the treasures found in the salt mines of Saxony and reported that "from 40,000 crates and other containers found in the mines," they had "selected 8,850 crates of literary and museum collections for which 85 wagons would be required" for shipment to Moscow.[4] In terms of archival materials, these included many manuscripts and early printed books from various German collections, several collections of Oriental manuscripts, drawings and engravings, negatives of art and architecture, ethnographic materials including folklore recordings, and a collection of charters and manuscript books from the Magdeburg City Archive.

The commission that seized the medieval Hanseatic archives from Bremen, Hamburg, and Lübeck from the same mines justified their action in terms of thinly masked relevance to Russian history, although in this case the trophy nature of the seizure was clearly predominant:

> The early part of the Lübeck archive deserves transport, since it reflects in great completeness the history of medieval cities belonging to the Hanseatic League and thus connected to the history of Novgorod. Similar materials in the USSR for the history of the Hansa are lacking to the extreme.[5]

---

additional signed copy is found in 5325/10/2030, fol. 35. In both cases a list of chosen fonds is attached.

[4]   G. Aleksandrov, N. Zhukov, and A. Poryvaev to TsK VKP(b) Secretary G. M. Malenkov, RGASPI, 17/125/308, fol. 41. The letter signed by G. Aleksandrov, N. Zhukov, and A. Poryvaev, accompanied a five-page list of cultural treasures the commission of Soviet experts had chosen. See also the additional cover letter to Malenkov with notice of additional copies to Molotov, Beria, and Mikoyan (13 November 1945), and Malenkov's endorsement regarding the urgency of the matter (23 November 1945).

[5]   GA RF, 5325/10/2030, fols. 14–30. The note about the Lübeck archive is found on fol. 19. Although not mentioned in that quote, medieval municipal archives were also brought from Bremen, Rostok, Magdeburg, and Halberstadt, most of which have been subsequently returned. A working copy of the Russian survey of cultural holdings in the mines is found in GA RF, A-534/2/4, fols. 234–250. Among archival materials marked with red checks for transport are, for example, 156 crates of Oriental manuscripts from the Library of the Prussian Academy of Sciences and 5 crates of manuscript books (13–15th cc.) from the Halberstadt City Archive.

The art treasures, library books, and archival materials selected for transport "would have great value for the Academy of Sciences of the USSR, central libraries, and museums," Grigorii Aleksandrov explained to Malenkov in December 1945. "[B]ringing them to the USSR might to some extent serve as compensation for the losses wrought by the German occupiers on scholarly and cultural institutions in the Soviet Union."[6] That same attitude is being expressed today by members of the Duma who refuse to permit their restitution.

Captured Nazi Records with Nazi Archival Loot

Records of Nazi Central Agencies. As noted earlier, the seizure of Nazi records was specifically authorized by the Allied Control Commission as part of the general policy of de-Nazification. A large part of the Nazi/German component within Soviet captured records came under the purview of the State Archival Administration under Beria's People's Commissariat for Internal Affairs (GAU pri NKVD) later known as Glavarkhiv. Most of those materials from high-level central Nazi agencies went directly to Moscow. Some went to specialized military or intelligence agencies. The Nazi Foreign Ministry materials went directly to the Commissariat for Foreign Affairs, although some of the materials were eventually turned over to the Special State Archive for captured records. Some materials were specifically designated for "operational" analysis. Among other aims, this involved establishing Nazi collaborators and other "enemies of the Fatherland." These materials then were worked over by investigatory units in the NKVD/MVD or those state archives themselves, which at that time were all under the NKVD.

A report dated July 1945 notes the capture of (among others) of:

(1) The Archive of the Intelligence Division of the German General Staff, in Wannsee—approximately 30 wagons of documents;

(2) The Archive of the Ministry of the Navy, in Berlin (ul. Kloster Ufer)—approximately 10 wagons of documents;

(3) Various records from the Reich Chancery in Berlin;

---

[6]   G. F. Aleksandrov to TsK VKP(b) Secretary G. M. Malenkov, RGASPI, 17/125/308, fols. 49–51 (the quote is from fol. 51).

   (4)   Various records in the building of the General Staff of the
         German Army in Berlin;
   (5)   A large military archive in Potsdam;
   (6)   The archive of the quartermaster service, taken from Berlin,
         in the city of Bad Freienwalde...[7]

Among the many other Nazi records captured by Soviet authorities, in the village of Kaput, near Potsdam, in April 1946, they found an additional collection of over 2,000 microcopies of high-level documents from the Reich Chancery, which merited a "special report" to Stalin.[8] Equally important to Beria, for example, they found some 200,000 personnel files of an SS intelligence branch, including "many who were German foreign ['fifth column'] agents abroad."[9]

   Some Nazi records went to other agencies. For example, the successful seizure of 30 sealed wagons of high-level scientific and technological files, including plans and drawings for rocket and atomic reactors from the Central Military-Technical Archive of the Wehrmacht, was reported to high CP authorities in August 1945. Those that had not already been taken by Czech authorities (the records were found in a Prague railway depot) were rushed to Moscow and transferred to specialized Soviet scientific institutes.[10] German factory records provide another example, since in some instances they were clearly seized along with the factories in which they had been produced.

---

[7]   As reported by the Deputy Chief of Staff of the First Belorussian Front, Zapevalin to Glavarkhiv chief Nikitinskii (20 July 1945), GA RF, 5325/2/1353, fol. 207. Two other collections listed were not of Nazi origin.

[8]   GA RF, 9401/2/135, fols. 272–273. The file (dated 12 April 1946) is described in *"Osobaia papka" I. V. Stalina: Iz materialov Sekretariata NKVD-MVD SSSR 1944–1953 gg.: Katalog dokumentov/The "Special File" for Stalin, From Materials of the Secretariat of the NKVD-MVD of the USSR, 1944–1953: A Catalogue of Documents*, comp. O. V. Edel´man, L. S. Kudriavtseva, E. D. Grin´ko, and M. E. Kolesova; ed. S. V. Mironenko and V. A. Kozlov (Moscow: "Blagovest," 1994), p. 165 [=Arkhiv noveishei istorii Rossii, Seriia katalogi, 1].

[9]   Nikitinskii to Beria, GA RF, 5325/2/1353, fol. 211. The draft report itself is undated by a handwritten endorsement is dated 12 October 1945. The same is repeated by Golubov to I. A. Serov (24 October 1945), GA RF, 5325/2/1353, fol. 115v. These materials were found in a suburban "dacha" near Wernigerode.

[10] L. Gaidukov to G. M. Malenkov (20 August 1945), RGASPI, 17/125/308, fol. 28. Pavel Kyneshevskii comments on this trophy technology and its utilization in the USSR, *Dobycha: Tainy germanskikh reparatsii* (Moscow: Soratnik, 1994), pp. 62–66.

Since such records seem to have been incorporated into the records of the receiving factories or research institutes, data is not available about the extent to which these were preserved, utilized, or eventually transferred to public state archives.

Some important groups of records from major Nazi agencies are best considered in conjunction with the foreign records that had been looted by that same agency. As long-suppressed Nazi records held in Russia and Ukraine are being examined, in conjunction with those long open in the West, many new facts are emerging about the pattern of Nazi looting in Eastern Europe as well as other parts of the European Continent. Understanding why and by what Nazi agencies particular groups of records were seized may also help establish their exact provenance and migratory paths, provide clues about contingent missing segments. This ultimately will help to reconstitute still lost archives and library collections.

Most of the Nazi records in Moscow and Kyiv unfortunately are not well arranged and described for this type of research, because Soviet authorities in the immediate postwar decades were interested in them principally for "operational" purposes. Soviet authorities had no interest in learning more about Nazi operations during the war *per se,* and hence had no need to record what groups of foreign records may have been found together with the records of a particular Nazi agency. Archives accessioning those records after the war had no time for the niceties of determining provenance, retaining their original order, or recording whence they came. In many cases it was safer, and more discreet, for archivists not to know or care. In some cases, manuscripts and printed books were destroyed.[11] Other record groups were left fragmentary when certain files were returned to East Germany, and microfilms were not retained. Almost all foreign records accessioned by Soviet archives were separated out in separate fonds according to their alleged institutional or individual provenance, with no attempt to preserve data about the record groups or collections from which they came. However, today, for our purposes of tracing migratory patterns and lost segments, which records were collected by which Nazi agency can be of crucial importance. A few examples pertaining directly to Ukraine illustrate the point.

---

[11] For example, the end of the year report for 1948 notes that 25,558 manuscripts and printed materials were destroyed (1 February 1949), GA RF, 5325/2/2447, fol. 188, and a summary report later in 1949 notes 7,765 files designated for destruction from 58 fonds, along with 67,000 books given away. Total destruction and transfers between 1946 and 1949 amounted to 509,600 file units, and 65,145 books—GA RF, 5325/2/3037, fols. 164v, 166, 167–169.

The Heeresarchiv and its Loot. Foreign military records were among the most voluminous trophy archives shipped to Moscow immediately after the war. No less than thirty freight cars came from the special German military archival intelligence center under the Heeresarchiv at Berlin-Wannsee. (The separate Military Archive [Heeresarchiv] had been split off from the Reichsarchiv in Potsdam in 1936.) The extent of plundered military records seized in the West in the early years of the war, and especially from France, was so great that the Heeresarchiv set up a special archival depository between Potsdam and Berlin in Berlin-Wannsee (*HA–Aktensammelstelle West*) for their captured foreign records. Documentation in large bulk was still coming into the Berlin-Wannsee depository in the fall of 1944 and early 1945.[12] The Wannsee Branch was still operating as late as 10 April 1945, a month before the Soviet seizure.[13]

Most of the Polish and western Ukrainian military records that the Nazis captured early in the war, including those that Soviet authorities found in Berlin-Wannsee, had first been shipped to a Heeresarchiv branch in Danzig-Oliva. Details about some of the evacuations from Lviv were mentioned earlier. Details of what looted records were sent to Danzig-Oliva are also recorded in the fragmentary administrative records of that branch archive now held in Moscow.[14] The Moscow files also contain a whole series of

---

[12] Heeresarchiv–Aktensammelstelle West, Berlin-Wannsee, Conradstr. 14. Report of Director von Hagen (9 December 1944), RGVA, 1256K/2/ 67, fols 18–19.

[13] Some of the fragmentary administrative records of this depository and finding aids the Germans prepared for materials gathered there are now preserved as a separate section (*opis´*) in the fond of the Chief of the Heeresarchiv (Potsdam) in Moscow, RGVA, fond 1256K, *opis´* 2. The latest outgoing letter found so far among the remaining files of this branch is datelined from Berlin-Wannsee (10 April 45), RGVA, 1256K/2/67.

[14] See for example the register of incoming predominantly Polish holdings (including a few from Lviv) in one of the storage areas, RGVA, fond 1387K/2, nos. 16 (1940–1943). Regarding the Lviv military archival seizures see above, Chap-. ter 5, p. 203n66. During the last half of 1944 the Danzig-Oliva facility was directed by Dr. Georg Strutz (1893–19??), who was later interrogated by Soviet military archival authorities after the war. In the end of March 1945, the Danzig branch archive was formally joined to the Berlin-Wannsee depository, where Major Johann Lubojacki was then serving as director—Aktensammelstelle Wannsee des Heeresarchiv (Potsdam), Berlin-Wannsee. HA (Danzig-Oliva) to HA (Potsdam) (15 September 1944), RGVA, 1387K/3/34, fols. 26–27. One file with correspondence dating from 1944 and 1945 is misplaced, since it is actually labeled as coming from the records of the HA (Potsdam) (now fond 1255), consisting of the correspondence received from the Danzig branch (all the incoming letters are original and bear receipt stamps).

detailed reports of the special Heeresarchiv archival scout sent to Poland first in 1939 and 1940, western Ukraine in July and August 1941, and then to the eastern Ukraine in the fall of that year.[15] Many military records from southeastern Poland and Galicia were sent to the additional Heeresarchiv branch in Vienna. Although we do not have the comparable incoming records from the Vienna branch, many of the outgoing shipments from Lviv are described in detail in the field reports and in the records of the Nazi Archival Administration of Galicia mentioned earlier.[16]

After the Danzig-Oliva branch was closed down in the fall of 1944, many of the captured Polish military records were transferred to Berlin-Wannsee. Some of the records collected in Danzig are believed to have perished in the intensive bombing there in late 1944 and early 1945; some were intentionally destroyed, and others were captured in that vicinity by the Red Army.[17] German administrative files from the Danzig-Oliva Branch also remain in Moscow. Since these files were transferred to TsGOA in 1953 from the MVD and MID, we do not know if they were captured with the materials from Berlin-Wannsee or were found in Poland.[18]

Available Soviet reports of the seizure of the Berlin-Wannsee facility provide no details about the foreign records recovered there. From one report we learn that the Red Army removed "200 Studebaker [truck] loads" in May

[15]   RGVA, 1256K/1/7a, 8, 28, 29, 34–37, for example.

[16]   For example, 1,600 bundles with protocols and registers from the fond of the General Military Command in Lviv, 1779–1914, were shipped to Vienna 5 February 1940, as noted in a report of Mündl, RGVA, 1256K/1/7a, fol. 57v; many other shipments followed, as apparent in other reports by von Hödl, TsDIAL, fond 755. See also Chapter 5, pp. 200–201, fns. 61 and 62.

[17]   Azarov reports to Glavarkhiv Chief Nikitinskii the seizure of 40,000 units of military materials (23 February 1945), presumably from the Danzig facility GA RF, 5325/10/1883, fol. 56. Tsaplin ("Arkhivy, voina i okkupatsiia [1941–1945 gody]" [Moscow, 1968], p. 359) quotes Sturtz as confirming the September shipment of "one wagon with Russian and Polish records" to Berlin-Wannsee and another 50 crates in January 1945—Strutz interrogation report (6 September 1947; fond 7317/17/16, fols. 246–247), but the original report itself among SVAG records was not accessible to me. See also Tsaplin, "O rozyske dokumentov, pokhishchennykh v gody voiny iz arkhivokhranilishch SSSR," *Otechestvennye arkhivy* 1997 (5): 13.

[18]   Heeresarchiv, Zweigstelle Danzig, in Danzig-Oliva (Zimmererstr. 8), had been established in 1936. Remaining records from TsGOA (now in RGVA) in 3 *opisi* are now grouped in fond 1387K. Among reports on the receipts of Polish records by the branch, *opis´* 2 includes reports on several Ukrainian nationalist organizations operating in Poland (1937–1939).

of 1945, and from another that "30 freight wagons" were required to transport the holdings to Moscow.[19] Of crucial importance today, many of the German general plans of the Wannsee repository and its holdings, and the careful inventories that the German military archivists had prepared of their archival loot came to Moscow as well, now interspersed in the former TsGOA holdings among the administrative records of the Heeresarchiv.[20] Soviet inventories in Moscow do not mention where those records were found, but many of the holdings listed in the German inventories match up with those brought back to Moscow. We do not yet know the extent of French and other European military records that were retained by Soviet military authorities, since quite possibly not all of them were turned over to Glavarkhiv. Many of the French military records recently returned to Paris have been reprocessed by French archivists. In the recently published survey, French archivists had no idea where the French records had been while they were in Nazi hands; they had not seen the detailed German inventories that are now interspersed among the records of the Heeresarchiv in Moscow.[21] These records also have not been adequately studied by Ukrainian specialists investigating the Nazi shipment of archives from occupied Ukrainian lands. This despite the fact that they provide many details concerning precisely what groups of records the Germans removed from specific repositories.

[19]   Reference was noted above (p. 283n7) of "30 wagon-loads of records from the archive of the Intelligence Command (Razvedupravleniia) of the former German General Staff in the region of Vonzie [Wannsee], southwest suburb of Berlin"—Zapevalin to Nikitinskii (20 July 1945), GA RF, 5325/2/1353, fol. 207. The same report lists the major seizure from Potsdam without any specific quantity. Tsaplin quotes Soviet seizures from the Berlin-Wansee repository, noting "200 studebakers," Tsaplin, "O rozyske dokumentov," *Otechestvennye arkhivy* 1997 (5): 13. Tsaplin did not know whether any of the military records captured from Soviet lands was included.

[20]   RGVA, 1256K/1—inventories from 1941 and 1942 covering French, Belgian, and Dutch materials are found in file nos. 68–73. Fond 1256K, *opis´* 2 includes inventories of military records from Holland, 1940–1941 (nos. 4–5) and France (nos. 6–8b, nos. 10–17). Other files contain German translation and annotations of the foreign military records held in Berlin-Wannsee. Interestingly, several of the draft (handwritten) German inventories were written on the back of French military letterhead and blanks, and in a few cases, on the back of actual French documents (e.g., 1256K/2/17).

[21]   Claire Sibille, "Les Archives du Ministère de la Guerre recupérées de Russie," *Gazette des Archives* 176 (1997): 64–77; Dominique Devaus, "Les Archives de la direction de la Sûreté rapatriées de Russie," ibid., pp. 78–86.

Loot from the Reich Security Main Office—RSHA. Another major group of Nazi-captured archival materials from many European countries that reached Moscow later in the fall of 1945 involved the relatively complete archival cache of the Seventh Office (Amt VII) for "ideological research and analysis" (*Weltanschauliche Forschung und Auswertung*) of the infamous Reich Security Main Office—RSHA (Reichssicherheitshauptamt). Similar to the Heeresarchiv (although for quite different purposes), in terms of plunder the RSHA was not interested in art. Rather it was principally interested in archives and library materials to aid its research operations on enemies of the Nazi regime. As organized by 1941, Amt VII had separate units researching Freemasonry; Jewry; the Catholic Church and other religious sects, including witchcraft; the European socialist movement, including Marxism and "the Bolshevik Menace"; and liberalism, along with other potential political opponents, in various European countries. We now know much more about Amt VII operations from an extensive British interrogation report on its last chief, Dr. Paul Dittel.[22] However, because that report gives very little information about the archival materials amassed by Amt VII, it needs to be studied in conjunction with the massive Amt VII archival trove found by Soviet, and especially Ukrainian, trophy scouts in Silesia after the war.

This represents another group of records of a major Nazi archival looting agency that were seized by Soviet authorities that now should be examined in connection with the massive RSHA loot from all over Europe.[23] Its archival loot must be understood in terms of the Amt VII research activities. Heinrich Himmler's tremendous interest in Freemasonry and plans for a Masonic Museum explains why Amt VII had collected materials from Masonic lodges all over the Continent, not only their archives and libraries, but regalia and portraits as well. Archives and liturgical materials were taken from Jewish

---

[22] "RSHA AMT VII (Ideological Research)" (British interrogation report on SS Obersturmbannführer Dr. Paul Dittel, Late Acting Leiter of Amt VII RSHA), US NA, RG 165 (OSS). Jürgen Matthäus, now a Senior Research Fellow at the United States Holocaust Museum, kindly furnished me with a copy of the Dittel interrogation that another researcher had found in the PRO; I later found a copy in US NA.

[23] I am preparing a more thorough study of RSHA Amt VII operations in Silesia and the archives they had collected. An initial report that I presented at a symposium in Amsterdam in 1996 appears as "New Clues in the Records of Archival and Library Plunder during World War II: The ERR Ratibor Center and the RSHA VII Amt in Silesia," in *Return of Looted Collections,* pp. 52–67. See also my forthcoming article "Twice Plundered or 'Twice Saved'? Russia's 'Trophy' Archives and the Loot of the Reichssicherheitshauptamt," in *Holocaust and Genocide Studies* 4(2) September 2001.

organizations, in competition with the Einsatzstab Reichsleiter Rosenberg (ERR), which had already amassed many Jewish treasures for its Institute for the Study of the Jewish Question, in Frankfurt. The RSHA had vast stores of records from European socialist groups and political parties, files for the study of communism, anarchist political parties or splinter groups, and other records of Russian and Ukrainian émigré organizations. Although by the end of the war, with their staffs seriously reduced, the various Amt VII units were not actively using most of the archival materials they had collected, most of their loot was intact.

To house the archival plunder collected at the beginning of the war, especially from France, the RSHA Amt IV established its own collection center in Berlin—*Auswertungsstelle Frankreich* (Neue Friedrichstr., 55), which principally held materials collected by the Nazi Security Service (SD) from other West European countries. An accession register for this facility for 1940–1942, held in the former TsGOA holdings in Moscow, presents a vivid picture of their varied exploits, ranging from the massive files (first recorded in 1940) from the Sûreté Générale (after 1934, Direction Générale de la Sûreté Nationale) to those of Ukrainian émigré organizations in Paris.[24] The Masonic, Jewish, and socialist archives under Amt VII were located in the cellar of an RSHA headquarters building in Berlin (Emserstr. 12).

Starting in 1943, many of the RSHA Amt VII operations, together with their extensive library and archives collected from many countries, were moved further east to Silesia and the Sudetenland (now part of Poland and the Czech Republic). One of the first major Amt VII centers was established in a spacious palace of the Schlesiersee (*Pol.* Jeziero Sławskie) near Glogau (*Pol.* Głogów), identified as the Ausweilstelle Schlesiersee already in 1943.[25] The Masonic archives were first moved in 1943 to the castle of Fürstenstein (*Pol.* Książ) near Waldenburg (*Pol.* Wałbrzych, 35 km. southwest of Breslau/ Wrocław). Later in April 1944, Amt VII moved major parts of its archival holdings to the Silesian castle of Wölfelsdorf (*Pol.* Wilkanów) of Count von

---

[24] "Tagebuch der Auswetungsstelle Frankreich" (18.8.1940—14.9.1942), RGVA, fond 500K/2/215. Ukrainian organizations are noted as having been received in 1942 (fol. 346v). More information about the materials forwarded to Berlin is found in contingent files in the same fond in Moscow.

[25] See the report by Rolf Mühler about evacuations from the Schlesiersee in January and February 1945, BAB, R 58 (RSHA)/1044. Głogów is a city on the Oder (*Pol.* Odra) River, northwest of Wrocław and southwest of Poznań. The lake Schlesiersee (*Pol.* Jeziero Sławskie), with the town (and palace) by the same name on its shore, is about 30 km. to the north.

Althann, near Habelschwerdt (*Pol.* Bystrzyca-Kłodzka) in May 1944.[26] The Masonic archives were also moved there from the castle of Fürstenstein. The press archive, parts of the Masonic library, and other operations remained in Schlesiersee, directed by Dittel and later by SS Sturmbannführer Rolf Mühler under the code name Brabant I. The Wölfelsdorf archive center was headed by SS Sturmbaunführer Walter Braune, under the code name Brabant II.[27]

In the summer of 1945, a Ukrainian Party historian, Ivan D. Shevchenko, had been sent to Germany, Silesia, and Czechoslovakia to assist in the recovery of collections that had been looted from Kyiv, and he was also on the lookout for prospective "trophies" for Ukraine. In the case of the Wölfelsdorf cache, Nazi inventories of the archival materials held by Amt VII have not been found, but Shevchenko's telegrams and subsequent consolidated report, found recently in the former Communist Party Archive (now TsDAHO) in Kyiv, provide the most extensive Soviet list to date of the materials discovered there in 1945.[28] These add considerable detail to data from other Soviet reports that surfaced earlier in Moscow.

Groups of records include those gathered for research and analysis by Nazi secret police and racist propaganda units—ranging from Cabinet files of Léon Blum to records of the Rothschild banks and Jewish rescue organizations from almost all European countries, to records of various families of European royalty, and even Dutch feminist organizations.[29] Meriting a coded

---

[26]   See notes about the transfer (13 May 1944), with correspondence and shipping details, in RGVA, fond 500K/1/304, fols. 1–2. The rental contract for the castle (dated 14 April 1944) is found in RGVA, 500K/1/304, fol. 3–3v. The castle itself is now in ruins.

[27]   A staff and operation list for the RSHA (15 December 1944) covers both these facilities. BAB, R 58/849, fol. 19(18). Another Division (Amt V) was then located in Mecklenburg (Fürstenberg), and there were at least seven other main operation centers including Potsdam. Wilhelm Lenz at the Bundesarchiv kindly made me aware of this document.

[28]   TsDAHO, 1/23/1484. Shevchenko's 8-page composite report is entitled "Spravka iz soobshchenii instruktora otdela propagandy i agitatsii TsK KP(b)U tov. Shevchenko, I. D., komandirovannogo v Germaniiu dlia vozvrashcheniia materialov i dokumentov" (fols. 2–9). His fragmentary incoming original telegrams follow. At that point Shevchenko was attached to the NKO to the 2nd Trophy Brigade of the 3rd Battalion of the 2nd Front. I am very grateful to Dr. Ruslan Pyrih, now Chief of the State Committee on Archives of Ukraine, for acquainting me with the existence of the Shevchenko file in TsDAHO.

[29]   Many of the foreign holdings at Wölfelsdorf are also listed in the initial reconnaissance and shipping reports found in GA RF, 5325/10/2027—see especially

telegram to Kyiv, Shevchenko found a "top secret file of the Special Division of the NKVD UkrSSR on the 15th and 169th Riflery Divisions (1938–1940)" and "some 1941 Gestapo documents on conspiracies in Kherson."[30] Of special interest was "the large library with interesting correspondence and masses of unpublished documents belonging to Pavel Miliukov," which was probably seized by the Nazis from Paris. "Among the documents were some that showed his relations with reactionary Ukrainian émigrés."[31]

The largest single collection of Masonic materials ever assembled in one place, "which will require 20 freight cars," came from lodges and other Masonic organizations located all over the Continent. The materials dated from the eighteenth century through 1940. Occupying two floors of the nearby building of a former brewery, they included regalia, portraits, and vast library collections, as well as archives from different lodges.[32] As later arranged in the Special Archive in Moscow, the Masonic collections totaled over half a million files. Some lodges were represented by only a few files, others, such as the Grand Lodge of Germany in Berlin by over 10,000 files. Some additional German Masonic materials were found by Soviet authorities in the basement of one of the buildings used earlier by the RSHA in Berlin, which had been an important lodge before the Nazis closed it down (Emerstrasse 12–13).[33] The Masonic materials were a low priority for the Soviet security services controlling the archives, and many of them were never divided up into fonds according to their lodge of origin. Many of the German

---

the list (21 September 1945), fol. 7–7v. But none of the lists in that folder are as complete as the one by Shevchenko found in Kyiv.

[30] Shevchenko to Litvin (TsK KP(b)U)–deciphered (8 August 1945), TsDAHO, 1/23/1484, fol. 10.

[31] Shevchenko, "Spravka," TsDAHO, 1/23/1484, fol. 6.

[32] The Masonic collections were first found in Wölfelsdorf and reported to the Institute of History in Moscow by G. Ginler, who hoped they "would be brought back to the Soviet Union as the property of the Academy of Sciences." G. Ginler to Institut istorii AN SSSR (6 August 1945), GA RF, 5325/10/2027, fol. 6–6v; L. M. Ivanov (Scientific Secretary of the Institute of History) to Nikitinskii (20 September 1945), fol. 7. Shevchenko reported that a detailed inventory had been prepared, but I have not found it.

[33] Retrieval of the Berlin materials (47 crates) is mentioned in the composite report of the Soviet Trophy Brigade, "Otchet o rabote…s 6 maia po 31 dek. 1946 g.," signed by A. D. Manevskii (31 March 1946), published in a German translation in *Die Trophäenkommissionen*, p. 105; the original is found in GA RF, A534/2/10, fols. 1–69.

Masonic materials were returned to East Germany during the Soviet period. Those returned to the GDR have, since reunification, now been brought together, arranged, and described in the Privy State Archive of Prussian Culture Property (Geheimes Staatsarchiv Preußischer Kulturbesitz) in Berlin-Dahlem.[34]

Of particular interest to Soviet trophy archive hunters, materials from socialist sources included records of the Second International and papers of various European socialist leaders, some of which had been plundered from the International Institute of Social History in Amsterdam and its Paris branch as well as from various labor institutions in Belgian, including papers of Friederich Adler and the Museum of Social and Labor History in Brussels. Among the papers of socialist leaders were those of Viktor Chernov, Pavel Aksel'rod, Karl Kautsky, Rosa Luxemburg, and Georgii Plekhanov, along with Russian and Georgian Menshevik materials, including papers of L. Martov (Iulii Tsederbaum), Fedor Dan, and Iraklii Tsereteli. There were 4 crates of the personal archive of the German Social-Democrat and former Foreign Minister, Walter Rathenau. A special prize for the Soviet scouts were "40 copies of letters of Lenin."[35]

A few Ukrainian collections came from the east, including "20 large sacks in good condition" from the Kirovohrad Oblast Communist Party Archive, "books and exhibits from the Museum of Revolution in Kyiv," and "Ukrainian émigré editions, along with files of political and social organizations from Transcarpathia."[36] By 12 August, Shevchenko had already

---

[34]   Most of those returned to the GDR now form part of a special collection in the Geheimes Staatsarchiv in Berlin-Dahlem; a two-volume finding aid has been prepared: Renate Endler and Elisabeth Schwarze, *Die Freimauererbestände im Geheimen Staatsarchiv Preußischer Kulturbesitz*, vol. 1: *Grosslogen und Protektor, Freimauerischen Stiftungen und Vereinigungen;* vol. 2: *Tochterlogen* (Frankfurt-am-Main: Peter Lang, 1994–1996) [=Schriften reihe der Internationalen Forschungsstelle "Demokratische Bewegungen in Mitteleuropa 1770–1850," 13, 18]. In addition to the materials returned from Moscow, the finding aid covers some files that remained in Poland after the war (AGAD) and were also returned to the GDR. See the brief report about the restitution of the Masonic collections by Ulrich Wolfgang, "The Material Losses of the German Freemasons," *Spoils of War: International Newsletter* 3 (1996): 18–21. He incorrectly assumes that most of the Masonic archives now in Moscow had been found by the Soviets in Berlin, since he was not aware of the RSHA Amt VII operations in Silesia, where Soviet authorities found most of the Masonic materials.

[35]   See the list of holdings dated 21 September 1945, GA RF, 5325/10/2027, fol. 7–7v, and a later variant list addressed to Beria (20 October 1945), fol. 22. Most of these are covered in more detail by Shevchenko's telegrams.

[36]   TsDAHO, 1/23/1484, fol. 15, fols. 16–17.

"packed and loaded 5 wagons with valuables," and he was "searching through the remains for materials for Kyiv, especially books for TsNB." Along with the archives, he reported finding many library holdings from Ukraine, looted by the Nazis from libraries in Kyiv, Kharkiv, and other cities. Later he was preparing to load 15 wagons. In one telegram to his Kyiv superiors, he regretted that he "didn't have an airplane available so he could send some samples home to Comrade Khrushchev," who was then the CP First Secretary in Kyiv.[37] In another message he expressed his frustration at having to await the arrival of specialists from Moscow before getting more shipments under way, as he was busily preparing things to be sent so they would "not have to leave anything for the Poles."[38]

When Beria was informed of the Wölfelsdorf materials by the head of the Ukrainian Archival Administration in September 1945, he personally ordered a group of NKVD archival workers to the spot to organize their transport to Moscow.[39] The Nazi RSHA archival and library loot was seized in its entirety—no less than 28 railroad freight cars reached Moscow. By the time the NKVD archival party arrived from Moscow, they reported that 7 freight cars had already been dispatched to Kyiv under Shevchenko's escort, but Beria ordered their immediate apprehension and redirection to Moscow.[40] The materials sent to Kyiv—1,295 crates and 26 containers with paintings—included printed books in French, German, and Russian, as well as manuscript materials; they arrived in Moscow in October 1945 in 13 railway cars. Another 15 wagons were sent directly to Moscow in November.[41]

One might assume that the materials looted from Ukraine by the Nazis and subsequently retrieved by the Soviets would have been offloaded in

---

[37] TsDAHO, 1/23/1484, fols. 51–52, fols. 100–101, and fol. 56. The incoming original telegrams from Shevchenko are not bound in chronological order. At another point, Shevchenko notes 8 wagons prepared, but I have been unable to determine exactly how many he actually sent to Kyiv.

[38] TsDAHO, 1/23/1484, fol. 14.

[39] Beria to Selivanovskii (11 September 1945), GA RF, 5325/10/2027, fol. 3; Beria to Riasov (11 September 1945), fol. 4.

[40] Kobulov to Beria (27 September 1945), GA RF, 5325/10/2027, fols. 9–10 (second copy fols. 11–12). Beria added his usual red pencil note to Kobulov on the first copy ordering the dispatch of a delegation to bring the materials to Moscow and to locate the wagons sent to Kyiv. See also the order from Kobulov to Selivanovskii (29 September 1945), fol. 13.

[41] Telegrams and further correspondence regarding the materials sent to Kyiv follow in the same folder—GA RF, 5325/10/2027, fols. 14–20.

Kyiv. This indeed seems to have been the case with those items that Shevchenko brought back from the Museum of Revolution and other Kyiv libraries (although at least part of the archives from the Museum of Revolution was later found in Vienna).[42] However, Shevchenko had also kept some Nazi files from their Historical Commission and other socialist related documents, including a couple of trophy letters of Marx, which had remained with the CPU Central Committee in Kyiv.[43] The records from the Kirovohrad CP Archive, which Shevchenko had retrieved in Wölfelsdorf, went to Moscow and then were officially transferred back to Kyiv in June 1946.[44] According to the official act of transfer, the 19 crates contained files from Party and Komsomol committees from 6 different raions of Kirovohrad Oblast, which were among "the 13 wagons received via Kyiv from the village of Vel'fol'dorf [*sic*] near the city of Gratz and from the castle of counts Al'toneu near Gavel'shberga (Germaniia) [*sic*]."[45] The socialist manuscripts that were "inadvertently" sidetracked in Kyiv were subsequently requisitioned by Moscow, but by the end of October 1945, Shevchenko had prepared a detailed inventory. They were subsequently all forwarded to Moscow.[46]

The collected documentation found in Wölfelsdorf that was brought to Moscow included fragmentary records of the RSHA Amt VII itself. This also

---

[42] No information has been found about exactly what materials were offloaded in Kyiv. A report about the archival materials from the Museum of Revolution found in Vienna is held in RGASPI, 17/125/579.

[43] See the exchange of correspondence between Nikitinskii in Moscow and Gudzenko in Kyiv regarding possible materials remaining in Kyiv from Shevchenko's 1945 shipment. Nikitinskii to Gudzenko (24 July 1946), and Gudzenko to Nikitinskii (1 August 1946), TsDAVO, 14/7/54, fols. 14–15.

[44] The report of the Special Archive (Osobyi Arkhiv—TsGOA SSSR) for 1946 dates the transfer to Kyiv as 25 June 1946, with reference to a letter from Kruglov to Khrushchev (30 May 1946), GA RF 5315/2/1640, fol. 82.

[45] Copies of the official acts of transfer to Kyiv from Moscow and from Kyiv to Kirovohrad are retained in TsDAHO, 39/3/507. During the war the Silesian area was in fact part of Germany. The Kirovohrad materials that were recovered included some Party files from one raion that was then part of Odesa Oblast.

[46] "Opis' rukopisei, kopii statei i drugikh materialov." The top secret list, including a more detailed survey of some files, was subsequently forwarded with a covering note to Beria by Riasnoi, People's Commissar of Internal Affairs UkrSSR (24 October 1945), TsDAVO, 14/7/54, fols. 2–13, and Gudzenko to Nikitskii (24 July 1946), fol. 15.

is of tremendous importance for the fate of looted collections. Although most of the RSHA files predate their move to Wölfelsdorf (many dating from the 1930s), they provide unique insights into RSHA operations and deserve more extensive analysis in the context of a full listing of the RSHA loot. Some of the RSHA documentary loot is mentioned precisely in these fragmentary operational files that remain in Moscow. As housed in RGVA (as part of former TsGOA records), the fond is not well arranged for research use, and the Russian-language inventories are inadequate, although nonetheless essential for researchers.[47] Data from the RSHA files held in Moscow obviously still need to be coordinated with those gleaned from the even larger group of RSHA records that were returned to Germany by American authorities, but those records only tangentially covered Amt VII operations.[48] Given the new Russian law nationalizing the "spoils of war," however, the prompt return of the RSHA files to Germany has become less likely.

Recently, another major group of RSHA Amt VII records surfaced in Warsaw. These were captured by Polish authorities, presumably from Schliesersee in Silesia, and were long held in secret by Polish security services. The United States Holocaust Museum in Washington, DC, acquired microfilms of the Warsaw RSHA records. As arranged in Warsaw, some of the foreign archival loot collected by various sectors of Amt VII were intermingled with the records themselves, including Masonic materials and files from West European socialist sources. The fact that the RSHA files themselves have not yet been separated out from the original documents collected by the RSHA makes this set of records important for further analysis of the types of activities with which Amt VII was involved. Those Warsaw RSHA records were restituted to Germany in 1997; they have been processed and are now held in the Bundesarchiv in its Berlin-Lichterfelde

---

[47] See also the brief German research report by Wolfgang Form and Pavel Poljan, "Das Zentrum für die Aufbewahrung historisch-dokumentarischer Sammlungen in Moskau—ein Erfahrungsbericht," *Informationen aus der Forschung* [Bundesinstitut für ostwissenschaftliche und internationale Studien] 7 (20 October 1992): 1–8. This important group of RSHA records deserve professional reprocessing and a microform edition in its entirety that could be available to interested researchers in different countries, particularly since archival materials looted from so many countries are mentioned in its files.

[48] A detailed published finding aid was prepared by the Bundesarchiv after these records were returned to Germany: *Reichssicherheitshauptamt: Bestand R 58*, comp. Heinz Boberach (Koblenz: Bundesarchiv, 1992) [=Findbücher zu Beständen des Bundesarchiv, 22]. More recently, these records have been transferred to the Bundesarchiv in Berlin-Lichterfelde (BAB).

facility.[49] Some additional RSHA records that were found in Poland were transferred to East Germany earlier and interfiled with other Stasi records relating to RSHA activities. At least one group of these records relate to Amt VII church-related research, and again, some of the original looted documentation is intermingled in the files. They are still being processed with a finding aid for researchers, and hence still await exploration in Berlin.[50]

Looted French Intelligence Records. Much more important for Beria, however, was the major Nazi archival cache of the French army military intelligence agency (Deuxième Bureau) and police and intelligence records from the Sûreté Générale which were found in May 1945 in a manor house in the village of Horní Libchava (*Ger.* Oberliebich) a few miles northwest of Česká-Lípa in Czechoslovakia (*Ger.* Böhmisch-Leipa, part of the Sudetenland under the Reich) by a SMERSH unit of the First Ukrainian Front.[51] The top secret unit operating with the French records there has now been identified with the RSHA Fourth Office (Amt IV–Gestapo). They managed to destroy their own operational files when they fled the village and, so far as is known, none of the Nazi personnel were captured for interrogation. Soviet reports on the seizure operation that have surfaced do not provide further information about the Nazi agency involved, and, apparently, no Nazi files

---

[49]   An English-language summary inventory, prepared by the Holocaust Museum is available on the Musuem website (<http://www.ushmm.org>); a Polish-language version is available on the first reel of microfilm at the Holocaust Museum; a German translation is available in BAB. Microfilms remain in Warsaw, in addition to the copies in the Holocaust Museum. An introduction to an initial publication of a few documents from this record group, edited by Jürgen Matthäus, provides some historical background on Amt VII operations— "'Weltanschauliche Forschung und Auswertung': Aus den Akten des Amtes VII im Reichssicherheitshauptamt," *Jahrbuch für Antisemitismus-Forschung* 5 [ed. Wolfgang Benz; Berlin] 1997: 287–96. Further exploration of other RSHA originals in Berlin is needed before the study of the RSHA Amt VII operations can be complete.

[50]   Jürgen Matthäus, now with the U.S. Holocaust Museum in Washington, DC, kindly informed me about these materials, with which he had become briefly acquainted during a recent trip to Berlin.

[51]   See the relevant communications dated May 1945 (fols. 7–11, 13) and 6 June 1945 (fol. 14), GA RF, 5325/10/2029. The latter to GAU director Major General Nikitinskii. When the present author and Ukrainian colleagues visited the site in August 1991, we found evidence of an abandoned air strip close to the manor house, which may indicate that a Nazi military intelligence unit have also been involved.

were found with the French records. Under personal orders from Beria, a special Soviet archival team was flown to Dresden and made their way to the abandoned Nazi hideout. They prepared for transport the approximately six-and-a-half kilometers of captured French intelligence and Paris police records, some going back to the late nineteenth century, together with extensive French card files with approximately two and a half million entries that the Nazis had left behind in the two-story building and attached shed.

The French records themselves had been captured at several different times from several different sources by Nazi agents, starting after the invasion of France in 1940.[52] The French archivists who processed the records after their return to France in 1994 did not know anything about their fate in Nazi hands, but we now know from other Nazi records in Moscow that at least some of the Sûreté Générale records had been initially logged in by the RSHA to their special Berlin repository and processed by that agency.[53] Records of the Deuxième Bureau were initially brought to the Berlin-Wannsee branch of the Heeresarchiv, but more thorough research in both those groups of records will be needed to determine their migration and if any parts were lost or destroyed along the way.[54] We still do not know if all of the French police and intelligence files that were captured by Soviet authorities were seized in the village near Česká-Lípa, but Soviet reports mention the records of the three different French agencies as being found there, and no reports have surfaced of additional French intelligence and police records found elsewhere.

We do know that 28 freight cars and one first-class wagon were dispatched from Česká-Lípa, and on 8 August 1945, the shipment arrived in Moscow under tight security.[55] A general description of the materials was prepared soon after their arrival in Moscow, and they were given high

---

[52] For the French analysis of where the records were before their capture, see the Sibille, "Les Archives du ministère," and Devaus, "Les Archives de la direction," which were prepared after most of the records were returned to France in 1994.

[53] See 'Tagebuch der Auswertungsstelle Frankreich, RGVA, 500K/2/215, fols. 1v, 7–9, 592, 676, 650, and 612. See also the RSHA references and reports on these materials in 500K/2, files 213 and 227. Additional research is still needed in the Moscow RSHA files on this subject.

[54] See, for example, the German inventories in RGVA, 1256K/2/15, and the later materials received as late as December 1944, as mentioned in 1256K/2/67, fols. 18–19.

[55] Reports on the shipment and its arrival in Moscow are found in GA RF, 5325/10/2029.

priority in processing even before they were moved to the Special Archive.[56] By the end of 1946 Soviet specialists had prepared a historical report on the Deuxième Bureau records and reported finding a registration book covering 2,060 units from 1914 to 1942. They were particularly pleased to find lists of French agents in various countries.[57]

Unfortunately, in Moscow, there is evidence that the collections were not all kept together. International archival principles, as we have seen, emphasize the obligation to preserve the "integrity of records (fonds)," which is often in direct conflict with intelligence needs. As apparently happened to many of the captured records, some of the French police and intelligence files were ruthlessly split from their original archival context. Many files and card files regarding the high-level Soviet leadership, including those on Stalin, Molotov, Kalinin, and Kaganovich, were removed for analysis by other agencies and there is no record of their present archival location.[58] Some documents reflecting French infiltration of Soviet diplomatic missions were given to MID. Reportedly, some French security files on the Hungarian communist leadership were even given to Hungary.[59] Quite probably the French intelligence file on Leon Trotsky that has been advertised in promotional literature for the Chadwyck-Healey microfilms of the Trotsky papers from the former Party Archive in Moscow came from the same source.[60]

[56]   As eventually processed in TsGOA SSSR (now part of RGVA), the Sûreté Générale records constituted fond no. 1, with an additional 3,554 files boxes of 2,427,370 cards; the Deuxième Bureau records were assigned to fond 7, with an additional 1,025 file boxes with 490,242 cards; and the Prefecture of the Paris Police was assigned fond no. 95, with 4 boxes of 3,837 cards. Most have been restituted to France.

[57]   See the 1946 report (25 January 1947), GA RF, 5325/2/1946, fols. 4–5, also fols. 25–27v, fols. 41–68 passim.

[58]   The existence of these files was noted in one of the early Soviet reports (21 August 1945), GA RF, 5325/10/2029, fols. 20–23.

[59]   Vitalii Iu. Afiani, "Dokumenty o zarubezhnoi arkhivnoi Rossike i peremeshchennykh arkhivakh v fondakh Tsentra khraneniia sovremennoi dokumentatsii," in *Problemy zarubezhnoi arkhivnoi Rossiki*, p. 96. Precise documentation regarding the transfer is not furnished.

[60]   The Trotsky papers microfilmed by Chadwyck-Healey came only from the former Central Party Archive, now RSASPI (*earlier* RTsKhIDNI) (fond 325), and, as indicated in RTsKhIDNI reference literature, some of the Trotsky papers in fond 325 came earlier from security service sources. We know from other sources, including the Volkogonov biography of Trotsky, that Soviet foreign intelligence agents had

At least one report was sent to Kyiv, namely a survey of the documentary materials of the Ukrainian People's Union in France, which had been found among the records of the French security agency. The GAU officer involved thought that it would be useful for operational work in Kyiv "to establish a report on the Prosvita Society."[61] As was Soviet archival practice at that time, files from various outside sources that had been acquired with the French records were filtered out. A group of files of the Union itself found among the French police records was established as a separate fond in TsGOA, where it remains today; in 1946 archivists were preparing a card file on the personal documents found in those files. They also reported finding "some documents of Hetman Skoropads'kyi."[62]

The "Special Archive," Dispersal, and Soviet Restitution

The "Special Archive." For Beria and other Glavarkhiv NKVD authorities, the French intelligence materials were the prize and the impetus for the foundation of the top secret Special Archive. As soon as they arrived in Moscow in August 1945, Glavarkhiv chief Nikitinskii reviewed their contents in a memorandum to Beria, and recommended:

> ...the formation of a special central state archive of foreign fonds, in which would be concentrated the above-mentioned materials from the French archives, as well as earlier received Romanian Siguranțe, former Polish military and political agencies, and various German occupation agencies [which he deemed of] great state interest for [the security agencies]...NKVD, NKGB, NKO, and NKID.[63]

---

succeeded in "retrieving" Trotsky papers from Paris and other sources in addition to those they may have received from the former TsGOA SSSR.

[61] Captain GAU NKVD SSSR Gur'ianov to Lieutenant Iaroshenko, Chief of the Division of Use AU NKVD UkrSSR (17 November 1945), GA RF, 5325/2/1423, fol. 93.

[62] The fond of the Ukrainian National Union in France (now RGVA, fond 65K, with 26 files) contains scattered documents from several Ukrainian émigré groups in Paris, dating from 1933–1939. Reference to the card file is in a report on operational archivities for 1946, GA RF, 5325/2/1640, fol. 97; see also fol. 78; reference to the Skoropads'kyi materials occurs on fol. 96.

[63] Nikitinskii to Beria, "Dokladnaia zapiska" (21 August 1945), GA RF, 5325/10/2029, fols. 20–23.

In support of the plan, the head of the GAU NKVD Acquisition Department, Captain Golubtsov, prepared a top secret report listing the received "documentary materials of foreign agencies in state archives of the USSR," totaling some "half a million files and card files with approximately a million and a half cards," including "documentary records of agencies in Germany, Italy, Romania, France, Poland, Japan, and Hungary." He explained that "the largest part of the materials dates from the second quarter of the twentieth century, but there are also materials from the sixteenth through the nineteenth centuries," and he listed the major groups of records from each country named above.[64]

Soviet leaders and archival specialists were not, however, of one opinion in regard to such a separate "special" archive and the extent to which it might serve scholarly as well as operational aims. The mentality and rationale of leading Glavarkhiv authorities, revealed in the minutes of a top secret meeting of archival leaders in August 1945, nevertheless showed Soviet awareness of international archival norms and continuing issues of archival restitution. For example, the historian-archivist Professor Vladimir V. Maksakov, who then directed the Central State Historical Archive in Moscow (TsGIAM), explained:

> Fonds such as those brought from Czechoslovakia...we only have a right to them until the international matters are regulated. [In any case the archive] would probably exist for only three, four, or maybe at most five years.[65]

NKVD Captain A. A. Iur'ev at the above-mentioned meeting, in contrast, best expressed what proved to be the ultimate government policy in regard to the Special Archive for foreign captured records:

> Use [of that archive], in my opinion, should have an exclusively specific, limited character, namely utilization only with the meaning of *operational aims* of the NKVD, VD, MO [Defense], and ID [Foreign Affairs]. No scholarly research whatsoever can be carried out on the basis of that archive, and to be sure, no access whatsoever can be permitted to that archive for representatives of any scholarly institutions. No, only uniquely operational use...There is no need for compiling full inventories (*opisi*), nor is

---

64   Golubtsov, "Spravka o dokumental'nykh materialakh inostrannykh uchrezhdenii, khraniashchikhsia v Tsentral'nykh gosudarstvennykh arkhivakh SSSR" (21 August 1945), GA RF, 5325/2/3623, fols. 9–11.

65   "Protokol soveshchaniia pri zam. nachal'nike Glavnogo arkhivnogo upravleniia NKVD SSSR—Izuchenie voprosa o sozdanii Osobogo Tsentral'nogo gosudarstve-nnogo arkhiva" (21 August 1945), GA RF, 5325/2/3623, fols. 2–3, 8.

there need for arranging the files [according to archival principles]. The only immediate need is to use the documents there for operational aims.

Captain Iur'ev was then directing the special operational research section in the Central State Historical Archive in Moscow (TsGIAM), where the French intelligence records were first deposited.[66]

The top secret Central State Special Archive—TsGOA (Tsentral'nyi gosudarstvennyi osobyi arkhiv) was formally established in March 1946, by which time a September 1945 draft of a founding decree to be signed by Stalin himself, and a subsequent one to be signed by Beria, were replaced by a more modest SNK decree dated 9 March 1946.[67] There were separate national divisions for French, German, and Polish materials. Initially a Romanian division was also planned, since the archive had received many police files from Northern Bukovyna, Bessarabia, and Transdnistria, including some from the wartime period (1941–1944). However, most of the extensive captured Romanian records were transferred to the Moldavian SSR in Chişinău (Kishinev), and others to the Ministry of Foreign Affairs. Many of them were later restituted to Romania.[68] A few groups of the records still remain in RGVA, and others remain in oblast archives in Odesa and Chernivtsi.

Captured Polish records were significant enough in Moscow's eyes to

---

[66] By mid-September, Iur'ev was already actively fulfilling his recommendation with reports to the Soviet high command documenting contacts of Laval and other high French government leaders with the Gestapo, in anticipation of their potential importance in French collaboration trials. See, for example, Maksakov to Nikitinskii (18 September 1945), GA RF, 5325/2/1788, fol. 5; A. A. Iur'ev report (17 September 1945), fol. 6; Nikitinskii to Beria (18 September 1945), fol. 7.

[67] The unsigned drafts are found in GA RF, 5325/2/3623. The implementing *prikaz* (22 March 1946) was signed by Internal Affairs Minister Major-General Sergei Kruglov (copy furnished by TsKhIDK).

[68] Reference to the receipt of 161 crates of Siguranţe files from these areas from the Control Commission for Romania, GA RF, 5325/2/1640, fols. 73–74; reference to their transfer to Moldova appears on fols. 81–82. Many other shipments from Romania are noted in GA RF, 5325/2/992–94, 1352, and 1704, among others. A full investigation about the extent and fate of trophy archives from Romania is needed. Although some of the 1945 records of Soviet trophy archival operations in Romania are available, many of the later files are still closed. Related files on both the retrieval of Romanian-looted archives and the Soviet plunder of Romanian archives are available in Kyiv in TsDAVO (see, for example, 14/7/54–57, and 90, among others). Regarding Romanian records in Moscow, see Gheorghe Buzatu, *Românii în Arhivele Kremlinului* (Bucharest: Univers enciclopedic, 1996).

form one of the three separate national divisions (together with French and German) in the Special Archive, reflecting the high political and operational priorities in dealing with the "Polish question" at the end of the war and early postwar years. Many of the Polish materials had been collected by the NKVD in 1939 and 1940 after the annexation from Poland of what are now the western oblasts of Belarus and Ukraine. Even before the establishment of the Special Archive, their operational use by Soviet security agencies had begun in Moscow. As TsGAOR SSSR director Prokopenko emphasized in a March 1944 report, these fonds included:

> Card files from police administrations in Warsaw and other Polish areas (compiled 1932–1939), with lists of Germans active in Poland (400), Russian White émigrés (400), Ukrainian nationalists (500), those with communist leanings (1,000), and those involved with Jewish-Zionist organizations (1,000). [Other files] compiled in the 1920 to 1939 period involved 600,000 names.[69]

Also of potential special Ukrainian interest among the Polish materials in the former TsGOA are a few files from the records of the Ukrainian Scientific Institute in Warsaw, which were previously thought to have been lost during the war.[70]

One of the few exceptions in terms of major government records of foreign states that went to Ukraine after the war was another important group of central Polish ministerial records that had been evacuated at the beginning of the war to Volhynia and was seized there by the Nazis and taken to Lviv.[71] Apparently taken to the Nazi archival center in Troppau (*Czech* Opava) in Czechoslovakia (at that time part of the Reich), then captured by Soviet authorities and taken back to Ukraine, they were first deposited in the Special Secret Division of the Central State Historical Archive of the UkrSSR in Kyiv. Apparently deemed of lesser operational interest, they were subse-

---

[69] Prokopenko to Starov, director, Glavarkhiv Division of "Utilization" (29 March 1944), GA RF, 5325/2/1045, fols. 1–8. The TsGAOR director recommended translation of the files into Russian, so they would be more immediately accessible to Russian agencies. More details about the work being carried out on the Polish materials are found in subsequent TsGOA reports and work plans, for example the plan for 1947, GA RF, 5325/2/2060, fols. 21, 86–87, 174–175.

[70] These files now comprise a separate fond among the holdings in RGVA, fond 431K, but only 7 units remain.

[71] See the Nazi report on high-level Polish governmental records that had been brought to Lviv and were being held there in 1942—signed by Buttkin (11 September 1942), TsDIAL, 755/1/265.

quently transferred to Lviv and long held in secret in the Central State Historical Archive there. Some of them were reportedly returned to Poland in 1959.[72]

Accessions to TsGOA continued during 1946 from the Secretariat of the MVD and, later, from different divisions of the MGB (Ministry of State Security).[73] However, in March 1947, the director was forced to protest when he heard that the Foreign Ministry intended to transfer records of the Nazi Ministry of Justice and two other fonds:

> [The archive (TsGOA)] could accept no significant new acces-
> sions due to the utter lack of storage space...46 crates from Ha-
> belschwerdt are piled up on the floor in disarray, along with 100
> crates from Danzig and 25,000 files from Liechtenstein..., the in-
> appropriateness of which was noted in a fire inspector's report
> from 23/25 December 1946.[74]

The archive moved into its present building in 1951. Vast quantities of these captured archives had been considered of the "utmost value to the Academy of Sciences" when Soviet authorities justified their seizure. Ironically, these same materials—even those of purely "historical signifi-cance" to the Soviet government—remained tightly closed to researchers.

As Captain Iur'ev had recommended, inventories were prepared in the Special Archive, but they were minimal and often highly inaccurate. Files were often inappropriately grouped together out of their normal order of creation.[75] Massive card files and operational reports were prepared for

---

[72]   See, for example, the list of high-level Polish governmental records that had been brought back to Kyiv after the war (later transferred to Lviv), "Spisok fondov osobogo otdela [TsDIA-K]," (1946), TsDAVO, 4703/2/6, fol. 34; (1948), fol. 82.

[73]   See Musatov, "Doklad o rabote TsGOA SSSR za 1946 god," GA RF, 532/2/1640, fol. 92.

[74]   Musatov to Nikitinskii (8 March 1947), GA RF, 5325/2/1946, fol. 24–24v. Golubtsov to Kuz'min (31 January 1947), fols. 12–13; he quotes the concluding sentence from his earlier report, "Ob"iasnitel'naia zapiska" (11 December 1946), fol. 29. Nikitinskii was obliged to explain to the Foreign Ministry (2 April 1947), fol. 28, that they could receive the materials only as soon as they got more space.

[75]   There were complaints about the quality of *opisi* in Glavarkhiv reports from the early years of the archive, and my experience in working there confirms the statement. In 1993, when a foreign publisher was interested in preparing complete microfiche editions of all of the *opisi* in the archive, the staff and current director turned the project down, due to the poor quality of the *opisi*, which they naturally felt would adversely reflect on the professional staff. I was engaged as a consultant and had to agree with their decision. In addition, poor-quality Russian *opisi* of German or

intelligence and counterintelligence purposes. As noted in a 1990 *Izvestiia* series that provided the first public knowledge about the existence of such an archive, many of the captured records:

> ...came under the agency which was least of all pursuing truth, history, or scientific interests—and most of all—was seeking internal enemies...That archive worked exclusively for catching "traitors to the Motherland."[76]

Police and gendarme records among the official government records from France, Belgium, Austria, and Poland received priority processing, and extensive card files were prepared indexing names there that might be of potential intelligence interest. Many of the Jewish and Masonic holdings that were of less operational interest to the Soviet regime than to the Nazis received only minimal arrangement and description. The chancery and personal papers of Léon Blum and those of various European royalty, for example, were all but forgotten for half a century, as was a collection of Greek and early Jewish documents on parchment (15th–17th centuries), and other materials of lesser "operational" interest.

Dispersal of Trophy Archives. It must be emphasized that the "Special Archive" was only one of the many destinations for trophy archives. Many of the archives that were first directed to the Special Archive were later dispersed to other institutions, as noted above in connection with the dispersion of the trophy French police and intelligence files. During the first year of its existence, for example, the Special Archive transferred to other repositories some 26 different groups of materials, ranging from individual files to major library or museum collections, all of which were deemed not to be suitable for the work of TsGOA or, in some cases, identified as belonging to other archives, such as the case of the Kirovohrad materials mentioned above.[77]

Many of the important archival materials from European socialist sources, as well as the International Institute for Social History in Amsterdam, were later transferred to the Institute of Marxism-Leninism in Moscow

---

French-language records might not be considered as commercially a salable project as the prospective publisher had anticipated. One hopes that when the records are returned to their countries of origin, the files will be more appropriately arranged and more professional finding aids will be prepared.

76   Ella Maksimova, "Piat' dnei v Osobom arkhive," *Izvestiia* 16 February 1990.

77   Musatov, "Doklad o rabote TsGOA SSSR za 1946 god," GA RF, 5325/2/1640, fols. 78, 80–87.

and are hence now held in the former Central Party Archive (RGASPI, *earlier* RTsKhIDNI). This was true, for example with the Fond of the Socialist Workers' International, with over 2,000 files (1923–1939/40), including the executive council of Friederich Adler and original autographs of August Bebel and Karl Kautsky. These materials, "have more limited scientific-historical significance and cannot be utilized in operation investigatory work," explained the TsGOA director in his transfer letter. The "Institute of Marxism-Leninism has already been expressing interest in the fate of trophy Party documents which relate to its profile."[78]

Some of the more purely Russian émigré fonds were transferred to Central State Archive of the October Revolution of the USSR—TsGAOR SSSR (now the State Archive of the Russian Federation—GA RF), where they joined the rich collections brought to Moscow from the Russian Historical Archive in Prague—RZIA. Such was the case with the Pavel Miliukov papers found in Wölfelsdorf, which the Nazis had seized from Paris.

Apparently TsGOA did not have specialists at that time for Ukrainian-language operational analysis, and hence at least some Ukrainian émigré files were sent to Kyiv, as was the case with documents on Hetman Skoropads'kyi. Also sent to Ukraine was a packet of "retrieved" NKVD operational documents from Mariupol and the twenty crates from local Communist Party archives in Kirovohrad, which the Nazis had managed to seize.[79] Some Ukrainian fonds from Poland and Paris, however, remained in TsGOA.

Many émigré literary files went directly to the Central State Archive of Literature and Art—TsGALI (now the Russian State Archive of Literature and Art—RGALI), and others were forwarded there by TsGOA. Some 334 Jewish Torah scrolls, along with 230 crates of Masonic portraits and regalia, were transferred to the State Historical Museum in Moscow (GIM) in 1946, but their subsequent fate has not been determined.[80] Many of the books and other published materials that came with the archives were turned over to the Lenin Library among others. As noted earlier, some were destroyed, while some are still held in a still uncatalogued collection in the archival stacks.

In addition to those later transferred from TsGOA, a number of trophy manuscript materials went directly to the Lenin Library. Of particular note

---

[78] Musatov to Nikitinskii (12 June 1947), GA RF, 5325/2/1946, fols. 49–51.

[79] Musatov, "Doklad o rabote TsGOA SSSR za 1946 god," GA RF, 5325/2/1640, fols. 97, 96, 86. Regarding the Kirovohrad return, see fns. 44–45, above.

[80] Musatov, "Doklad o rabote TsGOA SSSR za 1946 god," GA RF, 5325/2/1640, fols. 80–87.

because of its complicated migration and unfortunate dispersal was the Zamoyski archive and manuscript collection that Soviet authorities had recovered. In June 1947 the Zamoyski materials from the Lenin Library, including 20,000 books (with at least 1,000 early imprints) were transferred to Poland.[81] One group of 78 "charters and other state documents" from the Zamoyski archive, however, had not gone to the Lenin Library, but rather was deposited to the Central State Archive of Early Acts (TsGADA; *now* RGADA) in Moscow, where they remain today. According to a knowledge-able May 1945 inventory, those trophy documents had come "from the distinguished private Polish library of the Zamoyski counts, held in their Warsaw palace and then on their ancestral estate." They were turned over to TsGADA by the Committee for Cultural and Educational Institutions, given the fact that "most of them are previously unknown in historical literature and hence could provide a valuable source in historical science."[82] Details about the Soviet seizure of the Zamoyski materials has not surfaced, but it should be noted that another part of the Zamoyski archive had been held in the Kyiv Archive of Early Acts before it was taken by the Nazis in 1943.[83]

The manuscript materials received by the Lenin Library from Dresden were returned to East Germany in 1958, but some other manuscripts received from Germany remained there. The Lenin Library also received some 300 trophy Hebrew manuscripts that the Nazis had gathered from Jewish communities in many different countries, which as of 1999 have still not been fully described.[84]

---

[81]   See Krystyna Wróbel-Lipowa, *Rewindykacja archiwaliów polskich z ZSRR w latach 1945–1964* (Lublin, 1982), p. 74. Details about their return were published in *Wolność* 141 (27 June 1947), and reprinted in *Dokumenty i materialy po istorii sovetsko-pol'skikh otnoshenii,* vol. 9 (Moscow: "Nauka," 1976), pp. 197–98 (docs. 136 and 138).

[82]   See the draft memorandum and "top secret" inventory of the 78 charters, forwarded to GAU NKVD Chief I. I. Nikitinskii (17 May 1945), GA RF, 5325/2/1353, fols. 160–178. The first 8 charters were loose documents, the others were bound in an album, which bore the number 1792 from the Zamoyski Library. The album today is held as part of fond 31 in RGADA.

[83]   Several Polish magnate archives were removed by the Nazis from Kyiv to Kamianets-Podilskyi and then Troppau (*Pol.* Opawa). Although reportedly, not all of those materials were recovered after the war, the losses are difficult to calculate, because those suppressed fonds had not been well arranged and described before the war.

[84]   Some of the trophy Hebrew manuscripts have been examined by specialists from the Institute of Microfilmed Hebrew Manuscripts at the National and University

In the case of many fragmentary files that were accessioned by other state archives, the facts and whereabouts of their retrieval were likewise concealed; sometimes the receiving archivists did not themselves know and were never able to record from whence they came. Archivists today have no idea of the exact provenance or details of the migration of many of these materials. Equally tragic is that many of these trophy materials became subject to theft and dispersal either en route or due, in part, to their suspect and not fully registered status within the archives where they were placed. For example, a majority of the medieval records from the Bremen City Archive, found in a salt mine in Saxony, was deposited in the Central State Archive of Early Acts (TsGADA) in Moscow, but at least initially, the charters were split off from the rest of the collection and held in the Saltykov-Shchedrin State Public Library (now the Russian National Library—RNB) in Leningrad. Some were sold on the antiquarian market, which explains why two Bremen charters have recently been identified as part of the Tikhomirov Collection in Novosibirsk. When the Bremen City Archive was finally returned to Bremen in 1990, some 248 early charters and 1,387 maps were missing as a result of its migration.[85]

Soviet Archival Restitution. Gradually, Soviet authorities did return some of their looted records, but mostly to East Germany and other Eastern-bloc nations. A few summary details about those transfers were published at the time— in the late 1950s, for example, noting that the files had been "rescued by the Soviet Army."[86] A few fragmentary French files "rescued by the Soviet Army" were presented to France in March 1960, including a 1599

Library in Jerusalem (IMHM), and their existence has been recorded there, but apparently these materials were never officially registered in the Manuscript Division and a full list is not available.

[85] These figures are based on precise lists (data as of 11 February 1993) furnished to me by the deputy directory of the Bremen Stadtsarchiv. The Bremen charters were returned with identifying markings of GPB (now RNB) on their containers. See the earlier article by Hartmut Müller, "'... for safekeeping': Bremer Archivschutzmass nahmen im Zweiten Weltkrieg und ihre Folgen," in *Bremisches Jahrbuch* 66 (1988): 409–22 [=*Festschrift für Wilhelm Lührs und Klaus Schwarz*].

[86] See, for example, E. G. Baskakov and O. V. Shablovskii, "Vozvrashchenie arkhivnykh materialov, spasennykh Sovetskoi Armiei," *Istoricheskii arkhiv* 1958 (5): 175–79.

charter signed by King Henry IV.[87] There was an additional small transfer to France in 1966, and "in strict adherence to international legal norms and respectful of the sovereign law of peoples and their national historical and cultural legacy, the Soviet government transferred to the Democratic Republic of Germany archival materials rescued by the Soviet Army after the defeat of Hitlerite Germany...more than 2 million archival files (from the fourteenth century to 1945)."[88]

A 1969 Glavarkhiv report lists over two million file units of Soviet-captured archival materials (held predominantly by Glavarkhiv and the Ministry of Foreign Affairs) that were returned to various countries in the 1950s and 1960s, including some of the Hanseatic records.[89] Through additional restitution in the late 1970s, in the spirit of a resolution of the International Council of Archives Round Table in Cagliari, Italy, the Soviet Union was "helping other countries reunify their national archival heritage."[90] Unfortunately, however, in the process many fonds were split up and individual files broken out of integral groups of records. Microfilms were not retained in most cases.

During the late 1980s, some 40 tons of German archival documents were returned to East Germany.[91] In October 1990, remaining treasures from the medieval Hanseatic city archives of Bremen, Hamburg, and Lübeck (other parts of these collections had been transferred earlier to East Germany) were finally restored to their proper homes in direct exchange for the counterpart medieval treasures from the Tallinn City Archive that were returned to

[87] "Peredacha dokumentov Natsional'nomu arkhivu Frantsii," *Voprosy arkhivo-vedeniia* 1960 (6): 107.

[88] Mikhail Ia. Kapran, "Mezhdunarodnoe sotrudnichestvo sovetskikh arkhivistov," *Sovetskie arkhivy* 1968 (3): 33. Other restitution is mentioned to and from Socialist countries of Eastern Europe, including Poland and Czechoslovakia.

[89] "Spravka o dokumental'nykh materialakh, peredannykh pravitel'stvam inostran-nykh gosudarstv," typescript with handwritten corrections added and signed by V. V. Tsaplin (3 February 1969). These figures do not take into account archival materials and manuscript treasures restituted by libraries under other controlling agencies, such as the German and Polish materials restituted in 1957/58 by the Manuscript Division of the Lenin State Library and the Library of Moscow State University.

[90] S. L. Tikhvinskii, "Pomoshch' Sovetskogo Soiuza drugim gosudarstvam v vossozdanii natsional'nogo arkhivnogo dostoianiia," *Sovetskie arkhivy* 1979 (2): 11–16. Again, most went back to the GDR and other Eastern-bloc countries.

[91] See the report by Wolfram Schmidt, "Übernahme von Archivgut aus der UdSSR," *Archivmitteilungen* 39(5) 1989: 179–80.

Estonia from the Bundesarchiv in Koblenz.[92] The 1990 Soviet-German Pact of Friendship had a paragraph ensuring the further return of cultural treasures by both sides, but implementation has been frustrated at every turn. The long-suppressed "death books" from Auschwitz (*Pol.* Oświęcim), which listed deaths other than those of people who had perished in the gas ovens, were turned over to the museum in Oświęcim. (Microfilm copies of these registers were made available to the Red Cross only in 1989.) As the last archival restitution transfer to Germany, 2,200 music scores and related manuscripts were returned to the University of Hamburg from the Leningrad State Institute for Theater, Music, and Cinematography (now the Russian Institute for the History of Art) in 1991.

The Opening and Closing of the "Special Archive." The "Special Archive" was first mentioned in print in connection with that microfilm transfer to the Red Cross. But the extent of its holdings of trophy Nazi records was first publicly revealed in an interview with the director in a Moscow journalist's "Five Days in the 'Special Archive,'" which appeared in February 1990.[93] At that point, the only source of Nazi holdings mentioned was the castle of the Counts of von Althann in Wölfelsdorf (*Pol.* Wilkanów) near Habelschwerdt, although the Polish name was not mentioned, and the director implied it was in Germany (as it was before and during the war). Revelations of the even more extensive holdings in the "Special Archive" from other countries (and especially France) first came in October 1991 in my own interview with a Moscow journalist, whom I had first met earlier as the one who exposed the trophy books rotting in the church of Uzkoe, outside of Moscow.[94] A week

---

[92] "Vozvrashchenie ganzeiskikh arkhivov," *Sovetskie arkhivy* 1991 (1): 111. See also Evgenii Kuz′min, "Netrofeinaia istoriia," *Literaturnaia gazeta* 41 (1990): 10. Regarding the fate of the Tallinn City Archive, see Wilhelm Lenz, "Die Verlagerung des Revaler Stadtarchivs im Rahmen des 'Archivschutzes' während des Zweiten Weltkrieges," in *Reval: Handel und Wandel vom 13. bis zum 20. Jahrhundert*, ed. Norbert Angermann and Wilhelm Lenz (Lüneburg: Institut Norddeutsches Kulturwerk, 1997), pp. 397–443 [=*Schriften der Baltischen Historischen Kommission*, 8].

[93] See Ella Maksimova, "Piat′ dnei v Osobom arkhive," *Izvestiia* 49–53 (17–23 February 1990). A notice by Maksimova, "Arkhivnyi detektiv," *Izvestiia* 177 (24 April 1989), was the first mention of the archive in print. I was refused access to the archive until the spring of 1993.

[94] See Evgenii Kuz′min's interview with me, "Vyvezti…unichtozhit′… spriatat′…, Sud′by trofeinykh arkhivov," *Literaturnaia gazeta* 39 (2 October 1991): 13. Publication of that interview was delayed for almost a year, and in the interim, Kuz′min took

later, my story was confirmed when the former director of TsGOA admitted publicly that over a million files of French intelligence records, to say nothing of many other "lost" foreign archives, were indeed ensconced in the so-called "Special Archive" off the Leningrad Highway (Leningradskoe shosse).[95]

In June 1992, the Special Archive (TsGOA SSSR) was euphemistically renamed the Center for the Preservation of Historico-Documentary Collections—TsKhIDK (Tsentr khraneniia istoriko-dokumental'nykh kollektsii), and gradually started opening its doors. A number of Western researchers were quick to publish selected lists of holdings in Germany[96] and in Belgium.[97] A cursory English-language list of predominantly German fonds was published in America, with a supplement the following year.[98] An unauthorized, and not entirely accurate, brief guide appeared in Germany late in 1992, predominantly covering only the German and Austrian holdings, including Nazi records and summary listings of others that had earlier been returned to East Germany.[99] The Belgians followed their earlier survey with a more detailed guide to Belgian fonds, first prepared in Russian, and later in a Flemish edition in 1997, at which time the Belgian materials under review

---

great pains to verify my story by the examination of the archival files I had found., More details subsequently appeared in my "Beyond *Perestroika*: Soviet Area Archives After the August Coup," *American Archivist* 55(1) Winter 1992: 94–124; and my "The Fate of Ukrainian Cultural Treasures," pp. 72–79.

95   See the follow-up interview by Ella Maksimova with the former director of the Special Archive, Anatoli S. Prokopenko, "Arkhivy frantsuzskoi razvedki skryvali na Leningradskom shosse," *Izvestiia* 240 (3 November 1991). See also the article by Prokopenko, "Dom osobogo naznacheniia (Otkrytie arkhivov)," *Rodina* 1992 (3): 50–51.

96   Bernd Wegner, "Deutsche Aktenbestände im moskauer Zentralen Staatsarchiv. Ein Erfahrungsbericht," *Vierteljahrshefte für Zeitgeschichte* 40(2) 1992: 311–19; Kai von Jena and Wilhelm Lenz, "Die deutschen Bestände im Sonderarchiv in Moskau," *Der Archivar* 45 (1992, no. 3): 457–67.

97   *AMSAB Tijdingen*, n.s. 16 (Summer 1992), extra number: *Mission to Moscow. Belgische socialistische archieven in Rusland.*

98   George C. Browder, "Captured German and Other Nations' Documents in the Osoby (Special) Archive, Moscow," *Central European History* 24(4) 1992: 424–45; idem, "Update on the Captured Documents in the Former Osobyi Archive, Moscow," *Central European History* 26(3) 1993: 335–42.

99   Götz Aly and Susanne Heim, *Das Zentrale Staatsarchiv in Moskau ("Sonderarchiv"), Rekonstruktion und Bestandsverzeichnis verschollen geglaubten Schriftguts aus der NS-Zeit* (Düsseldorf: Hans-Böckler-Stiftung, 1992).

had been prepared in microform (at Belgian expense) and are now available in Ghent.[100]

There has been no similar listing, however, nor even a published survey of the French- and Polish-language divisions.[101] The archive does have its own internal part-typewritten, part-manuscript "List of French Fonds," which is not usually communicated to researchers.[102] Because it was prepared for the most part on the basis of language, rather than country of origin, it includes Belgian materials, as well as a number of fonds from other countries. Quite unexpectedly, the list includes nine Ukrainian émigré fonds, most of them from Paris, and among them part of the long-lost materials from the Petliura Library in Paris, which had been seized by the Nazis in January 1941; those materials were transferred to the Special Archive from Minsk in 1955/56.[103]

At the beginning of 1994, TsKhIDK itself reported holding a total of 870 trophy fonds, although that figure is somewhat misleading because some of the captured materials remain in large collections that have not been broken down into fonds according to their provenance. Such is the case, for example, of one large collection of Masonic files from all over Europe that was never

---

[100] *Fondy bel'giiskogo proiskhozhdeniia: Annotirovannyi ukazatel'*, comp. T. A. Vasil'eva and A. S. Namazova; edited by M. M. Mukhamedzhanov (Moscow, 1995; [Rosarkhiv, TsKhIDK, Institut vseobshchei istorii RAN]). Unfortunately, institutional and personal names are cited only in the Russian language without reference to original-language forms. A Flemish translation appeared in April 1997, edited by Michel Vermonte et al.: *Fondsen van Belgische Herkomst: Verklarende Index* (Ghent: AMSAB, 1997).

[101] See further notes on published finding aids for former TsKhIDK in my "Displaced Archives and Restitution Problems on the Eastern Front in the Aftermath of the Second World War." *Contemporary European History* 6(1) 1997: 27–74; and, more recently, "'Trophy' Archives and Non-Restitution: Russia's Cultural 'Cold War' with the European Community," *Problems of Post-Communism* 45(3) May/June 1998: 3–15. See also *Archives of Russia, 2000*, vol. 1, pp. 225–30.

[102] "Spisok frantsuzskikh fondov" (33 pp.) has been augmented at various times, usually indicating the year of receipt of the materials. It provides the most complete listing available other than the new general annotated list of fonds in preparation.

[103] See my "The Postwar Fate of the Petliura Library and the Records of the Ukrainian National Republic," *Harvard Ukrainian Studies* 21(3–4): 395–462. It was only when I was permitted to consult the normally closed list of French fonds in the archive that I discovered these Ukrainian listings. Another part of the library records and other archival materials from the Petliura Library in Paris are located in GA RF, while still others are now in Kyiv.

broken down according to their lodge of provenance.[104] Many other Masonic records were separated out into fonds, including files from close to 100 German Masonic lodges that were returned to East Germany in the 1950s.[105] Among the massive French Masonic holdings, is a fond for the "Grand Orient of France" and two separate "Consolidated Archival Fonds" for the "Daughter Lodges of the 'Grand Orient of France,'" which include files from subsidiary lodges ranging from Algiers to Dakar and Casablanca to Belgium, the Dominican Republic, and Indo-China.[106] Separate fonds were established for the Grand Lodge of France of the Scottish Rite and the Supreme Council of the Scottish Rite in Paris (Suprême Conseil de France du Rite Écossais Ancien et Accepté), but this latter fond also includes a number of files from the Grand Orient.[107] Separate composite collections remain for Belgian and Luxembourg Masonic documentation, although other files from lodges in those countries may also be found intermixed in other Masonic fonds.[108] Parts of several of these Masonic fonds, together with fragmentary personal papers of many French and German Jewish leaders had first come to Kyiv, but were subsequently sent to Moscow in 1957.

The Archive itself had long promised at least a brief list of fonds. In 1997 an outside semi-commercial group reached an agreement with the Archive for preparation of a CD-ROM guide and found funds to pay outside researchers to prepare annotations for many of the fonds. While billing

---

[104] Reference here is to fond 1412 "Dokumental'nye materialy masonskikh lozh (kollektsiia)." The fond contains six *opisi* with 14,394 numbered files, ranging in provenance from Germany, Austria, Greece, the Netherlands, and Norway, among other countries.

[105] Regarding the restituted German Masonic records, see above, pp. 291–92 and fn. 34.

[106] RGVA Fond 92K is assigned to the Grand Orient of France, Paris (17,214 units; 1712–1940). Fond 112K is assigned to daughter lodges of the Grand Orient of France (fond 112K; 4 *opisi*; 1,244 file units; 1784–1940), as is fond no. 113K. That collection has 4 *opisi*, totaling 5,429 file units (respectively 1,473; 1,393; 435; and 228 file units); 1740–1940.

[107] RGVA fond 93K (2,185 file units; 1723–1940) and fond 111K; 2 *opisi*; 804 file units; 1771–1940. Files from several other French Masonic lodges have been assigned to separate fonds, but there appears to be considerable intermixing, while some of the French fonds contain files from lodges in other countries.

[108] The Belgian Masonic collection (RGVA fond 114K) has been surveyed in the guide, *Fondy bel'giiskogo proiskhozhdeniia*. The relatively smaller Luxembourg collection bears the fond number 117K (2 *opisi*; 103 items; 1803–1939).

themselves as a "charitable foundation," as part of the project, they launched a preliminary, but still rough English-language list of fonds on the Internet in effort to sell research services and copies of documents. By the end of 1998, however, given complaints about the numerous errors involved, the Internet listings were removed at Rosarkhiv request.[109] The Archive itself has now prepared a more definitive, but still preliminary, list of fonds, due for publication in 2000.[110]

In recent years, the principal archive that houses foreign captured records in Moscow has been frequently without heat and electricity. As temperatures reached freezing in October, staff could only work a few hours a day, and researchers who ventured in had to keep on their gloves and overcoats. There were few qualified staff left, with only token salaries—if and when they were paid on time. (Like other Russian archives, the TsKhIDK average was about $50 per month.) With many in the staff lacking foreign languages and training in history and historiography, there has been little possibility for serious professional work.

In March 1999, as part of a larger Rosarkhiv reform and economy measure, TsKhIDK itself was abolished as a separate archive. As yet another symbol of their wartime fate and ill-defined status, the TsGOA/TsKhIDK trophy holdings became part of the neighboring Russian State Military Archive—RGVA, together with the records of the NKVD/MVD agencies of the Main Administration for Affairs of Prisoners of War and Internees (Glavnoe upravlenie po delam voennoplennykh i internirovannykh—GUPVI, 1939–1960), also held by TsKhIDK.

The dissolution of TsKhIDK as a separate repository does not lessen the

---

[109] The listing under the sponsorship of the Klassika/Classica Foundation, appeared during 1998 under the heading of "Russian Archives" within the website of the firm MediaLingua, a firm peddling various computer products, but it has since been withdrawn. Although the listing contains many errors and shortcomings, it was nonetheless the first, relatively comprehensive publicly available coverage of French and Polish holdings in the archive. The Klassika/Classica group had a contract with the Archive for the publication of a CD-ROM multimedia guide to the archive, but that project has been dropped due to the unprofessional quality of the product.

[110] According to Vladimir N. Kuzelenkov, who now directs the combined RGVA, German funding has been found for a small pressrun. The latest draft I saw in October 1999 attempts to provide the original language names and locations for all the creating agencies, and also lists fonds that were earlier restituted. While still not complete or comprehensive, it is nonetheless a considerable improvement over the Classica/Klassika 1998 Internet English-language listing. It is hoped that an English-language edition of the new fond list will soon follow.

need for a comprehensive guide to its foreign trophy holdings, as archival authorities in Moscow are well aware. Archivists and other specialists from affected countries, as well as researchers from throughout the world, still need accurate information about precisely which displaced archives were "rescued" by the Red Army and other Soviet agencies, where they were found, the extent to which their provenance has been identified, known facts about their migration, when and to whom they were transferred, whether or not microfilms are available, and where the originals are now preserved. As early as 1977, the ICA advocated open description of displaced archives. Since the TsGOA/TsKhIDK trophy holdings are now part of a public archive freely open to world scholarship and, especially, since Russia has agreed "to settle rapidly all issues related to the return of property claimed by Council of Europe member states, in particular the archives transferred to Moscow in 1945," accurate identification of the origin and fate of displaced archival materials from the former Special Archive has become acutely essential. Russia's trophy archives represent the national heritage and legal record of many European nations and organizations, but until their provenance, migration, and whereabouts have been professionally identified, it will be difficult, if not impossible, to establish potential claims and insure their appropriate restitution.

Captured Nazi Records in Ukraine

Nazi Occupation Records in Ukraine. Ukraine received only a very small share of Nazi agency records, predominantly those of occupation authorities in Ukraine. A considerable volume of local Nazi occupation records were found in Ukraine after the war, and, apparently, some locally relevant files from those Nazi occupation records captured abroad were also distributed to Ukrainian oblast-level archives. Some of these, however, were later destroyed in various archival "cleansing" operations. The 1998 publication of the report on "Nazi Gold" in and from Ukraine provides the most up-to-date survey of local Nazi occupation records remaining in Ukraine, but alas its listings are still not comprehensive.[111]

The core records of the Reich Commissariat for Ukraine (RKU), headed by Eric Koch, undoubtedly were destroyed by the Nazis in retreat from its Rivne headquarters to Königsberg and points west. Nazi destruction orders or

---

[111] Hennadii Boriak, Maryna Dubyk, and Nataliia Makovs´ka, *"Natsysts´ke zoloto" z Ukraïny: U poshukakh arkhivnykh svidchen´*, part 1 (Kyiv, 1998).

evacuation reports have been found in many instances. Only scattered central RKU files now remain in Ukraine.[112]

Cultural and Archival Administration Records. Records of the RKU cultural administration, the Provincial Authority for Archives, Libraries, and Museums (Landesverwaltung der Archive, Bibliotheken und Museen—LV ABM), nevertheless do survive in Kyiv. Relatively intact, they represent one of the most signification extant groups of records from a Nazi agency subordinate to the RKU. The records of the LV ABM, which had been headquartered in Kyiv, were found by Ukrainian archivists along with other evacuated Ukrainian archives in its final point of operation in Troppau (*Czech* Opava) and taken back to Kyiv in the fall of 1945.[113]

Professional archivist Dr. Georg Winter, who headed the LV ABM, had been sent to Ukraine in the fall of 1941. Directly responsible to the Reichsarchiv in Berlin-Dahlem, Winter had earlier served with Nazi archival operations in France. After the formation of the LV ABM at the end of 1942 as a political counterweight to the ERR (apparently in the power struggle between Eric Koch and Alfred Rosenberg), Winter also reported to Koch.

First opened for public research in 1989, the extensive LV ABM files provide many fresh details about Nazi organization and activities on the cultural front in eastern Ukraine.[114] Those records contain many important documents about archival developments during the war as well as those dealing with museums and libraries. They also contain many precise inventories and shipping lists for archival materials evacuated, including some that cover other Ukrainian cultural treasures looted by the Nazis. There is a

---

[112] Only a few other scattered central files of the Reich Commissariat (RKU) are held in TsDAVO (fond 3206), but these contain few original documents of importance.

[113] The LV ABM records were joined to the fond of the RKU (TsDAVO, fond 3206) as the fifth *opis´*—but within that fond only those LV ABM records recovered in Opava contain significant original files. The recovery by Ukrainian archivists in Opava in the summer of 1945 was first reported by Pavliuk to Nikitinskii (Prague, 9 August 1945), GA RF, 5325/2/1353, fol. 78 (another copy in Kyiv is found in TsDAVO, 4703/2/2, fol. 7).

[114] A report and good summary of the contents of this fond has been published in Kyiv: Maryna H. Dubyk, "Skhema sprav Kraiovoho upravlinnia arkhivamy, bibliotekamy ta muzeiamy pry Reikhskomisariati Ukraïny (1944 r.)," *Arkhivy Ukraïny* 1995 (1–3): 35–37. See also idem, *Arkhivna sprava v okupovanii Ukraïni (1941–1944 rr.)*, Avtoreferat dysertatsiï na zdobuttia naukovoho stupenia kandydata istorychnykh nauk (Kyiv, 1997; NANU IUA).

critical need for them to be studied carefully in conjunction with other Nazi records, given the clues they hold to the displacement and fate of many cultural treasures, including Ukrainian archives, during the war.

Unlike the Künsberg Commandos and the ERR, the LV ABM was more concerned with the preservation of archives and cultural treasures *in situ*. With the Nazi retreat in 1943—and concerned about the potential for archival, museum, and library damage as the Red Army advanced on Kyiv—the agency planned the evacuation of some of the remaining most valuable paintings from the Kyiv museums. These included first priority paintings from the Museum of Western and Oriental Art and the remaining icons from the Kyiv Museum of Russian Art (as it had been reorganized under the LV ABM). On 16 September, a three-ton truck with the most important paintings was dispatched to Rivne. The bulk of the museum shipment (two freight cars), however, went north to the Königsberg region and thence to Bavaria, rather than following the archival shipments from Kamianets-Podilskyi to Troppau.[115]

The LV ABM was involved in only limited evacuations of archival materials from Ukraine. It was Winter himself who personally supervised the evacuation of what was nearly the earliest half of the Kyiv Archive of Early Acts. As mentioned earlier, this was of particular importance for demonstrating early German influence through Magdeburg Law in Ukrainian lands.[116] After retreat from Kyiv, the LV ABM continued operations first in Kamianets-Podilskyi and then in Troppau until early 1945, before moving some of its most valuable archival loot to western Bohemia.

Also retrieved in Czechoslovakia, but taken to Lviv, were the records of the Nazi archival administration in Galicia, which according to Nazi administrative-territorial divisions during the war was part of the Polish General-Gouvernement. These records, evacuated by the German archivist Rudolf Fitz, who had directed the archival service there, contain documentation regarding archival operations and evacuations in western Ukraine. They include many archival inventories and detailed shipping lists for records

---

[115] See the scattered documentation regarding the shipment of art, which was accompanied by the Ukrainian art historian Pavlina Kul'chenko. She was lodged in the manor of Richau near Wehlau in East Prussia (now Kaliningrad Oblast). TsDAVO, 3206/5/8, esp. fols. 15–16, 116–123, 130–131, 138–139, 143–144, 150, 154, 191–192, and 197.

[116] There is considerable documentation about Winter's evacuation of the archive from Kyiv, especially in TsDAVO, 3206/5/8. See Chapter 6, above, p. 234.

removed during the entire wartime Nazi occupation.[117]

Records of the Nazi wartime archival authorities in Cracow, to whom in some cases Galician operations were subordinate, were incorporated into the files of the administrative archive of the State Archive in Cracow. Open for research there, they only tangentially relate to Ukraine, but they do contain documentation confirming Nazi shipments of archives during the war and postwar Soviet retrievals.

These three different groups of records of German provenance are now housed in Kyiv, Lviv, and Cracow, as records of local Nazi occupying authorities. Nevertheless, they are clearly of "joint" heritage, representing significant original files of the Nazi German occupation. While the agencies involved were subordinate to local occupying authorities, namely the RKU and, in the case of those from Lviv and Cracow, the General-Gouvernement, their directors, such as Georg Winter and Rudolf Fitz, were simultaneously responsible to the Nazi Reichsarchiv, headquartered first in Potsdam, but also during the war in Berlin-Dahlem, where it was directed by Ernst Zipfel (1891–1966).[118] Accordingly, for many purposes, these files need to be studied in connection with the central records of the Reichsarchiv. A significant body of Reichsarchiv records from the prewar and wartime period came into Soviet hands after the war and ended up in the Special Archive in Moscow.[119] These Reichsarchiv records, however, have been dispersed, since only part of the fond was restituted to East Germany in 1957 and copies were not kept in Moscow, while others were held in the West German Bundesarchiv.[120] Those files in Germany are now being consolidated in the new Bundesarchiv facility in Berlin-Lichterfelde.

---

[117] These records are now held in Lviv, TsDIAL (fond 755). An original Czech inventory, prepared before Soviet seizure of the fond, is to be found in the administrative file (*sprava fonda*) for fond 755.

[118] Regarding Reichsarchiv operations during the war, see the dissertation by Matthias Herrmann, *Das Reichsarchiv (1919–1945): Eine archivische Institution im Spannungsfeld der deutschen Politik*, Band II (Berlin: Humboldt-Universität, ca. 1993); and Torsten Musial, *Staatsarchive im Dritten Reich: Zur Geschichte des staatlichen Archivwesens in Deutschland, 1933–1945* (Potsdam: Verl. für Berlin-Brandenburg, 1996) [=Potsdamer Studien, Band 2]. Neither of these studies have used available documentation in the former USSR and Poland.

[119] These are now held in RGVA with the former TsKhIDK holdings, fond 1255K with 2 *opisi* (*opis'* 1; 23 file units, 1919–1945; *opis'* 2, 87 file units, 1711–1945).

[120] In 1957, 37 files were transferred to the GDR and, before German reunification, were held with other Reichsarchiv records in Potsdam (Bestand 15.06). A major group of Reichsarchiv records were held before unification in BAK (Bestand R 146).

Records of the Einsatzstab Reichsleiter Rosenberg (ERR). Undoubtedly, most important among Nazi records in Ukraine for our present subject are the extensive records from operations of the special propaganda and cultural plundering commando force headed by Hitler's henchman Alfred Rosenberg, the Einsatzstab Reichsleiter Rosenberg (ERR). The ERR functioned independently of Rosenberg's simultaneous post as Minister of the Reich Ministry for Occupied Eastern Territories—RMbO (Reichsministerium für die besetzten Ostgebiete). Operations in terms of art looting by the ERR, and their relations with competing Nazi agencies, especially in Western Europe, have been well documented by Jonathan Petropoulos in his insightful analysis of Nazi art policies and by Lynn Nicholas in her important work.[121]

Special units were established in Berlin soon after the foundation of the ERR itself for analyzing Bolshevism and preparing the propaganda battle against the reigning Soviet ideology. The ERR Main Task Force Groups (Hauptarbeitsgruppe; HAG) operating in Soviet lands, in addition to other cultural surveillance and looting operations, all had many specific assignments for research and writing regarding Bolshevism and related aspects of the Soviet political and cultural scene.[122] This was one of the reasons why the capture of Communist Party archives was a high priority for them.

During the summer of 1943, after Western bombing of Berlin had started, the ERR moved many of its operations out of Berlin to the East. Its Central Library for the planned Higher Party School (Hohe Schule), was already located in the Austrian Tyrol. At that point it was moved to the monastery of Tanzenberg, together with much of its choice ERR library loot.

The major ERR anti-Bolshevik propaganda and research center was transferred to the Silesian city of Ratibor (*Pol.* Racibórz). Also transferred were the major ERR library collections, including the specialized library for Eastern matters, the so-called *Ostbücherei*. Much of the captured loot from the West that remained in ERR hands, especially books and archival materials involving East European and socialist subjects were moved there. By the

---

[121] Jonathan Petropoulos, *Art as Politics in the Third Reich: The Collecting Policies of the Nazi Elite* (Chapel Hill: University of North Carolina Press, 1996), especially pp. 127–41 and passim. See also Lynn Nicholas, *The Rape of Europa: The Fate of Europe's Treasures in the Third Reich and the Second World War* (New York: Alfred A. Knopf, 1994).

[122] For example, a revealing lists of the studies planned and under way in Ukraine appears in the HAG-Ukraine circular report —"Rundschreiben," no. 9/43 (Kyiv, 23 March 1943), signed by Anton, TsDAVO, 3676/1/26a, fols. 204–218. Those being conducted in Vilnius were listed in a supplement to the HAG-O monthly report for November 1943 (Vilnius, November 1943), TsDAVO, 3676/1/171, fol. 185.

fall of 1943 many of the remaining ERR operations and specialized task forces, especially those relating to the East, were headquartered in Ratibor.[123]

ERR looting operations in other occupied western areas of the USSR enlarged the Ostbücherei. Ukraine was particularly well represented, with the most extensive holdings from the State Library (in the name of the Communist Party) in Kyiv and from the Korolenko Library in Kharkiv, among others. In April the extensive card catalogs from Kharkiv and another major shipment were directed to the castle of Thunskirch (*Pol.* Tworków) outside of Ratibor, but by the end of the year, the card catalogs from the Korolenko Library in Kharkiv were housed in a separate building in the city (Oderstr. 23).[124] Belarus was also well represented, as many of its richest libraries were virtually cleaned out. In fact, most of the Ostbücherei were volumes which the ERR had looted from Soviet lands, although the Turgenev Library and the Petliura Library from Paris were also held there, having been transferred up the Oder from Berlin.[125]

Archival materials were high on the priority list of ERR loot for the anti-Bolshevik study units in Ratibor. The ERR forces worked closely with the archival professionals sent by the state archival system (Reichsarchiv and Archivschutz) in tracking down those most politically and ideologically-sensitive materials most appropriate for their research units, including their anti-Bolshevik research in Ratibor. Working together with professional Nazi archival authorities, led by Dr. Georg Winter, who directed the Provincial Authority for Archives, Libraries, and Museums under the Reich Commissariat of Ukraine, the ERR collected significant fragments of four or five regional Communist Party archives from Ukraine—from Dnipropetrovsk, Kirovohrad, Zaporizhzhia, and Uman, although we do not have evidence that

[123] Regarding ERR operations in Ratibor and the fate of the archives involved, see my "New Clues in the Records of Archival and Library Plunder during World War II," pp. 52–67. See also the earlier commentary in my *Odyssey of the Smolensk Archive*, pp. 7–23, 42–48, 52–54; and the introductory chapters about the ERR in Willem de Vries, *Sonderstab Musik: Music Confiscations by the Einsatzstab Reichsleiter Rosenberg under the Nazi Occupation of Western Europe* (Amsterdam: Amsterdam University Press, 1996), especially pp. 30–33, 70–78, and 85–115.

[124] ERR quarterly report, 1 January 1944–4 March 1944 (17 April 44), BAB, NS 30/55; Lommatzsch report, 13 December 1944, NS 30/50. Details about the preparation and shipping of these materials are available in other ERR reports in Kyiv, TsDAVO, fond 3676, *opys* 1. I am currently documenting further library shipments from Ukraine for the Ostbücherei in Ratibor.

[125] ERR report, Ratibor, 14 February 44, BAB, NS 30/22, fol. 246.

all of them reached Ratibor.[126] The important fragments of the Party Archive in Dnipropetrovsk arrived in Ratibor the 5th of November 1943, consisting of "29 crates, 64 satchels, and 343 document packages."[127] In December 1944 the Dnipropetrovsk Party files were being held in the building of the former Lagerplatz Synagogue with the Russian-language part of the Ostbücherei (Niedertorstr. 3), but there is no available indication of the specific use that ERR researchers were making of the materials.[128]

The Nazis also brought a significant group of files from the Museum of Revolution in Kyiv for what they called the "Revolutionary Archive," containing politically sensitive materials regarding the Ukrainian anti-Bolshevik factions to establish an independent state during the revolutionary and Civil War period (1917–1923). By September 1942 in Kyiv, they had recorded 2,000 units, including original posters, handbills, and leaflets from the years 1917–ca.1920, along with "counterrevolutionary" materials collected in Ukraine (including Denikin and others as their subject)."[129] By

---

[126] See also references above, pp. 292–94; and more details in my *Odyssey of the Smolensk Archive*, esp. pp. 20–23.

[127] Its dispatch from Cracow in a freight car to Ratibor is confirmed by Hülle, "Halbmonatsberichte 9.–31.Okt.1943" (Cracow, 2 November 1943), with a copy of the shipping list—"29 Kisten 64 Schachteln und 343 Aktenpakete," together with "1 crate of books and atlases and 6 large crates [Verschläge] with paintings — 'die schon im Besitz des ERR waren,'" TsDAVO, 3676/1/225, fol. 296. Hülle to ERR HAG-Ukraine (8 November 1943), fol. 288, and his monthly report for November 1943 (fol. 268), in the same file both confirm that the shipment with the Dnipro-petrovsk material left for Ratibor 5 November 1943.

[128] Lommatzsch report (13 December 1944), BAB, NS 30/50. The Dnipropetrovsk files are identified in a poster announcement of ERR Ratibor activities reproduced in de Vries, *Sonderstab Musik*, p. 114, photo 10, from a copy in BAK. I have found another copy in an album held in US NA, Still Picture Division, RG 260–PHOAD-III-6.

[129] A number of other of ERR reports reference the collection. For example, an ERR cultural registration card (8 September 1942) notes a collection of 2,000 documents including original posters and other "counterrevolutionary" materials in the Museum of Revolution in the Lavra, with an inventory in progress, under the direction of Dr. Granzin—TsDAVO, 3676/1/56, fol. 1, and another card prepared by Lange (25 February 1942) with less detail, but also mentioning 2,000 units as fol. 2. An ERR 1942 quarterly report noted that Dr. Granzin (in Kyiv) was working on the collection with 3,000 documents, 200 of which he had worked over. "Vierteljahresbericht" (1 July–30 September) (Berlin, 9 October 1942), CDJC, CXLI-147, fol. 3. Neither of the cards mention shipping data, which corresponds to other reports that in September 1942, they were still working on the collection in Kyiv.

the time they shipped this collection to Ratibor, there were at least 3,000 plundered units relating to the various independent Ukrainian governments during the revolutionary and Civil War period.[130] At the end of the war, however, some of the archival materials from the Museum of Revolution in Kyiv were found in the RSHA VII research center mentioned above, while others were found in Vienna. It is not clear when these materials were sent to Wölfelsdorf, or if possibly the collection was split between the RSHA and the ERR.[131]

There also was a separate photographic archive in Ratibor, with some 8,000 photographs from the USSR and some 4,000 Soviet sound recordings. However, most of the extensive films and photographic archival collections plundered from Soviet lands had been sent earlier to Berlin for other centers in the Reich and were not transferred to Ratibor.[132] This is confirmed by various shipping instructions and by the example that some 500 crates with 37,000 negatives from the Central State Archive of Film and Photographic Documents of the Ukrainian SSR in Kyiv were recovered in Germany by Soviet authorities after the war and returned to Kyiv in 1946.[133]

The ERR center operated in Ratibor and in numerous castles and other buildings in its vicinity through the end of 1944, reaching its zenith in the summer and fall of 1944, with close to 350 specialists in ERR employ.[134] At its height, the Ostbücherei totaled over one million volumes, but it is not clear what this total included and whether all of these were held in Ratibor.[135] Figures given in different reports add up to divergent totals, and many shipments still remained unpacked in crates that may or may not have been included.

---

[130] The location of this collection in Ratibor (Flurstr. 12) is noted in the Lommatzsch ERR report (13 December 1944), BAB, 30/50. The holdings from the Kyiv "Revolutionary Archive" are listed in the same ERR poster notice with the Dnipropetrovsk files mentioned above, in fn. 128.

[131] See above, p. 292, and p. 294n42 and the paragraphs preceding them.

[132] ERR Ostbücherei report (October–November 1944), BAB, NS 30/29.

[133] This according to a July 1946 report, Pshenichnyi, "Dokladnaia zapiska o prodelannoi rabote TsGAFFKD MVD UkrSSR za 1-e polugodie 1946 g." (13 July 1946), GA RF, 5325/2/1620, fol. 113.

[134] ERR report (1 August–30 September 1944), BAB, NS 30/122. The totals in this report come to 343, but it is not clear if all of these individuals were on the professional staff.

[135] ERR report ([?1944]), CDJC, CXLI–158. Other sources suggest closer to two million.

The last reports from the Ratibor operation from late January 1945 attest to the fact that the ERR did not have sufficient rolling stock to evacuate many of their Ratibor holdings westward. A remaining ERR agent "was prepared to destroy the materials there with gasoline and canisters readied for the task." However, they decided not to destroy the Ostbücherei, as there was still some hope of evacuating it or of returning to use it again, if the war situation changed. Otherwise, they assumed the abandoned materials would be "captured by the Bolsheviks."[136] The Ukrainian Fourth Army liberated the Ratibor area in late February and March of 1945, but there are no reports that Soviet forces were aware that there had been a Nazi center there.

In fact, in the end, the ERR was unable to evacuate many of its Ratibor holdings, including the massive Ostbücherei. Parts of the library materials reached intermediary points on the evacuation route. The Nazis abandoned a large segment of their foreign archival and library loot near the castle of Pless (*Pol.* Pszczyna), which had housed one of the major ERR operational units in the Ratibor area. The Red Army found many of materials still in shipping crates in the railroad station in Pless, and a nearby rail junction, Czechowice-Dziedzice about 50 km. to the east of Ratibor. The shipment of books, periodicals, and other ERR-seized cultural treasures from the USSR required 12 full freight cars. Four freight cars alone were needed for the Communist Party Archive from Smolensk Oblast, which the ERR had moved to Pless from Vilnius in the summer of 1944. But none of the Red Army reports available mention any materials of Ukrainian provenance there, nor any ERR records or other archival loot.[137]

---

[136] ERR Stabsführer Gerhard Utikal to Rosenberg, "Aktenvermerk für den Reichsleiter—"Dienstgut in Oberschlesien" (25 January 1945), BAB, NS 8/261; another copy in NS 30/7 is cited in significant sections by de Vries, *Sonderstab Musik*, pp. 57–58. ERR evacuation sites in the Bamberg/Staffelstein area were headquartered in the nearby town of Lichtenfels at Schloss Banz, owned by Baron Kurt von Behr, who had directed ERR operations in Paris; they also included parts of the former Benedictine Abbey (or Convent—Kloster Banz), near Staffelstein, and another building within Staffelstein itself. Records found there, together with other Rosenberg ministerial (RMbO) records from Berlin, were recovered by the Western Allies and taken to the United States. Following further analysis and microfilming, they were returned to the Bundesarchiv in Koblenz in the 1950s, and are now held in the new archival facility in Berlin-Lichterfelde. Regarding the U.S. Army recovery, see my *Odyssey of the Smolensk Archive*, pp. 52–53.

[137] See the published Red Army reports about the library and archival materials found there, as edited by Valerii N. Shepelov, "Sud'ba 'Smolenskogo arkhiva,'" *Izvestiia TsK KPSS* 1991 (5): 135–38; the original documents are found in RGASPI, 17/125/308, fols. 11–18.

The segment of ERR records now in Kyiv, and more directly related to its eastern operations out of Berlin and Ratibor, had obviously not reached the ERR evacuation site in Castle Banz. The Kyiv records appear to have been acquired by TsDAVO from several different sources, although no reports of their "capture" have surfaced.[138] The largest group of ERR records in Kyiv (now *opys* 1 of the main record group) were officially transferred to the Central State Historical Archive in Kyiv (TsDIA URSR) in December 1945, having been received by the Committee on Cultural and Educational Institutions of the UkrSSR, reportedly among one of the trophy shipments from Dresden. It was placed in the Special Secret Division of TsDIA URSR (later TsDIAK).[139] Although much of Dresden itself was reduced to rubble in 1945, a major Soviet shipping unit had been established in the area. No reports have surfaced about where these ERR records were actually found, or confirmation about their recovery in Germany.

Three additional file units, predominantly with incoming reports to Berlin from the ERR Task Force in Belgium and the Netherlands are now are arranged as a separate fond in TsDAVO. These apparently were first deposited in TsDAZhR after the war. This may explain why they were not integrated with the more voluminous reports from that same Task Force that are currently interfiled in the first section (*opys* 1) of the main ERR record group from TsDIAK.[140]

A second group of files (*opys* 2), acquired from a different source and apparently also first deposited in TsDAZhR URSR, appears to contain fragmentary ERR administrative files from its Ratibor operations, predomi-

---

[138] Most of the ERR records now held in Kyiv are arranged in TsDAVO, fond 3676, with 5 *opysy*. A very helpful survey of the Ukrainian-related ERR materials held in fond 3676 in TsDAVO was prepared by Tat′iana M. Sebta, "Kyïvs′ka chastyna materialiv Ainzatsshtabu reikhsliaitera Rozenberga," *Arkhivy Ukraïny* 1997 (1–6): 53–73. See also the earlier, but generally inadequate survey published in Kyiv in 1994 cited above, Chapter 2, p. 52n5.

[139] The official acts of transfer when they were accessioned by the Special Secret Division of TsDIA URSR state that they were received from Dresden—Pashchin, Chairman of the Committee on Cultural and Educational Institutions of the SNK UkrSSR (Komitet po spravakh kul′turno-osvitnykh ustanov pry RNK URSR), to TsDIA URSR (12 December 1945), TsDAVO, 4703/2/3, fol. 1. That coincides with the official TsDIA URSR report for 1946 (12 January 1947) which notes the ERR records in the "Special Division of Secret Fonds [of TsDIA URSR]," TsDAVO, 4703/1/20, fol. 25.

[140] TsDAVO, fond 3674; but many more reports from that same Task Force are interfiled in fond 3676 (*opys* 1, nos. 139–239, passim).

nantly relating to housekeeping matters, lease of buildings, transport arrangements and personnel movements.[141] These may well have been captured in Silesia by Soviet forces, either near Ratibor or to the west on ERR evacuation routes.

There are three other groups of files in the main ERR fond in Kyiv, all of which were initially processed later in TsDAZhR. *Opys* 3 contains personnel files of ERR staff (48 files). The last two *opysy* in the fond, however, do not appear to belong with the ERR records, strictly speaking. *Opys* 4 contains extensive files of *Volksdeutsch* units operating in Ukraine, including maps and detailed information on many German settlements dating back to the eighteenth century, which German specialists had compiled. Of particular importance are the files of the RMbO Special Commando for *Volksdeutsch* headed by Dr. Karl Stumpp, one of the leading Nazi genealogists and author of several important works on German settlers in the Russian Empire. There are also a few other scattered ERR report files interfiled in this *opys* and some Gestapo files on numerous individuals and Ukrainian nationalist groups, all of which were transferred from MVD sources. *Opys* 5 contains a few fragmentary files from RMbO operations in Ukraine, including personnel files on teachers. This latter group was most probably abandoned in retreat by one of the RKU agencies.[142]

The main section of ERR operational records in TsDAVO (*opys* 1 and *opys* 2 of fond 3676 and fond 3674) include major runs of reports of the ERR Main Task Force Groups (HAG) in the Balkans, Belgium, the Netherlands, the Baltics, Western Russia, and Belarus, and of the HAG and subsidiary ERR units operating in Ukraine. The initial finding aid (*opys* 1) for fond 3676, prepared in TsDIA URSR after the war, includes rubrics for some of the ERR subgroups whose records are contained in that part of the fond (and even German names) and hence suggests more understanding of the contents and function of the agency than is apparent in more recent versions.[143]

---

[141] The first version of *opys* 2 was prepared in TsDAZhR in 1954 rather than TsDIAK.

[142] All of the last three *opysy* were also first processed in TsDAZhR and obviously came from different sources—*opys* 3 was first prepared in 1954, *opys* 4 in 1961, and *opys* 5 in 1964. Since 1991, new Ukrainian-language translated versions have been prepared for all five *opysy*, but there has been no attempt at rearrangement of the materials involved.

[143] The original *opys* 1 (now file no. 240 in *opys* 1) was in fact prepared in TsDIA URSR, as noted on the cover (with its original fond no. of 276s, corresponding to the fond no. listed for the ERR fond in TsDIA through 1949). Although integral blocks of files were kept relatively intact, many of the files from different ERR operations were

Hence the ERR records in TsDAVO are of pertinence to the entire occupied Soviet lands as well as many other European countries. Some of the records are apparently of Berlin provenance, although many ERR records from the early years of the war in the east (1941–1942) were destroyed in a Berlin bombing raid that destroyed one of the ERR headquarters buildings in 1943. Hence, many of these files may be of Ratibor provenance—that is, reports of field units to ERR headquarters—although some of the records were undoubtedly transferred from the earlier ERR headquarters in Berlin.

Of specific Ukrainian pertinence, numerous files contain reports and inventories prepared by ERR field units, including HAG Ukraine and its subsidiary groups, dealing with a wide range of cultural surveillance and looting operations. Many of them appear to be incoming reports or copies about ERR operations in Ukraine, which were addressed both to Berlin and Ratibor, and/or copies sent back and forth to other local ERR units. It is possible that these Ukrainian related sections were part of the operating records of ERR commando units in Ukraine that they sent out or brought with them during their retreat in 1943, when at least some members of the HAG Ukraine commando unit retired to the Austrian Tyrol after they left Ukraine.

Although still inadequately arranged for optimal research purposes, the Kyiv ERR files greatly expand the source-base for the study of ERR operations throughout occupied Soviet lands, as well as in the Balkans and Belgium. They are crucially important for documenting Nazi cultural seizures of all kinds, from archeological exhibits to films, paintings, and Soviet propaganda exhibits. The files include extensive documentation—often with precise inventories and shipping lists—on the shipment of libraries and archives from Ukraine, as well as similar activities in other parts of Europe.

In postwar decades, the ERR documentation, unfortunately, was inadequately analyzed and put to use by Soviet authorities for the purpose of tracing cultural loses. Although a few of the documents were extracted and published in documentary collections highlighting Nazi atrocities, there was no analysis of the ERR operations and the loot that the ERR removed from the USSR. NKVD archivists in that period had other priorities.

An eleven-page report prepared in 1947 on what is now *opys* 1 of the

---

intermingled when the documents were bound in seemingly helter-skelter order, and there are no sub-rubrics within the present *opys* 1. The most recent Ukrainian-language *opys* 1 is a translation of an earlier Russian one—both of them lack any rubric divisions or explanation about the source of the records or organization of the *opys*.

main ERR records shows the different groups of ERR materials involved.[144] The report emphasizes the value of the records to security services for "operational" purposes. It shows what segments of the ERR records might reveal or document wartime collaboration on the part of Soviet citizens with the Nazis. As is apparent in the marginal instructions throughout the report, the "operational" analysis principally involved preparation of reports on Soviet citizens who had been actively working with the Nazi occupation forces, and especially those whom the Nazis took with them westward in the process of retreat. There also is some evidence in the marginal annotations by V. P. Gudzenko, the Chief of Archival Administration of the NKVD UkrSSR, that Soviet authorities at that time were interested in analyzing the ERR documentation for identifying plundered cultural treasures and the shipments of library and archival materials from Soviet lands, but that would appear to have been a secondary concern. An endorsement on the top of one of the remaining archival copies instructs TsDIA Chief A. V. Bondarevskii that "the materials should be worked through and analyzed for operational and general state aims...[and that a report] on materials relating to other union republics should be sent to Moscow with an appropriate letter prepared for [the Chief of the Main Archival Administration of the MVD USSR] Nikitinskii."[145]

Not all the ERR materials and other documents acquired with them are still present in the two Kyiv ERR fonds. Some other original trophy archival materials and newspaper clippings that were received by TsDIAK with the ERR materials were listed in contemporary reports, but these were later siphoned off and arranged as separate fonds.[146]

When specialists in Kyiv processed the ERR materials in 1947, they separated out some 80 fragmentary fonds of Nazi-captured files of original French, German, and other Western provenance—predominantly personal papers that had been acquired together with the ERR materials. An initial list of 38 French-language fonds contained fragmentary records and personal papers of predominantly of French and Belgian Jewish and Masonic origin,

---

[144] "Kharakteristika dokumental'nykh materialov shtaba reikhsliaitera Rozenberga" (11 October 1947), presented over the signature of one of the deputy directors of TsDIA URSR, A. V. Bondarevskii—TsDAVO, 4703/2/12, fols. 3–13. The report clearly shows the different groups of ERR materials involved in what is now *opys* 1. The text of that 1947 TsDIA URSR survey together with a brief introductory commentary by the present author and Tan'ia Sebta is in preparation.

[145] Bondarevskii, "Kharakteristika," TsDAVO, 4703/2/12, fol. 3.

[146] Bondarevskii, "Kharakteristika dokumental'nykh materialov shtaba reikhsliaitera Rozenberga" (11 October 1947), TsDAVO, 4703/2/12, fols. 3–13.

including documentation of Jewish communities in France dating back to the eighteenth century.[147] A separate memorandum listed an additional 42 fragmentary fonds, identified later, that were predominantly of German and Austrian origin, and a forty-third group of "of manuscripts, letters, and photographs that had not been identified."[148]

It has recently come to light that some 150 kilograms of those ERR-looted files of foreign provenance were destroyed as waste paper, on orders from the Expert Appraisal Commission in Kyiv in 1953—"147 kg., 11 file units, and 10 cartons." A copy of the list of destroyed materials has recently come to light, showing most of them to be of French Jewish provenance, including fragmentary records of Jewish communities undoubtedly annihilated during World War II.[149] The rest of the original Western archival materials received with the ERR materials was sent to Moscow in 1956, although on the basis of administrative correspondence files of the archive, they were supposed to have been sent earlier in 1948.[150]

ERR Files in Moscow. Some additional scattered ERR files—with only a few original documents—are held in the former Special Archive (now part of

---

[147] A list of 38 fonds in the French language was presented with a descriptive memorandum by Bondarevskii to Gudzenko (11 July 1947), TsDAVO, 4703/2/10, fols. 19–20; with the separate list—"Spisok i kratkoe soderzhanie fondov i grupp dokumentov na frantsuzskom iazyke, vyiavlennykh v fonde 'Aenzatsshtaba Rozenberga'" [compiled by Vaisbergan?], signed by A. Bondarevskii (Kyiv, 26 November 1947), TsDAVO, 4703/2/10, fols. 33–40, 51–52 (cc fols. 41–50).

[148] The list was prepared over the signature of TsDIA director Oleinik [Oliinyk] and division head Skorokhedova (8 January 1948), TsDAVO, 4703/2/15.

[149] The official excerpt from the Commission protocol No. 026 is dated 30 June 1953; it designated 1 August 1953 as the date of destruction, but the promised copy of the list of ERR files to be destroyed is now missing in that file—TsDAVO, 4703/2/29, fols. 1–3. However, the eight-page list (in two copies) of the files destroyed was found among the TsDIAK appraisal commission records for 1953, TsDAVO, 4703/1/136, fols. 113–121 (a second copy follows, fols. 122–129). More details about these materials, and the published list, will appear in my forthcoming report on the ERR Silesian operations.

[150] See the official letter from the chief of the Archival Administration of the UkrSSR, Pil'kevich, to the director of TsDIA URSR, Oleinik (4 August 1953), complaining about the non-fulfillment of the 4 April 1948 transfer order—TsDAVO, 4703/2/17, fol. 69. Later records of the transfers in 1956 have been located elsewhere, together with detailed inventories of the transferred materials, TsDAVO, 4703/1/192, fols. 105–180.

RGVA) in Moscow. Although their exact provenance or point of capture has not yet been determined, over half of them were forwarded to TsGOA from Minsk in 1955, and hence undoubtedly were received there with some of the book shipments that had come from Silesia.[151] In contrast to the Kyiv ERR records, the fragmentary files in RGVA (former TsGOA holdings) contain only a few stray reports of book shipments and inventories of library and other materials being prepared for shipment, including some from Novgorod, Voronezh, Kursk, and more from Kyiv. They add little to what we know from the much more extensive reports and other materials in Kyiv and the other important collections of ERR records long available in the West.

Most intriguing in Moscow is the ERR inspection card file that was only added to the fond in TsKhIDK in April 1994, having earlier been held separate in one of the Glavarkhiv SSSR offices. Details about its recovery or transfer to Moscow are not available, but reportedly it was found in Silesia by the Poles and transferred at some point to Moscow, since all of the cards cover Soviet territories. The cards served to register cultural sites and their contents considered important by the ERR, including archives. The cards themselves provide only summary information, and just a few indicate ERR plans for evacuation. They thus need to be consulted in connection with the more detailed ERR reports and shipping lists found in the Kyiv ERR records. Most were compiled between the fall of 1941 and mid-1942. The cards cover cultural monuments and treasures, including archives, in former Soviet territories, ranging from the Baltic countries to Crimea. A facsimile of the cards covering Russian, Belarusian, and Ukrainian lands, with Russian translation was issued in printed format in 1998.[152] Commentary and annotations are provided with the Russian translations, including citations from numerous relevant documents from the Kyiv ERR records.

Like the RSHA and the Heeresarchiv records in Moscow discussed above, the ERR records in Kyiv need to be reprocessed (together with the few in Moscow) with more professional arrangement and description. Because these important groups of trophy archives in both Moscow and Kyiv involve the records of key Nazi agencies that were themselves involved in the

[151] The scattered ERR files in RGVA (former TsGOA holdings) now constitute fond no. 1401K (with 76 file units); 43 of them were received from Minsk in 1955, as reported to the author by TsKhIDK archivists.

[152] *Kartoteka "Z" Operativnogo shtaba "Reikhsliaiter Rozenberg": Tsennosti kul'tury na okkupirovannykh territoriiakh Rossii, Ukrainy i Belorusi, 1941–1942,* comp. and with an intro. by Mikhail A. Boitsov and Tat'iana A. Vasil'eva (Moscow: Izd-vo Moskovskogo universiteta, 1998) [="Trudy istoricheskogo fakul'teta MGU," 5; Istoricheskie istochniki, 1].

plunder and displacement of Europe's archives and other cultural treasures, they hold the clues to the record of that plunder and displacement. Not only do they require better arrangement and description, but they should also be made publicly accessible in their entirety on microform, at least as an interim step towards restitution to their homeland. Eventually, they need to be united with the contingent files of those same Nazi agencies that are now in Germany, along with other fragments that remain scattered throughout the Continent.

CHAPTER 9

Émigré Archival Ucrainica Retrieved: Prague, Kyiv, and Moscow

Émigré Rossica and Ucrainica and the End of the RZIA in Prague

Postwar Retrieval Incentives. The extensive Ukrainian émigré-related documentation that was brought to Kyiv after the war now constitutes the most significant component of Soviet postwar archival plunder for the archival heritage of Ukraine. At the time one large component was officially presented as a "friendship gift" of the Czechoslovak government to the Ukrainian SSR. And even today many would argue that the shipment of one freight wagon of materials from the Ukrainian Historical Cabinet (UIK) from Prague to Kyiv, like the much larger shipment to Moscow of nine wagons from the Russian Foreign Historical Archive (RZIA), should be considered neither "plunder" nor "trophy" archives. Others—this author in-cluded—demur and insist that its status as a gift should remain in quotation marks. As we will see, those shipments represent only a portion of the postwar retrieval of archival Ucrainica as well as Rossica. Yet, contrary to popular opinion, most of the émigré archival "Ucrainica" transferred from Prague and elsewhere in Europe in the wake of the war is now held in Kyiv, not in the Russian Federation.

The Soviet archival authorities in Moscow who ordered the seizures made no distinction between "Rossica" and "Ucrainica"—or sometimes more correctly "Sovietica" (also including Ucrainica). Those actual terms, however, were rarely used in the operations. The émigré component of the extensive postwar Soviet archival seizures consisted of two prime categories. First, the Soviets sought out twentieth-century émigré materials relating to the Civil War and foreign intervention, Ukrainian attempts to establish an independent state, the White political emigration, and records of Russian and Ukrainian émigré communities abroad during the interwar period.

A second high-level priority for the Soviet authorities was material relating to the international labor and revolutionary movement that was considered of prime "historical-scientific" value in the context of "Sovietica." These included records of Russian and Ukrainian non-Bolshevik factions, such as the Mensheviks and Socialist Revolutionaries (SRs), as well as non-Russian Marxist elements. Most of this second category of records were deposited in the former Central Party Archive (*now* RGASPI), although most of the non–later-CP émigré components went to the Central State Archive of the October Revolution of the USSR (TsGAOR SSSR, *now* GA RF) in Moscow.[1]

In neither category was the distinction made as to whether the files involved were of provenance within the lands of the former Russian Empire or Soviet Union and then alienated, or whether they had been created abroad in exile or emigration. These were retrieved by Soviet archival scouts everywhere they were found, from Prague and Poděbrady to émigré caches in Sofia and Manchuria. Other émigré materials that were seized had earlier been captured from West European sources by Nazi archival scouts for their "anti-Bolshevik" research operations mentioned earlier. In the policy of Soviet authorities, they were all subject to seizure.

The intellectual background and rationale for current archival Ucrainica retrieval efforts abroad are quite different. Today the aim is to open Ukrainian historical and cultural research in the broadest possible extent, and to reunite the Ukrainian diaspora with the now independent homeland. Present efforts and the rationale behind them should be seen first and foremost as stemming from the renaissance of a national historical and cultural identity in Ukraine in the wake of the collapse of the Soviet Union. Freed from the narrow shackles of Soviet ideology and its concomitant cultural iron curtain, Ukrainian scholars and cultural leaders have been acutely aware of the need to rewrite their political and cultural history based on newly opened archives at home and access to Western interpretive literature and divergent methodologies. Equally important, they are anxious to redefine their own historiographic and cultural context following decades of a political regime that sought to redefine Ukrainian culture in a narrow Soviet and often russified Soviet image. Today, Ukrainian intellectuals of all shades in the political spectrum are seeking reintegration with the "lost" or exiled Ukrainian history and culture in emigration.

---

[1] For a discussion of the search for Russian- and Ukrainian-related émigré materials and more details about some of the seizures and collections brought back to Moscow mentioned below, see also my *Archival Rossica—Rationalizing the Search and Retrieval of the Russian Archival Legacy Abroad* (Amsterdam: IISH, forthcoming). See also my earlier articles, "Archival Rossica/Sovietica Abroad: Provenance or Pertinence, Bibliographic and Descriptive Needs," *Cahiers du Monde russe et soviétique* 34(3) 1993, esp. pp. 449–52, 463–65, and the earlier Russian variant "Zarubezhnaia arkhivnaia Rossika i Sovetika. Proiskhozhdenie dokumentov ili ikh otnoshenie k istorii Rossii (SSSR): Potrebnost' v opisanii i bibliografii," *Otechestvennye arkhivy* 1993 (1): 20–53.

In the process today, however, Ukrainian political and intellectual leaders often tend to look abroad to try to find archival Ucrainica in exile, but they appear to be unaware of the even more important, and perhaps even sensational, Ucrainica that was seized by Soviet authorities and brought back to Kyiv after World War II. While they are anxious to travel abroad in search of Ucrainica, they overlook the exiled Ucrainica that was already retrieved in the postwar decades, but that was kept hidden for "utilization" only by the security services—and never described and made available to the public. Accordingly, we should survey these extensive postwar retrieval operations. In the decade since the archival doors were thrown open, not a single new guide or even brief list of fonds has appeared in print in Ukraine, not to mention preliminary electronic or typescript form. Once these extensive collections are made known, the public will have reason to appreciate the extensive archival Ucrainica that was brought back to Ukraine after the war. At the same time, one cannot avoid the realization of the sinister purpose of its retrieval and the operational, anti-Ukrainian purposes for which it was employed during its long suppression from the public eye.

In the 1940s, a few individuals in Moscow emphasized the scholarly and cultural as opposed to the operational value of seizing archival Rossica abroad. Most particularly, the well-known Bolshevik intellectual Vladimir V. Bonch-Bruevich, who survived the 1930s as director of the State Literary Museum in Moscow, wrote a now-famous letter to Stalin in February 1945 outlining the most aggressive possible plan for retrieval of Russian- (and by implication Ukrainian-) related archival and manuscript holdings.[2] Written as the victorious Red Army was advancing through Eastern Europe, he predicted, "Germany itself would soon be utterly routed and the time for reparations would be immediately at hand."[3] He identified major collections of Rossica "held within the aggressor countries and their satellites (i.e., Germany, Austria, Romania, Hungary, Finland, and Bulgaria)" and strongly recommended, "while it is possible, to confiscate such archives from abroad either in whole or in part and join them to our Soviet holdings." He

---

[2]   Bonch-Bruevich to Stalin (24 February 1945), RGASPI, 71/125/308, fols. 2–8 (unsigned copy, received by Zhdanov's office 5 March 1945). Initial manuscript and typewritten drafts remain among Bonch-Bruevich's papers in RGB OR, 369/206/11, fols. 28–34 and fols. 35–40. The original signed copy has not yet been located. In a September 1994 communication, the Archive of the President of the Russian Federation (AP RF) reported to me that neither a copy nor any related materials were found there. The text (from the RGASPI copy) is published by Pavel Knyshevskii, *Dobycha: Tainy germanskikh reparatsii* (Moscow: "Soratnik," 1994), pp. 89–94.

[3]   Bonch-Bruevich to Stalin (24 February 1945), fols. 2–8.

continued:

> I recommend that such archives should be confiscated from those
> countries completely and entirely—Russian manuscripts, docu-
> ments, correspondence, portraits, engravings, paintings, valuable
> rare books from libraries, substantial specialty objects among
> others, and even all Slavonic manuscript books. Most importantly
> from Germany—all Russian materials, all Slavic materials, with
> nothing left behind.[4]

In contrast to his NKVD and other archival imperialist contemporaries,
Bonch-Bruevich added the important caveat that such confiscation had as its
ultimate aim "thorough study, and—even more importantly—quality
scholarly publications." He emphasized "the extent to which such materials
are needed for our history, for our literature, and for our scholarship."[5] Had
his recommendations been followed, fewer medieval Slavic manuscripts or
important Rossica and Ucrainica would remain in Germany and other East
European repositories today.

Stalin's security henchman and Commissar of Internal Affairs, Lavrentii
Beria, and his archival scouts, in contrast, were most interested in Rossica
(and Ucrainica, although never so labeled), not because it represented "lost
elements" of Russian culture that would be the basis "for scholarly editions,"
but because it could serve as a tool for secret police and intelligence "operational" aims to identify members of various émigré factions involved in "anti-
Soviet" activities and those who had collaborated with the Nazis. Bonch-
Bruevich's letter went to Andrei Zhdanov, who headed one of the main
ideological and cultural offices in the CP Central Committee, and thence was
forwarded to Deputy Commissar of Foreign Affairs Lozovskii (pseud. of
Solomon A. Dzidzo).[6] Lozovskii approved Bonch-Bruevich's plan, although
in his formulation, the search for Rossica was understandably in third place
after the tasks of: "(1) retrieval of all documentary materials taken by the
Germans during the Great Patriotic War 1941–45," and "(2) retrieval of
documentation taken by the Germans from Russia during the First World
War and the period of intervention in Ukraine in 1918." Zhdanov agreed.[7]

---

4   Ibid., fol. 3.

5   Ibid. fols. 3, 7–8.

6   The copy of Bonch-Bruevich's letter cited above from RGASPI was stamped as
having been received by Zhdanov's office 5 March 1945. A resolution by Zhdanov at
the top notes that a copy was to be sent to Deputy Foreign Minister "t. Lozovskii with
the request to present his reaction."

7   As explained by Nikitinskii to Deputy Commissar of Internal Affairs S. N.
Kruglov (16 May 1945), GA RF, fond 5325/2/1353, fol. 33.

Even before the Nazi capitulation, the Ukrainian Commissar of Internal Affairs Valentin Riasnoi telegraphed Beria on 4 May 1945 that valuable archival materials removed by the Nazi authorities from Ukraine were being held in Troppau (*Czech* Opava) and Berlin. But of even higher political importance, he noted that "in Berlin and Prague, and other cities, there were Ukrainian-German nationalist organizations which held a tremendous quantity of documents having scientific and operational interest." In his traditional red crayon across the transcript of the top secret telegram, Beria ordered action.[8] A Ukrainian search team set out soon after to Czechoslovakia to retrieve materials plundered by the Nazis. Equally important, retrieval operations also targeted, in the euphemism of Moscow archival leaders, "archives of foreign provenance having operational and scientific-historical significance for our country."[9] Most valuable for "operational" aims were the Russian and Ukrainian émigré collections in Prague. Soviet authorities (especially those from Moscow), considered such émigré collections of top priority because they would potentially provide information about "counter-revolutionary nationalist elements" and their "anti-Soviet activities."

The End of RZIA in Prague. Bonch-Bruevich's most important prize was the Russian Foreign Historical Archive—RZIA (Russkii zagranichnyi istoricheskii arkhiv, sometimes translated as the "Russian Historical Archive Abroad"), the extensive "Russian Archive under the auspices of the Ministry of Foreign Affairs," which he had been able to visit during one of his trips to Czechoslovakia. He mentioned the "tremendous wealth of manuscript and epistolary literature of the nineteenth century" there and in the Prague museums with "many interesting documents relating to the Civil War." He had described this archive in a personal appeal to Stalin already in 1935 and quoted Edvard Beneš's agreement to assist with photocopying efforts:

> "...it would be nice for you to see all of those collections in one place," he [Beneš] said to me. "You can address the matter to me," and added that, "the matter should be included in our cultural agreement."[10]

---

[8]   Riasnoi telegram to Beria (4 May 1945), GA RF, 5325/10/2029, fol. 2; see the typed copy with Beria's instruction in red crayon (fol. 1).

[9]   "Spravka o rezul'tatakh raboty GAU NKVD SSSR po vozvrashcheniiu v Sovetskii Soiuz dokumental'nykh materialakh Gosudarstvennogo arkhivnogo fonda SSSR i o vyvoze v SSSR arkhivov inostrannogo proiskhozhdeniia," signed by Golubtsov and Kuz'min (15 December 1945), GA RF, 5325/10/2148, fol. 1.

[10]   Bonch-Bruevich to Stalin (5 July 1935), RGB OR, 369/206/10, fol. 47–47v (signed typewritten copy).

Having failed to obtain the funds needed for copying in the mid-1930s, ten years later, Bonch-Bruevich was much more aggressive in his plea for the acquisition of RZIA, which, he assured Stalin in 1945, "Beneš would be prepared to present to the Soviet Union."[11]

The Russian Foreign Historical Archive (RZIA), founded initially in 1923, came under the auspices of the Czech Ministry of Foreign Affairs in 1928. It was unquestionably the most important archival center for politically sensitive materials that were taken abroad after 1917 and created in exile by the Russian, Ukrainian, and Belarusian émigrés. Regular published reports starting in 1929 show the prewar development of the collections.[12] RZIA had agents throughout Europe actively searching out and soliciting archival materials for donations or purchase. The RZIA Documentary Division was long headed by Aleksandr Filaretovich Iziumov (1885–1951), who had served as an archivist in Russia in the early post-revolutionary years before he was arrested and exiled abroad in 1922 for his participation in the People's Socialist Party. He had been active in the development of RZIA after settling in Prague in 1925, and in 1935 was named Deputy Director, also continuing to head the Documentary Division.[13]

A separate Ukrainian Historical Cabinet (UIK) was organized in 1929, also under the Czech Foreign Ministry, which provided funding for the operation through the interwar period. While housed in the same building (Toskanský Palace, Prague IV, Loretánské nam. 109), the two archives

---

[11] Ibid., fol. 6. Bonch-Bruevich had been negotiating photocopies since the mid-1930s; his earlier activities in this regard are analyzed in the study in my *Archival Rossica—Rationalizing the Search.*

[12] Annual reports started with 1929, although not all of them were published separately: *Russkii zagranichnyi istoricheskii arkhiv pri Ministerstve inostrannykh del Chekhoslovatskoi respubliki v 1929 godu* (Prague, [1930]); through ...*v 1931* (Prague, 1932; [microfiche=IDC-R-11,233]), and ...*v 1936 g.* (Prague, 1936; [microfiche= IDC-R-11,236]). Archival materials collected during the first ten years were surveyed by Aleksandr F. Iziumov, *Otdel dokumentov. Russkii zagranichnyi istoricheskii arkhiv v Prage (1923–1932 gg.)* ([Prague, 1932]; [microfiche=IDC-R-11,232], updated from the article version published in *Ročenka slovanského ústavu,* vol. 4 (1931), pp. 228–45; his contribution to the 1936 annual report (pp. 12–21) updates the 1932 coverage, and lists recent acquisitions (p. 45). Copies of these reports and other typescript ones are filed with the RZIA administrative records, GA RF, 7030/1/20, 21, 28, 30, 39, 114, among others.

[13] Regarding Iziumov, see Tat'iana F. Pavlova, "A. F. Iziumov i RZIA," *Otechestvennye arkhivy* 1996 (4): 28–37. A few files from Iziumov's personal papers constitute a separate fond in GA RF (fond R-5962; 29 units; 1922–1940).

"worked independently," according to Iziumov, who claims he "did not even know the contents of the Ukrainian Archive," although "to be sure some Ukrainian documentation was also held in the Russian Archive."[14] A Belarusian Archive, established as a separate entity under the Czech Foreign Ministry in 1933 parallel to UIK, constituted a second, but much smaller, RZIA subsidiary.[15]

After the Nazi annexation of the Sudetenland in 1938, and establishment of the Nazi Protectorate of Bohemia and Moravia, control over the RZIA, UIK, and Belarusian collections was transferred to the Ministry of Internal Affairs. Efforts of the Russian and Ukrainian émigré community in Prague to evacuate the archive to the West were unsuccessful, including proposals for its sale or transfer to the United States.[16] The Nazis imprisoned Iziumov in June 1941, and hence were deprived of the most knowledgeable RZIA archivist.

During the war, the Nazis left the collections in Prague, although they removed most of the military-related materials from RZIA to a branch of the Reich Military Archive (Heeresarchiv) in the building of the Czech Military Museum in Žižkov in the outskirts of Prague.[17] The Nazis had detailed

---

[14] Aleksandr Iziumov, "Zapiska o Russkom Istoricheskom Arkhive," in Sergei Porfir'evich Postnikov, *Politika, ideologiia, byt i uchenye trudy russkoi èmigratsii: 1918–1945: Bibliografiia. Iz kataloga biblioteki RZI arkhiva*, ed. Sergei Blinov, 2 vols. (New York: Norman Ross Publishing, 1993), vol. 2, p. 406. The manuscript of Iziumov's July 1945 report on RZIA remained with the RZIA administrative records transferred to Moscow with the RZIA collections, GA RF, 7030/1/95, fols. 1–15.

[15] A brief notice about the Belarusian Archive in Prague prepared by its director, Tomash Hryb, "Belaruski zahranichny arkhiŭ u Praze," *Kalos'se: Belaruski literaturna-navukovy chasapis* (Vilnius) 1 (1935): 72, explains the organization of the archive along the lines of RZIA, but does not describe the holdings.

[16] Pavlova documents Iziumov's attempts to find a home for RZIA in America—"A. F. Iziumov i RZIA," p. 35. Iziumov recalls an offer of $1,000,000, which he considered inadequate—Iziumov, "Zapiska o Russkom Istoricheskom Arkhive," p. 407.

[17] A report filed with the RZIA transfer documents in GA RF provides more details of wartime developments—GA RF, 5325/10/2024. See also the earlier published article on wartime developments by Václav Pešák, "Zpráva o činnosti Ruského historického archivu, Ukrajinského historického kabinetu a Běloruského archivu v létech 1939–1946," *Ročenka slovanského ústavu v Praze*, vol. 12, *Za léta 1939–1946* (Prague, 1947), pp. 211–21, but there is no specific identification of important groups of holdings, nor reference to Nazi documentation and RZIA reports from the wartime period, which have since become available.

German-language inventories prepared of those files that were transferred.[18] Iziumov later suggested that the Germans removed one-fifth of the archive which was probably taken to Berlin.[19] However, no other available sources indicate any significant Nazi archival seizures that left Prague, and the majority of the collections remained in Prague when the Red Army liberated the city from Nazi control in May 1945.[20]

Belarusian émigrés, however, were more successful in removing the Belarusian Archive from Prague, although its fate is still unknown. Mikola Abramchyk, who headed the Belarusian People's Republic (BNR) after the death of its exiled president, Vasil' Zakharka, in Prague in 1943, reportedly managed to take "two suitcases" of BNR files to Paris in 1943. While Abramchyk's papers still remain in private hands in Paris, the rest of the Prague materials that had come to be known as the Krechevskii-Zakharka Archive have disappeared.[21] So far as is known, only a few Belarusian files that had been accessioned directly by RZIA itself were included in the RZIA transfers to Moscow, and none went to Minsk.[22] One Prague specialist

---

[18] The German typescript inventories describing the documents transferred are preserved with the RZIA administrative records in Moscow, GA RF, 7030/1/103a (1941, 390 p.), 103b (476 p.), and 119 (1942—through no. 10,265). The inventories reflect the order of the accession numbers by which they had been listed in RZIA.

[19] Iziumov, "Zapiska o Russkom Istoricheskom Arkhive v Prague," p. 406. Iziumov, who was freed from Nazi prison in June 1945, was apparently unaware of the extent of transfers to the branch Heeresarchiv in Prague, or may have been repeating rumors in Prague.

[20] In addition to sources available in Moscow, files and reports about the wartime operation of the archive itself are held in the records the Ministry of Internal Affairs in the State Archive in Prague—Státní ústřední archiv III, Ministerstvo vnitra, nová registratura (especially P 1411–P 1313, k. 5488–5489). My colleagues from the Institute of Ukrainian Archeography in Kyiv and I studied them in August 1991.

[21] See Hanna A. Surmach, "Belorusskii zagranichnyi arkhiv," in *"Russkaia, ukrainskaia i belorusskaia èmigratsiia" 1995,* vol. 1, pp. 85–90; and her later report, "Poshuki strachanykh arkhivaŭ pa historyi belaruskai dziarzhaŭnastsi (Praha, Maskva, Paryzh)," in *Restytutsyia kul'turnykh kashtoŭnastsei,* pp. 185–88. Mikola Abramchyk succeeded Vasil' Zakharka as president of the Council of the Belarus People's Republic (BNR) in exile. According to this account, Surmach reports—based on a memoir source—that the files taken to Paris in 1943, together with some of his own files from the government in exile for the period 1943–1970, remain with Abramchyk's widow Madame Liaŭkovich.

[22] See Nina Stuzhynskaia, "Materyaly pa historyi Belarusi u Ruskim zamezhnym histarychnym arkhive," in *Restytutsyia kul'turnykh kashtoŭnastsei,* pp. 188–92.

suggests that at least part of the Belarusian archive remained in Prague, but there is no information there about its subsequent fate.[23] Further efforts are needed to determine exactly what may have survived in Paris or elsewhere and to insure that it has found a suitable archival home.

Bonch-Bruevich may well have been one of the first to alert the Soviet leadership as early as the mid-1930s regarding RZIA's riches, and later recommend transfer to Moscow after the war. We do not know the extent to which his discussions with Beneš may well have been instrumental in preparing the way for the Czech "gift" of those collections to Russia and Ukraine, but official negotiations in 1945 were conducted without him. The Soviet appropriation of the RZIA and UIK holdings in 1945 and their shipment to Moscow and Kyiv illustrate well the nature of Soviet-style archival retrieval and repatriation and the traditional Soviet attitudes towards émigré archival Rossica and Ucrainica abroad during the Cold War years. In June 1945, an article in *Pravda* had already announced the "gift of the Czech government to the Academy of Sciences of the USSR."[24] A few days later, the Commissariat of Internal Affairs declared that "the documentary materials in RZIA should be considered an integral part of the State Archival Fond of the USSR and should be returned to the Soviet Union." Commissar of Foreign Affairs Viacheslav Molotov was requested "to make the appropriate official request to the diplomatic representation of the government of the Czechoslovak Republic for [its] return."[25]

The most detailed recent Russian study of RZIA does not reveal the still untold full story of the transfer negotiations, nor does it take into account the potential strong émigré objections to the transfer of RZIA to the USSR at that time.[26] American Slavist George Fischer visited Prague in the summer of

---

[23]   Vladimir Bystrov, "Konets Russkogo zagranichnogo istoricheskogo arkhiva v Prage," in *"Russkaia, ukrainskaia i belorusskaia èmigratsiia" 1995,* vol. 1, pp. 79–80.

[24]   The *Pravda* announcement appeared on 18 June 1945—"Dar Akademii nauk SSSR ot Chekhoslovatskogo pravitel'stva" (TASS, 17 June 1945), *Pravda* 18 June 1945.

[25]   Chernytsov to Molotov (22 June 1945), GA RF, 5325/2/1353, fol. 51; another copy is found in a top secret "special file" addressed to Molotov, GA RF, 9401/2/103, fols. 208v–209. RZIA had been declared part of the State Archival Fond of the USSR already on 27 March 1941, according to a SNK *postanovlenie* (no. 723).

[26]   See Tat'iana F. Pavlova, "Russkii zagranichnyi istoricheskii arkhiv v Prage," *Voprosy istorii* 1990 (11): 19–30, the first scholarly account about RZIA to appear in the period of glasnost. The most detailed study of RZIA is Pavlova's unpublished dissertation—I appreciate Pavlova making her typescript available to me. See also the

1948; by that time, the archive was already in Moscow, and his report presented few details about the fate of RZIA.[27] As he realized, however, the fate of the archive was caught up in higher politics, not unlike the documentation in its important contents. That point of view was voiced at a 1995 conference in Prague devoted to the Russian, Ukrainian, and Belarusian interwar emigration in Czechoslovakia. The "political" factors involved in the "End of RZIA in Prague" are well documented by Czech journalist and translator Vladimir Bystrov.[28]

The Russian émigré community in Prague that collected the archive undoubtedly intended for its eventual return to Russia. When RZIA came under the Czech Foreign Ministry in 1928, it was agreed that "that RZIA might be transferred to Russia "only when power would be changed from the Communist Party dictatorship" to a political power that would "guarantee legal order, personal freedom, societal self-government, and the legal return of the present emigration to Russia."[29] After the triumphal Red Army raised the Soviet flag in Berlin in May 1945, many among the émigré community were impressed with Stalin's victory over Hitler and had hopes for a better future in the USSR. Aleksandr Iziumov, recovering from incarceration under the Nazis, lent his support to the RZIA transfer to Moscow. In his memoir prepared after the transfer to Moscow had been decided, he realized that "sooner or later the archive would be returned to the Motherland." He considered that "the gift to the Academy of Sciences made my stay outside the Motherland appear as a business trip (*sluzhebnaia komandirovka*), which I had done all in my power to fulfill."[30] Nevertheless, Iziumov himself chose to remain in Prague.

Others undoubtedly would not have agreed that the time was ripe in 1945 for RZIA's transfer to Moscow, although at that point, they had no choice in the matter. Some, like Lev Magerovskii, who had headed the RZIA newspaper division, fled to the United States. Sergei Porfir'evich Postnikov (1883–1965), who headed the RZIA library, was tried, convicted for his

---

1990 interview by Natal'ia Davydova with MGIAI specialist Valerii Sedel'nikov, "Arkhiv, o kotorom dolgo molchali," *Moskovskie novosti* 15 (15 March 1990): 16.

[27] See George Fischer, "The Russian Archive in Prague," *American Slavic and East European Review* 8 (December 1949): 289–95.

[28] Bystrov, "Konets RZIA," pp. 70–84.

[29] Bystrov quotes from the 1928 protocol of transfer from Zemgor, "Konets RZIA," p. 75. A copy of the RZIA transfer papers from Zemgor are preserved with the RZIA records in Moscow.

[30] Iziumov, "Zapiska o Russkom Istoricheskom Arkhive v Prague," p. 407.

membership in the Socialist Revolutionary Party, and imprisoned in the USSR. Although he survived his years in prison and exile and returned to live his final years in Prague, two other RZIA librarians who were incarcerated perished.[31]

Bystrov raises the ugly specter of the politically incriminating documentation in the archive for these and many others of the Russian and Ukrainian émigré community in Czechoslovakia who were in fact imprisoned in the postwar decade. Bystrov reminds us that, indeed, such political and human factors need to be considered today in understanding the context of the "gifts," or what others would call "seizures," including the disregard for the wishes of émigrés whose papers were on "deposit" in RZIA and UIK. And it is not surprising to hear Czechs speak out today in complaint that they never received the promised microfilms of the materials after they arrived in Moscow and Kyiv.[32]

The Ukrainian Historical Cabinet (UIK) in Prague. When it was established in 1929 under the Czech Ministry of Foreign Affairs, the Ukrainian Historical Cabinet (UIK) was enriched by materials held earlier by the Ukrainian National Museum-Archive—UNMA (Ukraïns'kyi natsional'nyi Muzei-arkhiv) in Prague, which had been active during the 1920s. Receipts for the archive, earlier held in the museum, started in 1925. The first 29 collections (most received on deposit) had been received before the separate Ukrainian Cabinet was established in 1929.[33] A complete item-by-item inventory now held in Kyiv covers the archival materials and books from the museum (nos. 1–3232), over half of which are manuscripts, and photographs (nos. 1–1927), all of which were apparently kept together as a separate

---

[31]   Regarding Postnikov, see the biographical note in the posthumous publication of his bibliography—Sergei Porfir'evich Postnikov, *Politika, ideologiia, byt i uchenye trudy russkoi èmigratsii: 1918–1945: Bibliografiia. Iz kataloga biblioteki RZI arkhiva*, ed. Sergei Blinov, 2 vols., introduction by Edward Kasinec and Robert H. Davis, Jr. (New York: Norman Ross Publishing, 1993), vol. 1, pp. vii–ix. Bystrov names the librarians who perished, Petr Bovrovskii and Nikolai Tsvetkov, in "Konets RZIA," p. 79.

[32]   Although not included in the official act of transfer, the provision for microfilms was one of the items in the preliminary agreement. See the 22 August letter to Ambassador Zorin reproduced below in Appendix VIII. See "Konets RZIA," p. 78.

[33]   A separate handwritten summary register briefly lists the early collections received by name of the person responsible for transfer—owner, donor or from whom purchased—TsDAVO, 3866/1/23, fols. 1–9. For the other part of this register see fn. 52, below.

collection within UIK.[34] Additional detailed registers of the other documentary materials acquired by UIK were prepared. File-level descriptions remain for most archival groups (institutional records, personal papers, or collections) that were received later (i.e., those numbered 451 to 549). These were transferred to Kyiv with the collections themselves and could now serve as a comprehensive guide to the riches of UIK in the form in which they were originally arranged in Prague.[35] UIK, however, never took over all of the Ukrainian materials already deposited in RZIA. Important Ukrainian documentation, including many groups of UNR files, continued to be either purchased by or donated to RZIA as part of more general collections. This Ukraine-oriented collection activity in RZIA continued even after the formation of UIK.

During the first two years of operation, UIK was headed by the ethnographer and poet Mykhailo Obidnyi (Myxajlo Obidnyj), with Arkadii Zhyvotko (Arkadij Životko) and another assistant.[36] There had been a third assistant the first year, at the end of which a printed report of limited

[34] The handwritten inventory register covering the UNMA holdings is held with the other UIK records in TsDAVO, 3866/1/33. The printed and manuscript materials (nos. 1–3232, fols. 1–152) are listed with dates of receipt and designated accordingly. The 1,344 photographs are listed later in the volume, starting with 1927 acquisitions (nos. 1–1344).

[35] Two handwritten inventory registers (vols. 2 and 3) are held with the other UIK records in TsDAVO, 3866/1/34 and 36. No. 36 (labeled vol. II), covers archival groups nos. 451–487; no. 34 (labeled vol. III) covers archival groups nos. 488–549. Three inventory registers are mentioned in the act of transfer, although only two are specified as being transferred (nos. 451–588 [*sic*]). See the text in Appendix VIII, §5, and fns. 51 and 56, below). In July 1999, when I was first able to survey these materials, archivists could not find the first volume, which, as indicated in the act of transfer, covers archival groups nos. 1–450. The multiple manuscript corrections and lack of order or precision in the present *opys* of fond 3866 makes it very difficult to determine if the first volume is in fact missing or was never transferred. The inventory register covering the earlier UNMA collections (3866/1/33; see above fn. 34]) is now marked (in pencil) on its cover as "Documentary Division, vol. 1," although that could not be the missing first volume.

[36] Arkadii Zhyvotko (1890–1948) had been active in the Ukrainian Party of Socialist Revolutionaries during his student days in St. Petersburg, and in 1917–1918, he represented Voronezh in the Central Rada. After emigrating to Prague, he taught at the Ukrainian Pedagogical Institute. Zhyvotko fled to West Germany at the end of the war, where he directed the Aschaffenburg branch of the Museum-Archive of the Ukrainian Academy of Arts and Sciences until his death in 1948.

circulation was prepared.[37] By the years 1934–1936, however, Arkadii Zhyvotko was running UIK alone, or at least he had no paid assistant. He prepared a five-year report at the end of 1935, but it was not published. By that time the documentary fond numbered 78,895 folios.[38] Active accessioning continued of many important Ukrainian archival collections— acquired by gift or purchase or deposited under provisional arrangements— together with books, newspapers and journals, and photographs.

In 1940, while under Nazi occupation, Zhyvotko published a ten-year report, summarizing those activities and mentioning a few of the most important archival acquisitions.[39] The Documentary Division had brought together considerable documentation from the period of the struggle to establish an independent state, including materials from the Central Rada, the Hetmanate, and the Ukrainian National Republic (UNR), including collections of documents from Ukrainian military units and organizations, military internment camps in Poland and Czechoslovakia, and files from diplomatic missions. There were files from various Ukrainian political parties, such as the Revolutionary Ukrainian Party (RUP), the Ukrainian Party of Socialist Revolutionaries (UPSR), and the Ukrainian Social-Democratic Workers' Party (USDRP), among others. The collection had important groups of correspondence of Symon Petliura, Volodymyr Vynny-chenko, and Pavlo Skoropads'kyi. Already by the mid-1930s, among files of

[37] *Biuleten' Ukraïns'koho istorychnoho kabinetu v Prazi* 1 (Prague, 1932 [micro-fiche=IDC-R-14,895]), which lists newspapers and journals received and also mentions the archival holdings. Reports and correspondence for those years are found in TsDAVO, 3866/1/1–3. An archival copy of the 1932 bulletin (covering operations for 1931) is held as 3866/1/20 and another copy in 3866/3/4. See also the report on the Ukrainian collection in *Ročenka slovanského ústavu v Praze,* vol. 11 (Prague, 1938), pp. 159–60.

[38] That report is found in TsDAVO, 3866/1/6, which also includes correspondence and monthly reports for 1935. Reports and correspondence for other years comprise separate files in TsDAVO, 3866/1/4 (1933), 5 (1934), 7 (1936), 8 (1937), 9 (1938–1939).

[39] Arkadii Zhyvotko, *Desiat' rokiv Ukraïns'koho istorychnoho kabinetu (1930–1940)* (Prague, 1940 [microfiche=IDC-R-14,920; reprint ed.=New York: Norman Ross Publishing, 1994]) [=Inventari Arkhivu Ministerstva vnutrishnikh sprav, series S, 1]. The central section (pp. 12–19) describes the documentary holdings with emphasis on materials from the successive independent Ukrainian governments (1917–1919) and their collapse, with mention of official documentation, personal papers, and collections of letters, manuscripts, maps, and photographs. Drafts and proofs remain in TsDAVO, 3866/1/21 and 22; and also an untitled and undated copy as 3866/3/3.

Ukrainian émigré organizations, UIK had received at least part of the records and other collections from the Ukrainian Sociological Institute, the Ukrainian Higher Pedagogical Institute in Prague, the Ukrainian Agricultural Academy in Poděbrady, and the Ukrainian Community Committee in Czechoslovakia, along with files of student organizations and newspapers, among others.[40]

Some holdings had been transferred from the Shevchenko Scientific Society in Lviv and some from the Ukrainian Scientific Institute in Warsaw. In 1939, UIK received the records of the UNR diplomatic mission in Washington, DC, among others, and the personal collection of the writer, journalist, and publisher Yurii Tyshchenko. Among the many personal papers of Ukrainian émigrés acquired during the 1930s were those of the ethnographer and poet Mykhailo Obidnyi, Mykyta Shapoval, General O. Pil'kevych, and those of the civic and political activist and law professor Serhii Shelukhyn (Serhij Šeluxyn; Šeluchyn). More of Shelukhyn's archive was received on deposit later during the war.[41]

Zhyvotko continued to head UIK throughout the Nazi occupation; his last monthly report was signed in February 1945.[42] The wartime records preserved in Kyiv and Prague give no suggestion that the Nazis removed any of the archival materials from UIK, although a receipted list remains for 34 books taken in July 1939 for the Russian library under the high-level security services (SS) in Berlin.[43] There are no reports of transfers of UIK documentation to the Military Archive in Prague as was the case with RZIA. Dr. Georg Leibbrandt, Alfred Rosenberg's special assistant for Ukraine and the Soviet area, visited UIK in January and May of 1940, but apparently decided not to move or extract any of the archive.

The Nazis apparently increased the supporting staff, since there were again two, and sometimes three, assistants. Mykola Balash (*Czech* M. Balaš),

---

[40] Many of these are listed in various unpublished UIK reports, as well as the UIK registers mentioned above. Some of these receipts are also listed by Zhyvotko, *Desiat' rokiv UIK*, especially pp. 16–18.

[41] Many of the personal papers received are listed in unpublished UIK reports, as well as the UIK registers mentioned above. See, for example, for 1939, TsDAVO, 3866/1/9, fols. 73–75, fol. 85. Some of these receipts are also listed by Zhyvotko, *Desiat' rokiv UIK*, especially pp. 12–19. For a survey of the Shapoval papers (now held in TsDAVO, fond 3563), see N. Mironets, "Dokumenty fonda Nikity Shapovala kak istochnik dlia izucheniia ukrainskoi èmigratsii v Chekhoslovakii," in *"Russkaia, ukrainskaia i belorusskaia èmigratsiia" 1995*, vol. 2, pp. 565–71.

[42] Reports and correspondence for the years 1940–1945 remain in TsDAVO, 3866/1/10; the latest March 1945 report is found on fol. 189.

[43] TsDAVO, 3866/1/8, fol. 189.

was particularly active, and served briefly as the last head of UIK in Prague. He prepared the last report from the wartime period for March 1945.[44] Descriptive work continued during the war for the archival materials, including an inventory for the archive of the Ukrainian Pedagogical Institute (on deposit), the archive and library from the Ukrainian Sociological Institute and the Ukrainian Technical-Agricultural Institute in Poděbrady, the records of the Prosvita Theater from Uzhhorod, the Ukrainian Peasant Association (Ukraïns'ka selians'ka spil'ka), the Kuban Archive and Library, the archive and collection of Yurii Tyshchenko, some materials received from V'iacheslav Lypyns'kyi and Mykyta Shapoval, and the personal papers of the literary historian and critic Leonid Bilets'kyi.[45] Inventories had been prepared earlier for the materials received on deposit from Shelukhyn.[46] During the war, Nazi authorities also kept the staff busy preparing press summaries and analytic files for articles from journals and newspapers received by UIK.[47]

The End of UIK and Transfer to Kyiv. Soon after the agreement to transfer RZIA to Moscow, a Ukrainian archival mission arrived in Prague in July 1945 searching out Ukrainian archival materials that the Nazis had looted. It had as an additional special mission the retrieval of Ukrainian émigré collections located in Prague. Pavlo I. Pavliuk, Chief of the Main Archival Administration of the NKVD UkrSSR, headed the group, which also included Hordii S. Pshenychnyi, director of the Central State Archive of Films and Photographs, and Hryts'ko P. Neklesa, Chief of the Archival Administration of Lviv Oblast.[48] Before their arrival, they seem not to have

---

[44]   See UIK records for the years 1940–1945 in TsDAVO, 3866/1/10. The added staff during the war under Nazi occupation may explain why more detailed registers are preserved for archival collections numbered 451–549 (see fn. 35, above).

[45]   TsDAVO, 3866/1/10, fol. 1 and fol. 7.

[46]   These inventories, and possibly others are preserved among the UIK records in TsDAVO, 3866/1/39 and 41, but apparently they were never coordinated with later descriptions after those materials came to Kyiv. In Prague, most of the other descriptive work was simply recorded in the main UIK register books: vol. II, covering collections nos. 451–487 (fond 3866/1/36) and vol. III, covering nos. 488–549 (fond 3866/1/34); again, see above, fn. 35.

[47]   For example, the last almost half of the now-bound file with correspondence and reports for the wartime period (TsDAVO, 3866/1/10, fols. 189–306) contains press and radio summaries for 1938–1939.

[48]   The dispatch of the mission, listing the participants, was announced in a top secret "special file" addressed to Molotov, GA RF, 9401/2/103, fol. 254. In 1989, I

been well informed about the Ukrainian émigré community in Prague and the location and status of UIK. In early August 1945, Pavliuk reported that they:

> ...were able to establish the location of the so-called Ukrainian Cabinet (archive of the Bourgeois-Nationalist governments and well-known Ukrainian nationalists), and it turns out to be located under the jurisdiction of the Archive of the Ministry of Internal Affairs of the Czechoslovak Republic. With the help of the Soviet Embassy, negotiations are in process to receive this archive as a gift to Ukrainian Soviet archives.[49]

In terms of the Ukrainian materials involved, the August 1945 negotiations, according to Bystrov, led to a decision "to extract from RZIA the Ukrainian Historical Archive and send it in advance to the Ukrainian Soviet Socialist Republic to exemplify the sincere friendly relations of both countries."[50] That explanation, however, is somewhat misleading, because there is no indication that any Ukrainian materials were in fact extracted from RZIA for transfer to Kyiv. The Kyiv transfer involved only materials from the still separate Ukrainian Historical Cabinet (UIK), with the possible addition of materials from other Ukrainian émigré institutions in the Prague region, most of which were already on deposit in UIK. The official UIK transfer ceremony for the "gift of the Czechoslovak government to the Ukrainian people," took place in Prague on 4 September. The transfer was signed on the Czech side by Josef Borovičký, the Head of the Archive of the Czech Ministry of Internal Affairs, Mykola Balash, the last Head of UIK in Prague, and Václav Pešák, Special Advisor to the Archive of the Czech Ministry of Internal Affairs, and on the Ukrainian side, by the above-mentioned three representatives of the Archival Administration under the NKVD UkrSSR who were in Prague.[51]

---

had an opportunity to meet with Pavliuk and Pshenychnyi, under the auspices of the Ukrainian Archival Administration, and hear some (limited) reminiscences about the mission. They were, however, not prepared to discuss the UIK transfer at that time.

[49]   Pavliuk to Nikitinskii (Prague, 9 August 1945), GA RF, 5325/2/1353, fol. 81. Another copy of Pavliuk's report is preserved in Kyiv, TsDAVO, 14/7/56, fols. 37–39.

[50]   Bystrov, "Konets RZIA," p. 77.

[51]   Copies of the official act of transfer (30 August 1945) in Ukrainian and Czech, and a copy translated into Russian, are found in the recently opened secret *opys* of the administrative archive (AA) of TsDIAK, which is now officially cited as TsDAVO, 4703/2/2, fols. 15–23. When I first consulted these documents in 1994, they were held by TsDIAK. They were due for subsequent transfer to TsDAVO (fond 4703) with the other administrative records of TsDIAK, although the formal transfer had not taken

Different reports and registers have different figures for the total number of archival groups that had been acquired and registered by UIK by mid-1945, at which time the transfer negotiations were under way. The brief summary acquisition register for UIK lists 605 entries with indication of the person responsible for transfer and whether they were a donation, purchase, or deposit.[52] The latest (1946) published report about the activities of UIK, by the responsible archivist from the Ministry of Internal Affairs, Václav Pešák, indicated 604 archival groups.[53] However, some of those entries comprised only books or photographs, and so should not be counted as separate archival groups (records, personal papers, or collections).[54] The last volume of the more detailed register of the UIK documentary section, which in most cases includes file-level descriptions of the documentary holdings, extends through number 549.[55] It seems, though, that some of the later receipts had not yet been fully described in that register. It is clear that this particular register did not cover the acquisitions that were only printed books.

As indicated in the official act of transfer, the "gift" included all of the 588 archival collections (that is, groups of institutional records, personal papers, or collections) of the Ukrainian Historical Cabinet itself, as listed in its three inventory registers by 1945, including photographs and some unprocessed files. Related photographic materials, the three inventory registers themselves, and the relevant administrative records of UIK in Prague were also sent. The archival documents from the former Ukrainian National Museum-Archive (UNMA; nos. 1–3232) and the UNMA photographic collection (nos. 1–1344), which were both covered by a separate

---

place by the end of 1999; I cite the TsDAVO designations, as requested by archivists in Kyiv. As of fall 1998, this *opys* still requires special permission of the TsDIAK director for access. Another copy of the act of transfer is held in TsDAVO, 3866/3/1. The act itself and relevant transfer documents are reprinted herein as Appendix VIII.

[52]   A separate handwritten summary lists the collections from 1–605—TsDAVO, 3866/1/23, fols. 10–22. For the first part of this register covering UNMA collections, see fn. 33, above.

[53]   Pešák, "Zpráva o činnosti Ruského," pp. 218–19.

[54]   In fact the last receipt listed in the summary register (605) was a collection of photographs, which immediately explains the discrepancy of one number.

[55]   This register describes collections, record groups, or personal papers numbered from 488–549—TsDAVO, 3866/1/23, fols. 10–22. See fn. 35, above—including regarding the missing first part of this register.

register, were likewise included.[56]

In addition to the archival materials from UIK and UNMA listed in the inventory registers, the official act of transfer listed "unprocessed" archival materials from eleven other Ukrainian émigré institutions that were apparently still held in deposit status, or, in a few cases, all the files which had never been formally accessioned by UIK. These included the Ukrainian Workers' University, the Ukrainian Sociological Institute, the Ukrainian Party of Socialist Revolutionaries Abroad (UPSR), the Ukrainian Pedagogical Institute in Prague, and the Ukrainian Community Publishing Fund, among others.[57] Some of these materials, as is apparent from the wartime reports mentioned above, had already been processed in UIK and their contents are listed in the UIK inventory registers, but that was not true in all cases. A subsidiary document was issued by the Czech Foreign Ministry to prevent any potential claims in connection with those records and personal papers that had not been legally accessioned by UIK (i.e., that were still on deposit, and hence not legally owned by the archive), including some of the other materials of provenance in Ukrainian émigré institutions in Prague and Poděbrady.[58]

Ukrainian NKVD Chief Riasnoi proudly announced the UIK "gift" to Ukrainian Party Secretary and Chairman of the Council of People's Commissars Nikita Khrushchev and to Beria in Moscow:

---

[56] The figures cited here are those that appeared on the official transfer act. There is still some question as to whether any additional émigré collections from Prague were also transferred that had not been registered in UIK. The official act of transfer does not list any Ukrainian-related materials from RZIA itself that were transferred to Kyiv. The UNMA collections are listed in fn. 34, above.

[57] Listed separately in the official act of transfer (30 August 1945) were: Ukraïns'kyi robitnychyi universytet, Ukraïns'kyi sotsiolohichnyi instytut, Ukraïns'kyi hromads'kyi komitet, Ukraïns'ka Zahranychna Partiia Sotsialistiv-Revoliutsioneriv (UPSR), Ukraïns'ka selians'ka spilka, Ukraïns'ka vil'na spilka, Orhanizatsiia "Ukraïns'ka khata," Ukraïns'ka "knyhozbirnia" v Prazi (1927–1928), Kubans'kyi arkhiv, and the Ukraïns'kyi hromads'kyi vydavnychyi fond—see the act of transfer cited in Appendix VIII—TsDAVO, 4703/2/2, fol. 17 (Ukrainian). Most of these are in fact listed in the UIK register, and some of their records were processed and described in the more detailed registers, as is also apparent from UIK monthly reports.

[58] A copy of the separate document dismissing potential claims is held in TsDAVO, 4703/2/2, fols. 13 and 14. See the text in Appendix VIII. Czech documents regarding the Soviet appropriation and the status of the various fonds involved are to be found among the records of the Interior Ministry, Státní ústřední archiv III, Ministerstvo vnitra, nová registratura, P1412/ k. 5488.

...the so-called Ukrainian archive, formed on the basis of the Ukrainian University in Poděbrady (Czechoslovakia), [comprised] documentary materials of the ministries of the Ukrainian bourgeois-national "governments" of Skoropads'kyi, the Central Rada, Petliura, and others. The archive also holds a large quantity of personal fonds of known individuals in the Ukrainian national movement. Besides, the archive acquired documentary records formed from the activities of various Ukrainian nationalist organizations existing in Czechoslovakian territory. Among these are materials of the "Ukrainian Academic Society," the "Ukrainian Drahomanov Higher Pedagogical Institute," the editorial records of the newspapers "Nastup," "Nationalist" and others. Most of the documentary materials of the "Prague Ukrainian Archive" relate to the years 1918 to 1937.[59]

In October 1945 the important railroad freight car of materials from the Ukrainian Historical Cabinet was transferred directly from Prague to Kyiv.

A consolidated "Ukrainian Archive" as referenced in those official reports and others is something of a misnomer, because most of the materials transferred to Kyiv were either formally accessioned by, or were on deposit with, UIK in Prague. That most important collection of Ukrainian materials from Prague in fact came from UIK (as Pavliuk had indicated in his initial report in August), not the university in Poděbrady, so the Poděbrady reference is also misleading. (As far as can be determined, UIK was never associated with institutions in Poděbrady.) Some materials from Poděbrady that had already been processed in UIK were included in the official UIK transfer, but others were held in deposit status, and their transfer to Kyiv was undoubtedly not authorized. These included, for example, the administrative records of both the Ukrainian Agricultural Academy and its correspondence arm, the Ukrainian Technical-Agricultural Institute, some of which had already been processed in Prague and for which separate fonds were assigned in Kyiv, as well as those for organizations associated with these institu-

---

[59] The official announcements from Ukraine describe the "gift"—Riasnoi to Nikita S. Khrushchev (25 September 1945), TsDAVO, 4703/2/2, fols. 28–30, and to Beria, fols. 31–33. (Full text below, in Appendix VIII.) The official top secret Archival Administration report in Moscow follows the same text: Nikitinskii to S. N. Kruglov, "Spetsial'noe soobshchenie o sostave 'Ukrainskogo arkhiva'" (September 1945; received 29 September), GA RF, 5325/2/1353, fol. 88–88v. This same text was repeated in the year-end report, "Spravka o rezul'tatakh raboty GAU NKVD SSSR po vozvrashcheniiu v Sovetskii Soiuz dokumental'nykh materialov Gosudarstvennogo arkhivnogo fonda SSSR i o vyvoze v SSSR arkhivov inostrannogo proiskhozhdeniia," signed by Golubtsov and Kuz'min (15 December 1945), GA RF, 5325/10/2148, fol. 2–2v.

tions.[60] Part of the records of some of those institutions still remain in Prague, as is evident from the 1995 guide to Russian and Ukrainian émigré archival fonds and collections in the Czech Republic.[61]

There is no indication that the Ukrainian materials that had been interspersed in RZIA collections (rather than UIK) were brought to Kyiv, but were rather taken to Moscow. Accession registers for the Ukrainian materials in RZIA had not been kept separately, and Ukrainian materials acquired by RZIA, especially those accessioned before the founding of UIK in 1929, remained a part of RZIA. Besides, many later collections acquired by RZIA had intermixed Ukrainian and Russian documentation.

UIK had one of the largest collections of Ukrainian newspapers and émigré publications outside the USSR, but according to recent estimates, only approximately 35 runs of newspapers and approximately 2,100 books from the UIK newspaper and library collections went to Kyiv. None are indicated in the official act of transfer.[62] However, many library books and serials came to Kyiv along with the records and archival collections from other Czech Ukrainian institutions, which makes it more difficult to access the extent and nature of library holdings that came with the shipment to Kyiv. One 1945 report notes a total of 5,000 volumes received from Prague, but the source libraries are not indicated; presumably less than half of these were

---

[60] These records appear as separate fonds on the TsDIA URSR work plan for 1949. The Ukrainian Technical-Agricultural Institute (Ukraïns'kyi tekhnichno-hospodars'kyi instytut zaochnoho navchannia, Poděbrady), listed in Russian on the 1949 list (8,667 units; 1932–1945) had been assigned fond no. 3879 in TsDAZhR by 1960 (2 *opysy*, 8,250 and 250 units; 1927–1945). The Ukrainian Agricultural Academy (Ukraïns'ka hospodars'ka akademiia v Chekhoslovachchyni, Poděbrady) as listed in 1949 (2,135 units; 1922–1936) was assigned fond no. 3795 with four *opysy* by 1960 (2,298 units, 1922–1936; 339 units, 1922–1939; 104 units, 1922–1939; and 49 units, 1922–1927), apparently reflecting receipts from different sources. A fond with the same number is listed in TsDIA in 1962 with five *opysy* (780 units; 1922–1938). Later these materials were all consolidated in TsDAZhR.

[61] Václav Podaný and Hana Barvíková, et al., *Russkaia i ukrainskaia èmigratsiia v Chekhoslovatskoi respublike, 1918–1938: Putevoditel' po arkhivnym fondam i sobraniiam v Cheshskoi respublike*, trans. L'ubov Beloševská and Marina Luptáková (Prague: Euroslavica, 1995).

[62] Statistics for UIK books and newspapers transferred to Kyiv were listed by Pešák, "Zpráva o činnosti Ruského," p. 219. That figure has recently been confirmed by specialists in Prague, although possibly some additional collections that had not been catalogued by UIK were also transferred to Kyiv.

from UIK.[63] Some émigré internal agency publications were later processed as part of some of the archival fonds. Most of the library books, however, were deposited in the main archival library in Kyiv, later consolidated in the present building of the Main Archival Administration, although some were transferred to other libraries. Book markings or ex libris were understandably not recorded in library catalogs in Kyiv, so it is difficult now to determine how many books remain from what émigré collections. One recent preliminary survey conducted in the Holovarkhiv library identified over 500 volumes in Ukrainian and over 125 in foreign languages from the Ukrainian Free University and the Ukrainian Taras Shevchenko Library-Reading Room in Prague. A more thorough survey of the holdings in that library and others from Prague will be needed, especially to determine if any UIK printed holdings were received.[64]

Although more of the books and newspapers in the RZIA and UIK library collections were initially to be included in the shipments to Moscow and Kyiv, plans changed in the course of negotiations, and most of the RZIA library and newspaper division, along with those in UIK, remained in Prague.[65] Subsequently, those collections become part of the Slavonic Library (Slovanská knihovna); however, the RZIA collections were not integrated into the general library collections and their existence in Prague was kept quiet during the communist period. Some books had been removed by the censor during those years, and access generally was extremely limited. The collections are now part of the National Library of the Czech Republic, although they still remain intact as separate collections. A microfiche edition of the catalog of the RZIA library, recently filmed in Prague, is currently available commercially, together with several bibliographies covering parts of the collections. The UIK newspapers and book collections that had been kept separately in Prague are also covered by that catalog and are part of the RZIA library there.[66]

---

[63]   As quoted in the TsDIA URSR report for 1945 (12 January 1946), TsDAVO, 14/2/51, fol. 70.

[64]   As reported to the author by librarians in the HAU (now DAKU) Central Library in Kyiv. Since the library had been requested to search for only those markings, they were not prepared to report on others found in the process, and their search involved only the formerly classified "Special Fond" and not those in the open part of the library.

[65]   These developments, as reported by Bystrov, "Konets RZIA," p. 78, confirm reports from the Moscow and Kyiv representatives in Prague.

[66]   The microfiche catalog is *Katalog byvshei Biblioteki Russkogo zagranichnogo istorichnogo arkhiva/Catalog of the Former Library of the Russian Historical Archive*

An official Czech communiqué to the Soviet ambassador in Prague, V. A. Zorin, in August 1945, a week before the UIK "act" of transfer was signed specified two important Czech provisions for the "presentation to the Government of the Ukrainian SSR as testimony of the sincere friendly relations between our peoples, now close neighbors, of the Ukrainian part of the so-called 'Russian Archive.'" First, that "the Ukrainian Central Archive would supply Czechoslovakia with photocopies of the documentation transferred," and, second, that "the transferred archive would be retained in Kyiv in the Ukrainian Central Archive as an integral division to be named the 'Prague Ukrainian Archive.'" [67] Those provisions were not included in the official act of transfer (30 August 1945), and neither of them have been carried out since.

Several articles have appeared about the so-called "Prague Ukrainian Archive" in Kyiv. One brief report prepared by the director of TsDAVO in Kyiv, the archive where most of the archival materials from Prague are now housed, appeared in 1994. This was followed by a somewhat more detailed report by Liudmyla I. Lozenko. Lozenko, following the Czech communiqué, treats the Ukrainian émigré materials in Kyiv as if they constituted an integral "Ukrainian Archive" in Prague and a separate entity in Kyiv, but she gives few details about UIK and does not cite that document. More seriously, she unwittingly assumes that most of the UNR and other important Ukrainian émigré materials in Kyiv came from Prague.[68] A comprehensive study of the Ukrainian émigré archival materials as organized in Prague, and as transferred after the war from Prague and other countries, will require more thorough research, based on sources in Moscow and Prague, as well as those in Kyiv. The initial observations given here may provide the basis for further study.

Abroad (New York: Norman Ross Publishing, 1995). The printed guide includes introductory comments by Richard J. Kneeley and Edward Kasinec, based on their earlier article, "The Slovanská knihovna in Prague and its RZIA Collection," *Slavic Review* 51(1) Spring 1992: 122–30. See fn. 114, below, regarding other published bibliographies from RZIA. The Prague library director Milena Klimová recently kindly confirmed some of these details.

[67] See the full texts below, in Appendix VIII.

[68] Larysa Iakovlieva, "Praz'ki fondy v Kyievi," *Pam'iatky Ukraïny* 1994 (3–6[26]): 120–22. Liudmyla I. Lozenko, "Praz'kyi ukraïns'kyi arkhiv: Istoriia i s'ohodennia," *Arkhivy Ukraïny* 1994 (1–6): 18–30. Lozenko issued a second article, "Z istoriï Praz'koho ukraïns'koho arkhivu," in *Mizhnarodni zv'iazky Ukraïny: Naukovi poshuky i znakhidky* (Kyiv, 1997), pp. 85–94.

Ucrainica in Kyiv from Prague and Elsewhere

The Prague Ukrainian Collections in Kyiv. The Prague Ukrainian collections that arrived in Kyiv in October 1945 were immediately placed in the Special Division of Secret Fonds—OOSF (*Osobyi otdel sekretnykh fondov*) of the Central State Historical Archive of the Ukrainian SSR (TsDIA URSR, later TsDIAK). Some 1,496 photographic positives from the Prague collections were placed in the Central State Archive of Documentary Films, Photographs, and Sound Recordings (TsDAKFFD URSR). [69] Regrettably, however, and despite the above-mentioned Czech provisions, the UIK collections were not retained intact and their original arrangement was not taken into account when they were processed in Kyiv. Today it is almost impossible to identify their components in either archive.

The émigré documentary materials from UIK and other sources in Prague were initially broken down into over 280 fonds according to the agency from which the files initially came or the individual whose personal papers were involved. In UIK, by contrast, the materials had been kept together as an integral extensive collection, internally numbered in 588 archival groups roughly in the order of their acquisition. When the fonds—often artificial—were established in Kyiv, no reference was made, nor correlation to the earlier archival disposition, numeration, or existing finding aids for the materials in Prague.

The Soviet organization of the Prague materials into strict, but often highly fragmentary, fonds completely destroyed the UIK order and thereby completely disguised their archival provenance. If the Kyiv archivists understood that order, they had no time to reconstruct it out of the often miscellaneous and sometimes unsorted bundles that arrived from Prague. Unfortunately, they made no effort to preserve any record of it (such as the UIK acquisition numbers). This now makes it much more difficult to establish the provenance of the materials or the source of their acquisition by UIK in Prague. One reason for this may have been that the official "gift" of the Prague collections was principally identified with UIK, whereas in fact,

---

[69] According to a July 1946 report: Pshenichnyi, "Dokladnaia zapiska o prodelannoi rabote TsGAFFKD MVD UkrSSR za 1-e polugodie 1946 g." (13 July 1946), GA RF, 5325/2/1620, fol. 114. The report notes that an inventory *opis′* for that collection was already established. Archivists in TsGAFFKD have been unable to locate a separate inventory for the Prague photographic materials that were subsequently integrated into the general thematic organization of the archive.

many of the émigré materials retrieved from Prague and other sources had never been formally accessioned by UIK, and many of them did not even come from Prague. The administrative files of UIK in Prague that came to Kyiv with the 1945 transfer do contain the original detailed inventory registers in addition to reports and correspondence with important data about provenance and about the organization and development of the UIK collections, but they have not been thoroughly analyzed, either during initial processing of the materials in Kyiv or even today.[70]

"Operational" Utilization. NKVD/MVD archivists in Kyiv had more important priorities than prudent archival basics. As is apparent in now declassified archival reports from the immediate postwar period, some of the Ukrainian émigré "fonds of highest operational interest" brought from Prague and elsewhere were indeed already "prepared for immediate operational use," even during 1945 in Special Secret Division of the TsDIA URSR. "Others were to be ready by early 1946." The annual report promised full reports on:

(1)　the Ukrainian-White emigration in Czechoslovakia,
(2)　counter-revolutionary activities of Ukrainian political parties (especially UPSR and USDRP),
(3)　Ukrainian fascist organizations abroad, and
(4)　the Directorate of the UNR abroad.[71]

Extensive card index files on the Ukrainian emigration were compiled, and by the end of 1946 the Division had already prepared:

...card reports on a total of 190 Ukrainian-White emigrants who were engaged in anti-Soviet activities. Of those information on

---

[70]　The original UIK administrative records are now all held in TsDAVO, fond 3866 (ca. 230 units, 1930–1945). These materials were not mentioned by Larysa Iakovlieva and Liudmyla Lozenko in their articles about the Prague holdings, nor have they been thoroughly studied or referenced in other works.

[71]　"Otchet o rabote Osobogo sekretnogo otdeleniia TsGIA UkrSSR za 1945-i god," signed by Strel'skii (30 November 1945/27 December 1945), TsDAVO, 4703/2/1, fols. 3–4. The report gave the figure of 280 fonds from Czechoslovakia, at least 203 of which were from UIK. It singled out with annotations those of the first order of importance, including the Ukrainian Community Commission in Prague (1921–1939), and the personal archives of Mariia(?) Derkach, Spyrydon Dovhal' (1931–1942), Myroslav Hryhoriv (1943–1944), Nykyfor Hryhoriv (1919–1933), Pan'ko Kaluizhnyi, Professor Dmytro Antonovych (1943–1944), and Professor Borys Martos (1919–1944).

170 persons were sent to the MVD UkrSSR (in the form of reference lists and special reports). Personal appraisals (*kharakteristiki*) were prepared for 30 Ukrainian White emigrants (for those politically tainted). For the VKP(b) and the TsK(b)U, copies were prepared of documents relating to the activities of the Ukrainian Central Rada and M[ykhailo] Hrushevs'kyi…Systematization proceeded and reference lists were prepared for C[ounter]-R[evolutionary] elements.[72]

The 1946 report noted a total of 291 fonds devoted to "documentary materials of the Ukraino-Nationalist emigration," out of which by the end of the year they could already report on 188.[73] By 1948, they had prepared reports on 19,298 predominantly "Ukrainian bourgeois-nationalist émigrés," and sent the MGB detailed reports on several organizations of Ukrainian nationalists abroad.[74] Besides, in connection with their "utilization of archival materials in operational aims," they planned "to enlarge the scientific reference system (NSA) for 58 émigré fonds with three groups of historical reports on: (1) Ukrainian educational institutions in Czechoslovakia, (2) Ukrainian student organizations in Czechoslovakia, and (3) Ukrainian peasant associations (*selians'ki spilky*) in Czechoslovakia." For the MGB and MVD they were compiling a comprehensive card file of "Ukrainian White émigrés abroad, and reference lists with appended copies of the most important documents on counterrevolutionary elements, characterizing their activities."[75] The extent to which reports prepared in Kyiv were used for arrests or surveillance in Prague or elsewhere awaits further investigation.

By 1948, Kyiv archivists could list 75 émigré fonds and personal papers that had already been processed, most of them from Prague and Poděbrady,

---

[72] "Otchet o rabote TsGIA UkrSSR za 1946-i god," to Gudzenko (12 January 1947), TsDAVO, 4703/1/18, fols. 27–28.

[73] "Otchet o rabote TsGIA UkrSSR za 1946-i god," TsDAVO, 4703/1/18, fols. 27–28. The 188 fonds had 20,617 units and 350 kilos of unarranged materials (*rossypi*). Compare reports and work plans from the secret division of TsDIA URSR in the formerly secret *opys'* of the administrative records of TsDIA URSR—TsDAVO, 4703/2/7 (1946), and *sprava* 9 (1947).

[74] "Otchet o rabote Osobogo otdela sekretnykh fondov za 1948 god," TsDAVO, 4703/2/13, fol. 35.

[75] "Plan raboty Osobogo otdela sekretnykh fondov na 1948 god," signed by Oliinyk [Oleinik] (4 February 1948), TsDAVO, 4703/2/13, fols. 8–9. The TsDIAK Special Secret Division report for 1948 in the same folder (fol. 3) mentions six special cabinets in the archive containing these files and reference materials, but their present whereabouts has not been determined.

and an additional 41 they intended to process during that year.[76] By the end of the year they had 148 fonds that were still being worked over and 16 that they planned to process during 1949. By then, however, many fonds involving politically suspect "bourgeois-nationalist" organizations and individuals were being transferred from Lviv and other western Ukrainian centers for scrutiny by authorities in Kyiv.[77] In April 1949, they were reporting a total of 361 separate fonds in the Special Division of Secret Fonds of TsDIA UkrSSR.[78]

The "operational" analysis gained momentum. During 1949 the Special Secret Division of the archive reported that "for operational aims and use of documentation by agencies of the MGB and MVD," on the basis of some 13,781 files processed during the year, they had prepared "72,000 cards on White emigrants," "55,400 cards on C[ounter]-R[evolutionary] elements," and more detailed reports on 235 people in the SS "Halychyna" Division."[79]

Later Receipts from Prague. Archival retrieval shipments from Prague did not end with the 1945 "gift." Another important group of Ukrainian émigré archival materials was transferred from Prague in 1958 with the assistance of Czech security service authorities and the Slavonic Library. At least 25 fonds received were initially deposited in TsDIAK, and the current Chief of the Ukrainian Archival Administration gave orders for their "appropriate processing" during 1959.[80] Others came in 1962. A list of many of these and other materials received from Prague, which was prepared at the time of their

---

[76] Ibid., fols. 13–17.

[77] "Spisok fondov Osobogo otdela sekretnykh fondov TsGIA UkrSSR, podlezhashchikh uporiadocheniiu v 1949 g." (25 January 1949), TsDAVO, 4703/2/16, fols. 10–18; and "Spisok fondov Osobogo otdela sekretnykh fondov TsGIA UkrSSR, podlezhashchikh razrabotke v 1949 godu" (25 January 1949), ibid., fols. 19–20. These lists were both appendices to the official archival work plan for 1949. Almost half the fonds named in the first list are from Lviv, with personal papers and material from Ukrainian social, political, cultural, and religious organizations.

[78] "Spisok fondov Osobogo otdela sekretnykh fondov Tsentral'nogo gosudarstvennogo istoricheskogo arkhiva UkrSSR" (April 1949), TsDAVO, 4703/2/18, fols. 18–73.

[79] "Otchet o rabote Osobogo otdela TsGIA USSR za 1949 g." (5 January 1950), TsDAVO, 4703/2/16, fols. 47–48.

[80] Pil'kevich to TsDIA-K Chief Teslenko (18 December 1958), TsDAVO 4703/2/39, fol. 2 and fol. 8. A list of 25 fonds follows (fols. 3–7).

transfer, has recently come to light.[81]

Of particular significance, much of this documentation was earlier held by the interwar Museum of the Struggle for Liberation of Ukraine (sometimes translated as the "Museum of the Ukrainian Struggle for Independence") in Prague, founded by the well-known Ukrainian historian Dmytro Antonovych, but in 1945 it was rechristened the Ukrainian Museum in Prague for obvious political reasons. The museum activities and some of its rich documentation had been surveyed in interwar publications in Prague.[82] The fate of the museum and its holdings is the subject of a recent monograph by Mykola Mushynka.[83] According to one report, the materials from the museum that were transferred to Kyiv in 1958 and processed during the 1959–1963 period were divided into 173 fonds with 7,232 file units, providing an important supplement to those of the Ukrainian Historical Cabinet and earlier receipts from Prague (some materials from the museum came already with the UIK shipment in 1945). Other fragmentary archival materials from the Museum were distributed to other Ukrainian state archives including TsDIAL, and oblast archives in Volhynia, Rivne, Ternopil, and Kharkiv. Photographic albums from the Museum were transferred to the state audio-visual archive in Kyiv; library materials went to the TsDIAK library and other libraries; while some of the museum exhibits went to the Historical Museum. An additional 27 crates of documents were received in Kyiv from Prague in 1983, although some files from the museum still remain in Prague.[84] An item-level inventory of the holdings from the Ukrainian

---

[81]   TsDAVO, 4703/2/39. The 1958 and 1962 Prague receipts (fols. 58–62, and fol. 79), together with the lists of other fonds received from Prague earlier (fols. 65–78 and 85–98) are bound together in a recently declassified folder.

[82]   See the newsletters published in Prague, ed. D. V. Antonovych, *Visti Muzeiu vyzvol'noï borot'by Ukraïny*, 22 issues (Prague, 1925–1938 [microfiche=IDC-R-14,894]). Thirteen additional issues were published by the Museum through 1944, but copies were not available for inclusion in the microfiche edition at the time it was prepared.

[83]   Mykola Mushynka, *Muzei vyzvol'noï borot'by Ukraïny ta dolia ioho fondiv* (Melbourne: Monash University, Slavic Section, 1996). See also Mushynka's report, "Muzei vyzvol'noï borot'by Ukraïny u Prazi ta ioho ostannii dyrektor Symon Narizhnyi," in *"Russkaia, ukrainskaia i belorusskaia èmigratsiia" 1995*, vol. 1, pp. 806–815. That article provides a helpful list of publications relating to the history and fate of the Museum, which are given in more detail in monograph.

[84]   These details are noted, but not specifically documented, by Mushynka, "Muzei vyzvol'noï borot'by Ukraïny," pp. 806–815 (see esp. pp. 812–13). See more detail in Mushynka, *Muzei vyzvol'noï borot'by*. Mushynka's figures quoted from Kyiv reports

Museum remaining in the National Archives in Prague was published in Kyiv in 1996 in collaboration with the Prague compiler.[85]

In 1988, a considerable group of archival materials that had been held by the KGB or MVD (or both) in Ukraine were transferred by the MVD to the former Communist Party Archive in Kyiv, now known as the Central State Archive of Public Organizations—TsDAHO. Still being processed in TsDAHO, they are tentatively arranged as a consolidated fond under the title of the Ukrainian Museum in Prague. Not all the documents came from that source, having unfortunately been separated from the larger groups that went earlier to TsDAVO (and its TsDAZhR and TsDIAK predecessors).[86] Gathered by secret service agents from many sources, the collection contains many important documents of various Ukrainian émigrés, ranging from letters of Petliura and Volodomyr Doroshenko to the large collection of editorial files that had been compiled for a Ukrainian émigré encyclopedia, which was coordinated in Prague by Vasyl′ Symovych.

Some of the materials complement contingent documents held across the city by TsDAVO, and undoubtedly were withheld by the security service from incoming acquisitions or subsequently turned over to the MVD following analysis in the Special Secret Division of TsDIAK. Some of the materials came from other sources. Unlikely to be of provenance in Prague or UIK, for example, are some files from student societies in Berlin and Gdańsk, and some materials relating to the ZUNR leader Ievhen Petrushevych (which probably came either from Berlin or Vienna).[87] As important as it is that

---

about the number of fonds and units require further verification, because it is not clear if they all came from the Museum itself.

[85]   *Inventáře a katalogy fondů Státního ústředního archivu v Praze—Ukrajinské muzeum v Praze, UM, (1659) 1925–1948: Inventář/Inventari i katalohy fondiv Derzhavnoho tsentral′noho arkhivu v Prazi—Ukraïns′kyi muzei v Prazi, UM, (1659) 1925–1948: Opys fondu*, comp. Raisa Machatková (Kyiv, Prague: IUAD, 1996) [=Naukovo-dovidkovi vydannia z istoriï Ukraïny, 41].

[86]   These collections, along with several other fragments collected by the KGB and MVD from Czechoslovakia, were transferred from the Ukrainian MVD archive. An announcement to this effect was circulated on electronic mail by TsDAHO in February, 1994. TsDAHO director Ruslan Ia. Pyrih showed these materials to the present author in 1994. Initially, they had been assigned to fond no. 269, and a detailed card catalog of the collections was started. Their transfer from Prague is mentioned in Iakovlieva, "Praz′ki fondy v Kyievi," p. 121.

[87]   I am grateful to TsDAHO archivist Anatolii Kentii, who is currently processing these materials, for discussing the problems he is finding and the difficulties of

these Ukrainian émigré materials are now finding professional archival processing in TsDAHO in Kyiv, their countless transfers and fragmentation has
caused the unfortunate further dispersal of many earlier integral collections.

An example of the materials split between the two archives is the
correspondence of Ivan Rudychiv, the librarian of the Petliura Library in
Paris, who was summoned to Berlin by the Nazis in 1941. The few Rudychiv
letters now held in TsDAHO apparently came from the same source as some
of his other papers, which are intermingled with some files arranged as the
fond of the Petliura Library and now held in TsDAVO.[88] Although these
materials were either part of the Paris library holdings or Rudychiv's personal
papers before the war, most of them are his correspondence and writings
from the 1941–1942 period, during which he was in Berlin under Nazi
orders. In his report to the library board in Paris in December 1942 after his
return, he admits to having given some documentation from the library, along
with his own memoirs written in Berlin, to a colleague from Prague to be
safeguarded and some of them to be placed in the Museum of the Struggle for
the Liberation of Ukraine. Hence, quite possibly, the Rudychiv materials and
some other files from the Petliura Library may have come to Kyiv via
Prague, unless the Nazis had seized them in Berlin.[89]

Ukrainian Émigré Archives from Other Countries. Extensive archival
materials relating to post-revolutionary Ukrainian political and cultural
developments had been scattered throughout Europe with the Ukrainian
emigration during the interwar period. This included documentation relating
to the struggle to establish an independent Ukrainian state during and
Ukrainian opposition to Bolshevik rule. During World War II, almost all such
surviving documentation of the Ukrainian National Republic (UNR), the
Western Ukrainian National Republic (ZUNR), and other Ukrainian émigré
organizations throughout the Continent was targeted by the Nazis as of
potential propaganda use in its *Drang nach Osten* and anti-Bolshevik

---

attributing provenance. My report is based on his preliminary description prepared for
the forthcoming TsDAHO guide.

[88]   Details about these files are in my "The Postwar Fate of the Petliura Library from
Paris and the Records of the Ukrainian National Republic." *Harvard Ukrainian
Studies* 21(3–4): 395–462.

[89]   "Prymushenyi vyïzd bibliotekaria Ivana Rudycheva i ioho perebuvannia v Berlini
(Dopovid' na zasidanni Rady Biblioteky 3-oho hrudnia 1942 roku)"; a typescript copy
of this report was kindly furnished to me by Professor Arkady Joukovsky from the
Petliura Library in Paris. See fn. 98, below.

campaign. In fact, during the war, Nazi specialists succeeded in seizing and preserving much more of such materials than is realized. In many instances the materials were removed to Nazi research or storage centers, first in Berlin, then increasingly in more remote areas from Silesia to the Austrian Tyrol, but also in Prague and Cracow.[90]

The same types of émigré materials that had been seized by the Nazis were likewise a high priority for Beria's archival scouts—both those who, with the victorious Red Army, followed the Nazis to Berlin, and those who were sent out on special missions to retrieve looted archival materials. When Soviet agents found Nazi archival stores, Russian and Ukrainian émigré files were among their highest priority. The seizure of these collections and their transport to Kyiv and Moscow has been mentioned in print on several occasions, but a full scholarly account of those developments is long overdue.[91]

As seen previously, some collections came to Moscow from the RSHA Amt VII research centers in Silesia, while others came with the French security and intelligence files from the Sudetenland. Some had been seized by Nazi military intelligence and research agents and were found with remnants of the Heeresarchiv; still others came from ERR sources. By and large, most Ukrainian émigré archival materials seized by Soviet agents after the war went to Kyiv, especially the major shipments from Prague and Cracow. Soviet authorities were also on the lookout for politically sensitive archival Ucrainica of potential "operational" value elsewhere in Eastern Europe. Archival materials were brought in through intelligence or counter-intelligence agents in Vienna, Cracow, and other European centers after the war, and during the subsequent decade of Soviet control over Eastern Europe.

Of particular importance here was the shipment of a freight train wagon of UNR records from Cracow. In March 1945, a Red Army counterintelligence (SMERSH) unit located and seized the UNR Foreign Ministry and Finance Ministry records in the State Archive in Cracow.[92] The Nazis had

---

[90] Cf. my "The Odyssey of the Petliura Library and the Records of the Ukrainian National Republic during World War II," *Harvard Ukrainian Studies* 22 (1998): 181–208 [=*Cultures and Nations of Central and Eastern Europe: Essays in Honor of Roman Szporluk*, ed. Zvi Gitelman et al.].

[91] Cf. my "Ukrainian Cultural Treasures," *Jahrbücher für Geschichte Osteuropas* 39(1) 1991: 73–74; and my "Archival Rossica/Sovietica Abroad," *Cahiers du Monde russe et soviétique* 34(3) 1993: 463–65.

[92] See the report that in Cracow a SMERSH unit of the Ukrainian Fourth Army "was in the possession of Petliura documents in the Ukrainian language, 1918–1922," Gudzenko to Nikitinskii (Kyiv, 27 March 1945), GA RF, 5325/2/1353, fol. 17; see

brought the materials from Tarnów during the war and had them provisionally inventoried by a Ukrainian archivist brought from Lviv.[93] The UNR materials seized from Cracow were apparently joined to four wagon loads of Lviv archival holdings that the Nazis had evacuated early in 1944 to the Abbey of Tyniec near Cracow and which were retrieved by Red Army units and returned to Lviv in April 1945.[94] Another report to Moscow notes that "a freight-train wagon-load of documentary materials of the former Petliura Directorate and its ministries, under the jurisdiction of a counterintelligence 'SMERSH' unit of the Ukrainian Fourth Army transported from Vienna" had already arrived in Lviv at the end of May 1945.[95] With archival materials coming from many sources, some confusion—or else intentional camouflage—is evident in incoming Ukrainian reports between those materials received from Vienna and the UNR materials from Cracow. However, given the Nazi inventory of the UNR Foreign Ministry records in Cracow, Soviet reports of the SMERSH seizure, and several reports of its shipment, we know that these materials came to Kyiv from Cracow.

As evidenced in the postwar lists of fonds in the Special Secret Section

---

also the copy in a more recently declassified file in Kyiv, TsDAVO, 14/7/56, fol. 11. This confirms a penciled note regarding the March 1945 seizure by archivist Adam Kamiński on a report by Włodzimierz Budka, "Archiwum Państwowe w Krakowie podczas okupacji niemieckiej (6 September 1939–17 January 1945)" (Cracow, 2 March 1946), Archiwum Państwowe w Krakowie, fond APKr, 167, fol. 26v. See more details about these records in Grimsted, "Odyssey of the Petliura Library."

93   Details of these operations are found in the files of the Nazi Archival Administration in Cracow, which was headed by Dr. Randt. A copy of one of Randt's reports to Berlin and his detailed survey of these materials "Archiv der ukrainischen Nationalregierung (Petlura) aus den Jahren 1917–1922" (Cracow, 25 March 1942), also remains in the records of the Nazi Archival Administration in Kyiv, TsDAVO, 3206/5/26, fols. 2–5. The transfer and inventory work on the UNR records in Cracow are summarized in the Budka report mentioned immediately above, fols. 25–26. A copy of the Nazi inventory was found in the Bundesarchiv—"Verzeichnis des Archivs des Aussen-Ministeriums der Ukrainischen-Volks-Republik, 1918–1926," BAK, R 146/73.

94   Lists of the materials from Lviv returned from Tyniec and Cracow are included in a report dated 18 April 1945, TsDAVO, 14/7/55, fols. 10, 20–21. It is not clear in that report if the UNR materials from Cracow were included in that shipment or a later one.

95   Gudzenko and Grinberg to Nikitinskii (Kyiv, 30 May 1945), GA RF, 5325/2/1353, fol. 39. Several other separate references have been found referencing the Petliura materials from Cracow.

of TsDIAK, there were other Ukrainian émigré collections shipped from Vienna, although more specific reports of the seizures there have not surfaced.[96] Despite Soviet efforts to find some of the UNR and ZUNR materials known to be held there, as far as is known, no major groups of UNR records were seized by Soviet authorities in Vienna. For example, one freight car load with 78 crates was received in Kyiv from Vienna in July 1947, but the crates contained military service records for Austria-Hungary (1868–1945). A special report was prepared on these records with card files and alphabetical indexes for the registration books from the Consolidated Military Registration Bureau in Vienna.[97]

Elsewhere, Soviet authorities found many of the archival materials that the Nazis had removed in 1940 from the Petliura Library in Paris. Other larger portions of the Library have recently been identified in Moscow, some of which first went to Belarus and thence to Moscow. A small collection of documentation from and relating to the Petliura Library came to Kyiv via Berlin and Prague.[98] Another "half wagon load of documents" was found in 1947 "in a wagon that arrived from Germany, among which were some documents from Paris in French." Their contents have not been identified.[99]

Shipments came so frequently during 1945 and 1946 that archivists were overwhelmed. Some acquisitions from Prague were intermingled in the Special Secret Division of TsDIAK with materials received from elsewhere. Others went directly to TsDAZhR in Kharkiv. Although individual separate fonds—or those that could be so identified—were almost always assigned for institutional records, fonds that had been established for individuals often received materials from several different sources. Most of the materials involved have remained arranged in those same fonds, although some of

[96] Several collections from Vienna are listed among the fonds held by the Special Secret Division of TsDIA URSR in the immediate postwar years—TsDAVO, 4703/2/6, among others.

[97] Bondarevskii to V. P. Gudzenko (9 July 1947), TsDAVO, 4703/2/10, fols 9–13.

[98] See fn. 89, above. It has not as yet been possible to document where the Paris Petliura materials (seized by the Nazis from Paris in January 1940) were found by Soviet authorities, but fragmentary Petliura files from Paris and Geneva were noted as having been accessioned by TsDIA URSR on 10 January 1946 (after the Prague materials that had been received in October of 1945). In the 1947 list of secret fonds they appear as nos. 245–248, 250, 251, and 253—TsDAVO, 4703/2/6, fol. 35; in the 1949 list (fol. 35) they appear as fond nos. 243, 246–248, 250, and 256. Other parts of the same fonds have recently been identified in Moscow. See my "Odyssey of the Petliura Library" and "The Postwar Fate of the Petliura Library."

[99] Iaropenko to Gudzenko (4 April 1947), TsDAVO, 4703/2/11, fol. 6.

these have been reorganized several times. In almost all cases, fond numbers have changed as they were moved from one archive to another.

To give some idea of the range of sources for these materials, consider that the initial pages of the list of fonds being worked over in TsDIA URSR in Kyiv during 1949 included a small fond of a Ukrainian Teachers' Seminary in Vienna (1915–1918), the League of UNR Military Veterans in France from Paris, a Branch Ukrainian Military Aid Committee in Graz (*earlier* Gratz), Austria, a Committee to Aid Refugees from Ukraine in Uzhhorod, a Ukrainian Committee for Famine Relief in Ukraine from Prague, and the Society of Ukrainian Economists in Czechoslovakia from Poděbrady. Half of the fonds in line to be processed that year were of provenance in Poland, including several UNR prisoner-of-war camps (called in Russian "lageria internirovannykh petliurovtsev") in Poland (1919–1924) and a Society of UNR Veterans in Kalisz (1925–1932).[100]

Among the central Polish records that were held in Kyiv in 1946 were records from the Presidium of the Cabinet of Ministers (1921–1930), the Ministry of Internal Affairs (1925–1939), the Post and Telegraph Direction (1936–1939), the Ministry of Finance (1930–1939), the Polish Consulate in Kharkiv (1931), and other scattered local administrative records from Volhynia and Galicia during the interwar period. Some of these had been evacuated to Volhynia early in the war. Subsequently evacuated to Czechoslovakia by the Nazis, they came to Kyiv with other retrieved records. Most of them were later transferred to Lviv, but it has not been determined if any of them were revindicated with other materials to Poland in May 1959.[101]

TsDIA URSR reported in 1948 that it had finished processing the UNR Foreign Ministry fond, although they never noted it came from Tarnów, and they never had a copy of the German inventory prepared in Cracow. Indeed, their top secret list of fonds in 1949 indicates a UNR Foreign Ministry fond covering the years 1918–1923 with 858 file units. It also enumerates a number of contingent fonds for UNR diplomatic missions in several different countries, which suggests that the UNR records from Tarnów, which the Nazis had arranged and described in Cracow, were again reprocessed. Their

---

[100] "Spisok fondov...TsGIA UkrSSR, podlezhashchikh uporiadocheniiu v 1949 g," TsDAVO, 4703/2/16, fol. 10; and "Spisok fondov...TsGIA UkrSSR, podlezhashchikh razrabotke v 1949 godu" (25 January 1949), ibid., fols. 19–20.

[101] "Spisok fondov Osobogo otdela sekretnykh fondov TsGIA UkrSSR" (1946), TsDAVO, 4703/2/6, fol. 34; (1948), fol. 82. The 1959 revindications to Poland are mentioned by Krystyna Wróbel-Lipowa, *Rewindykacja archiwaliów polskich z ZSSR w latach 1945–1964* (Lublin, 1982; Uniwersytet Marii Curie-Skłodowskiej), pp. 103–104, but other indications suggest the materials all remain in Lviv. See Chapter 11.

arrangement completely revised, they were broken down and reorganized into many different fragmentary fonds in Kyiv. Because of this reorganization, it is virtually impossible to tell if all the UNR Foreign Ministry records from Tarnów remain today in Kyiv; nowhere is there reference to the fact that at least some of the materials came from Tarnów.[102] A group of 18 Ukrainian émigré fonds transferred to TsDAZhR URSR in October 1954 included at least some of the UNR Foreign Ministry records.[103] A 1962 list of émigré fonds in TsDIAK still lists one fond of the UNR Foreign Ministry (fond no. 3696; 17 units). Some fonds for UNR diplomatic missions in other countries were still there.[104] But how do those materials relate to the materials presently arranged as fond 3696 of the UNR Foreign Ministry in TsDAVO? Archivists claim no history of the fond or "*sprava fonda*" is available, and if it were, it would not be available to researchers.

TsDAVO has two other fonds containing Foreign Ministry files from the UNR that had been held in Ukraine before the war, but both of these represent the period while the UNR government was still in Ukraine. One is now entitled the Secretariat for National Questions of the Ukrainian Central Rada, with at least one *opys* devoted to Foreign Ministry files. Additional Foreign Ministry files are found in the current fond 3766 from 1918.[105] The same

---

[102] "Otchet o rabote Osobogo otdela sekretnykh fondov za 1948 god," TsDAVO, 4703/2/13, fol. 34. "Spisok fondov Osobogo otdela sekretnykh fondov Tsentral'nogo gosudarstvennogo istoricheskogo arkhiva UkrSSR" (April 1949), TsDAVO, 4703/2/18, fol. 51. The fond number cited for the main UNR Foreign Ministry records (346s) corresponds to the old number indicated on the present *opysy* for TsDAVO, fond no. 3696. However, there is no correlation possible with the German-language inventory of these records prepared in Cracow, a copy of which was found in BAK, NS 30. See more details about these records in my, "The Postwar Fate of the Petliura Library."

[103] The transfer protocol listed 18 émigré fonds including UNR MID records (26 October 1954), TsDAVO, 4703/2/31, fol. 38.

[104] "Spisok fondiv orhanizatsii, ustanov ta osobystykh fondiv ukraïns'kykh emihrantiv viddilu fondiv respublikans'kykh ustanov TsDIA URSR" (6 January 1962), TsDAVO, 4703/2/39, fol. 96.

[105] Fond 2592 (earlier 344s)—Sekretarstvo natsional'nykh sprav Ukraïns'koï tsentral'noï Rady (1917–1918; 4 *opysy*; 121, 10, 3, and 19 units), a part of which is devoted to the files of the Narodne ministerstvo sprav zakordonnykh, 1918—UNR. The first *opys* had been prepared in 1942 in Zlotoust, so had obviously been in Ukraine before the war; the second *opys* had earlier comprised fond no. 4614. Fond 3766—predominantly from the Hetmanate, 1918, has an even more complicated genealogy (3 *opysy*); the first 2 *opysy* had earlier comprised fond 345s/2593; *opys* 3 had earlier been the separate fond 46.

unresolved problems of undefined provenance are apparent there. And, as will be seen below, a few small fonds with UNR diplomatic files are now held in GA RF in Moscow, but those apparently came directly from RZIA.

Ucrainica and Rossica to Moscow

The RZIA Transfer to Moscow. Meanwhile, in Prague during the fall of 1945, preparations continued for the removal of remaining parts of RZIA and other Prague Russian collections to Moscow. Two Glavarkhiv representatives from Moscow had joined the Ukrainian delegation in July 1945.[106] After the UIK materials had left in October, a commission from Moscow was sent to Prague to negotiate final details of the RZIA transfer. Departing for Prague in November, that commission was headed by Glavarkhiv chief Major General Nikitinskii, with Corresponding Members Sergei K. Bogoiavlenskii and Isaak I. Mints representing the Academy of Sciences, and S. Sutotskii representing the Institute of Marxism-Leninism. Neither Bonch-Bruevich nor the literary specialist Ilia S. Zil'bershtein—whom the president of the Academy of Sciences recommended for the mission—were sent to Prague, because "the entire archive was being brought to Moscow…[and] Comrade Zil'bershtein will be able to work with the archive in Moscow."[107]

The official protocol of transfer signed 13 December 1945, carried the "Czech government's hope that the archive would subsequently be put to scholarly use by the Academy and contribute to strengthen the scholarly relations between Czechoslovakia and the USSR."[108] An appended verification protocol lists the 396 crates of materials to be sent to Moscow from RZIA. It was signed by Aleksandr Iziumov. Similar to the Ukrainian case, the shipment even included the materials technically "on deposit," which had not been officially signed over to RZIA by their legitimate owners. The shipment also included another 145 crates from the archive-museum of the Don

---

[106] According to the instruction of 11 July 1945, the official Glavarkhiv delegation consisted of Sergei Ivanovich Kuz'min, and TsGAOR SSSR director, Nikolai Romanovich Prokopenko, GA RF, 5325/10/2023, fol. 1; another copy is found in a top secret "special file" addressed to Molotov, GA RF, 9401/2/103, fol. 253.

[107] G. Aleksandrov to G. M. Malenkov, "Spravka" (6 December 1945), GA RF, 5325/2/1353, fol. 30; the Academy request a month earlier addressed to L. V. Beria (2 November 1945), had been signed by President S. I. Vavilov and Academic Secretary N. G. Bruevich, RGASPI, 17/125/308, fol. 29.

[108] The official leather bound, elaborately printed act of transfer is retained in GA RF, 5325/2/1354.

Cossacks, which had been taken from Novocherkassk during the Civil War, and which were then under the jurisdiction of the Military Archive in Prague. Archival materials from the interwar Russian Cultural-Historical Museum were also included as "a gift for the Academy of Sciences specially designated by the former secretary of L. N. Tolstoi, V. F. Bulgakov."[109] The Russian Cultural-Historical Museum had been established in 1935 under the Russian Free University in Zbraslav Castle near Prague. In addition to archival materials, that collection also included museum exhibits, books, and many runs of émigré newspapers. The RZIA administrative records, including acquisition correspondence, registers, and other related documentation accompanied the collections.[110]

The protocol and shipping lists only cursorily describe the materials transferred. They reference 18 RZIA inventory books covering 10,343 inventory units sent to Moscow, in some cases indicating the RZIA acquisition numbers; however, many of the items were simply described as "unprocessed archival materials."[111] Nevertheless, as GA RF archivists have recently discovered, these lists together with data from RZIA accession registers, correspondence and acquisition files, German wartime inventories, and other data among the RZIA administrative records in Moscow could help reconstruct the complex as it existed in Prague. Of particular importance for Ukraine, these data could also help establish more precise provenance of the Ukrainian materials held by RZIA that went to Moscow. The Belarusian holdings that came with RZIA and now remain in Moscow have been described in a 1997 conference report in Minsk.[112]

Many of the reference books from RZIA also went to Moscow, but as noted above with the UIK materials, the precise figures for library collections are difficult to establish. Some books are noted in the RZIA shipping lists, but these were supposed to be only the duplicates. Crates of newspaper were listed separately. According to official figures, approximately 1,100 books

---

[109] Kruglov to Stalin, GA RF, 9401/2/134, fols. 1–2. See also fn. 120, below.

[110] These records now constitute the separate fond of RZIA, GA RF, 7030. Related fonds in GA RF are also important for the history of RZIA, including the personal papers of the last RZIA archivist and deputy director, Aleksandr F. Iziumov (fond 5962; 29 units; 1922–1940).

[111] The verification protocol was also signed in Prague (13 December 1945), GA RF, 5325/10/2024, fols 3–4v; the shipping lists follow (fols. 5–32). Another copy is found among the RZIA records, GA RF, 7030/2/727.

[112] Nina Stuzhynskaia, "Materyialy pa historyi Belarusi u Ruskim zamezhnym historychnym arkhive," in *Restytutsyia kul'turnykh kashtoŭnastsei*, pp. 188–92.

and 879 volumes of newspapers were sent to Moscow from RZIA.[113] According to figures of the GA RF Central Library, on the other hand, where most of the printed acquisitions from RZIA were long held in the secret division (*spetskhran*), there are now approximately 30,000 books, brochures, journals, and newspapers (1917–1940) that came from Prague. Although card catalogs are now open to researchers in GA RF, it remains difficult to determine how many printed materials came from RZIA, since RZIA library holdings were integrated with printed materials from other sources. Besides, some of the printed materials were classified as file units within various archival fonds. It is possible that more books and newspapers were sent to Moscow from other sources than is apparent in the RZIA shipping lists. However, as noted above, the bulk of the RZIA library holdings remained in Prague and are now part of the Slovanská knihovna within the National Library of the Czech Republic. Aside from the microfiche edition of the of the RZIA library catalog, several recently reissued bibliographies cover parts of the RZIA library collections.[114]

RZIA in Moscow. Nine freight cars of RZIA collections arrived in Moscow just after New Year's Day 1946, officially a "gift" to the Soviet Academy of Sciences on the occasion of its 220th anniversary from the Czech "working classes." A "Special File" (*Osobaia papka*) from the NKVD Secretariat documents the immediate announcement of its arrival to Stalin. The importance attached to the RZIA collections by the Soviet leadership is demonstrated by that two-page document; among other notable items enumerated specifically mention was made of "documents of the government of Denikin and his staff [and] documents of the Petliura government."[115]

Once in Moscow, the materials never came under Academy custody, but rather were immediately delivered to the Main Archival Administration of

---

[113] As reported by V. Bystrov, "Konets RZIA," p. 78. Bystrov's figures come from the official transfer documents but do not involve shipments to Kyiv.

[114] See fn. 66, above, regarding the microfiche catalog available from Norman Ross Publishing in New York. The same publisher has recently issued reprint editions of the bibliography of newspapers from the revolutionary period held by RZIA, Lev Magerovskii, *Bibliografiia gazetnykh sobranii Russkogo istoricheskogo arkhiva za gody 1917–1921* (Prague, 1939), reprint ed. with an introduction by Richard Kneeley (New York: Norman Ross Publishing, 1994) [="Inventari Arkhiva Ministerstva vnutrennikh del v Prage," Ser. B, "Inventari RIA," no. 1], and the bibliography by Postnikov, *Politika, ideologiia, byt i uchenye trudy russkoi èmigratsii*, which survived only in typescript, but was published in New York in 1993.

[115] Kruglov to Stalin (3 January 1946), GA RF, 9401/2/134, fols. 1–2.

the NKVD and deposited in the secret division of the Central State Archive of the October Revolution of the USSR (TsGAOR SSSR).[116] At the end of January the president of the Academy of Sciences, Sergei I. Vavilov, signed an official transfer document, turning the collections over to TsGAOR SSSR "in light of their great value."[117]

A Soviet archival administration official in Moscow assured Stalin's ideological henchman Andrei Zhdanov that the Prague documents would be analyzed for "data on anti-Soviet activities of the White emigration to be used in operational work of agencies of the MVD and MGB SSSR." He added the assurance that there would be "no access to the materials by research institutions."[118]

Within TsGAOR itself, operational work was soon under way with the RZIA holdings. By October NKVD archivists in Moscow reported having completed 10,000 reference information cards from the "fonds of the White counterrevolutionary government and their military units," in addition "to preparing 4,560 reports (*spravki*) in answer to inquiries of operational agencies." They found files with photographs of 6,835 emigrants. By the end of the year, the plan included 17,000 individual cards, although not all of those came from RZIA.[119] This goal, and the qualified archivists devoted to it, may explain the extent of reference descriptive work for those records in Moscow—as witnessed by the two and a half million card files on Russian and Ukrainian émigrés and those who served in the White Army that remain today in GA RF. Unlike the counterpart files in Kyiv, these extensive card files in Moscow are open to researchers and provide in many cases a document-by-document reference aid—particularly for personal names—to many of the émigré fonds brought back to the USSR in postwar years.

---

[116] Details about the RZIA arrival in Moscow under tight security and its immediate transfer to TsGAOR SSSR appear in a report dated 3 January 1946, among Glavarkhiv records in GA RF, 5325/10/2023, fol. 40, with a further explanatory letter (15 May 1946), fol. 42.

[117] See the official letter of Vavilov to Nikitinskii (31 January 1946), GA RF, 5325/10/2023, fol. 42.

[118] Kruglov to Zhdanov (15 May 1946), GA RF, 5325/10/2023, fol. 46.

[119] A series of reports on the work of the archive during 1946 are found in the same file among Glavarkhiv records (GA RF, 5325/2/1791)—for example, Gur'ianov and Golikova to Nikitinskii (15 October 1946), fols. 8–11, with a list of fonds they had processed (10 October 1946), fols. 12–18; Golikova to Starov (27 October 1946), fols. 19–20; Prokopenko to Kuz'min (25 November 1946), fol. 23, and to Starov (23 December 1946), fol. 24. See also the 1946 report, covering specifically work on the Prague materials, GA RF, 3961/5/219, fols. 7–9.

As was the case in Kyiv, the RZIA materials in Moscow were separated out into many fragmentary fonds comprised of different groups of institutional files that could be identified as coming from government agencies, private émigré institutions and community organizations, and personal papers. In Prague by contrast, acquisition numbers had been retained, and archival materials for the most part had been kept intact with the collection in which it was received. When more detailed arrangement was undertaken, it usually was made by type of document (e.g., letters, manuscripts, etc.). Further confusion arises here because the materials removed to the Heeresarchiv by the Nazis were subsequently packed by the Soviets for transfer to Moscow before they had been reintegrated with the other remaining RZIA collections. Besides this fundamental problem, many of the materials acquired at the end of the 1930s or during the war by RZIA in Prague had hardly been processed, if at all. Since RZIA archivist Iziumov had been imprisoned by the Nazis and there had been considerable staff turnover, archivists were uncertain about the extent to which other materials may have been removed by the Nazis. Thus, when the materials were hastily prepared for shipment in 1945, finding aids were grossly inadequate, and the accompanying shipping lists with their frequent references to "unprocessed archival materials," were all the documentation that the Moscow archivists could use. The Prague acquisition numbers were never retained in Moscow. In some cases the RZIA materials were intermixed with documents acquired by TsGAOR from other sources. The various points of provenance of the Prague materials themselves, even to the extent that they might have been apparent, was not respected in Moscow. For example, some of the materials from the interwar Russian Cultural-Historical Museum in Zbraslav Castle were subsequently intermingled with those from RZIA, and many of those were transferred to TsGALI (now RGALI).[120]

A fond-level guide to the émigré materials in TsGAOR, including those from RZIA, was issued in a secret edition in 1952.[121] The main problem with

---

[120] A major group of the records of this museum also came from Prague and are held today in GA RF, fond R-6784, but many have been transferred to TsGALI (now RGALI). Other pertinent sources about the museum in GA RF are revealed in the report by M. Iu. Dostal', "Russkii kul'turno-istoricheskii muzei v Prage v tvorcheskoi sud'be V. F. Bulgakova (po novym arkhivnym dannym)," in *"Russkaia, ukrainskaia i belorusskaia èmigratsiia" 1995,* vol. 1, pp. 806–815. See also the brochure by E. S. Dokasheva, *Russkii kul'turno-istoricheskii muzei v Prage* (Moscow, 1993).

[121] *Tsentral'nyi gosudarstvennyi arkhiv Oktiabr'skoi revoliutsii i sotsialisticheskogo stroitel'stva SSSR: Putevoditel',* vol. 2 (Moscow, 1952). Published in a "secret edition" in 1952, that guide was not declassified until 1987, along with most of the

that guide and with the corresponding indications in the often hastily prepared *opisi* for individual fonds, is that details are not provided about the provenance of the fonds, nor the migratory pattern by which they reached TsGAOR SSSR.

Unfortunately, the dispersal of the Prague materials among different Soviet archives was even more tragic for the integrity of the collections than their processing in a multitude of separate fonds. Soon after the Prague shipment arrived, NKVD Chief Kruglov had assured Zhdanov that none of the "fonds or individual collections of documents would be transferred to other archives or research institutions."[122] Such assurances not withstanding, a large group of foreign-policy related materials from RZIA were transferred to the Ministry of Foreign Affairs at the end of the first year. Among those listed in the official transfer are important Ukrainian diplomatic files from the Petliura government, including documents of UNR representatives in Western Europe.[123] We still do not know how many of those Ukrainian files remain in MID archives, but UNR holdings there have not yet been publicly described.[124]

Ukrainian Components in RZIA. As RZIA archivist Aleksandr Iziumov noted, despite the existence in Prague of the separate Ukrainian Historical Cabinet, "some Ukrainian documentation was also held in the Russian

---

RZIA materials remaining in TsGAOR SSSR. One of the few remaining copies of that guide, now available in the GA RF reading room, has marginal notes indicating that the materials transferred elsewhere.

[122] Kruglov to Zhdanov (15 May 1946), GA RF, 5325/10/2023, fol. 46.

[123] An official request for transfer addressed to I. I. Nikitinskii from V. Khvostov from MID (24 December 1946), is accompanied by a seven-page list of the files involved—GA RF, 5325/2/1705a. The original typescript list with a covering letter from Madik to Kruglov (dated 24 June 1947) remains in another file, GA RF, 5325/2/2286a.

[124] During informal inquiries, MID archival officials in Moscow denied that any UNR files were still held in their archives. This may mean that they are still classified or were arranged as part of a composite collection. Other RZIA fonds that were transferred to MID and that can be identified now in AVPRI are listed in the new RZIA guide: *Fondy Russkogo zagranichnogo istoricheskogo arkhiva v Prage: Arkhivnyi putevoditel'*, comp. O. N. Kopyleva et al.; ed. T. F. Pavlova et al. (Moscow: ROSSPEN, 1999). See also the listings by Andrei V. Popov, *Russkoe zarubezh'e i arkhivy: Dokumenty rossiiskoi èmigratsii v arkhivakh Moskvy: Problemy vyiavleniia, komplektovaniia, opisaniia, ispol'zovaniia* (Moscow: IAI RGGU, 1998), p. 132 [="Materialy k istorii russkoi politicheskoi èmigratsii," 4].

Archive."[125] However, during the preparation in Prague for the hasty 1945 transfer of the RZIA and UIK to the USSR, no attempt was made to separate out the Ukrainian materials from the RZIA in order to ship them to Kyiv. Had the Ukrainians been aware of the situation, they probably would not have been successful, given the tremendous Moscow interest in UNR records (among others), as is apparent from the specific mention of the Petliura government documents in the arrival notice sent to Stalin in January 1946. This interest also is clear in the transfer of UNR diplomatic files to the Ministry of Foreign Affairs at the end of the year.

The intermingling of Ukrainian materials in the RZIA in Prague is readily apparent in the RZIA acquisition correspondence and related administrative records now held in GA RF. For example, a large file of letters and inventories of incoming materials during the years 1926–1939 clearly shows the extent to which Ukrainian and Belarusian materials were intermingled with Russian documentation. Sometimes the different materials would be acquired simultaneously—often as part of the same collection.[126]

Once the RZIA collections arrived in Moscow and were resorted into fonds in TsGAOR, designations of institutional provenance were not accurately or consistently made. A case in point: although most of the UNR diplomatic files were transferred to MID in late 1947, among Ukrainian fonds now held in GA RF is a small group of files designated as UNR Foreign Ministry records. TsGAOR and later GA RF archivists initially attributed their provenance to Tŭrnovo, Bulgaria, but in 1999 that was corrected to Tarnów, Poland.[127] According to the inventory of the fond in GA RF, three kilos of materials initially assigned to that fond were consigned to waste paper in 1956 as "having no scientific value," and six more files—more clearly of Foreign Ministry relevance—were then added to the fond from

---

[125] Iziumov, "Zapiska o Russkom Istoricheskom Arkhive," p. 406.

[126] See particularly the administrative records of RZIA itself, GA RF, fond 7030. Of particular interest in this respect is, for example, 7030/1/91, where clearly many Ukrainian and Belarusian receipts are intermingled.

[127] GA RF, fond R-6087. Recently GA RF archivists agreed with me that the Tŭrnovo attribution was inaccurate and changed it at the last minute in the RZIA guide. They kindly provided me with an advance copy of the proof page describing that fond (see above, fn. 124). In several GA RF publications the fond is listed erroneously under "Bulgaria, Diplomatic Missions," with its provenance in Tyrnovo [*sic,* for Търново], Bulgaria—see, e.g., the comprehensive list of fonds in *Perechen' fondov Gosudarstvennogo arkhiva Rossiiskoi Federatsii i nauchno-spravochnyi apparat k dokumentam arkhiva,* comp. L. G. Aronov, O. N. Kopylova, et al.; ed. S. V. Mironenko (Moscow: Red.-izd. otdel Federal'nykh arkhivov, 1998), p. 161.

unsorted materials.[128] The 17 files now in that fond (mostly dating from the early 1920s) most probably all came directly from RZIA (as part of three different groups of documents in 1924, 1926, and 1935), and were probably created either in Tarnów or Warsaw. They do not constitute an integral group of ministry records, and probably most of them would better have been assigned to the fond of the UNR Council (Rada) of Ministers, rather than the Foreign Ministry. Indeed, GA RF also has a separate fragmentary fond with files designated as of provenance in the Chancellery of the UNR Rada—which is now listed in GA RF as of Polish provenance. Archivists initially thought that these files also came from RZIA, and, indeed, a few documents bear RZIA stamps. Other documents possibly came with other archival materials from the Petliura Library in Paris that were transferred to TsGAOR from the Lenin Library in 1948.[129]

Another fragmentary UNR fond in GA RF is devoted to records of the UNR Embassy in Berlin. These records already were listed as such in the 1952 guide.[130] This fond also turns out to be artificial in its formation. It is quite certain that the documents came to RZIA in the late 1920s or early 1930s from several different sources. For example, notes in RZIA records confirm the receipt of a collection containing documents from the Berlin Embassy, also contained documents from the UNR delegation in France, UNR missions in England, Turkey, Italy, Vienna, and other countries, as well as a large packet from the UNR Ministry of Finance (1919–1920). However, the materials described cannot be matched up with current GA RF hold-

---

[128] See the preface to the *opis'* for GA RF, fond R-6087. See the description in *Fondy RZIA,* pp. 99–100.

[129] GA RF, R-7526 (16 units; 1920–1930). The original *opis'* covering file nos. 1–11 is dated 1957; nos. 12–16, were added in 1960. The fond is not listed in *Fondy RZIA.* In November 1948, TsGAOR received 170 crates of archival materials from the Lenin Library in Moscow, which included materials of "Ukrainian émigré organizations in Paris, among others." The official receipt in the records of TsGAOR SSSR was signed by Mikhail Il'ich Rubinskii, chief of the RZIA Division of TsGAOR SSSR (9 November 1948), GA RF, 5142/1/423, fols. 140–141.

[130] A fond of the UNR Embassy in Berlin remains in GA RF, as was indicated in the secret 1952 TsGAOR *Putevoditel'*—fond 5889 (28 units, 1918–1926). Presently, however, the fond has 35 units; file no. 36 is the original *opis'* of the fond (14 May 1947). Other fragments of these records are held in TsDAVO in Kyiv, probably that came with the UNR Foreign Ministry records from Tarnów that were seized by SMERSH in Cracow in March 1945. See the description in *Fondy RZIA,* pp. 54–55.

ings.[131] A folder later added to the Berlin Embassy fond in TsGAOR SSSR contains some personal letters from Petliura to Viktor V. Porsh, who served as the UNR ambassador in Berlin. One of those letters has a separate 1934 presentation note to RZIA attached. There is some indication that another had been sold to RZIA.[132] This particular fond was one of those listed among the UNR materials from RZIA to be transferred to the Ministry of Foreign Affairs of the USSR in December 1946; however, it was not included in the transfers.[133] Other RZIA materials held in the Foreign Ministry archives have been documented recently (although other UNR materials are not among them).[134]

A separate fond also remains in GA RF for the UNR Delegation to the Paris Peace Conference (fond R–7027; 40 units; 1919–1921). This is another group of records that is documented as having, at least in part, been acquired by RZIA. GA RF has separated these fragmentary files from the related files of the UNR Mission to France, which now forms a separate fond.[135] Other files from those records were known to have been held in the Petliura Library in Paris before the war. Some of these files, along with archival materials from the Petliura Library in Paris, most probably were transferred to TsGAOR from the Lenin Library in 1948.[136]

---

[131] See a descriptive list of a UNR collection received by RZIA, GA RF, 7030/1/91, fols. 7–8. The name of the collector or its source is not indicated, except that it was sent through "M.A."; nor was the exact date given. The printed 1931 RZIA report mentions that some files of the UNR Embassy in Berlin were received that year—GA RF 7030/114, 1931 report, p. 7. Several other RZIA annual reports in the same folder (1928–1931) also mention the receipt of UNR documentation.

[132] GA RF, 5889/1/34. One of the Petliura letters was sold to RZIA by V. L. Forna with a receipt for 600 crowns. There is also a letter of V. K. Vynnychenko (no. 26), and a 1919 letter about UNR funds in the Reichsbank (no. 29a).

[133] See the list that accompanied the official MID transfer request (24 December 1946)—GA RF, 5325/2/1705a. The fond does not appear in the official acts of transfer, as recorded in the *dela* fond, and recently verified for me by GA RF archivist Ol'ga Kopylova. The fond retained 28 units in 1948, *after* the transfers to MID.

[134] Further investigation in the MID archives is still required, since all of the UNR files are not listed in the RZIA guide.

[135] See the RZIA annual report listing receipts for 1928, with mention of 500 pages of documents of the Ukrainian delegation in Paris (1919–1922). GA RF 7030/1/114, p. 7. See the descriptions in *Fondy RZIA*, pp. 125–27.

[136] See fns. 129, above, and 148, below, and my "Postwar Fate of the Petliura Library."

The Dispersal of RZIA in the USSR. The transfer of RZIA materials to the Ministry of Foreign Affairs in 1946, despite earlier assurances that the collections would be kept intact, unfortunately set a precedent. Afterward, parts of the RZIA collections were dispersed to over 30 different repositories throughout the former USSR. Soon after their receipt, some Polish materials from RZIA were transferred to the Special Archive—TsGOA. Some Herzen and Ogarev manuscripts from Prague and Sofia had been transferred to the Manuscript Division of the Lenin Library. Then in 1956, 801 Herzen and Ogarev documents, including some from RZIA, were transferred to the Central State Archive of Literature and Art—TsGALI (now RGALI). Those were among the first of the retrieved émigré collections to be described openly in print with acknowledgment of their provenance.[137] They were followed to TsGALI later in the early 1960s, by many more fonds relating to literature and art, including numerous personal papers and materials from the Russian Cultural-Historical Museum in Prague.[138] White Army records went to the Soviet-period military archive, the Central State Archive of the Soviet Army—TsGASA (now RGVA), where they, along with those acquired from other sources, are described in a new 1998 guide.[139] The reference card catalogs compiled for White Army participants, however, remained in TsGAOR SSSR. Many RZIA materials of more local interest were sent to regional archives and other Soviet republics.

Although most military records from the pre-revolutionary and Soviet periods were traditionally concentrated in Moscow after World War II, fragments from 55 fonds from RZIA in TsGAOR SSSR—predominately files relating to UNR military units during the attempt to establish an independent

---

[137] L. R. Lanski and V. A. Putintsev, "Rukopisi proizvedenii Gertsena v 'Prazhskoi' i 'Sofiiskoi' kollektsiiakh: Opisanie," *Literaturnoe nasledstvo* 63 (1956): 725–52. Additional Herzen and Ogarev materials from Prague in TsGALI (fond 5770) were described in the same volume 752–92, 793–830, 831–54, 855–64. S. A. Makashin, "'Sofiiskaia' kollektsiia rukopisei' iz arkhiva Gertsena i Ogareva," *Izvestiia Akademii nauk SSSR. Otdelenie literatury i iazyka* 13 (1954) 5: 456–63.

[138] Many of the transfers are noted by Popov, *Russkoe Zarubezh'e i arkhivy*, pp. 132–33. Popov had access to TsGAOR SSSR acquisition and transfer registers that I have not consulted. I have found many transfers registered in annual reports and transfer correspondence; those given here are only a few examples.

[139] [Rossiiskii gosudarstvennyi voennyi arkhiv], *Putevoditel' po fondam Beloi Armii*, comp. N. V. Pul'chenko, N. D. Egorov, and L. M. Chizhova; ed. N. D. Egorov and L. V. Dvoinykh (Moscow: Russkoe bibliograficheskoe obshchestvo, 1998) [="Academia ROSSICA," vol. 4]. Some of the RZIA materials involved were earlier listed in the 1952 guide to TsGAOR SSSR.

Ukrainian state—were sent to Kyiv in 1964. In the late 1980s Kyiv archivists furnished descriptions of those fonds included in the Moscow RZIA guide, but their descriptions so far are not publicly available to researchers in Kyiv.[140] During the period when RZIA fonds were being dispersed, however, not all Ukrainian fonds were sent to Kyiv (as is evident from the RZIA Ukrainian materials discussed above). A few of the archival materials that came to Kyiv with the UIK collections went the other direction—from Kyiv to Moscow.

RZIA and Trophy Rossica and Ucrainica from Other Sources in Moscow. Most of the RZIA materials shipped to Moscow and deposited in TsGAOR SSSR formed what then became a special "RZIA Division" of the archive. Since they had been a "gift" to the Academy of Sciences of the USSR, and since they were officially considered to be part of the State Archival Fond of the USSR, they had a more "legitimate" status than the trophy fonds from other sources that preceded or followed their arrival in Moscow. Even today, most Russian archivists do not consider the RZIA collections to be "trophies."

Many other Russian émigré fonds from various countries that were acquired with the trophy archives after World War II were also deposited in TsGAOR SSSR. They joined the RZIA collections, and in some cases became intermingled with them. These included émigré records brought back from Bulgaria, from Germany, and from Yugoslavia later in 1948, to name only a few of the sources. As noted above, there was considerable documentation from Russian and Ukrainian "bourgeois-nationalist" political parties and émigré circles held by the RSHA Amt VII in Silesia. This included a large part of the archive of Pavel Miliukov from Paris that went to TsGAOR SSSR, together with the records of the journal *Poslednie novosti*, which Miliukov edited in Paris until 1940.[141] Popov's 1998 monograph on archival Rossica in Moscow archives has appended lists of fonds (some of them Ukrainian) in a number of Moscow archives and manuscript collections, providing the most complete listing to date of such holdings.[142]

---

[140] GA RF archivists earlier acquainted me with the list of transfers and the incoming descriptions from Kyiv. See *Fondy RZIA,* pp. 371, 430, 463, 466, 481–89.

[141] See the list of holdings dated 21 September 1945, GA RF, 5325/10/2027, fol. 7–7v. Regarding their capture in Silesia, see Chapter 8, p. 291.

[142] Popov, *Russkoe zarubezh'e i arkhivy.* Many of his descriptions must still be considered preliminary. The forthcoming fourth volume of the guide to GA RF will include annotated coverage of all of the émigré fonds held by that archive.

Soviet archival agents were already on the scene in Romania in February 1945. By spring the Soviet archival envoys reported the recovery from Bucharest of the archive of an International Refugee Office that was helping Ukrainian and other refugees after the October Revolution.[143] Most important were parts of the archive of the former imperial Russian Embassy and two crates of papers from the former Russian ambassador Aleksei Savinov, which had been seized by the Romanian security service (Siguranţe) after his death.[144]

Two years later, in May 1947, another special mission was directed to Yugoslavia, this time under joint Foreign Ministry auspices, where they found "records of the Yugoslav Commission for Affairs of the Russian emigration, files relating to the evacuation of emigrants from Crimea (1922–1923), and card files on the Russian émigrés in Yugoslavia (1922–1923)," among other materials "that have serious operational and historical significance for the Soviet Union."[145] They dispatched 82 crates, which arrived in Moscow in early February 1948. Most of the documentary materials went to TsGAOR SSSR, while a few files of literary materials were directed to TsGLA (*now* RGALI), some documentation on military-history to TsGVIA, and other documentation to the MID archive.[146] Materials from the special museum established in Belgrade by Russian émigrés to honor Nicholas II went to the State Historical Museum in Moscow in 1947, although it was 1998 before the rich documentation involved was described in print.[147]

In November 1948 the Lenin Library in Moscow transferred 170 crates of archival materials to TsGAOR SSSR, and the act of transfer specifically directing them to the RZIA Division. That document specifies files of the

[143] Susaikov to Kruglov (Bucharest, 19 May 1945), GA RF, 5325/2/992, fols. 209–210. The materials were received officially in Moscow on 10 May 1945, as indicated by a receipt found in fol. 207.

[144] Istomii and A. Iur′ev to E. I. Golubtsov (19 May 1945), GA RF, 5325/2/992, fol. 205.

[145] See the report of Deputy Foreign Minister A. Vyshinskii to S. N. Kruglov (19 May 1947), GA RF, 5325/2/2172, fol. 1; Nikitinskii to Kruglov (31 May 1947), GA RF, 5325/2/2172, fols. 2, 5, 7.

[146] See the report of Sofinov and Golubtsov to Riaskov (21 October 1947), GA RF, 5325/2/2172, fols. 14–17, with an appended list (fols. 18–20); and the official document of receipt (3 February 1948), GA RF, 5323/2/2172, fols. 24–26.

[147] M. B. Falaleeva, "Fond Romanovykh v sobranii OPI GIM," *Arkheograficheskii ezhegodnik za 1996 god* (Moscow, 1998), pp. 270–81 (see especially pp. 279–81).

Ukrainian National Committee in Paris, the Orthodox Church, records of the Turgenev Library, and materials of "Ukrainian émigré organizations in Paris, among others," that had been received by the Lenin Library from Berlin in 1946–1947.[148] Presumably, that transfer also included the records of the Petliura Library and the UNR journal *Tryzub*, which had been housed in the library before the war. The materials also include some of the administrative records and prewar catalogs of the library, as well as archival materials that had been collected by the library before 1940. Those Ukrainian émigré materials from Paris that had been found in Silesia together with major library holdings were shipped in part to Moscow and in part to Minsk. The archival materials from the Petliura Library that went to Minsk were later transferred to the Special Archive in Moscow in 1955, which explains why the collections are now divided. In both cases, they were broken down into six or eight splinter fonds following Soviet archival procedures.[149] Many of the materials from the Petliura Library now held in GA RF were earlier listed as having come to GA RF from RZIA.

When GA RF started preparing its guide to the RZIA archival collections transferred to Moscow—and even as late as several years ago—its staff still assumed that these Petliura Library materials, along with other UNR documentation held in GA RF, had all come from Prague. This is clear in a preliminary version of the RZIA guide annotations for those fonds.[150] It has

---

[148] The official receipt in the records of TsGAOR SSSR was signed by Mikhail Il'ich Rubinskii, chief of the RZIA Division of TsGAOR SSSR (9 November 1948), GA RF 5142/1/423, fols. 140–141. GA RF archivist Ol'ga Kopylova found this document and kindly showed it to me, after I had questioned the accuracy of attributing the provenance of the Petliura Library files to RZIA or other Prague sources. Although received in a shipment from Berlin, the Turgenev Library and other Ukrainian materials were actually found in Silesia and brought to Berlin for shipment.

[149] The "S. Petliura Ukrainian Library, Paris" itself constitutes fond R-7008 in GA RF with 141 units (1909, 1914–1917, 1919–1920, 1922, 1924–1939). The "Editorial Records of the Journal *Tryzub*, Paris" constitutes fond 7498 (earlier 3882s; 93 units). See more details about these and related archival materials from the library and the problems of their migration in my "The Postwar Fate of the Petliura Library."

[150] I was shown those preliminary annotations in the fall of 1997, which is when I started examining various files in those fonds in effort to determine their provenance. I found many stamps and dedicatory inscriptions to the Petliura Library in files in both those fonds, and I assured GA RF archivists that the library had been looted by the Nazis from Paris and that none of its materials had ever been in Prague. Possibly some publications (many are included now as files within the fond) might have been received or sent to RZIA/UIK on exchange. I appreciate the assistance of archivists in

since been determined that none of these Petliura Library materials were ever held in Prague, but were rather seized by the Nazis in Paris, along with the records of the Turgenev Library, that are also now held in GA RF.[151] Quite possibly, some of the files in a portion of the Ukrainian émigré archival fonds from Paris in GA RF were added to those fonds from other sources. Some of those fonds do indeed have stray file units, or even stray documents, of alternate provenance, including material that may well have been received with the Prague RZIA shipment (which itself also included materials from other émigré institutions in Czechoslovakia). Because of the multiple archival transfers in the postwar decades, and the fact that all of the incoming miscellaneous collections were broken down into artificially specific fonds without regard to the archive where they were last held or the collection with which they were received, considerable research and verification has been needed before any attributions can be accurately assigned.

Two additional Ukrainian émigré fonds of Swiss provenance in GA RF were also earlier thought to have come from RZIA: the Ukrainian Press Bureau in Lausanne and the editorial records of the journal *Ukraïna* (also received from Lausanne). Further research has revealed, however, that they were in fact received from the Lenin Library in 1949, having been earlier received by the Library from Geneva with the papers and library of the Russian bibliographer Nikolai Aleksandrovich Rybakin.[152]

The Intellectual Reconstruction: A New Guide to RZIA Holdings in the Former USSR. Following ten years of research and gathering data about the dispersed RZIA collections, archivists in GA RF completed a comprehensive guide to the RZIA collections that were transferred to Moscow in 1945/46. The guide covers all of the fonds as established after transfer of the RZIA

GA RF, who were willing to work with me in trying to correct the provenance attributions.

[151] Archivists in TsGAOR SSSR (now GA RF) first showed me the Turgenev Library records in 1990, when I questioned their provenance, after which it was clear to me that they all came from Paris and not Prague. A parallel article on the odyssey of the Turgenev Library is in preparation in collaboration with Hélène Kaplan in Paris.

[152] The Ukrainian Press Bureau now constitutes fond R-7050 (2 *opisi*; 2,011 units; 1902–1944); records of the journal *Ukraïna* are now grouped as fond R-7063 (257 units; 1911–1924). Their receipt by TsGAOR SSSR (16 August 1949) is documented in the archive of TsGAOR SSSR, GA RF, 5142/1/449, fol. 72. Ol'ga Kopylova kindly showed me the relevant documents she had found.

collections to Moscow, and after their subsequent dispersal to nearly thirty archives throughout the USSR. Funding for the publication was provided from international sources in Western Europe concerned about the fate of those collections.[153]

Preparation of the comprehensive fond-level guide to the RZIA collections started in 1989.[154] The project director, Tat'iana F. Pavlova, former deputy director of TsGAOR SSSR, was the first to publish openly about RZIA, after the collections had been declassified in the days of glasnost. She prepared what was intended to be completed as a candidate dissertation about RZIA.[155] At a 1995 international conference in Prague, one of the present GA RF archivists heading the project gave a presentation about the forthcoming guide.[156]

The new guide certainly will help fulfill a part of the responsibility and debt that Russian archivists must feel vis-à-vis the Russian diaspora for the dispersal of the RZIA collections. As if to compensate for such dispersal, the new guide provides an attempted intellectual reconstruction. At the same time it furnishes information of the collections' original content, current location, and their present division into fonds.

Russian specialists have already taken the lead in identifying the archival Rossica that was retrieved from Prague after World War II. But what about the Ucrainica? Now that the RZIA guide has been completed, it is time for Ukrainian specialists to keep pace with their Russian colleagues. If Ukrainian archivists and historians together would be willing to make similar efforts, it is quite likely that supporting funding could be found from foreign, if not domestic Ukrainian sources. Even the most preliminary list of the Ukrainian collections retrieved from the related Ukrainian Historical Cabinet in Prague (UIK) has not reached the planning stage in Kyiv. Ukrainian specialists have

---

[153] *Fondy RZIA.* See the bibliography (section VII) for the funding agencies.

[154] See *Metodicheskie rekomendatsii po sostavleniiu mezharkhivnogo spravochnika po fondam byvshego Russkogo zagranichnogo istoricheskogo arkhiva v Prage (b. RZIA)* (Moscow: TsGAOR SSSR, 1991); Tat'iana Pavlova kindly furnished me a copy for review when it was first published in limited edition for internal circulation. I appreciate the continuing opportunity for discussion about the project with Pavlova and her colleagues on numerous occasions since the project started in 1989.

[155] Pavlova, "Russkii Zagranichnyi istoricheskii arkhiv." Pavlova's administrative career prevented the research needed to complete and defend her dissertation (cf. fn. 26, above).

[156] L. I. Petrusheva, "Dokumenty prazhskoi kollektsii v nauchno-spravochnom apparate Gosudarstvennogo arkhiva Rossiiskoi Federatsii," in *"Russkaia, ukrainskaia i belorusskaia èmigratsiia" 1995,* vol. 1, pp. 91–97.

made no attempt to study the original acquisitions and composition of the UIK holdings with an aim of indicating the fonds into which they were subsequently divided in Kyiv. Neither have they traced the current location and archival designations of those materials, the vast majority of which are held in Ukraine. After half a century, it is time for these extremely valuable materials to be brought fully to light.

Ukrainian Émigré Files from Kyiv to Moscow. Despite popular belief, only a few of the Ukrainian émigré materials received in Kyiv from abroad were transferred to Moscow, although reports on "anti-Soviet" and "Ukrainian bourgeois-nationalist" elements were shared with the secret service agencies in the Soviet capital. In fact, relatively few transfers from Kyiv to Moscow of Ukrainian émigré files have been documented.

The most significant transfer took place in 1954, involving at least a dozen fonds with approximately 825 file folders of the Ukrainian Party of Socialist Revolutionaries (UPSR) and related left-wing political groups. Most of this had come from Prague with the UIK collections. These materials went to TsGAOR SSSR.[157] At least a major part of these files now form part of the GA RF fond established as "Collection of Materials of Foreign Organizations of the Ukrainian Party of Socialist Revolutionaries, 1919–1938." The files were obviously reprocessed in TsGAOR after arrival in Moscow, but that fond now has only 360 file units dating from 1919–1931.[158] Further research is needed to determine if other SR files from

---

[157] Notes to this effect are found penciled on one of the copies of the list of fonds then held in the Special Secret Division of TsDIA URSR—TsDAVO, 4703/2/6. Among materials requisitioned by TsGAOR SSSR in Moscow were those relating to different local operations of the Ukrainian Party of Socialist Revolutionaries (UPSR) in Prague and elsewhere abroad. Documentation regarding the transfers is found in the TsDIAK correspondence file for 1954 (TsDAVO, 4703/2/31), where there are references to transfers on 20 February 1954 (fol. 5) and 10 March 1954 (fol. 6) to TsGAOR SSSR (referencing a Soviet order dated 19 January 1954), encompassing 444 folders of Ukrainian SR fonds (and some files of Jewish committees) from Czechoslovakia, Austria, and Poland, and on 18 October 1954, referencing 381 folders of Ukrainian SR files. It is difficult to determine now if all of these came from UIK and what their status had been there.

[158] GA RF, R-7744, "Kollektsiia materialov zagranichnykh organizatsii ukrainskoi partii sotsialistov-revoliutsionerov, Prague, 1919–1938." As currently listed in GA RF, the fond is supposed to have 10 *opisi* (361 units). Within the first *opis′* (unit no. 3) is one of the original Kyiv *opisi* from TsDIAK—(*opys* 3, prepared 10 July 1946) indicating 122 units (1928–1938), under the Ukrainian title "Holovnyi politechnyi komitet Ukr.P.SR (za kordonom) v Prazi, Tsen. kom." (with the indication

Kyiv are held elsewhere, or if they were added to other fonds in TsGAOR SSSR after their arrival in Moscow.

Orders came to Kyiv from Moscow from the Central State Archive of the Soviet Army in 1956 for the transfer of the remaining files from Ukrainian Sich Riflemen Units (Sichovi Stril'tsi) although most such materials, of predominantly west Ukrainian origin, had earlier been returned to Lviv.[159] At the end of 1955, some 6,661 "printed editions" from TsDIA-K were transferred to the Special Archive (TsGOA SSSR).[160]

Another transfer occurred in 1957, involving a relatively small group of Ukrainian "bourgeois-nationalist" files, particularly relating to Ukrainian organizations operating in Poland. These included a few UNR files along with predominantly foreign-language military-oriented files regarding Poland. They were forwarded to the Special Archive (TsGOA SSSR).[161] It has not yet been possible to document the current location of these materials in Moscow in terms of specific fonds among the former TsKhIDK holdings. It should also be noted, however, that some materials of Ukrainian émigré origin came directly to Moscow in the course of various postwar archival retrieval operations, and some were later transferred to TsGOA SSSR from Belarus. So it is possible that the materials from Kyiv were interfiled in other

---

that it was earlier fond no. 86s/3956s). The fond number 86s corresponds to the fond of that title listed on the April 1949 and April 1952 TsDIAK lists, when that particular fond in TsDIAK had 116 units. Other parts of the GA RF collection may represent materials from TsDAZhR, although further verification is needed to determine if all of the original files sent from Ukraine are retained in the GA RF fond.

[159] See the Moscow communiqué claiming that according to their data, 7 fonds and 8 units were held in Kyiv (fol. 36), and the note confirming transfer (5 April 1956) from TsDIA URSR to TsGASA, TsDAVO, 4703/1/192, fol. 42.

[160] The act of transmittal to TsGOA (4 January 1956) notes an attached list, but a copy has not been retained in the TsDIAK records, TsDAVO, 4703/2/33, fol. 1. So far, an incoming copy of the list has not been available in TsKhIDK. We therefore do not know—although we may well suspect—that they involved émigré or other foreign-language materials.

[161] See the communiqué regarding the transfer from TsDIAK to TsGOA SSSR, listing 16 files in Polish and other languages (29 February 1957), TsDAVO, 4703/1/193, fol. 31. A few émigré files are also listed among 5 crates of materials of various foreign provenance transferred in another communiqué dated 29 March 1957, TsDAVO, 4703/1/193, fols. 39–51. Although most of the materials transferred mentioned in the above shipments were previously held in TsDIA URSR, some transfers were also made from TsDAZhR URSR, but it has not yet been possible to document them.

Moscow fonds. Again, it is difficult to tell now if those materials were acquired in Kyiv as part of the UIK collections.

Archival Ucrainica Retrieved in Kyiv

Ucrainica Reorganized in Kyiv. In 1960, when additional shipments were being received from Prague, the Special Secret Division of what was then TsDAZhR URSR in Kharkiv prepared an extensive list of all of the Ukrainian émigré fonds that it had received from Prague and other sources in Czechoslovakia. This list clearly shows that virtually all of the materials from UIK and other sources in Czechoslovakia had by that time been consolidated in TsDAZhR URSR with the same fond numbers that most of them preserve today. Upon receipt of a copy of the list in Kyiv, the director of the TsDIAK Special Secret Division was requested to verify their holdings and report any additional materials that should be part of these fonds.[162] Of importance in this list, archivists then were quite aware that other émigré archival materials in Kyiv had come from other countries, such as from Vienna, Berlin, and various cities in Poland, or the Petliura materials from Paris, because none of those are included in the TsDAZhR Czech list.

In the early 1970s a new archival building was constructed in Kyiv and the former Central State Archive of the October Revolution (TsDAZhR URSR—now TsDAVO) was moved from Kharkiv to Kyiv. The Prague and other émigré collections in the Special Secret Divisions of both TsDAZhR URSR from Kharkiv and TsDIA URSR in Kyiv (at that time TsDIAK) were then consolidated in the secret division of the newly-moved TsDAZhR URSR. There they continued to remain closed to public research, and even their existence was denied. Despite the protests of many Kyiv archivists, some brief references to these collections and notes about the lack of public information about their availability in Kyiv first appeared in my 1988 Ukrainian archival directory with additional bibliographic references to earlier descriptions from Prague.[163]

---

[162] "Spisok fondov uchrezhdenii i organizatsii ukrainskikh burzhuaznykh natsionalistov na territorii Chekhoslovakii" (5 February 1960), TsDAVO, 4703/2/39, fols. 9–23. The list and covering letter are signed by the TsDAZhR director, Vostrikova, and the chief of the Division of Special Secret Fonds, Chernov.

[163] Grimsted, *Archives: Ukraine,* pp. 244–45. Information about them and their existence was constantly denied to the author before the publication of that directory in 1988. Archival officials in Kyiv requested that I not include such references, but

Access to Ucrainica in Kyiv after Independence. It was not until 1994 that published reports openly admitted that most of the interwar Ukrainian collections from Prague were, in fact, in Kyiv. One report, as mentioned above, was prepared by TsDAVO director Larysa Iakovlieva. Two others were written by Liudmyla Lozenko.[164] None of these articles identified specific fonds, nor were they detailed enough to serve as finding aids for researchers. None discussed the other important Ukrainian émigré materials in Kyiv that came from sources other than Prague.

As we have seen earlier, in the course of their "operational" work with the archival Ucrainica retrieved, NKVD/MVD archivists in the Ukrainian SSR prepared careful lists of the fonds held and processed in the Special Secret Divisions of TsDIAK and TsDAZhR UkrSSR. Some of the earliest postwar lists of fonds in the secret division of TsDIA URSR do not indicate those that had been brought back from Czechoslovakia. They also do not distinguish UIK materials from those seized elsewhere (or seized by the Nazis elsewhere). Some of the lists do, however, have penciled annotations identifying their provenance as UIK. Others clearly note their origin as Paris, Vienna, Berlin, or Cracow. Some of the lists have penciled annotations indicating archival transfers and changes of fond numbers. Even if incomplete and needing verification, such lists and their annotations could provide the basis for an initial guide for researchers.[165] These early lists still need to be coordinated with later ones. The lists also need to be compared with similar ones that were undoubtedly prepared for TsDAZhR in Kharkiv to indicate archival transfers and organizational changes.

Most of the archival materials listed are now held in TsDAVO, although some have been transferred to other archives, including the Central State Archive-Museum of Literature and Art—TsDAMLM in Kyiv. Many of the fond numbers in TsDAVO have been changed from those originally assigned in Kyiv, particularly since the émigré materials in TsDIAK were later

---

numerous colleagues both in Ukraine and abroad assisted in tracking down earlier published descriptions.

[164] Iakovlieva, "Praz'ki fondy v Kyievi"; Lozenko, "Praz'kyi ukraïns'kyi arkhiv" and "Z istoriï Praz'koho ukraïns'koho arkhivu."

[165] TsDAVO, 4703/2/6. This folder contains lists of fonds dating from 1945 through 1949. Separate lists of processed fonds and those being worked on during 1949 give a relatively comprehensive idea of those being held by TsDIA URSR (TsDIAK) at that time—TsDAVO, 4703/2/16, fols. 10–20, 54–59. See references to other lists above in the notes, passim.

consolidated with those in TsDAZhR URSR. Undoubtedly, there are similar records covering the Special Secret Division of TsDAZhR (now TsDAVO) in postwar decades—both while it still was in Kharkiv and after it was transferred to Kyiv. Those files have not yet been made available to researchers.[166] TsDAVO needs both to verify the lists, in order to add current fonds numbers for those that remain in Kyiv, and to indicate fond numbers elsewhere for those sent to Moscow or returned to Lviv. The latest guide to TsDAZhR, published in 1984 and declassified only after independence, does not list any of the émigré fonds.[167]

The TsDIA lists and transfer documents also confirm the location in that same Special Secret Division of TsDIA URSR in Kyiv of many fonds of western Ukrainian nationalist and Ukrainian Greek Catholic (Uniate) organizations that were brought to Kyiv from Lviv and elsewhere in western Ukrainian oblasts during the immediate postwar years.[168] Almost all of those western Ukrainian materials were returned to Lviv in the 1950s or transferred to other archives. But it would be helpful for scholars to know about their fate and about their journey to Kyiv and back. It is possible that some "operational" card files and other reference materials for them remain in Kyiv.

The fact that important TsDIAK archival reference lists have survived and have now been declassified could provide the basis for a comprehensive list of the records of early Ukrainian governments and their various agencies (1917–1923), fragmentary files of Ukrainian émigré institutions and organizations, and the personal papers of many important Ukrainian political and cultural leaders—a clear boon to researchers interested in Ukrainian political, cultural, and intellectual development in the twentieth century. At the core of such a project should be the intellectual reconstruction of the Ukrainian Historical Cabinet (UIK) as it was brought together in Prague, parallel to the

---

[166] The administrative records of TsDAVO (*earlier* TsDAZhR) are available in TsDAVO as fond no. 4665. As of the summer of 1999, they could be viewed only with the special permission of the director. (I was unable to obtain at such permission at that time due to the director being on vacation.) The records of the Special Secret Division were not among the *opysy* publicly available in that fond when my Ukrainian colleagues and I were permitted to consult them earlier.

[167] *Tsentral'nyi gosudarstvennyi arkhiv Oktiabr'skoi revoliutsii, vysshikh organov gosudarstvennoi vlasti i organov gosudarstvennogo upravleniia Ukrainskoi SSR: Kratkii spravochnik*, comp. R. I. Tkach, V. M. Brozhek, V. V. Prokopchuk, and O. L. Rybalko (Kyiv: HAU, 1984) [microfiche ed.=East View Publications].

[168] These are seen especially starting with the reports of the Special Secret Division for 1947 and 1948—TsDAVO, 4703/2/9 (1947), 6 (1948), fols. 76–95, and 13 (1948). See the list of transfers from Lviv (6 April 1947), 4703/2/6, fols. 34, 54–65.

RZIA guide just completed in Moscow.

Starting with the period of glasnost and, especially, after Ukraine's independence, the change in the political climate meant that captured records from Prague and other Ukrainian émigré communities elsewhere in the West could at last be opened to the public. Despite this, many of the fonds in Kyiv archives could not be opened for research owing to their inadequate processing. In many cases the inventories that were made available had little relationship to the contents described, nor were they usable for public research, since they had been prepared hastily for the purposes of operational analysis. Most of the inventories prepared in Kyiv in the immediate postwar decade were prepared in Russian. After independence, TsDAVO started translating all of their earlier Russian-language inventories into Ukrainian. In some cases this has led to further confusion and occasional mistakes in translation. The original Russian-language inventories have since been added as file units within the particular *opys* of the fond in question, but they often are not readily accessible to researchers.[169]

Researchers throughout the world should know of the existence of these highly important materials, despite any hesitation that Ukrainian archivists might have about announcing them.[170] The crucial point is that most of these materials relate to the "blank spots" of Ukrainian history; many of them were long thought to have been lost or destroyed during the war. Even before further efforts to locate, describe, and retrieve more archival Ucrainica abroad, it is essential to describe those collections that already exist in Kyiv. There will be little credence in the seriousness of further retrieval and descriptive programs for archival Ucrainica abroad, particularly among the Ukrainian diaspora, before it is openly known what materials were seized by Soviet authorities and from whence they were taken during and immediately after World War II.

In preparing lists of Ukrainian émigré fonds, indications (to the extent possible) are needed regarding their provenance and migratory details, all of which may help to reveal related files held elsewhere. But even in independent Ukraine in 1999, not all the files regarding these materials, their acquisition, and their transfers are themselves open for scholarly research.[171] Many

---

[169] Usually, researchers are permitted to consult the original *opysy*, although often that has required special permission; many researchers may not even know about their existence.

[170] Which, especially in the case of TsDAVO, is due to the lack of adequate processing to make the materials immediately available to public researchers.

[171] After a long series of requests, I was shown for the first time in March of 1994 the hitherto secret files describing these materials that had been held in the secret

essential sources, as we have seen, remain in Moscow, where researchers may also find access problems or incomplete records covering the postwar years (or both). The story of postwar archival seizures and transfers has been suppressed far too long.

The referenced reports and card indexes for the Ukrainian émigré collections in Kyiv prepared in the archives for "operational use" by the Soviet secret services have not been located in Kyiv, although presumably they remain either in TsDAVO or in the MVD archive. It is to be hoped that those reports and indexes will be located and declassified soon, since they would be extremely helpful for scholarly research with the materials. The extensive counterpart card files in Moscow are already open to the public in the State Archive of the Russian Federation (GA RF).

*   *

*

Discussion of this long-suppressed episode in the fate of archival Ucrainica abroad, including its seizure by Soviet authorities, is crucial in the present context. We must not forget that the motivation for the seizure of these important collections was for use by Stalin's operational agencies against suspected "enemies of the state." It is hard for older émigrés and their families to forget this fact. We still do not know how many of their families and loved ones were arrested or adversely affected by information contained in these records. We do not yet know to what "operational" uses the information contained in those files were put.

Today, the search and identification of Ucrainica abroad is obviously being undertaken with sharply contrasting motivations. But the identification and proper description of the important materials seized after the war, aside

---

division of TsDIA URSR (now TsDIAK), before they were later consolidated with those in TsDAZhR. As explained above, the files are part of a hitherto top secret *opys* of the administrative records (AA) of TsDIA URSR/TsDIAK from the immediate postwar years (scheduled for deposit with the rest of the TsDIAK records in TsDAVO, fond 4703, as *opys* 2); some parts of that fond were reportedly destroyed. These data still need to be compared and coordinated with data from TsDAVO (TsDAZhR), i.e., the parallel secret *opysy* for the administrative records of TsDAZhR/TsDAVO (TsDAVO fond no. 4665), if they have been preserved. Access to only a few of the relevant postwar files among the secret section of the Ukrainian Holovarkhiv records (fond 14, *opys* 7) was granted in 1994, but other contingent files were still not declassified by 1998. At the end of 1998, the *opys* itself still was not available for consultation. It has been declassified since then.

from their obvious political and historiographic significance, is vital in a larger perspective. Such a descriptive effort would demonstrate that the purposes of the present national archival Ucrainica retrieval program are no longer linked with postwar Stalinist "operational" aims. Equally important, the publics both in Ukraine and in the diaspora need assurance that such archival materials—and related reference aids and "operational" card files—are open for public research at last, available for full scholarly examination by those who are interested in reconstructing Ukrainian history free from the blinders and blank spots of Soviet historiography. Published professional description of the rich stores of retrieved émigré archival Ucrainica in Ukraine today will encourage others in the Ukrainian diaspora harboring additional important archival materials to consider transferring or "returning" them to the Ukrainian homeland.

The Ukrainian community in Prague and its heirs that have subsequently been dispersed throughout the world may harbor pretensions on at least some of the materials seized. Some of the files may in fact be records of Ukrainian governments in exile, but many of them were the personal papers of Ukrainian émigrés or records of émigré communities created abroad. Hence, following our earlier typology, they would not be considered archival records of provenance in the present territory of Ukraine. Today, with Ukrainian independence, it may be considered most fitting that the materials remain in Kyiv, just as the RZIA collections now remain in Moscow and dispersed throughout the former USSR. However, it is fitting that microform copies, together with professional description, should make many of the most interesting fonds available to researchers elsewhere, besides providing security copies for the originals in Kyiv. It should also not be forgotten that the microfilm copies of the UIK holdings, promised to the Czechoslovak government at the time of their transfer in 1945, still have not been provided.

Aside from the intrinsic interest of the materials themselves, there is an added need for coordinating listings of related parts of the Prague Ukrainian collections that are now scattered in various repositories and contingent files held elsewhere abroad—some in Moscow, a few in Lviv, and some related materials of Prague émigré provenance still in Prague and Paris. Parts of the Ukrainian collections that remain in Prague—all of which are open to research—were surveyed in a report presented at the International Association for Ukrainian Studies world congress in Kyiv (August 1990).[172] In

---

[172] The Prague archivist Bohdan Zilyns'kyi's survey, "Ukraïnistyka v praz'kykh arkhivakh," has not been published, but is now less crucial, given the new guide compiled by Podaný and Barvíková, *Russkaia i ukrainskaia èmigratsiia v Chekhoslovatskoi respublike, 1918–1938.*

Prague, a comprehensive guide to remaining Ukrainian and Russian émigré fonds in the Czech Republic appeared in 1995; research in these collections is open to all.[173] Many examples of their riches and current research regarding the Russian, Ukrainian, and Belarusian emigration in Czechoslovakia between the wars were reported at a conference in Prague in 1995. The published proceedings include many revelations regarding the archival materials remaining in the Czech Republic and abroad, as well as a few in Ukraine.[174]

An item-level inventory of a major Ukrainian collection from the former Ukrainian Museum in Prague now held in the National Archives in Prague was published in Kyiv in 1996, under sponsorship of the Institute of Ukrainian Archeography in collaboration with the compiler in Prague.[175] It is a telling fact that a catalog of the Prague part of the collection appeared before even a simple list of fonds of the Kyiv materials has been made available to researchers. It is to no one's credit that a history of the Museum and the transfer of the rest of its documentary holdings has already appeared in Australia, before so much as even a *preliminary* list of those holdings—with the simple indication of their current fond numbers in the two archives currently holding them—has appeared in Kyiv.

The National Archives of Canada recently presented to Ukraine some files that had been deposited there from a Ukrainian government in exile. Others were transferred by members of the Ukrainian UNR government in exile in the United States; more came from the UNR mission in Switzerland. Other such sources are to be found in various countries of Western Europe, in Israel, and in the United States and Canada. It will grow increasingly harder to convince individuals in these countries to transfer these materials to the Ukrainian homeland if the government of Ukraine does not provide funding for a professional archival service to insure their processing, preservation, and public availability. Ukrainian émigré communities abroad should, correspondingly, be wary of advocating the return of archival treasures to Ukraine until information is publicly available about the extensive émigré

---

[173] Ibid.

[174] *"Russkaia, ukrainskaia i belorusskaia èmigratsiia" 1995.* In terms of Ukrainian materials, see there, for example, the report by N. Mironets, "Dokumenty fonda Nikity Shapovala."

[175] *Inventáře a katalogy fondů Státního ústředního archivu v Praze—Ukrajinské muzeum v Praze* (Kyiv/Prague, 1996). See also Václav Pešák, "Zpráva o činnosti Ruského historického archivu," pp. 218–19.

holdings already located in official Kyivan archives. There is no reason for such materials in Kyivan archives to remain hidden from Ukraine.

CHAPTER 10

The Nationalization of Cultural Trophies in Russia: A New Cultural Cold War in Europe

Russia's Cultural Cold War with the European Community

The case for unilateral restitution of archives, as the official records of State, institutions, and individual families, is much stronger than for art. This has been recognized by many of the international acts and resolutions discussed earlier. Public interest, though, runs counter to this fact. In the world of post-Cold War restitution politics, the public's imagination has been captured by the such treasures as the "Trojan Gold," excavated by the German archeologist Heinrich Schliemann and transported from Turkey to Germany—and in turn removed from its Berlin hiding place by Soviet authorities in 1945; the "Twice Saved" master canvases at the Pushkin Museum; and the looted Gutenberg Bibles held hostage in Moscow libraries. However, as we shall see, the long-hidden displaced West European archives in Moscow—and Russia's recalcitrance regarding their restitution— also became front-page items in France and other countries during the 1990s, after news about the "Special Archive" reached the West.[1]

Conditions for Russian Admission to the Council of Europe. While Ukraine had already been accepted as a member of the Council of Europe (CE) by November 1995 without obligations,[2] Russian acceptance was

---

[1]   See the first Paris news about the extensive French intelligence records that surfaced in Moscow in the fall of 1991, following the initial Russian newspaper accounts (e.g., Ella Maksimova, "Piat' dni v Osobom arkhive," *Izvestiia* 16 February 1990; see Chapter 8, pp. 296ff. For French reportage, see, e.g., Thierry Wolton, "L'histoire de France dormait à Moscou" (interview with Anatolii Prokopenko), *L'Express* (21 November 1991). See also later newspaper coverage cited below as negotiations developed.

[2]   Ukraine was accepted for membership in the Council of Europe on 25 October 1995 and acceded on 9 November 1995, but no statements of intent were required as was the case with Russia. "Invitation to Ukraine to become a member of the Council of Europe" (25 October 1995), Council of Europe/Conseil de

delayed. Russia's failure to resolve the appropriate restitution of cultural treasures and archives was the subject of hearings before the Council of Europe in the fall of 1995.[3] Some members went so far as to suggest that Russia should not be admitted before it made good on the cultural and archival claims of member States. As a compromise, two points with specific mention of archives—along with others regarding human rights as well as additional issues—were included in a statement of intent that Russia was required to sign in order to be admitted to membership in the CE in January 1996. These included the intent of Russia:

> xi. to negotiate claims for the return of cultural property to other European countries on an ad hoc basis that differentiates between types of property (archives, works of art, buildings etc.) and of ownership (public, private or institutional)...

> xiv. to settle rapidly all issues related to the return of property claimed by Council of Europe member states, in particular the archives transferred to Moscow in 1945.[4]

Since that document was signed, Russia's parliament has flagrantly disregarded those intents, culminating in the May 1997 passage of a law that nationalized all cultural treasures brought to Russia at the end of the Second World War. It was passed a second time almost unanimously by both houses of parliament over President Yeltsin's veto, and was finally signed into law by the president on 15 April 1998.[5] The *Spoils of War: International Newsletter*, a forum for discussing and gathering information about restitu-

---

l'Europe, Parliamentary Assembly/Assemblée parlementaire, Resolution (95) 22, ADOC 7420.

[3]   A background paper that I had developed was circulated by the ICA in connection with those hearings: *Displaced Archives on the Eastern Front: Restitution Problems from World War II and Its Aftermath* (Amsterdam: IISH, 1996) [=*IISG Research Papers*, 18]. A published version appeared in the ICA journal *Janus* 1996 (2): 42–77.

[4]   Council of Europe Parliamentary Assembly/Conseil de l'Europe Assemblée parlementaire, Opinion No. 193 (1996)—"On Russia's Request for Membership of the Council of Europe," adopted by the Assembly on 25 January 1996, when Russia was admitted to membership on its basis.

[5]   Federal'nyi zakon "O kul'turnykh tsennostiakh, peremeshchennykh v Soiuz SSR v rezul'tate Vtoroi mirovoi voiny i nakhodiashchikhsia na territorii Rossii-skoi Federatsii" (signed 15 April 1998–64-FZ), *Sobranie zakonodatel'stva Rossiiskoi Federatsii*, 1998, no. 16 (20 April 1998), statute 1879, pp. 3624–3628.

tion accomplishments and problems throughout Europe, published a preliminary English-language translation of the Russian law soon after it had been passed by both houses in May 1997. A more finalized English version is now available on the Internet.[6] The foreign policy impact for Russia should be seen in the context of what some would call Russia's new "cultural Cold War" with the European Community.[7]

Initial Post-Soviet Russian Restitution Agreements. Following the collapse of the Soviet Union, Russian archival authorities were initially receptive to open discussion of restitution of the vast quantity of foreign captured records that still remained in Moscow.[8] There was hope in 1992

[6]   The more authoritative English-language translation by Konstantin Akinsha and Lynn Visson, together with the original Russian text, is found at the website of the "Project for Documentation of Wartime Cultural Losses": "Federal Law on Cultural Valuables Displaced to the U.S.S.R. as a Result of World War II and Located in the Territory of the Russian Federation"—<http://docproj.loyola.edu>. That website also provides a succinct summary of the major provisions of the law and advice for prospective claimants.

A variant translation is published as "Federal Law No. 64-FZ of April 15, 1998 on Cultural Treasures Transferred to the Union of Soviet Socialist Republics as a Result of World War II and Located in the Territory of the Russian Federation," in *Washington Conference, 1998*, pp. 1049–1062. The initial version appears as "Federal Law on Cultural Valu[abl]es Removed to the U.S.S.R. as a Result of World War II and Located in the Territory of the Russian Federation," *Spoils of War: International Newsletter* 4 (August 1997): 10–19; and in Russian translation through <http://www.libfl.ras.ru>. Among the awkward phrasings, for example, "values" is used where "valuables" would be more appropriate in English, since the reference is not to abstract values. The *Newsletter* is available on the Internet at the Spoils of War website—<http://www.beutekunst.de>; the materials are to be moved to another site in the near future: <http://www.lostart.de>.

[7]   These developments through 1997, including the passage of the Russian law, are covered in finer detail in my "'Trophy' Archives and Non-Restitution: Russia's Cultural 'Cold War' with the European Community," *Problems of Post-Communism* 45(3) May–June 1998: 3–16. President Yeltsin signed the law just after that article went to press.

[8]   See, for example, the statement to this effect by Roskomarkhiv (later Rosarkhiv) Chairman Rudol'f G. Pikhoia, "Sotrudnichestvu s zarubezhnymi partnerami—ravnopravnuiu osnovu" (interview by A. V. Shavrov), *Otechestvennye arkhivy* 1992 (2): 15. See also Grimsted, "Beyond Perestroika: Soviet-Area Archives After the August Coup," *American Archivist* 55 (Winter 1992): 108–109.

when the Netherlands was the first to sign a restitution agreement for 60 groups of Dutch records identified in Moscow, and Dutch archivists started an extensive program of archival assistance to Russia.[9] Other countries were hopeful, too, as bilateral agreements were negotiated with Belgium, Hungary, and Norway, among others.

There was even reason to believe that restitution would follow a bilateral German cultural and archival agreement in 1992, which reinforced the 1990 Soviet-German Treaty of Friendship that had called for the return of "the works of art lost without a trace or unlawfully held, found in their territories."[10] The German government grudgingly came up with half a million deutsche marks (as the first of three promised installments) for microfilming equipment, when Russian archival authorities insisted that the captured German records be filmed before their return, as provided for by the 1992 bilateral agreement. Unlike the attitudes in the United States and Great Britain, where decisions were made in the 1950s to return almost all of the captured German records to Germany, there is a considerable body of opinion in Russia that the Nazi records held in Moscow, and especially those of Nazi security authorities, should not be returned at all.[11]

Newly improved relations between Russia and Poland also permitted raising the hitherto taboo problem of cultural property and archives removed by Soviet authorities from Polish territories at the end of World War II. An article in the new May 1992 "Treaty of Friendship and Good Neighborly Cooperation" resolved:

---

[9]   Regarding the 1992 agreement to return the Dutch materials, see "Scripta Manent," *Bulletin of Central and East-European Activities* (International Institute of Social History) 2 (August 1992): 3–4; and "Semper Manent" and "Aid Program for Russia Underway," *Bulletin of Central and East-European Activities* 3 (September 1992): 1–2 and 4.

[10]   The quotation is from article 16 of the 1990 treaty. Both the November 1990 "Treaty on Good-Neighborliness, Partnership, and Cooperation," and the relevant articles in the 1992 (ratified 1993) "Agreement on Cultural Cooperation," are reprinted as Appendix 14 and 15 in *The Spoils of War: WWII and Aftermath*, pp. 304–307.

[11]   Roskomarkhiv Chairman Pikhoia, apparently already under some pressure to slow down the restitution process to Germany, told me that he did not believe that the Americans really had returned the records of the Reich Security Main Office (RSHA) to Germany after the war, but the Bundesarchiv-published finding aid (see Chapter 8, p. 295n48), a copy of which I presented him, provided good evidence that such had in fact been the case. A major segment of that fond remains in RGVA (fond 500K).

> to reveal and unify, to introduce to the cultural currency and to insure the necessary legal, material and other protection regarding the assets, historical monuments and objects found in their territories that are related to the historic and cultural heritage of the nations of the other Side.

and more specifically:

> ...in accord with the international standards and agreements... the Sides will regard with favor the mutual efforts to reveal and return the cultural and historical goods, including archival materials which had been seized and unlawfully removed or that by some other unlawful manner had come to be found in the territories of the other Side.[12]

As one concrete result in the archival sphere, a formal exchange of Rossica and Polonica was put into effect, involving significant visits and archival surveys on each side and exchange of microfilms.[13]

On a higher political level, Rosarkhiv Chairman Pikhoia appeared frequently on television and in the press during his visit to Warsaw as Yeltsin's personal representative in October 1992 to deliver copies of the long-hidden "special files" about the Katyn massacre. The press interpreted the move as political maneuvering and opined that the action should have been taken long ago.[14] Given the politicization of the matter, many were skeptical about the extent to which the incident could raise hope that major restitution of more Polish records would follow. Token copies of documents

---

[12] The first quotation is from art. 13 §3 and the second from art. 13 §4 of the 22 May 1992 treaty, as quoted by Wojciech Kowalski, *Liquidation of the Effects of World War II in the Area of Culture* (Warsaw: Institute of Culture, 1994), p. 96.

[13] "Soglashenie arkhivnykh sluzhb Rossii i Pol'shi," *Otechestvennye arkhivy* 1992 (4): 120–21.

[14] Valerii Masterov, "Reshenie o rasstrele prinimalos' v TsK," and Natal'ia Govorkian, "Zakrytye arkhivy v otkrytoi bor'be," *Moskovskie novosti* 43 (25 October 1992): 9. See also Lev Elin, "Troe s paketom v Kremle—Katynskie igry," *Novoe vremia* 43 (October 1992): 12–14. The English version is "Three men in the Kremlin and a package—Katyn: Murder Will Out," *New Times International* 44 (October 1992): 30–32. See the Moscow report on Warsaw reactions by Vladimir Kiryianov, "Imena opekunov sovetskikh sekretnykh arkhivov stali izvestny v Varshave," *Rossiiskie vesti* 83 (4 October 1992): 1; and the interview on the subject with Polish President Lech Wałęsa by Rudolf Boretskii, "Katynskii krest na kommunizme," *Novoe vremia* 44 (October 1992): 22–23. See also the retrospective analysis by Vera Tolz, "The Katyn Documents and the CPSU Hearings," *RFE/RL Research Report* 1(44) 6 November 1992: 27–33.

involving other scandalous incidents of the Soviet regime and Cold War crises have been delivered by President Yeltsin and his deputies to various countries, including information about prisoners of war and persons missing in action. Often, however, these involved only isolated documents torn from their archival context and without reference to their contiguous files. They never included original documents.

At the same time that the Dutch were in despair over negotiations to recover the Koenigs Collection of early drawings, restitution had more hopeful results in the library world, with an exhibit in the fall of 1992 at the All-Russian State Library of Foreign Literature (VGBIL) of 300 trophy books in the Dutch language that the Nazis had looted from the Netherlands. The books, along with 300 others, all were returned and exhibited at the University Library in Amsterdam, and a full catalog was published indicating the libraries from which they had been seized.[15] They were joined in restitution to Germany and the Netherlands with another shipment of books from Moscow that had been looted by the Nazis from the International Institute of Social History in Amsterdam and other sources, and which Soviet authorities had uncovered and deposited in the library of the former Institute of Marxism-Leninism.

Russian librarians well understood the advantages and goodwill engendered by such restitution efforts, and there were even more hopeful prospects as the year 1992 culminated with the Russo-German round table of professional librarians discussing proposals for appropriate restitution.[16] Since the conference, however, reaction has set in on the part of zealous Russian nationalist politicians, who have put a stop to restitution efforts and have ignored professional agreements and the tremendous benefits to Russian libraries that could result from restitution.

The Scandal over French Archival Restitution. After the collapse of the Soviet Union, France was the first Western country to have received any of its archives back from Moscow. A high-level Franco-Russian diplomatic agreement was signed in November 1992 for the restitution of the estimated six-and-a-half linear kilometers of French records in the Special Archive in

---

[15] *Tentoonstellingcatalogus van de boeken uit het fonds van de VGBIL aanhorig bij de Nederlandse bezitters Amsterdam, Universiteitsbibliotheek, September 1992*, comp. M. F. Pronina, L. A. Terechova, N. I. Tubeeva, and E. E. Eikhman; ed. M. F. Pronina (Moscow: "Rudomino," 1992).

[16] See the description of and published proceedings from the roundtable cited above (Chapter 7, p. 258n28).

Moscow (TsKhIDK) by the end of 1994. The French side was required to pay three-and-a-half million francs for microfilming and an additional high charge for photocopies of the relatively primitive Russian-language *opisi*. Also, in exchange, France was to furnish Russia with a number of Russian-related archival holdings in France, some going back to the nineteenth century.[17]

Between January and May of 1994, approximately 75 percent (although the Russian sides claims approximately 90 percent) of the French records held in TsKhIDK were actually returned to France before the Russian parliament angrily halted the process in May 1994.[18] Two of the six French trucks sent to Moscow returned home empty. When the matter of French archival restitution was raised in parliamentary debate on 20 May 1994, one deputy went so far as to suggest that it would be appropriate to exact storage charges from France for the one million files that had been preserved in Moscow for fifty years—as if France had sanctioned, or even known about, the long-term storage of the records seized for Beria's operational purposes (or as if the large sum that the French had paid for microfilming was not a large enough ransom). In justifying the embargo on archival restitution to France, the Duma cited the example of the United States of America that has refused to return the "Smolensk Archive" to Russia.[19]

---

[17] Laurent Chabrun, "La France retrouve ses archives secrètes," *Le Parisien* 4 September 1992; Jacques Isnard and Michel Tatu, "Moscou accepte de restituer 20 tonnes de documents des Deuxièmes bureaux," *Le Monde* 14 November 1992. See also "Les archives secrètes du 2e Bureau sont demandées une nouvelle fois à la Russie par Paris," *Le Monde* 13 February 1992.

[18] According to figures provided by TsKhIDK, of the 1,100,00 French files held there, 995,000 were dispatched to Paris, first priority going to the military records, including the Deuxième Bureau, and those of the French security services (see, for instance, Claire Sibille, "Les Archives du Ministère de la Guerre recupérées de Russie," *Gazette des Archives* 176 [1997]: 64–77; and Dominique Devaus, "Les Archives de la direction de la Sûreté rapatriées de Russie," ibid., pp. 78–86). None of the French Masonic archives, nor those of Jewish organizations were then returned, and many fonds of personal papers remained in the former TsKhIDK (now part of RGVA). The transfers do not include any archival materials of French provenance that were transferred to other archives, but a thorough inventory of such holdings has yet to be prepared. I appreciate the assistance of then TsKhIDK director M. M. Mukhamedzhanov and archivists in verifying details.

[19] See the official transcript—Federal'noe Sobranie, parlament Rossiiskoi Federatsii, *Biulleten'* 34, "Zasedaniia Gosudarstvennoi Dumy, 20 maia 1994 goda" (Moscow, 1994): 4, 26–33. For more details about this discussion and the curious, but symbolic, involvement of the "Smolensk Archive" see my *The*

To make the scandalous situation even worse on the Russian side, the money received by Rosarkhiv from France for microfilming went into various speculative investments, which later turned sour. Not only did France not receive all of its archives, but TsKhIDK did not receive a kopeck for its efforts, and was accordingly only able to film part of the materials that were returned to France before the Duma embargo. Reportedly, the microfilming equipment furnished by Germany to be used for German filming was used to film the French materials.[20]

During the bitter debates, the Russian Duma cited the lack of international laws and the inadequacy of domestic legislation to justify its refusal to permit further restitution. Russian legislators, backed by legal specialists, now claim that all cultural treasures (including archives) "rescued by the Soviet Army" or brought to Moscow under government orders were transferred legally: Stalin and, later, his deputies signed the appropriate orders. A highly placed Academy of Sciences legal specialist and representative in the Russian legislature cried out, "We owe nothing to no one," offering in a later press account a Soviet-style legal justification for not surrendering wartime trophies, despite already signed bilateral agreements.[21] There have been, nevertheless, other circles in Russia, including the Yeltsin government, that have argued for better solutions. This is evidenced by the pro-government *Izvestiia* banner in September 1994, "A Scandal Not Fitting for Russia,"

Odyssey of the Smolensk Archive: Captured Communist Party Archives for the Service of Anti-Communism (Pittsburgh: REES, University of Pittsburgh, 1995), pp. 84–88 [="Carl Beck Occasional Papers in Russian and East European Studies," 1201].

[20]   To be sure this scandal does not appear in the account by Vladimir P. Tarasov, Deputy Chief of Rosarkhiv, "The Return of Archival Documents, Moved to the USSR as a Result of World War II," *Spoils of War: International Newsletter* 6 (February 1999): 53–55, but my information comes from reliable Rosarkhiv sources in Moscow.

[21]   Evgenii Stroev, "Pora poniat': My nikomu nichego ne dolzhny," *Rossiiskaia gazeta* 4 August 1994. Stroev is an RAN academician and is chairman of the Committee for Questions of Science, Culture, and Education of the Council of the Federation. The phrase was earlier used in an article by Pushkin Museum director Irina Antonova, who argued that her museum had in fact saved and preserved the artistic masterpieces, as indicated by the title of the 1995 Moscow exhibition, "Twice Saved." See Irina Antonova, "My nikomu nichego ne dolzhny, Eshche raz o vozvrate kul'turnykh tsennostei," *Nezavisimaia gazeta* 5 May 1994. See the commentary on Antonova and the exhibit in "Spoils of War," *The Economist* (15 April 1995): 80.

which denounced the parliamentary prohibition on French archival restitution.[22]

Cold War Revival. Revived Cold War attitudes have dominated restitution issues in Russia since revelations about the Soviet spoils of war brought the problem of displaced cultural treasures to world attention. When drawings from the Koenigs Collection from the Netherlands, brought back to the USSR from Germany by Soviet forces after the war, finally went on display in Moscow in October 1995, Russian Minister of Culture Evgenii Sidorov introduced the exhibit as symbolizing "a liberation of the last prisoners of war—the cultural valuables."[23] However, those words did not reverse the overwhelming April 1995 vote in the Russian Duma, which had declared a moratorium on restitution until a newly drafted Russian law could be passed. The Duma was urged on by a new collection of nationalist anti-restitution literature issued by the outspoken opponent of restitution, Vladimir Teteriatnikov (now an American citizen), arguing Russian legal rights to the Koenigs Collection.[24] The tract included the texts of captured German documentation on the "sale," but there was no mention of the January 1943 London Declaration, whereby the Soviet Union and 16 Allies declared "null and

---

[22] "Skandal, ne dostoinyi Rossii," headlines separate articles by Iurii Kovalenko (Paris) and Ella Maksimova (Moscow), *Izvestiia* 172 (8 September 1994): 5. The articles mention details of some of the archival Rossica presented to Russia in connection with the restitution process.

[23] Evgenii Sidorov, in the forward to the elaborate catalog, *Five Centuries of European Drawings: The Former Collection of Franz Koenigs: Exhibition Catalogue, 2.10.1995–21.01.1996* (Milan: Leonardo Arte, 1995), p. 5. A parallel Russian edition was available at half the price of the English one. The Koenigs collection was "sold" through Nazi art dealers in 1940 for Hitler's planned super museum in Linz.

[24] The initial text of the law was published in a nationalist tract in March 1996, together with Nazi documents and commentary justifying the Russian seizure of the Koenigs Collection, as a joint publication of *Obozrevatel'* and *Tverskaia starina*: V. M. Teteriatnikov, *Problema kul'turnykh tsennostei peremeshchennykh v rezul'tate Vtoroi mirovoi voiny: Dokazatel'stvo rossiiskikh prav na "kollektsiiu Kenigsa"* (Moscow and Tver: Obozrevatel', 1996). Ironically, Teteriatnikov, one of the most outspoken opponents of restitution, had emigrated to the United States in 1985 and is now an American citizen; see Ralph Blumenthal, "A Maverick Art Scholar Pursues a Tangled Case," *New York Times* 24 September 1996: C11, C13, particularly with reference to his writings against Dutch claims to the Koenigs drawings.

void" Nazi-style wartime "sales" and seizures.[25]

The Russian Battle over the Nationalization Law

Russia Nationalizes the "Spoils of War," 1995–1998. Meanwhile, on the political front in Russia, three years of parliamentary hassles produced a law nationalizing all of the cultural treasures with no distinction as to archives. During the three years following the fiftieth anniversary of the defeat of Nazi Germany, and even after Russia's "conditional" admittance to the Council of Europe, the parliamentary milieu hardly appeared conducive to further international accords that might encourage restitution of the "spoils of war" or completing "unfinished chapters" in restitution. Already in March 1994, the Russian archival Regulation defined the so-called "Archival Fond of the Russian Federation" to include "archival fonds...received through legal means into state proprietorship, including those from abroad."[26]

The Russian law "On Cultural Valuables Displaced to the U.S.S.R. as a Result of World War II and Located on the Territory of the Russian Federation" was first adopted by the Council of the Federation in March 1995 by an overwhelming majority, just before the exhibition of "Hidden Treasures" of trophy Impressionist art opened at the Hermitage. As initially stated in the preamble, the new law seeks, "to establish necessary legal bases for realistically treating said cultural valuables as partial compensation for the loss to the Russian cultural heritage as a result of the plunder and destruction of cultural valuables by the German occupation army and their allies in the course of the Second World War."[27] Of particular importance in this regard, the law makes no distinction between archives and art, and the law's supporters failed to recognize, as we have seen earlier, that many archives

---

[25] "Inter-Allied Declaration Against Acts of Dispossession Committed in Territories Under Enemy Occupation or Control," 5 January 1943, reprinted as Appendix 9 in *The Spoils of War: WWII and Aftermath*, p. 287.

[26] See the 17 March 1994 Archival Regulation, "Polozhenie ob Arkhivnom fonde RF," no. 552, *Sobranie aktov Prezidenta I Pravitel'stva RF*, 1994, no. 12 (21 March), statute 878, §I.1.

[27] I generally follow the translation from the Documentation Project cited above in fn. 6, although I have compared the translations by the U.S. Department of State and the *Spoils of War: International Newsletter* version. The initial version of the law was passed with a somewhat variant title, starting with "On the Right of Ownership of Cultural Valuables," but that phrase was dropped in the subsequent version.

were captured for "security operations" rather than "compensation."

The second article claims an international legal basis for the law with the citation of several postwar agreements and treaties, although there is mention neither of the Hague Conventions of 1907 and 1954, both of which Russia and the Soviet Union signed and both of which outlaw wartime cultural looting. Now some Russian political and legal experts are presenting the interpretation that their "reparations" or "compensation" shipments to Moscow were seized after the war was over, and hence the Hague Convention of 1907 did not apply.

Article 6 proclaims all cultural treasures transferred as a result of the war that are now in Russia as the property of the Russian Federation. Article 7 provides an exception for valuables taken from the territory of the Baltic republics, Belarus, Ukraine, and Moldova. Later paragraphs make provision for the restitution of cultural treasures claimed by those countries or religious groups who fought against the Nazi regime. More specific mention in Article 8 is made of "cultural valuables which were the property of religious organizations or private charitable organizations and which were used exclusively for religious or charitable purposes and did not serve the interests of militarism and [or] Fascism [Nazism]" (Art. 8 §2); and also "Cultural valuables which belonged to individuals who were deprived of those valuables because of their active struggle against Fascism [Nazism]...and [or] because of their race, religion or national affiliation" (Art. 8 §3). Claims may be filed only "by the government of the claimant states," however, not by individuals, religious groups, or social agencies. Foreign governments, in cases decided in their favor for legitimately established claims, are required to pay in compensation for restitution the full or "equivalent value" of the objects claimed (Art. 15), as well as "the expenses for its identification, expert examination, storage and restoration," and transportation costs (Art. 18). And claimants must certify that they have not received compensation for the items involved.

Personal family relics (including archives) may also be subject to restitution "except for those of individuals who were active in militarist and/or Fascist (Nazi) regimes." (Art. 12) Again, the law requires "the payment of its worth, as well as the costs of identification, appraisal, storage, restoration, and transfer costs (shipment, etc.)." (Art. 19 §2) Claims in this category may be filed "by duly authorized representatives of families to whom the valuables (heirlooms) formerly belonged" (Art. 19 §1).

The new law greatly complicates negotiations, since it requires an act of parliament for every act of restitution: "Without the adoption of an appropriate federal law, no removed cultural valuable may be the subject of an act of transfer, gift, exchange, or any other form of alienation for the benefit of any state, organisation, or individual" (Art 18 §3). The term "restitution" normally would not be used, especially now that all of the cultural treasures have been declared the national property of the Russian Federation. All claims are supposed to be finalized within eighteen months of the time the law takes effect (i.e., October 1999) (Art. 9), unless an extension (now being proposed) is granted. Such terms effectively prevent the settlement of many potential claims (let alone their rapid resolution), especially given the fact that there is no public listing of the cultural treasures and archives held by Russia, and in many cases, specialists from foreign countries investigating a potential claim have been denied access to the items under question and available documentation concerning them. Between the passage of the law and the fall of 1999, only two laws were passed by the Duma authorizing restitution. Both involved archives: one permitted the completion of the "exchange" with France, the other provided for the return of the Nazi-captured documentation of the British expeditionary forces.

Statements pointing out the inadequacies of the law were submitted to the Duma in April 1995 by the Ministry of Culture and the State Archival Service of Russia (Rosarkhiv), among others, but the politicians were not ready to listen. At the end of the summer of 1996, Minister of Culture Sidorov, who a year earlier had been burned in effigy by conservative nationalists for his support of restitution, summarized the deficiencies of the proposed law and its alternative variant. He set forth a convincingly reasoned summary of the importance of restitution for Russia on the international front—especially to countries other than Germany.[28] But the extent to which the Yeltsin government favored restitution was one more point of opposition, as the Communist and nationalist-oriented parties increased their strength in parliamentary elections.

In the heat of the 1996 presidential campaign, a week after Victory Day (9 May), the Duma passed a first reading of the proposed law. Indicative of extreme nationalist attitudes, a week later *Pravda* published another diatribe against restitution, "Will the Russian People Be Robbed Again?" It consisted of a full-page listing of various acts or proposals for restitution, naming many of the "offenders," including many current officials in the Yeltsin administration. That "black" list even included library books that had been transferred to western Ukraine in 1939 after annexation from Poland and other

---

[28] Evgenii Sidorov, "U zolota Shlimana ne mozhet byt´ 'khoziaina,' ne politicheskie spekulianty, a zakon i zdravyi smysl dolzhny reshit´ sud´bu peremeshchennykh tsennostei," *Izvestiia* 159 (25 August 1995): 9.

treasures that had been presented to Ukraine after the war.[29] It was as if compensation for wartime damage to the former Soviet republics was as offensive to Russian nationalists as the return of the cultural treasures of other European nations that had been seized first by the Nazis and then by Soviet authorities as "compensation."

After the Russian Duma passed the law almost unanimously on 5 July 1996, Germany and other European countries that were affected became understandably bitter. Official diplomatic protests were registered in Bonn and Moscow.[30] The foreign reaction may have had a sobering effect on Russian lawmakers. On 17 July, the Russian upper house turned down the law, with representatives from the victorious Yeltsin administration emphasizing the extent to which its passage would conflict with numerous international agreements, and would compromise "Russian international prestige." A delegate who was born in western Belarus reminded the chamber of patterns of plunder and counter-plunder in Belarus, Armenia, and Ukraine, agreeing with those who recommended rejection of the law: "We've had enough seizures [grabbing] and nationalization."[31]

Support for the law was nonetheless intense. Nikolai Gubenko, himself a native of Odesa and the former minister of culture under Soviet President Gorbachev, continued to push for passage of the law, emphasizing that all of the treasures brought back to the Soviet Union were transported "legally," according to Allied agreements. "The law indeed provides justice" and would be supported by "those who perished" in that war and their loved ones—"the votes of 22 million, if only they could speak." Lawmakers in both houses

29   Vladimir Teteriatnikov, "Ograbiat li vnov′ russkii narod? Tragicheskaia sud′ba kul′turnykh tsenostei, peremeshchennykh v rezul′tate Vtoroi mirovoi voiny," *Pravda* 73 (22 May 1996): 4.

30   For a good sense of the Duma attitudes to the law, see the published stenographic texts of the Duma sessions of 17 May and 5 July 1996—Gosudarstvennaia Duma, *Stenogramma zasedanii, Biulleten′*, no. 27 (169) (17 May 1996) and no. 37 (179) (5 July 1996). The textual changes in the law between the first and second reading are explained in the presentation by Nikolai Gubenko in the 5 July text (pp. 51–52), and likewise in the presentation to the Council of the Federation on 17 July. The intense and bitter German reaction to the Duma passage of the law is portrayed in the report from Germany by Valentin Zapevalov, "Igra v ambitsii: Na konu bol′shie kul′turnye tsennosti," *Literaturnaia gazeta* 32 (7 August 1996): 9, although it was not published until after the law had been rejected by the upper house.

31   See the text of the deliberations—Sovet Federatsii Federal′nogo Sobraniia, Zasedanie deviatoe, *Biulleten′*, no. 1 (107), 17 July 1996, pp. 55–63.

again cried out that Russia had received nothing back from Germany that was taken by the Nazi invaders.[32]

After the law was defeated in the upper house in July 1996, historian Igor' Maksimychev reasoned that, "the thesis 'We owe nothing to no one,' entails grave unpleasant consequences for our country. We do not live on the moon, but rather surrounded by other countries who always owe us something and to whom we have debts ourselves." His suggestion that Russia's "weakened moral authority" would be strengthened and restored by its "adherence to generally accepted norms of international law" brought strong counterreaction. The rare book specialist Aleksandr Sevast'ianov, who had written against restitution in the past, once again argued in favor of the law that the Council of the Federation threw out, and bitterly denounced the "anti-patriotic and liberal currents of the 1991–1993 period," which were favoring restitution of the "Spoils of War"—these, in his view, were much "more than trophies" for Russia.[33]

Minor editorial changes addressed some of the earlier technical criticism, but the only new article guaranteed ownership rights for the newly independent states on the basis of former Soviet union republics. On 5 February 1997—by an almost unanimous vote of 291 to 1, with 4 abstentions—the Duma again approved the law nationalizing all cultural treasures transported to Russia at the end of the Second World War.[34]

Overriding the Presidential Veto: Yeltsin's Last Stand. Aware of the potential international outcry about the violation of international law and agreements, and undoubtedly with an eye toward his upcoming visit to Germany, President Yeltsin vetoed the law on 18 March 1997. In his official message to the Duma, Yeltsin emphasized that the law contradicted the Constitution, and among other points, failed to distinguish "between former enemy, allied or neutral nations, and different categories of individuals in

---

[32]   Ibid. Quotations cited by Deputy Head of the Committee on Culture of the Duma Nikolai N. Gubenko (pp. 60–61).

[33]   Igor F. Maksimychev, "'Peremeshchennoe,' ne znachit 'nich'e': Nanesti ushcherb natsional'nym interesam mozhno i iz samykh blagorodnykh pobuzhdenii," *Nezavisimaia gazeta* 26 July 1996: 2; Aleksandr Sevast'ianov, "Bol'she, chem trofei—Polemika...s Igorem Maksimychevym," *Nezavisimaia gazeta* 14 September 1996: 6.

[34]   See the transcript of the 5 February Duma session with discussion of the law: *Gosudarstavenoi Dumy: Stenogramma Zasedanii, Biulleten'*, no. 74 (216) (5 February 1997), pp. 19–23, 56.

respect of their property rights."[35] When the law came back to the Duma on the 4th of April, the specific legal points raised by Yeltsin, and the Administration's view on the incompatibility of the law with international legal norms and Russian agreements, fell on deaf ears. Antagonism between the Duma and the president was apparent at every turn.

The Duma was much more prepared to listen to the law's chief patron, Nikolai Gubenko, who emphasized the "symbolic significance" of the struggle for "Victory" in adopting the law. This time, he suggested, "It could be appropriately compared to the Battle of Stalingrad." Fully justifying provisions that "restitution of cultural treasures" to the "aggressor nations" could "be possible only by exchange for Russian cultural treasures," he glossed over other presidential objections. Gubenko stated that he was thinking only of "the 27 million who perished [during the Great Patriotic War] and the graves on the Volga" and implied that even symbolic restitution to Germany would be like "spitting on those graves." Ultra-nationalist Vladimir Zhirinovskii bitterly complained about any prospective Yeltsin restitution to the German "fascist scoundrels."[36] International reaction was so intense that even the *New York Times* carried a front-page story with a picture of French records in the stacks of the former "Special Archive."[37]

The Council of the Federation then overrode the presidential veto on the 14th of May 1997 with 141 of 178 representatives voting in favor of the law.[38] With allegations of voting irregularities as well as conflict with Russia's international legal obligations, President Yeltsin defied the legislature by refusing to sign the law for another year, until the Constitu-

---

[35] The text of President Yeltsin's message to the Duma was not available to me. Excerpts were given by Svetlana Sukhova, "Iskusstvo dolzhno prinadlezhat´...," *Segodnia* 54 (19 March 1997), which correctly predicted that the Duma would quickly override the veto. Fragments of the presidential response are also quoted in the reports cited after the Duma vote on 4 April 1997.

[36] Quotations are from the press conference reported on Russian television, 16 March 1997, fragments from which were reported in the article by Boris Piiuk, "Ty mne–Ia tebe," *Itogi* 16(49) 22 April 1997: 13–14. See also the comments of Shvydkoi and Duma deputy Mikhail Selavinskii in *Kul'tura* 15 (17 April 1997): 1.

[37] Michael R. Gordon, "Hot Issue for Russia: Should It Return Nazi Plunder?" *New York Times* 17 April 1997.

[38] I quote from Itar-Tass wire service reports dated 13 and 14 May 1997. See the report by Michael R. Gordon, "Slap at Yeltsin as Legislators Veto Return of Art Booty," *New York Times* 14 May 1997: 3.

tional Court forced his hand in April 1998.[39]

The communist system and the Soviet empire it created may have collapsed at the end of 1991, but the image of the "Great Patriotic War of the Fatherland" created by the Stalinist regime still has a powerful sway on the public mind. The perceptive essay by Nina Tumarkin entitled "The Great Patriotic War as Myth and Memory" deserves attention by those monitoring the restitution debates in Moscow.[40] With considerable insight, Tumarkin demonstrates the extent to which the memory and horrors of the war were exploited by the postwar Stalinist regime through propaganda and half-truths about the Soviet role, all of which have intensified the "cult" of the war and the Soviet leaders in victory as glorified in museums and public statuary. Justification for Stalin's postwar "reparations" policy appears to be even stronger since the collapse of the Soviet empire, while the displaced cultural treasures and archives resulting from that policy and the rejection of cooperative restitution efforts remain part of the continuing Soviet legacy to the European continent.

Large segments of Russian public opinion appear unconcerned that many of the artistic and archival prisoners of that war remain in captivity. The "intents" Russia was forced to sign for admission to the Council of Europe were never mentioned in the course of debate nor in the vast press coverage of the "spoils of war" and restitution issues.[41] Many "blank spots" persist in

---

[39]   Postanovlenie Konstitutsionnogo Suda Rossiiskoi Federatsii, no. 1879: "Po delu o razreshenii spora mezhdu Sovetom Federatsii i Prezidentom Rossiiskoi Federatsii, mezhdu Gosudarstvennoi Dumoi i Prezidentom Rossiiskoi Federatsii ob obiazannosti Prezidenta Rossiiskoi Federatsii podpisat' priniatyi Federal'nyi zakon 'O kul'turnykh tsennostiakh, peremeshchennykh v Soiuz SSR v rezul'tate Vtoroi mirovoi voiny i nakhodiashchikhsia na territorii Rossiiskoi Federatsii'" (6 April 1998), *Sobranie zakonodatel'stva RF*, 1998, no. 16 (20 April 1998), statute 1879, pp. 3624–3628.

[40]   Nina Tumarkin, "The Great Patriotic War as Myth and Memory," *The Atlantic* 267 (June 1991) 6: 26–31. Tumarkin's recent book, *The Living & The Dead: The Rise and Fall of the Cult of World War II in Russia* (New York: Basic Books, 1994), expands her analysis on a personal memoir basis. See also Tumarkin's essay, "The War of Remembrance," in *Culture and Entertainment in Wartime Russia*, ed. Richard Stites (Bloomington: Indiana University Press, 1995), pp. 194–207, along with a number of other insightful essays in that collection.

[41]   See the reviews of Russian press opinion by Evgeniia Korkmasova (VGBIL), "Review of the Russian Press for 1997 on the Question of the Restitution of Cultural Valu[abl]es (Part 1)" *Spoils of War: International Newsletter* 4 (August 1997): 48–51; "Part 2," ibid., 5 (June 1998): 41–43; and "Part 3," ibid., no. 6 (February 1999): 22–24.

the historical record of the war and the postwar archival seizures for "operational" purposes that are now being viewed as "compensation" and symbols of "Victory."

When the Russian Constitution Court obliged President Yeltsin to sign the law in April 1998, it made it clear that in so doing, it had not passed judgment on the constitutionality of the law itself. The Russian high court could examine those issues only after the president had signed it into law. After the law was signed, President Yeltsin's case against the law went back for examination by the Constitutional Court, both on technical grounds in connection with alleged irregular voting procedures in the final passage of the law and with the conflict between the law and Russia's international legal obligations. A press commentary at the time suggested that such a "state of suspension suits Yeltsin. He knows the Russian people do not want to return the trophy art, but he has proved his own good intentions to his friend, German Chancellor Helmut Kohl."[42]

Ukrainian and Other International Reaction

Bitter Ukrainian Reaction to the Russian Law. While the strong support in both houses of the Russian parliament has fueled the largely positive Russian public reaction to the new law, criticism and dissenting voices have dominated Ukrainian reaction, most particularly from specialists who have been involved with restitution issues. As a successor State to the USSR, Ukraine is closely affected by the problems and fallout of displaced archives and other cultural treasures in Russia.

Even before President Yeltsin had signed the law, Ukrainian reaction was understandably strong. While there were a number of commentaries in the Ukrainian press, examples cited here were presented by experts in an international forum. For example, Viktor Akulenko, of the Korets'kyi Institute of State and Law of the National Academy of Sciences of Ukraine, took issue with the fact that the law:

> ...does not observe the constitutional principle of prime supe-riority of international law and fully ignores "The Hague Convention" of 1907, previous international agreements between

---

[42]   See the commentary on the situation by Konstantin Akinsha and Grigorii Kozlov, "Russian Deposits: No Return?" *ARTnews* 97(6) April 1998: 62.

the USSR and Germany, and the ones between the Russian Federation and Germany of 1990 and 1992.[43]

Akulenko suggested that the preamble of the law "stating that it creates 'favorable conditions for continuing development of international coopera- tion' is quite disputable in this sphere," because it fully ignores "the damage to the cultural valu[abl]es of Ukraine" and other former Soviet republics. He complained that the law is much too limited in recognizing Ukrainian rights to cultural treasures from Ukraine that had been seized by Germany and its allies and that were later transferred or returned to Russian territory. He further lamented "that even experts have no access to the valu[abl]es of Ukraine in the warehouses in Moscow, Saint Petersburg and Nizhny Novgorod." Following the refusal of the Russian parliament to ratify the February 1992 CIS agreement "On the Return of Cultural and Historical Valuables to the Countries of Origin," Akulenko "consider[ed] the practical realization of this law in the national interest of Ukraine to be very problem- atic, as it has been, by the way, during the previous 50 years of restitution stagnation since the war."[44] Akulenko also criticized the law in his address to the 1997 conference on cultural restitution in Minsk, and reminded the audience of the conditions regarding restitution imposed on Russian for admittance to the Council of Europe, which he considers to be further abrogated by passage of the new law.[45]

Later, after President Yeltsin signed the law, and even before the final legal judgment of the high court, Serhii Kot, a Ukrainian historian in the Academy of Sciences of Ukraine, considered "the most scandalous event in contemporary Russian history and history of international affairs, since this law has become a fait accompli."[46] By adopting a law nationalizing German

---

[43]   Viktor Akulenko, "A Bill which Faces the Past," *Spoils of War: International Newsletter* 4 (August 1997): 19.

[44]   Ibid., p. 20.

[45]   Viktor Akulenko, "O sootnoshenii mezhdunarodnykh pravovykh i moral'no- èticheskikh norm v sfere vozvrashcheniia i restitutsii kul'turnykh tsennostei," in *Restytutsyia kul'turnykh kashtoŭnastsei*, pp. 80–85.

[46]   Sergei [Serhii] Kot, "The Ukraine and the Russian Law on Removed Cultural Valu[abl]es," *Spoils of War: International Newsletter* 5 (June 1998): 9. I quote from the shorter English-language presentation, but Kot discusses the Russian law with more details about several important examples of pending restitution problems in his Ukrainian-language article "Restytutsiia chy konfiskatsiia?: Rosiis'kyi zakon pro peremishcheni pid chas Druhoï svitovoï viiny kul'turni tsinnosti ta Ukraïna," *Polityka i chas* 1998 (8), especially pp. 29–34.

state and private property and that of its allies, the law was also trying to establish a legal base for nationalizing "the cultural property of countries they occupied (i.e., essentially the allies of the USSR and the victims of aggression)." Such action:

> ...openly flout[s] international public opinion and infring[es] on a whole range of international conventions, declarations, agreements and treaties to which Russia, as one of the legal successors of the former Soviet Union, is a party.[47]

The enacting of such a law, Kot lamented, makes the "hopes for restitution of national relics" to many countries "appear most uncertain." He sees two principle problems in the law for Ukraine:

> The Russian law directly touches the national interests of the Ukraine, particularly in terms of the cultural property evacuated from the Ukraine to Russian territory during the war and not returned since, but also Ukrainian cultural property transferred to the USSR in the scope of postwar restitution and now kept in Russia.[48]

Kot cited a number of examples in both cases, and he raised other problems, such as the delineation of only "'national cultural valu[abl]es' that were situated within the territory of the former republics of the Soviet Union until February 1, 1950," because that would exclude the Crimea, which "was 'reunited' with the Ukraine in 1954."

Besides, under this law, in order to submit claims, Ukraine would have to compensate Russia for all of the expenses involved. He further is appalled by Russian nationalization to the exclusion of:

> Ukraine and other former Soviet republics which suffered in the war [and] must have a deciding voice in determining the fate of the stocks of art treasures stolen as war booty. These are enormous cultural assets which should be re-allocated fairly on the basis of international norms and democratic principles.[49]

Other International Criticism. The *Spoils of War: International Newsletter*, following publication of the complete text of the Russian law, also published extensive commentary on the law by specialists in several countries. Given that source and the analysis presented above, there is no

---

[47] Kot, "The Ukraine and the Russian Law," p. 10.

[48] Ibid.

[49] Ibid., pp. 14–15.

need to dwell on details here. Nevertheless, a few comments provide a flavor of the serious problems experts find in the new law.

Conclusions in the Ukrainian position stated above, for example, were reinforced in one of the resolutions of the "International Scientific Conference on the Return and Joint Use of Cultural Valuables" that gathered in Minsk in October 1997, a few months after the law was passed by the Russian parliament. As formulated in that resolution, in connection with the adoption of the new Russian law, "the following problems take on special significance:"

> —the role of Ukraine, Byelorussia, Lithuania, Latvia, Estonia, Moldavia in deciding the fate of these valu[abl]es; and their accessibility to the citizens of the above-mentioned states.

> —the problem of these valu[abl]es from the museums, archives and libraries of the above-mentioned states transferred to the territory of the Russian Federation as a result of World War II.[50]

Critical comments were heard from other countries. For example, a Hungarian lawyer pointed out the ways in which the law violates the Paris Peace Treaty with Hungary and other international conventions of which the Russian Federation is a signatory. An American lawyer who has been dealing with restitution cases in U.S. courts likewise pointed out the extent to which the Russian law and Russian "nationalization of the trophy art would be deemed a violation of international law as set forth in The Hague Conventions and the UNESCO Convention" and would probably not stand a challenge in United States courts.[51]

A Polish legal specialist on restitution law, Wojciech Kowalski, has claimed that in many provisions the "Law is entirely unclear and dubious," concluding that:

> What is known for sure is that such an act will not help to build new and better relations between "affected states" as it was many times declared to be the policy of the Russian Federation. With the passage of time people can certainly forgive

---

[50]   The English-, Russian-, and Belarusian-language text of the "Final Document—"Itogovyi dokument" was published with the conference proceedings in *Restytutsyia kul'turnykh kashtoŭnastsei*, pp. 258–62; it is also included in the report by Adam Mal'dzis, "Byelorussia," *Spoils of War: International Newsletter* 5 (June 1998): 74. See the additional report on the 1997 conference in Minsk by Aleksandr Fedoruk, in ibid., pp. 58–59.

[51]   Thomas R. Kline, "The Russian Bill to Nationalize Trophy Art: An American Perspective," *Spoils of War: International Newsletter* 4 (August 1997): 31–35.

even wanton destruction of towns and villages but will never forget lost heritage which constitutes a part of their national identity.[52]

Kowalski also took part in the Minsk conference on restitution issues, where he presented an informative and well-documented background discussion on legal issues involved with restitution, especially in Eastern Europe.[53]

An editor of the *International Journal of Cultural Property* likewise noted that none of the international instruments referred to "legalize pillage, or any confiscation of foreign cultural property," for indeed, "such behavior was forbidden under international customary law." Fully admitting the extent to which "Russia suffered severely from German occupation and plundering," he queried, "how can this be compensated or how can co-operation be guaranteed if Russia takes unilateral measures?" And he concluded in quoting the Wiesbaden Declaration of 7 November 1945, signed by American cultural officers in contempt of the U.S. decision to remove 202 German paintings to the United States:

> "No historical grievance will rankle so long, or be the cause of so much justified bitterness, as the removal, for any reason, of a part of the heritage of any nation, even if that heritage may be interpreted as 'a prize of war'." The same is true for keeping such a prize of war.[54]

German criticism, to be sure has been the most intense, because the law effectively prevents any restitution of art or archives to Germany and its allies (despite the earlier-mentioned 1990 and 1992 agreements with Germany), unless such a former enemy state "presents to the Russian Federation on the

---

[52] Wojciech Kowalski, "Russian Law: The Polish Perspective," *Spoils of War: International Newsletter* 4 (August 1997): 36–38.

[53] Wojciech Kowalski, "Repatriatsiia kul′turnykh tsennostei v situatsii ustupok territorii i raspada mnogonatsional′nykh gosudarstv," in *Restytutsyia kul′turnykh kashtoǔnastsei*, pp. 21–52; Kowalski's presentation, as published in the conference proceedings is very well-documented with notes to significant legal instruments and literature in the field in numerous languages.

[54] Kurt Siehr, "Comment on the Russian Federal Law of 1997 on Cultural Valu[abl]es," *Spoils of War: International Newsletter* 4 (August 1997): 38–39. See the recent account of the controversial U.S. exhibition tour of 202 German paintings, and the strong protests by U.S. Monuments officers by Lynn Nicholas, *The Rape of Europa: The Fate of Europe's Treasures in the Third Reich and the Second World War* (New York: Alfred A. Knopf, 1994), pp. 382–405. The full text of the Weisbaden Manifesto is reprinted in *The Spoils of War: WWII and Aftermath*, p. 133.

basis of the principle of reciprocity no less favorable legal conditions for the return of that part of the cultural treasures plundered by former enemy states and that are located in...the interested state." (art. 9)

The Constitutional Court Rules

A compromise and somewhat confusing if not contradictory ruling of the Russian high court was handed down on 20 July 1999, declaring parts of the law "unconstitutional," but refraining from invalidating the law. While it "ruled that parliamentary procedures were violated when the law was passed," the concluding article declared the enaction of the law "was not in conflict with the Constitution." The essence of the lengthy and seemingly self-contradictory ruling by the high court sounded more like an interpretive political pronouncement than a legal brief, as summarized in the press:

> The court determined that cultural valuables seized from Nazi Germany at the end of World War II and now located on Russian territory should not be returned to former "aggressor countries." At the same time, it said that countries that fought against Hitler as well as victims of the Holocaust and the Hitler regime are entitled to the restitution of their cultural heritage.[55]

That round in the political controversy over wartime trophies and restitution was hardly the last. Many questions were left unresolved by the Constitutional Court decision. At first there was hope that the legal grounds had been cleared to proceed with restitution under terms of the law to countries who fought against the Nazi regime and individuals who were repressed by it. But further delays in implementation followed. When politicians and bureaucrats were faced with interpreting the Court decision, they decided that the next step required a series of amendments to the law to be passed by the legislature before new acts of restitution could be imple-

---

[55] I quote from the text of the decision as available in printed form and immediate press commentaries. The quoted statement is from the "RFE/RL Newsline" (21 July 1999), found on the Internet. A similar story was filed the same day by Reuters, found on the news compilation "Russia Today." See also the statements by the Minister of Culture, Vladimir Egorov and several museum leaders in "Nachinaem restituirovat', no Germanii ne dadim nichego," *Kommersant* 127 (21 July 1999): 10, and "Spravedlivoe reshenie v nespravedlivykh obstoiatel'stvakh," *Kultura* 27 (29 July–4 August 1999): 1. See the text in *Rossiiskaia gazeta* 155 (2264) 19 August: 4–5; and in *Sobranie zakonodatel'stva RF*, no. 30 (26 August 1999), statute 3989, pp. 6988–7007.

mented. Accordingly, in November 1999 the Duma undertook a first reading of the draft amendments.[56] While passed by the legislature, further study and debate was required. A second reading was scheduled for spring, 2000.

While postponing the "eighteen months" deadline for restitution claims, the latest developments brought new problems and delays to restitution procedures. The restitution of archives still was not handled in a distinct manner. One of the changes proposed in the law sought to limit its applicability to trophy cultural treasures transferred to the USSR from Germany as "cultural compensation." That would, however, potentially limit applicability for archives and other cultural treasures seized by Soviet authorities outside of Germany, such as the archives brought back to Moscow from Poland and Czechoslovakia. Various other countries, including Belgium, the Netherlands, and Luxembourg, have been negotiating for the return of their archives. Yet further restitution negotiations carried out under Rosarkhiv auspices revealed new legal problems which had to await the proposed amendments to the law. The Russian side reportedly still was demanding high fees for processing restitution claims. Clearly the bitter struggles between Russia and other members of the European Community over cultural restitution are far from resolved.

Archival Restitution Qua Barter for Archival Rossica

Barter for Archival Rossica. Ukraine did not send a representative to the 1994 ICA Round Table in Thessalonica. But when the resolution favoring archival restitution and against considering archives as "trophies" or "objects of exchange" came to the floor, Russia was one of the three abstentions (Poland and Niger also abstained). Otherwise, the resolution passed unanimously. Now that Russia has passed a law nationalizing all of the spoils of war half a century after the end of hostilities, it is more prepared to barter for the return of certain categories of displaced records.

In fact, from the beginning of international reaction to the revelations of the foreign trophy archives held in Russia, Rosarkhiv (earlier Roskomarkhiv)

---

[56] See the resolution following the Duma session of 30 November, "O proekte Federal'nogo zakona 'O vnesenii izmenenii i dopolnenii v Federal'nyi zakon ot 15 aprelia 1998 goda No. 64-FZ 'O kul'turnykh tsennostiakh, peremeshchennykh v Soiuz SSR v rezul'tate Vtoroi mirovoi voiny i nakhodiashchikhsia na territorii Rossiiskoi Federatsii,'" in *Sobranie zakonodatels'stva RF,* no. 50 (13 December 1999), statute 6121, pp. 10925–10926. The text of the draft amendments was not published there, but was made available to me by Rosarkhiv.

viewed Russia's trophy archives, which they assumed would eventually be returned, as a chance to retrieve, or at least acquire more copies of, archival Rossica abroad. So important was this to archival leaders that they insisted on added barter arrangements to all of the restitution agreements negotiated. Even the Hoover project for microfilming internal finding aids (*opisi*) of Soviet-period records included the requirement for complete microfilms of all of the archival Rossica held by the Hoover Institution in California. As noted above, the 1992 French diplomatic agreement for the restitution of the twice-seized French archives in Moscow carried stipulation for the return of archival "Rossica" located in France.

Rosarkhiv sponsored a large conference on "archival Rossica abroad," which took place in Moscow in December 1993, with proceedings finally published in early 1997. The conference itself emphasized Rosarkhiv's concern with the issue of archival Rossica, and some speakers openly noted its importance as barter for the prospective return of Russia's trophy archives. Many of the Russian participants (representing different archives and other institutions) emphasized the need to retrieve archival Rossica from abroad—in copy if not in the original—although the need for identification and description also loomed large. There was little recognition that the vast majority of archival Rossica abroad is in fact "émigré Rossica," taken or kept abroad for its own protection against the potential destruction or suppression by a hostile regime at home. Russians today, and even professional archivists, also appear to overlook the issue of provenance.[57]

The other foreign participant at the 1993 conference, beside myself, was Jaap Kloosterman, Director of the International Institute of Social History in Amsterdam. He emphasized the role of IISH in rescuing and preserving many significant records of the Russian revolutionary struggle, for example. (Some of those archives rescued and preserved by IISH during the interwar period were seized during the war by the Nazis and are now among the trophy archives in the former Central Party Archive in Moscow.) Microfilms of almost all of the trophy Russian-related IISH holdings have already been exchanged with Russian archives, but some Russians still demand the "return" of the original archives from IISH to Russia. A legal concept such as the "Archival Fond of the Russian Federation" and state "proprietorship" of such private and social or political agency archives, Kloosterman explained, could not exist in the Netherlands, nor could it be recognized under the law

---

[57] *Problemy zarubezhnoi arkhivnoi Rossiki: Sbornik statei,* ed. V. P. Kozlov (Moscow: "Russkii mir," 1997). See my "Arkhivnaia Rossika/Sovetika: K opredeleniiu tipologii russkogo arkhivnogo naslediia za rubezhom," pp. 7–43.

of most other Western countries.[58] Russian archivists did not want to understand the implications of private ownership.

In November 1995, the Duma passed a resolution calling for international negotiations for the return to Russia of three private archives of émigré Russian jurists located abroad. Most of the personal papers involved were not even created in Russia and are now being well cared for in archives in New York, Prague, and Warsaw.[59] When, in turn, will Russian politicians be ready to adhere to international agreements, resolutions, and conventions that the unique archives of community, religious, and private bodies abroad now held in Moscow should be restored to their appropriate home and that they should not they be subject to "barter" or "exchange"?

The Liechtenstein "Exchange." Despite the then still prevailing Russian moratorium on restitution and its own endorsement of nationalization, in June 1996 the Duma did nevertheless approve provisions for the return of a major group of Nazi-looted archival materials to the Grand Duchy of Liechtenstein, which, seized by Soviet authorities in Vienna after the war, remained among the trophy archives in Moscow. The special exception by the Duma that permitted their return involved not only high diplomatic interventions. Most importantly, the royal family of Liechtenstein agreed to barter. At the suggestion of Rosarkhiv, they purchased through the auction house Sotheby's—reportedly for half a million dollars—some documents from the Okhrana investigator N. A. Sokolov relating to the death of the Russian imperial family to be traded for those parts of the Nazi-looted Liechtenstein archives now held in Moscow.[60] As presented in the Duma,

---

[58] Jaap Kloosterman, "Rossika za rubezhom: Arkhivy Mezhdunarodnogo instituta sotsial'noi istorii," *Problemy zarubezhnoi arkhivnoi Rossiki [RGGU]* 33 (1996): 121–23.

[59] "O vozvrate v Rossiiu nauchnykh arkhivov vydaiushchikhsia russkikh uchenykh-iuristov," Postanovlenie Gosudarstvennoi Dumy Federal'nogo sobraniia RF, 17 November 1995, no. 1339-I GD, *Sobranie zakonodatel'stva RF*, no. 49 (4 December 1995), statute 4713.

[60] Nikolai A. Sokolov was an investigator in the Okhrana who had been closely monitoring the imperial family. Some of the related documentation was published in his account, *Ubiistvo Tsarskoi sem'i* (Berlin: Slovo, 1925). Another set of Sokolov's reports is held in Houghton Library at Harvard University, but the materials purchased at Sotheby's are Sokolov's originals, which include additional evidence and photographs collected in the course of the investigation and the original telegram from Ekateringrad announcing the assassination of the imperial family. The Sokolov materials are described in detail with lavish

the issue was viewed as an "exchange" for Liechtenstein "family archives," which "had no bearing on the history of Russia" and "would not be contrary to the new law on restitution."[61]

Symptomatic of the strong and persistent anti-restitution attitudes in Russia, an outcry in another newspaper published by no less than the Presidential Administration appeared a month later, accusing the government of a "monstrous mistake," whereby "three raw notebooks of Nikolai Sokolov" were being exchanged for "over three tons" of valuable Liechtenstein manuscripts, "which Liechtenstein willingly gave to the Third Reich," thus involving a "tremendous detriment to Russian security, economy, and prestige." Russian critics seemed unaware of the favorable reaction to the exchange in international archival circles, where there was new hope that despite the "barter" involved, perhaps Russia was beginning to conform to international practice.[62]

The formal ceremonial delivery to Lichtenstein in Switzerland by Rosarkhiv Chairman and Chief Archivist of Russia, Vladimir P. Kozlov,

---

illustrations in the Sotheby's catalog, *The Romanovs: Documents and Photographs relating to the Russian Imperial House,* initially offered at auction in London, 5 April 1990. I am grateful to Ann Robertson for acquainting me with the Sotheby's catalog. I also thank colleagues in TsKhIDK and Rosarkhiv for verifying the details of this situation. According to Sotheby's press office, the advertised reserve price of £350,000 was not met when the collection was first offered at auction; they refuse to divulge the price of the private contract sale arranged with "an anonymous buyer" several years later. Newspapers alternatively quote the selling price as $500,000 or £500,000, but inside sources report considerably less, with one quotation given as just under £100,000.

[61] See the transcript of the Duma session of 13 June 1996 (p. 59), and the official "Postanovlenie Gosudarstvennoi Dumy—ob obmene arkhivnykh dokumentov Kniazheskogo doma Likhtenshtein, peremeshchennykh posle okonchaniia Vtoroi mirovoi voiny na territoriiu Rossii, na arkhivnye dokumenty o rassledovanii obstoiatel'stv gibeli Nikolaia II i chlenov ego sem'i (arkhiv N. A. Sokolova)," 13 June 1996 (No. 465–II GD). Earlier, the Duma had voted down the return of the Liechtenstein archive.

[62] See Natal'ia Vdovina, "Prizraki trofeinogo arkhiva: Kniaz' fon Likhtenshtein, shtabs-kapitan Sokolov i deputaty Gosdumy RF," *Rossiiskie vesti* 186 (2 October 1996): 1–2. According to TsKhIDK archivists, the Liechtenstein archive was actually transferred to the former Special Archive from the Library of the Academy of Sciences (BAN) in 1946. It had been found by Soviet authorities in Holleneck Castle in Vienna in 1945. A report of its seizure by Soviet authorities is in GA RF, 5325/2/.

marked one of the few recent significant steps forward in the much-disputed cultural restitution process with the European community. Prince Hans-Adam II may have had to "'purchase' back his own property," as the Liechtenstein newspaper in Vaduz described the transfer the next day.[63] But at the opening of the elaborate exhibit of the Sokolov materials in Moscow in September 1997, the Prince expressed tremendous satisfaction in having back his family archive and played down the much-criticized "barter" involved. Indeed without the "exchange" for a tantalizing tidbit of imperial Rossica, the Duma would have certainly not reversed its initial stand against restitution. The entire affair bodes ill for Ukraine and other countries trying to vindicate their own archival heritage.

Barter for French Restitution. Since the Russian law was passed, most countries seeking archival restitution are likewise faced with prospective "barter" arrangements. In May 1998, a month after President Yeltsin signed the Russian law nationalizing all of the "spoils of war," the Duma issued a directive (*postanovlenie*) authorizing continuation of the archival restitution process with France. The official wording authorized the "exchange of archival records of the French Republic, transferred to the territory of the Russian Federation as a result of the Second World War, for archival records of Russian provenance, located on the territory of the French Republic." In effect the new directive authorized the necessary preparatory work for the "continuation" of the "exchange." Notably the word "restitution" or "return" was not used and there was no reference to the formal diplomatic agreement signed between Russia and France in November 1992. Neither was there mention of the payment France had already made under terms of that agreement.[64] A year later, as of April 1999, preparations were still under way, but the authorized "continuation of the exchange" had not commenced. According to Rosarkhiv, the process is now "being curbed by the inadequacy of procedure mechanisms, mentioned in the Federal Law. For example, an Interdepartmental Council on Cultural Items, mentioned in §4, article 16 of

---

[63] Patrik Schädler, "Fürstliches Hausarchiv und Sokolov-Archiv/Gestern begann der Austausch: Fürst Hans-Adam 'kauft' sein Eigentum zurück," *Liechtensteiner Vaterland* 172 (31 July 1997): 1.

[64] "Ob obmene arkhivnykh dokumentov Frantsuzskoi Respubliki, pere-meshchennykh na territoriiu Rossiiskoi Federatsii v rezul'tate Vtoroi mirovoi voiny, na arkhivnye dokumenty rossiiskogo proiskhozhdeniia, nakhodiashchie-sia na territorii Frantsuzskoi Respubliki": Postanovlenie Gosudarstvennoi Dumy Federal'nogo sobraniia RF ot 22 maia 1998 g., no. 2504–II GD, *Sobranie zakonodatel'stva RF*, 1998, no. 24 (15 June), statute 2662.

the Federal Law, still has not been established."[65]

In effect, however, the French "exchange," which involves only archives and not art, had to be renegotiated. Disputes continue about many French records that were not returned in 1994 and the fate of many more captured French archival materials remaining in Russia, some of them undoubtedly dispersed among repositories other than the former "Special Archive." Nevertheless, given the Duma resolution already approved for France, there was new hope that another shipment of archival materials would be returned to Paris—although this still would not cover all those materials that earlier were determined to be of French provenance.

British Restitution. Similar bureaucratic impediments also delayed the return of records of the British World War II Expeditionary Forces and prisoner-of-war documentation that had been authorized by the Duma on 16 September 1998. Under the terms of the new Russian law these have been described as "family relics."[66] According to Rosarkhiv officials, the British archival materials were turned over to the Russian Foreign Ministry and ready for transport to London with the visit of Russian Foreign Minister Igor´ Ivanov in May 1999. However, at that point, Kosovo negotiations took a turn for the worse, and the plane was unloaded before departing—and the restitution of archives once again became an international political ploy. The British archival materials were returned, finally, in a ceremony in London in late July 1999 during a subsequent visit of Russian Foreign Minister Igor´ Ivanov. That act of restitution, it turned out, also involved archival "barter," since the British side handed over copies of some significant files with long-secret reports on the assassination of Nicholas II and his family in 1918, the reaction of his cousin King George VI, and related British documents that, according to press accounts, had just been declassified for the occasion.[67]

---

[65]   Vladimir P. Tarasov, "The Return of Archival Documents Moved to the USSR as a Result of World War II," *Spoils of War Intenational Newsletter* 6 (February 1999): 55. Another round of French negotiations took place in October 1999.

[66]   "O peredache Velikobritanii peremeshchennykh na territoriiu Rossiiskoi Federatsii v rezul´tate Vtoroi mirovoi voiny lichnykh dokumentov i dokumentov, udostoveriaiushchikh lichnost´ voennosluzhashchikh Britanskogo èkspeditsionnogo korpusa": Postanovlenie Gosudarstvennoi Dumy Federal´nogo sobraniia RF ot 16 sentiabria 1998 g., no. 2970–II GD, *Sobranie zakonodatel´stva Rossiiskoi Federatsii*, 1998, no. 39, statute 4862.

[67]   See, for example, the report by Paul Lashmar, "New Light Cast on the Romanovs' Final Hours," *The Independent* 23 July 1999: 1 and 3; and, "British POW Diaries Released," *The Independent* 23 July 1999: 3. The Public Record

The restitution act also involved the signing of a bilateral agreement on archival cooperation between Russia and the United Kingdom.

On the British side, specialists still are trying to document the fate of the cultural treasures involved in the immediate postwar British restitution efforts to the USSR, one important example of which took place in Austria. British authorities had identified thousands of exceedingly valuable library books from the Russian imperial palaces and other collections in Kyiv that were looted by the Künzberg commandos, and were found at the end of the war in the Monastery of Tanzenberg in the Austrian Tyrol (see Chapter 7). The British then tried to bargain with their Soviet counterparts: they wanted the Soviets to hand over the treasures of Schonbrunn Palace that they had been looting in Vienna in order to prevent their shipment to Moscow. We still do not know if all the books from Kyiv that the British army returned to the Soviets from that Rosenberg stash in the Monastery of Tanzenberg eventually reached Kyiv. But now that at least some inventories of the transferred books have surfaced in the Public Record Office, better documentation of the fate of the books may be possible.[68]

Russian Archival Information and Access Problems

Information Problems. In an effort that has continued despite legal developments in Russia, researchers from many countries have been trying to identify captured cultural treasures and displaced archives there. To Russian credit, there has been a tremendous opening of reference information about Russian archives since 1991 (although few copies of the new publications have been acquired in Ukraine). A new directory of previously secret unpublished internal reference facilities in federal archives appeared in

---

Office (National Archives) subsequently assured me that despite the press accounts, the British documents had long been publicly available, and emphasized that in any case, only copies were involved.

[68] See above Chapter 6, p.232n42. Regarding the attempted Schonbrunn Palace trade-off for the Russian imperial library books, see, for example, the letter from the Acting Deputy Commissioner Allied Commissioner to Austria, C. D. Packard to Sir Arthur Street (13 December 1945), PRO, FO 371/45771, file UE6509. I am very grateful to archivists at the PRO for their assistance in uncovering these files, details from which have not previously been published. A further study of these British restitution efforts is in progress.

1994.[69] A comprehensive new directory of close to 250 repositories in Moscow and St. Petersburg includes agency archives, independent non-governmental archives and archival materials in libraries and museums. It has an extensive bibliography of reference publications and, for our purposes, provides a starting point for identifying Ucrainica in the imperial capitals.[70] Comprehensive guides have appeared for many of the public federal archives that hold the central records of the Russian and Soviet empires, and hence the bulk of records pertinent to Ukraine, including many that were earlier removed from Ukrainian lands.[71] And, as noted above, even microform *opisi* are now available for several of the most important repositories with Soviet-era holdings, such as GA RF and the former Communist Party Central Archive, now the Russian State Archive of Socio-Political History (RGASPI).[72] Later in 2000, Rosarkhiv plans to inaugurate a website with up-to-date directory information about Russian archives and their reference publications, including information about recently declassified records.[73]

Despite new guides for many federal archives, including the agency archives of the Foreign Ministry and the post-1940 Central Naval Archive (TsVMA) in Gatchina, a comprehensive list of captured records in Moscow

---

[69]   *Federal'nye arkhivy Rossii i ikh nauchno-spravochnyi apparat: Kratkii spravochnik*, comp. O. Iu. Nezhdanova; ed. V. P. Kozlov (Moscow: Rosarkhiv, 1994).

[70]   *Arkhivy Rossii: Moskva i Sankt-Peterburg. Spravochnik-obozrenie i bibliograficheskii ukazatel'*, ed. V. P. Kozlov and P. K. Grimsted (Moscow: "Arkheograficheskii tsentr," 1997), with a second, updated English-language edition: *Archives of Russia, 2000.*

[71]   See the my survey, "Increasing Reference Access to Post-1991 Russian Archives," *Slavic Review* 56(4) Winter 1997: 718–59; coverage is updated in the revised chapter 12 of my *Archives in Russian Seven Years After: "Purveyors of Sensations" or "Shadows Cast to the Past"* (Washington, DC: Cold War International History Project, 1998) [=CWIHP Working Paper, 20].

[72]   Regarding the commercially available microfilmed *opisi*, see above Chapter 2, p. 76. Effective March 1999, the Russian State Archive of Socio-Political History—RGASPI (Rossiiskii gosudarstvennyi arkhiv sotsial'no-politicheskoi istorii), consolidates the former Center for Preservation and Study of Records of Modern History (RTsKhIDNI), earlier the Central Party Archive, and the Center for Preservation of Records of Youth Organizations (TsKhDMO, earlier the Central Archive of the Komsomol).

[73]   See more details about recent reference publications in *Archives of Russia, 2000;* in my "Increasing Reference Access" and *Archives in Russia Seven Years After*; and at the ABB website <http://iisg.nl/~abb>.

has never been prepared. Even within the former Special Archive (since March 1999 part of RGVA), a comprehensive list of fonds was not publicly available to researchers by the end of 1999. Because many trophy archives were dispersed to other facilities, even the promised list of trophy fonds in the former TsGOA would only be a start. The period for claims under the new Russian law on cultural treasures was slated to expire in October 1999, without a reliable list of trophy archives in Russia, let alone other cultural treasures. How can people even consider filing claims?

Access Problems. Increasing openness of reference literature about the archives in Russia has been accompanied by some, but not however, all of the desired progress in access to information regarding World War II losses, trophy archives, and restitution issues. As noted above, major groups of records, such as many of those of the Soviet Military Administration in Germany (SVAG) and of military trophy brigades and retrieval operations still remain closed. The administrative records of the former Special Archive have not been declassified, and the administrative files for individual fonds (*dela fonda*) in that archive and others, which might help determine provenance and archival migrations of captured records, are not open to researchers.[74]

A prominent Hungarian museum director, István Fodor, likewise complained in 1998 that:

> ...no agreement was reached concerning possible research in Russian archives, meaning that Hungarian experts are still barred from investigating formerly classified documents which might provide clues to the fate of Hungarian artworks.[75]

Professor Wolfgang Eichwede, who directs the major research program on World War II loses at the University of Bremen, commented to this effect in 1995, with words that bear on Ukraine as well:

> In a number of joint statements, Germany and Russia have promised each other unlimited information. It is simply absurd that several Russian archives, which could supply information on their own wartime losses, are inaccessible to Western researchers to this day. This policy of secrecy leaves unanswered a myriad of questions. We do not know, for example, what Soviet cultural goods previously plundered by Hit-

---

[74] Regarding access problems in Russian archives, see my *Archives in Russia Seven Years After*, especially chapters 1 and 13.

[75] István Fodor, "Hungary," *Spoils of War: International Newsletter* 5 (June 1998): 58.

ler's divisions the Red Army was able to recover during its advance. In addition, we do not know the location of hundreds of thousands of books and artworks from Russia and Ukraine which were restituted by the Americans to the USSR soon after 1945. In this respect, it is not only the Germans who are awaiting the opening of archives.[76]

Ukraine is waiting as well.

Even in connection with the preparation for this volume, Ukrainian colleagues tried to obtain a copy of reports about the location of trophy art and manuscripts prepared by the Ministry of Culture of the USSR in 1957 and related documents—only to be informed that the files were still classified! I also tried directly myself in Moscow. In that particular case, the related documents had already appeared in print in 1996 in German translation, but the originals remain closed to researchers in the former archive of the Central Committee, now known as the Russian State Archive for Contemporary History (RGANI) in Moscow![77] Another series of five documents dating from 1950 that describe trophy music held in several prestigious Moscow institutions, including the Tchaikovsky Conservatory in Moscow and the Glinka Central Museum of Musical Culture, also appear in the same 1996 German documentary collection. As of October 1999, those documents are among the only folios closed off to readers in the file cited from the records of the Agitation and Propaganda Sector under the CP Central Committee in the former Central Party Archive (now known as the Russian State Archive of Socio-Political History—RGASPI). In that same archive, I was shown a 1948 Glavlit (Soviet censorship agency) report regarding trophy library holdings in libraries and museums in July and again in October 1999. But the photocopy I ordered arrived with at least three paragraphs censored out.

At the major international conference on Holocaust era assets in Washington, DC, in December 1998, the Russian ambassador and other participants in the Russian delegation announced a new Russian policy of archival openness regarding Holocaust-related cultural treasures still held by Moscow. As a participant in the Archival Symposium at the U.S. National Archives following the conference, I remained skeptical when I heard the positive reaction of the State Department conference directors to the Russian proclamations. That skepticism has been confirmed: as this book goes to press, I

---

[76]   Wolfgang Eichwede, "Models of Restitution (Germany, Russia, Ukraine)," in *Spoils of War: WWII and Aftermath,* p. 219.

[77]   See above, Chapter 7, p. 261.

have had no answer from my letters of complaint and request for declassification from the two archives named above.

Two earlier examples in connection with this study likewise come to mind: I also wrote a letter several years ago objecting when I was not allowed to see the archival originals of recently published 1945 GKO documents relating to Stalin's "reparations" and "cultural trophy" policies in RGASPI (earlier RTsKhIDNI).[78] As well, a "special file" from the NKVD Secretariat addressed to Viacheslav Molotov in June 1945 relating to trophy cultural valuables is still wrapped in brown paper so that it cannot be seen by researchers in the State Archive of the Russian Federation (GA RF).[79]

In fairness, it should be noted that such problems do not occur only in Russia. I have found files relating to Nazi trophy seizures that are closed in France. And in Ukraine, as noted in earlier chapters, several groups of files relating to captured records and trophy books have still not surfaced; we thus do not even know if they have been preserved.

*   *

*

We conclude with very specific examples of restrictions on access to information about trophy cultural treasures now in Russia, because lack of information—and freedom of access to information—was a crucial ingredient in the earlier "Cold War" era. Those of us who were working closely in and with Russian archives in 1989, 1990, 1991, and immediately after the collapse of the USSR in late 1991 and 1992, imbibed the optimism, if not euphoria, that we were entering a "new era" of "rapprochement" between Russia and the West. With the collapse of the "Iron Curtain" and the Berlin Wall, archives were being thrown open and the "truth" about the past could be openly revealed. We were finally able to reveal details about the Western archival "trophies" still ensconced in the "Special Archive" off Leningrad

---

[78] See Chapter 7, p. 249n4. Knyshevskii also cites documents from military archives that are likewise still classified.

[79] The still-classified document (encased in a brown-paper cover in the file), dated 18 June 1945, in GA RF, 9401/2/103, fols. 202–204, is described in the inventory as "On the organization of registration of cultural valuables, acquired in repositories of the NKVD SSSR. Appendix: draft SNK USSR regulation 'On Trophy Valuables'."—See the published inventory, *"Osobaia papka" V. M. Molotova: Iz materialov Sekretariata NKVD-MVD SSSR 1944–1956 gg.: Katalog dokumentov/The "Special File" for V. M. Molotov: From Materials of the Secretariat of the NKVD–MVD of the USSR, 1944–1956: A Catalogue of Documents,* comp. E. D. Grin'ko et al.; ed. S. V. Mironenko and V. A. Kozlov (Moscow: "Blagovest," 1994) [=Arkhiv noveishei istorii Rossii, Seriia: Katalogi, 2], p. 38.

Highway. We were able to establish archival information systems and put information about Russian archives on the Internet, revealing many of their hitherto hidden treasures to an eagerly awaiting Western world.

However, the rise of a burgeoning rival current of traditional Russian national reaction against the West challenged those possibilities. Alternative political powers in the "new Russia" all too soon forgot the achievements of Soviet archival restitution (especially to the Communist Bloc) and turned inward. Hopes for restitution of the newly revealed archival treasures from Western Europe captured more than a half-century ago by Beria's scouts were dashed. Few paid heed to the fact that many of them were earlier seized by the Nazis from occupied countries, from Holocaust victims, or from others that were considered enemies of the Third Reich. Even information about World War II cultural "trophies" was again suppressed, although some traces had already leaked out (or been sold) to the West. The battle over the law nationalizing the cultural spoils from World War II was but another symbol of the emergence of a renewed claim to "Victory" over the "Fascist invader." Yet at the same time, it meant a renewed "Cold War" on the cultural front with the European Community—of which, ironically, Russia had just become a member by virtue of a promise of restitution.

CHAPTER 11

Independent Ukraine and Poland:
A New Climate for Restitution?

Post-1991 Ukrainian-Polish Restitution Issues

For Ukraine and Poland the mutual issues of restitution that linger are exceedingly complicated and deserve special attention. These result from centuries of shifting borders between the two nations and the millennial cohabitation of these two Slavic peoples with other nations in the same territory. Added to this is the rise and fall of empires whose rivalries brought the eclipse of both nations at various times, alternately splitting their lands or throwing them together under a single flag. As a result, many of the archival records of Poles and Ukrainians are intricately intermingled and often to be found among the records of previous regimes (including Polish and Polish-Lithuanian ones from the fourteenth through the end of the eighteenth century) that governed the lands that now constitute Ukraine.

One of many examples of the difficulties of trying to designate and separate the archival heritage of one or another national entity is the fate of provincial and municipal court records from eastern Galicia that before the Polish partitions were predominantly created by local Polish administrative and judicial authorities—and which now form the basis for the Central State Historical Archive in Lviv (TsDIAL).[1] The extensive survey of western Ukrainian archives in connection with the recent directory of records of the Austro-Hungarian Empire shows the extent to which the archival heritage of Ukraine is tied to yet another imperial legacy from the late eighteenth century through to the fall of that empire at the end of World War I.[2] Still another example of the difficulty of dividing "Polish" from "Ukrainian"-related

---

[1]   See, for example, my "The Fate of Early Records in Lviv Archives: Documentation from Western Ukraine under Polish Rule (Fifteenth Century to 1772)," *Slavonic and East European Review* 60(3) July 1982: 321–46. For a complete bibliography of other publications relating to pre-partition records in Lviv, see Grimsted, *Archives: Ukraine*, pp. 425–70.

[2]   See my "Ukraine," in *A Guide to East-Central European Archives,* ed. Charles W. Ingrao (Houston: Rice University Press, 1998), pp. 171–200 [=*Austrian History Yearbook* 29(2) 1998]. For more complete bibliography, see the related sections in Grimsted, *Archives: Ukraine.*

records and the inappropriateness of separating archives from their territorial provenance is prominently displayed in the now divided family (and estate) records from the Polish magnate elite. The local political and economic power of the Polish *szlachta* brought Ukrainians and Poles together on the same land for many centuries; their vast landholdings and the records generated by those landholdings transcended changing political regimes. In these and other cases the viability of the concept of "joint" archival heritage should more frequently come into play.[3]

On the other hand, many current problems of "displaced" Polish and Ukrainian cultural treasures remain a prime component of the immediate legacy of World War II. However, Ukrainian claims and Polish counter-claims for archival materials, libraries, and other cultural treasures displaced by Nazi wartime or Soviet postwar plunder are only a small part of the story that needs to be viewed in its historical context. Given the major Soviet redrawing of the Polish-Ukrainian border as a result of the war, with the incorporation of previously Polish western Ukraine into the Ukrainian SSR, major displacements of cultural treasures and revindication of archives was motivated by or came in the wake of the mass resettlement of Polish and Ukrainian populations. The horrific acts of "ethnic cleansing" on both sides of the border during and after the war have left bitter memories. (Only since the collapse of the Soviet regime and Ukrainian independence has it been possible to tell their story.) Documentation on the forced deportation of Ukrainians from Poland to the USSR and Polish atrocities against Ukrainians, such as Operation "Vistula" (*Akcja Wisła*) has found its archivist in the Polish-Ukrainian writer Eugeniusz Misiło. Ukrainian nationalist atrocities against Poles during the war, which under Soviet rule was often blamed on the Nazis and their collaborators, are also being documented in recent publications by Polish specialists.[4] A Western scholar, Timothy Snyder, has

---

[3]   See *Archiwa rodzinno-majątkowe w zbiorach państwowych we Lwowie: Informator*, comp. Stanisław Pijaj (Warsaw, Ministerstwo Kultury i Sztuki: 1995) [=Polskie dziedzictwo kulturalne, Seria B: Wspólne Dziedzictwo].

[4]   See, for example, Eugeniusz Misiło [Ievhen Misylo], *Akcja "Wisła"* (Warsaw: Archiwum Ukrainskie, 1993); and the related documents on forced repatriation edited by Misiło: *Repatriacja czy deportacja: Przesiedlenie Ukraińców z Polski do USRR 1944/1946*, 2 vols. (Warsaw: Ukraińskie, 1996–1999) and "Etnotsyd. Etap I: Pereselennia ukraïntsiv z Pol'shchi v URSR 1944–1946," *Slidamy pam'iati: Litopysnyi kalendar* 1 (Warsaw, 1996): 31–108. Misiło's recently established Ukrainian Archive in Warsaw serves as a resource center for collected related documentation. For a good example of the Polish perspective on Ukrainian atrocities, see Władysław Filar, *Eksterminacja ludności polskiej na Wołyniu w Drugiej wojnie światowej* (Warsaw, 1999).

been re-examining the atrocities in an historical and political perspective.[5] The dimensions of archival transfers and "cultural cleansing" still require further research and explication.

With the annexation of western Ukrainian lands as part of the Ukrainian SSR came the Soviet policy of "depolonization." Rabid "cultural cleansing" in the area was particularly strong in the city of Lviv itself, as the capital of eastern Małopolska. This "cleansing" included the destruction of all remnants of Polish culture—from street names to statues, from the liquidation of Polish cultural institutions and relics of all kinds to the suppression of the Roman Catholic Church. Despite the massive forced population transfers, there was never any intergovernmental agreement for the transfer of treasures of the Polish cultural heritage from the area. Each departing Polish family was allowed to take with them only two tons of possessions. Some limited postwar revindication of archival materials took place, such as immediately needed vital statistics records and local administrative and police files. In the face of Polish pressure, the Soviet side made limited gestures with postwar "gifts" of "Polish" cultural treasures, but the arrangements were predominantly fiats, lacking professional appraisal and binational consultations. The cultural devastation caused by the unprofessional division and transfers of library and archival materials has yet to be healed.

The Polish-Ukrainian political, economic, and cultural rapprochement following the dissolution of the USSR provides a new context for negotiation of cultural restitution issues.[6] Cultural and archival effects of the redrawn postwar boundaries are now coming into better focus in a new spirit of post-Soviet accommodation. A thorough study of the legal background of the cultural restitution and revindication issues involved was published in 1994 by Wojciech Kowalski, a Polish specialist in cultural restitution law.[7]

---

[5] See his "'To Resolve the Ukrainian Question Once and For All': The Ethnic Cleansing of Ukrainians in Poland, 1943–1947," *Journal of Cold War Studies* 1(2) 1999: 86–120.

[6] Timothy Snyder's seminar presentation at the Harvard Ukrainian Research Institute in February 1999 gave an excellent overview of the shifting Polish-Ukrainian relationship since WWII. In more complete form, his analysis will comprise the third chapter of his forthcoming book, *The Reconstruction of Nations: Poles, Ukrainians, Lithuanians, Belarusians, 1569–1999* (New Haven: Yale University Press, 2001). One phase of his analysis is represented by his "To resolve the Ukrainian Question."

[7] Wojciech Kowalski, *Liquidation of the Effects of World War II in the Area of Culture* (Warsaw: Institute of Culture, 1994), p. 100. The Polish version includes appended texts of many related documents: *Likwidacja skutków II Wojny Świato-*

In the context of this rapprochement, both sides have been making retrospective reviews of displaced Polonica and Ucrainica and their revindication desiderata. A well-documented study of the transfers of Polish cultural treasures and archives of all types from Lviv during and immediately after the war was published in 1996 by Maciej Matwijów, a professional manuscript specialist in the Ossolineum in Wrocław. Matwijów appended many revealing original documents on the issues from Polish sources. He indicates in his book that because of insufficient research opportunities abroad for him and the less than optimal cooperation of knowledgeable Ukrainian specialists, he was unable to avail himself of the vast relevant documentation in Lviv itself which would have further enriched his study and confirmed many of his findings.[8]

Ukrainian pretensions regarding the Ossolineum were also set forth in 1996 with a defensive collection of documents in Lviv, edited with an introduction by Larysa Krushel′nyts′ka. Krushel′nyts′ka now directs the Vasyl′ Stefanyk Scientific Library, the Lviv successor to the Ossolineum. The cover picture of the statue of Stefanyk in front of the original Ossolineum building sets the tone, with documents from the library history, demonstrating its role as a key Ukrainian institution, whose collections should remain put—and those previously removed returned to it.[9] Krushel′nyts′ka was apparently not aware of the above-cited studies by Kowalski and Matwijów, and generally did not cite any Polish sources, although she did include a brief extract from one of Matwijów's earlier

---

wej w dziedzinie kultury (Warsaw: Institute of Culture, 1994). As noted earlier, Kowalski also presented a well-documented background survey of the legal issues at the 1997 Minsk conference on restitution: "Repatriatsiia kul′turnykh tsennostei v situatsii ustupok territorii i raspada mnogonatsional′nykh gosudarstv," in *Restitutsyia kul′turnykh kashtoŭnastsei*, pp. 21–52. Kowalski's presentation, as published in the conference proceedings, cites significant legal instruments and literature in numerous languages.

8   Maciej Matwijów, *Walka o lwowskie dobra kultury w latach 1945–1948* (Wrocław: Towarzystwo Przyjaciół Ossolineum, 1996). See the author's prefatory note, p. 9. In addition to extensive citations from relevant archival and published sources, Matwijów includes 63 original documents from the period. In October 1999 he indicated to me that it was not the case that he was denied access (as implied in the book and as was the practice during the Soviet regime), but rather that he had limited time in Lviv and that cooperation of Ukrainian specialists was not as forthcoming as he would have desired.

9   *L′vivs′ka naukova biblioteka im. V. Stefanyka NAN Ukraïny: Dokumenty, fakty, komentari*, ed., with an intro. by Larysa Krushel′nyts′ka (Lviv: LNB, 1996).

articles. She also did not mention the problems of reference access to the now divided collections. The contrasting tone and approaches of the Ukrainian and Polish publications are indicative of the lingering problems and the distance that separates them from resolution.

It is a positive development that such matters can be aired at all; only since the fall of Soviet hegemony in Eastern Europe and Ukrainian independence has this been the case. The generally improved Ukrainian-Polish diplomatic and economic relations since then have encouraged more open discussion of unresolved issues of displaced cultural treasures and archives. In this spirit, we should briefly consider a few examples of the displaced archival and library materials involved and the future agenda of reconciliation that they will require.

New Cultural Agreements. Noteworthy in post-Soviet cultural developments, a "Treaty between Ukraine and the Republic of Poland on Good Neighborliness, Friendly Relations, and Cooperation," was signed 18 May 1992. Specific paragraphs in an additional "Preliminary Agreement for Cultural and Scientific Cooperation," signed at the same time call for the open description and access to archival materials and other historical treasures of interest to the other country and for the reuniting of dispersed collections:

> The Side on whose territories are found objects and historical treasures of culture, history and learning as well as archival materials and library collections of the other country...will act to disclose, inventory, bring together, preserve, restore (those objects) and give access to them. The Sides will cooperate in this area, especially in bringing together collections of art, libraries and archives that had been scattered due to historical events (art. 5, §1).

> In accord with the UNESCO international conventions and other international agreements and standards...the Sides will take steps to disclose and return the movable treasures of culture, history and archives of the other country (art. 5, §2).[10]

---

[10] I cite the English translation in Kowalski, *Liquidation of the Effects of World War II*, p. 100, quoting the text of Article 5 in the unpublished "Preliminary Agreement for Cultural and Scientific Cooperation." Similar wording appears as Article 13 in the "Treaty" of the same date, "Dohovir mizh Ukraïnoiu ta Respublikoiu Pol'shcheiu pro dobrosusidstvo, druzhni vidnosyny i spivrobitnytstvo," extracted in its Ukrainian version in document 130 in *Ukraïna v mizhnarodno-pravovykh vidnosynakh,* vol. 2, pp. 586–90.

These points were also announced in a communiqué from a meeting of the Consultative Committee of the Presidents of Ukraine and Poland in September 1995, which further affirmed that:

> The Sides recognize the desirability of undertaking a new inventorization of objects of their cultural heritage— Ukrainian in Poland and Polish in Ukraine, and likewise of attempting all possible means for the preservation and restitution of such objects of cultural heritage.[11]

More specific efforts at implementation have begun following the signature of an "Agreement on Cooperation in the Realm of Protection and Return of Cultural Property Lost or Illegally Displaced during the Second World War" in Warsaw on 25 June 1996.[12] A Joint Commission was subsequently established to deal with such problems; it had its first meeting in Lviv in mid-May 1997.[13] A second meeting of the Commission took place in Warsaw in mid-February 1999, and a third was scheduled in Ukraine for October 1999. Under the auspices of the Commission a group of archival experts was formed, the first meeting of which was scheduled for Cracow in June 1999. (A group of library specialists was also scheduled to meet in Wrocław at that time, but the Ukrainian side was represented only by Stefanyk Library Director Krushel′nyts′ka; hence, no working sessions were possible.) High among the aims of the Commission and working groups is the guarantee of access for specialists of both sides to the displaced materials and their precise identification.

Outside of official meetings, serious professional implementation of the "inventorization" provision has been progressing, especially on the Polish side. Of particular note in terms of archival materials in Ukraine is the 1995 repertory of Polish family estate archives which covers materials held in the

---

[11]   A Ukrainian version is published in the quoted extract as document 132 in *Ukraïna v mizhnarodno-pravovykh vidnosynakh*, vol. 2, p. 558.

[12]   The Ukrainian version is published as document 134 in ibid., vol. 2, pp. 559–62. The Polish text of the agreement appears in the internal Polish Ministry of Culture publication *Wnioski rewindykacyjne*, pp. 142–44. Copies of this Polish text are not publicly available, pending a more definitive edition.

[13]   The Polish text of the protocol signed at the conclusion of the meeting was printed as "Protokół z pierwszego posiedzenia Międzyrządowej Komisji Polsko-Ukraińskiej do spraw ochrony i zwrotu dóbr kultury utraconych i bezprawnie przemieszczonych podczas II wojny światowej," in *Wnioski rewindykacyjne*, pp. 145–46. See the summary report by a member of the Ukrainian delegation, Sergei [Serhii] Kot, "Ukraine," *Spoils of War: International Newsletter* 5 (1998): 71–72.

Central State Historical Archive (TsDIAL) and the Stefanyk Library (in LNB NAN) in Lviv.[14] A 1996 bibliography compiled by Urszula Paszkiewicz provides a repertory of manuscript inventories and catalogs of libraries in eastern lands of the former Polish-Lithuanian Commonwealth. A subsequent larger volume covers all types of library inventories and catalogs (published as well unpublished) from 1510 through 1939.[15] Both of these latter works cover many library collections in Ukraine, but no comparable reference studies by Ukrainian specialists have yet appeared.

The Symbolic Ossolineum Divided

The Rise and Fall of the Ossolineum in Lviv. Most significant in terms of the archival component in the cultural heritage of the area is the tragic fate and dispersal of what had been the most important library in pre-1939 western Ukraine—the Ossoliński National Institute (Zakład Narodowy im. Ossolińskich). Since the abolition of the Ossolineum (as it is usually known in English) by Soviet authorities in 1940, its fate has been the most serious bone of cultural contention between Ukraine and Poland. The Ossolineum was founded in Lviv (Lwów, Lemberg) in 1817 and was chartered by the Austrian emperor as a national library, according to the foundation bequest of the Polish nobleman Józef Maksymilian Ossoliński (1746–1826). Initially, the Ossolineum comprised a library and publishing house; the associated Lubomirski Museum was chartered in 1824 and presented to the city in 1870. Before 1918, the Ossoliński Institute served a major cultural and educational function, especially for the Polish population of the area, and indeed for all of Poland, during a century when Polish, like Ukrainian culture was brutally suppressed in the Russian Empire.

The Ossolineum was the most important library in Galicia and, later, Małopolska (after the area's incorporation into the Second Polish Republic following WWI), and continued to serve a crucial archival function up to

---

[14] See *Archiwa rodzinno-majątkowe*.

[15] Urszula Paszkiewicz, *Rękopiśmienne inwentarze i katalogi bibliotek z ziem wschodnich Rzeczypospolitej (spis za lata 1553–1939)* (Warsaw: Wyd-wo DiG, 1996; Ministerstwo Kultury i Sztuki) [=Polskie dziedzictwo kulturalne, Seria B: Wspólne Dziedzictwo]; and, idem, *Inwentarze i katalogi bibliotek z ziem wschodnich Rzeczypospolitej (spis za lata 1553–1939)* (Warsaw: Wyd-wo DiG, 1998; Ministerstwo Kultury i Sztuki) [=Polskie Dziedzictwo Kulturalne, Seria B: Wspólne Dziedzictwo]. Paszkiewicz is continuing this research and plans supplemental coverage.

1939, consolidating records of Polish cultural organizations, estate archives, and personal papers of the Polish elite in the area, along with literary manuscripts and other elements of Polish cultural heritage. Although Latin and Polish predominated, its archival holdings were hardly purely Polish, as would be expected in a multi-ethnic region. They included important Ukrainian, Jewish, Armenian, and other elements. The Shevchenko Scientific Society (NTSh) served a parallel archival function for the Ukrainian population, although it lacked the funding support and level of professional development of its Polish counterpart.

Soon after the annexation of western Ukraine under the terms of the Ribbentrop-Molotov Non-Agression Pact, the Ossolineum was abolished by the Soviet authorities. On 2 January 1940 it became one of the eighty formerly independent libraries to be amalgamated into the newly created Lviv Branch of the Library of the Ukrainian Academy of Sciences in Kyiv. Its "Polish" character was strictly repressed.[16] Independent Ukrainian cultural institutions, such as the library of the Shevchenko Scientific Society, suffered a parallel fate, and became part of the new Academy Library. Restored and reorganized as part of the centralized State Library (Staatsbibliothek) under Nazi occupation, many of the Polish staff were restored; the last director of the Lviv Ossolineum was Mieczysław Gębarowicz.

As the war turned against the Nazis and the front grew closer in 1944, evacuation of major cultural treasures from Lviv to Cracow, including archives and libraries, was started with the full agreement of the Polish directors of the various archives and libraries. (Their major role in the assignment of evacuation priorities may explain the emphasis on Polish treasures.) Evacuation intensified in the spring, with two shipments—18 March and 2 April—from the Ossolineum, totaling 2,298 predominantly Polish manuscripts, 2,198 charters, approximately 1,860 incunabula and early printed books, and 2,371 prints and drawings from the collections of the Pawlikowski Library and the Lubomirski Museum. The second shipment took place a week before a Soviet bomb fell on the main building of the Ossolineum on 9 April.[17] First taken to the Jagellonian Library in Cracow at

---

[16] Regarding the fate of the Ossolineum during 1939–1941, see, for example, the memoir account of Tadeusz Mańkowski, "Ossolineum pod rządami sowieckimi," *Czasopisma ZNiO* 1 (1992): 135–55.

[17] These figures were quoted by Matwijów, *Walka o lwowskie dobra kultury,* p. 30, and in his more recent article, "Ewakuzcja zbiorów polskich ze Lwowa w 1944 r.," *Rocznik Lwowski* 1995/1996: 31–46, which includes references to the diary of Karl Badecki, who had headed the City Archive in Lviv and helped the Nazis organize the evacuation. Additional evacuation details are provided by

the end of March and early April 1944, these materials were later moved to Silesia in July 1944 to an evacuation site on an estate in Kswary Świerkowski, near Złotoryja (*Ger.* Goldberg) and Adelina (*Ger.* Adelsdorf), eighty kilometers west of Wrocław.[18] After their recovery, the Lviv materials were taken to the Biblioteka Narodowa in Warsaw, while the collections of provenance in Polish postwar territories were returned to their homes. Later after the Ossolineum was reestablished in Wrocław, the Ossolineum holdings were transferred there from Warsaw.

Postwar Transfers to Poland. In the wake of the redrawn Polish-Ukrainian frontier and the forced resettlement of the Polish population, Polish authorities and cultural leaders campaigned for the revindication of Polish cultural treasures, including the symbolic Ossolineum. The last Polish director of the Ossolineum before the war, Mieczysław Gębarowicz, stayed in Lviv and refused repatriation. He subsequently was instrumental in acquainting Soviet authorities with its holdings.[19] These authorities recognized the political as

---

Matwijów's introduction to his publication of letters of Gębarowicz, "Lwowskie Ossolineum w listach Mieczysława Gębarowicza z lat 1943–1946," *Czasopismo ZNiO* 1 (1992): 159–62, although there are slight discrepancies in the evacuation statistics in the different accounts. See also Matwijów's more detailed coverage of the Ossolineum during the war, "Zbiory rękopismienne Zakładu Narodowego im. Ossolińskich we Lwowie w latach 1939–1946," *Czasopismo ZNiO* 10 (1999): 211–41.

[18] The shipment of about 5 freight cars, found in a shed on the estate was described in a 25 October 1945 report by Dr. Bohdan Horodyski of the Biblioteka Narodowa (Warsaw). The head of the Manuscript Division of the Biblioteka Narodowa kindly showed me a copy of the report and inventory. Abandoned by the Nazis in February 1945, the shipment also included books from the Polish Library in Paris along with other collections of Polish provenance and some materials from the NTSh in Lviv.

[19] See Matwijów, *Walka o lwowskie dobra kultury,* esp. pp. 33–38, 42–51, 67–69; and idem, "Zbiory rękopismienne," pp. 225–41. See also Matwijów's analysis in, "Mieczysław Gębarowicz (1893–1984), ostatni dyrektor lwowskiego Ossolineum," *Czasopismo ZNiO* 2 (1993): 9–71, together with an edition of some of Gębarowicz's correspondence in idem, "Lwowskie Ossolineum w listach." Some of this correspondence also is published in *Walka o lwowskie dobra kultury.* See, for example, Gębarowicz's memoranda of April and May 1945 there, pp. 169–76. The fourth volume of the same series was entirely devoted to a Gębrowicz memorial: *Poświęcony profesorowi Mieczysławowi Gębarowiczowi w setną rocznici urodzin* (Wrocław, 1994) [=*Czasopismo ZNiO* 4 (1994)].

well as cultural significance of the Ossolineum to the Polish nation. In October 1945, a decree of the Council of Commissars of the Ukrainian SSR, countersigned by Nikita Khrushchev, authorized the first shipment of "Polonica" from Ukraine to Poland, including 50,000 books and manuscripts, along with some 577 museum exhibits from three museums in Lviv and three in Kyiv.[20] That directive did not designate the source of the books and manuscripts to be sent from the Lviv Branch of the Library of the Academy of Sciences, but later orders from Kyiv, citing that directive, designated for transfer to Poland "all of the former Ossolineum library, with the exception of books, manuscripts, and archival materials that have a direct relationship to the history, science, literature, art, and economy of Ukraine." One hundred, fifty crates were to be ready for shipment by 1 August 1946.[21] But more precise guidelines for determining the "exception" were never drawn up.

Considerable fanfare and an official Soviet delegation accompanied the delivery of the "gift" of Ossolineum materials to Wrocław in July 1946, which in propagandistic wording was to "demonstrate the friendship and solidarity between the Soviet and Polish people born in the fight against the fascist Hitlerite Germany":

> ...With completion of the repatriation of Polish citizens from the UkrSSR, the Government of the UkrSSR declares as a sign of eternal friendship between our brotherly countries giving to the Polish people the Lviv "Ossolineum" book collection, the Racławicka Panorama, paintings by distinguished painters, many museum exhibits, valuable manuscripts, and also other artistic and historical monuments relating to the history of Polish national culture, science, and art.[22]

---

[20] Postanova SNK URSR, no. 1673 (18 October 1945), published in *Dokumenty i materialy po istorii sovetsko-pol'skikh otnoshenii,* vol. 8 (Moscow: "Nauka," 1974), p. 583 (doc. 337); also published in Matwijów, *Walka o lwowskie dobra kultury,* pp. 216–17.

[21] "Pro peredachu istorychnykh i kul'turnykh tsinnostei pol's'koho narodu Tymchasovomu Uriadovi Natsional'noï Pol's'koï Respubliky," Postanova Rada Ministriv URSR, no. 1182 (5 July 1945), signed by Nikita Khrushchev (M. Khrushchov), published in *L'vivs'ka naukova biblioteka: Dokumenty,* pp. 29–30 (doc. 7).

[22] The texts of the announcement appeared in *Kyïvs'ka pravda* 127 (25 June 1946), which was republished in *Dokumenty i materialy po istorii sovetsko-pol'skikh otnoshenii,* vol. 9 (Moscow: "Nauka," 1976), p. 131 (doc. 79); the Polish edition gives the Ukrainian text, pp. 138–39 (doc. 80). See also the announcement in *Głos Ludu* 209 (August 1946), which is found in *Dokumenty i*

Notably, the text gives the impression that the entire Ossolineum was involved, neglecting to mention that only "part" of the Ossolineum was being revindicated to Poland. According to the official act of transfer, the July 1946 shipment included 7,068 manuscripts and 34,464 early printed books, along with later imprints and other cultural treasures. This contrasts with the approximately 16,600 manuscripts, 3,200 charters, and 13,999 autographs that, together with approximately 85,000 early printed books (not including the Baworowski Library holdings and some others), comprised the Ossolineum archival holdings in 1945.[23] After the shipment reached Wrocław, the Ossoliński National Institute (Zakład Narodowy im. Ossolińskich) was reestablished there, although it then comprised no more than half of its prewar Lviv holdings. A second shipment followed in March 1947, but did not include any manuscripts.[24]

The postwar "Polish program" for Soviet authorities did not just include the redrawing of national boundaries. In addition to the political pacification of the Poles, the "ethnic cultural cleansing" of strong Polish cultural traditions in Lviv—as represented by the Ossolineum—was clearly a high priority for the Soviets. A major shipment of Polish-language books was sent to Moscow, and Jewish-language materials were sent to Kyiv.[25] Numerous proposals, including one from Gębarowicz, recommended the revindication of the entire Ossolineum to Poland; some rejected the idea of partial transfer. That point of view still finds strong Polish backing today.

As noted earlier, there are good grounds for transfers of cultural property and archives in connection with major resettlements of ethnic populations. Yet the transfer in toto of a cultural institution such as the Ossolineum, as

---

materialy as doc. 85, pp. 135–36. A thank you letter from Polish President Bolesław Bierut appears as doc. 88 (pp. 137–38).

[23] As listed in the official "act of transfer" (30 August 1946), published in Matwijów, *Walka o lwowskie dobra kultury*, pp. 280–81 (facsimile), p. 92. The estimated 1945 figures are those from an unpublished Gębarowicz report of June 1945, quoted by Matwijów, ibid., p. 31. In fact, however, according to Matwijów's actual figures sent, there were 6,471 manuscripts (in 6,790 volumes) and 35,565 early printed books (p. 101). Matwijów devotes considerable analysis to the background and publishes many related documents for the first time, with a separate chapter analyzing the Ukrainian "gift" of July 1946, including the materials from the Ossolineum (pp. 93–114).

[24] See Matwijów, *Walka o lwowskie dobra kultury*, especially pp. 145–55.

[25] The orders for those shipments are published in *L'vivs'ka naukova biblioteka: Dokumenty*, pp. 26–27 and pp. 31–32 (doc. 6 and 8).

important as it is symbolically to the Polish nation, is impossible without extracting the roots of the vast archives, library holdings, and cultural traditions of local provenance that it had created over almost a century and a half of its existence in the multi-ethnic city of Leopolis-Lemberg-Lwów-Lviv. However, given the Soviet policy of "cultural cleansing," the Ossolineum had already been abolished in Lviv, and so there was important reason to have it take fresh root in the newly polonized city of Wrocław. In the case of the division of the Ossolineum, there was no archivally "right" manner in which to proceed once Lviv (and its culture) was officially made "Soviet Ukrainian." The "wrong" that was committed was made even worse by the lack of principles and professional guidelines for the division of the archives- and manuscript collections that did take place.

We have analyzed the difficulties of using ethnic or linguistic criteria for archival, and let-alone cultural, divisions. Personal papers and manuscripts of acknowledged Polish writers, artists, and other cultural figures were prime candidates for transfer, given the Soviet authorities' desire to "depolonize" Lviv. Roman Catholic archives and collections were likewise selected, particularly with the Roman Catholic Church's close connection to the Polish population of the area and the Soviet authorities' policy to suppress that church and its culture.

Ukrainians tried to prevent the removal of books and archival materials that were closely related to Ukrainian lands, given the transfer act's official "exception." As noted earlier, though, territorial pertinence is a difficult principle to define and rarely in and of itself a valid principle for archival devolution or determining a nation's archival heritage. (And, at any rate, when the division took place, no one appeared to be interested in principles.) Contrary to expectation (but understandable in terms of Marxist historical principles), major Polish estate archives from the region that were directly related to the land and economy were deemed essential and retained in Lviv, even if they represented the legacy of primarily Polish gentry or "bourgeois nationalist" families. (Many were transferred to the Secret Division of TsDIAL.) Thus, problems naturally arose because many of the archives of Polish cultural institutions, the papers of Polish political and cultural leaders, and many manuscript treasures, even those written in Latin or Polish, were integrally tied to the land, history, and culture of the multi-ethnic city and region of their creation. These problems remain today.

The most disastrous aspect of the division of the Ossolineum manuscript collections was the lack of respect for the integrity of groups of records (fonds) or component collections—a cardinal principle in accepted international archival practice. An appropriate agreement on the selection of materials for transfer from the Ossolineum was never drawn up. A delegation from Poland worked by day while a local ad hoc committee worked by night.

As a result, the treasures were hastily, ruthlessly, and, seemingly willy-nilly divided. Many individual personal and family papers were hopelessly split. In some cases individual volumes of a single manuscript are now divided between Lviv and Wrocław.[26]

Soviet Attempts at Remediation. The Ossolineum case has been a poster child for how *not* to resolve revindication or archival transfers. It is little wonder that the division of the Ossolineum continued to be a source of friction between Poland and the USSR, or that many of the same issues arose when, later, there were considerations for additional transfers or attempts to repair the damage that had already occurred. In 1969, when the matter once more was raised in Moscow, two specialists from the Manuscript Division of the Lenin Library were sent to Lviv to appraise the situation. Their report emphasized the difficulties and "in many cases the inadequacies" involved in the choice of books and manuscripts transferred earlier, because "the major part of Ossolineum documents could not be clearly designated as bearing only on the history of Poland or only on the history of Ukraine, Lithuania, and Belarus: much too closely was the historical fate of those territories and peoples intertwined." However, they emphasized that since published catalogs and many scholarly citations had already indicated the division of the manuscripts, any further transfers "would be ill-advised" and "would make the use of the materials more difficult for research work." They recommended instead "wider information about the materials and the exchange of microfilms between the two repositories."[27]

Twenty years later, in 1989, a commission under the Academy of Sciences of Ukraine again looked into the issue of the divided Ossolineum. Their recommendations were included in the 1996 Lviv publication, undoubtedly because they went even a step further in presenting a Ukrainian nationalist position. In their conclusion, the transfer to Poland of "materials relating to the history, culture, science, and economy of Ukrainian lands had been done without any legal act of transfer"; they queried, "isn't it time for

[26] See many details in Matwijów, *Walka o lwowskie dobra kultury.* Matwijów suggests that one of the specialists involved in the selection process on the Ukrainian side did not even know Polish and Latin. My "The Stefanyk Library," *HUS* 5(2) June 1981: 210–23, provides many examples of personal papers and manuscript collections now split between Lviv and Wrocław. See also the coverage in my *Archives: Ukraine*, pp. 509–514, 535–48. As well, see Matwijów, "Zbiory rękopismienne ZNiO w latach 1939–1946," pp. 225–41.

[27] The 1969 report, signed by V. G. Zimina and O. I. Gerasimova, is published in *L'vivs'ka naukova biblioteka: Dokumenty*, pp. 58–61 (doc. 15).

the Soviet side to raise the question of the return of such treasures?"[28] Several other reports made by the current library director, Larysa Krushel'nyts'ka, were included in the 1996 Lviv collection, clearly chosen to represent a strong Ukrainian point of view. This point of view demonstrates the importance of the Stefanyk Library to Lviv and Ukraine, the necessity of the return of its holdings, and the ill-advised error of anyone who would consider further transfers to Poland.

Since the 1969 Moscow recommendation, however, no progress has been made in Lviv for wider reference access to the divided collections that still need to be correlated with the never-implemented (quality) microform exchange. What was understandably not emphasized in the Lviv presentation is that there were no published catalogs of the Ossolineum manuscripts remaining in Lviv during the Soviet period. Furthermore, the prior existence of the Ossolineum and its Polish character was usually suppressed in Soviet Ukraine, which would have made the publication of authoritative catalogs impossible.

None of the documentation presented recently by the Ukrainian side provides precise reference details about the actual fate of the now-divided Ossolineum manuscripts, nor about the dispersal of those manuscripts that remain in Lviv. Nor has any published appreciation been shown for the catalogs prepared in Wrocław, the manuscripts missing from component Lviv collections held there, or the cultural importance of the collections to Poland as well as Ukraine. Approximately half of the Ossolineum manuscripts remain in Lviv. Some specialists quote a figure of 47 percent remaining there, but exact figures are difficult to establish, with discrepancies resulting from the fragmentation of the original component collections and the fact that not all the manuscripts had been catalogued before 1939.

Only the first 1,504 manuscripts were thoroughly described in Lviv in the nineteenth century, but in an admirably detailed catalog by Wojciech Kętrzyński.[29] Manuscripts through no. 6000 were described in a summary catalog published in the interwar period, and typescript supplements prepared

---

[28] See the 1989 report, signed by 8 members of the commission, including such scholars as F. I. Steblii, Ia. D. Isaievych, and O. A. Kupchyns'kyi, among others; it is published in *L'vivs'ka naukova biblioteka: Dokumenty*, pp. 63–71 (doc. 18).

[29] Wojciech Kętrzyński, *Katalog rękopisów Zakładu Narodowego im. Ossoliń- skich/Catalogus codicum manuscriptorum Bibliothecae Ossolinianae Leo- poliensis*, 3 vols. (Lviv, 1881–1898); 80 percent of the manuscript covered are in Wrocław, but those remaining in Lviv are omitted in the Wrocław inventories. Present locations are indicated marginally in the special IDC microfiche edition, ed. P. K. Grimsted (Zug, Switzerland: IDC, 1987) [=IDC-R-14,485].

in the late 1930s and during the war continue even briefer coverage through to manuscript no. 8091 (in the case of the Lviv copy).[30] Card catalogs, acquisition registers, and some other partial manuscript lists and provisional inventories prepared through World War II cover many individual manuscripts in Lviv, but these are difficult to use, since they do not always conform to present library code numbers. Full manuscript descriptions with attributions of provenance were never completed for publication, nor were further catalogs prepared in Lviv. Thus, even by 1999 the rest of the Ossolineum manuscripts in Lviv still have not been adequately described and catalogued, nor have the 609 parchment charters (nos. 1421–1930) that remain there.

Following Soviet archival rules, the Ossolineum collection was not kept together as an integral collection and the provenance of its components was not usually identified. Many of the parchments, manuscript books, and personal papers were split up into separate fonds without full accounting for their collection of origin, and catalogs or correlation tables for the remaining Ossolineum manuscripts were never published. Many of the materials that were considered most blatantly Polish, or "bourgeois nationalist" in Soviet terminology, and particularly papers of Polish political leaders, were suppressed during the Soviet period, as were the many Ossolineum internal finding aids and library records that remained in Lviv. Some of the Polish estate archives were transferred to TsDIAL, along with other "politically sensitive" materials requiring special attention of the NKVD/MVD archival

---

[30] *Inwentarz rękopisów Biblioteki Zakładu Narodowego im. Ossolińskich we Lwowie*, 2 vols. (Lviv, 1926–1934; hectographed). The first typescript supplement continues the mimeographed list: "—— Nr 6001[6109]–6615 [with continuation to 6596 in one of the carbon copies]" (Lviv, 1937). A typescript original of the second supplement in ZNiO (Lviv, 1941–1945; 262 p.) covers manuscripts "[Nr 6616 do 7705]"; the copy in Lviv, "Inventar rukopysiv buvshoï biblioteky im. Ossolins'kykh u L'vovi, NoNo. 6597–8091," includes all but the last two Lubomirski manuscripts in the Ossolineum Collection remaining in Lviv. The ZNiO copies (to MS 7705) of the two supplements (based on microfilms furnished to HURI) are included in the special microfiche, ed. with preface by P. K. Grimsted (Zug, Switzerland: IDC, 1987) [=IDC-R-14,429], and indication of the present location of the manuscripts. Soviet authorities prohibited filming the Lviv copies, although I was permitted to consult them in order to verify the location of manuscripts. ZNiO in Wrocław has subsequently acquired a photocopy of the supplement covering MSS nos. 7706–8091. See the notes regarding LNB finding aids for the Ossolineum collection in *Archiwa rodzinno-majątkowe*, pp. 81–82.

authorities there.[31] At times even the existence of the Ossolineum was denied in Lviv and the proper identify of its manuscripts prohibited.[32]

By contrast, a professional new catalog series was prepared in Wrocław covering the parts of the collection transferred there. Its level of detail—and failure, in many cases, to assign provenance—may not satisfy all research needs, but it provides a start.[33] The original Lviv Ossolineum numbers have been retained in Wrocław for the manuscripts transferred, so by noting the missing numbers in the Wrocław catalog, and referring back to the available Lviv catalogs and supplements, a researcher can determine at least some of the volumes that remain in Lviv—that is for the manuscripts that had been listed in the Lviv typescript supplements through 1945. Parchment charters from the Ossolineum now in Wrocław are covered by a separate catalog.[34]

---

[31]   The first systematic survey of estate archives, which includes those from the Ossolineum collections is the recent Polish edition *Archiwa rodzinno-majątkowe*, pp. 81–163. The compiler, however, was unable to include some of the materials that were not catalogued before 1945. Although that survey also includes estate archives in TsDIAL, the compiler did not have complete data about the transfers to TsDIAL from the Ossolineum collections, namely parts of the Dzieduszycki, Lubomirski, and Treter archives, and possibly part of the Jabłonowski estate archive, among others.

[32]   I recall being told at one point in the 1970s, while gathering data for my archival directory, that I should not list the Ossolineum Library under the Stefanyk Library, nor should I mention its other Polish components such as the Lubomirski Museum that had been liquidated, nor should I try to describe the totality of the Ossolineum historical manuscript collections in Lviv, since the Ossolineum itself no longer existed there and had been moved to Wrocław. During the Soviet period, I had great difficulties even meeting with specialists in the Manuscript Division who knew about the Ossolineum collections, and for a long time, I was not given access to card catalogs and internal finding aids. I was never given open access to the records of the Ossolineum itself; and Gębarowicz was prohibited from meeting with me.

[33]   *Inwentarz rękopisów Zakładu Narodowego im. Ossolińskich we Wrocławiu*, ed. Jadwiga Turska et al., 9 vols. and index (Wrocław: ZNiO, 1948–1984) [microfiche=IDC-R-14,430]. Some details about the transfer of the manuscripts is found in the first volume and also in my prefaces to the IDC microfiche editions of the ZNiO catalogs. While the early volumes cover manuscripts that were previously held in the Ossolineum in Lviv, additional volumes through vol. 15 (Wrocław: ZNiO, 1997) cover later acquisitions through inventory no. 17260.

[34]   Feliks Pohorecki, *Catalogus diplomatum Bibliothecae Instituti Ossoliniani nec non Bibliothecae Pawlikowianae inde ab anno 1227 usque ad annum 1506* (Lviv: Sumptibus societatis amicorum Instituti Ossoliniani, 1937); and Adam

Special annotated microfiche editions of all available pre-1945 catalogs of the Ossolineum collections, including the typescript supplements, were prepared in connection with my Ukrainian archival directory at the Harvard Ukrainian Research Institute in the 1980s. Marginal indications identify the manuscripts in Lviv (through MS no. 8091) and those in Wrocław.[35] Specialists appear not to be aware of these microfiche editions and only a few have been sold; neither have these microfiche editions been mentioned in Ukrainian or Polish publications in Lviv or Wrocław and Warsaw. Nevertheless, they might now provide an example for a much needed coordinated reference effort between the two libraries. For reference purposes today, however, they can serve only as a preliminary starting point for a much needed, comprehensive electronic reference aid.

Post-1991 Surveys. In 1998, a brief but relatively comprehensive survey of the remaining Ossolineum manuscripts in Lviv prepared by Matwijów was printed in a preliminary edition connected with ongoing Polish revindication negotiations. Not formally published as of fall 1999, it still remains the most extensive recent coverage surveying the Ossolineum manuscripts in Lviv.[36] Matwijów also has prepared several surveys of the fate of the Ossolineum manuscript collections during and immediately after WWII, with analysis of the problems of its current divided status.[37] In terms of estate and family archives within the collections, his work is supplemented by the

---

Fastnacht, *Catalogus...Supplementum I. Inde ab anno 1279 usque ad annum 1506* (Wrocław: ZNiO, 1951). Only 5 of the 287 parchments in the initial catalog remain in Lviv, while only 11 of the 101 covered in the supplement came from Lviv. Present locations are indicated in the special IDC microfiche edition, ed. P. K. Grimsted (Zug, Switzerland: IDC, 1987; = R-14,537).

[35] See the special microfiche editions by Grimsted listed in the notes above. Microfiche editions are available for many other rare published finding aids for the Stefanyk Library, including the Ossolineum collections; see my *Archives: Ukraine*, pp. 535–48. A full catalog of the microfiche finding aids for Ukrainian archives and manuscript collections, including the Stefanyk Library is available from the publisher: "Archives and Manuscript Collections in the USSR: Finding aids on microfiche," Series 3: "Ukraine and Moldavia," ed. P. K. Grimsted (Leiden: IDC, 1988).

[36] Maciej Matwijów, "Wniosek rewindykacyjny zbiorów Zakładu Narodowego im. Ossolińskich—Rękopisy," in *Wnioski rewindykacyjne*, pp. 36–47.

[37] Maciej Matwijów, "Zbiory rękopismienne ZNiO we Lwowie," pp. 211–41; and his 1996 *Walka o lwowskie dobra kultury.*

1995 Polish compilation by Stanisław Pijaj.[38] No comparable reference work has appeared in Lviv since independence. Matwijów's and Pijaj's efforts could be the start of an appropriate finding aid for the Ossolineum manuscripts in Lviv, particularly if Ukrainian specialists were to collaborate on a future expanded version.

The lack of even a single professional finding aid from the Stefanyk Library for the Ossolineum collection—even 30 years after the 1969 review—remains a stain on the library and a great frustration for researchers throughout the world. One can only hope that the Ukrainian side will forego personal and parochial considerations and undertake, in a professional and principled manner, the collaboration envisaged by the bilateral agreements signed by the Ukrainian and Polish governments.

Divided Component Collections. A number of important former Polish libraries and their manuscript collections that had been consolidated with the Ossolineum before 1939 were also dispersed as a result of the war and subsequent postwar transfers. One prominent example is the Library of Gwalbert Pawlikowski, which was acquired by the Ossolineum in 1921. Today, only 55 manuscripts from the collection remain in Lviv, while 235 manuscript books and many of the parchments are in Wrocław.[39] The Dzieduszycki Library which had been moved to Lviv from the Dzieduszycki family estate in Potorytsia (*earlier Pol.* Poturzyca; now in Lviv Oblast) in 1857, remained a separate library open to the public before it was acquired by the Ossolineum in 1939, together with the family archive. Its holdings were integrated with the Ossolineum collections in 1940–1941 and then divided: 19 manuscripts removed by the Nazis in 1944 are now in the Biblioteka Narodowa in Warsaw; 157 manuscripts were transferred to Wrocław; 185 manuscripts remain in the Stefanyk Library; while large parts of the estate archive are held by TsDIAL in Lviv.[40]

---

[38] *Archiwa rodzinno-majątkowe*, pp. 81–163. See also above, fn 31.

[39] Details about the fate of this collection were first presented in my "The Stefanyk Library," p. 217, and later in my *Archives: Ukraine*, p. 512 (and no. NL-274). Of crucial importance is the catalog by Mieczysław Gębarowicz, *Katalog rękopisów Biblioteki im. Gwalberta Pawlikowskiego* (Lviv: ZNiO, 1929) [microfiche=IDC-R-14,536]; the second edition, issued as vol. 2 of the general Wrocław catalog of Ossolineum manuscripts (Wrocław: Wyd-wo ZNiO, 1949), omits the 55 manuscripts from the collection remaining in Lviv.

[40] See my "The Stefanyk Library," pp. 221–22, and in my *Archives: Ukraine*, pp. 513–14 (and nos. NL-356 to NL-358, pp. 561–62 there). A catalog of 360 manuscripts was prepared in 1943 before the collection was split (see NL-356,

Even more complicated, and somewhat suspect, is the fate of the private collection brought together by the Polish historian-archivist Aleksander Czołowski (1865–1944), over 2,525 manuscripts of which had been presented to the Ossolineum in Lviv in 1936 and 1939. Some parts of the Czołowski collection (and additional personal papers that had not been presented to the Ossolineum) were evacuated with other archives from Lviv to the Abbey of Tyniec near Cracow in 1944. They were removed before Soviet authorities retrieved the Lviv archives sequestered there in April 1945. As a result of wartime and postwar migrations, the whole collection is now dispersed in at least four different repositories: 1,062 manuscript units remain in the Stefanyk Library in Lviv (17th–19th cc.), while 266 manuscript units are now held by the Ossolineum in Wrocław. Czołowski's personal papers and parts of his historical collection were presented to the Biblioteka Narodowa by his heirs after his death in Poland, and the most valuable documentation, including original parchments, were subsequently transferred to the Archiwum Główne Akt Dawnych (AGAD) in Warsaw. Of particular importance, among the Czołowski collection in Warsaw are manuscript and typescript inventories of many personal, family, and estates archives which have remained in Lviv. Within the collection in AGAD, for example, are a series of original early nineteenth-century inventories and historical materials about and from the Bernardine Archive (now part of TsDIAL) in Lviv. The provenance of parts of this collection are suspect, since Czołowski allegedly had acquired and brought to Poland some original documents and finding aids from Lviv state archives and libraries.[41] Even if the bulk of his collection should remain in Poland, it would be essential that copies of those inventories and historical reference materials be returned to Lviv.

One Lviv collection involved with the Czołowski legacy brings us back to the larger problem of identifying Ossolineum materials that are clearly related to the history of western Ukraine. Demonstrating the multi-ethnic society and culture of the region, the revealing notebooks of the nineteenth-century historian and geographer Antoni Schneider (1825–1880) constitute

---

p. 561); 185 of those covered remain in Lviv, 157 are in Wrocław (listed in the Wrocław ZNiO catalog, vol. 2), while those removed with a Nazi shipment in 1944 are described in a typescript index in the Biblioteka Narodowa (Warsaw). See also note NL-358 (*Archives: Ukraine*, p. 562) and the special IDC microfiche edition (R-14,644).

[41] See details about the fate of this collection in my "The Stefanyk Library," pp. 217–18. Some of the reference materials from the early nineteenth century are described in my *Archives: Ukraine*, nos. NL-21 and NL-24, pp. 453–54.

extremely important sources for the local history of Galicia. However, because of their value, and the fact they result from the work of a non-Ukrainian and were prepared in Polish, their fate has resulted in another divided legacy. Their importance for local history was recognized even during the Soviet period with a survey description of the 222 notebooks remaining in LNB. The survey was prepared under a pseudonym by the now well-respected Ukrainian historian Iaroslav Dashkevych and was one of the few detailed descriptions of Ossolineum holdings in Lviv published in that period.[42] The most complete inventory of the collection as it existed before 1939 in Lviv was removed from there in 1944 and is now held within one of the bound manuscripts in the Czołowski collection in the Biblioteka Narodowa in Warsaw.[43] At the same time, one of the original Schneider notebooks from Lviv remains as part of the Czołowski collection in AGAD.[44] An even larger group of 282 Schneider notebooks are now held in the State Archive in Cracow (APKr).[45]

As yet another example among many other seriously divided Lviv collections, a similar, but even more complicated fate befell the rich archive and library of the Lviv Armenian Cathedral Chapter, part of which was acquired by the Ossolineum in 1866 and another part during World War II, and part of which was transferred to Vienna in the late nineteenth century. Of those manuscripts acquired by the Ossolineum, approximately half are now in Wrocław, a few are held in the Biblioteka Narodowa in Warsaw, and others are in the Matenadaran in Yerevan, while part of the archive was

[42]   See [Iaroslav Dashkevych] (pseud. S. Piskovyi) "L'vivs'ki 'teky' A. Shneidera iak istoryko-kraieznavche dzherelo," *Arkhivy Ukraïny* 1965 (4): 73–76. A review of the Dashkevych article by Adam Kamiński presents more details about the collection: *Archeion* 45 (1966): 238–40.

[43]   See the inventory, "Teki Antoniego Schneidera w Zakładzie Narodowym im. Ossolińskich we Lwowie," BN, Zbiór Czołowskiego, MS 5540, fols. 223–230.

[44]   The Schneider notebook entitled "Materiały dotyczące kościołów w Zółkowie," is found in AGAD, Zbiór Czołowskiego, no. 466. These details are presented in *Archives: Ukraine and Moldavia*, pp. 513 and 567 and nos. NL-373 and NL-374, p. 567.

[45]   The related collection of 282 Schneider notebooks in Cracow (Archiwum Państwowe w Krakowie) is covered by the typewritten inventory "Spis Tek Antoniego Schneidera." See Larysa Krushel'nyts'ka's comments in "Zbirky Ossolineumu restytutsiï ne uliahaiut'," *Halyts'ka brama* 12(36) December 1997: 6–7; she does not mention the Warsaw Schneider holdings, but believes that the Cracow holdings should be revindicated to Lviv.

transferred to the Central State Historical Archive in Lviv (TsDIAL) in the mid-1970s.[46] Some Armenian manuscripts from the collection are now held in the Hermitage, but details about their migration have not been established.

Post-1991 "Non-Solutions." A solution to these issues is not in sight, but even since independence, funds and personnel have not been available in Ukraine for the much needed cataloguing and preservation work. Matwijów represents the opinion of many Polish specialists, when he complains that, "efforts made after 1946 to integrate the entire Ossolineum collection—considered a cultural heritage of the Polish nation—have not been successful."[47] The troubled "symbolism" of the relationship is evident in the very location of the Ossoliński holdings in Lviv—they are now integrated into the Stefanyk Library (as the Scientific Library of the Ukrainian Academy of Sciences in Lviv has been known since 1971.) Symbolically, the main administration and Manuscript Division of that library, named in honor of the Ukrainian progressive writer Vasyl' Stefanyk, now occupies the original nineteenth-century building of the Ossoliński Institute.

During a visit to Poland in early 1996, Ukrainian President Leonid Kuchma suggested transferring the remaining displaced parts of the Ossolineum collection to Poland in exchange for some of the Ukrainian materials in Warsaw from the Library of the Shevchenko Scientific Society. But his intended goodwill gesture, which was naturally welcomed by the Poles, occasioned bitter protest demonstrations on the Ukrainian side. Soon after Kuchma's offer, Krushel'nyts'ka issued an angry denunciation of the president in local newspaper interviews.[48] In answer to Polish claims for the remainder of the Ossolineum put forth by Matwijów in the *Spoils of War: International Newsletter*, Krushel'nyts'ka complained in a later issue that,

---

[46] Details are presented in my *Archives: Ukraine*, pp. 511–12 (and nos. NG-393–NG-395, pp. 576–7 and NL-330–NL-331, p. 554). A manuscript catalog of 360 manuscripts was prepared in 1943 before the collection was split (see PKG-NL-356); 185 of those covered remain in Lviv, 157 are in Wrocław (listed in the Wrocław ZNiO catalog, vol. 2), while 19 (removed with a Nazi shipment in 1944) are described in a typescript inventory in the Biblioteka Narodowa (Warsaw).

[47] Maciej Matwijów, "Ossolineum. The Case of the Dispersed Library," *Spoils of War: International Newsletter* 3 (1996): 71–72.

[48] See Krushel'nyts'ka's open letter to the Minister of Justice of Ukraine (4 July 1996), published in *L'vivs'ka naukova biblioteka: Dokumenty,* pp. 92–94 (doc. 28); and her article "Zbirky Ossolineumu restytutsiï ne uliahaiut'," *Universum* 3-4 (1997): 42–45. See also her, "Pravdyvo pro Ossolineum," *Pam'iatky Ukraïny* 1994 (3-6 [26]): 85–86.

"against legal rules, there were six removals of books, manuscripts, and art collections to Poland." In fact some of the most valuable Ossolineum manuscript treasures were removed in 1944 under Nazi auspices, as noted above, not as loot, but as a wartime safety evacuation measure with the supervision of Polish specialists, just before Soviet forces started bombing Lviv. Krushel′nyts′ka ignored the fact that those Polish treasures that had been recovered in Silesia were subsequently transferred to Wrocław to rejoin the Ossoliński Institute, after its legal reestablishment there, and as far as is known there never was a formal Soviet claim for their return. Krushel′nyts′ka emphasized that "Count Ossoliński donated his collection to the city of Lviv," but she fails to mention that he did so to form a center of Polish culture in Lviv "on behalf of the Polish people," who since had been driven out by Stalin. Nor does she mention that the Ossolineum and the related Lubomirski Museum were liquidated and nationalized by Soviet authorities in 1940, following the initial annexation of western Ukraine in 1939. And she ignores the fact that Khrushchev and other Soviet leaders authorized the official Ukrainian "gift" as part of the recognized cultural heritage of the Polish people who had been forcibly resettled following the redrawn postwar boundaries, and whose culture was subsequently bitterly suppressed in Lviv.[49]

The Stefanyk Library today might like to see more of the Ossolineum collections returned and to keep those that remain, although the reestablishment of the Polish Ossoliński Institute would be now inconceivable in Lviv. Even the dispersed manuscript holdings of the Ukrainian-oriented library of the Shevchenko Scientific Society (NTSh) have not been reunited in Lviv, after their own division and suppression under Soviet rule. And even the archive of the current library's namesake, Vasyl′ Stefanyk was transferred to Kyiv in 1950 and never returned to Lviv.[50] To the discredit of any potential claims from the Stefanyk Library (and its budgetary supporters), reports have been circulating about the abysmal condition of the remaining rare Ossolineum manuscripts, archival materials, and early imprints in Lviv, the lack of specialists conversant with Polish traditions in the area (and with a knowledge of Latin and Polish to describe them), to say nothing of the physical disrepair of the Ossolineum building and considerable recent theft from it. Indeed, according to numerous allegations from librarians abroad,

---

[49]   Larysa Krushel′nyts′ka, "The Case of the Ossolineum Collection," *Spoils of War: International Newsletter* 5 (1998): 25.

[50]   Krushel′nyts′ka also emphasizes this fact with the publication of the transfer order (24 January 1950) in *L′vivs′ka naukova biblioteka: Dokumenty*, pp. 36–38 (doc. 12).

early printed books with Ossolineum markings recently have been appearing on the commercial antiquarian market. Half a century has passed since the Ossolineum was reestablished in Wrocław, but its priceless manuscripts, rare library holdings, and other unique components remain divided, information about them is still suppressed, and the world of scholarship does not have a working catalog of the manuscripts remaining in Lviv.

With improved Polish-Ukrainian relations and a new commission in operation on the cultural front, a special working group has been established to consider the problem of the divided Ossolineum. As of the end of 1999, however, no working session has been possible. It is nonetheless to be hoped that what has become a virtual crisis can be resolved in a professional manner in keeping with the world-class status and cultural importance of the Ossoliński legacy. The most urgent step is that those parts of the manuscript, rare book, print, and cartographic collections and the extensive archives that remain in Lviv will be professionally preserved and described, with full account of their provenance and due attributions to the original Ossoliński collections of which they once formed part.

Even if the manuscripts and rare books are to remain physically dispersed, at least, intellectually, they could be reunited in a virtual electronic catalog. Once that has been accomplished—or perhaps at the same time—the long-awaited microforms (or, now, digitized copies even) could make quality reproductions of at least the most important manuscripts readily available to researchers on both sides of the frontier. The symbolic importance of the Ossolineum to both countries, and the political importance of a resolution of the disputed cultural heritage, should ease the search for funding. But until such steps are undertaken, researchers throughout the world can only vent their frustration at the disrespect for international principles of provenance and the integrity of collections that produced the ruthless division of one of the most important libraries in Eastern Europe.

Other Divided Polish Collections from Lviv

The Baworowski Library. The Ossolineum and its earlier component collections are hardly alone as a divided manuscript collection from Lviv. Several other collections of predominantly Polish manuscript materials and rare books were also evacuated from Lviv in 1944 as part of Nazi shipments. Another prominent example were some of the Polish treasures from the former private library of Wiktor Baworowski (1826–1894), later opened to the public as the Baworowski Library. Like the Ossolineum, that library had been abolished in 1940 by Soviet authorities, and its holdings nationalized as part of what is today the Stefanyk Library. Over 100 of the most valuable early manuscripts (including a copy of the First Lithuanian Statute), approximately 115 individual parchments, and over 400 early printed books were evacuated to Cracow in 1944; later moved further west, they were abandoned by the Nazis in Silesia, where they were recovered by the Poles.[51]

The Baworowski Library represents another exceedingly important, predominantly Polish complex of manuscript collections that had been gathered in Lviv from many parts of Poland, but which have been dispersed since the end of the war. From the original Lviv collection, 136 manuscripts are now held in the Biblioteka Narodowa and another 31 in AGAD in Warsaw, while the vast majority are still held in the Stefanyk Library (1,581 units in the main Baworowski collection alone). However, after the original collection was nationalized by the Academy Library it was broken up and dispersed among a number of different fonds within the library.[52]

Lviv University Library Manuscripts. Already mentioned in passing was the evacuation of the predominantly Polish and other Roman Catholic manuscripts, along with some Armenian Catholic manuscripts, from the University Library in Lviv. Most of these are now held in the Biblioteka Narodowa in Warsaw, having followed the same evacuation route as the Baworowski Library.[53] Although Ukrainian ChGK reports and more recent sources may claim that these were looted by the Nazis (and there were even allegations that they were taken to Germany), the shipments were actually

---

[51] These figures were quoted by Matwijów, in his introduction to letters of Gębarowicz, "Lwowskie Ossolineum w listach Mieczysława Gębarowicza z lat 1943–1946," pp. 159–62. The evacuated materials from the Bawrowski Library were recovered with the shipment from Cracow that also included the Ossolineum and other Polish library collections. See also above, p. 431n18.

[52] See my, *Archives: Ukraine*, pp. 531–35 (nos. NL-250 to NL-261, pp. 532–35); listed there are also original manuscript inventories of some of the component collections acquired by the Baworowski Library. See also my, "The Stefanyk Library," pp. 208–210.

[53] I earlier documented their evacuation in one of the shipments to the Archival Administration in Cracow, probably on 17 March 1944—TsDIAL, 755/1/285, fols. 118–126 (352/44), but a complete inventory has not been found in Lviv files. Matwijów, "Lwowskie Ossolineum w listach Mieczysława Gębarowicza," pp. 159–60, quotes the figure of 40 crates of manuscripts from the University Library. My figures total over 100 manuscripts now in Warsaw, which presumably were all evacuated in the March and April Cracow shipments; additional incunabula and early printed books were apparently also involved in the shipment, which would explain the Soviet claim mentioned above in Chapter 5, pp. 210–12.

made as a preservation measure in anticipation of Soviet bombing, with the cooperation of Polish archivists, who were themselves fleeing to Cracow or elsewhere in Poland in advance of the Red Army. The manuscripts involved are for the most part Polish Roman Catholic medieval and Renaissance Latin texts, some with priceless illuminations from the Abbey of Tyniec near Cracow, along with some Oriental and Armenian Catholic religious manuscripts, and Polish literary manuscripts from later centuries. Several other Oriental manuscripts and five Church Slavonic texts are among them. Their evacuation assured the preservation of such treasures in Poland, because their protectors feared their fate in the hands of the returning Soviet regime in Lviv.

Official requests were later made from the Soviet side for the return of the manuscripts, rare books, and cartographic materials from the University of Lviv Library, but official Soviet restitution requests exempted the Polish materials involved, which in fact made up the bulk of those evacuated. At one point in 1949, preparations were made in Warsaw for the return of some of the materials, but then, given the negotiated exemption, it is not clear from available documentation if any were returned, given the secrecy in which diplomatic negotiations were conducted at that time. We do know that none of the manuscripts were returned and, most probably, none of the incunabula and early imprints as well, since most of them could be identified as "Polish."[54] The Polish, Armenian, and other Oriental manuscripts that remain in the Biblioteka Narodowa have not been described in print, but they are covered by card catalogs and can be precisely identified with reference to their prewar Lviv University call numbers and catalog listings.[55] If there

---

[54]   Regarding the Soviet claims and negotiations over the transfer from Poland, see Matwijów, *Walka o lwowskie dobra kultury*, pp. 156–57. Matwijów has been unable fully to document this matter, and suspects that none of the materials were returned in 1949. See also Krystyna Wróbel-Lipowa, *Rewindykacja archiwaliów polskich z ZSRR w latach 1945–1964* (Lublin, 1982), pp. 77–78, who implies that some of the materials were restituted to Lviv. Halyna Svarnyk, in briefly discussing this issue, also quotes a 1948 Soviet document and suggests the Soviet claim was withdrawn, since the materials were determined to be of predominantly Polish cultural origin: "Arkhiv Naukovoho tovarystva im. Shevchenka v Natsional'nii bibliotetsi u Varshavi," in *Z istoriï Naukovoho tovarystva imeni Shevchenka* (Lviv: NTSh, 1998) [=*Pratsi sesii, konferentsii, sympoziumiv, kruhlykh stoliv*, 10].

[55]   See the correlation table I established in the 1980s for these manuscripts on the basis of their earlier Lviv numbers and card catalog listings in the Manuscript Division of the Biblioteka Narodowa in Grimsted, *Archives: Ukraine*, pp. 574–75; references to earlier published catalogs follow (especially nos. NL-390–NL-396,

remain specific manuscripts that Ukrainian scholars might want to claim on the grounds of their provenance or closer association with Ukrainian culture, such as the early Cyrillic ones, there are grounds for barter with new Polish interest in the revindication to Poland of the library collection of Witold Kazimierz Czartoryski (1876–1913), which remains at the library of Lviv University (see below).

Roman Catholic Collections. It should also be noted in connection with divided collections and earlier archival transfers that some official Roman Catholic Church archives and manuscript collections from Lviv were revindicated to Poland at the end of 1945 and 1946, when Soviet authorities were again starting to suppress Roman Catholic interests in Lviv. As mentioned earlier, most of the remaining records of the Roman-Catholic archdiocese of Lviv, which were revindicated to Poland at the end of 1945, are now held in Lubaczów, Poland.[56] Preservation microfilm copies have been prepared under the auspices of the Church archival program at the Catholic University of Lublin, and a detailed published catalog of the microfilms serves as a comprehensive description of the remaining records themselves.[57] Part of the archive was destroyed in Lviv in 1939 at the time of the Soviet takeover. Some other parts remain in TsDIAL; they have not yet been appropriately identified or described following their recent declassification.

Similarly, in May 1946, the departing friars of the Dominican Order were permitted to take a large part of their archival materials and manuscript

---

pp. 576–77). Among the predominantly Roman Catholic and Polish literary manuscripts are five Church Slavonic manuscripts (15th–17th cc.), one Moldavian manuscript (mid-18th c.), one Turkic (17th c.), two Arabic (17th–18th cc.), and 13 Armenian manuscripts (15th–18th cc.). Although the Armenian manuscripts were of provenance in the Lviv region, the Armenian rite was prohibited in Lviv under Soviet rule; that rite has not been restored in Lviv.

[56]   See Chapter 4, p. 153n12, and the annotations to the finding aids prepared before 1939, when they were still in Lviv: Grimsted, *Archives: Ukraine,* pp. 480–81. See also the account of the revindication in Matwijów, *Walka o lwowskie dobra kultury,* pp. 123–24; Matwijów dates the revindication as 1946.

[57]   Regarding the holdings in Lubaczów and the preservation microfilms prepared by the Catholic University in Lublin, see ks. Janusz Kania, "Katalog mikrofilmów Ośrodka Archiwów, Bibliotek i Muzeów Kościelnych przy Katolickim Uniwersytecie Lubelskim," no. 5 (Lublin, 1985) [=*Archiwa, Biblioteki i Muzea Kościelne* 51 (1985): [5]–115], and the survey article by Mariusz Leszczyński, "Archiwum Archidiecezji w Lubaczowie," *Archiwa, Biblioteki i Muzea Kościelne* 53 (1986): 57–66.

collections from Lviv, which are now located in Cracow.[58] However, many Roman Catholic archives from the Archbishopric, Diocese, and monastic orders remained in Lviv, some in what is now the Stefanyk Library and some in the Central State Historical Archive (TsDIAL). Again, many collections and integral groups of records remain fragmented with no professional descriptions available for researchers.

The predominantly Polish cultural orientation of these and other private and religious collections that had been nationalized after 1939 and were taken in part to Poland during and immediately after the war exempt them as a target for Ukrainian claims. But given the fact that they all constitute the common heritage of the multi-ethnic history of Halych–Galicia–Małopolska–western Ukraine, their fragmentation is unfortunate and their multicultural value deserves recognition. Most of those fragments in Poland have already been or are in the process of being microfilmed and described. The fate of those remaining in Lviv, however, is more dubious. Security provisions (including the production of preservation microfilms) are essential for their survival and access abroad, while professional description is urgently needed to promote intellectual as well as physical access.

Archival Ucrainica in Poland

Archival Materials from the NTSh Library. Mention has already been made of some of the manuscripts and archival materials that were evacuated from Lviv during the war and ended up in the Manuscript Division of the Biblioteka Narodowa, such as parts of the Baworowski and Czołowski collections, among others. The Ukrainian collection, which Ukrainian President Kuchma suggested exchanging with Poland for the remainder of the Ossolineum manuscripts, comprises some 28 boxes of sensitive twentieth-century Ukrainian documentation from the former Library of the Shevchenko Scientific Society (Naukove Tovarystvo im. Shevchenka NTSh). Hidden in the basement of the Krasiński Palace (undoubtedly because they were Ukrainian rather than Polish), they were first identified by the Ukrainian specialist in Warsaw, Eugeniusz Misiło (Ievhen Misylo), after their chance discovery during building renovations in the late 1980s; some of them were on the point of being destroyed as loose papers scattered in the park outside

---

[58] See Chapter 4, p. 161n17. See also the newspaper article by Zygmunt Mazur, "Dominikanie we Lwowie (1939–1946)," *Tygodnik Powszechny* 1990 (38).

the Krasiński Palace that houses the Manuscript Division.[59] There is evidence that 35 to 40 crates from the NTSh Library were evacuated from Lviv with one of the Nazi shipments to Cracow in March or early April 1944.[60] However, an outgoing inventory of the NTSh materials has not been found, nor has a full correlation with previous NTSh catalogs or inventories been established.[61] Possibly, they were intermingled in Cracow with Ukrainian, and especially UNR, materials from other sources that the Nazis had been gathering there. Subsequently evacuated to Silesia in June 1944, they were found there in 1945 with the same shipment mentioned above that included books from the Baworowski Library and the Ossolineum, among

[59] This is described in his unpublished account, "Kolekcja naukowego Towarzystwa im. T. Szewczenki ze Lwowa w zbiorach Biblioteki Narodowej w Warszawie." Polish authorities had apparently tried to suppress the details of the discovery. See Misylo's article "Ukraïns'ki tsinnosti u varshavs'komu skhovyshchi," in *Slidamy pam'iati* (1996), pp. 109–12. *Slidamy pam'iati* is a new Ukrainian series published in Poland. A supplemental memoir follows (by Stanisław Kryciński who was working with the restoration crew) that describes finding some of the papers scattered in the park outside the building—"Svidchennia Stanislava Krytsins'koho pro obstavyny vyiavlennia arkhivu Naukovoho tovarystva im. Shevchenka v budynku Natsional'noï biblioteky u Varshavi," pp. 112–13.

[60] Inventories or even box lists of the contents of the NTSh materials evacuated have not been found. The shipment may have included some politically sensitive Ukrainian materials in Lviv that had not been accessioned by the NTSh before the war. It is not possible to correlate these materials with an all-too-primitive war-time inventory of the NTSh collections in Lviv—"Rukopysy, shcho shche bulo v Bibliotetsi pry provirtsi v dniakh 1.X.1944 r.," which shows some of the hold-ings crossed out; many of the numbered positions, however, are simply listed as "collection of manuscripts" or other such unidentifiable indication—TsDIAL, 309/2/25. The NTSh materials are also not listed in any of the Nazi orders or shipping lists regarding these evacuations that I have seen in Lviv and Cracow.

[61] I have not found inventories identifying all of these materials in the NTSh library in 1944, nor has Halyna Svarnyk, who has been describing them. Possibly some of the UNR materials in the collection may have been among the scattered UNR military records that had been brought to Lviv in 1925/26 and housed with the Sheptys'kyi archive. As is evident from a wartime report, the Nazis knew about those records of the UNR General Staff and two Ukrainian divisions and had been anxious to take them to the West in their final evacuations from Lviv—ERR report (March 1942–March 1943), TsDAVO, 3206/5/26, fols. 4–5. Since that shipment also included books from several different libraries in Poland, as well as the Polish Library in Paris (then in Cracow), it is possible that some of the included Ukrainian archival materials could have come from other sources.

others. The Manuscript Division first admitted their existence in the late 1980s, and since then they have become the focus of considerable attention.[62] A call for restitution by the Ukrainian historian Iaroslav Dashkevych first appeared in print in 1991.[63]

Described subsequently in a survey by Lviv archivist Halyna Svarnyk, the rather fragmentary materials include scattered records of the Ukrainian National Republic (UNR), including a few Foreign Ministry files (1918–1919), military files of the Ukrainian Galician Army (1918–1920) and the Ukrainian Sich Riflemen (*Ukraïns'ki Sichovi Stril'tsi;* 1914–1918); some scattered documentary files from the Western Ukrainian National Republic (ZUNR); and records of the Prosvita Society from Lviv and the Ukrainian National-Democratic Association (1922–1938), among others.[64] Personal papers includes those of Dmytro Dontsov (1907–1939), who had edited the journals *Literaturno-naukyi vistnyk* and *Vistnyk* in Lviv; Olena Kysilevs'ka, the editor of the journal *Zhinocha dolia* and a senator in the Polish parliament (1928–1939); Andrei Zhuk, the editor of a Ukrainian cooperative journal (1907–1939); and Ivan and Iurii Lypa (1902–1938), writers who were also active in the UNR army, among others.[65] Undoubtedly, Ukrainians in Lviv were anxious to get these sensitive materials out of Lviv before the return of the Red Army. It is possible that some of the materials included here (which would also have been of interest to the Nazis) were not

---

[62] Colleagues in the Manuscript Division first showed me the 1948 report with a rough inventory of these materials in the late 1980s. I prepared a cursory list of the contents at the time, and, suspecting they were from the NTSh, I encouraged Ukrainian colleagues to prepare a full description in anticipation of preservation microfilming and their hoped-for restitution to Ukraine.

[63] See Iaroslav Dashkevych, "Dolia i nedolia nashoï Biblioteky," *Visnyk NTSh* (Lviv) March 1991 (1): 2.

[64] Halyna Svarnyk, "Arkhiv Naukovoho tovarystva im. Shevchenka v Natsional'nii bibliotetsi u Varshavi," in *Z istoriï NTSh*, pp. 232–41. See also the shorter article by Svarnyk, "Arkhiv Naukovoho tovarystva im. Shevchenka zi L'vova v Natsional'nii bibliotetsi u Varshavi," in *Slidamy pam'iati* (1996), pp. 114–23, followed by "Spysok materialiv z arkhivu Naukovoho tovarystva im. Shevchenka u L'vovi, iaki teper zberihaiut'sia u Viddili rukopysiv Natsional'noï biblioteky u Varshavi," pp. 124–27; and "L'vivs'ki zbirky u Varshavi (Arkhiv Naukovoho tovarystva im. Shevchenka v Natsional'nii bibliotetsi u Varshavi)," *Halyts'ka brama* 12(36) December 1997: 12.

[65] See Halyna Svarnyk, "Arkhiv Dmytra Dontsova," *Pam'iatky Ukraïny* 1994 (3–6 [26]): 122–28.

accessioned by the NTSh before the NTSh Library was abolished by Soviet authorities in 1940.

Given the fragmentary nature of the materials, some apparently have been lost or destroyed in the course of migration. Others may have disappeared in the course of their subsequent unfavorable secret storage conditions in the basement of the Krasiński Palace, where they were sequestered for 40 years. During a state visit to Ukraine in 1993, Polish President Lech Wałęsa presented six books of original protocols of the Prosvita Society (1868–1923) to Ukraine, and they are now held in the Historical Archive in Lviv (TsDIAL). Negotiations for the restitution of other parts of the collection are under way as part of the larger Polish-Ukrainian restitution efforts. Most of the materials have already been microfilmed, copies of which are available in Lviv.[66]

Przemyśl Capitula Manuscripts. Another important Ukrainian collection in the Biblioteka Narodowa was acquired under completely different circumstances and cannot be considered a direct result of wartime displacements. Considered by many a unique part of the Ukrainian archival heritage, although long held outside of what now constitutes Ukrainian lands, is the library of the Przemyśl (*Ukr.* Peremyshl) Ukrainian Greek Catholic Capitula. Frequently persecuted in Poland for its Ukrainian focus, the Greek Catholic Church has had a difficult history, but, thanks to support in the Vatican, the diocese remained alive, lending aid to the underground Church in western Ukraine during the decades it was outlawed by the Soviet regime as representative of Ukrainian "bourgeois nationalism." Although briefly part of the Ukrainian SSR in 1939–1941, Przemyśl, the seat of the diocese, now remains in Poland.

When intolerance was at its height, most of the valuable collection of early manuscripts from Przemyśl was transferred to Warsaw, where they were given the protection of the National Library, although open access was not always permitted.[67] During the 1970s, while the Greek Catholic Church was still outlawed by Soviet authorities and suspect to the Poles, many of the manuscript treasures in Warsaw were described by a Basilian scholar from

---

[66]   Microfilms are available for purchase from the Biblioteka Narodowa, Oddział Mikrofilmów and are available in Lviv in TsDIAL.

[67]   See the 1946 report on the library made by a specialist from the Biblioteka Narodowa—"Sprawozdanie z wyjazdu do Przemyśla w dn. 23.X.–1.XI.46 r." (4 February 1946), in *Slidamy pam'iati* (1996), pp. 134–35; the original document is from the Archive of the Biblioteka Narodowa in Warsaw, 2663/46.

Rome.[68] Some fragmentary parts of the library remain in Przemyśl and some manuscripts are held among the diocesan records in the state archive in Rzeszów. A number of early printed books and a few manuscripts from the library are held in the library of the Catholic University in Lublin. Although most of the diocese, and its episcopal center of Przemyśl, are now part of Poland, part of the diocese is in Ukraine itself. Some eighteenth-century visitation protocols and other fragmentary files from the diocesan records are held in the Museum of Ukrainian Art in Lviv.[69] For the most part, parish registers from the archive involving vital statistics for areas now in Ukraine were already transferred to ZAHS archives in Lviv with postwar archival revindications. Now that the Greek Catholic (Ukrainian Catholic, Uniate) Church has been officially reestablished in Ukraine, Ukrainians are seeking the revindication of this library, which they consider a vital part of their cultural heritage.

Other Polonica in Ukraine

Displaced Polish Archives in Lviv. In terms of other displaced archives, Lviv still retains several groups of records of interwar central Polish government agencies, which had been evacuated to western Ukraine early in WWII. The Nazis had evacuated them westward, but the Soviets found them in Czechoslovakia. In the late 1940s these Polish records were transferred to Kyiv and then to Lviv.[70] No documentation has been found to the effect that some of the records were returned to Poland during the Soviet period.[71] Recently, a list of those that remain in Lviv has been furnished to Polish archival authorities. These records clearly should be restituted to Poland in connection with other appropriate archival revindications on both sides of the

---

[68] "Rukopysy Peremyshl'skoï hreko-katolyts'koï kapituly v Narodnii bibliotetsi u Varshavi," *Bohosloviia* 37(1–4) 1973: 193–213; and 38(1–4) 1974: 237–43. An expanded description of the Przemyśl collection is now in progress in Poland.

[69] Ivan Franko, "Prychynok do istoriï halyts'ko-rus'koho pys'menstva XVIII v.," *Zapysky NTSh* 107 (1912): 110–15; and Melaniia Bordun, "Z zhyttia ukraïns'koho dukhovenstva l'vivs'koï eparkhiï v druhii pol. XVIII v. (na osnovi vizytatsii M. Shadurs'koho 1759–1763)," *Zapysky NTSh* 134–135 (1924): 137–60.

[70] These records were listed among the holdings of the Special Secret Division of TsDIAK in 1948. See Chapter 9, p. 382n165.

[71] See Wróbel-Lipowa, *Rewindykacja archiwaliów polskich*, pp. 103–104.

frontier, but it is only with the recent goodwill gesture on the part of Lviv archivists that it is possible for Polish archivists to formulate a claim.[72]

The Witold Czartoryski Collection. Poles have also formulated a claim for the library collection of Witold Kazimierz Czartoryski (1876–1913), which remains in the University Library of Lviv. The collection had been earlier held by the family in the Côte de Grace Palace in Honfleur, France, but was deposited in the Lviv library in 1923. A description was prepared in Lviv in 1928.[73] Approximately 22,450 volumes from the library with the Czartoryski *ex libris* remain in the Lviv University Library, including over 2,500 manuscripts. The Polish claim was formulated in 1997, but the legal status of the collection as a "donation" is still being debated.[74]

The Polish Royal Library in Kyiv. Another cultural issue of even greater symbolic value to Polish national identity is the part of the library of the last Polish King Stanislaus Augustus that had been held before the Partitions of Poland in Warsaw Castle. At the time of the Partitions (in the late eighteenth century), the remaining library that had not been seized by the Russians came under the control of the bibliophile collector Tadeusz Czacki, and then part of the library of the renowned lyceum in Kremenets in Volhynia. After the revolution, the Kremenets collection was transferred to Kyiv and deposited in the newly established Library of the Academy of Sciences (now NBU NAN, formerly TsNB). A large part of the Polish royal collection was evacuated by the Nazis during World War II. Now out of hiding, it is held by NBU NAN, along with some of the original library cabinets from the Royal Castle in Warsaw.

During the last decade, Polish library specialists have at last been permitted to see and describe the collections, which is a step forward from Soviet denials of its whereabouts. A full catalog is being prepared for

---

[72]   Władysław Stępniak, deputy director of the Polish State Archival Directorate, informed me in October 1999 about the list received and the claim that is in preparation.

[73]   S. Mękarski and K. Remerowa, "Księgozbiór z Honfleur ks. Witolda Kazimierza Czartoryskiego w lwowskiej Bibliotece Uniwersyteckiej" (Lviv, 1928).

[74]   The Polish claim appears formulated in the Ministry of Culture collection by Jan Pruszyński, "Wniosek rewindykacyjny księgozbioru Witolda K. Czartoryskiego z Oddziału Rzadkiej Książki Biblioteki Uniwersytetu im. Iwana Franki," in *Wnioski rewindykacyjne*, pp. 103–106. See also the brief note about the collection by Jacek Miler, "Zbiory lwowskie (II): Księgozbiór z Honfleur," *Cenne, bezcenne/utracone— Valuable, priceless/lost* 4(16) August 1999: 23.

publication in Poland under the auspices of the Biblioteka Narodowa, with the first volume expected early in the year 2000. In the meantime, several summary descriptions have appeared prepared by the Polish librarian heading the catalog project.[75] The national importance of this unique collection makes it of archival significance and its fate today in Kyiv, where there are insufficient funds for the preservation and descriptive work it needs and deserves, bring it to international attention.

New Prospects for Negotiations

A number of important restitution issues under negotiation with Poland lie ahead for Ukraine. The examples mentioned here do not exhaust the list. Most fundamental is a detailed review of the background of the various cases and a preliminary scholarly description of the materials under consideration on both sides. The context of these issues needs to be seen, not primarily in terms of captured Nazi records or the "spoils of war," but rather under the category of necessary cultural and archival transfers growing out of changes of boundaries with the forced resettlement of ethnic populations and respect for their cultural heritage. The multi-ethnic culture of western Ukraine—along with the frequent changes of sovereignty over the centuries—has greatly complicated the archival heritage and the history of the illustrious institutions that housed it in Ukrainian lands. What is most needed now is careful, professional description of the displaced records and dispersed collections, recognition of their component elements, appreciation for their historical development, and the location and reproduction of earlier inventories. This all should be undertaken in an attempt to, at least intellectually, reunite the dispersed archival heritage and unique manuscript collections, even if it may prove unfeasible under present circumstances to unite all of them physically.

On the Polish side there has been a fundamental change away from the totalizing demands for the transfer of Polish cultural treasures from the western regions of the former USSR that were annexed from Poland as a result of the Nazi-Soviet pact in 1939 and re-annexed to the Soviet Union at

---

[75] Hanna Laskarzewska, "Księgozbiór króla Stanisława Augusta Poniatowskiego w Kijowie: Historia, stan obecny, rejestracja," *Biuletyn Informacyjny Biblioteki Narodowej* 1996 (2[137]): 7–12; and "Biblioteka króla Stanisława Augusta Poniatowskiego przechowywana w Kijowie," *Cenne, bezcenne /utracone—Valuable, priceless/lost* 1997 (4): 10–11. The published catalog series is being prepared under the editorial direction of Laskarzewska (of the Biblioteka Narodowa).

the end of the war. As explained by Wojciech Kowalski, a Polish law professor, who long has been involved with issues of cultural restitution and is now a consultant to the Polish-Ukrainian Cultural Commission and the Polish Ministry of Foreign Affairs:

> In view of the postwar boundary changes and the mass repatriation of the populations, [in 1945] the Bureau of Revindication and Reparations of the Ministry of Culture and Art, assumed that all of Poland's cultural treasures that could be transported should be returned [i.e., transported to Poland].... [In the immediate postwar period,] although many of Poland's historical objects were brought back, yet not even a small part of the plan was carried out due to political circumstances. Today, we view the problem in a basically different light, we cannot forget the rights of our compatriots living in their historical settlements. Consideration must also be given to the cultural heritage that bears important witness to our contribution to the development of the civilization and culture of that area. Seen in this context, the large scale repatriation of the cultural objects, as laid down in the postwar plans, would lead to a cultural cleansing and a gross misrepresentation of the history of the former Eastern Territories of the Polish Republic.[76]

Even after setting forth that basically internationalist, cosmopolitan perspective, Wojciech Kowalski puts forward the position that among "cultural objects that are of special significance to our heritage and whose fate attracts an understandable public interest" are "the Ossolineum collection in Lvov and part of the library of King Stanislaus Augustus in Kiev."[77] Obviously, more negotiations lie ahead, but a spirit of compromise and respect for the national cultural heritage and especially the archival legacy of both nations remains essential in such cases.

Despite many thorny problems and lack of adequate public information about the historical background of some of the archives and manuscript collections involved, resolution of cultural claims and restitution issues appear much easier to come by in Ukraine than in Russia. The resolution of restitution issues with Poland may be more difficult, and serious stumbling blocks remain. By the same token, Poland has yet to resolve many of its cultural restitution and wartime reparations claims with Germany. Nevertheless, with Ukrainian independence and improved diplomatic, economic, and

---

[76]   Kowalski, *Liquidation of the Effects of World War II*, pp. 99–100. [Polish version: *Likwidacja skutków II Wojny Światowej*, p. 101.]

[77]   Kowalski, *Liquidation of the Effects*, p. 100.

cultural relations with Poland, there is hope that a spirit of cooperation and mutual respect for the cultural and archival heritages of individual national States—as well as for their common multinational cultural heritage—will in the end prevail.

CHAPTER 12

Independent Ukraine, Germany, and the International Context of Restitution

The International Context of Displaced Archives for Ukraine

Ukraine was accepted as a member of the Council of Europe in November 1995 with no obligations with respect to cultural restitution. That same year Ukraine became a member of the UNESCO Intergovernmental Committee for Promoting the Return of Cultural Property to its Country of Origin or its Restitution in the Case of Illicit Appropriation. In 1996 it was given an alternate seat on the European Executive Committee of the International Council on Archives. One of the factors in Ukraine's increased stature—and its favorable impression as a member of the European Community—has been its policy regarding restitution of trophy cultural treasures to Germany and other countries. Independent Ukraine has pursued an independent foreign policy from Russia: it needs potential economic and cultural benefits from friendly new foreign relationships. Yet its close ties and debts to Russia as the prime successor to the USSR forces Ukraine to walk a narrow tightrope when it comes to viable international arrangements with respect to culture—and especially cultural restitution.

As we have already seen, as a successor State to the USSR, Ukraine is closely affected by the problems of displaced archives and other cultural treasures in Russia, further complicated by foreign reaction to the new Russian law, and fallout from the Russian policy of non-restitution to the European Community. The special problems of Ukrainian-Polish relations in this sphere showed the complexity of cultural transfers qua restitution in the face of shifting international borders and the complex legacy of World War II. Although Ukrainian restitution negotiations are pending with several other countries, including a formal claim to the United States, the remaining major set of problems in restitution issues for Ukraine resides in its relationship with Germany. Such issues come into focus in the context of a series of international conferences devoted to these matters, where internationally applicable principles are being formulated that may provide future guidelines in resolving some of the problems involved.

German-Ukrainian Restitution Gains. There may be relatively few German cultural trophies left in Ukraine and even fewer Ukrainian ones in Germany. Still, the positive steps in restitution that have developed as a result of recent German-Ukrainian cooperation deserve special note. Ukraine considers itself an heir to the 9 November 1990 "Treaty on Good Neighborliness, Partnership, and Cooperation between the USSR and the Federal Republic of Germany," signed after German reunification, whereby in Article 16 the Sides "agree that lost or unlawfully transferred art treasures which are located in their territory will be returned to their owners or their successors."[1] That principle was reinforced in the 15 February 1993 "Agreement between the Government of Ukraine and the Government of the Federal Republic of Germany on Cultural Cooperation."[2]

Several acts of restitution between Germany and Ukraine in 1993 and 1994 had been elaborated in protocols of joint meetings regarding displaced cultural treasures following the intergovernmental agreement.[3] In May 1993, then Ukrainian Premier Leonid Kuchma handed over to Germany some letters and sketches of Johann Wolfgang von Goethe. And in June 1993, Ukraine returned some archeological relics to the Landesmuseum in Berlin from Soviet postwar booty that were identified in the Institute of Archeology in Kyiv. In exchange, in March 1994, some Bronze-Age relics were returned from the Berlin Museum of Early and Pre-History to the Regional Studies Museum in Kherson, where they had been seized by Nazi trophy brigades. At the time of the first transfer, German President Richard von Weizsäcker declared that "the return of this cultural property is a symbol which attests to the end of a dark chapter in history and to the beginning of a new era of friendly relations between Germany and Ukraine."[4]

[1] The complete English text of the treaty is published in *The Spoils of War: WWII and Aftermath*, pp. 304–306. A Ukrainian translation of Article 16 appears in *Ukraïna v mizhnarodno-pravovykh vidnosynakh*, bk. 2, pp. 528–29.

[2] Extracts of the Ukrainian text of the agreement appears as document 152 in *Ukraïna v mizhnarodno-pravovykh vidnosynakh*, bk. 2, p. 582.

[3] The Ukrainian text of the protocol of the February 1993 delegation meeting under the auspices of the Ukrainian National Commission on Restitution appears as document 153 in *Ukraïna v mizhnarodno-pravovykh vidnosynakh*, bk. 2, pp. 583–84, and the text of the February 1994 meeting follows as document 154 (pp. 584–86).

[4] These exchanges were described, and Weizsäcker's remarks quoted, by Valentina Vrublevskaia and Sergei [Serhii] Kot, "Cultural Property of the Ukraine Lost as a Result of World War II—Problems of Research and Restitution," in *Cultural Treasures Moved Because of the War—A Cultural Legacy of the Second*

A few notable celebrations of restitution marked the fiftieth anniversary of the end of World War II in Ukraine in line with these agreements. During the state visit of Ukrainian President Kuchma to Germany in June 1995, a charter issued by Peter I in 1700 to Kyiv Metropolitan Varlaam Iasyns'kyi (which had been seized by Nazi agents and later found by an American GI in a ruined bunker in Vienna) was returned to Kyiv.[5] Earlier that year, during a German-Ukrainian round table on "Culture and War" in Odesa at the end of April, 723 books from the nineteenth and early twentieth centuries were returned to the Historical Museum in Kyiv from a museum on the shores of the Bodensee. They had been taken there by one of the leaders of the Ukrainian brigade of the Einsatzstab Reichsleiter Rosenberg (ERR). At the same time, a self-portrait by the German artist Hans von Marées was returned to the Bremen Kunsthalle by a young Ukrainian whose father had found it in 1945 in a castle in Brandenburg (where it had been shipped for safekeeping during the war). The importance of the latter symbolic event was noted halfway around the world as "the first official return to Germany of World War II art booty by one of the former Soviet republics since the collapse of the USSR."[6]

A further important exchange of displaced cultural treasures took place during the state visit of German Chancellor Helmut Kohl to Kyiv in early September 1996. Three albums of lithographs and engravings which had been missing since 1945 were returned to the Department of Prints and Drawings

---

World War: Documentation and Research on Losses: Documentation of the International Meeting in Bremen (30.11.–2.12.1994), ed. Jost Hansen and Doris Lemmermeier (Bremen, 1995), pp. 120–21.

[5] See commentary on the return of the 1700 charter by O. V. Muzychuk, "Nove nadkhodzhennia TsDIAK Ukraïny," *Arkhivy Ukraïny* 1995 (1–3): 77–78. It has not yet been determined exactly when the charter was removed from Kyiv nor from which collection it was taken.

[6] Jamey Gambrell, "First Return of War Booty," *Art in America* 6 (June 1995): 31. These events were also appreciatively noted by Professor Wolfgang Eichwede, who was instrumental in the restitution efforts, in his address to the round-table—Eichwede, "Ukraina idet svoim putem," *Kul'tura i viina: Pohliad cherez pivstolittia* (Kyiv: Adrys, 1996), p. 10 [=*Povernennia kul'turnoho nadbannia Ukraïny: Problemy, zavdannia, perspektyvy,* 7]. The return of the Ukrainian books is described by Gunter Schöbel from the Pfahlbaumuseum, "Eine kleine Geste an die Ukraine: Rückgabe von verschleppten Büchern," in *Displaced Books: Bücherrückgabe*, pp. 68–74. The official 28 April 1995 protocol for the return of the books printed with the report gives the figure as 724, but Eichwede and other publications cite 723.

of the Dresden Galley from the Museum of Western and Oriental Art. At the same time the German chancellor presented to Ukrainian President Leonid Kuchma an eighteenth-century icon, an antique Scythian mirror, and 173 books that included imprints from the Kyiv Monastery (Lavra) of the Caves and the library of Kyiv Metropolitan Flavian, which were among those removed by the Künsberg Commandos. The Dresden albums were part of the trophy shipment to Kyiv described earlier. Representatives of the Dresden Gallery were delighted to receive the albums—one with 57 early nineteenth-century lithographs after a Saxon artist, one entitled "Scenes of Switzerland" with 69 eighteenth- and nineteenth-century color etchings, and a third with 95 engravings by Johann Bläu with scenes of festivities, ceremonies, and residences of the Dukes of Savoy (dating back to 1700).

There was, nevertheless, serious disappointment on the German side, because, as German museum officials subsequently reported, they had earlier been shown five albums in the Museum of Western and Oriental Art in Kyiv in July 1996, and had understood that all would be returned.[7] According to published estimates, there may be many more (see Chapter 7). While the act of restitution had "deep historical meaning and symbolic significance," as noted during the ceremony by Ukrainian Deputy Prime Minister Ivan Kuras, we still do not know how much more trophy German art remains in that museum or others in Kyiv known to have received significant spoils of war, major portions of which were not returned in the 1950s.[8] Nor do we know how many more cultural treasures looted from Ukraine may still be found in Germany. A preliminary catalog of 475 lost paintings from the Museum of Western and Oriental Art in Kyiv mentioned earlier, was handed over to the German side in 1996, but as of the end of 1998, when the full catalog was published, Professor Wolfgang Eichwede, the director of the Bremen project, reports that none of them have been located, nor sources on their migration uncovered.[9]

[7]   Wolfgang Holler, "Return of Three Albums from the Ukraine to the Department of Prints and Drawings, Dresden," *Spoils of War: International Newsletter* 3 (1996): 63. The Ukrainian text of the protocol of the February 1996 delegation meeting agreeing to the exchange appears as document 155 in *Ukraïna v mizhnarodno-pravovykh vidnosynakh*, bk. 2, pp. 586–90.

[8]   As reported in a Kyiv newspaper as part of a larger article on the state visit by Tat′iana Kovalevskaia, "Gel′mut Kol′ vidit luchshee budushchee Ukrainy," *Rabochaia gazeta: Ukrainy* 132 (5 September 1996): 1.

[9]   A published version of the catalog appeared in 1998: *Catalogue of Works of Western European Painters Lost during Second World War*, comp. Olena Roslavets; ed. Oleksandr Fedoruk et al. (Kyiv, 1998). Wolgang Eichewede

From the German side in 1997 came an important act of goodwill restitution to Ukraine with the transfer of a major collection of photographs from the Bundesarchiv in Koblenz, part of it from the Ukrainian photograph archive that had been looted during the war.[10]

Earlier in February that year, four drawings found by a Soviet soldier in 1945 were returned to the Bremen Kunsthalle from anonymous private sources in Ukraine. Again, this act of restitution from Ukraine contrasts markedly with the refusal of Russian authorities to permit the planned return of the collection of 362 drawings and 2 paintings from the Kunsthalle that had been rescued after the war by the Russian art historian Viktor Bataldin. The Bataldin collection was exhibited in the Hermitage in 1995, and President Yeltsin had assured Bataldin that his often repeated desire for their return would be respected, but Bataldin died in 1997 without the realization of that restitution.[11]

The Bremen Connection and the 1994 Symposium. One important element in post-1991 German-Ukrainian restitution developments has been the serious effort of German specialists, especially those at the University of Bremen, who have been working with Ukrainian specialists to document losses and transfers during the war on both sides. Their work has especially focused on art and other cultural treasures from museums. As part of the Bremen project mentioned earlier in the book, German researchers have had good access to Ukrainian archives. Several Ukrainian graduate students have been brought into the project and have enjoyed fellowships for research in Germany, opportunity for research in German archives, and open access to copies of documentation collected in Bremen. Results now are available through important published investigations of displaced cultural treasures and related wartime sources.

A 1994 symposium in Bremen, in which Ukrainian representatives took part, was one of the first international gatherings of specialists on cultural

---

discussed with me the difficulties—and lack of success—in trying to trace the lost paintings in December 1998. See my comments on this catalog above, Chapter 2, pp. 58–59.

[10] Elena Mashchenko, "Ukrainskie arkhivy vozvrashchaiutsia na rodinu," *Zerkalo nedeli* 48 (165) 29 November 1997: 15; Ihor Petrov, "Nimets'ki foto vykryvaiut' zlochyny NKVS," *Chas* 27 February–5 March 1997: 71; Olena Hrynchenko, "Chy potribne nam zoloto skifiv?" *Den'* 119 (25 June 1997): 7.

[11] Doris Lemmermeier, "Germany," *Spoils of War: International Newsletter* 4 (1997): 78. See also the note on Bataldin's death, ibid., p. 96.

displacements and restitution issues arising from World War II.[12]

Restitution Progress with Germany

In 1999 the priceless collection from the Sing-Akademie in Berlin that includes long-lost music scores of the Bach family and other predominantly eighteenth-century German composers was located and identified in Kyiv in the Central State Archive-Museum of Literature and Art (TsDAMLM). Discussion of possible restitution was immediately aired.[13] Soon after the discovery was publicized, a new law, "On the Import, Export, and Return of Cultural Valuables," was rushed through the Ukrainian parliament and signed by President Leonid Kuchma on 21 September 1999. Like the Russian law, cultural treasures of Ukraine were defined to include those "transferred to Ukrainian territory as a result of World War II as partial compensation for destruction during occupation" (article 3). But unlike the Russian law, there are no provisions or mechanisms for restitution. Also following the earlier Russian law, export of cultural treasures is prohibited if the treasures involved are legally part of the "National Archival Fond…, the Museum Fond of Ukraine," or those listed in the "National Register of the National Cultural Heritage" (article 14).[14] Thus, unless there is further legislation on the subject, any further restitution of cultural treasures would require special measures to ensure their exclusion from those legal entities.

Meanwhile—of more cultural significance—a project for cataloguing and creating preservation microfilms of the collection so it can be made publicly

---

[12] See above, Chapter 5, p. 181, and the published symposium proceedings: *Cultural Treasures Moved Because of the War*.

[13] Regarding the discovery, see above, Chapter 5, and my article, "Bach Scores in Kyiv: The Long-Lost Sing-Akademie Collection Surfaces in Ukraine," *Spoils of War: International Newsletter* 7 (August 2000): 23–35. Regarding restitution possibilities, see the statement by a representative of the National Commission for the Restitution of Cultural Treasures to Ukraine, as quoted in a Kyiv story by Agence France Presse (10 August 1999). That point of view was also expressed by Ukrainian archival leaders during our visit to Kyiv when the collection was discovered. See also Joseph P. Kahn, "A Bach Score: Accident and adventure lead to a collection long thought lost," *Boston Globe* 30 September 1999: E1, E7; and Sarah Boxer, "International Sleuthing Adds Insight About Bach," *New York Times* 16 August 1999: B1, 4.

[14] "Pro vyvezennia, vvezennia ta povernennia kul'turnykh tsinnostei," Law of Ukraine, 1068–14, 21 September 1999, in *Ofitsiinyi visnyk Ukraïny,* no. 42 (Kyiv, 1999), statut 2072. The text first appeared on the official website of the Ukrainian parliament <http://alpha.rada.kiev.ua/sgi-bin/putfile.cgi>.

available for study and performance is under way in collaboration with the National Academy of Music in Kyiv, the Bach Archive in Leipzig, the Sing-Akademie in Berlin, and the Ukrainian Research Institute at Harvard University; the project is being directed by Harvard music Professor Christoph Wolff, who identified the collection in Kyiv after a search of twenty-five years.[15] The saga of the transfer of the Sing-Academie collection to Kyiv and the fate of its still missing parts have not been resolved.

The new revelation in Kyiv is an important and positive step in restoring long-hidden treasures of the European music heritage to what we might hope is a now more civilized world. But wartime and postwar plunder and restitution politics still keep too many music treasures as prisoners of war in Eastern Europe. The most famous Berlin musicalia collection held before the war in the Staatsbibliothek was evacuated to Silesia before the bombing of Berlin. Following its "rescue" by Polish authorities from the Benedictine Monastery of Grüssau (*Pol.* Krzeszów) in Silesia, it was long secretly ensconced in the Jagellonian Library in Cracow.[16] Knowledge of its whereabouts and restitution negotiations between Poland and Germany became public only in 1977, when Polish Communist Party First Secretary Edward Gierek presented GDR President Erich Honecker with three symbolic red boxes with the original autograph manuscript scores of Bach's *Concerto for*

---

[15] Christoph Wolff, an internationally recognized Bach scholar, earlier described another important Berlin music collection rich in Bach scores, see his "From Berlin to Łódź: The Spitta Collection Resurfaces," *Notes* (December 1989): 311–27. That collection still remains in Poland.

[16] Regarding the losses from the Prussian Staatsbibliothek, see *Verlagert—verschollen—vernichtet: Das Schicksal der im 2. Weltkrieg ausgelagerten Bestande der Preußischen Staatsbibliothek* (Berlin: Staatsbibliothek zu Berlin, Preußischer Kulturbesitz, [1995]), which includes extensive bibliography regarding the missing manuscripts and updates reconnaissance efforts. Regarding the thirty-five year search for the German music collections in Poland, leading up to the 1977 presentation, see the intriguing account by Nigel Lewis, *Paperchase: Mozart, Beethoven, Bach. The Search for Their Lost Music* (London: Hamish Hamilton, 1981). See also Dieter Henrich, "Beethoven, Hegel und Mozart auf der Reise nach Krakau: Der Übergang des Grüssauer Depots der Preußischen Staatsbibliothek in die Hand der Volksrepublik Polen," *Neue Rundschau* 88 (1977): 165–99; "Bestände aus der früheren Preußischen Staatsbibliothek in Polen," *Jahrbuch für preußischer Kulturbesitz* 29 (1995): 339–64; and P. J. P Whitehead, "The Lost Berlin Manuscripts," *Notes* 33(1) September 1976: 7–15. Regarding non-music manuscripts see, for example, Deborah Hertz, "The Varnhagen Collection is in Krakow," *American Archivist* 44(3) Summer 1981: 223–28.

Two Harpsichords, Mozart's *Magic Flute*, and Beethoven's *Ninth Symphony*. The rest of the musicalia collection and other long-lost manuscript treasures from that Berlin library remain in Cracow. Since the late 1970s, their survival has been known to the world and they have been fully open to scholarship. Restitution negotiations have made no progress since 1977; this is due, unquestionably, to the reality of the incalculable Polish cultural losses during the war and the Polish desire for compensation.

By contrast, identification or even survey descriptions are still not publicly available for the extensive trophy music and many other manuscript treasures held in Moscow and St. Petersburg, although their receipt by a number of repositories after the war has been confirmed in the 1996 publication of German translations of Soviet documents (the Russian originals are now classified).[17] As the last act of Soviet-period restitution (in contrast to Russian non-restitution), a large collection of manuscript music scores and other music literature were returned to the University of Hamburg in 1991 from the Leningrad State Scientific Research Institute of Theater and Music (now the Russian Institute for the History of Art).

Unlike the situation in Russia, the Ukrainian press and public opinion react favorably to the official Ukrainian government policy of restitution. For example, in a front-page story a Kyiv correspondent notes the positive attitudes in restitution discussions between Germany and Ukraine as going hand and hand with a German business mission with representatives of several important German firms that could mean improved economic relations.[18] The Ukrainian historian Serhii Kot has been researching

---

[17] For example, music materials, along with parts of the Sanskrit collection from the Prussian Staatsbibliothek (Berlin), were among the trophy collections that were reported by the Lenin Library in Moscow (now the Russian State Library—RGB), according to a document signed by director V. Olishev (12 May 1948) in *Die Trophäenkommissionen*, no. 36, p. 214 (the document comes from the RGB archive, but no file numbers are provided). According to other documents in the same published collection, larger German trophy music collections were received by the Central Museum of Musical Culture and the Moscow State Conservatory, while other Soviet recipients included the Leningrad Conservatory, the Moscow Philharmonic, and the Saltykov-Shchedrin State Public Library—see documents nos. 37–40 (ibid., pp. 218–32; archival signatures are not provided, although they are listed as being held with Communist Party records in RTsKhIDNI [now RGASPI], 17/132/418). When I tried to verify the originals in October 1999, I found that the relevant documents in that file in RGASPI are now classified.

[18] Vasyl' Zaiets', "Svoia maty naidorozhcha," *Kul'tura i zhyttia* 11 (September 1996): 1.

seriously Ukrainian cultural treasures abroad and restitution problems resulting from wartime displacements. His recognition of the extent of "goodwill" that can be engendered on the international front by cooperative efforts in the restitution of cultural treasures is finding an audience in Kyiv.[19] In July 1999, when the discovery of the Sing-Akademie collection was announced, the *Kyiv Post* declared in an editorial that "Ukraine should set the standard for the West and return the Bach archive to Berlin's Sing-Akademie. Besides, it is obliged to do this by the treaty with Germany for the mutual return of wartime cultural trophies."[20]

Most important, both sides are starting to make serious efforts to determine wartime losses and displacements. Ukraine has agreed (at least on paper) to prepare a register of the German spoils of war held in Ukraine, and free access for German specialists to the depositories involved, which before independence were all held in secrecy. Oleksandr Fedoruk, who heads the National Commission for the Restitution of Cultural Treasures to Ukraine (now a "State Service"), has stated that "the current state of opinion gives grounds for hope that the return of cultural property on both sides (or compensation in the restitution process) will become a stable bridge uniting Western and Eastern Europe." He urges that "the tragic conflicts of the war...should be put aside." He also advocates that more open research be undertaken: "The facts, however unpleasant they may be, should not be ignored, because they can foster the establishment of the truth on the path to an agreement on the problem of restitution."[21]

Since independence, Ukraine may be better prepared for restitution to Germany than Russia, but it should be remembered that Ukraine holds many fewer cultural treasures from Germany than Russia. This, perhaps, makes symbolic acts easier. Yet it is also true, as Oleksandr Fedoruk has reminded us, that Ukraine suffered proportionately much more destruction and cultural plunder than Russia. Now that a collection of great value has surfaced, more questions are being asked. It is unlikely that the priceless collection of the

[19]   See, for example, Serhii Kot, "Povernuty kul'turni nadbannia mozhna, bula b dobra volia," *Viche* n.s. 5(50) May 1996, esp. pp. 129–44.

[20]   "Return Bach to Germany," *Kyiv Post* 32 (12 August 1999). See also the statement by a representative of the National Commission for the Restitution of Cultural Treasures to Ukraine, as quoted in a Kyiv story by Agence France Presse (10 August 1999). That point of view was also expressed during our visit to Kyiv when the collection was discovered.

[21]   Oleksandr [Alexander] Fedoruk, "Ukraine," *Spoils of War: International Newsletter* 2 (July 1996): 37. See also the corresponding report by Doris Lemmermeier, "Germany," ibid., pp. 25–26.

Sing-Akademie in Berlin will be returned without considerable debate and without some equivalent compensation from the German side. In the meantime, since its discovery, colleagues in Kyiv report a new under-current of anti-restitution sentiment in some Kyiv cultural and political circles, as was apparent in the passage of the Ukrainian law on cultural treasures.

Despite the opening of the Sing-Akademie collection, it is clear from attempts to document other trophy receipts in connection with this study that a considerable hesitancy continues in Ukraine to opening hitherto secret storage areas to public scrutiny. Besides, many relevant archival files either still are not openly available or cannot be located.

Remaining Captured Nazi Records in Ukraine. Most of the seized Nazi-looted and German trophy archives that did come to Ukraine after the war were subsequently transferred to Moscow and, as noted earlier, remain in the former imperial capital. Kyiv still retains, however, a major group of ERR records of Europe-wide significance. Since those ERR records also involve Nazi exploits in, and the cultural property of, many countries of Europe in addition to former territories of the USSR, they should be made more accessible through professional multi-language finding aids and complete microfilming, at the very least. Several other important groups of Nazi occupation records in Ukraine undoubtedly should be classed as part of the "joint" archival heritage with Germany. Given international archival precedents, however, they ideally should be reunited with the contingent ERR records now in the Bundesarchiv, which were returned from the United States in the 1960s.

Trophy Books in Ukraine? Georgian and Armenian Library Restitution. Facts and figures are not yet complete about Ukrainian holdings of trophy books. Further efforts on the part of librarians in Ukraine may lead to the discovery of the fate of some of the two (rather than the otherwise published three) million trophy books that were allegedly sent to Ukraine after the war. Perhaps more displaced books from Ukrainian libraries will be found in Germany, or more information about their migration may aid in tracking down their fate.

Library issues in Ukraine resulting from World War II displacements were aired at several conferences, as noted earlier in this book. Research is complicated by the fact that the issue of trophy German books in Ukraine has not been adequately investigated, and precise information about the fate of German trophy books sent to Ukraine is still not available to the public.

Unlike the impasse over library restitution in Russia discussed above, both Georgia and Armenia have recently made significant restitution of trophy library books to Germany. Mention was made earlier of the unwanted shipment of 100,000 trophy German books to the Library of the Georgian Academy of Sciences in the 1950s; in August 1996, the first of several containers brought at least 96,000 trophy books back to Berlin, where they were identified as having come from a number of different German libraries, including those in Bremen, Magdeburg, Halle, Hamburg, and Berlin.[22] Among the 575 books returned by Armenia in May 1998, primarily from Bremen, Hamburg, and Lübeck, were several manuscripts, including four folio volumes of church music scores by Johann Christian Bach and a twelfth-century missal from Hamburg.[23] The goodwill these restitutions have engendered in Germany is already leading to plans for library assistance to both Georgia and Armenia.

International Forums on Restitution Issues

Many of the issues connected with displaced cultural treasures and restitution come into focus in the context of a series of international conferences, the first of which were held in Bremen and Chernihiv in 1994. While providing an international context for discussion, they in turn reflect many of the twists and complexities in international restitution politics and diplomacy.

Bard 1995 Symposium—"The Spoils of War." The depth and complexity of restitution problems, and particularly those involving Russia, were apparent in the major symposium entitled "The Spoils of War," in New York City in January 1995, opening commemorations of the fiftieth anniversary year of the end of World War II. The elegantly published proceedings of the symposium, organized by the Bard College Center for the Visual Arts, bring perspective to many issues in the continuing "Cold War" debate over restitution or non-restitution half a century later.[24] The volume editor, Elizabeth Simpson, put it well in her "Introduction":

> Not only was this the first public meeting on the subject ever held, but it was also the first time that so many of those in-

---

[22] "A Splendid Gesture, Chronology of a Restitution": pt. 1 by Ingo Kolasa, and pt. 2, by Juri Mosidse, *Spoils of War: International Newsletter* 3 (1996): 53–58.

[23] "Books from Armenia Returned to Germany," *Spoils of War: International Newsletter* 5 (1998): 85.

[24] *The Spoils of War: World War II and Its Aftermath. The Loss, Reappearance, and Recovery of Cultural Property*, ed. Elizabeth Simpson (New York: Henry N. Abrams, 1997).

volved had been together in one place—in a less formal and more congenial setting than that of the courtroom or negotiating table.[25]

Ukraine was represented by Oleksandr Fedoruk, who spoke forcefully of the "stolen cultural treasures" that were:

> ...taken by force from their legal owners and subjected to forced migration, [and] are still being held in various places as 'prisoners of war'... Forcibly excluded from cultural life, these 'prisoners of war' still await a better fate. We sincerely hope that the conference organized by the Bard Graduate Center will bring us at least one step closer to a successful solution, based on the legal norms governing the restitution to their countries of origin of the cultural treasures lost during World War II and its aftermath.[26]

In concluding, Fedoruk recommended the creation of an international "data bank on all (or at least the most outstanding) cultural property lost during the war. Such information could be shared by all participating countries."[27]

Before the Bard symposium, there was scant public appreciation of the dimension of cultural loss and plunder on the Eastern Front and the bitterness of emotions that plague discussion of restitution half a century later. Appended texts of important international agreements and conventions relating to cultural property provide further background for discussion of the law recently passed over presidential veto in Russia.

Of particular importance were the commentaries by various international lawyers with clarification of legal issues involved in a number of specific cases as well as more general matters. The breakdown and failure of the quadripartite legal agreement on cultural restitution within the Allied Control Council in Germany after the war, according to Michael Kurtz, explains why restitution was handled on a zonal basis—or non-restitution and cultural reparations, as was the case in the Soviet zone of occupation. Kurtz also emphasized that the Control Council never authorized the type of cultural seizures or cultural "reparations in kind" that took place in the Soviet zone.[28]

---

[25] Elizabeth Simpson, "Introduction," in *The Spoils of War: WWII and Aftermath*, pp. 12–13.

[26] Oleksandr (Alexander) Fedoruk, "The Lost Cultural Treasures and the Problem of their Return," *The Spoils of War: WWII and Aftermath*, p. 72.

[27] Ibid., p. 76.

[28] Michael Kurtz, "The End of the War and the Occupation of Germany, 1944–1952: Laws and Conventions Enacted to Counter German Appropriations,

In contrast were the presentations of the Russian legal positions by several specialists from Moscow, emphasizing the legality of Russian seizures, given the breakdown of the quadripartite agreements.[29] Pushkin Museum director Irina Antonova defended her museum's role in "safeguarding" art and continued to emphasize the restoration and preservation accomplished by the Soviet Union. Such arguments hardly satisfied German officials who again cited the 1907 Hague Convention, the 1990 Soviet-German Treaty of Friendship, and the 1992 Russo-German cultural agreement, all of which provide for the restitution of cultural plunder.

Another question was raised for Russia when the conference presented a special session on the fate of the Quedlinburg treasures stolen from Germany by an American GI, which were only recently returned to Germany after a long search, court battle, and payment of a large ransom. Valerii Kulishov from the Russian Ministry of Culture appropriately asked:

> ...how can we explain to the ordinary Russian man in the street why, in the case of the Quedlinburg treasures, Germany raised the necessary funds to buy the works back from an American owner—when Russians for some reason are only blamed or pressured to return art treasures as a "gesture of good will"? And not only that, but give them back with apologies for having retained these things for so long.[30]

At the same time, like many from other countries, he emphasized the need to open the special depositories in Russia:

> To my mind, the return of these long-considered lost art treasures to the world is a much more urgent task than resolving the

---

the Allied Control Council," in *The Spoils of War: WWII and Aftermath*, pp. 112–16.

[29]   Nikolai Nikandrov, Department of Restitution, Ministry of Culture RF, "The Transfer of the Contents of German Repositories into the Custody of the USSR," in *The Spoils of War: WWII and Aftermath*, pp. 117–20; and Mark Boguslavskii, "Legal Aspects of the Russian Position in Regard to the Return of Cultural Property," ibid, pp. 186–90.

[30]   Valerii Kulishov, "The History of the Soviet Repositories and Their Contents," in *The Spoils of War: WWII and Aftermath*, p. 173. The figure of $3 million as a "finding fee" was mentioned as having been received by the Texas family for only one part of the medieval treasure, including the ninth-century Carolingian "Samuhel Gospels"; an editor's note sets the fee at $2.75 million in an out-of court settlement, all of which brought a public outcry in the United States. See the reports from the special session on the Quedlinburg treasures, in ibid., pp. 148–58.

difficulties surrounding their ownership and settling the various and often conflicting claims. The most important objective is the return of these works of art to humanity.[31]

The final session heard an emotional appeal for reason and restitution from Wolfgang Eichwede, who has been assembling an extensive database of source descriptions of captured art and archives that were removed by Nazi authorities from the former Soviet Union. Eichwede assured the Bard symposium that "Germany today holds almost no treasures from the Soviet Union and possesses nothing (or very little) that it could return." Yet he agonizes to find a creative solution to the restitution impasse between the German government and Russia:

> It is true that Russia has the German "trophies" to make up for its losses, but at the same time it knows that it is operating outside of international norms...What is needed here is a 'new thinking': gestures of reconciliation instead of a mutual standoff, a willingness to embark upon joint projects, instead of reviving the Cold War on the cultural front.[32]

Eichwede most especially praised the Ukrainian efforts to research their losses and the trophy German cultural treasures still in Ukraine. In contrast to Russia, he emphasized:

> These goods, however, are not about to be declared Ukrainian state property. What is on the agenda is the question of how a balance can be struck between compensation for one's own losses and restitution to Germany...The situation is favorable to progress.[33]

Ekaterina Genieva, the Russian director of the Library of Foreign Literature (VGBIL) in Moscow—in marked contrast to more official defensive presentations by many of her fellow countrymen—gave examples of the sad fate of many plundered books, courageously advocating the restitution process (with books at the forefront of that process). She pleaded that if restitution issues for art were still going to divide the European continent, perhaps the further restitution of library books, as planned by her

---

[31] Kulishov, in *The Spoils of War: WWII and Aftermath*, p. 173.

[32] Wolfgang Eichwede, "Models of Restitution (Germany, Russia, Ukraine)," in *The Spoils of War: WWII and Aftermath*, p. 217.

[33] Ibid., p. 219.

library, could "make us friends."[34] Indicative of the bitterness directed against alternative Russian attitudes by those opposed to any restitution, a full-page diatribe against the Bard symposium in *Pravda* (now the newspaper of the Russian Communist Party) considered Genieva's "anti-Russian rhetoric" a disgrace to the Russian delegation.[35]

UNESCO representative Lyndel Prott gave the closing address, noteworthy for its calm appeal to law and reason beyond law. Aiming to find a solution and rise above the lingering wartime passions evident in earlier symposia presentations, Prott was aptly skeptical that international law could prescribe settlements in many hotly contested issues. However, she appealed to law as a framework for working out negotiated settlements, and to a series of principles or reasoned guidelines that could and should be brought to bear in resolving restitution issues. She further proposed the UNESCO committee on restitution as a court of appeal if bilateral negotiations prove not to be conclusive. Although her remarks and recommendations in this case were directed towards freeing cultural treasures generally from treatment as war booty, they coincide with the ICA Thessalonica resolution in October 1994 against such treatment for archives.[36] The April 1995 ICA Position Paper discussed earlier also recommends international consultation and an eventual new convention to rectify the matter of displaced archives.

Amsterdam 1996 Symposium on Restitution. We have seen the beneficial results of small acts of restitution for Ukraine. Proof of the prospective friendship and goodwill engendered for Russia by restitution efforts was demonstrated at an Amsterdam symposium in April 1996, to which Genieva was invited to hear a movingly appreciative report on the fate of the 600 books symbolically returned by her library to the University of Amsterdam in 1992. In ironic contrast to the earlier New York symposium, the smaller

---

[34]   Ekaterina Iu. Genieva, in *The Spoils of War: WWII and Aftermath*, pp. 221–24. Genieva's remarks were featured in the conclusion of several newspaper accounts of the Bard symposium. See especially Catherine Foster, "Stolen Art as War Booty: Hostages or Harbingers of Peace?" *Christian Science Monitor* 8 February 1995: 1, 10; and an editorial in the *New York Times* by Karl E. Meyer (1 February 1995).

[35]   Vladimir Teteriatnikov, "'Kholodnaia voina' za muzeinymi shtorami—Kak rossiiskie iskusstvovedy sdaiut v plen shedevry, okazavshiesia v SSSR posle pobedy nad Germaniei v 1945 godu," *Pravda* 29 March 1995: 4.

[36]   Lyndel Prott, "Principles for the Resolutions of Disputes concerning Cultural Heritage Displaced during the Second World War," in *The Spoils of War: WWII and Aftermath*, pp. 225–30.

Amsterdam conference concentrated "On the Return of Looted Collections," honoring the fiftieth anniversary of the restitution of Dutch and other European collections from the U.S. Zone of Occupied Germany. The coincidence that the symposium opened the same day that the "Trojan Gold" went on display in Moscow did not escape notice by participants.

The Netherlands was occupied completely by Nazi Germany, and many of the Dutch archives now in Moscow were seized by the Germans during the period when Stalin was still allied with Hitler. As was reported again at the symposium, the Dutch have returned all of the Nazi occupation records found there to Germany (with copies retained in Amsterdam). But who in Moscow will ever read, or let alone appreciate, the long-lost records (described at the conference) of the Dutch feminist movement that were captured by the Nazis but now remain sequestered in Moscow? Such archival trophies in the Russian capital hardly serve as "compensation" for Russian historical records destroyed in Pskov or Novgorod.

Other reports underscored the importance of the Nazi records in Moscow and Kyiv that describe the Nazi's cultural plunder. For example, the large complex of records in Kyiv from the ERR operations were noted in several reports. While two reports converged on ERR Silesian activities in and near Ratibor (*Pol.* Racibórz) on their basis, the ERR files in Kyiv include reports from various work brigades in the Netherlands and Belgium, as well as Ukraine and other former republics of the USSR. A Belgian report at the symposium referred to the precise descriptions found in those files of archival and other cultural seizures from Belgian Masonic lodges.

The proceedings of the Amsterdam symposium, published in July 1997, focused on books and archives rather than art. The "unfinished chapters" involving books and archives still held on the Eastern Front loom large.[37]

Symposia in Kyiv in 1996 and in Minsk in 1997. The December 1996 UNESCO-sponsored international conference in Kyiv on international legal issues of restitution has already been mentioned several times.[38] Likewise, reference has been made to the international symposium in Minsk that addressed other restitution issues in the wake of passage of the Russian nationalization law. Dialog continues on an international level in Eastern

---

[37] *The Return of Looted Collections (1946–1946). An Unfinished Chapter: Proceedings of an International Symposium to Mark the 50th Anniversary of the Return of Dutch Book Collections from Germany*, ed. F. J. Hoogewoud, E. P. Kwaardgras et al. (Amsterdam, 1997).

[38] See the conference resolutions in Appendix X.

Europe, but a consensus over international guidelines for the restitution of displaced cultural treasures and archives has yet to emerge.

Washington, DC, 1998 Conference on Displaced Holocaust-Era Assets.
Still another dimension of the issue of cultural treasures displaced during World War II and the related problems of restitution and compensation came to the fore in the Washington Conference on Holocaust-Era Assets in December 1998. Following the 1997 London Conference on Nazi Gold, and encouraged by the generous early 1998 settlement of claims with Swiss banks, the focus was clearly on further compensation for Holocaust survivors by the identification of other Nazi-confiscated assets. The extensive "assets" involved in "insurance claims," art, and "communal property" emerged as the targets for more in-depth investigation. The broader issues of displaced cultural treasures and restitution were clearly subsidiary to the aim of direct "compensation" for Holocaust survivors and their heirs.[39] Within this framework, Nazi-confiscated art emerged as a major issue. The head of the U.S. delegation, then Under Secretary of State Stuart E. Eizenstat, said in his opening remarks that he was "hopeful that the Conference can achieve consensus on ways to bring about a speedier and far less confrontational resolution to the problem of looted art."[40]

Also in response to the 1997 London Conference on Nazi Gold, the Ukrainian delegation prepared a short book with preliminary revelations about "Nazi Gold" from Ukraine.[41] Based on extensive archival research, and surveying many of the available sources in central and local archives, the Ukrainian team suggested a number of important new directions for potential study of the accumulation of Nazi capital at the expense of occupied nations,

[39] *Washington Conference, 1998.* The proceedings of the conference also appeared in CD-ROM format and are available on the Internet at <http://www.state.gov/www/regions/eur/holocaust/heac.html>.

[40] Stuart E. Eizenstat, "Opening Remarks," in *Washington Conference, 1998,* p. 41.

[41] Hennadii Boriak, Maryna Dubyk, and Natalia Makovs'ka, *"Natsysts'ke zoloto" z Ukraïny: U poshukakh arkhivnykh svidchen',* pt. 1 (Kyiv, 1998). An appropriate English-language abstract was not included. A hastily prepared English-language summary rendition, "Accumulation of 'Nazi Gold' on the Occupied Territory of Ukraine during World War II: Information of the Ukraine's Delegation" (Washington, DC, 1998), was available for conference participants with an introductory position paper "Main Principles of Ukrainian Position's Determination" (pp. 3–4); the awkward English translation, however, obscured some of the most important points.

which intensified the horrors of Nazi exploitation of the population. One particular example in Ukraine was the exploitation of even the minimal wages and insurance benefits received by forced laborers from the East (*Ostarbeiteren*), a subject that had never been investigated during the Soviet regime. New Ukrainian research shows further economic exploitation of the *Ostarbeitery* and other segments of the Ukrainian population and their meager assets during occupation, together with extensive confiscation of capital assets through the Reich banking and monetary system in Ukraine.

The issue of forced laborers in Germany also involves the issue of forced repatriation at Stalin's insistence by the Western Allies after the war, whereby many of those who survived the horrors of transport and labor in Germany were forced back to the Soviet Union, only to meet persecution and in many cases incarceration as "collaborators."[42] Since the United States actively participated in the forced repatriation program after the war, the State Department had some reason to avoid that issue, and forced labor was not on the conference agenda.[43]

The conference nevertheless took notice of statements by both Russian and Ukrainian delegations that in those countries (and others of Eastern Europe) many non-Jewish survivors were affected by Nazi exploitation and those survivors and their heirs should be included in the search for appropriate compensation. Viewing the issue of Nazi atrocities primarily in terms of Jewish Holocaust victims does not address the most significant wartime effects in Russia, Ukraine, Belarus, and other former Soviet republics, as those delegations pointed out in official statements to the conference.[44] Furthermore, as the Ukrainian statement indicated, because the existence of private or community assets was not possible under the communist system

---

[42] See the important recent Russian study of this matter by Pavel Polian, *Zhertvy dvukh diktatur: Ostarbaitery i voennoplennye v Tret'em reikhe i ikh repatriatsiia* (Moscow: "Vash vybor TsIRZ," 1996).

[43] See the published documents on U.S. repatriation and related documents in *Ukraine during World War II: History and its Aftermath. A Symposium*, edited by Yury Boshyk (Edmonton: CIUS, 1986), especially pp. 203–232. Greg Bradshaw, the organizer of the post-conference symposium on archives at the U.S. National Archives told me he was asked to cancel the session that had been planned to discuss archival sources on forced labor and repatriation.

[44] See especially Appendix I: "Appeal by the Representatives of Former Prisoners of Fascism from Belarus, Russia, and Ukraine to the Participants in the Washington Conference on Holocaust-Era Assets," in *Washington Conference, 1998*, pp. 1003–1005, and Appendix J: "Report of the Government of the Russian Federation Cooperation and Conciliation Fund," ibid, pp. 1007–1018.

in eastern Ukraine (as part of the Soviet Union before the war), only western Ukrainian lands (Galicia, Bukovyna, and Transdnistria) came under the purview of conference concerns for insurance claims and communal property. Given the horrendous Ukrainian experience in the Holocaust era (not only in connection with the extermination of Jews), Ukraine considered that it has good grounds to seek compensation from the Federal Republic of Germany for many of its citizens who survived the war and ordeals of the Nazi occupation. The Ukrainian closing statement concentrated on issues of defining "Nazi Gold" more broadly as "capital formation" and establishing a means of "compensation" for "all categories of victims of National Socialist persecution."[45]

Several sessions dealt with the issues of identification and Nazi-confiscated art issues, especially those involving collections of Jewish victims of the Holocaust. The opening statement by Russian Ambassador Valentin Koptel'tsev emphasized that "Russia will continue the search for cultural valu[abl]es confiscated by the Nazis from their victims, and continue publishing their list." He suggested that Russia would be open to discussion of retrieval of art now located in Russia even after the eighteen-month period expires under the new law (October 1999). In closing, he emphasized the hope that additional missing art from Russia would be found abroad, and he presented the conference with the first of what is expected to be a series of catalogs of cultural valuables looted from Russian territory.[46]

The Russian law nationalizing cultural property transferred to the USSR understandably came into focus, and appears as an appended document in the published conference proceedings.[47] Most significantly, Nikolai Gubenko, mentioned above as the key spokesman for the new Russian law, participated in the Russian delegation. Gubenko spoke defensively about the law, when conference organizers requested him to clarify it. With some irony he commented on "the unanimity with which certain European countries supported Germany in its negative reaction to the Law." He stressed that "Russia has a normal right to compensation," particularly "because the Soviet

---

[45] "Ukraine: Delegation Statement," in *Washington Conference, 1998*, pp. 403–409.

[46] Valentin Koptel'tsev, "The General Goals of the Conference and the Looted Art Problem," in *Washington Conference, 1998*, pp. 319–20.

[47] See above, Chapter 10, p. 390n5 and p. 391n6. An English-language text is published as "Federal Law No. 64-FZ of April 15, 1998 on Cultural Treasures Transferred to the Union of Soviet Socialist Republics as a Result of World War II and Located in the Territory of the Russian Federation," in *Washington Conference, 1998*, pp. 1049–1062.

Union suffered the most," in the war which "was genocide against the Slavic, as well as Jewish races." He emphasized what in his view was an international legal basis for the new Russian law, under which "the Soviet Union had the right to confiscate and own the cultural treasures of former hostile states." Furthermore, he quoted an Allied Control Council resolution that "The right for restitution is granted only to the states, which were completely or partially occupied." And consequently, Gubenko affirmed that "Germany has no right to claim restitution, because it carries the biggest responsibility for waging the cruelest war in the history of mankind." His view that "the language of this Law is the language of justice" is obviously not accepted as widely in other European countries as in Russia, where Gubenko claims that "86% supported the Law."[48] Nevertheless, the fact of his participation in the Washington conference and the presentation of his views in a high-level international forum represents an encouraging step forward in the necessary Western dialogue on cultural restitution issues with the Russian political elite.

While Ukraine was not involved with presentations in the panels on art issues, Russia was well represented. Valerii Kulishov from the Russian Ministry of Culture expressed his doubt that art from Jewish Holocaust victims in the West would be found in Russia: "Everything that either disappeared or was not found in the American Zone should be sought in the West. It is unlikely that these works could have found their way to the East." He nevertheless affirmed Russia's readiness to participate in establishing a database on art confiscated from Holocaust victims, and assured conference participants that the archives in Russia were open.[49]

In a subsequent session, Konstantin Akinsha, the Ukrainian art specialist who helped expose the Russian secret repositories, took strong issue with Kulishov's claim "that Russian archives are open to researchers. It is not true," Akinsha retorted. "They are even more closed than in the beginning of the 90s." Akinsha proceeded to enumerate a number of examples of Jewish cultural property still held in Russian special depositories. While he welcomed Kulishov's commitment to Russian participation in an international database, he called upon Russia to open its art depositories to foreign specialists and to reveal its captured archives from Nazi and other Western

---

[48]   Nikolai Gubenko in *Washington Conference, 1998,* pp. 513–18.

[49]   Valerii D. Kulishov, addressing the Plenary Session on Nazi-Confiscated Art Issues, in *Washington Conference, 1998,* pp. 559–63. Kulishov has since left the Ministry of Culture and is now working with an independent, Western-funded Holocaust foundation in Moscow.

sources, which "could be of great help for the researchers working to create databases of looted art."[50] The extent to which the Russian delegation announced its intent for active cooperation "in resolving outstanding issues related to Holocaust-era art" was particularly welcome to the American conference organizers, and the extent to which the Russian delegation pledged to increase archival openness was likewise encouraging, as Eizenstat commented in several statements.[51]

Criticism of some of the Russian statements, however, also came from the press. Moscow was inviting "victims of the Nazis to reclaim their looted art," but as one art commentator remarked, "the Russians have revealed only a fraction of what they have in their depositories...How many Holocaust victims will still be alive to file a claim by the time the Russians complete their list of loot?"[52] Aside from this, Russia's first priority has been to compile an accurate list of their own losses, and they are having great difficulties even with that, as revealed by Nikolai Nikandrov, another key representative of the Ministry of Culture.[53]

Displaced archives and library books were raised in the conference as well, but those issues became auxiliary to the research needs for the other displaced Holocaust-era assets more centrally under consideration. The International Council on Archives (ICA), the International Federation of Library Associations (IFLA), and UNESCO all were *not* invited to send representatives. The former Archivist of the Netherlands, Eric Ketelaar, spoke about the need for archival access, and especially information access, and described a new research guide to archival sources for research on Holocaust-era just published in the Netherlands. In discussing research problems involved for Holocaust-era assets, he—diplomatically—did not even mention the many displaced Dutch archives still held in Moscow.[54]

Nazi confiscations in Soviet lands were predominantly from state institutions and hence, in terms of the conference focus, also appeared more

---

[50]   Konstantin Akinsha, addressing the "Break-Out Session on Nazi-Confiscated Art Issues," in *Washington Conference, 1998*, pp. 543–46.

[51]   For example, Stuart E. Eizenstat, in op. cit., pp. 415–16.

[52]   Sylvia Hochfield, "The Russian Surprise: Moscow Invites Victims of the Nazis to Reclaim their Looted Art. But Who Exactly is a Victim?" *ARTNews* 98(1) January 1999: 56.

[53]   Nikolai Nikandrov, "Russia," *Spoils of War: International Newsletter* 6 (February 1999): 50–52.

[54]   Eric Ketelaar, "Understanding Archives of the People, by the People, and for the People," in *Washington Conference, 1998*, pp. 749–61.

remote from "Holocaust-Era Assets." In fact, very little art or other "communal" assets were confiscated from individual Holocaust victims in Russia and eastern Ukraine, given the comprehensive nationalization of private and communal assets (including those of religious communities) before the Nazi invasion. As was clear in all of the conference presentations from Russia and Ukraine, displaced Holocaust-era assets must be seen in a broader context, because Jews were rarely the direct victims in the Nazi cultural looting that took place in Soviet lands. However, the resolution of such problems from the Eastern Front territories cannot be accomplished without also involving the foreign cultural treasures recently nationalized in Russia, together with the archives of many nations that may hold clues to the resolution of transfers and claims. In addition to the long-hidden art already mentioned, many archives taken to the USSR after the war had been earlier confiscated by the Nazis from other countries, and many of them also were from Jewish sources.

The conference did not deal with many critical cultural losses and "restitution" issues, such as came into focus at the New York "Spoils of War" symposium. The organizers had sought to avoid the type of Cold War confrontations between Russia and Germany that had characterized the New York gathering. That led to considerable criticism of the closed nature of the conference—the influential *Art Newspaper* reported it to be "closed to the press, to Holocaust victims, and to many recognized experts on art restitution."[55] The conference proceedings, however, were published within a half of a year and in multiple formats, as noted above.

The "Washington Conference Principles on Nazi-Confiscated Art" were set forth as a cornerstone conference achievement by Eizenstat, who personally provided a key "moral force" behind the Conference and made appropriate statements in many of the sessions. Because the principles are narrowly limited to "Nazi-confiscated art," they cannot help us in dealing with many of the other displaced cultural treasures in Russia and Ukraine.

---

[55] David D'Arcy, "Report on the Washington Conference on Holocaust Era Assets: Much Piety and Hot Air," *The Art Newspaper*, no. 88 (January 1999): 3. D'Arcy's subhead: "No binding agreements were reached and little effect on restitution is expected," reinforced his view that the conference "is expected to have little effect on the processes of art restitution internationally," especially given its insular nature. I can attest to way in which the conference was closed: Although invited to participate in the planning session and official opening at the Holocaust Museum, and a participant in the related archival symposium at the National Archives, I was refused a pass for any of the conference sessions at the State Department.

Yet, notably, they are not limited to art owned by "victims of the Holocaust," thereby broadening the extent to which they could be serviceable in Russia and Ukraine with regard to displaced cultural treasures generally, including archives. Particularly crucial were the points—with Eizenstat's supporting statements—on the underlying need for more open access to relevant archival information and the need for international databases.[56] Deliberations at the conference and conversations in the corridors on these and related issues thus did provide an important international diplomatic forum for some of the important cultural restitution issues under consideration here.

The Washington conference organizers were pushing for faster solutions, but it likely will take many more decades before the conference goals, particularly with respect to restitution of Nazi-confiscated art and archives, and archival openness, can be implemented, especially in Ukraine and Russia. Nevertheless, given the high-level diplomatic status of the conference and the participation of so many countries, it represents an important milestone in the context of our discussion. And it is to be hoped that the "Holocaust-Era" focus it provided might prove to be one more avenue on the international political front for approaching the goals of locating and identifying displaced cultural treasures and their appropriate restitution.

Displaced Art versus Displaced Archives

American conference organizers and those drafting the "Declarations" and "Principles" understandably paid little heed to the Nazi-confiscated art and archives now held in the United States. Yet two symbolic examples, both of which came up at the time of the Washington conference, show some of the complexities of displaced cultural treasures and claims amidst the international "politics" of restitution.

A Ukrainian Component of the "Smolensk Archive" from Kyiv. In the same building of the U.S. National Archives where the post-conference symposium on "Records and Research Regarding Holocaust-Era Assets" was held, over 500 "Smolensk Archive" files have long been prepared for their

---

[56] "Washington Conference Principles on Nazi-Confiscated Art," *Washington Conference, 1998*, pp. 971–72. See also Stuart E. Eizenstat, "Concluding Statement," in *Washington Conference, 1998*, pp. 125–32; and idem, "Explanation of the Washington Conference Principles on Nazi-Confiscated Art," ibid., pp. 415–20; "Art Databases and Archives," pp. 421–23; and "Archival Openness," pp. 429–31.

return to their archival home. Although these were not taken from Holocaust victims, they have become a symbolic legacy of wartime archival displacements. As noted earlier, their status was emphasized by Russian legislators to justify the non-restitution of French archives in 1994. Interestingly enough, those files in Washington known as the "Smolensk Archive" also contain a group of files identified as having been seized by the Nazis from the Institute of Jewish Proletarian Culture in Kyiv. Even if American politicians are not now prepared to return the "Smolensk Archive" to Smolensk, at least that small group of symbolic files should be returned to Ukraine.[57] There can be no question about their provenance; although the institute that created them no longer exists, other parts of those records are held by the National Academy of Sciences of Ukraine in Kyiv.

A Symbolic Dürer Drawing from Lviv. The Washington conference also was not prepared to deal with East European claims for art treasures that have ended up in the United States. Yet that subject was very much on the agenda of the Ukrainian delegation. On the eve of the Washington, DC, Conference on Displaced Holocaust-Era Assets, the director of the Stefanyk Library in Lviv, Larysa Krushel'nyts'ka, faxed a claim to the National Galley of Art for "Male Nude," one of the Albrecht Dürer drawings that Hitler's personal envoy, Kajetan Muhlmann, had seized from Lviv in July 1941, a few days after the Nazi invasion.[58] During their visit to Washington, the Ukrainian delegation to the Conference followed up with an appeal to the State Department for assistance in supporting the Ukrainian claim. The State Department recommended that they hire an attorney and seek legal remediation through the courts.[59]

---

[57] See Grimsted, *The Odyssey of the Smolensk Archive: Plundered Communist Records for the Service of Anti-Communism* (Pittsburgh, 1995) [=Carl Beck Papers in East European Studies, 1201]. I presented a formal plea to U.S. Vice President Albert Gore and Archivist of the U.S. John Carlin that strongly recommended reconsideration of this matter. An answer dated 9 April 1997, signed by Vice President Gore gave no tangible encouragement to the resolution of the restitution dilemma. A reply from Carlin suggested more willingness to pursue the matter, but since then there has been no progress.

[58] The act of confiscation signed by Muhlmann (2 July 1941) is reproduced in Matwijów, *Walka o lwowskie dobra kultury*, p. 29.

[59] D'Arcy, "Report on the Washington Conference," p. 3, notes "The Ukrainian delegation came to Washington to further its efforts to trace and recover drawings from the Lubomirski Collection," but that "Mr. Eizenstat's response to the Ukrainian bid for his help was not altogether in the spirit of the conference, at

Before 1939, the drawing, along with 23 others, had been part of the Dürer collection that had a place of honor in the Lubomirski Museum, which had been bequeathed to the city of Lviv in 1866 by the Lubomirski family "for the benefit of the Polish nation," as an auxiliary of the Ossolineum cultural center.[60] Hitler had a special interest in the Lviv Dürer drawings, as a representative masterpieces of the German national tradition, and kept them with him throughout the war. The drawings were sequestered in the Alt Ausee salt mine in the Austrian Tyrol at the end of the war, where they were found by American Army art specialists and taken to the Munich Collecting Point, one of the U.S. art restitution centers.

Prince Georg Lubomirski, having himself escaped to Switzerland, claimed the Dürer drawings, because the terms of the family donation in Lviv had been abrogated when Soviet authorities had abolished the Lubomirski Museum, nationalized the Polish collections after the annexation of western Ukraine to the USSR in 1939, and turned the Dürer drawings over to the newly established Library of the Academy of Sciences of the Ukrainian SSR. According to the 1866 deed of bequest, the family was to retain some hereditary rights as the "literary collectors" of the Lubomirski Museum, and if those rights were abrogated, the collections were to revert to the eldest male heir. Following considerable State Department investigation, Lubomirski won his appeal to American authorities. Although Lubomirski had told American authorities he would offer the collection to the National Gallery in Washington, he was not legally bound to do so. He later sold the Dürer drawings at auction in London and New York, and they were dispersed in various museums in Great Britain and the United States.[61]

---

which participants were urged to seek alternatives to litigation...In a letter, Mr. Eizenstat offered his advice to the Ukrainians vis-à-vis American museums: 'get a lawyer.'" That response has been confirmed to me by one of the Ukrainian delegates, who was quite surprised at the State Department attitude.

[60] See the catalog of the collection by Mieczysław Gębarowicz and Hans Tietze, *Albrecht Durers Zeichnungen im Lubomirskimuseum in Lemberg* (Vienna: A. Schroll, 1929), presented in a folio edition with reproductions of all 24 drawings. See also the article by H. S. Reitlinger, "An Unknown Collection of Durer Drawings," *Burlington Magazine for Connoisseurs* (London), March, 1927, pp. 153–55, which includes plates with reproductions of nine of the drawings and brief descriptions of the rest. See also Stepan Kostiuk and Vita Susak, "L′vivs′ka kolektsiia rysunkiv Al′brekhta Diurera," *Halyts′ka brama* 12(36) (December 1998): 11.

[61] The drawings themselves subsequently became pawns on the international art market and helped support the lifestyle of the displaced Polish aristocrat, who

The Dürer masterpieces will undoubtedly remain cultural ambassadors of the German Renaissance in museums around the world, although more lawyers may well benefit from efforts to reclaim them. As *Washington Post* correspondent Michael Dobbs phrased it recently, in what has been to date the most thorough investigation of the case:

> ...it is unlikely that any of the Lubomirski Durers, "Male Nude" included, will ever be pried away from American and European museums through legal action. But the secrecy surrounding the Durers' restitution and the complexity of the legal issues involved guarantee continuing controversy.[62]

At that time no formal claim for any of the drawings had been filed by Poland on behalf of the Ossolineum, which was reestablished in Wrocław. Noticeably, as is normal in the case of works of art, since the time of Hitler's seizure there has been no claim from Germany as the country of provenance. The National Gallery did not mention Adolf Hitler as one of the previous possessors, when the "Male Nude" was last displayed in 1997. Even if a Western museum that purchased and preserved it were prepared to bargain for compensation for any of the Dürers' return to Lviv, the Stefanyk Library has insufficient funds to ransom even one of the drawings, let alone pay the legal fees involved.

The U.S. State Department's suggestion that Ukraine should "hire an attorney" if it wanted pursue the "Male Nude," should have been no surprise to the conference delegation from Ukraine. It was the State Department in

---

retired to the French Riviera. Among the recent investigations of the case, see David D'Arcy, "Hitler, The Prince, and the Dürers," *The Art Newspaper* 47 (April 1995): 1, 6; and Martin Bailey, "The Lubomirski Durers: Where Are They Now?" *The Art Newspaper* 48 (May 1995): 5; Bailey gives the locations of all the drawings now in public collections, except for the one in the National Gallery of Art in Washington, DC, and mentions the titles of those in private hands and cities where they are located. D'Arcy concluded with the quoted opinion of U.S. art restitution officer Bernard Taper, "it was quite wrong not to return the Dürers to Lviv," suggesting that politics had intervened in the U.S. decision to turn the Dürer drawings over to Prince Lubomirski. There is no question about the growing Cold War politics of the decision, but the recent article by Michael Dobbs takes a more realistic position, "Stolen Beauty: Hitler Looted an Albrecht Durer Masterpiece; It Ended Up at the National Gallery of Art. But Where It Really Belongs Is Now in Dispute," *Washington Post Magazine* 21 March 1999: 12–18, 29.

[62] Dobbs, "Stolen Beauty," p. 29.

1949 that had decided, in secret, in favor of the Lubomirski claim. Besides, in the art world today, claims for individual works of art in the West are traditionally being handled in the courts, and not through diplomatic channels. Although the claim came from a Ukrainian state institution and could not be considered a "Holocaust" victim, clearly the drawings do constitute "Nazi-confiscated art," in the terms of the Conference "Principles." More recently the matter has been referred to the National Archives and the newly appointed Presidential Advisory Commission on Holocaust-Era Assets.

In fact, later in 1999, J. D. Bindenagel, who then held the rank of ambassador in the U.S. Department of State for dealing with Holocaust-Era Assets, raised the issue of the Ukrainian claim to the "Male Nude" in a more serious vein: "Ukraine asserts that the city of Lviv was the rightful owner of the drawings rather than the prince, because the Lubomirski family had earlier donated the drawings to the city." However, there is no mention in a published journalistic account of the pronouncement that there were "strings attached" to the donation, including explicitly Polish-oriented ones, nor that Soviet authorities following annexation of western Ukraine to the Ukrainian SSR, nationalized and abolished the Lubomirski Museum in Lviv. Quite appropriately, further legal and "provenance" research on the issue is under way in Washington and elsewhere. And now, according to this account, there is a formal claim from the Ossolineum in Wrocław.[63]

The examples of the "twice-seized" "Smolensk Archive" and the "twice-displaced" Dürer drawing—and the Ukrainian claim for it—thus further show the extent to which cultural restitution issues as they affect East Central and Eastern Europe, and especially the successor States of the former USSR such as Ukraine, need to be understood and dealt with in a broader international context. These two examples also make clear the differentiation needed in dealing with issues of displaced archives and art.

Beyond the New York and Washington Conferences

Washington Conference Fallout. A year has passed since the Washington Conference, and it is clear that, even if in Russia there has been no progress on declassification in Communist Party archives, there may be even more fallout than might initially have been expected. The presentation of the Russian nationalization law and the extent of public support for it in Russia,

---

[63]   See Martin Bailey, "Growing Unease over Lubomirski Dürers," *The Art Newspaper* 93 (June 1999): 3.

as emphasized by Nikolai Gubenko, was confirmed with the Russian Constitutional Count decision upholding the law in July of 1999. Yet there is now more optimism in the West about the possibilities of identification of the extensive trophy art, and other cultural treasures, in the former USSR. Although opinions differ as to how many trophy cultural treasures in Russia may have come from Holocaust victims, there is a new commitment to their description, both in Russia and abroad.

A new blue-ribbon U.S. Presidential Commission on Holocaust-Era Assets has created more public attention and research funds. There appears now to be extensive non-governmental funding in connection with "Holocaust-era assets," which promises to aid location and cataloging of trophy art and other cultural valuables in Russia. Perhaps the increased monetary incentives will encourage Russian officials to open still-classified archives and still-closed trophy storage collections. In such ways, the search for "Holocaust-era assets" may indeed promote description and cataloguing of all trophy art and archives in Russia and Ukraine.

For those of us working recently on the ground with the repositories in Russia and Ukraine that hold the often "twice-plundered" cultural treasures, including books and archives (which many of their post-Soviet holders still consider to have been "twice-saved"), there is a long, rocky road ahead in terms of the identification and assignment of provenance. Before even preliminary migration routes can be determined, it will be difficult in many cases to determine provenance and/or previous ownership, and even more difficult to know if those treasures may have come initially from Holocaust victims. With trophy archives, identification and assignment of provenance is usually tantamount to assigning original ownership to the country of origin (i.e., the creation of the records). But that is hardly the case for paintings or pianos. Nevertheless, more professional archival description could mean more open access to the clues about the migration and present locations of all displaced cultural treasures.

The most important cultural treasure to be revealed this past year in Ukraine is actually a collection of archival materials (although not official state records). The Sing-Akademie Collection in Kyiv is a trophy German private collection that has nothing to do with Jewish or "Holocaust-era assets." Yet since its "rediscovery" in Kyiv, funding has already been assured by foreign sources for its professional description and for preservation microfilming. No known Jewish-related cultural treasures have surfaced in Kyiv, and it is unlikely that they will, because most of them were removed to Moscow long ago. The Ukrainian delegation to Washington was notably silent in terms of cooperation in uncovering Nazi-seized cultural treasures in Ukraine. Yet, despite a lack of data, it remains possible that some art from German private collections still in Kyiv may have been in Jewish possession before the war. Indeed, not even a preliminary inventory of what trophy art remains in Kyiv has been made public, and the reports about it sent to Moscow during the Soviet regime are still classified in former Communist Party archives.

Since data about trophy books presently located in Ukraine are also not available, there is no way of determining if any of them came from Western Jewish sources. Given our knowledge of movements of Jewish-related library collections during the war, however, that is unlikely. If any are of Jewish provenance, then certainly there are not any such collections in significant quantities. In terms of archives, lists have surfaced for Jewish holdings brought to Kyiv, but the relatively limited numbers of files from West European Jewish sources that came to Ukraine after the war were, as far as is known, transferred to Moscow in the 1950s—with one symbolic exception. Confirmation about the destruction in Kyiv in 1953 of fragmentary trophy documentation from Jewish communities in France that came to Kyiv with the Rosenberg (ERR) records is first appearing in print in this volume (see Chapter 9), but that represented only 150 kilograms out of the approximately more than 40 tons of ERR documents received. There are no further indications that any other archives from Holocaust victims were found in Ukraine, nor other foreign trophy archives other than occupation records of the Nazi regime.

Revival of the 1995 New York Conference Principles. While the non-binding "Washington Conference Principles on Nazi-Confiscated Art" are gaining at least verbal "consensus" in the endorsements of many countries, they are noticeably limited to art, and they are limited to "Nazi-Confiscated Art," thus excluding by definition much of the "captured" or trophy art now in the former Soviet Union, most of which has yet to be identified as to provenance and previous ownership. Hence, for dealing with issues covered here, these principles still need to be supplemented by broader principles to include other types of cultural treasures and those captured by other countries during and after the war. And there are still somewhat variant specific points that need to be dealt with in identifying and providing for the restitution of displaced archives.

While the United States still refuses to resume participation in UNESCO, many European countries, and especially Ukraine and others in Eastern Europe look to that international forum for assistance and hope in the resolution of questions of "restitution" or "return" in connection with displaced cultural treasures. Yet the successive resolutions passed by UNESCO and the United Nations on that issue have brought no concrete results. As a new positive step on the international front, in January 1999, UNESCO issued a report and updated version of the "Principles for the

Resolution of Disputes Concerning Cultural Heritage Displaced during the
Second World War," enunciated at the 1995 New York symposium by
international cultural property lawyer Lyndel Prott.[64]

A conference is being organized in spring 2000 to discuss these "Principles," which are now being considered for adoption by the Council of
Europe.[65] Earlier chapters have shown the problems that arise from lack of
international principles and accepted procedures for dealing with these issues,
so such a prospect represents another positive step in resolving some of the
still-pending issues involved.

The UNESCO "Principles" are not limited to art, and they differ in a
number of points from the "Washington Conference Principles." The
UNESCO principles are intended to apply beyond "Nazi-confiscated Art" to
those items "seized" or "saved" by other countries. Given the extensive, still
unresolved issues of displaced cultural treasures on the Eastern Front
stemming from the war, this might be the occasion to consider the two
formulations together and seek an integration with important points to be
added from each. For example, the Washington "Principles" include a point
calling for open access to archives (not included in the UNESCO principles),
even mentioning that access should be "in accordance with the guidelines of
the International Council on Archives." Such a principle regarding public
access to archives and related other scientific information about displaced
cultural treasures might well be considered for addition to the UNESCO
principles. Since the "Washington Conference Principles" are not entirely
applicable to the situation in Eastern Europe, since they do not embrace all
cultural treasures (rather, only art), and since they are limited to "Nazi-
confiscated" ones, they are not adequate for the present situation in Eastern
Europe. The UNESCO principles, while broader in scope, could at least help
fill that gap.

Neither of the formulations are fully adequate for displaced archives.

---

[64] Intergovernmental Committee for Promoting the Return of Cultural Property
to its Countries of Origin or its Restitution in Case of Illicit Appropriation,
"Principles for the Resolution of Disputes Concerning Cultural Heritage
Displaced during the Second World War" (Paris: UNESCO, 1999) (CLT-
99/CONF.203/2). The publication, growing out of the Tenth Session of the
Committee (Paris, 25–28 January 1999), now posted on the UNESCO website,
includes an updated report on developments (although with no mention of the
Washington Conference) and recommendations that the Committee consider
adopting the Principles, with citations to appropriate earlier international legal
instruments.

[65] That development was reported to me by Lyndel Prott.

Given the still extensive displaced archives on the Eastern Front stemming from the war, this might also be the occasion for the ICA to formulate its own a set of "principles" that might better apply to archives. Alternatively, the UNESCO Committee might try, with the cooperation of the ICA, to include wording that would extend the relevance of its Principles to archives as well.

A spring 2000 conference on displaced cultural treasures and their identification is being planned in Moscow. Rather than a diplomatic forum, such as the one in Washington, it is being hosted by the All-Russian State Library of Foreign Literature (VGBIL), with emphasis on the books that have not yet gone home from the wars. Perhaps such a stage in Russia itself will be able to provide additional—less official and less political—input to discussions in an international context. Perhaps it can serve to bring Russians and Germans together again on the cultural front, with new strides in the identification of cultural treasures that still remain as "prisoners of war." And perhaps it can provide in broader perspective a counterpart and continuation of the strides made by previous conferences over the past decade, in addressing international issues of displaced cultural treasures, including those "twice plundered" and those "twice saved."

Conclusion

Consideration of the archival heritage of Ukraine and archives displaced during World War II has come full circle. We have seen in the final chapter the positive international effects of Ukrainian policy of restitution vis-à-vis Germany, as opposed to the more negative effects of the Russian policy of non-restitution. The broader international context of a series of conferences during the 1990s brought Ukraine into contact with other countries and allowed Ukrainian specialists to discuss issues of displaced cultural treasures and restitution and to help shape principles arising from those discussions. Émigré Ukrainian communities in the diaspora have been enthusiastically transferring archival materials and other cultural treasures to the newly independent Ukrainian homeland.

Devolution Following the Succession of States. Meanwhile, as a successor State to the USSR, Ukraine remains closely affected by the problems of displaced archives and other cultural treasures in Russia itself. The most important considerations for Ukraine relating to potential claims against Russia are the international legal precedents relating to the succession of States and those relating to redrawn national frontiers. But unlike other post-imperial accommodations in the course of the twentieth century, there was no archival devolution following the "fall" of the Soviet empire. With state debts, energy demands, and jockeying over the Black Sea Fleet all stealing the diplomatic and political limelight, cultural restitution issues were pushed aside during most of the 1990s. The only example of cultural "restitution" is symbolic: as I write this, Ukraine is slated to receive a few (but not the most important) frescoes or mosaics from St. Michael's Cathedral of the Golden Domes—a first for successor States to the USSR. In terms of archival transfers, there has been only a single, private arrangement for purchase of the "leftovers" of the archival legacy of the Ukrainian film director Oleksandr Dovzhenko.

Issues of appropriate archival devolution for independent Ukraine have not generally become a substantial political or diplomatic issue. In those cases where they have, they have become intertwined in the public mind and in politics with more specific international issues of restitution of displaced cultural treasures resulting from World War II and its aftermath. Restitution issues with Russia are further complicated by foreign reaction to the new Russian law nationalizing cultural "trophies," and fallout from the Russian policy of non-restitution to the European Community. Indeed the juxta-position of these issues greatly complicates the potential resolution of archival devolution in the post-Soviet environment. The two different parts of my analysis may have demonstrated their own inner logic—and understanding their interrelated issues requires a practical level of analysis of the two problems in turn—but they can remain separate only on a theoretical level.

Restitution—or devolution—of post-imperial archives in Eastern Europe became a major issue within the international archival community with the collapse of the Austro-Hungarian Empire and the Russian Empire after the First World War. Then, with the collapse of colonial empires after the Second World War, archival devolution became a major issue for former colonial powers of Western Europe, with a supportive role from the International Council of Archives. After the collapse of the Soviet Empire and federated states such as Czechoslovakia and Yugoslavia, the ICA—although its leadership was aware of the pending problems—was not in a position to interject itself. Archival devolution was handled only on an internal or bilateral basis. It was handled professionally and smoothly in the case of Czechoslovakia, while in the post-Soviet case, it was not handled at all.

World War II Displaced Archives and the Restitution Component for Ukraine. Only at the time of the collapse of the USSR did the extent of captured records "remaining on the Eastern Front" become known in the West. "Five Days in the 'Special Archive'" hit the headlines in February 1990, but it was a year and a half before the director of the Osobyi Arkhiv admitted the existence of the captured West European records that were still held there. It was only then that the ICA took up the issue of displaced European archives, and the issue of archival transfers appropriate to the succession of States became merged with issues of restitution of archives that had still not gone home from the wars.

While we started with an emphasis on defining the legitimate archival heritage of newly independent Ukraine, discussion of specific war-related examples and their international context has been important for a number of reasons:

First, Ukraine is currently negotiating with several countries, including Germany and Poland, regarding archives and other cultural treasures displaced as a result of the war and its legacy.

Second, Ukraine still hopes to determine the fate, and see the restitution, of Nazi-seized cultural treasures that were returned to the USSR but that did not come back to Ukraine. Opening of long-secret Soviet records are essential to this process, but the new Russian law creates substantial complications.

Third, although Kyiv took a secondary role to Moscow in the Soviet archival seizures after the war, some displaced archival Ucrainica in Russia resulted from wartime or immediate postwar seizures by Soviet authorities, and contingent files from integral record groups or archival collections are now split between Moscow and Kyiv.

Fourth, Nazi records now held in Kyiv, like others now displaced in Moscow, are important for tracing migration and identifying plundered cultural treasures from many European countries besides Ukraine. These remain prime candidates for further professional finding aids and microfilming to increase their availability to the international community.

Fifth, while Ukraine without question suffered proportionately more cultural losses during the war than Russia, its share of the Soviet "spoils of war" was very limited. Now with Russian nationalization, Ukraine has little or nothing to say about the fate of the vast cultural treasures of foreign countries captured by Soviet authorities that remain in the Russian Federation and are subject to the provisions of the new 1998 Russian law.

Sixth, the fate of wartime captured records held in Russia and other former republics of the USSR has been politically linked to the retrieval of archival Rossica (and, potentially, Ucrainica) abroad, but Ukraine has no voice in such negotiations.

Seventh, most of the politically sensitive Ukrainian émigré archival materials from the former Czechoslovakia, Poland, and other European countries now held in Kyiv that were seized by Soviet authorities for "operational" purposes during or soon after the war—still have not been appropriately described and opened for scholarship. Nor have the appropriate microfilms been made available to the countries of their provenance. In many cases integral collections have been fragmented, and files remain split between Kyiv and Moscow.

Eighth, Ukrainian discussion of wartime displacements is linked in the public mind to the broader discussion of the identification of parts of the Ukrainian archival heritage held in Russia—as has been evident in presentations and public reaction in recent conferences devoted to World War II displacements held in Ukraine.

Diversion of Potential Archival Claims from Russia. Since the revelations in 1990 and 1991 about the long-secret Russian depositories of trophy cultural treasures brought to the USSR in the wake of World War II, attention on international restitution issues that arise from the Soviet period has diverted attention from prospective claims or restitution issues in connection with the succession of States after the break-up of the Soviet Union. Russian preoccupation with the explosive political issues, diplomatic complications, legal technicalities, and other problems of restitution or non-restitution of foreign cultural treasures held in Russia has both overshadowed and become entangled with issues of potential restitution to successor States, including Ukraine. Furthermore, Russian attitudes with respect to non-restitution of records of foreign countries captured during and in the aftermath of World War extend to the non-restitution of records seized and/or transferred to the metropolis from former territories of the Russian and Soviet empires.

Despite any increase in the accessibility of Russian archives, there has been no concomitant progress in restitution of archival materials seized from former republics. Neither has there been adequate advance in the restitution of those archival materials of provenance in foreign countries seized in the wake of World War II—and there is only minimal progress in their identification. Since the collapse of the Soviet Union, as we saw in the first chapter, Russia considers itself the heir to virtually all archival records and manuscript collections remaining on the territory of the Russian Federation, and most specifically all those that were created or collected by Soviet authorities and those nationalized from the Russian Empire before it. The 1992 agreement signed by the heads of CIS archival authorities, ratifies that position.

Russian archival authorities, nonetheless, have assured Ukraine that they are open to archival claims on a bilateral basis. As of mid-1999, however, there have been no formal archival claims on behalf of Ukraine to Russia and no serious bilateral discussion of possible devolution. A bilateral agreement on cultural cooperation and exchange was signed between the Russian Federation and Ukraine on 26 March 1994 in which the somewhat contested fifth article obliges cooperation in the return of lost or illegally displaced cultural treasures.[1] It is likely that the Russian side or Russian courts would consider virtually all "removals" by imperial Russian or Soviet authorities "legal" under the terms of that article, so neither that agreement nor the subsequent cultural agreement of 26 July 1995 provides any help in the matter of "restitution" or "devolution" in the case of the succession of States. The July 1995 agreement does provide for mutual access to state archival, library, and museum holdings, although there are no provisions covering the identification of displaced cultural treasures, or access to otherwise still classified documentation.[2] The possibility of retrieving parts of the Ukrainian national cultural and archival legacy now held in Russia is also not

[1]   "Uhoda pro kul′turne spivrobitnytstvo mizh Ministerstvom kul′tury Rossiis′koï Federatsiï ta Ministerstvom kul′tury Ukraïny" (14 May 1994), in *Ukraïna v mizhnarodno-pravovykh vidnosynakh,* bk. 2, pp. 523–28.

[2]   "Uhoda mizh Uriadom Ukraïny ta Uriadom Rossiis′koï Federatsiï pro spivrobitnytstvo v haluzi kul′tury, nauky i osvity" (26 July 1995), in *Ukraïna v mizhnarodno-pravovykh vidnosynakh,* bk. 2, pp. 528–29.

mentioned in the 1998 treaty between Ukraine and Russia, nor in the 1998 Ukrainian-Russian agreement on archival cooperation.[3]

Deficiencies of Archival Reference Work. Our treatment of Ukrainian restitution issues with Poland has revealed yet another example where professional archival description is needed for such an essential component of the archival heritage of Ukraine as those manuscripts, groups of archival records, and personal papers from the Ossolineum that remain in Lviv. In Lviv in the nineteenth century, wealthy Polish aristocrats donated their art, manuscript collections, and their archives to the city. Public support led to the type of professional description provided by manuscript scholars such as Wojciech Kętrzyński in the late nineteenth century and cultural luminaries such as Mieczysław Gębarowicz in the interwar period, with resulting intellectual access to the priceless cultural legacy in western Ukraine.[4] While international interest and foreign funding has motivated archival reference publications in Russia since 1991, professional archival reference work has come to a virtual standstill in Ukraine. Even in the case of the Ossolineum, as we saw earlier, those surveys that have appeared were prepared in Poland, not Ukraine.

Lack of archival reference work since 1991 has also prevented intellectual access in Ukraine to much of the sensational émigré archival Ucrainica that was seized for anti-Ukrainian surveillance and other Soviet "operational" purposes after World War II. In Ukraine today, a high priority and much public attention is being given to the retrieval and restitution from abroad of archival Ucrainica to the newly independent Ukrainian homeland. But at the same time archives retrieved 50 years ago from Prague and other points in Europe remain displaced for the nation, because they are not professionally preserved or described, and are not publicly accessible.

Archives Should Go Home from the War. As has been made clear in presenting international legal traditions in earlier chapters, the case for restitution (and revindication) of archives is even stronger than for art. Paintings or sculpture may appropriately serve as cultural ambassadors in

---

[3]   The December 1998 archival agreement between Russia and Ukraine has not yet been published, and a copy was not available to me for consultation (see Chapter 1, p. 40n36).

[4]   See, for example, the Kętrzyński catalog cited in Chapter 11, p. 436n29 and the Gębarowicz catalog of the Dürer drawings and the Pawlikowski Collection as part of the Ossolineum cited above, Chapter 11, p. 430n17; and Chapter 12, p. 482n60.

museums throughout the world, but archives always deserve restitution to the countries where they belong as the official record, and the inalienable heritage of nations that created them. Archives have no place on the auction blocks and the black and gray markets of the art world, although the commercial value of charters and autographs may also make them likely targets. The Sokolov files purchased at Sotheby's to exchange with Russia for the trophy Liechtenstein archive are a clear example of this.

The long-term political and historiographic consequences of displaced archives are much greater than that of their artistic fellow prisoners. Like the Ossolineum collections in Lviv and the NTSh archives in Warsaw, most of the displaced foreign archives still held in Moscow have been withdrawn from the world of scholarship and culture for half a century. Lost letters from Beneš, Sikorski, or Petliura and the UNR regime, or the displaced records of French Jewish communities annihilated by the Nazis in the Holocaust are no less important to historians than the long-suppressed Auschwitz construction files, and long-hidden files from the Reich Foreign Office.

Equally significant to the European historical record—and even more significant to the retrieval of displaced cultural treasures and archives—are the Nazi records in Moscow and Kyiv that describe their cultural plunder, such as the RSHA Berlin archival accession register for receipts of files from the Sûreté Nationale and Ukrainian émigré organizations pilfered in Paris; and the Heeresarchiv reports of military archival seizures throughout Ukraine and other former Soviet lands, as well as Poland and other European countries. Of special importance in this regard are the ERR files in Kyiv, which even include seizure reports from Belgian Masonic lodges (some with drawings and inventories), plans of the Silesian castle rented by the Nazis to house the Sonderstab Musik with trophy music collections that were seized in France and other countries from Holocaust victims (and now presumed to be in Russia), along with extensive reports of ERR operations throughout the former USSR and the Balkans. The ERR records in Kyiv, alas, still are sewn together out of order in hastily prepared file units. Many of them are incorrectly or inadequately labeled and described. Other ERR fragmentary files are divided between Moscow, Riga, and Paris. These records all urgently need to be reunited (at least in copy) with the other major part of the ERR records, that are appropriately held in the Bundesarchiv in Berlin (earlier Koblenz), after their return to Germany in 1963 from the U.S. National Archives. Until that time, the appropriate contextual analysis of these materials remains exceedingly difficult. Moreover, until they are professionally arranged and described, the facts and clues they contain about the displacement of archives and other cultural treasures during and after the war will remain hidden from the world.

Many other groups of records that constitute the legitimate archival heritage of Ukraine remain in Moscow and St. Petersburg. An appropriate mechanism has not yet been devised for their restitution or devolution, while the Russian Federation has declared itself the legal heir to all records and manuscript collections of the entire Soviet Union that proceeded it. In that connection our theoretical concerns to define the archival heritage of Ukraine, and examples of the types of materials that remain outside of present Ukrainian territorial boundaries will still need practical implementation. An agenda is needed, particularly for potential archival claims from Russia. Given present political realities, though, such claims will likely remain theoretical, at least in the foreseeable future.

Professional archivists throughout the world, as evidenced in the ICA Round Table Conference in Thessalonica in 1994, are committed to professional standards, and most agree that archives—as the remaining official record and unique heritage of nations—should be returned to the countries of their provenance and should not be treated as "trophies" or objects of exchange. Despite this, in Russia today millions of files from all over the European Continent are trapped by politicians in the twin metropolises of the former Russian and Soviet empires, where they were brought together far from their homes. These files remain prisoners due to the emotive legacy "in myth and memory" of those empires as well as the wars they fought.

Archives deserve to be liberated from the status of trophies of empire or prisoners of war, and not simply despite the fact that under imperial regimes—in wartime or Cold War—they may have served intelligence, political, or propaganda purposes. Nearly ten years have passed since Ukraine at last achieved independence, but its legitimate archival heritage remains intellectually and physically dispersed. Appropriate archival devolution or "restitution" from the capitals of empire have yet to find priority on the political agenda. And, on the home front, professional archival description of that dispersed heritage is still in its infancy.

Documentary Appendices

APPENDIX I

UNESCO. "Report of the Director-General on the Study of Problems Involved in the Transfer of Documents from Archives in the Territory of Certain Countries to the Country of their Origin" 25 August 1978 (20C/102). Original: English*

SUMMARY

In pursuance of the resolution 5.1 adopted by the General Conference at its nineteenth session and the Programme and Budget for 1977–1978 (paragraph 5048) approved by the General Conference at its same session, a detailed study was undertaken on the transfer of documents from archives in the territory of certain countries to the country of their origin.

In the light of this study, the Director-General has prepared, and hereby submits to the General Conference, the present report on the problems involved in the transfer of documents from archives in the territory of certain countries to the country of their origin. This report summarizes the conclusions and recommendations of the study and of a series of consultations with specialists on the problems involved in the transfer of such documents.

It contains a plan of action and a statement of principles and guidelines intended to facilitate negotiations and agreements between or among Member States in respect of matters concerning the transfer of archives.

Point for decision: paragraph 37.

---

* Also reproduced in *Dossier on Archival Claims,* pp. 25–32.

I. INTRODUCTION

1. At its eighteenth session the General Conference adopted 18 C/Resolution 4.212 by which it, inter alia, invited "Member States of Unesco to give favourable consideration to the possibility of transferring documents from archives constituted within the territory of other countries or relating to their history, within the framework of bilateral agreements". By the same resolution, the General Conference recommended that, "in consultation with the appropriate non-governmental organizations, the Director-General envisage the possibility of a detailed study of such transfers and that he inform the nineteenth session of the General Conference thereof".

2. In pursuance of this resolution, the Secretariat organized at Headquarters, from 16 to 18 March 1976, a consultation with a group of experts in order to have a preliminary exchange of experience and to obtain the views of specialists on this subject. The group of experts identified the main issues of the problem and recommended to the Director-General the need for a preliminary investigation of the issues before undertaking a detailed study.[1]

3. The Secretariat then requested the International Council on Archives to undertake a preliminary investigation, and the Director-General presented a progress report on these activities to the nineteenth session of the General Conference (document 19 C/94). Since the preliminary investigation[2] was expected to report favorably on the need for a detailed study of the question, the attention of the General Conference was directed to the intention of the Director-General, expressed in 19 C/5 (paragraph 5048), to prepare a follow-up action through a detailed study of the transfer of documents from archives in the territory of other countries to the country of their origin, the results of which would be communicated to the twentieth session of the General Conference.

4. Following approval of this proposal (19 C/5 Approved, paragraph 5048), the Secretariat asked the International Conference of the Round Table on

---

[1]   *Final Report* of the "Consultation group to prepare a report on the possibility of transferring documents from archives constituted within the territory of other countries, Paris, 16–18 March 1976," 1 April 1976 (Paris: UNESCO, 1976) (CC-76/WS/9.)

[2]   Charles Kecskeméti, *Archival Claims: Preliminary Study on the Principles and Criteria to be Applied to Negotiations* (Paris: UNESCO, 1977) (PGI 77/WS/1); published in English and French.

Archives for the detailed study.[3] The publication of the draft of this study was subsequently approved by the Secretariat for use as the working document for the Seventeenth Conference of the Round Table on Archives, which met in Cagliari 5–8 October 1977. To ensure adequate representation of the views of developing countries on this problem, the Secretariat through its subvention to the International Council on Archives provided financial assistance to the national archivists of a number of Member States so that they could participate in the Cagliari Round Table.

5, In concluding its follow-up action the Secretariat organized at Headquarters, from 29 to 31 March 1978, a second consultation with a group of experts to consider the conclusions and recommendations of the detailed study in light of the discussions and findings of the Cagliari Round Table, and to advise the Director-General on the nature of the report which he might wish to submit to the General Conference at its twentieth session.

6. This report summarizes the conclusions and recommendations of the preliminary and detailed studies and of a series of consultations with experts on problems involved in the transfer of archives. It relates these problems to the broader question of restitution of other types of cultural property, proposes a statement of principles and guidelines to facilitate negotiations and agreements between Member States in cases involving conflicting claims to archives, particularly after decolonization, and recommends a programme of international and national action to assist in the solution of these problems.

II. ARCHIVES AND CULTURAL PROPERTY

7. Archives are universally recognized as an essential part of the heritage of every national community. Since they are indispensable in the development of national awareness and identity, they constitute a basic part of the cultural property of States.

8. The inclusion of archives within the broad definition of cultural property is fully recognized. The "Convention on the means of prohibiting the illicit import, export, and transfer of ownership", adopted at its sixteenth session by the General Conference, specified archives as one of the major categories of such property (Article I (j)). In addition, archives are one of the types of

---

[3]   Christian Gut, "Constitution et reconstitution des patrimoines archivistiques nationaux," in *Actes de la 17ème CITRA*, pp. 39–69.

cultural property covered by the proposals which, in accordance with 19 C/Resolution 4.128, the Director-General is Submitting to the General Conference in connection with the establishment, by the General Conference at its current session, of an inter-governmental committee to be entrusted with the task of seeking ways and means of facilitating bilateral negotiations for the restitution or return of cultural property to States having lost them result of colonial and foreign occupation.[4]

9. At the same time, however, it must be recognized that archives have an official and legal status different from that of most types of cultural property. Archives which were originally created to accomplish administrative transactions also serve as the evidence of those transactions. Both as evidence and because of the information they contain, they are indispensable for the continuing administration of all activities within the jurisdiction of the State. They not only document the experience of the people, but they also record and safeguard the rights and interests of the government and of individual citizens. Archives thus constitute irreplaceable legal titles and evidence which is essential to guarantee continuity in the exercise of the functions incumbent on public authorities.

10. This special status of archives has been expressed by the International Law Commission of the General assembly of the United Nations as follows: "While one can conceive of a State without a navy, for example, it is impossible to imagine one without a currency, without a treasury, without funds, and without archives . . . which constitute . . . these kinds of State property which are most essential and most widespread so much so that they can be said to derive from the very existence of the State."[5]

11. The International Law Commission further observes that "State archives, jealously preserved, are the essential instrument for the administration of a community. They both record the management of State affairs and enable them to be carried on, while at the same time embodying the ins and outs of human history; consequently, they are of value to both the researcher and the administrator. Secret or public, they constitute a heritage and public property which the State generally makes sure is inalienable and imprescriptible."[6]

---

[4]   The proposals will be examined under item 12 of the provisional agenda of the twentieth session of the General Conference. See document 20 C/86.

[5]   Bedjaoui, Mohammed, Special Rapporteur, *Eighth Report on Succession of States in Respect of Matters Other than Treaties: Draft Articles with Commentaries on Succession to State Property* (A/CN.4/292, and A/CN.4/322), p. 25.

[6]   Ibid., p. 54.

12. In dealing with problems of restitution of and access to cultural property, it is therefore essential that, where appropriate, the legal and official character of archives, and their special status as public property of the State deriving from the basic sovereignty of the State itself, be taken fully into account.

13. In discussions of archival claims a distinction is sometimes made between public and private archives. This is a legal distinction that not only differs significantly from State to State, but that has undergone change from time to time in the same State. Furthermore, in some States, archives that were once regarded as private have been or are now accorded the status of official records, for example, church registers of births, marriages, and deaths that have been used to establish citizenship rights or eligibility for certain public benefits. The proposed principles and guidelines contained in this report should therefore be understood to apply to all categories of archives within the jurisdiction of the State. The concepts relating to the general protection of cultural property, which may in particular cases be supplemented by specific national legislation, are applicable to all other categories of archives.

III. MAIN ISSUES OF THE PROBLEM

14. Changes in territorial boundaries and sovereignty have deprived a number of countries of ownership or convenient access to at least part of their archival heritage. It is therefore important to all nations, and to mankind generally, that the restitution of archives and the problems of providing access to archives should be dealt with urgently.

15. The studies and reports referred to above indicate that problems involving archives usually, arise in one of the following circumstances:

- (a) changes in sovereignty over a given territory without the creation of a new State;
- (b) transfers which took place during wars, or as an effect of military occupation;
- (c) the emergence of new States through the splitting of former political entities;
- (d) the effects of colonization and decolonization, which require consideration of the following categories of archives:
  - (i) archives created and retained in the metropolitan countries;

    (ii)   archives created in the colonies and transferred
           to other colonies;

   (iii)   archives of a colonial administration created in
           the former colony and removed to the metro-
           politan country at the time of independence;

   (iv)   archives of a regional colonial administration
           which relate to more than one now independent
           State;

    (v)   archives created in the colonies during the met-
           ropolitan administration and inherited by now
           successor States.

16. An analysis of more than 200 treaties, conventions, acts, agreements, and other legal instruments relating to the cession and transfer of archives[7] indicates the existence of a variety of routine policies and procedures for the transfer of and access to current records and archives in cases of cession of territory between existing States, for the restitution of archives evacuated or removed during war time or military occupation, and for the reconstitution of the archival heritage of formerly sovereign or autonomous States. However, no policies and procedures have been developed for the transfer ownership of archives to new States created through decolonization.

17. With regard to the creation of new States, there has been general recognition of the principle that such States have a right to certain archives, but there has been no generally accepted doctrine or criteria for determining such transfers. Nor has there been any consistent policy or procedures for implementing such transfers in the very few cases where multilateral and bilateral agreements have been concluded and implemented. Moreover, a significant portion of the existing source materials relating to the history of those countries which, for extended periods, have been under foreign administration, has been created and therefore automatically located outside the national territories of these new States. To the problems of ownership of archives must therefore be added related problems of access. Those involved in conflicting claims have asserted a wide variety of principles and criteria, which in turn have been variously interpreted and frequently subordinated to political, economic, and other considerations. It is this lack of generally accepted principles and guidelines to assist in the formulation of multilateral and bilateral agreements that has made essential the international consideration of these problems.

---

[7]   See the works cited in notes 3 and 5 above, and the updated ILC version in Appendix II.

IV. STATEMENT OF PRINCIPLES AND GUIDELINES

18. Objective

In light of the above considerations, the objective of this proposed statement of principles and guidelines is to provide to all Member States an instrument of reference intended to facilitate negotiations leading to the conclusion of special agreements, either bilateral or, if appropriate, multilateral, with a view to the resolution of conflicting archival claims.

19. Bilateral and multilateral negotiations and agreements

Because the patrimonial character of archives as State property derives from the basic sovereignty of the State itself, problems involved in the ownership and transfer of State archives are fundamentally legal in character. Such problems should therefore be resolved primarily through bilateral or multilateral negotiations and agreements between the States involved. The agreements should specify all practical and financial responsibilities with respect to their implementation.

20. International law principles, policies and procedures

During bilateral or multilateral negotiations, recourse should be had, to the maximum extent possible, to the relevant principles of international law and the policies and procedures developed thereunder, especially those relating to succession of States in respect of matters other than treaties.

21. National laws and regulations

Since State property, and especially the alienation of State property, is subject to specific legislation and procedures in most countries, due regard should be given to such legislation and procedures to help facilitate the formulation of transfer agreements. It is particularly important that attention be given to the definition and status of archives as provided by the laws and regulations of the particular States involved at the time of the removal or the transfer of the archives.

22. Retroactive sovereignty

In accordance with United Nations resolution 1514 (XV) of 1960, and resolution 2625 (XXV) of 1970, it is essential that the legal status of new States should be extended backwards to the period preceding their independence. This will materially assist in negotiations in cases of decolonization and the creation of new States because of the absence of any clear precedents from international law in such cases.

23. Provenance (respect for the integrity of archives groups)

It is equally essential that to the fullest possible extent the archival principle of provenance or respect for the integrity of archives groups should be observed in all proposed transfers of archives. In accordance with this principle all archives accumulated by an administrative authority should be maintained as a single, indivisible, and organic unity in the custody of that authority or its legally designated successor. This is necessary to preserve the integrity and value of archives as titles, as proofs, and as both legal and historical evidence.

24. Functional pertinence

The only significant exception to the principle of provenance derives from the application to archives of the concept of functional pertinence. The transfer of powers, responsibilities, and competencies to a new State must necessarily be accompanied by the transfer of titles, proofs, and information which will render the exercise of these powers and responsibilities possible. With regard to archives, there must be a transfer of those which are functionally pertinent in order to provide administrative continuity for all parties concerned. This concept makes it possible to determine the ownership of archives groups accumulated by administrations responsible solely for the affairs of a given non-sovereign political entity, whether or not the administrations operated within and were located within the territory of that political entity. Archives groups accumulated in such cases form part of the heritage of the successor to the political entity concerned, and not of the State or administration which was exercising sovereignty at the time the archives group was created or in the place where it was created.

25. Joint heritage

Where an archives group or a body of archives results from the activity of an administration where succession is shared between the predecessor State and two or more successor States—i.e. where the archives form part of the national heritages of two or more States but cannot be divided without destroying its juridical, administrative, and historical value—as a realistic solution recourse should be had to the concept of joint heritage. The practical result of the application of this concept is that the archives group is left physically intact in one of the countries concerned, where it is treated as part of the national archival heritage, with all of the responsibilities with respect to security and handling implied thereby for the State acting as the owner and custodian of that heritage. The States sharing this joint heritage should then be given rights equal to those of the custodial State.

26. Right to historical continuity

In the application of the above principles and guidelines it should be understood that every national community has the right to an identity acquired from its history. In the name of human solidarity, national communities are required to assist each other in the search for historical truth and continuity. Access to archives is indispensable in this search and in the establishment of a national identity.

27. International co-operation and understanding

It is well recognized that the foregoing legal and archival principles and concepts will not necessarily result in the successful resolution of problems involved in the transfer of archives without a background of a spirit of international co-operation and a recognition of moral principles and obligation by the Member States involved. Also in negotiations and the formulation of agreements between nations, special attention should be given to the international contribution toward the establishment of the new economic order which can be promoted directly through more liberal access to the informational content of archives and generally through the cultural development of the developing countries. The role of archives in such development does not need to be reiterated.

V. A PLAN OF ACTION

28. It is within the competence of Member States to solve problems relating to archival claims through bilateral or multilateral negotiations and agreements taking into account the principles and guidelines detailed above. In addition, Unesco should carry out a programme of action which would promote and facilitate the negotiations and implementation of agreements between Member States in this area. This programme was discussed at the Consultation on Archival Claims held in Paris in April 1978 and received the unanimous support of its members.

29. The programme, to be undertaken in co-operation with the International Council on Archives and other competent non-governmental organizations, is briefly summarized below.

30. Inventorying of sources

Unesco assistance would be continued for existing projects for the compilation and publication of guides to the sources of history of the nations of Africa, Asia, and Latin America. In these projects particular attention will be given to the identification and listing of both displaced archives and of documents relating to a nation's history that are properly located in foreign archives. The inventorying of sources is regarded as a basic action in promoting the solution of problems in this area.

31. Feasibility study for data base of sources

A feasibility study would be undertaken of the possibilities and problems involved in applying automated storage and retrieval systems and techniques to information on sources of national histories located in foreign archives.

32. Model agreements

To facilitate the negotiation of new agreements, financial support would be given for the compilation and publication of model bilateral and multilateral agreements and conventions concerning the transfer of archives, the establishment of joint heritages, and regulations providing for access thereto.

33. Pilot project

As a means of studying the procedures and techniques to be applied in actual situations involving the transfer of archives or the establishment of a joint heritage, action would be taken, upon the request of governments involved in current bilateral or multilateral arrangements, to establish a pilot project so as to share this experience with other interested Member States. The project would include a study of the formal agreement; surveys and studies of the procedures and techniques for identifying, testing and copying documents; and possible financial assistance for the above activities and for related fellowships and study grants.

34. Feasibility study for establishment of a microfilming fund

Because of the numerous proposals that have been made for the creation of an internationally-financed and managed microfilm fund to assist in the solution of problems involved in the transfer of archives and in obtaining access to sources of national history located in foreign archives, a feasibility study would be undertaken to define the dimensions of the problem, to determine all relevant cost factors, and to study administrative, procedural, and technical problems in the establishment and operations of such a fund.

35. Infrastructure development

Assistance would continue to be provided, chiefly through existing programmes toward creating in Member States the conditions required for the proper housing, preservation, and general administration of restituted archives. The assistance would include providing to these to these countries the equipment and manpower training necessary to provide copies of documents required by other Member States, and appropriate language training and training in foreign administrative procedures and record-keeping systems and practices so that restituted archives would be fully accessible to all users.

36. Budget implications

If the plan of action outlined above is to be launched in 1979-1980, additional resources, estimated in the order of $50,000 under the regular programme would be required. The Director General will make efforts to provide the necessary sum within the existing provision of draft document 20 C/5 through internal adjustments.

37. Draft resolution

The General Conference may wish to adopt the following resolution:

The General Conference,

Recalling resolution 212 adopted by the General Conference at its eighteenth session,

Having examined the Report of the Director-General on the Study regarding Problems involved in the Transfer of Documents from Archives in the Territory of Certain Countries to the Country of Origin (20 C/102),

Notes the Statement of Principles and Guidelines contained in paragraphs 19-27 of document 20 C/102, as instrument of reference intended to facilitate negotiations leading to the conclusion of bilateral and/or multilateral agreements, with a view to solving conflicting archival claims,

Invites Member States to take into consideration this Statement of Principles and Guidelines in matters relating to such archival claims,

Notes the plan of action contained in paragraphs 30–35 of document 20 C/102,

Invites the Director-General to make efforts to find the necessary funds to implement the above-mentioned plan of action through appropriate adjustments within the Programme and Budget foreseen for 1979–1980 (document 20 C/5).

APPENDIX II

UN. International Law Commission, "Non-Exhaustive Table of Treaties Containing Provisions Relating to the Transfer of Archives in Cases of Succession of States" *

No.	Date of Treaty	Title of treaty and indication of pertinent articles	Signatory States	Object of Treaty
1.	17 January 1601	Treaty of Lyons	France/Savoy	Cession by the Duchy of Savoy of the territories of Bresse, Bugey, Gex and Valromey to France. Handing over of legal documents.
2.	26 January 1622	Peace of Nikolsburg	Holy Roman Empire/ Transylvania	Return by Transylvania of the archives of the Chamber of Szepes seized during the military campaign and agreement for the exchange of authentic copies in respect to the archives of the seven counties of north-eastern Hungary ceded to Transylvania.
3.	13 August 1645	Treaty of Brömsebro, art. 29	Sweden/ Denmark	Handing over of archives to Sweden (upon the cession of various provinces).
4.	30 January 1648	Treaty of Münster, art. 69	Spain/ United Provinces of the Netherlands	Handing over of archives to the United Provinces.
5.	24 October 1648	Treaty of Münster, art. 110	France/ Holy Roman Empire	Status quo as regards archives removed.
6.	24 October 1648	Treaty of Osnabrück, art. 16	Sweden/Holy Roman Empire	Reciprocal handing over of archives.

*   As published in the *Yearbook of the International Law Commission*, 1979, II, pt. 1, *Documents of the Thirty-First Session (Excluding the Report of the Commission to the General Assembly)*, pp. 82–93.

7.	22 July 1657	Treaty of Wehlau	Poland/ Transylvania	Return of cultural property.
8.	25 February 1658	Treaty of Roskild, art. 10	Sweden/ Denmark	Handing over of archives to Sweden (upon the cession of various provinces).
9.	7 November 1659	Treaty of the Pyrenees, art. 54	France/Spain	Specifies a time-limit of three months for the handing over of archives to the successor State.
10.	3 May 1660	Treaty of Oliva, art. 9	Sweden/ Poland	Return of the archives of the Polish Chancellery (Treaty implemented in 1798: archives handed over to Prussia).
11.	27 May 1660	Treaty of Copenhagen, art. 14	Sweden/ Denmark	Handing over of archives to Sweden (upon the cession of various provinces).
12.	26 December 1661	Treaty of Partition of territories beyond the Meuse, art. 6	Spain/United Provinces	Return of archives removed.
13.	17 September 1678	Treaty of Nimeguen, art. 20	France/Spain	Reciprocal handing over of archives (following the cession and return of the territories). Distinction drawn between historical documents (which the 17th century treaties called "literary"), which remain with the predecessor State, and administrative archives which pass to the successor State (treaty of 5.2.1679, art. 22; treaty of 17.7.1.679, art 6). Return of the Lille and Ghent archives (treaty of 17.9.1678, art 20); of Lorraine archives (treaty of 5.21679, art. 22).
14.	5 February 1679	Treaty of Nimeguen, art. 22	France/Holy Roman Empire	
15.	17 July 1679	Treaty of Nimeguen, art. 6	France/Holy Roman Empire	
16.	26 September 1679	Treaty of Lund, art. 12	Denmark/ Sweden	Handing over to the annexing State of letters and papers, irrespective of their nature, concerning administration (justice, the militia, taxes).
17.	20 September 1697	Treaty of Ryswick, art. 16	France/Spain	Reciprocal handing over of archives (upon the cession and return of territories).
18.	11 April 1713	Treaty of Utrecht, art. 22	France/Austria/ United Provinces	Mutual cession of archives with the ceded provinces.

19.	15 November 1715	Barrier Treaty	England/ Holy Roman Empire/ United Provinces	Roermond archives left intact, after the partition of Gelderland; handing over of inventories; issues of copies.
20.	20 November 1719	Treaty of Stockholm, art. 3	Sweden/ Hannover	Handing over of Bremen-Verden archives to Hannover.
21.	21 January 1720	Treaty of Stockholm, art. 11	Sweden/Prussia	Reciprocal handing over of archives.
22.	3 June 1720	Treaty of Stockholm, art. 11	Sweden/ Denmark	Return of archives removed.
23.	30 November 1721	Treaty of Nystad, art. 3	Sweden/Russia	Mutual cession of archives (operation continued until 1825).
24.	28 August 1736	Convention of Vienna	Austria/France	Upon the cession of Lorraine and the Duchy of Bar to France, the archives followed the provinces, the Duke retaining his personal papers.
25.	7 August 1743	Treaty of Abo, art. 11	Sweden/Russia	Return of archives removed.
26.	20 February 1746	Capitulation of Laeken, art. 14	France/Austria	Maintenance of archival collections intact.
27.	18 October 1748	Treaty of Aachen, art. 11	France/Austria	Mutual cession of the archives of territories ceded and returned.
28.	24 March 1760	Treaty of Limits, art. 16	France/ Sardinia	Handing over by both parties in good faith, within a period of six months, of documents and title deeds concerning reciprocal cessions and those of territories exchanged under the treaties of Utrecht, Lyons and other earlier treaties.
29.	November 1762	Negotiations	France/Savoy	Division of the archival collection of the Chambéry Accounts Office (one of two).
30.	10 February 1763	Treaty of Paris, art. 22	France/ England	Handing over of archives on the basis of the principle of functional connection (not implemented).
31.	15 February 1763	Treaty of Hubertsburg	Prussia/Poland	Handing over by Prussia to Poland of archives belonging to Polish offices.

32.	15 February 1763	Treaty of Hubertsburg	Prussia/Austria	Demand by Frederick II that Austria faithfully return all archives of Silesian localities, which were returned to him.
33.	16 May 1769	Treaty of Versailles, art. 38	France/Austria	Reciprocal handing over of archives for all ceded provinces.
34.	11 September 1772	Declaration of the Empress Maria Theresa (Vienna)	Austria/Poland	Declaration of claims to Polish cultural property.
35.	13 September 1772	Declaration of King Frederick II (Berlin)	Prussia/Poland	Declaration of claims to Polish cultural property.
36.	18 September 1772	Declaration of St. Petersburg	Russia/Poland	Declaration of claims to Polish cultural property.
37.	16 March 1775	Treaty of Warsaw (first partition of Poland)	Austria/Poland	Archives remained in the ceded territories; commissioners were given responsibility for determining what was to be sent to Poland; authentic copies issued to Polish nationals for fixed charge.
38.	20 October 1795	Treaty of St. Petersburg (third partition of Poland)	Russia/Prussia/ Austria	Archives taken to Russia and then divided on the basis of territorial connection.
39.	17 October 1797	Treaty of Campoformio, art. 13	France/Austria	Return by Austria of archives taken from the Austrian Netherlands.
40.	9 February 1801	Treaty of Peace of Lunéville, art. 17	France/Austria	Return by Austria of archives taken from the Austrian Netherlands.
41.	1 October 1801	Treaty of San Ildefonso	Spain/France	Cession of Louisiana to France: archives repatriated, except papers relating to frontiers.
42.	30 April 1803	Treaty of Paris	France/United States of America	Handing over deeds of ownership and sovereignty to the United States of America.
43.	7 July 1807	Treaty of Tilsit	France/Prussia	Handing over of archives to the Grand Duchy of Warsaw and to the Netherlands (local archives and Berlin documents).
44.	17 September 1809	Treaty of Fredrikshamm	Sweden/Russia	Transfer of archives by Sweden upon the cession of Finland to Russia.

45.	2 December 1813	Secret Treaty of Frankfurt	Austria and its allies/ Elector of Hesse	Devolution of archives centralized at Cassel under the Kingdom of Westphalia; establishment of a Commission to separate the papers, instruments and documents belonging to the provinces formerly part of the Kingdom of Westphalia and to hand over to each sovereign those relating to the territories governed by him.
46.	14 January 1814	Treaty of Kiel, art. 21	Sweden/ Denmark	Handing over of archives upon the cession of Norway to Sweden.
47.	30 May 1814	Treaty of Paris	France/ Allied Powers	Return of archives assembled in Paris by Napoleon I.
48.	29 March 1815	Protocol on the cessions by the King of Sardinia to the Canton of Geneva	Sardinia/ Switzerland	Undertaking by the King of Sardinia to cede to the Canton of Geneva "the deeds, land registers and documents concerning things ceded as soon as possible" (art. 4).
49.	29 March 1815	Treaty between Prussia and Hannover, art. 8	King of Prussia and the King of England in his capacity as King of Hannover.	Reciprocal handing over within two months of "Crown deeds, documents and papers of the ceded territories."
50.	3 May 1815	Treaty of Vienna, art. 38	Russia/Prussia for their respective territories in former Poland	Reciprocal return of archives concerning ceded territories; any document concerning both parties to be held by the party in possession of it, but an attested and authenticated copy to be given to the other party.
51.	18 May 1815	Convention	Prussia/ Saxony	The originals to be retained by Saxony, which shall hand over authenticated copies to Prussia.
52.	7 June 1815	Treaty of Vienna, art. 14	Sweden/Prussia	Handing over of archives to Prussia (upon the cession of Swedish Pomerania).

53.	16 March 1816	Treaty of Turin	Sardinia/ Switzerland	Upon the delimitation of the frontiers between Sardinia and the Canton of Geneva, division of archives (including the apportionment of memoranda) on the basis of the principle of territorial connection.
54.	7 October 1816	Boundary Treaty signed at Cleves, art. 44	Prussia/ Netherlands	Handing over of administrative archives to the new authorities of the ceded territory; the administrative archives of communes divided by the new boundary to be handed over to the State receiving the chief town of the commune, which must "give access thereto to the other party whenever necessary."
55.	11 November 1817	Treaty of Berlin	Prussia/Sweden	Reciprocal return of archives concerning the ceded territories.
56.	22 February 1819	Treaty of Washington	Spain/United States of America	Handing over to the United States of America documents relating to the ownership and sovereignty of Florida.
57.	1 September 1819	Convention	Sweden/ Denmark	Confirmation of the Treaty Kiel (handing over of archives upon the cession of Norway to Sweden).
58.	19 April 1839	Treaty of London, arts. 13, para. 5	Netherlands/ Belgium	Handing over of archives to Belgium (administrative files of the period 1815–1830).
59.	5 November 1842	Convention	Netherlands/ Belgium	Handing over of archives to Belgium pursuant to the Treaty of London.
60.	13 September 1851	Convention	Denmark/ Sweden/ Norway	Handing over of documents by Denmark to Norway.
61.	10 November 1859	Treaty of Zurich, art. 2 and 15	France/Austria/ Sardinia	Handing over by Austria of documents concerning Lombardy.
62.	24 March 1860	Treaty of Turin	France/ Sardinia	Cession of Savoy and Nice to France; establishment of a joint commission to prepare the transfers.

63.	23 August 1860	Convention of Paris	France/ Sardinia	Agreement on the cession to France of administrative, religious and judicial archives, the French Government to return Sardinian royal archives; provision made for copies of documents.
64.	21 November 1860	Convention (Turin)	France/ Sardinia	Handing over of archives; negotiations continued until 1949; transfers completed in 1952.
65.	30 October 1864	Treaty of Vienna, art. 20	Prussia/Austria/ Denmark	Handing over by Denmark of current files and archives taken from the Duchies (Schleswig, Holstein, Lauenburg); implemented in 1876.
66.	3 October 1866	Treaty of Vienna, art. 18	Austria/Italy	Reciprocal handing over of administrative files on the basis of respect of archival collections.
67.	30 March 1867	Convention on the cession of territory (Alaska)	United States of America/ Russia	Handing over to the United States of America of local archives existing in Alaska.
68.	14 July 1868	Convention of Florence	Austria/ Italy	Concluded upon completion of the work of the bilateral commission responsible for the implementation of the Treaty of Vienna.
69.	10 June 1871	Treaty of Frankfurt, arts. 3 and 18	Germany/ France	Reciprocal handing over of administrative files (however, documents transferred from Strasbourg and Colmar to other German provinces in accordance with the principle territorial connection).
70.	11 December 1871	Supplementary Convention of Frankfurt	Germany/ France	Cession of archives in pursuance of the Treaty of Frankfurt.
71.	26 April 1872	Convention of Strasbourg	Germany/ France	Special Convention concerning the archives of the Strasbourg Academy.
72.	10 December 1898	Treaty of Paris, art. 8	Spain/ United States of America	Handing over to the United States of America of deeds of sovereignty concerning Puerto Rico, Guam and the Philippines. Cession to Cuba of local archives.

73.	27 April 1906	Exchange of Notes constituting a Convention	Sweden/ Norway	Division of previously joint archives of consulates.
74.	4 August 1916 (published on 25 January 1917)	Convention for the purchase of territory, art. 1, para 3.	Denmark/ United States of America	Upon the cession of the Virgin Islands by Denmark to the United States of America.
75.	24 January 1918	Decree of People's Commissars (Moscow)	USSR/Poland	Decree on the preservation of monuments belonging to the Polish nation; return of cultural property.
76.	28 June 1919	Treaty of Versailles, part III, sect. I, art. 78	Germany/ Belgium	Cession of archives; in addition, article 158 concerns the handing over of the archives of Kiaochow by Germany to Japan.
77.	28 June 1919	Treaty of Versailles, part III, sect. V, art. 52	Germany/ France	Cession of archives.
78.	10 September 1919	Treaty of Saint-Germain-en-Laye, arts. 93, 97, 192, 193, 194, 196, 249 and 250	Austria/ The Allied Powers	Handing over by Austria of the archives of ceded territories; return of archives removed (Italy, Czechoslovakia, Romania, Poland, Yugoslavia).
79.	27 November 1919	Treaty of Neuilly-sur-Seine, art. 126	Bulgaria/ Kingdom of the Serbs, Croats and Slovenes	Handing over by Bulgaria of archives removed from the territory of the former King of Serbia.
80.	9 January 1920	Financial Agreement (Paris Agreement)	Germany/ Poland	Return of collections of archives to Poland.
81.	2 February 1920	Treaty of Tartu	FSRSR (Federal Socialist Republic of Soviet Russia)/Estonia	Awarding the archives of local institutions to Estonia.
82.	4 May 1920	Convention, arts. 5, 6 and 7	Austria/Italy	In pursuance of article 196 of the Treaty of Saint-Germain-en-Laye, Austria to cede to Italy all historical archives originating from territories transferred to Italy, with the exception to those removed to Austria before 1790 and those not meeting the criteria of territorial connection to origin.

83.	18 May 1920	Convention	Austria/ Czechoslovakia	Handing over of historical collections of Bohemia concentrated in Vienna, and of files subsequent to 1888.
84.	2-4 June 1920	Treaty of Trianon, art. 77, paras. 175-178	Hungary/ The Allied Powers	Cession of files less than 30 years old to Czechoslovakia and to the Kingdom of the Serbs, Croats and Slovenes, and to Romania (uniting of Transylvania and Banat to Romania).
85.	12 July 1920	Treaty of Moscow, art. 9	FSRSR/ Lithuania	Awarding the archives of local institutions to Lithuania.
86.	10 August 1920	Treaty of Sèrves, art. 1	Italy/Poland/ Romania/ Kingdom of the Serbs, Croats and Slovenes	States which were formerly part of the Austro-Hungary monarchy or whose territories include part of the monarchy's former domain, to return to each other's military, civil, financial and legal archives and provide for mutual exchange of information.
87.	10 August 1920	Treaty of Sèrves, art. 1	Turkey/ The Allied Powers	Handing over of the archives of ceded territories by Turkey and return of archives removed.
88.	11 August 1920	Treaty of Moscow, art. 11	FSRSR/ Latvia	Awarding of archives of local institutions to Latvia.
89.	14 October 1920	Treaty of Dorpat (Tartu), art. 29	FSRSR/ Finland	Mutual handing over of archives concerning solely or mainly the other party and its history.
90.	12 November 1920	Treaty of Rapallo, art. 2	Italy/Kingdom of the Serbs, Croats and Slovenes	Delimitation of the territory of Zara with provision, in a separate convention, for the division of the archives between the territory assigned to Italy and that remaining attached to the Kingdom of the Serbs, Croats and Slovenes.

91.	18 March 1921	Treaty of Riga, art. 11	Poland/ FSRSR	Return of archives removed; handing over to Poland of archives of central administrations responsible mainly for Polish affairs.
92.	5 October 1921	Convention of Vienna arts. 1-22	Austria/ Romania	Handing over by Austria to Romania of archives, objets d'art and scientific and bibliographical material.
93.	6 April 1922	Convention, arts. 1-6	Austria/ Hungary/Italy/ Poland/ Romania/ Czechoslovakia/ Kingdom of the Serbs, Croats and Slovenes	Intended to settle various difficulties arising as a result of the application of the Treaty of Saint-Germain-en-Laye, the convention provides for exchanges of copies of documents, the allocation of archives relating to industrial property, refers to the obligation to respect of collections and contemplates the preparation of lists of claims.
94.	10 April 1922	Convention	Germany/ Denmark	Mutual cession of administrative archives.
95.	18 June 1922	Agreement of Oppeln	Germany/ Poland	Handing over of administrative documents to Poland.
96.	14 October 1922	Agreement of Vienna	Romania/ Czecho-slovakia	Mutual handing over of archives concerning the other party (inherited from the former Austro-Hungarian monarchy).
97.	23 October 1922	So-called "Santa Margherita" Protocol and Exchange of Notes, arts. 23, 25, 26, 27 28, 29, 30 and 31	Italy/ Kingdom of the Serbs, Croats and Slovenes	Settlement of practical questions relating to the application of clauses of the Treaty of Rapallo, respect of archival collections (but reciprocal access and copies), principle of functional connection, the archives of the Republic of Venice relating to Zara remaining intact in the possession of the Kingdom of Italy.
98.	27 February 1923	Agreement	France/Austria	Reciprocal handing over of documents.

99.	3 May 1923	Convention of Danzig	Italy/France/ Japan/United Kingdom	Archives building and its contents returned to the city of Danzig, with the exception of archives returned to Poland; agreements may be made between Poland and Danzig for the conservation and management of these documents.
100.	14 June 1923	Agreement of Poznán	Germany/ Poland	Handing over of documents of waterway co-operatives and dike conservation associations.
101.	26 June 1923	Convention	Austria/ Kingdom of the Serbs, Croats and Slovenes	Pursuant to application of the Treaty of Saint-Germain-en-Laye: handing over by the Kingdom of the Serbs, Croats and Slovenes of archives removed and of archives of administrations of ceded territories; a start was made with the implementation of this convention.
102.	24 July 1923	Treaty of Lausanne, arts. 67 and 139	United Kingdom/ France/Italy/ Japan/Greece/ Romania/ Kingdom of the Serbs, Croats, and Slovenes/ and Turkey	Reciprocal handing over of administrative documents concerning Turkey, Greece, Romania, the Kingdom of the Serbs, Croats and Slovenes, and former Turkish territories, with provision for the making of copies and photographs.
103.	24 November 1923	Convention of Belgrade	Romania/ Kingdom of the Serbs, Croats and Slovenes	Reciprocal handing over of archives.
104.	16 April 1924	Convention of Bucharest	Hungary/ Romania	Reciprocal handing over of archives.
105.	12 August 1924	Convention of Belgrade	Italy/Kingdom of the Serbs, Croats and Slovenes	An instrument of general scope relating to the return of cultural property, documents, etc., the handing over of which had suffered some delay.

106.	31 October 1924	Protocol of Vienna, arts. 1-9	Italy/Austria	Protocol supplementary to the Convention of 6 April 1922 on archives: archives having a functional connection to be ceded to Italy, those on sovereignty remaining in Austria; provision for reciprocal free access and copies, agreement on communications to individuals and their limits; agreement on military archives.
107.	3 December 1924	Convention of Bucharest, arts. 1 (para 5) and 18	Hungary/ Romania	Exchange of papers relating to judicial proceedings, land registers and registers of births, marriages and deaths.
108.	17 January 1925	Protocol of Vienna	Italy/Austria	Convention supplementary to that of 31 October 1924 (No. 105), settling certain points relating to lists of documents to be returned to Italy by Austria and to the conditions of the return itself.
109.	23 April 1925	Treaty of conciliation and arbitration	Poland/ Czecho- slovakia	Mutual handing over of archives inherited from the Austro-Hungarian monarchy concerning either party.
110.	20 July 1925	Convention of Nettuno, arts. 1-15	Italy/Kingdom of the Serbs, Croats and Slovenes.	Convention made pursuant to the treaty concerning Fiume signed at Rome on 27 January 1924: agreement on the maintenance at Fiume of the archives of the town and district, and handing over of the archives relating to Fiume kept in the territory of the Kingdom of the Serbs, Croats and Slovenes; conversely, the Kingdom to receive all archives concerning the territory transferred to it.

111.	28 May 1926	Convention of Baden	Austria/ Hungary	Handing over of collection of archives to Hungary; establishment of a permanent Hungarian delegation at Vienna.
112.	27 December 1926	Agreement of Berlin	Germany/ Poland	Handing over to Poland of administrative documents and registers of births, marriages and deaths.
113.	15 October 1927	General Arbitration Convention	Denmark/ Iceland	Reciprocal handing over of documents.
114.	26 October 1927	Convention	Poland/ Czecho-slovakia	Mutual handing over of archives inherited from the Austro-Hungarian monarchy concerning either party.
115.	23 May 1931	Convention of Rome, arts. 1-9	Italy/ Czecho-slovakia	Settlement concerning an exchange of documents or copies relating to military personnel who had been members of the former Austro-Hungarian army.
116.	26 October 1932	Agreement of Vienna	Austria/Poland	Handing over of archives to Poland (implementation in 1938).
117.	30 January 1933	Convention of Belgrade, arts 1-11	Romania/ Yugoslavia	Reciprocal exchange of archives.
118.	15 December 1933	Convention	Germany/ Denmark	Mutual cession of archives.
119.	1934	Decision of Congress of the United States of America	United States of America/ Philippines	Transfer to the Philippines of archives seized in 1902.
120.	2 February 1935	Agreement of Rome, arts. 15-16	Austria/Italy	General cultural agreement providing, as regards archives, for exchanges of originals or copies, subject to observance of the rule on respect of collections; direct loans between repositories of the two States.
121.	16 February 1935	Cultural Convention, arts. 13-15	Hungary/Italy	Containing clauses, with regard to Hungary, analogous to those relating to Austria in the Agreement mentioned above.
122.	31 May 1935	Protocol of Return	Romania/USSR	Return of 1,443 crates of archival documents and securities evacuated to Moscow by the Romanian Government in 1917.

123.	1937	Exchange of Notes	Denmark/ Norway	Transfer of archives from Denmark to Norway.
124.	23 November 1938	Cultural Agreement, art. 27	Germany/Italy	Agreement for facilitating the reciprocal loan of documents between both States in the interest of scientific research.
125.	23 March 1939	Agreement of Tokyo	Italy/Japan	Convention of cultural collaboration.
126.	7 September 1940	Treaty of Craiova, annex B, item 2	Bulgaria/ Romania	Cession of archives of the southern Dobrudja and issue of authentic copies of central archives to Bulgaria.
127.	December 1940	Exchange of letters constituting an Agreement	Spain/France	Handing over to Spain of the Simancas archives, which had been transferred to France by Napoleon I and had remained in Paris after 1814 (implemented in May-July 1941).
128.	8 April 1943	Agreement of Bucharest	Italy/ Romania	Convention on cultural collaboration (denounced on 4 March 1950).
129.	11 February 1945	Yalta Conference	USSR/ United States of America/ United Kingdom	Laid down the principles governing reparations.
130.	2 August 1945	Potsdam Agreements	USSR/United States of America/ United Kingdom/ France	Specified the terms for the return of property looted in the occupied territories, particularly Poland.
131.	20 February 1945	Act No. 10 of the Allied Control Council (Germany), art 2, para. 1(b)	Allied Powers	Any looting of public property declared to be a war crime.
132.	12 February 1946	Mutual Agreement	Poland/ Czecho-slovakia	Reciprocal return of archives.
133.	27 January 1947	Aide-mémoire relating to the Peace Treaty with Germany	Poland/United Nations	Documents transmitted to the United Nations by the Polish Government, for the Conference of Deputy Ministers for Foreign Affairs preceding the Peace Treaty with Germany; reaffirmation of Poland's claims to the return of collections of archives.

134.	10 February 1947	Treaty of Paris, arts. 7, 12, 23, 25, 29, 37, 75, 77 and 78; Annex X, art. 4; Annex XIV, arts. 1 and 7	Italy/ Allied Powers	Return by Italy to France of archives relating to Savoy and Nice antedating 1860 and not yet returned, pursuant to the instruments of 24 March and 23 August 1860. Return by Italy to China of archives and cultural property relating to Tientsin. Cession or return to Yugoslavia of archives which had been removed or those which should be ceded to Yugoslavia pursuant to the Agreement of 1924 and 1928, and those relating to newly ceded terrorizes (Istria, Zara, etc.). Cession to the territory of Treiste of all archives and property concerning it. Return by Italy to Albania and to Ethiopia of archives removed from those territories.
135.	10 February 1947	Treaty of Paris, particularly chap. V, art. 22	Bulgaria/ Finland/ Romania/ Allied Powers	Return to Bulgaria, Finland and Romania of all looted documents and property, or compensation by articles of equal value (principal Powers concerned: Poland, Czechoslovakia, Yugoslavia).
136.	10 February 1947	Treaty of Paris, art. 11	Hungary/Allied Powers	Handing over to Czechoslovakia and Yugoslavia of historical archives constituted on territories ceded between 1848 and 1919.
137.	19 October 1947	Protocol of Sofia	Bulgaria/ Romania	Return by Romania to Bulgaria of archives and official documents.
138.	28 August 1948	Convention	Hungary/ Romania	Exchange of court papers and administrative documents.
139.	8 March 1949	Exchange of letters constituting an Agreement	France/ States of former Indochina	Status quo with respect to possession of archives.

140.	1 August 1949	Exchange of letters constituting an Agreement	France/Italy	Protocol concluding the work of the joint Franco-Italian commission appointed pursuant to article 7 of the Treaty of Paris: Handing over to France of documents of local interest (Savoy, Nice, Bresse, Bugey, Gex), extracted from collections maintained in Italy. Handing over of documents relating to Italian local history maintained in French archives. Provision for the preparation of a protocol on reciprocal loans.
141.	6 August 1949	Exchange of letters constituting an Agreement	Italy/ Yugoslavia	Settlement of questions pending between the two countries, under article 67 and paras. 16 and 17 of annex XIV to the Treaty of Paris; procedure to be followed in the case of claims relating to archives.
142.	4 November 1949	Agreement of Paris	France/ Italy	Cultural convention providing for exchanges of information and documentary material.
143.	14 January 1950	Declaration	United Nations	Concerning the devolution to the various States concerned of material of artistic, historical and bibliographical interest recovered in Germany by the allied armies.
144.	15 January 1950	Exchange of letters constituting an Agreement	France/ States of former Indochina	Agreement on the division of archives.
145.	22 November 1950	Agreement on the importation of educational, scientific and cultural materials	States Members of the United Nations and of UNESCO	General agreement on the free circulation of documents.
146.	15 December 1950	Resolution 388 A (V) of the General Assembly of the United Nations, art. 1, para. 2	Italy/ Libya/ United Nations	Independence of Libya; transfer to Libya of relevant documents of an administrative character or of technical interest.

147.	23 December 1950	Agreement of Rome, arts. 1–9	Italy/ Yugoslavia	Agreement relating to the division of archives and documents of administrative and historical interest relating to the territories ceded pursuant to the Treaty of Paris; criteria of functional relevance to be observed, but also those of territorial origin; establishment of a joint commission with headquarters at Gorizia.
148.	2 February 1951	Agreement of Paris	France/India	Agreement made in consequence of the cession by France to India of the former comptoir of Chandernagore; France to maintain the historical archives and India to receive archives necessary for administration.
149.	8 November 1951	Agreement of London	Italy/ United Kingdom	Agreement laying down identical conditions in both countries for the access of research workers to documents.
150.	5 December 1951	Agreement of Rome	Italy/ Netherlands	General agreement on cultural collaboration.
151.	24 March 1952	Agreement of Rome, art. 12	Austria/ Italy	Confirmation of the provisions of articles 15 and 16 of the cultural agreement of 2 February 1935; general agreement on cultural collaboration.
152.	25 April 1952	Protocol of agreement	Norway/ Sweden	Cession of archives to Norway.
153.	30 June 1953	Exchange of letters constituting an Agreement	Federal Republic of Germany/ France	Settlement of the Alsace-Lorraine dispute; maintenance of the status quo and microfilming.
154.	8 September 1953	Exchange of letters constituting an Agreement	Federal Republic of Germany/ France	Same object as the above-mentioned exchange of letters.
155.	30-31 October 1953	Standing convention	Belgium/ Netherlands	Exchange of archives on the basis of the principle of functional connection.

156.	5 October 1954	Memorandum of agreement signed at London	United Kingdom/ United States of America/ Italy/ Yugoslavia	Italy to resume possession of the territory of Trieste and the zones hitherto administered by the allied military government; Italy thus legitimately retains custody of the archives relating to the region.
157.	6 October 1954	Agreement of Paris, arts. 1–5	France/Italy	Handing over by Italy to France of administrative, functional, domanial, notarial (original) and historical archives (in the form of microfilm) relating to the ceded territories of Tenda and Briga.
158.	21 October 1954	Agreement of New Delhi, art. 33	France/India	Agreement identical with that concerning Chandernagore and relating to the former French comptoirs of Yanaon, Pondicherrry, Karikal and Mahé; France to retain custody of the historical archives.
159.	15 May 1955	Treaty of State signed at Vienna	Austria/ four Occupying Powers (United States/United Kingdom, USSR, France)	Return of archives and cultural property (Austria, Italy, Yugoslavia).
160.	2 October 1956	Convention	Hungary/ Yugoslavia	Handing over of documents to Yugoslavia.
161.	28 March 1958	Exchange of letters constituting an Agreement	Poland/ Czechoslovakia	Settlement of various questions in dispute, some of them concerning archives.
162.	19 April 1958	Protocol of agreement	Hungary/ Yugoslavia	Handing over of documents to Yugoslavia.
163.	8 April 1960	Frontier Treaty signed at The Hague, art. 8	Netherlands/ Federal Republic of Germany	Reciprocal cession of archives corresponding to ceded territories.
164.	28 September 1960	Exchange of letters (Moscow)	Romania/USSR	Handing over of archives by the USSR to Romania.
165.	3 December 1960	Agreement of Rome	Italy/ Yugoslavia	The contracting parties undertake to facilitate the access of each other's research workers to archives, libraries and museums, very particularly in the case of documents relating to the history of either of the States concerned.

166.	29 May 1961	Protocol of agreement	Poland/ German Democratic Republic	Mutual return of archives which had been removed.
167.	15 September 1961	Protocol of agreement, arts. 1, 2 and 3	Italy/ Yugoslavia	Agreement for the settlement of questions relating to the return of archives to Yugoslavia, providing for the handing over of the last documents (many of them from the archives of Trieste) and payment of a sum to meet the cost of the microfilming of documents relating to Yugoslav territory of the period from 1718 to 1918, which will remain in Trieste.
168.	17 May 1965	Protocol	France/Italy	Amendment of article 1 of the Agreement of 4 November 1949.
169.	21 September 1965	Protocol	Italy/Hungary	The contracting parties will facilitate study of archival material in both countries, in the interest of historical research and within the limits allowed by the respective regulations.
171.	7 June 1967	Protocol of Return	France/Algeria	Handing over to Algeria of a first batch of historical archives concerning the period prior to 1830.
172.	1 September 1972	Convention of the Hague	The Netherlands/ Indonesia	Mutual microfilming.
173.	9 April 1973	Agreement of Mogadishu	Italy/ Somalia	Addendum to the cultural agreement of 26 April 1961.
174.	31 December 1974	Treaty of Lisbon	Portugal/India	Recognition of India's sovereignty over Goa, Damān, Diu, Dadra and Nagar Aveli; cession to India of administrative, judicial and other archives; transfer to Portugal of other documents; provision for authentic copies.

175.	14 March 1975	Exchange of Notes constituting an Agreement	Portugal/India	Conservation in India of archives originating in the ceded territories which concern other Indian territories; conversely, archives in Portugal concerning the ceded territories but also in other Indian territories will remain in the former metropolitan country.
176.	10 April 1975	Protocol of Return	France/Algeria	Handing over of a second batch of archives concerning the period prior to 1830.
177.	22 April-20 May 1975	Exchange of diplomatic correspondence	France/Algeria	Algeria reserves its rights to its historical archives antedating colonization; France declares that it has returned everything that was returnable and declares itself prepared to permit the microfilming of its collections, both of documents dated before 1830 and those of later date.
178.	5 July 1975	General Co-operation Agreement, art. 6	Portugal/ Cape Verde	Each country will deliver to the other authentic copies of documents held in its archives.
179.	12 July 1975	General Co-operation Agreement, art. 5	Portugal/ Sao Tome and Principe	Each country will deliver to the other authentic copies of documents held in its archives.
180.	2 October 1975	General Co-operation Agreement, art. 5	Portugal/ Mozambique	Same provisions as under No. 178 above.
181.	10 November 1975	Agreement of Osimo	Italy/ Yugoslavia	Convention on cultural collaboration.
182.	22 November 1975	Recommendation of Djakarta	Netherlands/ Indonesia	Joint recommendation by experts concerning cultural co-operation (including the transfer of archives).
183.	28 January 1977	Memorandum of Willemstad	Netherlands/ Antilles	Convention on cultural collaboration prepared by the Inter-Governmental Commission of the Antilles.

APPENDIX IIIa

UN. *"Vienna Convention on Succession of States in Respect to State Property, Archives and Debts,* Part III, *'State Archives' (art. 19 to 31),"* April 1983 *(A/Conf.117/14; has not come into force)*

PART III. - STATE ARCHIVES

Section I. - Introduction

Article 19   *Scope of the Present Part*

The articles in the present Part apply to the effects of a succession of States in respect of State archives of the predecessor State.

Article 20   *State Archives*

For the purposes of the articles in the present Part, "State archives of the predecessor State" means all documents of whatever date and kind, produced or received by the predecessor State in the exercise of its functions which, at the date of the succession of States, belonged to the predecessor State according to its internal law and were preserved by it directly or under its control as archives for whatever purpose.

Article 21   *Effects of the Passing of State Archives*

The passing of State archives of the predecessor State entails the extinction of the rights of that State and the arising of the rights of the successor State to the State archives which pass to the successor State, subject to the provisions of the articles in the present Part.

---

*   Also published in *Dossier on Archival Claims.* Regarding the conditions of enactment, see Chapter 3, pp. 96–97.

Article 22   *Date of the Passing of State Archives*

Unless otherwise agreed by the States concerned or decided by an appropriate international body, the date of the passing of State archives of the predecessor State is that of the succession of States.

Article 23   *Passing of State Archives without Compensation*

Subject to the provisions of the articles in the present Part and unless otherwise agreed by the States concerned or decided by an appropriate international body, the passing of State archives of the predecessor State to the successor State shall take place without compensation.

Article 24   *Absence of Effect of a Succession of States on the Archives of a Third State*

A succession of States shall not as such affect archives which, at the date of the succession of States, are situated in the territory of the predecessor State and which, at that date, are owned by a third State according to the internal law of the predecessor State.

Article 25   *Preservation of the Integral Character of Groups of State Archives*

Nothing in the present Part shall be considered as prejudging in any respect any question that might arise by reason of the preservation of the integral character of groups of State archives of the predecessor State.

Article 26   *Preservation and Safety of State Archives*

For the purpose of the implementation of the provisions of the articles in the present Part, the predecessor State shall take all measures to prevent damage or destruction to State archives which pass to the successor State in accordance with those provisions.

SECTION 2. - PROVISIONS CONCERNING SPECIFIC CATEGORIES OF SUCCESSION OF STATES

Article 27   *Transfer of Part of the Territory of a State*

1. When part of the territory of a State is transferred by that State to another State, the passing of State archives of the predecessor State to the successor State is to be settled by agreement between them.
2. In the absence of such an agreement:

(a) the part of State archives of the predecessor State, which for normal administration of the territory to which the succession of States relates should be at the disposal of the State to which the territory concerned is transferred, shall pass to the successor State;

(b) the part of State archives of the predecessor State, other than the part mentioned in subparagraph (a), that relates exclusively or principally to the territory to which the succession of States relates, shall pass to the successor State.

3. The predecessor State shall provide the successor State with the best available evidence from its State archives which bears upon title to the territory of the transferred territory or its boundaries, or which is necessary to clarify the meaning of documents of State archives of the predecessor State which pass to the successor State pursuant to other provisions of the present article.
4. The predecessor State shall make available to the successor State, at the request and at the expense of that State, appropriate reproductions of its State archives connected with the interests of the transferred territory.
5. The successor State shall make available to the predecessor State, at the request and at the expense of that State, appropriate reproductions of State archives of the predecessor State which have passed to the successor State in accordance with paragraph 1 or 2.

Article 28   *Newly Independent State*

1. When the successor State is a newly independent State:

(a) archives having belonged to the territory to which the succession of States relates and having become State archives of the predecessor State during the period of dependence shall pass to the newly independent State;

(b) the part of State archives of the predecessor State, which for normal administration of the territory to which the succession of States relates should be in that territory, shall pass to the newly independent State;

(c) the part of State archives of the predecessor State, other than the parts mentioned in subparagraphs (a) and (b), that relates exclusively or principally to the territory to which the succession of States relates, shall pass to the newly independent State.

2.   The passing or the appropriate reproduction of parts of the State archives of the predecessor State, other than those mentioned in paragraph 1, of interest to the territory to which the succession of States relates, shall be determined by agreement between the predecessor State and the newly independent State in such a manner that each of those States can benefit as widely and equitably as possible from those parts of the State archives of the predecessor State.

3.   The predecessor State shall provide the newly independent State with the best available evidence from its State archives which bears upon title to the territory of the newly independent State or its boundaries, or which is necessary to clarify the meaning of documents of States archives of the predecessor State which pass to the newly independent State pursuant to other provisions of the present article.

4.   The predecessor State shall co-operate with the successor State in efforts to re cover any archives which, having belonged to the territory to which the succession of States relates, were dispersed during the period of dependence.

5.   Paragraphs 1 to 4 apply when a newly independent State is formed from two or more dependent territories.

6.   Paragraphs 1 to 4 apply when a dependent territory becomes part of the territory of a State other than the State which was responsible for its international relations.

7.   Agreements concluded between the predecessor State and the newly independent State in regard to State archives of the predecessor State shall not infringe the right of the peoples of those States to development, to information about their history, and to their cultural heritage.

Article 29   *Uniting of States*

When two or more States unite and so form one successor State, the State archives of the predecessor States shall pass to the successor State.

Article 30   *Separation of Part of* [sic] *Parts of the Territory of a State*

1.   When part or parts of the territory of a State separate from that State and form a State, and unless the predecessor State and the successor State otherwise agree:

(a) the part of State archives of the predecessor State, which for normal administration of the territory to which the succession of States relates should be in that territory, shall pass to the successor State;

(b) the part of State archives of the predecessor State, other than the part mentioned in subparagraph (a), that relates directly to the territory to which the succession of States relates, shall pass to the successor State.

2. The predecessor State shall provide the successor State with the best available evidence from its State archives which bears upon title to the territory of the successor State or its boundaries, or which is necessary to clarify the meaning of documents of State archives of the predecessor State which pass to the successor State pursuant to other provisions of the present article.

3. Agreements concluded between the predecessor State and the successor State in regard to State archives of the predecessor State shall not infringe the right of the peoples of those States to development, to information about their history and to their cultural heritage.

4. The predecessor and successor States shall, at the request and at the expense of one of them or on an exchange basis, make available appropriate reproductions of their State archives connected with the interests of their respective territories.

5. The provisions of paragraphs 1 to 4 apply when part of the territory of a State separates from that State and unites with another State.

Article 31   *Dissolution of a State*

1. When a State dissolves and ceases to exist and the parts of the territory of the predecessor State form two or more successor States, and unless the successor States concerned otherwise agree:

(a) the part of the State archives of the predecessor State which should be in the territory of a successor State for normal administration of its territory shall pass to that successor State;

(b) the part of the State archives of the predecessor State, other than the part mentioned in subparagraph (a), that relates directly to the territory of a successor State shall pass to that successor State.

2. The State archives of the predecessor State other than those mentioned in paragraph 1 shall pass to the successor States in an equitable manner, taking into account all relevant circumstances.

3. Each successor State shall provide the other successor State or States with the best available evidence from its part of the State archives of the predecessor State which bears upon title to the territories or boundaries of that other successor State or States, or which is necessary to clarify the

meaning of documents of State archives of the predecessor State which pass
to that State or States pursuant to other provisions of the present article.
4.   Agreements concluded between the successor States concerned in regard
to State archives of the predecessor State shall not infringe the right of the
peoples of those States to development, to information about their history
and to their cultural heritage.
5.   Each successor State shall make available to any other successor State, at
the request and at the expense of that State or on an exchange basis, appropriate reproductions of its part of the State archives of the predecessor State
connected with the interests of the territory of that other successor State.

ICA. *"Professional Advice on the Vienna Convention on Succession of States in Respect of State Property, Archives, and Debts,* Part III, *'State Archives' (art. 19 to 31)"**

This professional advice has been formulated at the request of the French Ministry of External Relations, Division of Archives and Documentation, by an ad hoc Working Group appointed by the President of the International Council on Archives. The Working Group was composed of

Dr. Leopold AUER,   ICA representative at the United Nations Centre, Vienna, Austria,

Dr. Eckhart G. FRANZ,   Secretary of the International Archival Round Table Conference (CITRA),

Dr. Oscar GAUYE,   Former President of the ICA,

Dr. Charles KECSKEMÉTI,   Executive Secretary of ICA, Rapporteur of the Working Group,

Dr. Eric KETELAAR,   ICA Secretary for Standardization,

Dr. Evert van LAAR,   ICA Secretary for Development,

Mr. Peter WALNE,   ICA Secretary for Publications.

The Working Group was commissioned to study (i) Section III, "State Archives" of the text of the <u>Convention adopted in Vienna On 7th April 1983 by the UN Conference on Succession of States in respect of State property, archives and debts</u>, (ii) the documentation produced during the

---

* Prepared as an official report of the International Council on Archives (ICA). Paris, 1983 (CE/83/12). Reproduced in *Dossier on Archival Claims*, pp. 39–45. Reproduced with the permission of the ICA.

Conference (Provisional Summary Records, articles as amended by the Drafting Committee, draft amendments submitted by the Member States, report of the Committee on the whole), (iii) the background documentation, especially the Report of the International Law Commission on the work of its thirty-third session (UN document A/36/10), with a view to assessing whether the aforementioned Convention might contribute effectively to the settlement of existing or potential archival claims resulting from successions of States and whether the clauses of the Convention are compatible with internationally recognized principles and practices of archival administration.

Comments of the Working Group

1. General comments

1.1. The Working Group was greatly impressed by the comprehensive historical research carried out by the International Law Commission in formulating the draft Convention and in explaining each clause contained in it. This extensive historical compilation and analysis will be of invaluable help to any State in negotiating the settlement of disputed archival claims.

1.2. The Working Group was also greatly impressed by the comprehensive character of the Convention identifying all types of succession of States in respect of archives.

1.3. The Working Group recognized the difficulties inherent in the task of the International Law Commission and the Vienna Conference, which consisted in formulating a Convention composed of three distinct parts relating respectively to State property, State archives and State debts. The concern to achieve the harmonization of the three parts prevailed, in some cases, over the respect for the specific legal status and nature of State archives.

1.4. While acknowledging the extreme care which was taken to achieve a consistent and precise legal wording, the Working Group concluded that the text of the Convention adopted in Vienna does not provide an adequate basis for dealing with succession of States in respect of archives. The reasons of this conclusion are explained in Section 2, "Special comments" of the present document.

The fact that a significant number of Member States abstained or voted against the adoption of the text at the Vienna Conference indicates that the Convention may not fulfill its objective.

1.5. It has to be remembered that the report submitted by the Director General of Unesco to the 20th session of the General Conference on the Study regarding problems involved in the transfer of documents from archives in the territory of certain countries to the country of their origin (Unesco document 20C/102), which offers a comprehensive set of principles and criteria to be observed for the settlement of disputed archival claims was unanimously approved by the Member States. The consensus achieved by the Director General of Unesco on this subject is evidence that a similar consensus could have been attained at the Vienna Conference.

1.6. Commissioned to carry out a professional duty by an international non-governmental organisation, the Working Group decided to abstain from commenting on the deliberations of the Vienna Conference. It noted however the essentially political character of the debates, which partially explains why the Conference did not succeed in achieving a consensus.

2. Specific comments

2.1. Special agreements on State archives in cases of succession of States

2.1.1. Although the Convention declares in article 27 paragraph 1 that

> "When part of the territory of a State is transferred by that State to another State, the passing of State archives of the predecessor State to the successor State is to be settled by a special agreement",

paragraph 2 of the same article describes which parts of the States archives should be transferred "in the absence of such an agreement."

Similarly, article 30 relating to the case of "Separation of part or parts of the territory of a State" and article 31 relating to the case of "Dissolution of a State" set forth criteria for the sharing of archives "unless the predecessor State and the successor State otherwise agree." Article 28, relating to the case of "Newly independent States", reduces specifically in its paragraph 2 the scope of the agreement between the predecessor State and the successor State to the "passing or the appropriate reproduction of parts of the State archives the predecessor State other than those mentioned in paragraph 1", i.e. the main bulk of the archives to be transferred. It means that should a case of succession of States occur between two States which ratified or acceded to the Convention, no special agreement will be necessary, but State archives shall be transferred according to the provisions of the relevant article of the Convention.

Such a conception disregards the very nature of archives as well as the rationale of an international Convention on the succession of States in respect of archives.

2.1.2. Transfer of the Property of State archives cannot take place according to all existing national archival laws without a special legal instrument duly approved by the competent authorities of the States concerned and listing specifically and precisely the record/archive groups and/or sub-groups (and, if necessary, records) which shall pass from one State to the other.

Any Member State of the UN can accept, under an international convention, the binding rule that, in cases of succession of States, it will conclude a special agreement on the passing of State archives. On the other hand, it is unlikely that any State which has archival legislation be in a position to accede to a Convention which prescribes passing of parts of State archives without a special agreement or, should it accede to the Convention, the application of the Convention will prove impossible in the light of that existing legislation.

2.1.3. It can be objected to this approach that an International Convention containing clear and precise criteria and principles that shall govern the apportionment of State archives is a sufficient legal instrument for the settlement of successions of States in respect of archives since any State which accedes to the Convention accepts, ipso facto, to modify its legislation so as to be in a position to implement the provisions therein. Allowing it be granted, a list specifying the archive/record groups, sub-groups and items to be transferred, in original or copy, must still be agreed upon. Hence the agreement will be concluded or no transfer will take place for want of knowing what to transfer. It is possible to conclude an agreement in the spirit of a Convention but "in the absence of such an agreement", only the part of the archives of the predecessor State which is located within the territory of the successor State may pass to the latter.

If the predecessor State and the successor State, failing to make a special agreement, are satisfied, at the moment of the succession of States, with sanctioning the status quo, they will be led later to negotiate the transfer of copies and, possibly, of originals. The agreement will only be deferred as to the moment of the succession of States. The Convention will thus generate archival claims, instead of preventing them.

2.1.4. The major current disputed archival claims, with the exception of those originating from removal of archives as a result of warfare, are due to the absence of archival agreements, either because the general instrument relating to the change of sovereignty did not prescribe the conclusion of such an agreement, or because the archival agreement provided for in the general instrument was not actually concluded through the opposition of one (or more) of the parties concerned.

One of the Convention's basic objectives would consist in introducing in the international law, as a principle, that the succession of States with respect to archives is to be settled by way of concluding an agreement. It certainly may happen that a State, although a Party to the Convention, will refuse to enter into negotiations on the archival agreement. So may it happen with any provision of any international Convention, Procedures to be followed in such cases are specified in international law (see articles 42 to 45 of the Vienna Convention).

2.1.5. For the above reasons, the Working Group considers that one of the essential articles of the Convention could and should have been worded as follows:

> "In all cases of succession of States, the passing of State archives from the predecessor State to the successor State shall be settled by agreement between them. The agreement shall conform to the principles and criteria set forth in articles o to o of the present Convention."

2.2. Criteria for determining the categories of State archives which shall pass from the predecessor State to the successor State

Provided that the rule of concluding special agreements be included in the Convention, articles specifying which categories of archives should be subject to the bi-lateral (or pluri-lateral) negotiations in each type of succession of States would certainly help in reaching a mutually acceptable settlement.

The Working Group examined whether the definitions of the various categories of archives to be transferred according to the Convention could be instrumental in facilitating such negotiations.

(i) All four articles concerned (27, 28, 30 and 31) mention one of these categories: "the part of State archives of the predecessor State which, for normal administrations of the territory to which the succession of States relates, should be in that territory" (or, in article 27 "should be at the disposal of the State to which the territory concerned is transferred").

(ii) All four articles identify another category defined as follows "the part of State archives of the predecessor State other than the part mentioned in subparagraph (a) [subparagraph (b) in article 28, i.e. the category mentioned hereabove] that relates exclusively or principally to the territory to which the succession of States relates."

(iii) Article 28 contains in its paragraph 1 a subparagraph (a) worded as follow[s]:

"archives having belonged to the territory to which the succession of States relates and having become State archives of the predecessor State during the period of dependence . . . ."

Remarks on the above definitions

ad (i) The definition is consistent with internationally recognized principles and practices of archive administration and thus can be referred to when negotiating an archival agreement.

ad(ii) The second definition merely rewords the "principle of territorial pertinence" which has been rejected by the studies conducted under the auspices of Unesco as incompatible with the principle of provenance and inapplicable because of its ambiguity. The ownership of archives cannot be determined by or on the basis of the information contained in them, but only by their provenance.

The proper wording for the definition of the category archives referred to in the subparagraph should read as follows:

"the part of State archives of the predecessor State created by the transactions of administrations and institutions responsible exclusively or principally for the affairs of the territory to which the succession of States relates."

The above definition requires two additions:

a) "in cases where, in the process of change of sovereignty, a significant part of the population leaves the territory of the successor State and settles in the territory of the predecessor State, this fact shall be taken into account when negotiating the succession of States in respect of archives."

b) "unless otherwise agreed by the parties concerned, the definition hereabove does not cover the archives created by military occupation authorities."

ad (iii) The third category introduces the concept of "archives belonging to a territory." This concept is not sufficiently precise.

The category of archives to which the subparagraph refers to and which certainly shall pass, under an archival agreement, from the predecessor State to the successor State, is in fact:

"the archives constituted within the territory before it became dependent from the predecessor State and subsequently integrated in the State archives of the predecessor State whether preserved in situ or removed from the territory and entrusted to custodial institutions (archives, libraries, museums) located within the territory of the predecessor State."

Paragraph 4 of article 28 contains also the expression "archives . . . having belonged to the territory." The term "constituted within the territory" is more appropriate.

2.3. Date of the passing of State archives

The Working Group can make no comment on the legal principle set forth in article 22 regarding the date of passing of State archives. It considers however that, in order to make the Convention applicable, a second paragraph should be added to the article, worded as follows:

" 2. The time table for the transfer of archives from the territory of the predecessor State to the territory of the successor State and from the territory of the successor State to the territory of the predecessor State shall be specified in the agreement concluded in accordance with article o" (see above, comment 2.1.5.).

2.4. The preservation of the integrity of archive groups

The odd wording of the title of article 25 in English version (Preservation of the integral character of groups of State archives) is certainly due to a wrong translation from the French: "Sauvegarde de l'intégrité des fonds d'archives d'État." The text of the article is not clear. An understandable wording might have been:

> "In the settlement of the succession of State archives, the predecessor State and the successor State shall observe, as far as possible, the principle of respect for the integrity of archive groups."

2.5. The concept of joint heritage

In document A/CONF.117/C.1/L-29/Rev.1, Switzerland proposed an amendment to article 24 (renumbered 25 in the final text) for inserting a paragraph 2 introducing the concept of "joint heritage", already approved by the General Conference of Unesco. This amendment was rejected by 32 votes to 17 with 14 abstentions.

In some cases of succession of State archives, no settlement can be reached without recourse to the concept of joint heritage, since all parties concerned (the predecessor State and the successor State or States) have equal titles to the ownership of archive groups, but the latter cannot be dismembered without destroying their legal, historical and evidential value.

The paragraph of the Convention on joint heritage could have been worded as follows :

> "Archive groups created by administrations, functions of which are shared between the predecessor State and the successor State or States, as a result of the succession of States, may be declared in the special archival agreement "joint heritage." Rights and responsibilities connected with the custody of and access to the joint archival heritage shall be specified in the agreement."

2.6. Principles and dispositions which require no amendment for being applicable

Principles and dispositions contained in articles 21, 23, 24 26, paragraphs 3–5 of article 27, paragraphs 3–7 of article 28, article 29, paragraphs 2–5 of article 30 and paragraphs 2–5 of article 31 are applicable in their present wording.

The definition of the term "State archives" as worded in article 20 does not exclude divergent interpretations. However, since it is consistent with the other articles of the Convention and its intent is clear enough, it can be used during negotiations by <u>bona fide</u> parties.

3. Conclusions

3.1. The Working Group could not but conclude that the problems raised above could have been avoided, had the International Law Commission and the Vienna Conference called for archival expertise in wording the text.

The text, as it now stands, except for the articles and paragraphs listed above in special comment 2.6., is inapplicable.

3.2. Until the development under the auspices of the UN, of an applicable Convention on succession of States in respect of archives, States faced with problems of this type may refer, during bi-lateral or pluri-lateral negotiations, to the report of the Director General of Unesco quoted in general comment 1.5. of the present document.

APPENDIX IV

UN Resolution "Return or Restitution of Cultural Property to the Countries of Origin" 22 October 1991 (46/10)*

Return or Restitution of Cultural Property to the Countries of Origin

The General Assembly,

Recalling its resolutions 3026 A (XXVII) of 18 December 1972, 3148 (XXVIII) of 14 December 1973, 3187 (XXVIII) of 18 December 1973, 3391 (XXX) of 19 November 1975, 31/40 of 30 November 1976, 32/18 of 11 November 1977, 33/50 of 14 December 1978, 34/64 of 29 November 1979, 35/127 and 35/128 of 11 December 1980, 36/64 of 27 November 1981, 38/34 of 25 November 1983, 40/19 of 21 November 1985, 42/7 of 22 October 1987 and 44/18 of 6 November 1989,

Recalling also the Convention on the Means of Prohibiting and Preventing the Illicit Import, Export and Transfer of Ownership of Cultural Property adopted on 14 November 1970 by the General Conference of the United Nations Educational, Scientific and Cultural Organization,

Taking note with satisfaction of the report of the Secretary-General submitted in cooperation with the Director-General of the United Nations Educational, Scientific and Cultural Organization,

Noting with satisfaction that, following its appeal, other Member States have become parties to the Convention,

Aware of the importance attached by the countries of origin to the return of cultural property which is of fundamental spiritual and cultural value to them, so that they may constitute collections representative of their cultural heritage,

---

* United Nations, "Return or Restitution of Cultural Property to the Countries of Origin," 22 October 1991 (46/10), *Official Records of the General Assembly, Forty-Sixth Session,* Supplement No. 49. (A/46/49), p. 14. [Also available in a Russian edition.]

Reaffirming the importance of inventories as an essential tool for the understanding and protection of cultural property and for the identification of dispersed heritage and as a contribution to the advancement of scientific and artistic knowledge and intercultural communication,

Deeply concerned at the clandestine excavations and illicit traffic in cultural property that continue to impoverish the cultural heritage of all peoples,

Again supporting the solemn appeal made on 7 June 1978 by the Director-General of the United Nations Educational, Scientific and Cultural Organization for the return of irreplaceable cultural heritage to those who created it,

1. Commends the United Nations Educational, Scientific and Cultural Organization and the Intergovernmental Committee for Promoting the Return of Cultural Property to Its Countries of Origin or Its Restitution in Case of Illicit Appropriation on the work they have accomplished, in particular through the promotion of bilateral negotiations, for the return or restitution of cultural property, the preparation of inventories of movable cultural property, the reduction of illicit traffic in cultural property and the dissemination of information to the public;

2. Reaffirms that the restitution to a country of its objets d'art, monuments, museum pieces, archives, manuscripts, documents and any other cultural or artistic treasures contributes to the strengthening of international cooperation and to the preservation and flowering of universal cultural values through fruitful cooperation between developed and developing countries;

3. Recommends that Member States adopt or strengthen the necessary protective legislation with regard to their own heritage and that of other peoples;

4. Requests Member States to study the possibility of including in permits for excavations a clause requiring archeologists and palaeontologists to provide the national authorities with photographic documentation of each object brought to light during the excavations immediately after its discovery;

5. Invites Member States to continue drawing up, in cooperation with the United Nations Educational, Scientific and Cultural Organization, systemic inventories of cultural property existing in their territory and of their cultural property abroad;

6. Also recommends that Member States should ensure that inventories of museum collections include not only the items on display but also those in storage, and that they comprise all necessary documentation, particularly photographs of each item;

7. Also invites Member States engaged in seeking the recovery of cultural and artistic treasures from the seabed, in accordance with international law, to facilitate by mutually acceptable conditions the participation of States having a historical and cultural link with those treasures;

8. Appeals to Member States to cooperate closely with the Intergovernmental Committee for Promoting the Return of Cultural Property to Its Countries of Origin or Its Restitution in Case of Illicit Appropriation and to conclude bilateral agreements for this purpose;

9. Also appeals to Member States to encourage the mass information media and educational and cultural institutions to strive to arouse a greater and more general awareness with regard to the return or restitution of cultural property to its country of origin;

10. Requests States parties to the Convention on the Means of Prohibiting and Preventing the Illicit Import, Export and Transfer of Ownership of Cultural Property to keep the Secretary-General of the United Nations and the Director-General of the United Nations Educational, Scientific and Cultural Organization fully informed of the measures taken to ensure implementation of the Convention at the national level;

11. Welcomes the steady increase in the number of States parties to the Convention;

12. Invites once again those Member States that have not yet done so to sign and ratify the Convention;

13. Requests the Secretary-General of the United Nations, in cooperation with the Director-General of the United Nations Educational, Scientific and Cultural Organization, to submit to the General Assembly at its forty-eighth session a report on the implementation of the present resolution;

14. Decides to include in the provisional agenda of its forty-eighth session the item entitled "Return or restitution of cultural property to the countries of origin".

APPENDIX V

Agreement on the Right of Succession in Relation to State Archives of the Former USSR: *"Soglashenie o pravopreemstve v otnoshenii gosudarstvennykh arkhivov byvshego Soiuza SSSR,"* Moscow, 6 July 1992*

СОГЛАШЕНИЕ

О правопреемстве в отношении государственных
архивов бывшего Союза ССР

Государства—участники Содружества Независимых Государств,
именуемые далее Стороны,

признавая, что одним из последствий прекращения существования
Союза ССР является вопрос о правопреемстве в отношении государственных архивов,

считая необходимым определить общий подход к решению данного
вопроса,

придавая важное значение созданию полноценных архивных фондов
государств—участников,

согласились о следующем:

Статья 1

Стороны, исходя из принципа целостности и неделимости фондов,
образовавшихся в результате деятельности высших государственных
структур бывших Российской Империи и Союза ССР, которые хранятся
в государственных архивах, находящихся за пределами их территорий,

*   Russian version published in *Vestnik arkhivista* 10(4) 1992: 3–5, and
reprinted in *Arkhivy Ukraïny* 1992 (1–3): 4–5. An unofficial English translation
follows the Russian original in this appendix.

не претендуют на право владения этими комплексами документальных материалов.

Статья 2

Стороны взаимно признают осуществленный в соответствии с их национальным законодательством переход под их юрисдикцию государственных архивов и других архивов союзного уровня, включая государственные отраслевые архивные фонды бывшего Союза ССР, находящиеся на их территории.

Статья 3

Стороны имеют право на возвращение тех фондов, которые образовались на их территории и в разное время оказались за их пределами.

Статья 4

В случае, когда отсутствует возможность физического выделения комплекса документов, каждая из Сторон имеет право доступа к ним и получения необходимых копий. При проведении работ по выявлению и копированию документов для государств—участников Содружества официальным представителям государственной архивной службы предоставляются максимально благоприятные условия для работы.

Статья 5

Представители государственных архивных служб Сторон проводят регулярные консультации на многосторонней или двусторонней основе для обсуждения вопросов сотрудничества в данной области.

Статья 6

Стороны обеспечивают доступ исследователей к документам их государственных архивов в соответствии с порядком, установленным их национальным законодательством.

Статья 7

Стороны признают на своих территориях юридическую силу архивных справок, выданных государственными архивными учреждениями других государств—участников Содружества.

Статья 8

В тех случаях, когда какие-либо документы, хранящиеся в государственных архивах одного государства, затрагивают интересы другого или других государств—участников Содружества, заинтересованные Стороны принимают дополнительные согласованные меры по использованию и обеспечению сохранности этих документов и предотвращению их уничтожения.

Статья 9

Вопросы, связанные с возвращением документов, с порядком обмена копиями и расчетов за предоставление копий, в каждом конкретном случае должны быть предметом двусторонних соглашений.

Статья 10

В случаях, когда Стороной—владельцем передается право использования архивных документов, затрагивающих интересы другой Стороны, иностранным государствам, юридическим или физическим лицам, право на использование этих документов сохраняется за Стороной, интересы которой затрагивает этот документ.

Статья 11

Соглашение вступает в силу с момента его подписания.

Совершено в городе Москве 6 июля 1992 года в одном подлинном экземпляре на русском языке. Подлинный экземпляр хранится в Архиве Правительства Республики Беларусь, которое направит государствам, подписавшим настоящее Соглашение, его заверенную копию.

[signatures]

[English Translation]

AGREEMENT

on the right of succession in relation to state archives
of the former Soviet Union

The Participatory Governments of the Commonwealth of Independent States, hereinafter referred to as the "Sides,"

Recognizing that one of the results of the cessation of the existence of the Union of Soviet Socialist Republics is the question of succession in relation to state archives,

Considering it necessary to define a common approach to the resolution of this question,

Assigning important significance to the creation of optimal archival fonds of the participatory States,

Have agreed to the following:

Article 1

The Sides, basing themselves in the principle of the integrity and indivisibility of the archival fonds that were created as a result of the activity of the highest governmental agencies of the former Russian Empire and Union of Soviet Socialist Republics and are now housed in state archives that are located outside of a given Side's territory, have no pretensions to the right to control these complexes of documentary materials.

Article 2

The Sides reciprocally recognize the transfer under their jurisdiction, and according to their respective national legislations, of state archives and other archives of all-Union significance, including state branch archival fonds of the former Union of Soviet Socialist Republics, that are located on their territories.

Article 3

The Sides have the right of the return of those fonds which were created on their territories but at some other time have appeared outside their borders.

Article 4

In such cases where it is impossible to physically divide a complex of documents, each of the Sides has the right of access to said documents and the receipt of any necessary copies. During the execution of the work for the retrieval and copying of documents for participatory states of the Commonwealth of Independent States, official representatives of a state archival service will be accorded maximally beneficial conditions for said work.

Article 5

Representatives of the state archival services of the Sides will conduct regular consultations on a multilateral or bilateral basis for the discussion of questions of collaboration in this field.

Article 6

The Sides will facilitate the access of researchers to documents of their state archives in accordance with regulations established by their national legislatures.

Article 7

The Sides recognize on their territories the legal validity and force of archival certificates [or attestations] issued by the state archival institutions of other participatory governments of the Commonwealth.

Article 8

In those cases where documents located in the archives of one government might affect the interests of one or another participatory governments of the Commonwealth, the interested Sides may take supplementary measures by mutual agreement on the use and preservation of these documents as well as the prevention of their destruction.

Article 9

Questions regarding the return of documents as well as the regime for exchanging copies and fiscal responsibility for the provision of copies shall be the subject of bilateral agreements in each concrete case.

Article 10

In those cases where the interests of a Side are affected by the right to use archival documents that may be furnished by the proprietary Side to foreign governments, legal entities, or individuals, the right to use these documents shall remain with the Side whose interests are affected by that document.

Article 11

This Agreement enters into force from the moment of its signing.

Completed in the city of Moscow on 6 July 1992 in one original copy in the Russian language. The original copy will be stored in the Archive of the Government of the Republic of Belarus, which will provide certified copies to the signatory governments of the present Agreement.

[signatures]

[*English translation—Robert De Lossa*]

Resolutions of the XXXth International Conference of the Roundtable on Archives (CITRA). Thessalonica, 12–16 October 1994

RESOLUTION 1

The XXX International Conference of the Round Table on Archives

Considering that it is in the interests of all peoples that solutions be found to disputed claims arising from the displacement of archives as a result of the Second World War and of the process of decolonisation,

reaffirms the mission of archives in guaranteeing every nation's right to historical continuity,

recalls the accepted archival principles that archives are inalienable and imprescriptible, and should not be regarded as "trophies" or as objects of exchange,

confirms the support of the archival community for the principles embodied in the report of the Director General to the 20th session of the General Conference of UNESCO (20C/102),

calls upon the Executive Committee of ICA to keep CITRA informed of the results of the work of the Committee on Archival Legal Matters,

invites the Executive Committee of ICA to formulate at its next meeting, on the basis of and in the spirit of the deliberations of the present conference, a position paper stating the views of the archival community on the resolution of disputed claims, with principles to be followed and concepts to be rejected in accordance with existing legal practice,

recommends the Executive Committee of ICA to lend its support to bilateral and multilateral professional efforts aimed at ending disputed claims inherited from the period 1923–1989 and at resolving new problems confronting states formerly parts of federations which have dissolved,

expresses the wish that relevant intergovernmental organisations, in particular the United Nations, UNESCO and the Council of Europe, support, with their member States, non governmental initiatives intended to settle disputed claims and reconstitute the historical heritage of each nation.

RESOLUTION 2

The XXX International Conference of the Round Table on Archives

Considering the value of microfilm and other forms of imaging technology in reconstituting the archival heritage,

further considering the reciprocal obligations of former colonial powers and former colonies to co-operate in identifying and copying relevant material,

recognising that excellent work has already been done to implement the decision taken by the General Conference of UNESCO at its 23rd session held in Sofia in 1985 (23C/5 appr.07208) on the reconstitution of the archival heritage,

recalling that clear legal and technical standards for microfilming already exist,

calls on the Executive Committee of ICA, in co-operation with UNESCO, to reactivate and review the International Microfilming Programme, and in particular to investigate fully existing and new sources of funding, and to encourage regional branches and national archives to co-ordinate efforts to establish priorities for further reprography, including imaging technologies, and to distribute copies of material of joint interest.

RESOLUTION 3

The XXX International Conference of the Round Table on Archives

Recognising the particular role and responsibilities of those archival institutions which have in their custody holdings created during periods of common history with other nations, encourages these institutions to pursue or initiate a policy that gives equal access to all countries participating in the joint heritage,

further recognising the important role and responsibilities of the major international custodial institutions that collect and preserve dispersed archives which might otherwise have been destroyed,

emphasises that, in addition to optimal preservation and free access to these archives, there is an overriding need for full intellectual control of them, and underlines the value of ISAD (G) in achieving this, and further emphasises the value of using modern methods of information storage and retrieval to improve and widen access to these archives.

"The View of the Archival Community on the Settling of Disputed Claims": Position Paper Adopted by the Executive Committee of the International Council on Archives at Its Meeting in Guangzhou, 10–13 April 1995*

1. The Diplomatic Practice Followed until the Second World War

Despite the absence of generally applicable legal instruments, a diplomatic routine for settling disputed archival claims was progressively established from the time of the Treaty of Westphalia onwards.

The following rules were, in practice, implicitly respected

i) all treaties relating to changes of sovereignty over a given territory included clauses dealing with the surrender or exchange of archives;

ii) lists of archives to be transferred or copied as a result of such treaties were specifically agreed between the two parties;

iii) documents necessary for the conduct of current business and for administrative continuity were almost invariably handed over by the predecessor state to the successor State either in original form or as copies;

iv) archives captured and displaced during hostilities were returned once peace was concluded;

v) archives of temporary military authorities of occupation remained the property of the occupying powers.

2. The Break with Tradition after the Second World War

The traditional practice of devolution and restitution of archives was abruptly abandoned in 1945.

---

* Reprinted with permission of the ICA. Originally reprinted in *CITRA 1993–1995*, pp. 256–58; and *Dossier on Archival Claims*, pp. 45–47.

Despite the normalisation of relations since then, no peace treaty has been concluded with the main power defeated in 1945, the repatriation of archives seized during hostilities has not been systematically dealt with and, at the global level, the emergence of a hundred or so sovereign States through the process of decolonisation has occurred without there being specific instruments for the devolution of archives.

The abandonment of traditional practice has led to an unprecedented accumulation of unresolved problems concerning the restitution and devolution of archives. The legal vacuum thus created is all the more pernicious as it has been tacitly accepted by all governments.

3. *The International Imperative*

The International Council on Archives believes the time has come to put an end to the exceptional conditions which have lasted fifty years and to begin getting rid of disputed archival claims arising from the Second World War, decolonisation and the breakup of federations following the events of 1989.

The experience of the 1983 Vienna Intergovernmental Conference shows that an international convention is useless if it is established without a consensus among states at the price of a contradictory political debate and without regard to how applicable the proposed measures are.

Given the multitude of claims, of different types and origins, which have built up during fifty years of inaction, only a pragmatic approach offers a reasonable chance of breaking the deadlock.

The objective is to resume, as quickly as possible, the traditional practice of dealing with disputed claims by mean of negotiations between the interested parties. However, in view of the number of cases and the complex interrelations between the problems however, an international consultation seems essential if the situation is to get back to normal.

The consultation would aim to secure the agreement of States to the objective of settling the claims, to establish a typology of cases, to devise a conceptual framework acceptable to all and to draw up principles to be observed during the preparation of bi-lateral agreements.

The consultation could take place within the framework or under the aegis of international and regional inter-governmental organisations with responsibilities in the archival field.

The consultation would also have to take account of the international regulation of the movement and return of cultural property, which is evolving rapidly. Instruments dealing with the transfer of cultural assets and with the return of cultural assets which were illegally taken, such as the Unesco Convention of 14 November 1970 and the Unidroit draft Convention currently under consideration explicitly include archives in their field of competence.

The International Council on Archives is ready to lend its support to co-ordinating initiatives which might be taken by the different organisations and expresses the hope that the conclusion of a new International Convention could be examined after the traditional practice has been re-established.

4. *Concepts and Principles*

The body of documents relating to the settling of disputed archival claims which Unesco and ICA produced between 1974 and 1994, provides a sufficient basis to open up the desired consultation.

The consensus that is being sought could be built up from a number of concepts and principles appearing in these documents.

a) The inalienability and imprescriptibility of public records

National laws agree in conferring the status of inalienable and imprescriptible public property on public records. The transfer of ownership of public archives especially in the case of succession of States can therefore only occur through a legislative act of the State which created them.

b) Provenance and respect for the integrity of archival fonds

Archives are not groups of documents assembled at the whim of collectors, but instead are accumulated through the operation of their creating institutions. Their definitive place of preservation is determined by the national law of each country.

Archival doctrine, which is founded on the principle of provenance, there-fore excludes, on the one hand, the possibility of dismembering fonds, and on the other hand, the acquisition by any archive institution of fonds which do not fall within its jurisdiction.

c) The right of access and the right of reproduction

Fonds created by institutions where succession is shared between several States, and which cannot be broken up, should be physically integrated into the archival heritage of one of the States.

A state of permanent litigation can however be avoided if the other States sharing a common history see recognised a right of access to these fonds and a right to copy them.

To give effect to these rights, Unesco has, since 1979, recommended the introduction of the concept of common heritage, which means that identical rights of access are given, on the one hand to the States concerned and on the other hand to the citizens of those States.

d) Equity and international cooperation

Useful though recourse to the above principles is, it is not sufficient. The settlement of each claim raises particular problems which the parties concerned have to overcome by common agreement and in a spirit of fairness and mutual respect.

The International Council on Archives is convinced that a shared willingness to co-operate can, within a reasonable time, set right the abnormal situation which has resulted from political constraints in the post-war decades.

APPENDIX VIII

Official Act of Transfer from Prague and Select Communiqués Concerning the Ukrainian Historical Cabinet (UIK) under the Ministry of the Interior of the Czechoslovak Republic (October 1945)

[in English Translation]

Embassy of the USSR   25 August 1945
in Czechoslovakia,   No. 205.
Prague

To The Minister of Internal Affairs of the Republic of Czechoslovakia
Mr. V. Nosek.

The USSR Embassy in the Republic of Czechoslovakia reports that all legal norms resulting from responsibilities taken on by the Archive of the Ministry of the Interior of the Republic of Czechoslovakia with regard to private owners of deposits upon acceptance of their documents for safekeeping in the Ukrainian, Russian historical archive (that have been presented to the Soviet Union) will be upheld by Soviet agencies that acquire said archives and all complaints by private individuals related to said deposits should be directed to the Soviet agencies.

The Ambassador of the USSR in Czechoslovakia –

V. Zorin *

---

*   Translated from the Russian by Roman Altshuler from the copy retained in the recently declassified secret *opys* of the administrative records of TsDIAK in TsDAVO, 4703/2/2, fol. 13.

[No header]   Copy: 3 ~~17~~ [handwritten and struck out]
Honorable Mister Ambassador,   12 [handwritten]

I have the honor of bringing to your attention the fact that the Government of the Republic of Czechoslovakia, at its session on 14 August of the present year, has decreed the presentation to the Ukrainian Soviet Socialist Republic of the Ukrainian part of the so-called Prague "Russian Archive," as testimony to the sincere friendship between our people, now close neighbors,

The conditions for the transfer of the "Russian Archive," which is transferred to the Academy of Science of the USSR, must also be fulfilled in the case of this transfer, i.e., wherein the Ukrainian Central Archive will present Czechoslovakia with photocopies of the transferred documents, and that the transferred archive will be kept in Kyiv in the Ukrainian Central Archive as an independent division entitled the "Prague Ukrainian Archive."

The Ministry of Foreign Affairs would be highly grateful to you, Mister Ambassador, for specifying the date on which the archive will be actually transferred, so that all essential conditions for the archive's transfer may be undertaken.

In this connection, I will permit myself to note that materials from the aforementioned archive that are indubitably the property of the "Czechoslovak State Archive," can be transferred immediately, whereas materials that are on deposit can be transferred only upon the settling of pertinent legal preconditions.

On this occasion, I ask you, Mister Ambassador, to be assured of my high regard for you.

Prague, 22nd August 1945

[signed] p.p. [*] Klementis

To:
Mister   certified [signature not deciphered]
V.A. ZORIN   Eliukei
Ambassador of the Union of Soviet Socialist
Republics.

Prague.
---------- **

---

* The first initial is blurred.

** Translated from the Russian by Roman Altshuler from the original in the recently declassified secret *opys* of the administrative records of TsDIAK, in TsDAVO, 4703/2/2, fols. 11–12.

0001 5 [handwritten and stricken through]

<u>ACT</u>

30th August 1945, Prague.

We the undersigned are, on one hand, the Representatives of the Republic of Czechoslovakia in the person of the director of the Archive of the Ministry of Internal Affairs University Professor Doctor Iosyp Borovychka [Josip Borovička] and special advisor to the Archive of the Ministry of Internal Affairs Doctor Vatslav Peshak [Vaclav Pešak] and Head of the Ukrainian Historical Cabinet of the Archive of the Ministry of Internal Affairs Mykola Balash [Mikola Balaš]; on the other hand, the Representatives of the Ukrainian Soviet Socialist Republic in the person of the Deputy Chief of the Administration of State Archives of the People's Commissariat of Internal Affairs of the Ukrainian SSR—Captain Pavlo Ivanovych Pavliuk, Director of the Central State Archive of the Ukrainian Soviet Socialist Republic—Captain Hordii Semenovich Pshenychnyi, and Deputy Chief of Administration of the Department of State Archives of the of the People's Commissariat of Internal Affairs of Lviv Oblast—Sr. Lieutenant Hryts'ko Prokopovych Neklesa, have established the present act concerning the transfer of Ukrainian documentary materials in Prague on 18–30 August 1945 in accordance with the resolution of the Council of Ministers of the Republic of Czechoslovakia of 14 August 1945 concerning the transfer, as a gift to the Ukrainian Soviet Socialist Republic, of Ukrainian documentary materials, retained in the Ukrainian Archive of the Ministry of Internal Affairs in Prague.

Representatives of the archival agencies of the Ministry of Internal Affairs in Prague—CzSR transferred, while Representatives of the archival agencies of the Ukrainian Soviet Socialist Republic received:

1. Archival documents, recorded in the first inventory book from No. 1 through No. 450, with the exceptions of Nos. 44–111, 140–159, 161–164, 201–210, 252–272, 305–320, 353–354, 405–406.

2. Archival documents, recorded in the second volume of the inventory book under Nos. 451–488.

3. Archival documents, recorded in the third volume of the inventory book under Nos. 488–459, with the exception of Nos. 502–508, 510–513.

Points 1 and 3 indicate Nos. present in the *opys* that were not present among the documents at the time of receipt.

Representatives of the archival agencies of the Ministry of Internal Affairs in Prague explain that the missing documents under the numbers stated above are photographic documents that were described together with other documents, but are stored separately with documents that have not yet been processed and are contained in unnumbered boxes.

4. Archival documents, recorded in the inventory book of the former Ukrainian National Archive-Museum from No. 1 through No. 3232.

Conducting an actual verification of documents with the *opysy* is not deemed possible, inasmuch as every document is described, but all are stored together in boxes that are not marked with inventory numbers.

5. Reference apparatus, consisting of 2 volumes of inventory *opys* (451–588), inventory *opys* UNAM (1–3232), and 12 thematic *opysy* for photo-documents.

6. Photographic documents—negatives and positives according to the inventory *opys* v. I, II, III and the *opysy* of UNAM.

7. Besides the above-mentioned, archival documents of the following institutions were accepted unordered and not described:

1. Ukraïns'kyi Robitnychyi Universytet [Ukrainian Workers' University]—5 boxes.

2. Ukraïns'kyi Sotsiolohychnyi Instytut [Ukrainian Sociological Institute].—3 boxes.

3. Ukraïns'kyi Hromads'kyi Komitet [Ukrainian Community Committee].

4. Ukraïns'ka Zahranychna Partiia Sotsialistiv-Revoliutsioneriv [Ukrainian Party of Socialist-Revolutionaries Abroad].—11 boxes.

5. Ukraïns'ka Selians'ka Spilka [Ukrainian Peasant Association].—5 packages.

6. Ukraïns'ka Vil'na Spilka [Ukrainian Liberation Association]—3 packages.

7. Orhanizatsiia "Ukraïns'koï Khaty" ["Ukrainian House" Organization]—1 package.

8. Ukraïns'ka "Knyhozbirnia" v Prazi [Ukrainian "Library Collections" in Prague]—1 package.

9. Ukraïns'kyi Pedahohychnyi Instytut v Prazi / 1927–1932 / [Ukrainian Pedagogical Institute in Prague (1927–1932)].

10. Kubans'kyi Arkhiv [Kuban Archive].

11. Arkhiv Ukraïns'koho Hromads'koho Vydavnychoho Fondu [Archive of the Ukrainian Community Publishing Fund].

12. Dilovodstvo Ukraïns'koho Kabineti za 1927–1945 r.r.r. [*sic*] kotre stosuiet'sia peredavaemykh [*sic*] arkhivnykh materialiv [Records of the Ukrainian Cabinet for 1927–1945 concerning the archival materials transfered].

The Present act is compiled in two [identical] copies in the Ukrainian and Czech languages.

Representatives of the Republic of Czechoslovakia:
[with signatures]
Professor Dr. I. Borovychka [Borovička] (s.r.)
Special advisor Dr. V. Peshak [Pešak] (s.r.)
Head of the Ukrainian Archive M. Balash [Balaš] (s.r.)

Representatives of the Soviet Socialist Republic:
[with signatures]
Captain P. Pavliuk (s.r.)
Captain H. Pshenychnyi (s.r.)
Sr. Lieutenant H. Neklesa

Certified:*

*   Translated by Roman Altshuler, Patricia Grimsted, and Robert De Lossa from the Ukrainian-languaged signed original retained in the recently declassified secret *opys* of the administrative records of TsDIAK, in TsDAVO, 4703/2/2, fols. 15–17. A Czech-language original copy is retained as fols. 18–20, and a copy in Russian translation follows fols. 21–23. *See* Ch. 9, p. 345n51.

Top secret.

TO THE CHAIRMAN OF THE COUNCIL OF THE PEOPLE'S COMISSARS OF THE UKRAINIAN SSR

to Com[rade] N.S. KHRUSHCHEV

City of Kyiv

REPORT

concerning the gift by the Government of the Republic of Czechoslovakia to the Government of the Ukrainian SSR of documentary materials of the "Ukrainian Archive."

In accordance with the orders of the People's Commissar of Internal Affairs of the USSR—Marshal of the Soviet Union C[omrade] L. P. Beria, a group of personnel of the Archival Administration under the NKVD UkrSSR consisting of four people: Captain PAVLIUK, Captain PSHENICHNYI, Captain OLEINIK, and Sr. Lieutenant NEKLESA, was dispatched to Czechoslovakia for search and retrieval of documentary materials of the archival fond of the Soviet Union, taken by German-fascist conquerors to the territory of the Czechoslovak Republic.

The group established the existence under the Archive of the Ministry of Internal Affairs, of the so-called "Ukrainian Archive," consisting essentially of documents of the "Ukrainian Historical Cabinet," organized in its time in Prague by the Ukrainian nationalist emigration.

The group's personnel, through the Soviet ambassador in Prague, Com[rade] ZORIN, posed to the Government of the Republic of Czechoslovakia the question of transferring said documents to the Ukrainian SSR. After lengthy and persistent negotiations with Prime-Minister Mr. FIRLINGER, Minister of Education Mr. NEEDLY, and Minister of Internal Affairs Mr. NOSEK, the Government of Czechoslovakia, at its session on 14th August 1945, at the suggestion of Minister of Education Prof. NEEDLY, the decision was made: as a sign of sincere friendship between the Czech and Ukrainian peoples and friendly relations between both neighboring lands—to transfer the so-called Ukrainian Archive as a gift to the Ukrainian Soviet Socialist Republic.

The ceremonial transfer of the archive and signing of the act of transfer took place on 4 September 1945 in Prague in the building of the Archive of the Ministry of Internal Affairs.* Speeches were read at the signing of the act by: Minister of Internal Affairs Mr. NOSEK, Minister of Education Mr. NEEDLY, Ambassador of the USSR to Czechoslovakia C[omrade] ZORIN, and Deputy Chief of the Archival Administration under the NKVD UkrSSR Captain PAVLIUK.

Present at the transfer ceremony: from the Republic of Czechoslovakia: Minister of Internal Affairs Mr. NOSEK, Minister of Education Mr. NEEDLY, Minister of Information Mr. KOPETSKII [Kopecký], Director of the Archive of the Ministry of Internal Affairs Professor Borovichka [Borovička], Special Advisor to the Archive of the Ministry of Internal Affairs Dr. PISHAK, Head of the Ukrainian Historical Cabinet BALASH [Balaš], et al., present from the Soviet side: Ambassador of the USSR in Czechoslovakia V. A. ZORIN, political advisor to the Embassy Second Deputy Councilor I. A. CHICHAEV, Deputy Chief of the Archival Administration under the NKVD UkrSSR Captain P. I. PAVLIUK, and Director of the Central State Archive of the UkrSSR Captain H. S. PSHENICHNYI.

"The Ukrainian Historical Cabinet" was composed from the following sources:

a)   donations—from nationalist organizations and institutions abroad and private individuals—Ukrainian nationalists-émigrés.

b)   purchase of historical documents from various persons.

c)   documents accepted for safekeeping—deposits—from nationalist organizations and various persons under specific conditions—e.g. until the death of the depositor, for a period of 15–20 years, "until the moment of transfer to Ukraine under favorable circumstances," etc.

This group of documents was transferred to Ukraine only after the Soviet Ambassador to Czechoslovakia C[omrade] Zorin gave a written statement of obligation to the effect that all obligations undertaken by the Ministry of Internal Affairs of the Republic of Czechoslovakia will be adhered to by Soviet agencies.

---

*   See picture below, on p. 580.

Among the documents received are important materials of Ukrainian bourgeois-nationalist organizations, institutions, and their activists, e.g.—the records of the Ukrainian Party of Socialist-Revolutionaries, the Ukrainian Peasant Association, the Ukrainian Liberation Association, the Ukrainian Community Committee, the Ukrainian Sociological Institute, the Ukrainian Pedagogical Institute, the "Ukrainian Workers" University, et al., as well as documents and letters of outstanding activists of Ukrainian bourgeois-nationalist parties and governments—M. SHAPOVAL, M. TKACHENKO, M. GALAGAN, ZHYVOTKO, OBIDNYI, Prof. HRYHORIIV, Prof. TYMCHENKO, Prof. S. SHELUKHYN, VYNNYCHENKO, etc. In addition to this, there are individual letters of famous Ukrainian writers—M. KOTSIUBINSKYI, V. STEFANYK, P. MYRNYI, et al.

Among all these materials there is a large number of documents of the period of the October Revolution and the Civil War in Ukraine, as well as a sizeable group of documents concerning activities of the Ukrainian emigration abroad.

In total, one freight carload of documentary materials was received and has been already delivered to Kyiv.

Detailed information about their content and quantity will be presented to you after their processing.

People's Commissar of Internal Affairs
of the Ukrainian SSR

(RIASNOI)

25 September 1945
No. 6/3/121932
Kyiv[*]

---

[*]   Translated from the Russian by Roman Altshuler from the original, TsDAVO, 4703/2/2, fols. 28–30; a similar letter to L. V. Beria in Moscow follows, fols. 31–33.

OMGUS Report on Restitution of Soviet Cultural Property, Property Division, Restitution Branch, Richard F. Howard, Deputy Chief for Cultural Restitution (MFA&A), Karlsruhe, Germany, 20 September 1948

The following three pages represent facsimile reproduction from digitized files supplied by National Archives of the United States from RG260 (OMGUS), Records of the Property Division, Reparations and Restitution Branch, MFA&A Section, Records Pertaining to Restitution, Soviet–General, box 723.

HP/rf

OFFICE OF MILITARY GOVERNMENT FOR GERMANY (U.S.)
Property Division
Restitution Branch
APO 403
Karlsruhe, Germany

PD 007 (RES/MFAA)   20 September 1948

SUBJECT: Status of Applications for the Restitution of
Soviet Cultural Property Filed with MFA&A Section,
Restitution Branch, Karlsruhe

TO   : Restitution Branch, Property Division
Attn: USSR Restitution Mission

     1. Reference is made to conversation between Captain
G.P. Sidorin, your Mission, and Mr. H.E. Pilliod, MFA&A
Section, on 16 September 1948.

     2. Attached herewith are three (3) lists concerning
Soviet claims and restitution shipments to the USSR forwarded
to you for information as requested:

          List 1: Completed Soviet Claims
          List 2: Restitution Shipments to the USSR
          List 3: Dropped Soviet Claims (Unknown Location)

     3. Remarks about these Lists

          a. List 1

               The fifty-five (55) Soviet claims of this list
have been the object of an investigation, the items, when
found, have been brought to either the Munich or the Wiesbaden Central Collecting Point and restituted to the USSR
from there in one of the Restitution Shipments reported
in List 2.

               It should be noted that out of the 603 items
restituted, 250 were originating from KIEW.

          b. List 2

               Thirteen (13) Restitution Shipments of Cultural
Material have been made to the USSR:

1179x
2H612

Status of Applications for the Restitution of Soviet Cultural
Property Filed with MFA&A Section, Restitution Branch, Karlsruhe.
PD 007 (RES/MFAA), OMGUS, 20 Sep 48

    Five   (5)   from Munich
    One   (1)   from Nürnberg
    Two   (2)   from Wiesbaden
    Three   (3)   from Offenbach
    One   (1)   from Berlin
    One   (1)   from Trypist

    These shipments included 534,120 items (paint-
ings, icons, drawings, prints, furniture, ceramics, sculptures,
weapons, textiles, coins, books, scientific collections,
foto-negatives, archives, woodwork, glass, porcelain and
numismatics).

    Out of these 534,120 items restituted, 157,717
items were originating from KIEW.

    c. List 3

        556 Soviet claims with no LOCATION given have
been dropped; they represented 751 items. Out of these
556 claims dropped, 512 were for KIEW material (516 items).

        As already stated, all the KIEW material found
in the U.S. Zone of Occupation has been restituted to the
USSR (167,717 items).

        As it was impossible to identify the Kiew material
according to the dexcription given in the Soviet claims,
they have been dropped, but all the KIEW material located
in the U.S. Zone has been restituted. It amounted to a far
greater number of items than the number of items officially
claimed. No doubt, the 516 items claimed were included in
the 167,717 actually restituted.

    4. Status of Soviet Claims still active to date:

        Bavaria   37 claims
        Wuerttemberg-Baden   5 claims
        Hesse   9 claims

        FOR THE CHIEF:

3 Incls: a/s   RICHARD F. HOWARD
                                        Deputy Chief
Mr. Pilliod   for Cultural Restitution
Tel. 247   (MFA&A)

                              2

List 2

Restituted Russian Property

						IEW
Munich	28 August 46	Lt.Col.Alexander J. SLAVIN	1178 items:	paintings & icons		-
"	15 April 47	Major Alexander BOLTANOW	2400	"	paintings, icons drawings. prints, furniture, ceramics, sculptures, weapons	17
"	15 April 47	Major Alexander BOLTANOW	136800	"	paintings, books, ceramics, weapons, coins, sculptures, textiles	110000
"	22 July 47	Major A.D. KOROVKIN	4008	"	paintings and foto-negatives	-
"	30 January 48	Major Alexander BOLTANOW	322	"	paintings, books, chemical equipment	"
"	13 October 47	Lt.Col. Alexander BOLTANOW	1	"	Neptun Fountain	-
Wiesbaden	4 October 47	Major A.J. BOLTANOW	7012	"	paintings, insects pair of elk antler	-
"	16 September 48	Capt. G.P. SIDORIN	4	"	paintings	-
Offenbach	10 June 46	Lt.Col. N.P. NOVIK	160000	"	books and documents	50000
"	31 July 46	Lt.Col. A.J. SLAVIN	65000	"	books and brochures	5000
"	24 October 47	Major A.J. BOLTANOW	40395	"	library and archival material	-
Berlin	20 September 45	Lt.Col. Constantin PIARTLEY	1000	"	archival material	-
Prypiat	25 October 45	Major Lev.Grogorovich PODOLSKY	116000	"	archives, paintings, wood-work, leatherwork, glass, porcelain, numismatics	2700

Total: 534.120   Kiev: 167.717

APPENDIX X

Recommendations of the UNESCO Conference on Cultural Return, Kyiv, December 1996 *

Рекомендації науково-практичного симпозіуму "Правові аспекти реституції культурних цінностей: теорія і практика"

Учасники науково-практичного симпозіуму "Правові аспекти реституції культурних цінностей: теорія і практика",

Усвідомлюючи негативні наслідки для розвитку культури кожної країни та кожного народу незаконного відчуження їх історичних та релігійних реліквій;

Враховуючи, що справедливе вирішення проблеми повернення культурних цінностей у разі незаконного присвоєння є важливою та актуальною сферою міжнародного культурного співробітництва, сприяє встановленню відносин довіри та взаєморозуміння між людьми різних націй та народів;

Високо оцінюючи зусилля ЮНЕСКО та Міжурядового комітету із сприяння поверненню культурних цінностей країнам їхнього походження або їх реституції в разі незаконного привласнення по підтримці ідеї повернення культурних цінностей країнам їх походження;

Відзначаючи непересічне значення для досягнення взаєморозуміння та узгоджень позицій урядових та неурядових організацій різних держав, проведення міжнародних зустрічей з питань повернення культурних цінностей, зокрема Будапештської 1993 р., Бременської 1994 р., Нью-Йоркської 1995 р. та національного семінару у Чернігові 1994 р.;

Розуміючи, що лише на засадах доброї волі та тісної спільної праці можливо подолати руйнівні наслідки для національних культур незаконного відчуження та втрат культурних цінностей;

*   Reprinted from *Povernennia kul′turnoho nadbannia Ukraïny: Problemy, zavdannia, perspektyvy,* vyp. 10, *Materialy Naukovo-praktychnoho symposiumu "Pravovi aspekty restytutsiï kul′turnykh tsinnostei: teoriia i praktyka." Kyïv, hruden′ 1996* (Kyiv, 1997), pp. 192–93 (Ukr.) and 194–95 (Engl.).

Закликаючи всі держави-члени ЮНЕСКО співпрацювати в обміні інформацією про предмети культури, котрі підлягають реституції, та сприяти процесу повернення культурних цінностей країнам їх походження;

Розглянувши правові аспекти проблеми, наголошують, що чинні міжнародні норми та правові акти щодо захисту, повернення та реституції культурних цінностей не повною мірою відповідають потребам міжнародного культурного співробітництва;

Погодились на таке:

Звернутися до Генерального Директора та Секретаріату ЮНЕСКО, а також Ради Європи щодо:

продовження зусиль по вдосконаленню міжнародно-правових норм у сфері захисту, повернення та реституції культурних цінностей, [та по] створенню ефективних механізмів міжнародного співробітництва в даній галузі,

приведення у відповідність до норм міжнародного права національних законодавств у сфері захисту, повернення та реституції культурних цінностей, посилення відповідальності країн за невиконання взятих на себе багатосторонніх та двосторонніх угод, зобов'язань у сфері захисту, повернення та реституції культурних цінностей;

сприяння міжнародному обміну інформацією про втрачені та незаконно переміщені культурні цінності, які мають підлягати поверенню та реституції, створення дієвих механізмів їх розшуку на рівні міжнародного співробітництва.

Підтримати ініціативу України, Білорусі щодо проведення спеціальної сесії Міжурядового комітету ЮНЕСКО зі сприяння поверненню культурних цінностей країнам їх походження або їх реституції в разі незаконного привласнення, присвяченої проблемам розшуку та реституції культурних цінностей, втрачених під час другої світової війни, а також питанням повернення культурних цінностей, які складають невід'ємну частину національної спадщини, державам, що отримали незалежність, необхідності окремого вивчення та публікації усього комплексу документів і правових актів, пов'язаних з проблемами переміщення культурних цінностей під час другої світової війни та в результаті її наслідків.

Засудити навмисні дії проти культурних цінностей, що мають місце під час збройних конфліктів та підтримати ідею кваліфікації таких дій як злочинів проти людства, підтримати підготовку міжнародних документів, що застерігатимуть від таких злочинів.

Підтримати зусилля по виданню в Україні збірника міжнародно-правових актів з питань збереження культурних цінностей, їх повернення і реституції, а також щодо створення спеціального сектору міжнародного права і національного законодавства в Інституті держави і права ім. В. М. Корецького НАН України;

Учасники науково-практичного симпозіуму звертаються до всіх фахівців у галузі міжнародного права, вчених, працівників музеїв, бібліотек, архівів об'єднати зусилля у розшуку та поверненні втраченої національної історико-культурної спадщини, [та] сприяти тим самим зближенню народів і культур, їх взаємозбагаченню та процвітанню.

Київ, 13 грудня 1996 р.

* *
*

Recommendations of Scientific and Practical Symposium "Legal Aspects of Restitution of Cultural Treasures: Theory and Practice"

The participants of the scientific and practical symposium "Legal aspects of restitution of cultural treasures: theory and practice",

Being aware of the negative consequences of illegal alienation of historical and cultural property for the development of culture of every country and nation;

Having in mind that the just solution of the problem concerning the return of cultural treasures in case of their illicit appropriation is an important and vital sphere of international cultural cooperation and fosters the establishment of confidence and mutual understanding between different people and nations;

Highly appreciating the efforts of UNESCO and the "Intergovernmental Committee for Promoting the Return of Cultural Property to its Countries of Origin or its Restitution in Case of Illicit Appropriation" towards the support of the idea of the return of cultiral [*sic*] treasures to the countries of their origin;

Noting the utmost importance of international meetings and conferences, symposia, "round-table" talks, meetings dedicated to the repatriation of cultural treasures and, in particular—in 1993—in Budapest, 1994—in Bremen, 1995—in New York and the National Seminar in Chernihiv in 1994 for attaining mutual understanding and combination of efforts of governmental and non-governmental organisations of different countries;

Realising that only on the basis of good will and close mutual cooperation it is possible to overcome the disastrous consequences for the national cultures of the illegal alienation and loss of cultural treasures;

Calling upor [*sic*] all UNESCO Member-States to co-operate in the sphere of exchange of information on cultural objects liable to restitution and to foster the return of cultural treasures to the countries of their origin;

Considering the problem's legal aspects and stating that the current international norms and legal acts on protection, repatriation and restitution of cultural treasures do not fully correspond to the demands of international cultural co-operation;

Have agreed as follows:

To call upon the General Director and Secretariat of UNESCO:

to continue efforts for further updating international legal norms in the sphere of protection, repatriation, restitution of cultural treasures and creation of effective mechanisms of international co-operation in this sphere,

to bring national laws in the sphere of protection, repatriation and restitution of cultural treasures in line with the norms of international law, to emphasise Member States' liability for the non-fulfillment of their obligations in the sphere of protection, repatriation and restitution of cultural treasures as parties to international conventions and agreements,

to promote international exchange of information on the lost or illegally transferred cultural treasures which are subject to repatriation.

To support the initiative of Ukraine, Byelorus [*sic*]...to hold a special session of UNESCO Intergovernmental Committee for Promoting the Return of Cultural Property to its Countries of Origin or its Restitution in Case of Illicit appropriation dedicated to the problems of search and restitution of cultural treasures lost during W.W.II as well as the problems of return of cultural treasures which constitute an inseparable part of the national heritage to the countries which have become independent.

The Participants of the scientific and practical symposium call upon all working in the sphere of international law, scientists, people working in the museums, libraries and archives to pool their efforts in finding and returning of lost national historical and cultural heritage thus promoting closer ties between nations and cultures and ensure their mutual enrichment and prosperity.

Kyiv, 13 December 1996

SELECTED ILLUSTRATIONS

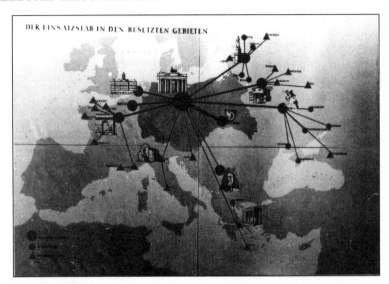

ERR schematic map showing routes of systematic archival and library looting throughout Europe. US NA Still Pictures Division, RG 260—PHOAD-III-3. Photo courtesy of the National Archives.

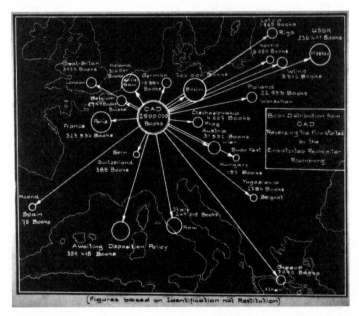

Schematic map of book restitution for the Offenbach Archival Depot (Frankfurt). From the album "Offenbach Archival Depot: Photographic History," Isaac Benkowitz, Captain S.R., Director. US NA Still Pictures Division, RG 260—POAD-II-49. Photo courtesy of the National Archives.

German archival officials load materials for transit out of Lviv to the Abbey of Tyniec in 1944. Photo courtesy of the Jagiellonian Library of Jagiellonian University, Cracow.

The Abbey of Tyniec (see, esp., pp. 360, 441, and 447), near Cracow, where German authorities stored archival treasures. Photo courtesy of the Jagiellonian Library of Jagiellonian University, Cracow.

September 4, 1945. Signing ceremony in Prague of the act transfering the Ukrainian
Historical Cabinet to the Soviet Union. Standing, from l to r: (for Czechoslovakia) Min.
of Education Zdenek Nejedlý; Min. of Internal Affairs Václav Nosek; Dir. of the Archive
of the Ministry of Internal Affairs Prof. Borovík; Advisor to the Archive Václav Peščak;
(for the USSR) Ambassador of the USSR to Czechoslovakia V. I. Zorin; Head of
TsDAFFK UkrSSR H. S. Pshchenychnyi. Signing is the head of the Archival Administration
of the NKVD of the UkrSSR, P. I. Pavliuk. Photo courtesy of TsDAKFFD, Kyiv.

Two Soviet officers and Capt. Isaac Benkowitz at the transfer of materials to the Soviet
Union. From the album "Offenbach Archival Depot: Photographic History," Isaac
Benkowitz, Captain S.R., Director. US NA Still Pictures Division, RG 260—POAD-II-
35. Photo courtesy of the National Archives.

Bibliography

I. Archival Sources

Individual record groups [fonds] actually consulted in the research for this book are listed by country and archive; in the case of large fonds, series or sections (such as *opisi/opysy* in Russia and Ukraine) are singled out where appropriate. Only those published guides and finding aids that actually bear on this study are included, although obviously many more have been used in the process of my varied archival research over several decades. Unpublished guides and other finding aids are listed only if they are referred to in the text or footnotes or have a direct bearing on the research involved, although *opisi* for individual fonds, for the most part, are not cited.

The archival research for this study has been done at various times over the past quarter century, during which time there have been many changes in names and designations of institutions. Efforts are made in the footnotes and the bibliography that follows below to provide current designations. Names and fond numbers have accordingly been updated where possible, although where deemed appropriate, earlier names are also cited. For the most part, only fonds are listed if their files have actually been cited in the footnotes. Many fonds, and especially trophy records and collections have been cited in passing in numerous instances, but not all of those are listed individually below. For abbreviations of archives (including previous names) and full references for short-titled works see above, pp. xvii–xxix.

General Archival Directories and Bibliographies of Reference Aids

Boberach, Heinz. *Inventar archivalischer Quellen des NS. Staates: Die Überlieferung von Behörden und Einrichtungen des Reichs, der Länder und der NSDAP*. 2 vols. Munich: K. G. Saur, 1991–1995. [=Texte und Materialien zur Zeitgeschichte, Band 3/1 and 2.]
   Vol. 1: *Reichszentralbehörden, regionale Behörden und wissenschaftliche Hochschulen für die zehn westdeutschen Länder sowie Berlin*. Comp. Dietrich Gessner, Kurt Metschieg, Gustav-Hermann Seebold, et al. Ed. Werner Röder and Christoph Weisz.
   Vol. 2: *Regionale Behörden und wissenschaftliche Hochschulen für die fünf ostdeutschen Länder, die ehemaligen preußischen Ostprovinzen und eingegliederte Gebiete in Polen, Österreich unter der Tschechischen Republik mit Nachträgen zu Teil 1*. Comp. Oldrich Sladek, Günter Weber, Wolfgang Weissleder, et al.
   The second volume includes coverage of many of the Nazi records in the former TsKhIDK (now part of RGVA) in Moscow.

"A Preliminary Bibliography of Descriptions of Archival Materials Originating in or Relating to Estonia, Latvia, Lithuania, and Belorussia now in Collections Outside the USSR." In Grimsted, *Archives: Estonia, Latvia, Lithuania, and Belorussia*, Appendix 5, pp. 717–830.
That survey itself (prepared in 1978–1979), to be sure, now requires updating and augmenting to serve as reference aid for specialists in these newly independent countries.

Vanrie, André, ed. *Les Archives en Europe depuis la Seconde Guerre Mondiale*. Brussels, 1984. [=*Archives et Bibliothèques de Belgique* 55 (1984): 3–291.]

—. *Les Archives en Europe Centrale et Orientale depuis la Seconde Guerre Mondiale*. Brussels, 1987. [=*Archives et Bibliothèques de Belgique* 58 (1987): 375–559.]

—, et al., eds. *International Bibliography of Directories and Guides to Archival Repositories/Bibliographie internationale des guides et annuaires relatifs aux dépôts d'archives*. Munich: Saur, 1990. [=*Archivum*, 36.]

BALTIC COUNTRIES AND BELARUS

Grimsted, Patricia Kennedy. *Archives and Manuscript Repositories in the USSR: Estonia, Latvia, Lithuania, and Belorussia*. Princeton: Princeton University Press, 1981.
(Hereafter: Grimsted, *Archives: Estonia, Latvia, Lithuania, and Belorussia*)

Dakumenty pa historyi Belarusi, iakiia zberahaiutstsa u tsentral'nykh dziarzhaŭnykh arkhivakh SSSR. Ed. and comp. A. M. Mikhal'chanka and T. A. Varab'iova. Minsk: Belaruskaia Savetskaia èntsyklapedyia imia Petrusia Brouki, 1990.

CZECH REPUBLIC (earlier Czechoslovakia)

Referenced general published guides and finding aids:

Podaný, Václav, and Hana Barvíková, et al. *Russkaia i ukrainskaia èmigratsiia v Chekhoslovatskoi respublike, 1918–1938: Putevoditel' po arkhivnym fondam i sobraniiam v Cheshskoi Respublike*. Trans. L'ubov Beloševská and Marina Luptáková. Prague: Euroslavica, 1995. [=Trudy po istorii Cheshskoi Akademii nauk/Studia Historiae Academiae Scientiarum Bohemicae; sponsors: Arkhiv Akademii nauk Cheshskoi Respubliki; Literaturnyi arkhiv Muzeia natsional'noi literatury; and

Slavianskii institut AN ChR. A Czech edition was issued simultaneously.]

Státní ústřední archiv v Praze, III
[State Central Archive in Prague]

Published finding aids:

Inventáře a katalogy fondů Státního ústředbího archivu v Praze—Ukrajinské muzeum v Praze, UM, (1659) 1925–1948: Inventář/Inventari i katalohy fondiv Derzhavnoho tsentral'noho arkhivu v Prazi—Ukraïns'kyi muzei v Prazi, UM, (1659) 1925–1948: Opys fondu. Comp. Raisa Machatková (Makhatkova). Kyiv and Prague, 1996. [=Naukovo-dovidkovi vydannia z istoriï Ukraïny, 41.]

Fonds cited:

Ministerstvo vnitra, nová registratura
[Ministry of Internal Affairs, new administrative records]
Especially P 1313–P 1411, k. 5488–5489.

1659. Ukrajinské muzeum v Praze (UM)
[Ukrainian Museum in Prague]

Slovanská knihovna [Slavonic Library], Prague

Published catalogs:

For RZIA reports, see under Russian Federation, GA RF. For UIK reports, see under TsDAVO, Kyiv.

Katalog byvshei Biblioteki Russkogo zagranichnogo istoricheskogo arkhiva/Catalog of the Former Library of the Russian Historical Archive Abroad. New York: Norman Ross Publishing, 1995. Microfiche edition.
Printed guide with introduction by Richard J. Kneeley and Edward Kasinec.

Magerovskii, Lev. *Bibliografiia gazetnykh sobranii Russkogo istoricheskogo arkhiva za gody 1917–1921.* Prague, 1939. Reprint ed. with an introduction by Richard Kneeley. New York: Norman Ross Publishing, 1994. [=Inventari Arkhiva Ministerstva vnutrennikh del v Prage, Ser. B, Inventari RIA, 1.]

Postnikov, Sergei P. *Politika, ideologiia, byt i uchenye trudy russkoi èmigratsii: 1918–1945: Bibliografiia. Iz kataloga biblioteki RZI arkhiva.* New York: Norman Ross Publishing, 1993.

FRANCE

Centre de Documentation Juive Contemporaine (CDJC)
[Center for Contemporary Jewish Documentation], Paris

Published finding aid:

Billig, Josef. *Alfred Rosenberg dans l'action idéologique, politique et administrative du Reich hitlérien. Inventaire commenté de la collection de documents conservés au C.D.J.C. provenant des archives du Reichsleiter et Ministre A. Rosenberg.* Paris, 1963. [=Les inventaires des archives du Centre de Documentation Juive Contemporaine, Paris, vol. 1).

A register of selected ERR documents held by CDJC with commentary (especially pp. 123–71).

Bibliothèque Ukrainienne Simon Petlura
[Symon Petliura Library in Paris], Paris

"Prymushenyi vyïzd bibliotekaria Ivana Rudycheva i ioho perebuvannia v Berlini (Dopovid´ na zasidaniiu Rady Biblioteky 3-ho hrudnia 1942 roku)." Typescript.

GERMANY

General directories and bibliographies of finding aids cited:

Website: Bundesarchiv: <http://www.bundesarchiv.de>. See also the "Kurzinformation über das Bundesarchiv und seine Bestände": <http://www.uncg.edu/~lixlpurc/GIP/BundArch.html>.

Bundesarchiv, Berlin-Lichterfelde (BAB)
(including some Nazi-era records formerly held in the **Bundesarchiv, Koblenz**)

N.B. Most of the records from the period of the Third Reich that had been returned from the United States and that were long held in the Bundesarchiv in Koblenz have since reunification been transferred to the Bundesarchiv Berlin-Lichterfelde (BAB). In some cases, they are now being combined with other files from the same record groups that previously had been held in East Germany.

Some confusion may be experienced in trying to coordinate the holdings in Germany with the microfilms prepared while the Nazi records were in the USA. The RMbO records captured by American authorities were intermingled and microfilmed together with the records of the Einsatzstab Reichsleiter Rosenberg (ERR) as temporary record group EAP 99; thus, the microfilm publication series (EAP 99) includes files from both groups of records. See *Guides to German*

Records Microfilmed at Alexandria, VA, no. 28: *Records of the Reich Ministry for the Occupied Eastern Territories, 1941–1943.* All of those records were subsequently returned to Germany in 1963. After they were turned over to the Bundesarchiv (BAK), they were reprocessed as several separate record groups, representing different Rosenberg agencies. The records of the Reich Ministry (RMbO) are now arranged in their own record group (R 6), while scattered remaining records of the Rosenberg chancellery have also been separated out (now R 8).

The ERR records themselves were processed in BAK as Bestand NS 30. They are now held in the new archival facility in Berlin-Lichterfelde (BAB). The introduction to the Bundesarchiv typescript finding aid (Findbücher) for NS 30 and those for other fonds provide more details about the history of the fonds and include correlation tables for the U.S.-produced microfilms; because of the most appropriate rearrangement, the films are exceedingly difficult to use. A more detailed description of many of the files was prepared by specialists from the Institut für Zeitgeschichte in Munich and copies of the resulting card files and inventories are available there.

Referenced published guides and finding aids:

Former Koblenz holdings:

Boberach, Heinz, comp. *Reichssicherheitshauptamt: Bestand R 58.* Koblenz: Bundesarchiv, 1992. [=Findbücher zu Beständen des Bundesarchivs, 22.]
The introduction includes a concise institutional history of the various divisions of the RSHA and considerable details about where the various parts of the records were found after the war. Typescript supplements available in BAB cover several groups of files received from GDR archives and those received from Poland in 1997.

Hagner, Hartmut, comp. *Reichsministerium für die besetzten Ostgebiete: Bestand R6.* Koblenz: Bundesarchiv, 1987. [=Findbücher zu Beständen des Bundesarchivs, 26.]

Former Potsdam holdings:

Übersicht über die Bestände des Deutschen Zentralarchivs Potsdam. Ed. Helmut Lötzke and Hans-Stephan Brather. Berlin: Rütten & Loening, 1957. [=Schriftenreihe des Deutschen Zentralarchivs, 1.]

Records cited:

NS 8. Kanzlei Rosenberg [Rosenberg Chancellery]

NS 30. Einsatzstab Reichsleiter Rosenberg (ERR)
[Reichsleiter Rosenberg Special Command]

R 6. Reichsministerium für die besetzten Ostgebiete (RMbO)
[Reich Ministry for the Occupied Eastern Territories]
Files from former GDR archives are being reprocessed as supplemental sections
of this record group.

R 58. Reichssicherheitshauptamt (RSHA)
[Reich Security Main Office]
As reprocessed in Berlin, this record group now includes the large group of
RSHA records received from Poland in 1997 as well as other RSHA records from
archives in the former GDR, including some large groups previously transferred
from Moscow.

R 138. Reichssippenstelle
[Reich Genealogical Office]

R 146. Reichsarchivverwaltung
[Reich Archival Administration]

Records formerly held in the Bundesarchiv, Abteilung Potsdam (BAP)
Now in Berlin-Lichterfelde (BAB)
Earlier: Deutsches Zentralarchiv Potsdam [German Central Archive, Potsdam]

15.06. Reichsarchiv [State Archive]

62 Di 1. Dienststellen Rosenberg [Rosenberg offices]
Mostly documentation from US NA microfilms, T454.

11.01. Reichsministerium für die besetzten Ostgebiete (RMbO)
[Reich Ministry for the Occupied Eastern Territories]
Mostly files received from the USSR and US NA microfilms.

12.01. Generalgouvernement Polen. Hauptverwaltung der Bibliotheken
[General Government–Poland, Head Administration for Libraries]

Bundesarchiv, Koblenz (BAK)

B 323. "Treuhandverwaltung für Kulturgut"
[Restitution Administration for Cultural Treasures]
Primarily includes remaining U.S. restitution files from the U.S. Collecting Points
in Munich and Wiesbaden.

N 1333. Nachlass Georg Winter (1895–1961)
[Papers of Georg Winter]

Geheimes Staatsarchiv Preußischer Kulturbesitz
[Secret State Archive of Prussian Cultural Property], Berlin-Dahlem

Rep. 178 A. Archivabteilung des Staatsministeriums
[Archival Administration of the State Ministry]

Politisches Archiv des Auswärtigen Amtes (PA AA)
[Political Archive of the Foreign Office], Bonn (now Berlin)

Referenced published guides and finding aids:

Kent, George O. "The German Foreign Ministry's Archives at Whaddon
Hall, 1948–58." *American Archivist* 24 (January 1961): 43–54.

—, comp. and ed. *A Catalogue of Files and Microfilms of the German
Foreign Ministry Archives, 1867–1920*. Oxford, 1959.

Records cited:

Sonderkommando von Künsberg Files
R 27542–R 27621

Inland, IIg, 441

GREAT BRITAIN

Public Record Office (National Archives) (PRO), Kew Gardens

Records cited:

FO 371/45771, file UE6509

FO 1020/1793, 2549, 2878 and 2879
Post–World War II Foreign Office records, Austria, including records regarding
cultural treasures and restitution

HUNGARY

Open Society Archive, Budapest

Records cited:

Arkhiv Samizdata Collection
A collection of *samizdat* materials from the USSR, including Russian, Ukrainian,
and other underground materials from Radio Liberty, earlier operating out of
Munich.
Most of the holdings from the original published series *Arkhiv Samizdata* are
available in a special microfiche collection from IDC.

THE NETHERLANDS

Nederlands Instituut voor Oorlogsdocumentatie (NIOD)
[Netherlands State Institute for War Documentation], Amsterdam
Previous name: Rijksinstituut voor Oorlogsdocumentatie (RIOD)

Records cited:

Einstatzstab Reichsleiter Rosenberg files

Miscellaneous reports on trophy libraries and archives (predominantly
copies)

POLAND

Referenced published directories:

Archiwa w Polsce: Informator adresowy (stan z 1 lipca 1998 roku). Warsaw:
NDAP, 1998.

Czachowska, Jadwiga, and Roman Loth. *Przewodnik polonisty: Bibliografie.
Słowniki. Biblioteki. Muzea Literackie.* 3rd ed. Wrocław, 1989.

Wyczawski, Hieronim Eugeniusz, OFM. *Przygotowanie do studiów w
archiwach kościelnych.* Wyd-wo "Calvarianum," 1989[1990].

Zbiory rękopisów w bibliotekach i muzeach w Polsce: Przewodnik. Comp.
Danuta Kamolowa and Krystyna Muszyńska. Warsaw: Biblioteka
Narodowa, 1988.

Warsaw

Archiwum Główne Akt Dawnych (AGAD)
[Main Archive of Early Records]

Referenced finding aids:

Zielińska, Teresa. "Zbiór archiwalny Aleksandra Czołowskiego w zasobie
Archiwum Głównego Akt Dawnych." *Archeion* 89 (1991): 38–60.

Manuscripts and other archival materials cited:

Zbiór Wiktora Baworowskiego (1826–1894)
[Wiktor Baworowski Collection]

Zbiór Aleksandra Czołowskiego (1865–1944)
[Aleksander Czołowski Collection]

Biblioteka Narodowa, Dział Rękopisów
[National Library]. Manuscript Division

Referenced finding aids:
Most of the Polish, Armenian, and other Oriental manuscripts from prewar Lviv University that remain in the Biblioteka Narodowa have not been described in print, but they are covered by card catalogs that reference their prewar Lviv University call numbers and catalog listings. See more details and a full bibliographic listing of prewar catalogs in Grimsted, *Archives: Ukraine*, pp. 573–77, including a provisional list of the Lviv manuscript numbers (pp. 74–75) for those manuscripts identified in Warsaw.

Svarnyk, Halyna. "Arkhiv Dmytra Dontsova." *Pam'iatky Ukraïny* 1994 (3–6[26]): 122–28.

—. "Arkhiv Naukovoho tovarystva im. Shevchenka v Natsional'nii bibliotetsi u Varshavi." In *Z istoriï Naukovoho tovarystva imeni Shevchenka*. Lviv: NTSh, 1998. [=*Pratsi sesii, konferentsii, sympoziumiv, kruhlykh stoliv*, 10.]

—. "Arkhiv Naukovoho tovarystva im. Shevchenka zi L'vova v Natsional'nii bibliotetsi u Varshavi." In *Slidamy pam'iati: Litopysnyi kalendar* 1 (Warsaw, 1996): 114–23.

—. "L'vivs'ki zbirky u Varshavi (Arkhiv Naukovoho tovarystva im. Shevchenka v Natsional'nii bibliotetsi u Varshavi)." *Halyts'ka brama* 12(36) December 1997: 12.

—, comp. "Spysok materialiv z arkhivu Naukovoho tovarystva im. Shevchenka u L'vovi, iaki teper zberihaiut'sia u Viddili rukopysiv Natsional'noï biblioteky u Varshavi." In *Slidamy pam'iati: Litopysnyi kalendar* 1 (Warsaw, 1996): 124–27.

"Rukopysy Peremys'koï hreko-katolyts'koï kapituly v Narodnii bibliotetsi u Varshavi." *Bohosloviia* 37(1–4) 1973: 193–213; and 38(1–4) 1974: 237–43.

"Teki Antoniego Schneidera w Zakładzie Narodowym im. Ossolińskich we Lwowie: [Summary inventory]." Czołowki collection, MS 5540, folios 223–30.

Manuscripts and other archival materials cited:
Microfilms of many of the materials cited are available for purchase from the Biblioteka Narodowa, Oddział Mikrofilmów

Zbiór Wiktora Baworowskiego (1826–1894)
[Wiktor Baworowski Collection]

Zbiór Aleksandra Czołowskiego (1865–1944)
[Aleksander Czołowski Collection]

Miscellaneous Collection of Ukrainian archival materials (evacuated from
Lviv in 1944)
Presumably from the NTSh, but possible partially from other sources.

Manuscripts from prewar Lviv University Library, evacuated in 1944

Manuscripts from the Przemyśl (*Ukr.* Peremyshl) Greek-Catholic Capitula

Cracow
Archiwum Państwowe w Krakowie (APKr)
[State Archive in Cracow]

Referenced finding aids:

"Spis Tek Antoniego Schneidera."

Records cited:

Zespól APKr [Administrative Records of the State Archive in Cracow]

Teki Antoniego Schneidera (1825–1880), 282 manuscripts

Biblioteka Jagiellońska, Cracow
[Jagellonian Library]

Materials cited:

Personal papers of Karl Badecki (1886–1953), Polish archivist from Lviv

Archive of the Dominican Order, Cracow

Lubaczów
Archiwum Archidiecezji w Lubaczowie
[Archive of the Archdiocese in Lubaczów]
Consists of the records held by the Episcopal Administrator for the Archdiocese
of Lviv, most of which were transferred from Lviv immediately after World War
II.

Published finding aids cited:
Since preservation microfilms of the archival materials held in Lubaczów are held
in the Catholic University of Lublin, the catalogs of the microfilms also serve as a
catalog of the originals.

Kania, Janusz, Rev. "Katalog mikrofilmów Ośrodka Archiwów, Bibliotek i
Muzeów Kościelnych przy Katolickim Uniwersytecie Lubelskim," no. 5.

Lublin, 1985. [=*Archiwa, Biblioteki i Muzea Kościelne* 51 (1985): [5]–115.]

Leszczyński, Mariusz. "Archiwum Archidiecezji w Lubaczowie." *Archiwa, Biblioteki i Muzea Kościelne* 53 (1986): 57–66.

Wrocław

Zakład Narodowy im. Ossolińskich (ZNiO), Manuscript Division,
Wrocław
[Ossoliński National Institute; or usually in English, Ossolineum]

Published finding aids cited:

> For more details about the previously published and manuscript finding aids for
> the Ossolineum manuscripts and other component collections such as the
> Dzieduszycki Library and the Baworowski Library, see the text and annotated
> bibliography in Grimsted, *Archives: Ukraine*, pp. 500–569. Most of the finding
> aids listed are available on IDC microfiche, including some special microfiche
> editions with prefaces and annotations by P. K. Grimsted, especially covering the
> divided collections. Only the most important ones covering the Ossolineum and a
> few selected other ones specifically cited in the text and footnotes are listed
> below. As explained above in Chapter 11, many of the collections are today
> divided between Lviv and Wrocław, but parts of some of them are also today held
> in the Biblioteka Narodowa and AGAD in Warsaw and in other repositories as
> indicated. For updates on coverage and a bibliography, see the ZNiO website:
> <http://www.oss.wroc.pl/>.

Gębarowicz, Mieczysław. *Katalog rękopisów Biblioteki im. Gwalberta
Pawlikowskiego.* Lviv: ZNiO, 1929. [Microfiche ed.: IDC-R-14,536.]
2nd edition: In *Inwentarz rękopisów ZNiO we Wrocławiu.* Ed.
Jadwiga Turska et al., vol. 2. Wrocław: Wyd-wo ZNiO, 1949.
The second edition omits the 55 manuscripts from the collection remaining in Lviv.

*Inwentarz rękopisów Biblioteki Zakładu Narodowego im. Ossolińskich we
Lwowie.* 2 vols. Lviv, 1926–1934. Hectographed.
Supplement 1: "—— [Nr 6001[6109]–6615 [with continuation to 6596
in one of the carbon copies]." Lviv, 1937. Typescript.
Supplement 2: "Inventar rukopysiv buvshoï biblioteky im. Ossolins'kykh
u L'vovi, NoNo. 6597–8091. Typescript. [Special microfiche ed. with
preface by P. K. Grimsted: IDC-R-14,429.]
The Special Microfiche edition includes the two supplements, based on ZNiO copies
(to MS 7705) and based on microfilms furnished to HURI. Annotations in the special
microfiche edition indicate the present location of the manuscripts. ZNiO since has
acquired a xerox copy of the supplement covering manuscripts 7706–8091.

Inwentarz rękopisów Zakładu Narodowego im. Ossolińskich we Wrocławiu.
Ed. Jadwiga Turska et al. 9 vols. and index. Wrocław: ZNiO,

1948–1984. [Special microfiche ed. with preface by P. K. Grimsted: IDC-R-14,430.]

Later volumes cover manuscripts acquired from Polish sources, although some manuscripts of Lviv provenance are included.

Kętrzyński, Wojciech. *Katalog rękopisów Zakładu Narodowego im. Ossoliń-skich/Catalogus codicum manuscriptorum Bibliothecae Ossolinianae Leopoliensis*, 3 vols. Lviv, 1881–1898. [Special microfiche ed. with preface by P. K. Grimsted: IDC-R-14,485.]

Pijaj, Stanisław, comp. *Archiwa rodzinno-majątkowe w zbiorach państwowych we Lwowie*. Warsaw: Ministerstwo Kultury i Sztuki, 1995. [=Polskie dziedzictwo kulturalne, Seria B: Wspólne Dziedzictwo.]

The compiler was unable to include some of the materials that were not catalogued before 1945 and did not have complete data about the transfers to TsDIAL from the Ossolineum collections.

Pohorecki, Feliks. *Catalogus diplomatum Bibliothecae Instituti Ossoliniani nec non Bibliothecae Pawlikowianae inde ab anno 1227 usque ad annum 1505*. Lviv: Sumptibus societatis amicorum Instituti Ossoliniani, 1937. Supplement: [—, and Adam Fastnacht]. *Catalogus...Supplementum I. Inde ab anno 1279 usque ad annum 1506*. Wrocław: Institutum Ossolinianum, 1951. [Special microfiche ed. with preface by P. K. Grimsted: IDC-R-14,537.]

Only 5 of the 287 parchments in the initial catalog remain in Lviv, while only 11 of the 101 covered in the supplement came from Lviv. Present locations are indicated in the special IDC microfiche edition.

RUSSIAN FEDERATION [*before 1991*, RSFSR and USSR]

General directories and bibliographies of finding aids cited:

Rosarkhiv website: <http://www.rusarchives.ru>
"Archives of Russia." ArcheoBiblioBase website: <http://www.iisg.nl/~abb>.

With updated information on Russian archives, now maintained by IISH, can be accessed through the IISH/IISG website out of Amsterdam.

Russian version: <http://www.openweb.ru/rusarch/>

Archives of Russia: A Directory and Bibliographic Guide to Holdings in Moscow and St. Petersburg. Comp. Patricia Kennedy Grimsted, Lada V. Repulo, and Irina D. Tunkina. Ed. Mikhail D. Afanas'ev, Patricia Kennedy Grimsted, Vladimir P. Kozlov, and Vladimir S. Sobol'ev. English edition, ed. Patricia Kennedy Grimsted. Armonk, NY: M.E. Sharpe, 2000.
(Hereafter: *Archives of Russia*, 2000)

Updated English-language edition of the following.

Arkhivy Rossii: Moskva i Sankt-Peterburg. Spravochnik-obozrenie i bibliograficheskii ukazatel'. Comp. Patritsiia Kennedi Grimsted [Patricia Kennedy Grimsted], Lada V. Repulo, and Irina V. Tunkina. Ed. Mikhail D. Afanas'ev, Patricia Kennedy Grimsted, Vladimir P. Kozlov, and Vladimir S. Sobol'ev. Moscow: "Arkheograficheskii tsentr," 1997.

Federal'nye arkhivy Rossii i ikh nauchno-spravochnyi apparat: Kratkii spravochnik. Comp. Ol'ga Iu. Nezhdanova. Ed. Vladimir P. Kozlov. Moscow: Rosarkhiv, 1994.

Archives of the Soviet Communist Party and Soviet State: Catalogue of Finding Aids and Documents from the Three Key Archives on Microfilm. Published jointly by the Russian State Archival Service (Rosarkhiv) and the Hoover Institution on War, Revolution and Peace, distributed by Chadwyck-Healey. Cambridge, UK, and Alexandria, VA: Chadwyck-Healey, 1995.
Electronic update: available on the Chadwyck-Healey website— <http://www.chadwyck.com>; or (outside USA)— <http://www.chadwyck.co.uk>.
Russian edition: *Arkhivy KPSS i Sovetskogo gosudarstva: Katalog opisei i dokumentov*. Cambridge, UK: Chadwyck-Healey, 1995.
[Limited distribution.]
Covers the microfilmed *opisi* and documentary series prepared since 1992 of post-1917 records in GA RF, RGASPI, and RGANI. Complete depository copies of the films are available at both the Hoover Institution and the Library of Congress; in addition, other libraries or library consortia have purchased copies.

Popov, Andrei V. *Russkoe zarubezh'e i arkhivy: Dokumenty rossiiskoi èmigratsii v arkhivakh Moskvy: Problemy vyiavleniia, komplektovaniia, opisaniia, ispol'zovaniia*. Moscow: IAI RGGU, 1998. [=Materialy k istorii russkoi politicheskoi èmigratsii, 4.]

"Spisok arkhivnykh materialov, rukopisei, proizvedenii iskusstva, otnosiashchikhsia k istorii i kul'ture Ukrainskoi SSR i khraniashchikhsia v arkhivakh, bibliotekakh, muzeiakh i kartinnykh galereiakh Moskvy i Leningrada." RGANI, 5/17/544 (film roll 5732), fols. 77–79.

Gosudarstvennyi arkhiv Rossiiskoi Federatsii (GA RF)
[State Archive of the Russian Federation], Moscow
Formerly TsGAOR and TsGA RSFSR.

Referenced published guides and finding aids:
For the microfilmed *opisi*, see the Chadwyck-Healey catalog above.

Perechen' fondov Gosudarstvennogo arkhiva Rossiiskoi Federatsii i
nauchno-spravochnyi apparat k dokumentam arkhiva. Comp.
L. G. Aronov, A. I. Barkovets, A. V. Dobrovskaia, O. N. Kopyleva,
T. N. Kotlova, et al. Ed. S. V. Mironenko. Moscow: Redaktsionno-izd.
otdel federal'nykh arkhivov, 1998. [=*Gosudarstvennyi arkhiv Rossiiskoi*
Federatsii: Putevoditel', 6; Russian Archive Series, 8 (Rosarkhiv;
GA RF).]

Tsentral'nyi gosudarstvennyi arkhiv Oktiabr'skoi revoliutsii i sotsialisti-
cheskogo stroitel'stva: Putevoditel'. Part 2. Ed. N. R. Prokopenko.
Moscow: GAU, 1952.

> A detailed guide to the fonds transferred to Moscow after World War II from
> RZIA in Prague and other foreign émigré holdings. Published in a "secret" edition
> in 1952, declassified in 1987. One of the few remaining copies of that guide, now
> available in the GA RF reading room, has marginal notes indicating the materials
> were transferred elsewhere.

"Osobaia papka" I. V. Stalina: Iz materialov Sekretariata NKVD-MVD SSSR
1944–1953 gg.: Katalog dokumentov/The "Special File" for I. V. Stalin,
From Materials of the Secretariat of the NKVD-MVD of the USSR,
1944–1953: A Catalogue of Documents. Comp. O. V. Edel'man,
L. S. Kudriavtseva, E. D. Grin'ko, and M. E. Kolesova. Ed.
S. V. Mironenko and V. A. Kozlov. Moscow: "Blagovest," 1994.
[=Russian Archive Series. Arkhiv noveishei istorii Rossii, Seriia:
Katalogi, 1 (Rosarkhiv; GA RF).]

"Osobaia papka" V. M. Molotova: Iz materialov Sekretariata NKVD-MVD
SSSR 1944–1956 gg.: Katalog dokumentov/The "Special File" for
V. M. Molotov: From Materials of the Secretariat of the NKVD-MVD of
the USSR, 1944–1956: A Catalogue of Documents. Comp.
O. V. Edel'man, L. S. Kudriavtseva, and E. D. Grin'ko. Ed.
S. V. Mironenko and V. A. Kozlov. Moscow: "Blagovest," 1994.
[=Russian Archive Series. Arkhiv noveishei istorii Rossii, Seriia:
Katalogi, vol. 2.]

Fondy Russkogo zagranichnogo istoricheskogo arkhiva v Prage:
Mezharkhivnyi putevoditel'. Comp. Ol'ga N. Kopyleva et al. Ed.
Tatiana F. Pavlova et al. Moscow: ROSSPEN, 1999.

> A reconstruction of the collections from RZIA that were transferred to Moscow
> from Prague in 1945/46 and subsequently dispersed to approximately 30 archives
> throughout the former USSR. Provides annotated descriptions of current fonds.

[Russkii zagranichnyi istoricheskii arkhiv (RZIA)]. *Russkii zagranichnyi*
istoricheskii arkhiv pri Ministerstve inostrannykh del Chekhoslovatskoi
respubliki v 1929 godu. Prague, [1930] through —*v 1931.* Prague, 1932.

[Microfiche ed.: IDC-R-11,233.]

—*v 1936*. Prague, 1936. [Microfiche ed.: IDC-R-11,236.]

Copies of these reports and other typescript ones are filed with the RZIA administrative records, GA RF, 7030/1/20, 21, 28, 30, 39, 114, among others. RZIA was
founded in Prague and transferred to TsGAOR SSSR in 1945/46, then dispersed
throughout the USSR. Its largest section and main records, however, are still held
in GA RF.

—. *Otdel dokumentov. Russkii zagranichnyi istoricheskii arkhiv v Prage
(1923–1932 gg.)*. Comp. Aleksandr F. Iziumov. [Prague, 1932.]
[Microfiche ed.: IDC-R-11,232.]

Fonds cited:

A-534, *opis'* 2. Komitet po delam kul'turno-prosvetitel'skikh uchrezhdenii pri
Sovete Ministrov RSFSR
[Committee on Cultural and Educational Institutions under the Council
of Ministers of the RSFSR]

R-5142. Tsentral'nyi gosudarstvennyi arkhiv Oktiabr'skoi revoliutsii,
vysshikh organov gosudarstvennoi vlasti i organov gosudarstvennogo
upravleniia SSSR (TsGAOR SSSR)
[Central State Archive of the October Revolution, Highest Agencies of
State Power and Agencies of State Administration of the USSR]
Administrative records of TsGAOR SSSR.

R-5325, *Opisi* 2 and 10. Glavnoe arkhivnoe upravlenie pri Sovete Ministrov
SSSR (Glavarkhiv SSSR). Glavnoe arkhivnoe upravlenie pri Kabinete
Ministrov SSSR
[Main Archival Administration under the Council/Cabinet of Ministers
of the USSR]

R-5889. Posol'stvo Ukrainskoi Narodnoi Respubliki v Germanii, Berlin
[Embassy of the Ukrainian National Republic (UNR) in Germany]

R-5962. Aleksandr F. Iziumov (1885–1951), Personal Papers

R-6087. Ministerstvo inostrannykh del Ukrainskoi Narodnoi Respubliki
[Ministry of Foreign Affairs of the Ukrainian National Republic]

R-6784. Russkii kul'turno-istoricheskii muzei v Prage pri Russkom
narodnom universitete
[Russian Cultural-Historical Museum in Prague under the Russian
People's University]

R-6846. Turgenevskaia obshchestvennaia biblioteka v Parizhe
[Turgenev Community Library, Paris]

R-7008. Ukrainskaia biblioteka im. S. Petliury v Parizhe
[S. Petliura Ukrainian Library, Paris]

R-7021. Chrezvychainaia Gosudarstvennaia Komissiia po ustanovleniiu i
rassledovaniiu zlodeianii nemetsko-fashistskikh zakhvatchikov i ikh
soobshchnikov i prichinennogo imi ushcherba grazhdanam,
kollektivnym khoziaistvam (kolkhozam), obshchestvennym
organizatsiiam, gosudarstvennym predpriiatiiam i uchrezhdeniiam SSSR
(v gody Velikoi Otechestvennoi voiny) (ChGK)
[Extraordinary State Commission for the Establishment and
Investigation of Crimes of the German-Fascist Aggressors and Their
Accomplices and Appraisal of the Losses Incurred by Citizens,
Collective Farms, Social Organizations, State Enterprises and
Institutions of the USSR (during the years of the Great Patriotic War)]

R–7027. Delegatsiia Ukrainskoi Narodnoi Respubliki na mirnoi konferentsii
v Parizhe
[Delegation of the Ukrainian National Republic at the Paris Peace
Conference]

R-7030. Russkii zagranichnyi istoricheskii arkhiv, Praga (RZIA)
[Russian Foreign Historical Archive, Prague]
RZIA administrative records from the period of its operation in Prague.

R-7050. Ukrainskoe press-biuro v Lozanne
[Ukrainian Press Bureau in Lausanne]

R-7063. Redaktsiia zhurnala "Ukraina," Lozanna
[Editorial records of the journal *Ukraïna* in Lausanne]

R-7317. Sovetskaia voennaia administratsiia v Germanii (SVAG)
[Soviet Military Administration in Germany]
(Records of other related SVAG agencies and regional administrations
are now arranged as separate fonds)
All the requested records from this fond were still classified, although I did have
the opportunity, briefly in 1990 and 1991, to use the card catalogs for parts of the
fond.
        Some of the SVAG records and the related card catalogs held in GA RF had
been open for limited research in the early 1990s, but were closed again by a
secret presidential decree in August 1992, pending the removal of Russian troops
from Germany. Another secret presidential decree at the end of August or early
September 1995 called for the declassification of SVAG records, except for those
relating to property.

R-7445. Mezhdunarodnyi voennyi tribunal dlia glavnykh nemetskikh
prestupnikov (Niurnbergskii protsess)
[International War Tribunal for the Chief German Criminals (Nuremburg
Trials), Nuremberg]

R-7526. Kantseliariia Rady Ukrainskoi Narodnoi Respubliki
[Chancellery of the Council (Rada) of the Ukrainian National Republic]

R-7744. Kollektsiia materialov zagranichnykh organizatsii Ukrainskoi partii
sotsialistov-revoliutsionerov, Praga
[Collection of materials of the organizations abroad of the Ukrainian
Party of Socialist-Revolutionaries, Prague]

R-9401. Ministerstvo vnutrennikh del SSSR
[Ministry of Internal Affairs of the USSR; and preceding Commissariat]
Opis' 2. Special Files of the NKVD/MVD Secretariat

Rossiiskii gosudarstvennyi arkhiv drevnikh aktov (RGADA)
[Russian State Archive of Early Acts], Moscow

Referenced published guides and finding aids:

*Tsentral'nyi gosudarstvennyi arkhiv drevnikh aktov SSSR [Rossiiskii...for
later volumes]: Putevoditel'.* Comp. E. F. Zhelokhovtseva, M. V. Babich,
and Iu. M. Eskin. Ed. S. M. Dushinov, N. P. Eroshkin, M. I. Avto-
kratova, et al. 4 vols. (in 5); publishers vary. Moscow, 1991–1999.

Tsentral'nyi gosudarstvennyi arkhiv drevnikh aktov: Putevoditel'. Comp.
V. N. Shumilov et al. 2 vols. Moscow: GAU pri NKVD, 1946–1947.
[Microfiche ed.: IDC-R-10,706]
Vol. 1: Ed. S. K. Bogoiavlenskii.
Vol. 2: Ed. A. I. Iakovlev.

Grimsted, Patricia Kennedy. "The Ruthenian (Volhynian) Metrica: Polish
Crown Chancery Records for Ukrainian Lands, 1569–1673." *Harvard
Ukrainian Studies* 14(1–2) June 1990: 7–83.

—. With the collaboration of Irena Sułkowska-Kurasiowa. *The "Lithuanian
Metrica" in Moscow and Warsaw: Reconstructing the Archives of the
Grand Duchy of Lithuania, Including an Annotated Edition of the 1887
Inventory Compiled by Stanisław Ptaszycki.* Cambridge, MA: Oriental
Research Partners, 1984.

Koval's'kyi, Mykola Pavlovych (Nikolai Pavlovich Koval'skii). *Istochniki po
istorii Ukrainy XVI–pervoi poloviny XVII v. v Litovskoi metrike v*

fondakh prikazov TsGADA: Uchebnoe posobie. Dnipropetrovsk: DGU, 1979. [Microfiche ed.: IDC-in R-14,562]

Malynovs′kyi, A. O. "Ohliad arkhivnykh materialiv z istoriï zakhidno-rus′koho prava, shcho perekhovuiut′sia u Drevlekhranylyshchi Moskovs′koho Tsentral′noho arkhivu (po 1-she liutoho roku 1926)." In *Pratsi Komisiï dlia vyuchuvannia istoriï zakhidn′o-rus′koho ta ukraïns′koho prava* (Kyiv) 2 (1926): 1–49.

Rus′ka (Volyns′ka) metryka: Rehestry dokumentiv koronnoï kantseliariï dlia ukraïns′kykh zemel′ (Volyns′ke, Bratslavs′ke, Kyïvs′ke, Chernihivs′ke voievodstva), 1569–1673/The Ruthenian (Volhynian) Metrica: Early Inventories of the Polish Crown Chancery Records for Ukrainian Lands (1569–1673). Comp. Patricia Kennedy Grimsted, Hennadii V. Boriak, Kyrylo Vyslobokov, Irena Sułkowska-Kurasiowa, and Natalia Iakovenko. 2 vols. Kyiv, forthcoming. With an introduction by Patricia K. Grimsted.
An English edition of the introduction by Grimsted is being published separately by the Harvard Ukrainian Research Institute.

Rossiiskii gosudarstvennyi istoricheskii arkhiv (RGIA)
[Russian State Historical Archive], St. Petersburg

Referenced published guides and finding aids cited:

Fondy Rossiiskogo gosudarstvennogo istoricheskogo arkhiva: Kratkii spravochnik. Comp. D. I. Raskin and O. P. Sukhanova. Ed. D. I. Raskin and V. V. Lapin. St. Petersburg: RGIA, 1994. [RGIA]

Tsentral′nyi gosudarstvennyi istoricheskii arkhiv v Leningrade: Putevoditel′. Ed. S. N. Valk and V. V. Bedin. Leningrad: GAU, 1956. [Microfiche ed.: IDC-R-10,722]

Opisanie dokumentov arkhiva zapadno-russkikh uniatskikh mitropolitov. 2 vols. St. Petersburg, 1897–1907. [Microfiche ed.: IDC-R-10,729.]

Rossiiskii gosudarstvennyi arkhiv Voenno-Morskogo Flota (RGAVMF)
[Russian State Archive of the Navy], St. Petersburg

Referenced published guides:

Mazur, Tamara Petrovna. *Rossiiskii gosudarstvennyi arkhiv Voenno-Morskogo Flota: Annotirovannyi reestr opisei fondov.* Ed. M. E. Malevinskaia. St. Petersburg: "Blits," 1996. [RGAVMF.]
Describes the pre-revolutionary holdings in RGAVMF.

Malevinskaia, Marina Evgen'eva, comp. *Rossiiskii gosudarstvennyi arkhiv VMF: Spravochnik po fondam (1917–1940).* Ed. T. P. Mazur. 2 vols. St. Petersburg: "Blits," 1995.

Lozenko, Liudmyla. "O. Ohloblyn pro arkhiv Chornomors'koï floty." *Pam'iatky Ukraïny* 1994 (3–6[26]): 116–19.

Rossiiskii gosudarstvennyi voenno-istoricheskii arkhiv (RGVIA)
[Russian State Military History Archive]

Referenced published guides and finding aids:

Rychkov, P. A. "Dzherela Rosiis'koho derzhavnoho voienno-istorychnoho arkhivu do istoriï mistobuduvannia u Pravoberezhnii Ukraïni." *Arkhivy Ukraïny* 1992 (5–6): 52–61.

Rossiiskii gosudarstvennyi voennyi arkhiv (RGVA)
[Russian State Military Archive], Moscow

Referenced published guides and finding aids:

Tsentral'nyi gosudarstvennyi arkhiv Sovetskoi Armii: Putevoditel'. Comp. O. V. Brizitskaia, N. D. Egorov, T. F. Kariaeva, et al. Ed. L. V. Dvoinykh and M. V. Stegantsev. 2 vols. Minneapolis: East View Publications, 1991–1993.

Putevoditel' po fondam Beloi Armii. Comp. L. M. Chizhova, N. D. Egorov, and N. V. Pul'chenko. Ed. N. D. Egorov and L. V. Dvoinykh. Moscow, "Vostochnaia literatura," 1998. [=Academia ROSSICA, 4; sponsors: Russkoe bibliograficheskoe obshchestvo; RAN; Rosarkhiv; RGVA.]

Trophy records from the former Tsentr khraneniia istoriko-dokumen-tal'nykh kollektsii (TsKhIDK/TsGOA):
[Center for Preservation of Historico-Documentary Collections]
In March 1999 TsKhIDK (earlier, TsGOA) was abolished as a separate archive, and its holdings are now combined with those of RGVA.

Referenced published guides and finding aids:

Kratkii spravochnik fondov byvshego Osobogo arkhiva. Moscow, forthcoming. [Sponsors: Rosarkhiv, RGVA]
A short listing of foreign trophy fonds, GUPVI records, and foreign fonds already returned to their country of provenance that were held by former TsKhIDK, prepared by the archive. Omits some fonds that had not been adequately processed. Prepared for publication in 2000.

Fondy bel'giiskogo proiskhozhdeniia: Annotirovannyi ukazatel'. Comp.
A. S. Namazova and T. A. Vasil'eva. Ed. M. M. Mukhamedzhanov.
Moscow, 1995. [Sponsors: Rosarkhiv; TsKhIDK; In-t vseobshchei istorii
RAN.]
Flemish edition: *Fondsen van Belgische Herkomst: Verklarende Index.*
Ed. Hendrik De Conninck, Piet Creve, Michel Vermote, and M. M.
Mukhamedzhanov. Translated by E. Saelmaekers. Ghent: AMSAB,
1997.

> A short annotated list of captured records of Belgian provenance held in former
> TsKhIDK covering 35 fonds (20,154 units). In the original edition, institutions
> and individuals involved are cited only in Russian, and there is no explanation of
> where the materials were recovered. The Flemish edition corrects that problem,
> although there is still no migratory information. Microfilms of some of the
> materials described have been prepared and are now held at AMSAB in Ghent.

Aly, Götz, and Susanne Heim. *Das Zentrale Staatsarchiv in Moskau
("Sonderarchiv"), Rekonstruktion und Bestandsverzeichnis verschollen
geglaubten Schriftguts aus der NS-Zeit.* Düsseldorf: Hans-Böckler-
Stiftung, 1992.

> A brief list of predominantly German fonds (only starting with no. 500) in former
> TsKhIDK.

Jena, Kai von, and Wilhelm Lenz. "Die deutschen Bestände im Sonderakhiv
in Moskau." *Der Archivar* 45(3) 1992: 457–67.

Wegner, Bernd. "Deutsche Aktenbestände im Moskauer Zentralen
Staatsarchiv: Ein Erfahrungsbericht." *Vierteljahreshefte für
Zeitgeschichte* 40(2) 1992: 311–19.

> A survey of predominantly German-related holdings in former TsKhIDK with
> helpful annotations characterizing some of the most important fonds.

Form, Wolfgang, and Pavel Poljan (Polian). "Das Zentrum für die Aufbewahrung historisch-dokumentarischer Sammlungen in Moskau—ein
Erfahrungsbericht." *Informationen aus der Forschung* (Bundesinstitut
für ostwissenschaftliche und internationale Studien) 7 (20 October
1992): 1–8.

Prokopenko, Anatolii Stefanovich. "Dom osobogo naznacheniia (Otkrytie
arkhivov)." *Rodina* 1992 (3): 50–51.

> A popularized survey history of the archive by the former director.

Fonds cited:

265K. Ukrainskii narodnyi soiuz vo Frantsii (Èmigrantskaia natsiona-
listicheskaia organizatsiia), Paris
[Ukrainian National Union in France (Nationalist émigré organization)]

> The 26 files in this fond (documents dating from 1933–1939) were apparently

pulled out of French security service records and established as a separate fond in TsGOA.

431K. Ukrainskii nauchnyi institut v Varshave
[Ukrainian Scientific Institute in Warsaw]

500K. Reichssicherheitshauptamt.
[Reich Security Main Office]

1255K. Reichsarchiv, Potsdam
[Reich Archive]

1256K. Chef des Heeresarchivs, Potsdam
[Chief of the Military Archive]

1358K. Reichsministerium für die besetzten Ostgebiete (RMbO)
[Reich Ministry for the Occupied Eastern Territories]

1387K. Heeresarchiv, Zweigstelle Danzig
[Military Archive, Danzig Branch Office]

1401K. Einsatzstab Reichsleiter Rosenberg
[Reichsleiter Rosenberg Special Command]

1412K. Dokumental'nye materialy masonskikh lozh (kollektsiia)
[Documentary materials of Masonic Lodges (Collection)]

Rossiiskii gosudarstvennyi arkhiv sotsial'no-politicheskoi istorii (RGASPI), Moscow
[Russian State Archive of Socio-Political History], Moscow
Previous names:
until 1991: Tsentral'nyi partiinyi arkhiv (Central Party Archive)
1992– March 1999: Rossiiskii tsentr khraneniia i izucheniia dokumentov
noveishei istorii (RTsKhIDNI) [Russian Center for Preservation and Study of
Records of Modern History]

Referenced published guides:
For the microfilmed *opisi,* see the Chadwyck-Healey catalog above (p. 593).

Rossiiskii tsentr khraneniia i izucheniia dokumentov noveishei istorii: Kratkii putevoditel'. Fondy i kollektsii, sobrannye Tsentral'nym partiinym arkhivom. Comp. Zh. G. Adibekova, Iu. N. Amiantov, S. S. Ivanova, et al. Ed. Iu. N. Amiantov, V. P. Kozlov, O. V. Naumov, et al. Moscow: "Blagovest," 1993. [="Spravochno-informatsionnye materialy k dokumental'nym fondam RTsKhIDNI," 1.]

Rossiiskii tsentr khraneniia i izucheniia dokumentov noveishei istorii: Kratkii putevoditel': Fondy i kollektsii, sobrannye Tsentral'nym partiinym arkhivom/Research Guide to the Russian Center for the Preservation and Study of Documents [Records] of Modern [Contemporary] History [Former Central Party Archive]. Comp. O. V. Naumov, Iu. N. Amiantov, et al. Ed. J. A. Getty, V. P. Kozlov, et al. Moscow: "Blagovest," 1993. ["Russian Archive Series," 1.]

Putevoditel' po fondam i kollektsiiam lichnogo proiskhozhdeniia. Comp. Iu. N. Amiantov and Z. N. Tikhonova. Ed. Iu. N. Amiantov, O. V. Naumov, Z. N. Tikhonova, and K. M. Anderson. Moscow, 1996. [=Spravochno-informatsionnye materialy k dokumental'nym fondam RTsKhIDNI, 2; sponsors: Rosarkhiv, RTsKhIDNI.]

Fonds cited:

17. Tsentral'nyi Komitet KPSS (TsK KPSS)
    [Central Committee of the Communist Party of the Soviet Union] (CPSU Central Committee)
    Opis' 125—Upravlenie propagandy i agitatsii TsK (1939–1948)(Agitprop) [Agitation and Propaganda Administration of the Central Committee]
    Opis' 132—Otdel propagandy i agitatsii TsK (1948–1956) (Agitprop) [Department of Agitation and Propaganda of the Central Committee]
    The potentially most revealing documents that I requested from this latter *opis'* were classified at the time of my request.

71. Institut Marksizma-Leninizma pri TsK KPSS (IML)
    [Institute of Marxism-Leninism under the CPSU Central Committee]
    Opis' 6. Records of the Central Party Archive (TsPA), files containing reports from local CP archives in Ukraine.

644. Gosudarstvennyi komitet oborony (GKO)[State Committee on Defense]
    None of the requested files from this fond were declassified.

Rossiiskii gosudarstvennyi arkhiv noveishei istorii (RGANI), Moscow
[Russian State Archive of Contemporary History]
Previous name, before March 1999: Tsentr khraneniia sovremennoi dokumentatsii (TsKhSD) [Center for the Preservation of Contemporary Documentation]

Referenced surveys:
For the microfilmed *opisi*, see the Chadwyck-Healey catalog above (p. 593).

Afiani, Vitalii Iu. "Dokumenty o zarubezhnoi arkhivnoi Rossike i peremeshchennykh arkhivakh v fondakh Tsentra khraneniia sovremennoi dokumentatsii." In *Problemy zarubezhnoi arkhivnoi Rossiki: Sbornik statei*. Ed. V. P. Kozlov. Moscow: Informatsionno-izd. agentstvo "Russkii mir," 1997, pp. 92–99.

Fonds cited:

4. Sekretariat TsK KPSS [CPSU Central Committee Secretariat]
The files requested including reports on trophy holdings in the USSR were closed in 1999, although this fond had been open to researchers briefly in 1992, which may explain why some of the related documents involved could have been published in Germany.

5. Apparat TsK KPSS [CPSU CC Apparatus], *Opis'* 17

Institut rossiiskoi istorii RAN, Sankt-Peterburgskii filial. Arkhiv, St. Petersburg
[St. Petersburg Branch of the Institute of Russian History, Archive]

Referenced guides:

Putevoditel' po arkhivu Leningradskogo otdeleniia Instituta istorii. Comp. I. V. Valkina et al. Ed. A. I. Andreev, et al. Moscow and Leningrad: AN SSSR, 1958. [Microfiche ed.: IDC-R-10,957.]

[Institut rossiiskoi istorii RAN, Sankt-Peterburgskii filial.] *Fondy i kollektsii arkhiva: Kratkii spravochnik*. Comp G. A. Pobedimova and N. B. Sredinskaia. St. Petersburg: "Blits," 1995.

Rossiiskaia gosudarstvennaia biblioteka (RGB), Otdel rukopisei (OR), Moscow
[Russian State Library, Division of Manuscripts]
Previous name: 1945–1992: Gosudarstvennaia biblioteka SSSR im. V. I. Lenina (GBL)
[V. I. Lenin State Library]

Fonds cited:

369. Vladimir V. Bonch-Bruevich Papers

Vserossiiskaia gosudarstvennaia biblioteka inostrannoi literatury im. M. I. Rudomino, Arkhiv (Arkhiv VGBIL)
[M. I. Rudomino All-Russian State Library for Foreign Literature, Archive]

Fonds cited:

1/29–37/20. Administrative records of VGBIL

Private Collections

Rudomino Family Papers, in the possession of Adrian V. Rudomino, Moscow Oblast

UKRAINE [*before 1991,* UKRAINIAN SSR]

General Directories and Specialized Interrepository Archival Finding Aids:

The website of the State Committee on Archives of Ukraine (DKAU) is found at <http://www.scarch.kiev.ua/>.

Arkhivni ustanovy Ukraïny: Dovidnyk. Ed. Ruslan Ia. Pyrih, Liubov A. Dubrovina, Hennadii V. Boriak, et al. Kyiv, 2000. [=Arkhivni zibrannia Ukraïny, Spetsial'ni dovidnyky.]
> A comprehensive updated directory of archival repositories in Ukraine, including those under various federal agencies, NAN, and major libraries. Includes an updated list of museums with archival holdings.

"Archives of Ukraine": <http://www.huri.harvard.edu/ukrarch>.
> The ArcheoBiblioBase website with updated English-language information on Ukrainian archives, now maintained by the Harvard Ukrainian Research Institute website at Harvard University.

Boriak, Hennadii, Maryna Dubyk, and Nataliia Makovs'ka. *"Natsysts'ke zoloto" z Ukraïny: U poshukakh arkhivnykh svidchen'.* 2 vols. Kyiv, 1998–2000.
Pt. 1. Kyiv, 1998.
Pt. 2: *Materialy do reiestru vyluchenykh u naselennia koshtovnostei.* Kyiv, 2000.
> Provides listings of record groups (fonds) available in Ukrainian archives from the World War II period (esp. section 1, pp. 23–51), including Nazi records in oblast-level archives in Ukraine. The second volume provides some sample shipment data and lists of confiscations from individual Ukrainian citizens and analysis of the authenticity of the sources, based on several specific wartime Nazi files.

Grimsted, Patricia Kennedy. *Archives and Manuscript Repositories in the USSR: Ukraine and Moldavia,* Book 1: *General Bibliography and Institutional Directory.* Princeton: Princeton University Press, 1988.

—. "Ukraine." In *Austrian History Yearbook* 29(2) 1998: 171–200 [=*A Guide to East-Central European Archives*].

Ivanov, Ievhen Mykolaiovych [Evgenii Nikolaevich Ivanov]. "Ukraïns'ki fondy, perevezeni z Moskvy." *Arkhivna sprava* 4 (1927): 44–65.

Kyiv

Derzhavnyi komitet arkhiviv Ukraïny (DKAU)
[State Committee on Archives of Ukraine]
Previous names:1991–2000: Holovne arkhivne upravlinnia pry Kabineti
Ministriv Ukraïny (HAU) [Main Archival Administration under the Cabinet of
Ministers of Ukraine]; *1974–1991:* Holovne arkhivne upravlinnia pry Radi
Ministriv URSR [Main Archival Administration under the Council of Ministers
of the UkrSSR]

Tsentral′nyi derzhavnyi arkhiv vyshchykh orhaniv vlady i upravlinnia Ukraïny (TsDAVO)
[Central State Archive of Highest Agencies of Power and Administration
of Ukraine], Kyiv
Previous names: 1980–1991: Tsentral′nyi derzhavnyi arkhiv Zhovtnevoï
revoliutsiï, vyshchykh orhaniv derzhavnoï vlady i orhaniv derzhavnoho
upravlinnia URSR (TsDAZhR URSR) [Central State Archive of the October
Revolution, Highest Agencies of State Power, and Agencies of State
Administration of the UkrSSR]
1943–1980: Tsentral′nyi derzhavnyi arkhiv Zhovtnevoï revoliutsiï ta
sotsialistychnoho budivnytstva URSR (TsDAZhR URSR) [Central State Archive
of the October Revolution and Socialist Development of the UkrSSR]

Basic published guides:

*Tsentral′nyi gosudarstvennyi arkhiv Oktiabr′skoi revoliutsii, vysshikh
organov gosudarstvennoi vlasti i organov gosudarstvennogo upravleniia
Ukrainskoi SSR: Kratkii spravochnik.* Comp. R. I. Tkach,
V. M. Brozhek, V. V. Prokopchuk, and O. L. Rybalko. Kyiv: HAU,
1984. [Microfiche ed.: East View Publications, no. B0060533.]
A basic, short Russian-language guide to TsDAZhR, much more extensive than
the 1960 guide. Initially issued for restricted use ("DSP"/*dlia sluzhebnogo
pol′zovaniia*), it is now openly available. Does not cover recently declassified
fonds or any of those from émigré sources.

*Tsentral′nyi derzhavnyi arkhiv Zhovtnevoï revoliutsiï i sotsialistychnoho
budivnytstva URSR: Putivnyk.* Ed. L. V. Husieva, M. K. Kolesnyk,
S. I. Rozin, I. K. Rybalka, V. I. Riabko, and P. V. Zamkovyi. Kharkiv:
Kharkivs′ke knyzhkove vyd-vo, 1960. [Microfiche ed.: IDC-R-14,348]

Zhyvotko, Arkadii. *Desiat′ rokiv Ukraïns′koho istorychnoho kabinetu
(1930–1940).* Prague, 1940. [=Inventari Arkhivu Ministerstva
vnutrishnikh sprav, series S, 1. Microfiche ed.: IDC-R-14,920. Reprint
ed.: New York: Norman Ross Publishing Inc., 1994.]
The central section (pp. 12–19) describes the documentary holdings of UIK in

Prague with emphasis on materials from the successive independent Ukrainian governments (1917–1919) and their collapse, with mention of official documentation, personal papers, and collections of letters, manuscripts, maps, and photographs. Drafts and proofs remain in TsDAVO, 3866/1/21 and 22, and also an untitled and undated copy as 3866/3/3. See also the report on UIK in *Ročenka slovanského ústavu v Praze* 11 (1938): 159–60.

Biuleten' Ukraïns'koho istorychnoho kabinetu v Prazi, no. 1 (only one published). Prague, 1932. [Microfiche ed.: IDC-R-14,895.]
An archival copy of the 1932 bulletin (covering operations for 1931) is held as 3866/1/20 and another copy in 3866/3/4.

Myronets', N. "Dokumenty fonda Nikity Shapovala kak istochnik dlia izucheniia ukrainskoi èmigratsii v Chekhoslovakii (Tsentral'nyi gosudarstvennyi arkhiv vysshikh organov vlasti i upravleniia Ukrainy, g. Kiev)." In *"Russkaia, ukrainskaia i belorusskaia èmigratsiia," 1995*, vol. 2, pp. 565–71.

Fonds cited:

14. Holovne arkhivne upravlinnia pry Kabineti Ministriv URSR (and its predecessors) (HAU; Holovarkhiv)
[Main Archival Administration under the Cabinet of Ministers of the UkrSSR]
Opysy 1, 7.

2592 (earlier 344s). Sekretarstvo natsional'nykh sprav Ukraïns'koï tsentral'noï Rady; Narodne ministerstvo sprav zakordonnykh, 1918—UNR
[Secretariat for Nationality Affairs of the Ukrainian Central Rada; National Ministry of Foreign Affairs, 1918—UNR]

3206. Reichskommissariat Ukraine (RKU) [Reich Commissariat for Ukraine]
Opys 5. Landesverwaltung der Archive, Bibliotheken und Museen (LV ABM)
[Provincial Administration of Libraries, Archives, and Museums]

3674. Einsatzstab Reichsleiter Rosenberg [Westen]
[Reichsleiter Rosenberg Special Command (for Occupied Western Regions and the Netherlands; Belgian Working Group)]
Comprises 3 files, predominantly from ERR operations in Belgium. However, more voluminous reports from that same Task Force are currently interfiled in the first section (*opys* 1, nos. 139–239, passim) of the main ERR record group (3676) earlier held in TsDIAK.

3676. Einsatzstab Reichsleiter Rosenberg
[Reichsleiter Rosenberg Special Command]

See more details about this fond above in Chapter 8. A few highly selected portions of files have been filmed by the U.S. Holocaust Museum and are available to researchers in Washington, DC.

Opsy 1, 2, 4.
The fourth *opys,* unlike *opsy* 1 and 2, appears not to be part of the ERR records. It contains files of the RMbO Special Commando for *Volksdeutsch* headed by Dr. Stumpp, one of the leading Nazi genealogists and author of several important works on German settlers in the Russian Empire. It also includes other trophy documentation from Nazi concentration camps and related materials received from the MVD.

3766. Ministerstvo sprav zakordonnykh, 1918
[Ministry of Foreign Affairs, 1918]

3866. Ukraïns'kyi istorychnyi kabinet v Prazi (UIK)
[Ukrainian Historical Cabinet in Prague]

4665. Tsentral'nyi derzhavnyi arkhiv Zhovtnevoï revoliutsiï, vyshchykh orhaniv derzhavnoï vlady i orhaniv derzhavnoho upravlinnia URSR (TsDAZhR URSR)
[Central State Archive of the October Revolution, Highest Agencies of State Power and Agencies of State Administration of the UkrSSR]
Administrative records of TsDAZhR URSR. During the summer of 1999, even the *opysy* of this fond were not available for consultation, making it impossible to verify earlier references. The records of the Special Secret Division were not among the *opysy* publicly available in that fond when I was permitted to consult them earlier.

4703. Tsentral'nyi derzhavnyi istorychnyi arkhiv URSR, Kyïv (TsDIAK)
[Central State Historical Archive of Ukraine, Kyiv]
Opysy 1 and 2.
Administrative records of TsDIAK. When I first consulted the formerly "secret" files in *opys* 2 in 1994, they were held by TsDIAK. They were due for subsequent transfer to TsDAVO (fond 4703) with the other administrative records of TsDIAK, although the formal transfer had not taken place by the end of 1999; I cite the TsDAVO designations, as requested by archivists in Kyiv. As of fall 1999, this *opys* still required special permission of the TsDIAK director for access.

4762. Komitet kul'turno-osvitnikh ustanov pry Radi Ministriv URSR
[Committee on Cultural and Educational Institutions under the Council of Ministers of the UkrSSR]
The secret section of the fond, which presumably would retain at least some files on postwar cultural transfers, is either not available or has not been preserved or located.

Tsentral'nyi derzhavnyi istorychnyi arkhiv Ukraïny, m. Kyïv (TsDIAK)
[Central State Historical Archive of Ukraine, Kyiv]

Basic guides:

Tsentral'nyi gosudarstvennyi istoricheskii arkhiv USSR v Kieve: Putevoditel'.
Comp. E. M. Apanovych, A. V. Bondarevskii, and M. A. Varshavchik.
Ed. A. V. Bondarevskii et al. Kyiv: TsGIA UkrSSR, 1958. [Microfiche
ed.: IDC-R-14,350]

> Now considerably out of date and incomplete, covering only approximately half
> the fonds in the archive, this guide is supplemented by a 1986 unpublished list of
> fonds (see below), including those that have been recently declassified and those
> transferred to other archives. The rich library holdings listed now form part of the
> HAU Central Library.

"Dopolneniia k putevoditeliu po TsGIA UkrSSR v g. Kieve"/"Dodatok do
putivnyka [po TsDIA URSR v m. Kyievi]." Comp. V. S. Konovalova.
Kyiv, 1986. Typescript. [TsGIA UkrSSR v g. Kieve]

Tsentral'nyi derzhavnyi arkhiv hromads'kykh ob'iednan' Ukraïny (TsDAHO)
[Central State Archive of Public Organizations of Ukraine]

> *Previous names: 1989–1991:* Arkhiv TsK Kompartii Ukrainy (Arkhiv KPU)
> [Archive of the Central Committee of the Communist Party of Ukraine];
> *1945–1989:* Partiinyi arkhiv Instytutu istoriï partiï pry TsK Kompartiï
> Ukraïny—Filial' Instytutu Marksyzmu-Leninizmu pry TsK KPRS (Arkhiv KPU)
> [Party Archive of the Institute of Party History under the Central Committee of
> the Communist Party of Ukraine—Branch of the Institute of Marxism-Leninism
> under the Central Committee of the Communist Party of the USSR]

Basic guide:

*Tsentral'nyi derzhavnyi arkhiv hromads'kykh ob'iednan' Ukraïny: Putivnyk-
dovidnyk.* Ed. R. Ia. Pyrih et al. Kyiv, forthcoming.

> A comprehensive guide to the archive has been completed, but not yet finalized
> for publication. The guide is not normally available to researchers.

Fonds cited:

1. Tsentral'nyi Komitet KPU (TsK KPU)
   [Central Committee, Communist Party of Ukraine]

> Includes a file (1484) with telegrams and a composition report of I. D. Shev-
> chenko about the archival holdings found in Wölfelsdorf (*Pol.* Wilkanów) near
> Habelswerdt (*Pol.* Bystrzyca-Kłodzka) in Silesia.
> Also includes files with reports of Ukrainian Trophy Brigade activities in
> Germany and Romania (e.g., files 1481 and 1482).

39. Partiinyi arkhiv Instytutu istoriï partiï pry TsK Kompartiï Ukraïny
    [Party Archives of the Institute of Party History, Central Committee
    CPU]
    O*pys* 3 (1929–1986). Reports from local Ukrainian CP archives.

269. Ukraïns'kyi muzei v Prazi [Ukrainian Museum in Prague]
    A partially processed collection of émigré materials received from MVD/KGB
    sources, most of which are of provenance in Prague, with some from Berlin,
    Paris, and other places.

**Tsentral'nyi derzhavnyi arkhiv-muzei literatury i mystetstva Ukraïny
(TsDAMLM)**
[Central State Archive-Museum of Literature and Art of Ukraine]

Fonds cited:

441. Kolektsiia rukopysiv diiachiv Zakhidnoievropeis'koï literatury i
    mystetstva, XVII–XIX vv.
    [Collection of Manuscripts of Representatives of West European
    Literature and Art from the 17th Century through the 19th Century]
    Trophy collection with over 5,100 music scores from the Sing-Akademie in
    Berlin.

**Tsentral'nyi derzhavnyi kinofotofonoarkhiv Ukraïny im. H. S.
Pshenychnoho (TsDKFFA)**
[H. S. Pshenychnyi Central State Archive of Films, Photographs, and
Sound Recordings of Ukraine]
    Previous name: 1943–1992: Tsentral'nyi derzhavnyi arkhiv
    kinofotofonodokumentiv URSR (TsDAKFFD URSR; *Rus.* TsGAKFFD UkrSSR)
    [Central State Archive of Documentary Films, Photographs, and Sound
    Recordings of the UkrSSR]

Holdings cited:

Film and photographic collections from UIK, Prague, and others relating to
    World War II.

Derzhavnyi arkhiv Kyïvs'koï oblasti (DAKO)
[State Archive of Kyiv Oblast]

Basic guide:

Gosudarstvennyi arkhiv Kievskoi oblasti: Putevoditel'. Comp. Iu. F. Borshch,
    V. S. Levin, H. I. Milova, F. M. Radomysl's'ka, and Iu. P. Khonineva.
    Kyiv: Izd-vo politicheskoi literatury Ukraïny, 1965. [Microfiche ed.:
    IDC-R-14,364]

Fonds cited:

R-2412. Muzei-Arkhiv Perekhodovoï doby m. Kyieva
[Museum-Archive of the Transitional Period]
Opys 1. Office records of the museum
Opys 2. Selected documentation collected for the musuem exhibits

Natsional´na biblioteka Ukraïny im. V. I. Vernads´koho, Instytut rukopysiv (IR NBU)

[V. I. Vernads´kyi National Library of Ukraine, Institute of Manuscripts]

Agency: Natsional´na Akademiia nauk Ukraïny [National Academy of Sciences of Ukraine]

Previous names: 1994–1996: Ukr. Tsentral´na naukova biblioteka im. V. I. Vernads´koho NAN Ukraïny (TsNB NAN Ukraïny), Viddil rukopysiv; *Rus.* Tsentral´naia nauchnaia biblioteka im. V. I. Vernadskogo NAN Ukrainy/TsNB NAN Ukrainy; Otdel rukopisei) [Vernads´kyi Central Scientific Library of the National Academy of Sciences of Ukraine, Manuscript Division]

1992–1994: Tsentral´na naukova biblioteka im. V. I. Vernads´koho AN Ukraïny (TsNB AN Ukraïny) [Vernads´kyi Central Scientific Library of the Academy of Sciences of Ukraine]

Ivano-Frankivsk

Derzhavnyi arkhiv Ivano-Frankivs´koï oblasti

[Ivano-Frankivsk Oblast State Archive]

Basic guide:

Gosudarstvennyi arkhiv Ivano-Frankovskoi oblasti: Putevoditel´, 2nd ed., Comp. V. I. Gritsenko et al. Kyiv: GAU pri SM UkrSSR, 1983.

Lviv

Tsentral´nyi derzhavnyi istorychnyi arkhiv Ukraïny, m. L´viv (TsDIAL Ukraïny)

[Central State Historical Archive of Ukraine, Lviv]

Specialized catalogs and finding aids cited:

Pijaj, Stanisław. *Archiwa rodzinno-majątkowe w zbiorach państwowych we Lwowie.* Warsaw: Ministerstwo Kultury i Sztuki, 1995. [=Polskie dziedzictwo kulturalne, Seria B: Wspólne Dziedzictwo.]

The compiler was unable to include some of the materials that were not catalogued before 1945 and did not have complete data about the transfers to TsDIAL from the Ossolineum collections.

Fonds cited:

755. Arkhivne upravlinnia v m. L′vovi, 1941–1944
[Records of the Nazi Archival Administration for Galicia]

L′vivs′ka naukova biblioteka im. V. Stefanyka NAN Ukraïny, Viddil rukopysiv (LNB NAN)
[V. Stefanyk Lviv Scientific Library of the National Academy of Sciences of Ukraine, Manuscript Division]

Basic guide:

Osobysti arkhivni fondy viddilu rukopysiv. Anotovanyi pokazhchyk. Comp. P. H. Bab'iak, O. O. Dz′oban, et. al. 2nd ed. Lviv: LNB NAN, 1995. 1st edition: Lviv: LNB NAN, 1977. Rotaprint. [Microfiche ed.: IDC-R-14,530.]

Specialized catalogs and finding aids cited:

For more details about the previously published and manuscript finding aids for the Ossolineum manuscripts and other component collections such as the Dzieduszycki Library and the Baworowski Library, see the text and annotated bibliography in Grimsted, *Archives: Ukraine*, pp. 500–569. Most of the finding aids listed are available on IDC microfiche, including some special microfiche editions with prefaces and annotations by P. K. Grimsted, especially covering the divided collections. Only the most important ones covering the Ossolineum and a few selected other ones specifically cited in the text and footnotes are listed below. As explained in chapter 11, many of the collections are today divided between Lviv and Wrocław, but parts of some of them are also today held in the Biblioteka Narodowa and AGAD in Warsaw and in other repositories as indicated.

Gębarowicz, Mieczysław. *Katalog rękopisów Biblioteki im. Gwalberta Pawlikowskiego.* Lviv: ZNiO, 1929. [Microfiche ed.: IDC-R-14,536.] Second edition: In *Inwentarz rękopisów ZNiO we Wrocławiu.* Ed. Jadwiga Turska et al. Vol. 2. Wrocław: Wyd-wo ZNiO, 1949. The second edition omits the 55 manuscripts from the collection remaining in Lviv.

Inwentarz rękopisów Biblioteki Zakładu Narodowego im. Ossolińskich we Lwowie. 2 vols. Lviv, 1926–1934. Hectographed. Supplement 1: "— [Nr 6001[6109]–6615 [with continuation to 6596 in one of the carbon copies]." Lviv, 1937. Typescript. Supplement 2: "Inventar rukopysiv buvshoï biblioteky im. Ossolins′kykh u L′vovi, NoNo. 6597–8091. Typescript. [Special microfiche ed. with preface by P. K. Grimsted: IDC-R-14,429.] The special microfiche edition includes the two supplements from ZNiO copies (to MS 7705), based on microfilms furnished to HURI. Annotations in the special

microfiche edition indicate the present location of the manuscripts. ZNiO has since
acquired a xerox copy of the supplement covering manuscripts 7706–8091.

Kętrzyński, Wojciech. *Katalog rękopisów Zakładu Narodowego im.
Ossolińskich/Catalogus codicum manuscriptorum Bibliothecae
Ossolinianae Leopoliensis*, 3 vols. Lviv, 1881–1898. [Special microfiche
ed. with preface by P. K. Grimsted: IDC-R-14,485.]

Pijaj, Stanisław. *Archiwa rodzinno-majątkowe w zbiorach
państwowych we Lwowie.* Warsaw: Ministerstwo Kultury i
Sztuki, 1995, pp. 81–163. [=Polskie dziedzictwo kulturalne,
Seria B: Wspólne Dziedzictwo.]
The compiler was unable to include some of the materials that were not
catalogued before 1945 and did not have complete data about the transfers to
TsDIAL from the Ossolineum collections.

Pohorecki, Feliks. *Catalogus diplomatum Bibliothecae Instituti Ossoliniani
nec non Bibliothecae Pawlikowianae inde ab anno 1227 usque ad annum
1505.* Lviv: Sumptibus societatis amicorum Instituti Ossoliniani, 1937.

[—, and] Adam Fastnacht, *Catalogus…Supplementum I. Inde ab anno 1279
usque ad annum 1506.* Wrocław: Institutum Ossolinianum, 1951.
[Special microfiche ed., with preface by P. K. Grimsted: IDC-R-14,537.]

Matwijów, Maciej, et al. "Wniosek rewindykacyjny zbiorów Zakładu
Narodowego im. Ossolińskich—Rękopisy." In *Wnioski rewindykacyjne*,
pp. 36–47.

Fonds cited:

Fond 5. Ossolineum Collection (and parts dispersed in other collections)

L′vivs′kyi muzei Ukraïns′koho mystetstva (LMUM)
[Lviv Museum of Ukrainian Art]

Specialized catalogs and finding aids cited:

Bordun, Melaniia. "Z zhyttia ukraïns′koho dukhovenstva l′vivs′koï eparkhiï v
druhii pol. XVIII st. (Na osnovi vizytatsii M. Shadurs′koho
1759–1763)." *Zapysky NTSh* 134–135 (1924): 137–60.

Franko, Ivan. "Prychynok do istoriï halyts′ko-rus′koho pys′menstva XVIII
st." *Zapysky NTSh* 107 (1912): 110–15.

Poltava

Derzhavnyi arkhiv Poltavs′koï oblasti
[Poltava Oblast State Archive]

Fonds cited:

R-1505. Derzhavnyi arkhiv Poltavs′koï oblasti
[Records of the Poltava Oblast State Archive], *opys* 1, file 118 (1943)

UNITED STATES OF AMERICA

General Guides and Finding Aids:

Grant, Steven A. *Scholars' Guide to Washington, D.C. for Russian, Central Eurasian, and Baltic Studies*. 3rd ed. revised by William E. Pomeranz with the assistance of Gina R. Ottoboni. Washington, DC, 1994.

U.S. National Archives, Washington, DC, and College Park, MD

Guides and Finding Aids:

Guide to Federal Records in the National Archives of the United States. 3 vols. Washington, DC: GPO, 1996.
  Electronic version: <http://www.nara.gov/guide/>.

Holocaust Era Assets: A Finding Aid to Records at the National Archives at College Park, Maryland. Comp. Greg Bradsher. Washington, DC: National Archives and Records Administration, 1999.
  Electronic version: <http://www.nara.gov/publications/assets/>.

U.S. Adjutant General's Office, Administrative Services Division, Departmental Records Branch. *Guide to Captured German Records in the Custody of the Department of the Army Agencies in the United States, Washington, D.C.* Washington, DC, April 1950.

U.S. Adjutant General's Office, Administrative Services Division, Departmental Records Branch. *Guide to Seized Records*. Washington, DC, December 1957. [Reference Aid Nr. 17 (revised).]

U.S. Central Intelligence Agency. *The Collections and Indexes of the German Military Documents Section (AG0)*. Washington, DC: CIA, May 1953. [=CIA/CD Research Aid #5.]

U.S. National Archives. *Guides to German Records Microfilmed at Alexandria, VA*. 97 vols. Washington, DC: U.S. National Archives, 1958–1996. [Mimeographed; also available in microfilm edition.]

No. 28: *Records of the Reich Ministry for the Occupied Eastern Territories (Reichsministerium für die besetzten Ostgebiete), 1941–1943.* Washington, DC, 1961.
Covers the microfilm series T454, 107 rolls. These records were subsequently rearranged after their return to Koblenz (see under "Germany" above), since they cover files from the Einsatzstab Reichsleiter Rosenberg (ERR) and other agencies, as well as the Reichsministerium (RMbO).
No. 97: *Records of the Reich Ministry for the Occupied Eastern Territories (Reichsministerium für die besetzten Ostgebiete) and Other Rosenberg Organizations,* Part II. (Microfiche ed.) Washington, DC, 1996.

Record groups cited:

RG 64. Administrative records of the National Archives and Records Service

RG 165. Office of Stategic Services (OSS). Scattered interrogation reports

RG 239. American Commission for the Protection and Salvage of Artistic and Historic Monuments in War Areas (Roberts Commission)
Extensive documentation regarding preservation and restitution issues, including copies of many MFF&A reports.

RG 242. National Archives Collection of Foreign Records Seized

Records of the All-Union Communist Party, Smolensk District, 1917–1941
Also available on microfilm.

Records of the Reich Commissioner for the Strengthening of Germandom, 1939–1945

Records of the Reich Ministry for the Occupied Eastern Territories (RMbO), 1942–1945

German Military Documents Section. Reference collection

AGAR-S. A special collection of copies of documents relating to U.S. captured records policies, prepared as reference files in the Captured Records Branch (most by Seymour J. Pomrenze)

RG 260. Office of Military Government, United States (OMGUS)

Office of Military Government for Germany, U.S. Zone, Reparations and Restitution Branch, General Records
Especially: Ardelia Hall Collection, Records Concerning Central Collecting Points

Records of the Military Government for Austria (USFA), Reparations and Restitution Branch

U.S. Holocaust Memorial Museum (USHMM)

Finding Aids :
> See more details of different record groups available and their finding aids at the
> USHMM website: <http://www.ushmm.org>.

Inventories of captured Nazi agency records microfilmed in Eastern Europe

Inventory of RSHA records acquired from Poland (see below), RG–15.007M
> An English-language finding aid for these records, prepared by George C.
> Browder (July 1995) is available on the USHMM website. The original Polish
> inventory is available on the first reel of the microfilm.

Record groups cited:

RG–15.007M–Records of the RSHA—Reichssicherheitshauptamt
[Office of the Reich Security Main Office.] Microfilm (78 reels)
> The records were filmed in Poland, when they were in the custody of the Main
> Commission for the Investigation of Hitlerite Crimes in Poland (Główna Komisja
> Badań Zbrodni Hitlerowskich w Polsce), now in the Institute of National Memory
> (Instytut Pamięci Narodowej), Warsaw as record group (*zespól*) 362. They
> primarily constitute fragmentary parts of the archives held by RSHA, Amt VII,
> including scattered office records along with miscellaneous archival materials that
> had been seized. In 1997, the originals were transferred to Germany and are being
> reprocessed in the Bundesarchiv–Berlin-Lichterfelde (BAB).

Fragmentary captured Holocaust-era Nazi records acquired on microfilm
from the Russian Federation and Ukraine
> The originals are listed above under Russia and Ukraine.

Library of Congress, Manuscript Division

Deutsches Ausland Institut [Institute for Germans Abroad]
Microfilms, together with inventories of the records

II. International Legal Documentation

A. Collections/Compendia

Council of Europe. *Reference Dossier on Archival Claims*. Comp. Hervé
    Bastien. [Paris]: ICA Legal Matters Committee, 1995.
    (Hereafter: *Dossier on Archival Claims*)
    French edition: *Dossier de référence sur les Contentieux Archivistiques*.
    Strasbourg: Conseil de l'Europe, 1997. (CC LIVRE [97] 1)
    Reprinted in its entirety (in both French and English) as an appendix to
    CITRA 1993–1995.

UNESCO. *Conventions and Recommendations of Unesco Concerning the
    Protection of the Cultural Heritage*. Paris: Unesco, 1983.
    (Hereafter: *Conventions and Recommendations of Unesco*)
    French edition: *Conventions et recommandations de l'Unesco relatives à
    la protection du patrimoine culturel*. Paris, 1983.

Mezhdunarodnaia okhrana kul'turnykh tsennostei. Ed. Mark Moiseevich
    Boguslavskii. Moscow: Mezhdunarodnye otnosheniia, 1979.
    (Hereafter: *Mezhdunarodnaia okhrana*)

*Mizhnarodna okhorona, zakhyst i povernennia kul'turnykh tsinnostei (zbirnyk
    dokumentiv)*. Ed. Iurii K. Kachurenko. Kyiv, 1993. [Sponsors:
    Ministerstvo zakordonnykh sprav Ukraïny; Natsional'na komisiia z
    pytan' povernennia v Ukraïnu kul'turnykh tsinnostei pry Kabineti
    Ministriv Ukraïny; IUA.]
    (Hereafter: *Mizhnarodna okhorona*)

*The Spoils of War: World War II and Its Aftermath. The Loss, Reappearance,
    and Recovery of Cultural Property*. Ed. Elizabeth Simpson. New York:
    Henry N. Abrams, 1997. Documentary Appendixes.
    (Hereafter: *The Spoils of War: WWII and Aftermath*)

Ukraïna v mizhnarodno-pravovykh vidnosynakh. 2 vols. Kyiv: Iurinkom
    Inter, 1996–1997.
    Book 1: *Borot'ba iz zlochynnistiu ta vzaiemna pravova dopomoha*. Ed.
    V. L. Chubariev and A. S. Matsko. Kyiv: Iurinkom Inter, 1996.
    Book 2: *Pravova okhorona kul'turnykh tsinnostei*. Ed. V. I. Akulenko
    and Iu. S. Shemshuchenko. Kyiv: Iurinkom Inter, 1997.
    (Hereafter: *Ukraïna v mizhnarodno-pravovykh vidnosynakh*)

United Nations Treaty Series. Treaties and international agreements registered or filed and recorded with the Secretariat of the United Nations. New York.
(Hereafter: *U.N.T.S.)*

B. International Legal Documents
(Multilateral Treaties, Conventions, and Resolutions)

1. Pre-1945 Conventions and Treaties

"Convention Respecting the Laws and Customs of War on Land." (Also known as "The Hague Convention of 1907"). Signed at The Hague, 18 October 1907. Entered into force, 26 January 1910. (36 Stat. 2277; 1 Bevans 631)
Significant excerpts in *The Spoils of War: WWII and Aftermath*, Appendix 3, pp. 278–79.

"Treaty of Peace with Germany." (Also known as the "Treaty of Versailles.") Signed at Versailles, 28 June 1919. (T.S. 658; 2 Bevans 43)
Significant excerpts in *The Spoils of War: WWII and Aftermath*, Appendix 4, pp. 280–81.

"Treaty of Peace between the Allied and Associated Powers and Austria." (Also known as the "Treaty of St. Germain.") Signed at St. Germain-en-Laye, 10 September 1919; entered into force 8 November 1921. (T.S. 659; 112 B.F.S.P. 317)
Significant excerpts in *The Spoils of War: WWII and Aftermath*, Appendix 5, pp. 282–83.

"Treaty of Peace between the Allied Powers and Hungary." (Also known as the "Treaty of Trianon." Signed at Trianon, 4 June 1920; entered into force 17 December 1921. (T.S. 660; 112 B.F.S.P. 486)
Significant excerpts in *The Spoils of War: WWII and Aftermath*, Appendix 6, pp. 283–84.

"Treaty of Peace between Poland, Russia, and The Ukraine." (Also known as the "Treaty of Riga." Signed at Riga, 18 March 1921; entered into force upon signature. (6 L.N.T.S. 123)
Significant excerpts in *The Spoils of War: WWII and Aftermath*, Appendix 7, pp. 284–85.

"Inter-Allied Declaration Against Acts of Dispossession Committed in Territories under Enemy Occupation or Control." (Also known as the "Declaration of London").
In the U.S. Department of State *Bulletin*, 21 (1943).
In *The Spoils of War: WWII and Aftermath*, Appendix 9, p. 287.

2. UN [United Nations] Conventions and Resolutions

United Nations. "Convention on Succession of States in Respect to State
Property, Archives and Debts." Adopted at the United Nations
Conference on Succession of States in Respect to State Property,
Archives and Debts, Vienna, 1 March–8 April 1983. (A/Conf.117/14)
Known as the "Vienna Convention." Not entered into force (not ratified). The text
of Pt. III (" State Archives") is reproduced in Appendix IIIa above.

—. *Resolutions*

The following series of UN resolutions "Return or Restitution of Cultural Property to
the Countries of Origin," have been issued in somewhat variant form at one- or two-
year intervals. The preamble of each successive resolution lists preceding resolutions
on the subject adopted by the General Assembly. All are printed in the *UN General
Assembly Official Records*, and the corresponding published records in the other four
official UN languages, including Russian, of the session in which they were adopted.
In most cases, only the UN document reference numbers are cited here, except for the
later ones that are cited in the text individually. All of them are available through the
UN website, and the electronic facility "AccessUN," available through many libraries.

UN. "Return or Restitution of Cultural Property to the Countries of Origin,"
Resolution 3026 A (XXVII), 18 December 1972.

—. Resolution no. 3148 (XXVIII), 14 December 1973.

—. Resolution no. 3187 (XXVIII), 18 December 1973.

—. Resolution no. 3391 (XXX), 19 November 1975.

—. Resolution no. 31/40, 30 December 1976.

—. Resolution no. 32/18, 11 November 1977.

—. Resolution no. 33/50, 14 December 1978.

—. Resolution no. 34/64, 29 November 1979.

—. Resolution nos. 35/127 and 35/128, 11 December 1980.

—. Resolution no. 36/64, 27 November 1981.

—. Resolution no. 38/34, 25 November 1983.

—. Resolution no. 40/19, 21 November 1985.

—. Resolution no. 42/7, 22 November 1987.

—. Resolution no. 44/18, 6 November 1989.

UN. "Return or Restitution of Cultural Property to the Countries of Origin," 22 October 1991 (46/10), *Official Records of the General Assembly, Forty-Sixth Session*, Supplement No. 49. (A/46/49), p. 14.

—. "Return or Restitution of Cultural Property to the Countries of Origin," 2 November 1993 (A/RES/48/15), *UN General Assembly Official Records: Forty-Seventh Plenary Meeting* (2 November 1993), Supplement No. 49.
Electronic version: Available through "AccessUN"; and at <http://www.tufts.edu/departments/fletcher/multi/texts/a-res-48-15.html>.
Ukrainian edition: in *Ukraïna v mizhnarodno-pravovykh vidnosynakh*, bk. 2, pp. 68–71.]

—. "Return or Restitution of Cultural Property to the Countries of Origin," 11 December 1995 (A/RES/50/56), *UN General Assembly Official Records: Fiftieth Session*, Supplement No. 49. (A/50/49)
Ukrainian edition: in *Ukraïna v mizhnarodno-pravovykh vidnosynakh*, bk. 2, pp. 71–72.

—. "Return or Restitution of Cultural Property to the Countries of Origin," 25 December 1997 (A/RES/52/24), *UN General Assembly Official Records: Fifty-Second Session*, Supplement No. 49. (A/52/49)

3. UNESCO [United Nations Educational, Scientific and Cultural Organization] and the International Institute for the Unification of Private Law (UNIDROIT)

—. *Conventions*

UNESCO. "Convention for the Protection of Cultural Property in the Event of Armed Conflict." (Also known as the "Hague Convention and Protocol of 1954.") Adopted as "Protocol to the Convention and the Conference Resolutions." The Hague, 14 May 1954; entered into force, 7 August 1956. (no. 3511, *U.N.T.S.*, vol. 249, pp. 215–386)
In *Conventions and Recommendations of Unesco*, pp. 13–56.
In *The Spoils of War: WWII and Aftermath*, Appendix 10, pp. 293–97, together with accessions as of 15 June 1996.
The text is reprinted with further discussion in the *International Journal of Cultural Property* 5 (1996): 55ff; and *Zeitschrift für vergleichende Rechtswissenschaft* 95 (1996): 203ff.
Electronic version: <http://www.unesco.org/culture/legalprotection/>.
Russian text: "Konventsiia o zashchite kul'turnykh tsennostei v sluchae vooruzhennogo konflikta ot 14 maia 1954 g." (Also known as the

"Gaagskaia Konventsiia 1954 goda o zashchite kul'turnykh tsennostei v sluchae vooruzhennogo konflikta.")
In *Mezhdunarodnaia okhrana*, pp. 145–55; and, including the protocol, in *Ukraïna v mizhnarodno-pravovykh vidnosynakh*, book 1, pp. 393–416.

Ukrainian edition: "Konventsiia pro zakhyst kul'turnykh tsinnostei u vypadku zbroinoho konfliktu."
In *Mizhnarodna okhorona*, pp. 5–20, together with the supplemental regulation and protocol (pp. 21–36); and in *Ukraïna v mizhnarodno-pravovykh vidnosynakh*, book 2, pp. 85–118.

"Second Protocol to the Hague Convention of 1954 for the Protection of Cultural Property in the Event of Armed Conflict," The Hague, 26 March 1999.
Electronic version: <http://www.unesco.org/culture/legalprotection/war/html_eng/protocol2.htm>.

UNESCO. "Convention on the Means of Prohibiting and Preventing the Illicit Import, Export and Transfer of Ownership of Cultural Property." Adopted 14 November 1970; entered into force, 24 April 1972. (*U.N.T.S.*, vol. 823, p. 231)
In UNESCO, *Records of the General Conference, 16th Session*, vol. 1: *Resolutions*, pp. 135–41.
In *Conventions and Recommendations of Unesco*, pp. 157–74, together with "State of ratifications and accessions as of 31 July 1982."
In *The Spoils of War: WWII and Aftermath*, Appendix 11, pp. 297–301, together with accessions through 15 June 1996.

Electronic version: <http://www.unesco.org/culture/legalprotection/>.
Russian text: "Konventsiia o merakh, napravlennykh na zapreschchenie i preduprezhdenie nezakonnogo vvoza, vyvoza i peredachi prava sobstvennosti na kul'turnye tsennosti."
In IuNESKO, *Akty General'noi konferentsii*, 16-ia sessiia, *Rezoliutsii*, pp. 146–58.
In *Mezhdunarodnaia okhrana kul'turnykh tsennostei*, pp. 166–73.
In *Ukraïna v mizhnarodno-pravovykh vidnosynakh*, book 1, pp. 417–28.

Ukrainian edition: "Konventsiia pro zakhody, spriamovani na zaboronu i zapobihannia nezakonnomu vvezeniu, vyvezenniu ta peredachi prava vlasnosti na kul'turni tsinnosti."
In *Mizhnarodna okhorona*, pp. 41–50; and in *Ukraïna v mizhnarodno-pravovykh vidnosynakh*, book 2, pp. 119–28.

UNIDROIT Convention on Stolen and Illegally Exported Cultural Objects. Adopted 4 June 1995. (34 I.L.M., 1322 [1995])
In *The Spoils of War: WWII and Aftermath*, Appendix 17, pp. 308–11 (includes signatories through 29 June 1996).
In Lyndel V. Prott, *Commentary on the UNIDROIT Convention on Stolen and Illegally Exported Cultural Objects, 1995*. Leicester: Institute of Art and Law, 1997.

Electronic version: <http://www.unidroit.org> and <http://www.city.ac.
uk/artspol/unidroit.html>
Ukrainian edition: (proposed draft): "Proekt konventsiï pro vykradeni
abo nezakonno vyvezeni za kordon predmety kul'tury." *Pam'iatky
Ukraïny* 1994 (1–2[25]): 7–9.
However, note that there were subsequent modifications in the adopted text.

—. Resolutions

—. "Statutes of the Intergovernmental Committee for Promoting the Return
of Cultural Property to its Countries of Origin or its Restitution in Case
of Illicit Appropriation." Resolution of the 20th Session of the General
Conference (October–November 1978). (20 C/Res 4/7.6/5)
In *The Spoils of War: WWII and Aftermath,* Appendix 13, pp. 302–303.
Ukrainian edition: "Statut Mizhuriadovoho komitetu zi spryiannia
povernenniu kul'turnykh tsinnostei kraïnam ïkh pokhodzhennia abo ïkh
restytutsiï v razi nezakonnoho pryvlasnennia."
In *Ukraïna v mizhnarodno-pravovykh vidnosynakh,* book 2, pp. 237–41.

—. Intergovernmental Committee for Promoting the Return of Cultural
Property to its Countries of Origin or Its Restitution in Case of Illicit
Appropriation. "Principles for the Resolution of Disputes Concerning
Cultural Heritage Displaced during the Second World War." Paris:
UNESCO, 1999. (CLT-99/CONF.203/2)
The publication grew out of the 10th Session of the Committee, Paris, 25–28
January 1999; it is found at the UNESCO website <http://www.unesco.org/>.

4. Resolutions of Other International Agencies

Fifth Conference of Heads of State or Government of Non-Aligned
Countries, 1976. Resolution reaffirming the UN Resolution "On the
Return or Restitution of Cultural Property."
In *Documents of the Fifth Conference of Heads of State or Government of Non-
Aligned Countries,* annex IV, Resolution 17 (A/31/197: 136). Quoted in *Yearbook
ILC 1979,* II, pt. 1: 82.

European Economic Community. "Resolution on the Right of Nations to
Information Concerning their History and the Return of National
Archives," 24 January 1991. (A3-0258/90) In *Dossier on Archival
Claims,* pp. 4–6.
Reprinted in *CITRA 1993–1995,* pp. 231–33.

—. "Council Directive 93/7/EEC of 15 March 1993 on the Return of Cultural
Objects Unlawfully Removed from the Territory of a Member State."
Official Journal L 074, 27/03/1993: 0074–0079.
Amendments are found in *Official Journal* L 060, 01/03/97: 59.

5. Agreements of the Commonwealth of Independent States (SNG/SND)

"Soglashenie o pravopreemstve v otnoshenii gosudarstvennykh arkhivov
byvshego Soiuza SSR." Moscow, 6 July 1992. *Vestnik arkhivista* 1992
(4[10]): 3–5 (Russian); and in *Arkhivy Ukraïny* 1992 (1–3): 4–5.
Ukrainian edition: "Uhoda pro povernennia kul'turnykh i istorychnykh
tsinnostei derzhavam ïkh pokhodzhennia." In *Mizhnarodna okhorona,*
pp. 66–67.
Printed above as Appendix V.

**C. Proceedings and Reports of International Agencies
(UN, UNESCO, and ICA)**

1. United Nations [UN].

—. *Yearbook of the United Nations*, vol. 35 (1981); vol. 36 (1982); and
vol. 37 (1983).

United Nations [UN]. Conference on Succession of States in Respect to State
Property.

—. "Analytic Compilation of Comments of Governments on the Final Draft
Articles on Succession of States in Respect to State Property, Archives
and Debts." 24 January 1983. (A/Conf. 117/5)

—. "Final Act of the United Nations Conference on Succession of States in
Respect to State Property, Archives and Debts." (A/Conf. 117/15)

—. Reports of individual meetings of the 1983 conference and related
conference materials. In mimeographed format and on microfiche. Most
bear the series identification A/Conf. 117.

United Nations [UN]. International Law Commission (ILC)

—. *Yearbook of the International Law Commission, 1979* (New York, 1981),
I; II, pts. 1, 2.

—. *Yearbook ILC, 1980* (New York, 1982), I; II, pt. 1.

—. *Yearbook ILC, 1981* (New York, 1983), I; II, pt. 1.

Bedjaoui, Mohammed, Special Rapporteur. *Eighth Report on Succession of
States in Respect of Matters Other than Treaties: Draft Articles with
Commentaries on Succession to State Property.* (A/CN.4/292, and
A/CN.4/322)

—. "Eleventh Report on Succession of States in Respect of Matters Other than Treaties." *Yearbook ILC, 1979* (New York, 1981), II, pt. 1, pp. 67–124.

—. "1979 Report." In *Yearbook ILC, 1979* (New York, 1981), II, pt. 2, pp. 77–78.

—. "Non-Exhaustive Table of Treaties Containing Provisions Relating to the Transfer of Archives in Cases of Succession of States." *Yearbook ILC 1979*, II, pt. 1, *Documents of the Thirty-First Session (excluding the report of the Commission to the General Assembly)*, pp. 82–93.
   Printed above as Appendix II.

Report of the International Law Commission on Work of its Thirty-Third Session, May 4–June 24, 1981, published as *Official Records of the General Assembly, Thirty-Sixth Session*, Supplement 10. (A/36/10)

2. United Nations Educational, Scientific and Cultural Organization [UNESCO].

Individually authored reports or working papers are listed under the authors in the list of Secondary Literature, Section VI below, although many of these were published under ICA or UNESCO auspices. Many of the listings below are available at UNESCO's website: <http://www.unesco.org>.

—. *Final Report* of the "Consultation group to prepare a report on the possibility of transferring documents from archives constituted within the territory of other countries, Paris, 16–18 March 1976." 1 April 1976. Paris: UNESCO, 1976. (CC-76/WS/9)

—. *Museum* 31(1) 1979.
   A special issue devoted to the establishment of the Intergovernmental Committee for Promoting the Return of Cultural Property and related issues of return and restitution of cultural property.

—. General Conference, Nineteenth Session, Nairobi, 1976. "Report by the Director General on the Study of the Possibility of Transferring Documents from Archives Constituted within the Territory of Other Countries or Relating to Their Territory, within the framework of bilateral agreements." 6 August 1976. (19C/94)

—. General Conference, Twentieth Session, Paris, 1978. "Proposals of the Director-General with a View to the Establishment of an Intergovernmental Committee Entrusted with the Task of Seeking Ways and Means of Facilitating Bilateral Negotiations for the Restitution or Return of Cultural Property to the Countries Having Lost Such Property as a Result of Colonial or Foreign Occupation." 29 September 1978. (20 C/86, Annex II)

—. General Conference, Twenty-First Session, Belgrade, 1980, "Report of the Intergovernmental Committee for Promoting the Return of Cultural Property to its Countries of Origin or its Restitution in Case of Illicit Appropriation" [First Session]. (21 C/83)

—. "Report of the Director-General on the Study of Problems Involved in the Transfer of Documents from Archives in the Territory of Certain Countries to the Country of Their Origin." 24 August 1978. (20 C/102)
    The report was initially prepared by Charles Kecskeméti for the 17th CITRA at Cagliari, and published as *Les contentieux archivistiques. Étude préliminaire sur les principes et les critères à retenir lors des négociations* (Paris, 1977) (PGI-77/WS/1), and also published in condensed form in *Actes de la 17ème CITRA*. Reprinted above as Appendix I.

—. "Report of the Director-General of UNESCO on the Action Taken by the Organization On the Return of Cultural Property to the Countries of Origin or its Restitution in Case of Illicit Appropriation." 25.VI.1997. (A/52/211)

—. "Retour et restitution de biens culturels: Aperçu succinct." Paris: UNESCO, 1987. (CLT-85/WS/41)
    List of cases handled by courts outside of the Intergovernmental Committee for Promoting the Return of Cultural Property to Its Countries of Origin or Its Restitution in Case of Illicit Appropriation, as well as resolutions of the UN and UNESCO on the subject.

UNESCO. Intergovernmental Committee for Promoting the Return of Cultural Property to its Countries of Origin or its Restitution in Case of Illicit Appropriation/Comité intergouvernemental pour la promotion du retour de biens culturels à leur pays d'origine ou de leur restitution en cas d'appropriation illégale

—. First Session. In UNESCO. General Conference, Twenty-First Session, Belgrade 1980. "Report of the Intergovernmental Committee for Promoting the Return of Cultural Property to Its Countries of Origin or Its Restitution in Case of Illicit Appropriation." (21 C/83)

—. Second Session, Paris, 14–18 September 1981. (CC-81/CONF.203/10)

—. Third Session, Istanbul, Turkey, 9–12 May 1983. (CLT-83/CONF.216/8)

—. Fourth Session, Athens and Delphi, Greece, 2–5 April 1985. (CLT-85/CONF.202/7)

—. Fifth Session, Paris, 27–30 August 1987. (24 C/94)

—. Sixth Session, Paris, 24–27 April 1989. (25 C/91)

—. Seventh Session, Athens, Greece, 22–25 April 1991. (26C/92)

—. Eighth Session, Guatemala City, 7–10 June 1993. (CLT-93/CONF.203/2)

—. Ninth Session, Paris, 16–19 September 1996. (29C/REP.12)

—. Tenth Session, Paris, 25–28 January 1999. (CLT-98/CONF.203.2)

—. "Guidelines for the Use of the 'Standard Form Concerning Requests for Return or Restitution'"; reprinted 1992. (CC-86/WS/3)
The printed "Guidelines" also include a copy of the "Standard Form," the "Statutes" of the Committee, and the 1970 UN convention mentioned above.

—. "Principles for the Resolution of Disputes Concerning Cultural Heritage Displaced during the Second World War." Draft Recommendation. Paris: UNESCO, January 1999. (CLT-99/CONF.203.2)

—. "Rules of Procedure" (1989). (CC-89/CONF-213/COL-3)

—. "Standard Form Concerning Requests for Return or Restitution/ Formulaire type pour les demandes de retour ou de restitution." UNESCO, Intergovernmental Committee for Promoting the Return of Cultural Property to Its Countries of Origin or Its Restitution in Case of Illicit Appropriation/Comité intergouvernemental pour la promotion du retour de biens culturels à leur pays d'origine ou de leur restitution en cas d'appropriation illégale, (CLT-86/WS/1) and "Guidelines"; reprinted 1992. (CC-86/WS/3)

—. "Statutes of the Intergovernmental Committee for Promoting the Return of Cultural Property to Its Countries of Origin or Its Restitution in Case of Illicit Appropriation." *Resolution of the 20th Session of the General Conference (October-November 1978)* (20 C/Res 4/7.6/5).
In *The Spoils of War: WWII and Aftermath*, Appendix 13, pp. 302–303.
Ukrainian edition: "Statut Mizhuriadovoho komitetu zi spryiannia povernenniu kul'turnykh tsinnostei kraïnam ïkh pokhodzhennia abo ïkh restytutsiï v razi nezakonnoho pryvlasnennia."
In *Ukraïna v mizhnarodno-pravovykh vidnosynakh*, book 2, pp. 237–41.

3. International Council on Archives (ICA and CITRA)

Note that individually authored reports or working papers are listed under the authors in the list of Secondary Literature below, although many of these were published under ICA or UNESCO auspices.

International Council on Archives/Conseil international des archives. *Actes de la Sixième conférence internationale de la Table ronde des archives. Les archives dans la vie internationale.* Paris: ICA, 1963.

—. *Actes de la Dix-septième conférence de la Table ronde des archives.*

Cagliari 1977. La constitution et la reconstitution des patrimoines archivistiques nationaux. Paris: ICA, 1980.
English edition: *ICA Bulletin* 9 (December 1977): 7; and in *CITRA 1993–1995*, p. 245.
(Hereafter: *Actes de la 17ème CITRA*)

—. *CITRA 1993–1995. Interdependence of Archives: Proceedings of the Twenty-Ninth, Thirtieth and Thirty-First International Conferences of the Round Table on Archives. XXIX Mexico 1993, XXX Thessaloniki 1994, XXXI Washington 1995/L'interdépendance des archives: Actes des vingt-neuvième, trentième et trente et unième Conférences Internationales de la Table ronde des Archives.* Ed. Joan van Albada et al. Dortrecht, 1998.
(Hereafter: *CITRA 1993–1995*)

—. "Les Archives du Komintern: Une histoire qui intéresse le monde." Paris, 1997.

—. "Opinion of the International Council on Archives Relating to the Unidroit Draft Convention, 20 April 1995." In *CITRA 1993–1995*, pp. 206–207.

—. "Professional Advice on the Vienna Convention on Succession of States in Respect of State Property, Archives and Debts. Part III, State Archives (art. 19 to 31)." Paris: ICA, 1983. Typescript original (document CE/83/12).
Also in *CITRA 1993–1995*, pp. 250–55; and in *Dossier on Archival Claims*, pp. 39–45. Included above as Appendix IIIb.

—. "The View of the Archival Community on the Settling of Disputed Claims," Position Paper adopted by the ICA Executive Committee ICA at its meeting in Guangzhou, 10–13 April 1995. Reprinted in *Dossier on Archival Claims,* pp. 45–47; and in *CITRA 1993–1995*, pp. 256–58.

—. *List of ICA Publications/Liste des publications du CIA.* 1992. Paris: ICA/CIA Secretariat, 1992.
Recent ICA publications are found on the ICA website: <http://www.ica.org>.

D. Documents of Other International Agencies

Allied Control Commission (post-WWII)

Allied Control Council. *Official Gazette of the Control Council for Germany*, no. 1 (2nd ed., corrected) (Berlin, 29 October 1945), Law no. 2, as published in German, Russian, French, and English.

Council of Europe
See also *Dossier on Archival Claims* under "Collections" (p. 616, above).

Council of Europe Parliamentary Assembly/ Conseil de l'Europe Assemblée parlementaire. "Invitation to Ukraine to become a member of the Council of Europe." 25 October 1995. Resolution (95) 22, ADOC7420.

—. "On Russia's request for membership of the Council of Europe." 25 January 1996. Opinion No. 193 (1996).
Includes the "Statement of Intents" that the Russian Federation was required to sign when admitted to membership on its basis.

E. Bilateral Treaties and Agreements

"Treaty between the Federal Republic of Germany and the Union of Soviet Socialist Republics on Good-Neighborliness, Partnership, and Cooperation." Signed at Bonn, 9 November 1990. In *The Spoils of War: WWII and Aftermath*, pp. 304–307 (FGR–USSR, 30 I.L.M. 505). Ukrainian edition of extracts (including Article 16): *Ukraïna v mizhnarodno-pravovykh vidnosynakh*, book 2, pp. 528–29.

"Agreement between the Government of the Federal Republic of Germany and the Government of the Russian Federation on Cultural Cooperation." Signed at Moscow, 16 December 1992. Ratified 18 May 1993. Excerpts in *The Spoils of War: WWII and Aftermath,* Appendix 15, pp. 306–307.

"Treaty between Ukraine and the Republic of Poland on Good Neighbor-liness, Friendly Relations, and Scientific Cooperation," signed 18 May 1992.
Ukrainian text: "Dohovir mizh Ukraïnoiu ta Respublikoiu Pol´shcheiu pro dobrosusidstvo, druzhni vidnosyny i spivrobitnytstvo." Extracted in *Ukraïna v mizhnarodno-pravovykh vidnosynakh*, book 2, pp. 586–90.

"Agreement between the Government of Ukraine and the Government of the Federal Republic of Germany on Cultural Cooperation," signed 15 February 1993.
Ukrainian text: Extracts in *Ukraïna v mizhnarodno-pravovykh vidnosynakh*, book 2, p. 582.

"Agreement between the Government of Ukraine and the Government of the Russian Federation Regarding Cooperation in the Spheres of Culture, Science, and Education," signed 26 July 1995.
Ukrainian text: in *Ukraïna v mizhnarodno-pravovykh vidnosynakh*, book 2, pp. 528–29.

"Agreement on Cooperation in the Realm of Protection and Return of Cultural Property Lost or Illegally Displaced during the Second World War," signed in Warsaw, 25 June 1996.
Ukrainian text: in *Ukraïna v mizhnarodno-pravovykh vidnosynakh*, book 2, p. 558.
Polish text: in *Wnioski rewindykacyjne*, pp. 142–44.

III. National Legal Documentation

A. Laws, Decrees, Regulations (by country, in chronological order)

Belarus

"Ab Natsyianal'nym arkhiŭnym fondze i arkhivakh u Respublitsy Belarus'."
6 October 1994.

Lithuanian SSR

"Postanovlenie Verkhovnogo Soveta Litovskoi SSR" (No. XI–3688)."
1 September 1990.

"Zakon Litovskoi Sovetskoi Sotsialisticheskoi Respubliki ob arkhivakh."
(No. XI–3687), 13 February 1990.

RSFSR/Russian Federation

While basically listed in chronological order, amendments, modifications, or
replacement laws are listed immediately after the law affected. For a full list
of Russian laws affecting archives, and further explanation of the types of
Russian legal instruments, see *Archives of Russia* (2000), vol. 2,
pp. 1213–1227.

"O partiinykh arkhivakh." Ukaz Prezidenta RSFSR [Decree of the President],
24 August 1991, no. 83, *Vedomosti S"ezda Narodnykh deputatov RSFSR
i Verkhovnogo Soveta RSFSR*, 1991, no. 35 (29 August), statute 1157.
Reprinted in *Otechestvennye arkhivy* 1992 (1): 3.

"Ob arkhivakh Komiteta gosudarstvennoi bezopasnosti SSSR." Ukaz
Prezidenta RSFSR [Decree of the President], 24 August 1991, no. 84.
Reprinted in *Otechestvennye arkhivy* 1992 (1): 3.

"Ob operativno-rozysknoi deiatel'nosti": Zakon RF [Law of the Russian
Federation], 29 April 1992, no. 2506–1. *Vedomosti S"ezda Narodnykh
deputatov RF i Verkhovnogo Soveta RF*, 1992, no. 17 (23 April),
statute 892.
Amendments to the law are recorded in *Vedomosti S"ezda*, 1992, no. 33, p. 1912.
Replaced by: "Ob operativno-rozysknoi deiatel'nosti": Federal'nyi zakon
[Federal Law], 12 August 1995, no. 144–FZ. *Sobranie zakonodatel'stva
RF*, 1995, no. 33 (14 August), statute 3349.
Revises and amends the 1992 law. A paragraph in the law places all information
about current agents and their informants of the FSB and its predecessors in the
category of "confidential," in a slightly modified form from the earlier 1992
edition, but still requiring written permission for access.
Modifications: "O vnesenii izmenenii i dopolnenii v Federal'nyi zakon
'Ob operativno-rozysknoi deiatel'nosti'": Federal'nyi zakon [Federal

law], 5 January 1999, no. 6–FZ. *Sobranie zakonodatel'stva RF*, 1999, no. 2 (11 January), statute 233.

"Vremennye polozheniia o poriadke zakliucheniia litsenzionnykh dogovorov na ispol'zovanie dokumentov gosarkhivov i tsentrov dokumentatsii RF v kommercheskikh tseliakh." Adopted by the Rosarkhiv Collegium 10 February 1993. Published in *Otechestvennye arkhivy* 1993 (2): 112.

"Osnovy zakonodatel'stva [Basic Legislation] Rossiiskoi Federatsii ob Arkhivnom fonde Rossiiskoi Federatsii i arkhivakh," 7 July 1993, no. 5341-I. *Vedomosti S"ezda Narodnykh deputatov RF i Verkhovnogo Soveta RF*, 1993, no. 33 (19 August), statute 1311.
    In *Rossiiskaia gazeta* 156 (14 August 1993): 5. Reprinted in *Otechestvennye arkhivy* 1993 (3): 3–10; and *Novaia i noveishaia istoriia* 1993 (6): 3–11 (with analysis by Rosarkhiv Chairman V. P. Kozlov, pp. 12–15).
    Draft modifications: "O vnesenii izmenenii i dopolnenii v Osnovy zakonodatel'stva Rossiiskoi Federatsii ob Arkhivnom fonde Rossiiskoi Federatsii i arkhivakh." Proekt Federal'nogo zakona [Draft federal law].
    Published in *Otechestvennye arkhivy* 1998 (6): 22–33.

"O realizatsii gosudarstvennoi politiki v arkhivnom dele." Postanovlenie Soveta Ministrov–Pravitel'stva RF [Directive of the Council of Ministers–Government of the Russian Federation], 23 August 1993, no. 838. *Sobranie aktov Prezidenta i Pravitel'stva RF*, 1993, no. 35 (30 August), statute 3342.

"Polozhenie ob Arkhivnom fonde Rossiiskoi Federatsii" and "Polozhenie o Gosudarstvennoi arkhivnoi sluzhbe Rossii." With executive confirmation: Ukaz Prezidenta RF [Decree of the President], 17 March 1994, no. 552. *Sobranie aktov Prezidenta i Pravitel'stva RF*, 1994, no. 12 (21 March), statute 878.
    In *Rossiiskaia gazeta* 1994 (1 April): 4.
    Reprinted in *Otechestvennye arkhivy* 1994 (3): 3–12.

["Ob obrazovanii Komissii po rassekrechivaniiu dokumentov, sozdannykh KPSS"]: Rasporiazhenie Prezidenta RF [Directive of the President], 22 September 1994, no. 489–rp. *Sobranie zakonodatel'stva RF*, 1994, no. 22 (26 September), statute 2498.
    Published as "O poriadke rassekrechivaniia dokumentov: Rasporiazhenie Prezidenta Rossiiskoi Federatsii." *Rossiiskaia gazeta* 185 (27 September 1994): 4.
    Reprinted in *Otechestvennye arkhivy* 1995 (1): 3, followed by a commentary by V. P. Kozlov (pp. 4–5).
    English edition and analysis by Mark Kramer appears in *Cold War International History Project Bulletin* 4 (Fall 1994): 89.

"O Ministerstve inostrannykh del Rossiiskoi Federatsii": Ukaz Prezidenta RF [Decree of the President], 14 March 1995, no. 271. *Sobranie zakonodatel'stva RF*, 1995, no. 12 (21 April), statute 1033.
Article 5 gives the Ministry of Foreign Affairs the right to retain its archives permanently.

"Polozhenie o litsenzirovanii deiatel'nosti po obsledovaniiu sostoianiia arkhivnykh fondov, ekspertize, opisaniiu, konservatsii i restavratsii arkhivnykh dokumentov." Postanovlenie Pravitel'stva RF [Directive of the Government], 24 July 1995, no. 747. *Sobranie zakonodatel'stva RF,* 1995, no. 31 (31 July 1995), statute 3134.
Reprinted in *Otechestvennye arkhivy* 1995 (5): 3–6.

"O vozvrate v Rossiiu nauchnykh arkhivov vydaiushchikhsia russkikh uchenykh-iuristov." Postanovlenie Gosudarstvennoi Dumy Federal'nogo sobraniia RF [Directive of the State Duma], 17 November 1995, no. 1339-I GD. *Sobranie zakonodatel'stva RF*, no. 49 (4 December 1995), statute 4713.

"Ob obmene arkhivnykh dokumentov Kniazheskogo doma Likhtenshtein, peremeshchennykh posle okonchaniia Vtoroi mirovoi voiny na territoriiu Rossii, na arkhivnye dokumenty o rassledovanii obstoiatel'stv gibeli Nikolaia II i chlenov ego sem'i (arkhiv N. A. Sokolova)": Postanovlenie Gosudarstvennoi Dumy Federal'nogo sobraniia RF [Directive of the State Duma], 13 June 1996, no. 465–II GD. *Sobranie zakonodatel'stva RF*, 1998, no. 26 (24 June), statute 3043.

"O kul'turnykh tsennostiakh, peremeshchennykh v Soiuz SSR v rezul'tate Vtoroi mirovoi voiny i nakhodiashchikhsia na territorii Rossiiskoi Federatsii." Federal'nyi zakon [Federal Law], 64–FZ, signed 15 April 1998. *Sobranie zakonodatel'stva RF*, 1998, no. 16 (20 April 1998), statute 1879.
English editions: (1) "Federal Law on Cultural Valuables Displaced to the U.S.S.R. as a Result of World War II and Located in the Territory of the Russian Federation." Trans. Konstantin Akinsha and Lynn Visson.
Electronic version (English and Russian): at the website "Project for Documentation of Wartime Cultural Losses": <http://docproj.loyola. edu>.
(2) "Federal Law No. 64-FZ of April 15, 1998 on Cultural Treasures Transferred to the Union of Soviet Socialist Republic as a Result of World War II and Located in the Territory of the Russian Federation." In *Washington Conference, 1998,* pp. 1049–1062.
Electronic version: <http://www.state.gov/www/regions/eur/holocaust/ heac.html>

(3) "Federal Law on Cultural Valu[abl]es Removed to the U.S.S.R. as a Result of World War II and Located in the Territory of the Russian Federation." In *Spoils of War: International Newsletter* 4 (August 1997): 10–19; also available electronically.

Among the awkward phrasings there, "values" is used throughout, where "valuables" would be more appropriate in English.

Constitutional court commentaries: Postanovlenie Konstitutsionnogo Suda RF [Directive of the Constitutional Court], no. 1879: "Po delu o razreshenii spora mezhdu Sovetom Federatsii i Prezidentom Rossiiskoi Federatsii, mezhdu Gosudarstvennoi Dumoi i Prezidentom Rossiiskoi Federatsii ob obiazannosti Prezidenta Rossiiskoi Federatsii podpisat´ priniatyi Federal´nyi zakon 'O kul´turnykh tsennostiakh, peremeshchennykh v Soiuz SSR v rezul´tate Vtoroi mirovoi voiny i nakhodiashchikhsia na territorii Rossiiskoi Federatsii,'" 6 April 1998. *Sobranie zakonodatel´stva RF*, 1998, no. 16 (20 April 1998), statute 1879, pp. 3624–28.

Postanovlenie Konstitutsionnogo Suda RF [Directive of the Constitutional Court]: "Po delu o proverke konstitutsionnosti Federal´nogo zakona ot 15 aprelia 1998 roda 'O kul´turnykh tsennostiakh, peremeshchennykh v Soiuz SSR v rezul´tate Vtoroi mirovoi voiny i nakhodiashchikhsia na territorii Rossiiskoi Federatsii,'" 20 July 1999. *Sobranie zakonodatels´stva RF,* no. 30 (26 August 1999), statute 3989. Also published in *Rossiiskaia gazeta*, 19 August, no. 155 (2264), pp. 4–5.

Amendments: "O vnesenii izmenenii i dopolnenii v Federal´nyi zakon ot 15 aprelia 1998 goda —64-FZ 'O kul´turnykh tsennostiakh, peremeshchennykh v Soiuz SSR v rezul´tate Vtoroi mirovoi voiny i nakhodiashchikhsia na territorii Rossiiskoi Federatsii.'" *Sobranie zakonodatels´stva RF,* no. 22 (29 May 2000), statute 2259.

"Ob obmene arkhivnykh dokumentov Frantsuzskoi Respubliki, peremeshchennykh na territoriiu Rossiiskoi Federatsii v rezul´tate Vtoroi mirovoi voiny, na arkhivnye dokumenty rossiiskogo proiskhozhdeniia, nakhodiashchiesia na territorii Frantsuzskoi Respubliki": Postanovlenie Gosudarstvennoi Dumy Federal´nogo sobraniia RF [Directive of the State Duma of the Russian Federation] ot 22 maia 1998 g., no. 2504–II GD. *Sobranie zakonodatel´stva RF*, 1998, no. 24 (15 June), statute 2662.

"O peredache Velikobritanii peremeshchennykh na territoriiu Rossiiskoi Federatsii v rezul´tate Vtoroi mirovoi voiny lichnykh dokumentov i dokumentov, udostoveriaiushchikh lichnost´ voennosluzhashchikh Britanskogo ekspeditsionnogo korpusa": Postanovlenie Gosudarstvennoi Dumy Federal´nogo sobraniia RF [Directive of the State Duma of the Russian Federation] ot 16 sentiabria 1998 g., no. 2970–II GD. *Sobranie zakonodatel´stva RF*, 1998, no. 39 (29 September), statute 4862.

Ukraine/Ukrainian SSR

Postanova SNK URSR, no. 1673 (18 October 1945). In *Dokumenty i materialy po istorii sovetsko-pol'skikh otnoshenii*, vol. 8 (Moscow: "Nauka," 1974), p. 583 (doc. 337).

Decree of the Council of Commissars of the Ukrainian SSR, countersigned by Nikita Khrushchev, authorizing the first shipment of "Polonica" from Ukraine to Poland. Also published in Matwijów, *Walka o lwowskie dobra kultury*, pp. 216–17.

"Pro peredachu istorychnykh i kul'turnykh tsinnostei pol's'koho narodu Tymchasovomu Uriadovi Natsional'noï Pol's'koï Respubliky," Postanova Rada Ministriv URSR, no. 1182 (5 July 1945), signed by Nikita Khrushchev [Mykyta Khrushchov].

Published in *LNB: Dokumenty*, pp. 29–30 (doc. 7).

"Pro utvorennia Natsional'noï komisiï z pytan' povernennia v Ukraïnu kul'turnykh tsinnostei." 28 December 1992. Postanova Kabinetu Ministriv Ukraïny No. 732. In *Ukraïna v mizhnarodno-pravovykh vidnosynakh,* book 2, pp. 687–92.

"Zakon Ukraïny 'Pro Natsional'nyi arkhivnyi fond i arkhivni ustanovy'" [Law of Ukraine], 24 December 1993, no. 3814–XII, §1.1. *Vidomosti Verkhovnoï Rady Ukraïny*, 1994, no. 15, p. 394.

Reprinted in *Arkhivy Ukraïny*, 1994 (4–6): 4–15. Reprinted in *Ukraïna v mizh-narodno-pravovykh vidnosynakh*, book 2, pp. 626–42.

"Polozhennia pro Natsional'nu komisiiu z pytan' povernennia v Ukraïnu kul'turnykh tsinnostei'" (18 October 1996). In *Ukraïna v mizhnarodno-pravovykh vidnosynakh,* book 2, pp. 687–92.

"Pro vyvezennia, vvezennia ta povernennia kul'turnykh tsinnostei," Law of Ukraine, 1068–14, 21 September 1999. *Ofitsiinyi visnyk Ukraïny,* no. 42 (Kyiv, 1999), statute 2072.

Electronic version: Website of the Ukrainian Verkhovna Rada: <http://alpha.rada.kiev.ua>.

Union of Soviet Socialist Republics (USSR)

"O reorganizatsii i tsentralizatsii arkhivnogo dela." 1 June 1918.

English edition: "Decree on the Reorganization and Centralization of Archival Affairs in the Russian Socialist Federated Soviet Republic. (Issued by the Council of People's Commissars of the RSFSR, 1 June 1918.)" Trans. P. K. Grimsted. *American Archivist* 45(4) Fall 1982: 441–43.

B. Parliamentary Proceedings

Russian Federation

Federal'noe Sobranie, Parlament Rossiiskoi Federatsii, *Biulleten'*, no. 34, *Zasedaniia Gosudarstvennoi Dumy, 20 maia 1994 goda* [20 May 1994], pp. 4, 26–33.

—, no. 27 (169), 17 May 1996, pp. 4, 30–39.

—, no. 33 (175), 13 June 1996, pp. 3, 58–59.

—, no. 37 (179), 5 July 1996, pp. 3, 51–53.

Federal'noe Sobranie. Zasedanie deviatoe, *Biulleten'*, no. 1(107), 17 July 1996, pp. 55–63.

Federal'noe Sobranie. Gosudarstavennaia Duma. *Stenogramma Zasedanii, Biulleten'*, no. 74(216), 5 February 1997, pp. 19–23, 56.

—, no. 89(231), 4 April 1997, pp. 14–19.

United States of America

U.S. Congress, 83rd, 1st Session. House of Representatives. *Report No. 1077*: Disposition of Sundry Papers.
Legal action authorizing the return of Nazi German records to the Federal Republic of Germany.

U.S. Congressional Record–Senate (Daily Record) 138(47) 31 March 1992: S 4537–40.
Sen. Albert Gore's introduction into the *Daily Record* of material on the Schneerson Aguda Shabad Collection in the Russian State Library, Moscow.

C. Government Reports and Official Protocols

Great Britain

British Committee on the Preservation and Restitution of Works of Art, Archives, and Other Material in Enemy Hands. *Works of Art in Austria (British Zone of Occupation): Losses and Survivals in the War*. London: HMSO, 1946.

Russian Federation/USSR/CIS [SNG/SND]

Embassy of the USSR, *Information Bulletin* 138 (19 November 1942).

Soobshchenie Chrezvychainoi Gosudarstvennoi Komissii po ustanovleniiu i rassledovaniiu zlodeianii nemetsko-fashistskikh zakhvatchikov i ikh soobshchnikov i prichinennogo imi ushcherba grazhdanam, kolkhozam,

obshchestvennym organizatsiiam, gosudarstvennym predpriiatiiam i uchrezhdeniiam SSSR. O razrusheniiakh i zverstvakh, sovershennykh nemetsko-fashistskimi zakhvatchikami v gorode Kieve. Moscow: Gospolitizdat, 1944.
Also published in *Pravda*, 1 March 1944 (no. 52).
A Ratibor German translation of the *Pravda* article remains filed with an ERR report—Stabsführung IV/3 (Ratibor, 15 April 1944), BAB, R 6/170, fols. 47ff; a photocopy is held in US NA, EAP 99/1085.

"Predlozheniia gruppy ekspertov gosudarstv-uchastnikov SNG dlia resheniia voprosov, sviazannykh s pravopreemstvom v otnoshenii gosudarst-vennykh arkhivov," Minsk, 23 April 1992.
Published in *Vestnik arkhivista* 1992 (3[9]): 10–11.

"Protokol zasedaniia predstavitelei obshchestv arkhivistov nezavisimykh gosudarstv," 14 October 1993. In *Otechestvennye arkhivy* 1993 (6): 92–94.

Ukraine/Ukrainian SSR/UNR

"Protokol zasidannia arkhivnoï sektsiï Komisiï dlia pidhotovky materialu do Myrnoho dohovoru z Rosiieiu Ministerstva narodnoï osvity UNR (Kyiv, 12.IV.1918)." In *Ukraïns'ki kul'turni tsinnosti v Rosiï. Persha sproba povernennia, 1917–1918.* Ed. Serhii Kot and Oleksii Nestulia. Kyiv: Soborna Ukraïna, 1996. [=*Povernennia kul'turnoho nadbannia Ukraïny. Dokumenty svidchat'*, 1.]

United States of America

U.S. Military Government Austria, *Report of the U.S. Commissioner*, no. 2 (December 1945).

IV. Symposia and Conference Proceedings, Collective Volumes, Series, and Serial Publications Relating to Cultural Valuables and Restitution

Arkhivna ta rukopysna Ukraïnika. Materialy rozshyrenoï mizhvidomchoï narady po obhovorenniu Derzhavnoï prohramy "Arkhivna ta rukopysna Ukraïnika" v Kyievi, 17 zhovtnia 1991 roku. Ed. Ol'ha Todiichuk, Vasyl' Ul'ianovs'kyi, and Hennadii Boriak. Kyiv: IUA, 1992. [=Naukovo-dovidkovi vydannia z istoriï Ukraïny, 18; Problemy edytsiinoï ta kameral'noï arkheohrafiï: Istoriia, teoriia, metodyka, 1.]
(Hereafter: *Arkhivna ta rukopysna Ukraïnika*)

"Betr: Sicherstellung" : NS-Kunstraub in der Sowjetunion. Ed. Wolfgang Eichwede and Ulrike Hartung. Bremen: Edition Temmen, 1998.
(Hereafter: *"Betr: Sicherstellung"*)

Captured German and Related Records: A National Archives Conference. Ed. Robert Wolfe. Athens, OH: Ohio University Press, 1974. [=National Archives Conferences, 3.]
(Hereafter: *Captured German Records*)

Cultural Treasures Moved Because of the War—A Cultural Legacy of the Second World War. Documentation and Research on Losses: Documentation of the International Meeting in Bremen (30.11.–2.12.1994). Ed. Jost Hansen, Dieter Opper, and Doris Lemmermeier. Bremen: Koordinierungsstelle der Länder für die Rückführung von Kulturgütern beim Senator für Bildung, Wissenschaft, Kunst und Sport, 1995.
(Hereafter: *Cultural Treasures, 1994*)

Displaced Books: Bücherrückgabe aus zweierlei Sicht: Beiträge und Materialien zur Bestandsgeschichte deutscher Bibliotheken im Zusammenhang von NS-Zeit und Krieg. 2nd ed. Hannover: Laurentius Verlag, 1999. [=Laurentius Sonderheft.]
(Hereafter: *Displaced Books: Bücherrückgabe*)

Kul'tura i viina: Pohliad cherez pivstolittia. Ed. Viktor Akulenko and Valentyna Vrublevs'ka, et al. Kyiv: Adrys, 1996. [=*Povernennia kul'turnoho nadbannia Ukraïny: Problemy, zavdannia, perspektyvy*, 7.]
(Hereafter: *Kul'tura i viina*)
  Publishes some of the reports from the Ukrainian-German Roundtable in Kyiv
  and Odessa, 25–27 April 1995.

Materialy natsional'noho seminaru "Problemy povernennia natsional'no-kul'turnykh pam'iatok, vtrachenykh abo peremishchenykh pid chas Druhoï svitovoï viiny." Chernihiv, veresen' 1994. Ed. Oleksandr K. Fedoruk, Hennadii V. Boriak, Serhii I. Kot, et al. Kyiv, 1996.

[=*Povernennia kul′turnoho nadbannia Ukraïny: Problemy, zavdannia, perspektyvy*, 6.]
(Hereafter: *Materialy natsional′noho seminaru, Chernihiv, 1994*)
See especially: "Rekomendatsiï Natsional′noho seminaru z problem povernennia natsional′no-kul′turnykh pam'iatok, vtrachenykh abo peremishchenykh pid chas Druhoï svitovoï viiny," pp. 321–29.

Materialy naukovo-praktychnoho sympoziumu "Pravovi aspekty restytutsiï kul′turnykh tsinnostei: Teoriia i praktyka" : Kyïv, hruden′ 1996. Ed. Oleksandr K. Fedoruk, Iurii S. Shemshuchenko, et al. Kyiv, 1997. [=*Povernennia kul′turnoho nadbannia Ukraïny: Problemy, zavdannia, perspektyvy*, 10]
(Hereafter: *Pravovi aspekty restytutsiï*)
See especially: "Recommendations of scientific and practical symposium 'Legal aspects of restitution of cultural treasures: Theory and practice'," pp. 194–95.

Materyialy mizhnarodnaha "kruhlaha stala" "Lesy Belaruskikh materyial′nykh i dukhoŭnykh kashtoŭnastsei u chas Druhoi susvetnai vainy i paslia iae (peramiashchenne, vyiaŭlenne, viartanne)." Ed. Adam Mal′dzis. Minsk: Belaruski fond kul′tury, 1996. [=*Viartanne*, 3.]
(Hereafter: *Lesy Belaruskikh materyial′nykh*)

Mezhdunarodnaia konferentsiia "Russkaia, ukrainskaia i belorusskaia èmigratsiia v Chekhoslovakii mezhdu dvumia mirovymi voinami. Rezul′taty i perspektivy issledovanii. Fondy Slavianskoi biblioteki i prazhskikh arkhivov," Praga, 14–15 avgusta 1995 g.: Sbornik dokladov/International Conference "Russian, Ukrainian and Belorussian Emigration between the World Wars in Czechoslovakia. Results and Perspectives of Contemporary Research. Holdings of the Slavonic Library and Prague Archives," Prague, August 14–15, 1995: Proceedings, 2 vols. Prague, 1995. [Sponsors: Slavianskaia biblioteka pri Natsional′noi biblioteke Cheshskoi respubliki; Slavianskii institut AN ChR; Obshchestvo po izucheniiu Vostochnoi i Srednei Evropy v Cheshskoi respublike.]
(Hereafter: *"Russkaia, ukrainskaia i belorusskaia èmigratsiia," 1995*)

Mezhdunarodnaia nauchnaia konferentsiia "Kul′turnoe nasledie Rossiiskoi èmigratsii: 1917–1940-yi god." Sbornik materialov, Moskva, 8–12 sentiabria 1993 g. Ed. E. P. Chelyshev and A. N. Sakharov. Moscow: RAN, "Kongress sootechestvennikov," 1993.

Pervyi kongress sootechestvennikov, 19–31 avgusta 1991 g.: Nauchno-informatsionnye materialy. Comp. A. V. Lupyrev. Ed. E. P. Chelyshev and M. N. Tolstoi. Moscow, 1992.

Povernennia kul'turnoho nadbannia Ukraïny: Dokumenty svidchat', 2.
Ukraïns'ki kul'turni tsinnosti v Rosiï: Arkheolohiia kolektsiï Ukraïny.
Comp. S. Beliaeva et al. Ed. P. Tolochko et al. Kyiv, 1997. [Sponsors:
Natsional'na komisiia z pytan' povernennia v Ukraïnu kul'turnykh
tsinnostei pry Kabineti Ministriv Ukraïny.]
(Hereafter: *Povernennia kul'turnoho: Dokumenty, 2)*

*Povernennia kul'turnoho nadbannia Ukraïny: Problemy, zavdannia,
perspektyvy.* Kyiv, 1993. [Sponsors: Natsional'na komisiia z pytan'
povernennia v Ukraïnu kul'turnykh tsinnostei pry Kabineti Ministriv
Ukraïny; Ministerstvo Kul'tury Ukraïny; Derzhavna biblioteka Ukraïny.]
(Hereafter: *Povernennia kul'turnoho, 1993)*

*Povernennia kul'turnoho nadbannia Ukraïny: Problemy, zavdannia,
perspektyvy*, no. 4. Comp. N. O. Hudimova. Ed. Olena Aleksandrova,
Hennadii V. Boriak, V. P. Ishchenko, and V. B. Vrublevs'ka. Kyiv,
1994. [Sponsors: Natsional'na komisiia z pytan' povernennia v Ukraïnu
kul'turnykh tsinnostei pry Kabineti Ministriv Ukraïny; Ministerstvo
kul'tury Ukraïny; IUA.]
(Hereafter: *Povernennia kul'turnoho, 4)*

*Povernennia kul'turnoho nadbannia Ukraïny: Problemy, zavdannia,
perspektyvy*, no. 5. Kyiv, 1994. [Sponsors: Natsional'na komisiia z pytan'
povernennia v Ukraïnu kulturnykh tsinnostei pry Kabineti Ministriv
Ukraïny; Holovne arkhivne upravlinnia pry kabineti Ministriv Ukraïny;
TsDAVO; Ministerstvo kul'tury Ukraïny; IUA.]
(Hereafter: *Povernennia kul'turnoho, 5)*

Povernuto v Ukraïnu. Kyiv: Natsional'na komisiia z pytan' povernennia v
Ukraïnu kul'turnykh tsinnostei pry Kabineti Ministriv Ukraïny. 2 issues
available through 1999.
No. 1: Comp. Valentyna Vrublevs'ka and Liudmyla Lozenko. Ed.
Oleksandr Fedoruk et al. Kyiv: Tov. "Tanant," 1997.
No. 2: Comp. Valentyna Vrublevs'ka, Iaroslava Muzychenko, and
Larysa Borodenkova. Ed. Oleksandr Fedoruk et al. Kyiv: Tov. "Triumf,"
1999.
(Hereafter: *Povernuto v Ukraïnu)*
Lists and describes Ukrainian cultural treasures received from abroad.

Problemy zarubezhnoi arkhivnoi Rossiki: Sbornik statei. Ed. Vladimir P.
Kozlov. Moscow: Informatsionno-izd. agentstvo "Russkii mir," 1997.
(Hereafter: *Problemy zarubezhnoi arkhivnoi Rossiki)*
Proceedings of the conference *"Zarubezhnaia arkhivnaia Rossika,"* Moscow,
December 1993.

Restitutsiia bibliotechnykh sobranii i sotrudnichestvo v Evrope. Rossiisko-germanskii "kruglyi stol," 11–12 dekabria 1992 g., Moskva: Sbornik dokladov. Ed. S. V. Pushkova. Moscow: Rudomino, 1994.
(Hereafter: *Restitutsiia bibliotechnykh sobranii*)
German edition: *Restitution von Bibliotheksgut. Runder Tisch deutscher und russischer Bibliothekare in Moskau am 11. und 12. Dezember 1992.* Ed. Ingo Kolasa and Klaus-Dieter Lehmann. Frankfurt-am-Main: Vittorio Klostermann, 1993. [=*Zeitschrift für Bibliothekswesen und Bibliographie*, Sonderheft 56.]

Restytutsyia kul'turnykh kashtoŭnastsei: Prablemy viartannia i sumesnaha vykarystannia (iurydychnyia, navukovyia i maral'nyia aspekty): Matery-ialy Mizhnarodnai navukovai kanferentsyi, iakaia adbylasia ŭ Minsku pad ehidai UNESCO 19–20 chervenia 1997 h. Ed. Adam Mal'dzis et al. Minsk: Natsyianal'ny navukova-asvetny tsentr imia F. Skaryny, 1997. [=*Viartanne,* 4.]
(Hereafter: *Restytutsyia kul'turnykh kashtoŭnastsei*)
Proceedings of the conference "The Restitution of Cultural Treasures: Problems of Repatriation and Common Usages (Legal, Scientific, and Ethical Aspects)." Minsk, 19–20 July 1997.

—. 1997 Minsk conference on "The Restitution of Cultural Treasures: Problems of Repatriation and Common Usages (Legal, Scientific, and Ethical Aspects)." "Final Document" (in Belarusian, Russian, and English). In *Restytutsyia kul'turnykh kashtoŭnastsei,* pp. 258–62.
Reprinted in Adam Mal'dzis, "Byelorussia." *Spoils of War: International Newsletter* 5 (June 1998): 74.

"The Return of Looted Collections (1946–1996). An Unfinished Chapter": Proceedings of an International Symposium to Mark the 50th Anniversary of the Return of Dutch Book Collections from Germany. Ed. F. J. Hoogewoud and E. P. Kwaardgras. Amsterdam, 1997.
(Hereafter: *Return of Looted Collections*)

Sbornik materialov po mezhdunarodnoi konferentsii "Arkhivy byvshikh kommunisticheskikh partii v stranakh tsentral'noi i vostochnoi Evropy." Stara Ves', 28 sentiabria–1 oktiabria 1995 goda. Warsaw: Naczelna Dyrekcja Archiwów Państwowych, 1996.
(Hereafter: *Arkhivy byvshikh KP*)

The Spoils of War: World War II and Its Aftermath. The Loss, Reappearance, and Recovery of Cultural Property. Ed. Elizabeth Simpson. New York: Henry N. Abrams, 1997.
Proceedings of the symposium "The Spoils of War," Bard Graduate Center for the Visual Arts, New York, NY, January 1995.
(Hereafter: *The Spoils of War: WWII and Aftermath*)

Spoils of War: International Newsletter. Bremen; Magdeburg. 6 issues available through 1999.
    Electronic version: <http://www.lostart.de> and <http://www.beutekunst.de>.
    Russian edition: *Voennye trofei: Mezhdunarodnyi biulleten'.* Moscow. 5 issues available through 1998.
    Electronic version: <http://Spoils.libfl.ru/>.

Ukraine during World War II: History and its Aftermath: A Symposium. Ed. Yury Boshyk. Edmonton: Canadian Institute of Ukrainian Studies, 1986.

Ukraïns'ka arkheohrafiia: Suchasnyi stan ta perspektyvy rozvytku. Tezy dopovidei respublikans'koï narady hruden' 1988 r. Kyiv; Arkeohrafichna komisiia AN URSR, 1988.
    (Hereafter: *Ukraïns'ka arkheohrafiia 1988*)

Viartanne: Dakumenty i arkhiŭnyia materyialy pa prablemakh poshuku i viartannia natsyianal'nykh kashtoŭnastei, iakiia znakhodziatstsa za mezhami Respubliki Belarus'. 4 vols. Minsk, 1992–1997.
    (Hereafter: *Viartanne*)
    Collected, along with lists, inventories, and other documents regarding displaced Belarusian cultural treasures, including archives, taken out of Belarus in various periods.

Washington Conference on Holocaust-Era Assets, November 30–December 3, 1998: Proceedings. Ed. J. D. Bindenagel. Washington, DC: U.S. GPO, 1999 [=U.S. Department of State, Publication 10603].
    Electronic version: <http://www.state.gov/www/regions/eur/holocaust/heac.html>.
    (Hereafter: *Washington Conference, 1998*)
    Also available in CD-ROM format. See especially the "Principles on Nazi-Confiscated Art" (pp. 971–72), which have been reproduced in several places.

Wnioski rewindykacyjne księgozbioru Ossolineum oraz Dzieł sztuki i zabytków ze zbiorów lwowskich. Ed. Jan Pruszyński. Warsaw: Ministerstwo Kultury i Sztuki, 1998. [=Polskie dziedzictwo kulturalne, Seria C: Materiały i Dokumenty].
    (Hereafter: *Wnioski rewindykacyjne*)
    A collection of materials relating to Polish–Ukrainian restitution negotiations prepared by Polish specialists for the Ministry of Culture and Art for internal circulation, but not publicly available.

V. Collections of Published Documents

Adibekova, Zh. G., ed. "Pervye dni voiny: Èvakuatsiia (po materialam 'osobykh papok' Politburo TsK VKP[b])." *Otechestvennye arkhivy* 1995 (2): 28–37.

Boitsov, Mikhail A., and Tat'iana A. Vasil'eva, comps. *Kartoteka "Z" Operativnogo shtaba "Reikhsliaiter Rozenberg" : Tsennosti kul'tury na okkupirovannykh territoriiakh Rossii, Ukrainy i Belorusi, 1941–1942*. Moscow: Izd-vo Moskovskogo universiteta, 1998. [="Trudy istoricheskogo fakul'teta MGU," 5; Istoricheskie istochniki, 1.]

Dokumenty i materialy po istorii sovetsko-pol'skikh otnoshenii.
Vol. 8: Moscow: "Nauka," 1974.
Vol. 9: Moscow: "Nauka," 1976.

Istoriia predosteregaet. Kyiv: Politizdat Ukrainy, 1986.
English edition: *History Teaches a Lesson: Captured War Documents Expose the Atrocities of the German-Fascist Invaders and Their Henchmen in Ukraine's Temporarily Occupied Territory during the Great Patriotic War (1941–1945)*. Ed. Iu. Iu. Kondufor et al. Kyiv: Politvidav Ukraini [*sic*], 1986.
Also issued in German translation.

Kolasa, Ingo, and Klaus-Dieter Lehmann, eds. *Die Trophäenkommissionen der Roten Armee: Eine Dokumentensammlung zur Verschleppung von Büchern aus deutschen Bibliotheken*. Frankfurt-am-Main: Vittorio Klostermann, 1996. [=*Zeitschrift für Bibliothekswesen und Bibliographie*, Sonderheft 64.]
(Hereafter: *Die Trophäenkommissionen*)

Kot, Serhii, and Oleksii Nestulia, eds. *Ukraïns'ki kul'turni tsinnosti v Rosiï. Persha sproba povernennia, 1917–1918*. Kyiv: Soborna Ukraïna, 1996.

Krushel'nyts'ka, Larysa, ed. *L'vivs'ka naukova biblioteka im. V. Stefanyka NAN Ukraïny: Dokumenty, fakty, komentari*. Lviv: LNB, 1996.
(Hereafter: *LNB Dokumenty*)

Matthäus, Jürgen. "'Weltanschauliche Forschung und Auswertung': Aus den Akten des Amtes VII im Reichssicherheitshauptamt." *Jahrbuch für Antisemitismus-Forschung* 5. Ed. Wolfgang Benz (Berlin, 1997): 287–96.

Misiło, Eugeniusz [Ievhen Misylo]. *Akcja "Wisła" : Dokumenty*. Warsaw: Archiwum Ukrainskie, 1993.
Ukrainian edition: *Aktsiia "Visla" : Dokumenty*. Trans. Ivan Svarnyk.

Lviv and New York: NTSh, 1997. [=Ukraïnoznavcha biblioteka NTSh, 8.]

—. "Etnotsyd. Etap I: Pereselennia ukraïntsiv z Pol′shchi v URSR 1944–1946." *Slidamy pam'iati: Litopysnyi kalendar* 1 (Warsaw, 1996): 31–108.

—, ed. *Repatriacja czy deportacja: Przesiedlenie Ukraińców z Polski do USRR 1944–1946.* 2 vols. Warsaw: Archiwum Ukrainskie, 1996–1999.

Sbornik rukovodiashchikh materialov po arkhivnomu delu (1917–iiun′ 1941 gg.). Moscow, 1961.

Shepelev, Valerii N., ed. "Sud′ba 'Smolenskogo arkhiva.'" *Izvestiia TsK KPSS* 1991 (5): 135–38.

Teteriatnikov, Vladimir M. *Problema kul′turnykh tsennostei peremeshchennykh v rezul′tate Vtoroi mirovoi voiny: Dokazatel′stvo rossiiskikh prav na "kollektsiiu Kenigsa."* Moscow and Tver: Obozrevatel′, 1996. [=Special issue of *Obozrevatel′/Observer: Informatsionno-analiticheskii zhurnal.*]

VI. Catalogs of Lost, Displaced, and Trophy Culture Treasures

See archival guides and finding aids under specific archives in Section I
above, pp. 581ff.

Exhibition Catalogs

Hoover Institution of War, Revolution, and Peace, and the Committee on
Archival Affairs of the Russian Federation (Roskomarkhiv). *Chtoby dela
shli: Rossiisko-amerikanskie èkonomicheskie otnosheniia, 1900–1930
gg./Making Things Work: Russian-American Economic Relations, 1900–
1930. An Exhibition Catalog for a Joint Historical Exhibit of Documents
and Photographs Organized by the Hoover Institution of War, Revolution, and Peace and the Committee on Archival Affairs of the Russian
Federation (Roskomarkhiv).* Stanford: Hoover Institution Press, 1992.

Katalog vystavki "Nemetskie trofeinye knigi v fondakh VGBIL." Comp. and
ed. E. E. Eikhman et al. Moscow: "Rudomino," 1992.

Sotheby's. *The Romanovs: Documents and Photographs relating to the
Russian Imperial House*, initially offered at auction in London, 5 April
1990. London: Sotheby's, 1990.
An elaborate catalog with colored illustrations of the collection of original
materials relating to the assassination of the Russian imperial family in 1918,
collected by Nikolai Sokolov.

*Five Centuries of European Drawings: The Former Collection of Franz
Koenigs: Exhibition Catalogue, 2.10.1995–21.01.1996.* Milan: Leonardo
Arte, 1995. [Sponsors: Ministry of Culture of the Russian Federation;
Pushkin State Museum of Fine Arts, Moscow.]

Catalogs of Library Collections

*Dark Mirror: Romanov and Imperial Palace Library Materials in the
Holdings of the New York Public Library: A Checklist and Agenda for
Research.* Comp. Robert H. Davis, Jr. New York: Norman Ross
Publishing, 1999.
See especially the introduction by Davis and Edward Kasinec.

*Katalog der Drucke des XVI.Jahrhunderts aus den Beständen des VGBIL/
Katalog nemetskoiazychnykh izdanii XVI veka v fondakh VGBIL/ Catalogus librorum sedecimi saeculi qui in totius Rossiae Reipublicae literarum externarum Bibliotheca asservantur.* Comp. I. A. Korkmazova and
A. L. Ponomarev. Ed. N. V. Kotrelev. Moscow: "VGBIL," 1992, 1996.
[Preface and introduction in German and Russian; annotations in German. Added Latin title page: *Catalogus librorum sedecimi saeculi qui in*

totius Rossiae Reipublicae literarum externarum Bibliotheca asservantur.]
Describes 427 books, including those from the Preußische Staatsbibliothek and the Esterhazy collecion. See also the *Katalog vystavki* above.

Tentoonstellingcatalogus van de boeken uit het fonds van de VGBIL aanhorig bij de Nederlandse bezitters Amsterdam, Universiteitsbibliotheek, September 1992. Comp. E. E. Eikhman, M. F. Pronina, L. A. Terechova, N. I. Tubeeva. Ed. M. F. Pronina. Moscow: "Rudomino," 1992.

Trofeinye knigi iz biblioteki Sharoshpatakskogo reformatskogo kolledzha (Vengriia) v fondakh Nizhegorodskoi gosudarstvennoi oblastnoi univer-sal'noi nauchnoi biblioteki: Katalog. Comp. E. A. Korkmazova, E. V. Zhuravleva, and N. N. Zubrov. Moscow: "Rudomino," 1997. Added English title page: *Displaced books from Sárospatak Calvinist College Library (Hungary) in the collections of Nizhny Novgorod Regional Research Library.*
Also available electronically at the VGBIL website.

Catalogs of Wartime Cultural Losses and Displaced Cultural Treasures

Catalogue of Works of Western European Painters Lost during the Second World War. Comp. Olena Roslavets´. Ed. Oleksandr Fedoruk et al. Kyiv, 1998. [Sponsors: National Commission for the Restitution of Cultural Treasures to Ukraine; Ministry of Culture and Arts of Ukraine; International Foundation "Renaissance"; Museum of Occidental and Oriental Art.]
Added Ukrainian title page: *Kataloh tvoriv zakhidnoievropeis´koho zhyvopysu, vtrachenykh pid chas Druhoï svitovoï viiny,* "Vtracheni skarby Ukraïny."

Katalog proizvedenii Kievskogo muzeia russkogo iskusstva, utrachennykh v gody Velikoi Otechestvennoi voiny 1941–1945 gg. (zhivopis´, grafika). Comp. Mikhail D. Faktorovich, Ekaterina I. Ladyzhenskaia, and Lidiia A. Pel´kina. Ed. Mikhail D. Faktorovich. Kyiv, 1994. [Sponsors: Ministerstvo kul´tury Ukraïny; Kyïvs´kyi muzei rosiis´koho mystetstva.]

Svodnyi katalog kul´turnykh tsennostei, pokhishchennykh i utrachennykh v period Vtoroi mirovoi voiny, vol. 4: *Gosudarstvennye arkhivy Rossiiskoi Federatsii: Utrachennye arkhivnye fondy,* book 1. Comp. Elena E. Novikova, V. I. Zvavich, et al. Ed. Pavel V. Khoroshilov, Nikolai I. Nikandrov, and Anatolii I. Vilkov. Moscow "IKAR," 1999.
English edition: *Summary Catalogue of the Cultural Valuables Stolen and Lost during the Second World War,* vol. 4: *State Archives of the Russian Federation: Lost Archives Funds,* book 1. Moscow and St. Petersburg: Ministry of Culture, 1999.

VII. Secondary Literature

Reports or articles published in conference proceedings or other collective volumes listed above (e.g., sections II.C, p. 622–26, and IV, pp. 636–40) are cited individually below in abbreviated form. Some proceedings and other collective volumes are repeated below under their editors. Archival reference literature, if covering an archive cited in section I, is only cited there if it is an official publication of the archive itself. It is repeated below under the compiler or editor if it has been prepared independently.

Note that publications of primary sources, such as editions of collected documents are also cited above in section IV, pp. 641–42, and catalogs of "trophy" or "lost" archival, library, or art collections are listed in section V, pp. 643–46.

Individual Works

Adibekova, Zh. G., ed. "Pervye dni voiny: Èvakuatsiia (po materialam 'osobykh papok' Politburo TsK VKP[b])." *Otechestvennye arkhivy* 1995 (2): 28–37.

Afiani, Vitalii Iu. "Dokumenty o zarubezhnoi arkhivnoi Rossike i peremeshchennykh arkhivakh v fondakh Tsentra khraneniia sovremennoi dokumentatsii." In *Problemy zarubezhnoi arkhivnoi Rossiki*, pp. 92–99.

Akinsha, Konstantin. "Bol' otechestva—Pechal'naia istoriia 'Adama i Evy.'" *Ogonek* 1988 (51) 17–24 December: 32–33.

—. "The Turmoil over Soviet War Treasures." *ARTNews* December 1991: 110–15.

—, and Grigorii Kozlov, with Sylvia Hochfield. *Beautiful Loot: The Soviet Plunder of Europe's Art Treasures*. New York: Random House, 1995.

—. "Die Beute lag auf dem Flugplatz im Schnee." *Art* (Hamburg) May 1993: 60–64.

—. "Russian Deposits: No Return?" *ARTNews* 97(6) April 1998: 62.

—. "Spoils of War: The Soviet Union's Hidden Art Treasures." *ARTNews* April 1991: 130–41.

—. "The Soviets' War Treasures: A Growing Controversy." *ARTNews* September 1991: 112–19.

—, and Clemens Toussaint. *Operation Beutekunst: Die Verlagerung deutscher Kulturgüter in die Sowjetunion nach 1945.* Nuremberg: Germanisches Nationalmuseum, 1995.

Akulenko, Viktor. "A Bill which Faces the Past." *Spoils of War: International Newsletter* 4 (August 1997): 19–20.

—. "O sootnoshenii mezhdunarodnykh pravovykh i moral'no-èticheskikh norm v sfere vozvrashcheniia i restitutsii kul'turnykh tsennostei." In *Restytutsyia kul'turnykh kashtoŭnastsei*, pp. 80–85.

—, and Iurii S. Shemshuchenko, eds. *Ukraïna v mizhnarodno-pravovykh vidnosynakh, vol. 2: Pravova okhorona kul'turnykh tsinnostei.* Kyiv: Iurinkom Inter, 1997.

Aleksandrov, Emil. *International Legal Protection of Cultural Property.* Sofia: Sofia Press, 1979.

Aleksandrova, Olena. "Poteri bibliotek Ukrainy: Problemy vyiavleniia i poiska." In *Restytutsyia kul'turnykh kashtoŭnastsei*, pp. 92–98.

—, Hennadii V. Boriak, Valentyna B. Vrublevs'ka, and V. P. Ishchenko, eds. *Povernennia kul'turnoho nadbannia Ukraïny: Problemy, zavdannia, perspektyvy*, no. 4. Comp. by N. O. Hudimova. Kyiv, 1994. [Sponsors: Natsional'na komisiia z pytan' povernennia v Ukraïnu kul'turnykh tsinnostei pry Kabineti Ministriv Ukraïny; Ministerstvo kul'tury Ukraïny; IUA.]

Alford, Kenneth D. *The Spoils of World War II: The American Military's Role in the Stealing of Europe's Treasures.* New York: Birch Lane Press (Carol Publishing Group), 1994.

Aly, Götz, and Susanne Heim. *Das Zentrale Staatsarchiv in Moskau ("Sonderarchiv"): Rekonstruktion und Bestandsverzeichnis verschollen geglaubten Schriftguts aus der NS-Zeit.* Düsseldorf: Hans-Böckler-Stiftung, 1992.

Anderson, Kyrill M. "Novyi oblik Arkhiva Kominterna." *Otechestvennye arkhivy* 1998 (1): 17–20.

Antonova, Irina. "Instances of Repatriation by the USSR." In *The Spoils of War: WWII and Aftermath*, pp. 145–46.

—. "My nikomu nichego ne dolzhny: Eshche raz o vozvrate kul'turnykh tsennostei." *Nezavisimaia gazeta* 5 May 1994.

Arkheohrafichna komisiia ta Instytut ukraïns'koï arkheohrafiï Akademiï nauk Ukraïny, 1987–1993. Kyiv, [1993].

Arkhivy v kapitalisticheskikh stranakh. Moscow: MGIAI, 1941.

Arpishkin, Iurii, et al. "Spravedlivoe reshenie v nespravedlivykh obstoiatel'-stvakh." *Kul'tura* 27 (29 July–4 August 1999): 1.
Includes interviews and statements about the Constitutional Court decision regarding the law on cultural treasures by Minister of Culture Vladimir Egorov, Mikhail Shvydkoi, and others.

Auer, Leopold. *Disputed Archival Claims. Analysis of an International Survey: A RAMP Study*, Paris: UNESCO, 1998.
Electronic version: Located at the UNESCO website.
French edition: *Les contentieux archivistiques, analyse d'une enquete internationale. Une étude RAMP*. [UNESCO microfiche no. 98.50737.]

—. "Restitution of Removed Records Following War." In *CITRA 1993–1995*, pp. 172–78.

—. "Staatennachfolge bei Archiven." In *Miscellanea Carlos Wyffels*, published as *Archives et bibliothèques de Belgique/Archief-en Bibliotheekwezen in Belgie* 57(1–2) 1986: 51–68.

—, and Christiane Thomas. "The Execution of the Austro-Yugoslavian Convention on Archives: A Case Study in State Succession." *Information Development* 1(3) 1985: 169–75.

Bahalii, Dmytro, and Viktor Barvins'kyi. "Ukraïns'ki arkhivni fondy v mezhakh RSFRR." *Arkhivna sprava* 1 (1925): 34–44.

Bailey, Martin. "Growing unease over Lubomirski Dürers: A sheet of paper found in a second-hand book by *The Art Newspaper* details valuations of the drawings when sold by Colnaghi." *The Art Newspaper* 93 (June 1999): 3.

—. "The Lubomirski Dürers: Where Are They Now?" *The Art Newspaper* 48 (May 1995): 5.

—. "Nazi Art Loot Discovered in Russia." *The Observer* 24 March 1991: 1.

—. "Search for Trojan Treasure Leads to Moscow Vault." *The Observer* 31 March 1991: 15.

Banasiukevich, Viacheslav D. "O pravovykh aspektakh mezhdunaronogo peremeshcheniia arkhivnykh dokumentov." *Otechestvennye arkhivy* 1994 (2): 6–10.
Presents the text of his report at the Rosarkhiv conference on Rossica in Moscow, December 1993

—. "Pro metodychne zabezpechennia peremishchennia arkhiviv." In *Materialy natsional'noho seminaru, Chernihiv' 1994*, pp. 182–87.

—, et al. "Mezhdunaronoe arkhivnoe pravo i zarubezhnaia praktika peremeshcheniia arkhivnykh dokumentov (Nauchnyi doklad)." Typescript. Moscow: VNIIDAD, 1993.

Baskakov, E. G., and O. V. Shablovskii. "Vozvrashchenie arkhivnykh materialov, spasennykh Sovetskoi Armiei." *Istoricheskii arkhiv* 1958 (5): 175–79.

Bastien, Hervé. "About Archival Claims." In *CITRA 1993–1995*, pp. 62–68.

—, ed. *Reference Dossier on Archival Claims.* Strasbourg: Council of Europe, 1997. (CC LIVRE [97] 1)
French edition: *Dossier de référence sur les Contentieux Archivistiques.* Strasbourg: Conseil de l'Europe, 1997. (CC LIVRE [97] 1)
Reprinted (in both French and English) as an appendix to *CITRA 1993–1995*, pp. 209–68. Originally sponsored by the ICA, Legal Matters Committee, 1995.

Bauer, Karl J. "Ein Quellenführer zu Geschichte der Nationen." *Historische Zeitschrift* 255 (1992): 667–706.

Bautier, Robert-Henri. "Les archives et le droit international." In *Actes de la 17ème CITRA*, pp. 11–56.

Beliaeva, S., et al., comp. *Ukraïns'ki kul'turni tsinnosti v Rosiï: Arkheolohiia kolektsiï Ukraïny.* Ed. P. Tolochko et al. Kyiv, 1997. [=*Povernennia kul'turnoho nadbannia Ukraïny: Dokumenty svidchat'*, 2.]

"Bestände aus der früheren Preußischen Staatsbibliothek in Polen." *Jahrbuch für preußischer Kulturbesitz* 29 (1992): 339–64.

Blumenthal, Ralph. "A Maverick Art Scholar Pursues a Tangled Case." *New York Times* 24 September 1996: C11, C13.

Boguslavskii, Mark M. "Legal Aspects of the Russian Position in Regard to the Return of Cultural Property." In *The Spoils of War: WWII and Aftermath*, pp. 186–90.

—, ed. *Mezhdunarodnaia okhrana kul'turnykh tsennostei.* Moscow: Mezhdunarodnye otnosheniia, 1979.
(Hereafter: *Mezhdunarodnaia okhrana*)

Boitsov, Mikhail A., and Tat'iana A. Vasil'eva, comps. *Kartoteka "Z" Operativnogo shtaba "Reikhsliaiter Rozenberg": Tsennosti kul'tury na okkupirovannykh territoriiakh Rossii, Ukrainy i Belorussii, 1941–1942.* Moscow: Izd-vo Moskovskogo universiteta, 1998. [=Trudy istoricheskogo fakul'teta MGU, 5; Istoricheskie istochniki, 1.]

"Books from Armenia Returned to Germany." *Spoils of War: International Newsletter* 5 (1998): 85.

Bordun, Melaniia. "Z zhyttia ukraïns´koho dukhovenstva l´vivs´koï eparkhiï v druhii pol. XVIII st. (na osnovi vizytatsii M. Shadurs´koho 1759–1763)." *Zapysky NTSh* 134–135 (1924): 137–60.

Boretskii, Rudolf. "Katynskii krest na kommunizme" (Interview of Lech Wałęsa). *Novoe vremia* October 1992 (44): 22–23.
English edition: "The Katyn Cross on Communism's Tomb." *New Times International*, October 1992 (45): 26–27.]

Boriak, Hennadii. "Bremens´kyi proekt 'Dolia kul´turnykh tsinnostei, vyvezenykh z SRSR v roky druhoï svitovoï viiny' (FRN): Kameral´ni metodyky i problemy doslidzhennia istoriï arkhivnykh dokumentiv." In *Materialy natsional´noho seminaru, Chernihiv, 1994*, pp. 251–60.

—. *Natsional´na arkhivna spadshchyna Ukraïny ta derzhavnyi reiestr "Arkheohrafichna Ukraïnika": Arkhivni dokumental´ni resursy ta naukovo-informatsiini systemy.* Kyiv, 1995. [Sponsors: NAN, IAUD, IR TsNB, HAU.]
(Hereafter: *Natsional´na arkhivna spadshchyna Ukraïny*)

—. "Proekt komp'iuternoho dovidnyka 'Arkheo-BiblioBaza' iak skladova 'Arkhivnoï ta rukopysnoï Ukraïniky.'" In *Natsional´na arkhivna informatsiina systema "Arkhivna ta rukopysna Ukraïnika" i komp'iu-terizatsiia arkhivnoï spravy v Ukraïni*, Pt. 1: *Informatizatsiia arkhivnoï spravy v Ukraïni: Suchasnyi stan ta perspektyvy: Zbirnyk naukovykh prats´* (Kyiv: IUAD, 1996): 189–92.

—. "U ramkakh proektu 'Dolia kul´turnykh tsinnostei, vyvezenykh z Ukraïny pid chas Druhoï svitovoï viiny.'" *Arkhivy Ukraïny* 1993 (1–3): 83–84.

—, Maryna Dubyk, and Natalia Makovs´ka. *"Natsysts´ke zoloto" z Ukraïny: U poshukakh arkhivnykh svidchen´.* 2 vols. Kyiv, 1998–2000.
Pt. 1. Kyiv, 1998.
Pt. 2: *Materialy do reiestru vyluchenykh u naselennia koshtovnostei.* Kyiv, 2000.
English summary: "Accumulation of 'Nazi Gold' on the Occupied Territory of Ukraine during World War II: Information of the Ukraine's Delegation" (Washington, DC, 1998). Typescript handout with an intro-ductory position paper "Main Principles of Ukrainian Position's Deter-mination" (pp. 3–4) for distribution at the Conference on Holocaust-Era Assets, November 30–December 3, 1998, Washington, DC.
Provides detailed listings of record groups (fonds) available in Ukrainian archives

from the World War II period (esp. section 1, pp. 23–51) and facsimiles of sample documents. The awkward English summary translation obscures some of the most important points. See also the Ukrainian delegation's presentation at the Washington conference in the official State Department translation, "Ukraine: Delegation Statement," in *Washington Conference, 1998*, pp. 403–409. The second volume provides some sample shipment data and lists of confiscations from individual Ukrainian citizens and analysis of the authenticity of the sources, based on several specific wartime Nazi files.

—, Patricia Kennedy Grimsted, and Natalia Iakovenko. "Memorial'na arkheohrafichna ekspedytsiia po Chekho-Slovachchyni: Slidamy kul'turnykh tsinnostei, vyvezenykh z Ukraïny pid chas Druhoï svitovoï viiny." *Ukraïns'kyi arkheohrafichnyi shchorichnyk*, n.s. 2 (1993): 437–45.

—, Patricia Kennedy Grimsted, Natalia Iakovenko, Irena Sułkowska-Kurasiowa, and Kyrylo Vyslobokov, comps. *Rus'ka (Volyns'ka) metryka. Rehesty dokumentiv koronnoï kantseliariï dlia ukraïns'kykh zemel' (Volyns'ke, Bratslavs'ke, Kyïvs'ke, Chernihivs'ke voievodstva), 1569–1673/The Ruthenian (Volhynian) Metrica: Early Inventories of the Polish Crown Chancery Records for Ukrainian Lands 1569–1673*. With an introduction by Patricia K. Grimsted. Kyiv, forthcoming.

—, Ol'ha Todiichuk, and Vasyl' Ul'ianovs'kyi, eds. *Arkhivna ta rukopysna Ukraïnika. Materialy rozshyrenoï mizhvidomchoï narady po obhovorenniu Derzhavnoï prohramy "Arkhivna ta rukopysna Ukraïnika" Kyïv, 17 zhovtnia 1991 roku*. Kyiv, 1992. [=Naukovo-dovidkovi vydannia z istoriï Ukraïny, 18; Problemy edytsiinoï ta kameral'noï arkheohrafiï: Istoriia, teoriia, metodyka, 1.]

Borisova, Elena P. "Vlast' i istoriko-kul'turnoe nasledie natsii: Organi-zatsionno-pravovoe oformlenie èksporta muzeinykh tsennostei v kontse 1920–30-kh gg." In *Rossiiskaia gosudarstvennost': Opyt i perspektivy izucheniia: Materialy mezhvuzovskoi nauchnoi konferentsii, 1–3 iiunia 1995 g. Chteniia pamiati professora T. P. Korzhikhinoi*. Moscow: IAI RGGU, 1995, pp. 95–99.

Born, Lester. "The Ministerial Collection Center." *American Archivist* 13 (July 1950): 237–58.

Borodin, Oleg, and Tat'iana Dolgodrova. "Kollektsiia Nemetskogo muzeia knigi i shrifta v sobranii Rossiiskoi gosudarstvennoi biblioteki." *Nashe nasledie* 32 (1994): 97–106.

Borsa, Ivan. *Feasibility Study on the Creation of an Internationally Financed and Managed Microfilm Assistance Fund to Facilitate the Solution of*

Problems Involved in the International Transfer of Archives and in Obtaining Access to Sources of National History Located in Foreign Archives. Paris: UNESCO, 1981. (PGI-81/WS/10)
Arabic, French, Russian, and Spanish editions are also available from UNESCO.

Boshyk, Yury, ed. *Ukraine during World War II: History and its Aftermath: A Symposium.* Edmonton: Canadian Institute of Ukrainian Studies, 1986.

Boxer, Sarah. "International Sleuthing Adds Insight About Bach." *New York Times* 16 August 1999: B1, B4.

Browder, George C. "Captured German and Other Nations' Documents in the Osoby (Special) Archive, Moscow." *Central European History* 24(4) 1992: 424–45.

—. "Update on the Captured Documents in the Former Osobyi Archive, Moscow." *Central European History* 26(3) 1993: 335–42.

Brown, John H. "The Disappearing Russian Embassy Archives, 1922–1939." *Prologue* 14 (Spring 1982) 1: 5–13.

Butych, Ivan L., and Liudmyla Lozenko. "Povernuty viis'kovi arkhivy." *Uriadovyi kur'ier* 1992 (59): 3.

Butych, Ivan L., and V. I. Strel'skii, eds. *Uchrezhdeniia Zapadnoi Ukrainy do vossoedineniia ee v edinom ukrainskom sovetskom sotsialisticheskom gosudarstve: Spravochnik.* Lviv: Izd-vo LGU, 1955.

Buzatu, Gheorghe. *Românii în Arhivele Kremlinului.* Bucharest: Univers enciclopedic, 1996.

Bystrov, Vladimir. "Konets Russkogo zagranichnogo istoricheskogo arkhiva v Prage." In *"Russkaia, ukrainskaia i belorusskaia èmigratsiia," 1995,* vol. 1, pp. 79–80.

Camphausen, Gabriele. *Die wissenschaftliche historische Russlandforschung im Dritten Reich 1933–1945.* Frankfurt-am-Main: Peter Lang, 1990. [=Europäische Hochschulschriften, series 3: Geschichte und ihre Hilfswissenschaften, 418]

Chabrun, Laurent. "La France retrouve ses archives secrètes." *Le Parisien* 4 September 1992.

Chelyshev, E. P., and A. N. Sakharov, eds. "Rossiiskoe nasledie: Razdelennye arkhivy." In *Mezhdunarodnaia nauchnaia konferentsiia "Kul'turnoe nasledie Rossiiskoi èmigratsii: 1917–1940-ye gody." Sbornik materialov, Moskva, 8–12 sentiabria 1993 g.* Moscow: RAN; "Kongress sootechestvennikov," 1993, pp. 145–66.

Chernov, A. V. *Istoriia i organizatsiia arkhivnogo dela v SSSR (Kratkii ocherk)*. Ed. D. S. Baburin. Moscow: GAU NKVD SSSR, 1940.

Chernykh, Vadim A. "Bonch-Bruevich i poluchenye iz-za granitsy dokumenty po istorii russkoi kul'tury." *Arkheograficheskii ezhegodnik za 1973 god* (Moscow, 1974): 133–46.

Danko, Osyp. "Vkradena Bibliia: Rosiis'ki arkheohrafichni ekspedytsiï v Ukraïni i naslidky ïkhn'oï diial'nosti." *Pam'iatky Ukraïny* 1994 (3–6[26]): 74–79.

D'Arcy, David. "Hitler, The Prince, and the Dürers." *The Art Newspaper* 47 (April 1995): 1, 6.

—. "Report on the Washington Conference on Holocaust Era Assets— Much Piety and Hot Air: No Binding Agreements were Reached and Little Effect on Restitution is Expected." *The Art Newspaper* 88 (January 1999): 3.

Dashkevych, Iaroslav. "Dolia i nedolia nashoï Biblioteky." *Visnyk NTSh* (Lviv) March 1991 (1): 2.

— (pseud. S. Piskovyi). "L'vivs'ki 'teky' A. Shneidera iak istoryko-kraieznavche dzherelo." *Arkhivy Ukraïny* 1965 (4): 73–76.
    A review of the Dashkevych article by Adam Kamiński presents more details
    about the collection—*Archeion* 45 (1966): 238–40.

Davis, Robert H., Jr., and Edward Kasinec. "Introduction." In *Dark Mirror: Romanov and Imperial Palace Library Materials in the Holdings of the New York Public Library: A Checklist and Agenda for Research*. Comp. Robert H. Davis, Jr. New York: Norman Ross Publishing, 1999.

—. "Witness to the Crime: Two Little-Known Photographic Sources Relating to the Sale and Destruction of Antiquities in Soviet Russia during the 1920s." *Journal of the History of Collections* 3(1) 1991: 53–59.

Decker, Andrew. "A Worldwide Treasure Hunt." *ArtNEWs* Summer 1991: 130–38.

Deich, Mark. "Dobycha—Restitutsiia po-sovetski, ili 'Sploshnaia Chemodaniia.'" *Moskovskii komsomolets* 25 April 1998: 5.

—. "Podpisano Stalinym: 'Dobycha tainy germanskikh reparatsii.'" *Stolitsa* 191 (1994) 29: 18.
    An article based on some of the new revelations in the book by Pavel Knyshev-
    skii.

Dement'eva, Mariia. "Osobaia sud'ba osobogo arkhiva." *Obshchaia gazeta* 4 May 1993 (13): 8.

Devaus, Dominique. "Les Archives de la direction de la Sûreté rapatriées de Russie." *Gazette des Archives* 176 (1997): 78–86.

Dobbs, Michael. "Stolen Beauty: Hitler Looted an Albrecht Durer Masterpiece; It Ended Up at the National Gallery of Art. But Where It Really Belongs Is Now in Dispute." *Washington Post Magazine* 21 March 1999: 12–18, 29.

Dokasheva, E. S. *Russkii kul'turno-istoricheskii muzei v Prage.* Moscow, 1993.

Dolgodrova, Tat'iana. "Sobranie perepletov Iakoba Krauze v Rossiiskoi gosudarstvennoi biblioteke." *Nashe nasledie* 49 (1999): 97–102.

—. "Unikal'nye zapadnoevropeiskie pechatnye knigi XV–XVI vekov iz trofeinogo sobraniia Rossiiskoi gosudarstvennoi biblioteki." *Nashe nasledie* 42 (1997): 113–19.

Dostal', M. Iu. "Russkii kul'turno-istoricheskii muzei v Prage v tvorcheskoi sud'be V. F. Bulgakova (po novym arkhivnym dannym)." In *"Russkaia, ukrainskaia i belorusskaia èmigratsiia,"* 1995, vol. 1, pp. 806–15.

Dubrovina, Liubov A. "Kodykohrafiia—Arkheohrafiia—Kodykolohiia (vzaiemozv'iazky ta rozmezhuvannia)." In L. A. Dubrovina and O. M. Hal'chenko, *Kodykohrafiia ukraïns'koï ta skhidnoslov'ians'koï rukopysnoï knyhy i kodykolohichna model' struktury formalizovanoho opysu rukopysu/Kodikografiia ukrainskoi i vostochnoslavianskoi rukopisnoi knigi i kodikologicheskaia model' struktury formalizovannogo opisaniia rukopisi.* Kyiv: IUA, 1992, pp. 7–31 (Ukrainian) and pp. 76–102 (Russian). [=Problemy edytsiinoï ta kameral'noï arkheohrafiï: Istoriia, teoriia, metodyka, 9.]

—. "Statuty Vsenarodnoï biblioteky Ukraïny pry VUAN iak dzherelo z istoriï rozvytku ta transformatsiï ideï Natsional'noï biblioteky (1918–1934)." *Ukraïns'kyi arkheohrafichnyi shchorichnyk,* n.s. 3/4 (1999): 308–30.

—. Review of *Grimsted, Archives: Ukraine.* In *Ukraïns'kyi arkheohrafichnyi shchorichnyk,* n.s. 2 (1993): 399–401

—, ed. (with O. V. Sokhan'). *Natsional'na arkhivna informatsiina systema: Struktura danykh (Materialy dlia obhovorennia.)* Kyiv, 1994. [Sponsors: HAU, NAN, TsNB, IUA.]

—, and O. M. Hal'chenko. *Kodykohrafiia ukraïns'koï ta skhidnoslov'ians'koï rukopysnoï knyhy i kodykolohichna model' struktury formalizovanoho opysu rukopysu/Kodikografiia ukrainskoi i vostochnoslavianskoi rukopisnoi knigi i kodikologicheskaia model' struktury formalizovannogo opisaniia rukopisi.* Kyiv: IUA, 1992. [=Problemy edytsiinoï ta kameral'noï arkheohrafiï: Istoriia, teoriia, metodyka, 9].

Dubyk, Maryna H. *Arkhivna sprava v okupovanii Ukraïni (1941–1944 rr.).* Avtoreferat dysertatsiï na zdobuttia naukovoho stupenia kandydata istorychnykh nauk. Kyiv: IUA NANU, 1997.

—. "Skhema sprav Kraiovoho upravlinnia arkhivamy, bibliotekamy ta muzeiamy pry Reikhskomisariati Ukraïny (1944 r.)." *Arkhivy Ukraïny* 1995 (1–3): 35–37.

Eichwede, Wolfgang. "Models of Restitution (Germany, Russia, Ukraine)." In *The Spoils of War: WWII and Aftermath*, pp. 216–20.

—. "Ukraina idet svoim putem." In *Kul'tura i viina*, p. 10.

—, and Ulrike Hartung, eds. *"Betr: Sicherstellung": NS-Kunstraub in der Sowjetunion.* Bremen: Edition Temmen, 1998. (Hereafter: *"Betr: Sicherstellung"*)

—. "Sowjetische Kulturgutverluste im Zweiten Weltkrieg: Zahlen, Odysseen und Rätsel. *Osteuropa* 48 (1998): 225–38.

—, et al., eds. *Property Cards Art, Claims and Shipments. Amerikanische Rückführungen sowjetischer Kulturgüter an die UdSSR nach dem Zweiten Weltkrieg"—Die CD der Arbeitsstelle "Verbleib der im Zweiten Weltkrieg aus der Sowjetunion verlagerten Kulturgüter."* Bremen: Forschungsstelle Osteuropa, 1996.

Eizenstat, Stuart E. "Archival Openness." In *Washington Conference, 1998,* pp. 429–31.

—. "Art Databases and Archives." In *Washington Conference, 1998,* pp. 421–23.

—. "Concluding Statement." In *Washington Conference, 1998,* pp. 125–32. Electronic version: <http://www.state.gov/ www/policy_remarks/1998/ 981203_eizenstat_heac_conc.html>.

—. "Explanation of the Washington Conference Principles on Nazi-Confiscated Art." In *Washington Conference, 1998,* pp. 415–20.

—. "In Support of Principles on Nazi-Confiscated Art."
Electronic version: <http://www.state.gov/www/policy_remarks/
1998/981203_eizenstat_heac_art.html>.
See also the principles, which Eizenstat played a major role in drafting, ibid.,
pp. 971–72. These are likewise posted at: <http://www.state.gov/www/regions/
eur// 981203_heac_art_princ.html>.

Elin, Lev. "Troe s paketom v Kremle—Katynskie igry." *Novoe vremia* 1992
(43) October: 12–14.
English version: "Three Men in the Kremlin and a Package—Katyn:
Murder Will Out." *New Times International* 1992 (44) October: 30–32.

Endler, Renate, and Elisabeth Schwarze. *Die Freimauererbestände im
Geheimen Staatsarchiv Preußischer Kulturbesitz*, vol. 1: *Grosslogen und
Protektor, Freimauerischen Stiftungen und Vereinigungen;* vol. 2:
Tochterlogen. Frankfurt-am-Main: Peter Lang, 1994–1996. [=Schriften
reihe der Internationalen Forschungsstelle "Demokratische Bewegungen
in Mitteleuropa 1770–1850," 13 and 18.]

Engstler, Ludwig. *Die territoriale Bindung von Kulturgütern im Rahmen des
Völkerrechts*. Köln–Berlin: Carl Heymanns Verlag, 1964. [=Annales
Universitatis Saraviensis, Schriftenreihe der Rechts- und Wirtschafts-
wissenschaftlichen Fakultät der Universität des Saarlandes, Heft 8.]

Evans, Frank B. "The Action by Unesco and ICA since 1976." *CITRA
1993–1995*, pp. 69–78.

Falaleeva, M. B. "Fond Romanovykh v sobranii OPI GIM." *Arkheograficheskii ezhegodnik za 1996 god* (Moscow, 1998): 270–81.

Farrington, Anthony. "The ICA's International Microfilming Project—Is
There A Future?" *CITRA 1993–1995*, pp. 120–24.

Fedoruk, Oleksandr K. "Natsional′na kul′turna spadshchyna—skarbnytsia
narodu." In *Ukraïns′ki kul′turni tsinnosti v Rosiï: Arkheolohiia kolektsiï
Ukraïny*. Ed. P. Tolochko et al. Kyiv, 1997, pp. 6–11. [=*Povernennia
kul′turnoho nadbannia Ukraïny: Dokumenty svidchat′*, 2.]

—. [Aleksandr.] "Net sroka davnosti vozvrashcheniiu natsional′nogo
naslediia." *Moskovskii komsomolets v Ukraine* 1–8 July 1999: 14.

—. [Aleksandr.] "Restitutsiia i vozvrashchenie kul′turnykh tsennostei—
vazhnyi faktor mezhdunarodnogo sotrudnichestva." In *Restytutsyia
kul′turnykh kashtoŭnastsei*, pp. 15–20.

—. "Treasures Plundered during World War II Not Yet Returned." *Ukrainian
Weekly* 9 (26 February 1995): 2, 12; 10 (5 March 1995): 2, 12.

—. [Alexander.] "Ukraine." *Spoils of War: International Newsletter* 2 (July 1996): 37.

—. "Ukraine: The Lost Cultural Treasures and the Problem of their Return." In *The Spoils of War: WWII and Aftermath*, pp. 72–76.

—. "Zberezhennia natsional′nykh kul′turnykh tsinnostei—na koryst′ suchasnoï tsyvilizatsiï." *Halyts′ka brama* 1997 (12[36]): 3.

Filar, Władysław. *Eksterminacja ludności polskiej na Wołyniu w Drugiej wojnie światowej*. Warsaw, 1999.

Fischer, George. "The Russian Archive in Prague." *American Slavic and East European Review* 8 (December 1949): 289–95.

Fodor, István. "Hungary." *Spoils of War: International Newsletter* 5 (June 1998): 58.

Form, Wolfgang, and Pavel Poljan (Polian). "Das Zentrum für die Aufbewahrung historisch-dokumentarischer Sammlungen in Moskau—ein Erfahrungsbericht." *Informationen aus der Forschung* [Bundesinstitut für ostwissenschaftliche und internationale Studien] 7 (20 October 1992): 1–8.

Forstreuter, Kurt. *Das Preußische Staatsarchiv in Königsberg. Ein geschichtlicher Rückblick mit einer Übersicht über seine Bestände.* Göttingen, Vandenhoeck & Ruprecht, 1955. [=*Veröffentlichungen der Niedersächsischen Archivverwaltung*, 3.]

—. "Das Staatsarchiv Königsberg als Quelle für Allgemeine Geschichte." *Hamburger Mittel- und Ostdeutsche Forschungen* 6 (1967): 9–35.

Foster, Catherine. "Stolen Art as War Booty: Hostages or Harbingers of Peace?" *Christian Science Monitor* 8 February 1995: 1, 10.

Franko, Ivan. "Prychynok do istoriï halyts′ko-rus′koho pys′menstva XVIII v." *Zapysky NTSh* 107 (1912): 110–15.

Fraoua, Ridha. *Convention concernant les mesures à prendre pour interdire et empêcher l'importation, l'exportation et le transfert de propriété illicites des biens culturels (Paris, 1970). Commentaire et aperçu de quelques mesures nationales d'exécution.* Paris: UNESCO, 1986. (CC–86/WS/40)

—. *Le trafic illicite des biens culturels et leur restitution. Analyse des réglementations nationales et internationales. Critiques et propositions.* Fribourg: Université de Fribourg Suisse, 1985. [=Travaux de la Faculté de droit de l'Université de Fribourg Suisse, 68.]
Puts many of the problems of traffic in and restitution of cultural treasures in

broader perspective and emphasizes the need for a more comprehensive
convention dealing with matters of cultural restitution.

Freitag, Gabriele. "Okhrana pamiatnikov iskusstva v amerikanskoi zone i
politicheskaia restitutsiia." In *Kul'tura i viina*, pp. 27–32.

—. "Die Restitution von NS-Beutegut nach dem Zweiten Weltkrieg." In
"Betr: Sicherstellung," pp. 170–208.

—, and Andreas Grenzer. "Der deutsche Umgang mit sowjetischem
Kulturgut während des Zweiten Weltkrieges: Ein Aspekt
nationalsozialistischer Besatzungspolitik." *Jahrbücher für Geschichte
Osteuropas* 45(2) 1947: 223–72.

—. "Die Evakuierung von sowjetischen Kulturgütern im Zweiten Weltkrieg."
Osteuropa 47(1) 1997: 922–31.

Gambrell, Jamey. "First Return of War Booty." *Art in America* 6 (June
1995): 31.

Genieva, Ekaterina. "German Book Collections in Russian Libraries." In *The
Spoils of War: WWII and Aftermath*, pp. 221–24.

Gordon, Michael R. "Hot Issue for Russia: Should It Return Nazi Plunder?"
New York Times 17 April 1997: A1.

—. "Slap at Yeltsin as Legislators Veto Return of Art Booty." *New York
Times* 14 May 1997: 3.

Gorfunkel', Aleksandr, and Nikolai Nikolaev. "Kak vozvrashchat' 'trofeinye
knigi': Eshche raz o zakhvachennykh vo vremia voiny kul'turnykh
tsennostiakh." *Nevskoe vremia* 8(163) 14 January 1992.

"Gotskaia biblioteka, kazhetsia gotova k otpravke v Germaniiu—knigi to
pakuiut, to raspakovyvaiut." *Nezavisimaia gazeta* 6 June 1994: 5.

Govorkian, Natal'ia. "Zakrytye arkhivy v otkrytoi bor'be." *Moskovskie
novosti* 25 October 1992 (43): 9.

Grabowicz, George G. "Ukrainian Studies: Framing the Contexts." *Slavic
Review* 54(3) Fall 1995: 674–90.

Greenfield, Jeanette. *The Return of Cultural Treasures*. 2nd ed. New York-
Cambridge: Cambridge University Press, 1996.
First edition: New York and Cambridge: Cambridge University
Press, 1989.
Weaves together international legal consideration of diverse cases from the
Icelandic medieval saga manuscripts to the Elgin Marbles, although manuscript
and archival materials are seen as elements of the larger cultural heritage.

Grenzer, Andreas. "Report on the Archive Situation in Russia as It Relates to Researching the Losses of Cultural Property." In *Cultural Treasures, 1994,* pp. 142–45.

—. "Research Project 'Fate of the Treasures of Art Removed from the Soviet Union during World War II.'" In *Cultural Treasures, 1994,* pp. 124–32.

—, and Gabriele Freitag. "Die Evakuierung von sowjetischen Kulturgütern im Zweiten Weltkrieg." *Osteuropa* 47 (1997): 922–31.

Grimsted, Patricia Kennedy. "Archeography in the Service of Imperial Policy: The Foundation of the Kiev Archeographic Commission and the Kiev Central Archive of Early Record Books." *Harvard Ukrainian Studies* 17(1–2) June 1993: 27–44.
Ukrainian version: "Arkheohrafiia na sluzhbi impers'koï polityky: Zasnuvannia Kyïvs'koï arkheohrafichnoï komisiï ta Kyïvs'koho tsentral'noho arkhivu davnikh aktiv." In *Materialy iuvileinoï konferentsiï, prysviachenoï 150-richchiu Kyïvs'koï arkheohrafichnoï komisiï (Kyïv, Sedniv, 18–21 zhovtnia 1993 r.).* Ed. Hennadii Boriak. Kyiv, 1997, pp. 11–33. [="Problemy edytsiinoï ta kameral'noï arkheohrafiï: Istoriia, teoriia, metodyka," 30.]

—. "The Archival Legacy of the Soviet Ukraine: Problems of Tracing the Documentary Records of a Divided Nation." *Cahiers du Monde russe et soviétique* 28 (January-March 1987): 95–108.
Preprint: Kennan Institute for Advanced Russian Studies Occasional Paper, no. 203 (Washington, DC, 1986).
An earlier French version of this article was presented at a seminar at the Centre d'études sur l'URSS, L'Europe orientale et le domaine turc, in November 1985, and an English version at HURI.

—. "Archival Rossica/Sovietica Abroad—Provenance or Pertinence, Bibliographic and Descriptive Needs." *Cahiers du Monde russe et soviétique* 34(3) 1993: 431–80.
Russian version: "Zarubezhnaia arkhivnaia Rossika i Sovetika. Proiskhozhdenie dokumentov ili ikh otnoshenie k istorii Rossii (SSSR), potrebnost' v opisanii i bibliografii." *Otechestvennye arkhivy* 1993 (1): 20–53.

—. "Archival Rossica—Rationalizing the Search and Retrieval of the Russian Archival Legacy Abroad." *Cahiers du Monde russe et soviétique,* forthcoming.

—. "Archives and Manuscript Collections in the Belorusian SSR: Soviet Standards and the Documentary Legacy of the Belorussian Nation."

Zapisy Belaruskaha instytutu navuki i mastatstva/Quarterly of the Byelo-russian Institute of Arts and Sciences 17 (New York, 1983): 85–102.

—. *Archives and Manuscript Repositories in the USSR: Estonia, Latvia, Lithuania, and Belorussia.* Princeton: Princeton University Press, 1981. (Hereafter: Grimsted, *Archives: Estonia, Latvia, Lithuania, and Belorussia*)

—. *Archives and Manuscript Repositories in the USSR: Ukraine and Moldavia,* Book 1: *General Bibliography and Institutional Directory,* Princeton: Princeton University Press, 1988. (Hereafter: Grimsted, *Archives: Ukraine*)

—. *Archives of Russia Seven Years After: "Purveyors of Sensations" or "Shadows Cast to the Past."* Washington, DC: Cold War International History Project, 1998. [=CWIHP Working Paper, 20.] Electronic version: <http://www.cwihp.si.edu/publications.htm>. Earlier version: *Archives of Russia Five Years After—"Purveyors of Sensations" or "Shadows Cast to the Past"?* Amsterdam: IISH, 1997. [=IISG Research Paper, 26]. Electronic version: <http://www.iisg.nl/publications/grimsted.pdf>.

—. "Arkhivnaia Rossika/Sovetika. K opredeleniiu i topologii russkogo arkhivnogo naslediia za rubezhom." In *Trudy Istoriko-arkhivnogo instituta* 33 (Moscow, 1996): 262–86. Alternate version: *Problemy zarubezhnoi arkhivnoi Rossiki,* pp. 7–43.

—. "Bach Scores in Kyiv: The Long-Lost Sing-Akademie Collection Surfaces in Ukraine." *Spoils of War: International Newsletter* 7 (August 2000): 23–35. Electronic version: HURI website <http://www.huri.harvard.edu/workpaper/grimsted/grimsted.html>.

—. "Beyond Perestroika: Soviet-Area Archives after the August Coup." *American Archivist* 55 (Winter 1992): 94–124.

—. "Biblioteka–arkhiv: Shliakh do intehruvannia (Avtomatyzovanyi dostup do arkhivnoï informatsiï dlia Rosiï, Ukraïny ta inshykh nezalezhnykh derzhav kolyshn'oho Soiuzu)." *Bibliotechnyi visnyk* 1994 (5–6): 26–29.

—. "Captured Archives and Restitution Problems on the Eastern Front: Beyond the Bard Graduate Center Symposium." In *The Spoils of War: WWII and Aftermath,* pp. 244–51.

—. "Czym jest i czym była Metryka Litewska? (Stan obecny i perspektywy odtworzenia zawartości archiwum kancelaryjnego Wielkiego Księstwa Litewskiego)." *Kwartalnik Historyczny* 92(1) 1985: 55–85.

—. *Displaced Archives on the Eastern Front: Restitution Problems from World War II and Its Aftermath.* Amsterdam: IISH, 1995 [=*IISG Research Papers,* 18.]
Republished by the ICA in *Janus: Revue internationale des archives/International Archival Journal* 1996 (2): 42–77. A summary version appears in *The Spoils of War: WWII and Aftermath,* pp. 244–51.

—. "Displaced Archives and Restitution Problems on the Eastern Front in the Aftermath of the Second World War." *Contemporary European History* 6(1) 1997: 27–74.
Updates the earlier 1995 Amsterdam edition of *Displaced Archives* above.

—. "The Fate of Early Records in Lviv Archives: Documentation from Western Ukraine under Polish Rule (Fifteenth Century to 1772)." *Slavonic and East European Review* 60(3) July 1982: 321–46.

—. "The Fate of Ukrainian Cultural Treasures during World War II: The Plunder of Archives, Libraries, and Museums under the Third Reich." *Jahrbücher für Geschichte Osteuropas* 39(1) 1991: 53–80.
Expanded Ukrainian edition (with Hennadii Boriak): *Dolia skarbiv ukraïns'koï kul'tury* (see below).

—. "Foreign Collections and Soviet Archives: Russian Archaeographic Efforts in Great Britain and the Problem of Provenance." In *The Study of Russian History from British Archival Sources.* Ed. Janet M. Hartley. London and New York: Mansell, 1986.

—. *A Handbook for Archival Research in the USSR.* Washington, DC: IREX; Kennan Institute for Advanced Russian Studies, 1989.

—. "Increasing Reference Access to Post-1991 Russian Archives." *Slavic Review* 56(4) Winter 1997: 718–59.
Based on chapter 12 of the original edition of Grimsted, *Archives of Russia Five Years After.* Updated in the revised chapter 12 of Grimsted, *Archives of Russia Seven Years After.*

—. *Intellectual Access and Descriptive Standards for Post-Soviet Archives: What Is to Be Done?* Princeton: IREX, 1992.

—. "Lenin's Archival Decree of 1918: The Bolshevik Legacy for Soviet Archival Theory and Practice." *American Archivist* 45(4) Fall 1982: 429–43.

—. "L'viv Manuscript Collections and Their Fate." *Harvard Ukrainian Studies* 3–4 (1979–1980): 349–75.

—. "New Clues in the Records of Archival and Library Plunder during World War II: The ERR Ratibor Center and the RSHA VII Amt in Silesia." In *Return of Looted Collections*, pp. 52–67.
An expanded, annotated edition with selected documents is in preparation for publication in *Holocaust and Genocide Studies*.

—. "The Odyssey of the Petliura Library and the Records of the Ukrainian National Republic during World War II." *Harvard Ukrainian Studies* 22 (1998): 181–208. [=*Cultures and Nations of Central and Eastern Europe: Essays in Honor of Roman Szporluk*. Ed. Zvi Gitelman et al.]

—. *The Odyssey of the Smolensk Archive: Plundered Communist Records for the Service of Anti-Communism*. Pittsburgh: REES, University of Pittsburgh, 1995. [=Carl Beck Occasional Papers in Russian and East European Studies, 1201.]
Abbreviated version: In *Zeitschrift für Sozialgeschichte des 20. und 21. Jahrhunderts*, 1997, Heft 4; 1998, Heft 2; 1999, Heft 1.

—. "The Postwar Fate of the Petliura Library and the Records of the Ukrainian National Republic." *Harvard Ukrainian Studies* 21(3–4): 395–462.

—. "Rus'ka metryka: Knyhy pol's'koï koronnoï kantseliariï dlia ukraïns'kykh zemel', 1569–1673 rr." *Ukraïns'kyi istorychnyi zhurnal* 1989 (5): 52–62.

—. "Russian Archives in Transition: Caught between Political Crossfire and Economic Crisis." *American Archivist* 56 (Fall 1993): 614–62.
Earlier edition published as the introduction to *Archives in Russia 1993: A Brief Directory*. Washington, DC: IREX, 1993.
Russian edition: "Rossiiskie arkhivy v perekhodnyi period posle avgusta 1991 g." *Novaia i noveishaia istoriia* 1994 (1): 63–83.

—. "The Ruthenian (Volhynian) Metrica: Polish Crown Chancery Records for Ukrainian Lands, 1569–1673." *Harvard Ukrainian Studies* 14(1–2) June 1990: 7–83.

—. "The Stefanyk Library of the Ukrainian Academy of Sciences: A Treasury of Manuscript Collections in Lviv." *Harvard Ukrainian Studies* 5(2) 1981: 195–229.

—. "'Trophy' Archives and Non-Restitution: Russia's Cultural 'Cold War' with the European Community." *Problems of Post-Communism* 45(3) May/June 1998: 3–16.

—. "Twice Plundered or 'Twice Saved'? Russia's 'Trophy' Archives and the Loot of the Reichssicherheitshauptamt." *Holocaust and Genocide Studies* 4(2) September 2001.

—. "Układ i zawartość Metryki Litewskiej." *Archeion* (Warsaw) 80 (1986): 121–82.

—. "Ukraine." In *A Guide to East-Central European Archives*. Ed. Charles W. Ingrao. Houston, Rice University Press, 1998, pp. 171–200. [=*Austrian History Yearbook* 29(2) 1998.]

—. "Zarubezhnaia arkhivnaia Rossika i Sovetika. Proiskhozhdenie dokumentov ili ikh otnoshenie k istorii Rossii (SSSR), potrebnost' v opisanii i bibliografii." *Otechestvennye arkhivy* 1993 (1): 20–53.
A preliminary shorter edition appeared as a chapter in *Intellectual Access to Soviet-Area Archives: What Is to Be Done?* Princeton: IREX, 1992. An expanded, English-language version appeared as "Archival Rossica/Sovietica Abroad—Provenance or Pertinence, Bibliographic and Descriptive Needs." *Cahiers du Monde russe et soviétique* 34(3) 1993: 431–80.

—, comp. U.S. Restitution of Nazi-Looted Cultural Treasures to the USSR, 1945–1959: Facsimile Documents from the National Archives of the United States. Foreword by Michael J. Kurtz. Intro. by P. K. Grimsted. Washington, DC: GPO, 2001 (CD-ROM edition).

—, ed. "Archives and Manuscript Collections in the USSR: Finding aids on microfiche." Series 3: "Ukraine and Moldavia." Leiden: IDC, 1988.

—, ed. *Archives in Russia 1993: A Brief Directory*. Part 1: *Moscow and St. Petersburg*. Ed. with an intro. by P. K. Grimsted. Pref. by Vladimir P. Kozlov. Washington, DC: IREX, 1993.
Reviewed by Liubov A. Dubrovina and Konstantin Ie. Novakhats′kyi in *Arkhivy Ukraïny* 1993 (1–3): 106–108.

—, ed. *Archives of Russia: A Directory and Bibliographic Guide to Holdings in Moscow and St. Petersburg*. Armonk, NY: M.E. Sharpe, 2000. (Hereafter: *Archives of Russia, 2000*)

—, and Hennadii Boriak. *Dolia skarbiv ukraïns′koï kul′tury pid chas Druhoï svitovoï viiny: Vynyshchennia arkhiviv, bibliotek, muzeïv*. Kyiv: Arkheohrafichna komisiia AN URSR, 1991.
A revised and expanded edition of Grimsted, "The Fate of Ukrainian Cultural Treasures"; 2nd ed.= Lviv, 1992, under the title *Dolia ukraïns′kykh kul′turnykh tsinnostei pid chas Druhoï svitovoï viiny*. This material appeared most recently as a summary article in the magazine *Pam′iatky Ukraïny* 1994 (3–6[26]): 92–105.

—, and Hennadii V. Boriak, Kyrylo Vyslobokov, Irena Sułkowska-Kurasiowa, and Natalia Iakovenko, comp. *Rus′ka (Volyns′ka) metryka:*

Rehestry dokumentiv koronnoï kantseliariï dlia ukraïns'kykh zemel'
(Volyns'ke, Bratslavs'ke, Kyïvs'ke, Chernihivs'ke voievodstva),
1569–1673/The Ruthenian (Volhynian) Metrica: Early Inventories of the
Polish Crown Chancery Records for Ukrainian Lands (1569–1673).
Kyiv, forthcoming.
Introduction by Grimsted.

—. With the collaboration of Irena Sułkowska-Kurasiowa. *The "Lithuanian*
Metrica" in Moscow and Warsaw: Reconstructing the Archives of the
Grand Duchy of Lithuania, Including an Annotated Edition of the 1887
Inventory Compiled by Stanisław Ptaszycki. Cambridge, MA: Oriental
Research Partners, 1984.

Gut, Christian. "Constitution et reconstitution des patrimoines archivistiques
nationaux." In *Actes de la 17ème CITRA,* pp. 39–69.
Initially issued separately: fascicule 3, appendice 2, pp. 1–30.

Hartung, Ulrike. "Der deutsche Umgang mit sowjetischen Archiven und
Bibliotheken im Zweiten Weltkrieg." In *Displaced Books: Bücher-*
rückgabe, pp. 42–51.

—. *Raubzüge in der Sowjetunion: Das Sonderkommando Künsberg*
1941–1943. Bremen: Edition Temmen, 1997.

—. "Die Weg zurück: Russische Akten bestätigen die Rückführung eigener
Kulturgüter aus Deutschland nach dem Zweiten Weltkrieg. Probleme
ihrer Erfassung." In *"Betr: Sicherstellung,"* pp. 170–208.

Henke, Josef. "Das amerikanisch-deutsche OMGUS-Project: Erschliessungund Verfilmung der Akten der amerikanischen Militärregierung in
Deutschland 1945–1949." *Der Archivar* 35(2) 1982: 149–57.

Henrich, Dieter. "Beethoven, Hegel und Mozart auf der Reise nach Krakau:
Der Übergang des Grüssauer Depots der Preußischen Staatsbibliothek in
die Hand der Volksrepublik Polen." *Neue Rundschau* 88 (1977): 165–99.

Herrmann, Matthias. *Das Reichsarchiv (1919–1945): Eine archivische*
Institution im Spannungsfeld der deutschen Politik, Band II. Ph.D.
Dissertation. Berlin, Humboldt-Universität, ca. 1993.

Hertz, Deborah. "The Varnhagen Collection is in Krakow." *American*
Archivist 44(3) Summer 1981: 223–28.

Heuss, Anja. "Archives in the Federal Republic of Germany on Art
Theft—An Overall View." In *Cultural Treasures, 1994,* pp. 135–41.

—. "Die 'Beuteorganisation' des Auswärtigen Amtes: Das Sonderkommando Künsberg und der Kulturgutraub in der Sowjetunion." *Vierteljahrshefte für Zeitgeschichte* 45(4) October 1997: 535–56.

Hewryk, Titus D. *The Lost Architecture of Kiev*. New York: Ukrainian Museum, 1982.
Ukrainian edition: *Vtracheni arkhitekturni pam'iatky Kyieva*. New York: Ukraïns'kyi muzei, 1982.
Republished in *Pam'iatky Ukraïny* 1990 (1): 25–40; 1990 (2): 19–38; and 1990 (3): 25–39.

Hochfield, Sylvia. "The Russian Surprise: Moscow Invites Victims of the Nazis to Reclaim their Looted Art. But Who Exactly is a Victim?" *ARTNews* 98(1) January 1999: 56.

Holler, Wolfgang. "Return of Three Albums from the Ukraine to the Department of Prints and Drawings, Dresden." *Spoils of War: International Newsletter* 3 (1996): 63.

Hoogewoud, Frits J. "The Nazi Looting of Books and Its American 'Antithesis': Selected Pictures from the Offenbach Archival Depot's Photographic History and Its Supplement." *Studia Rosenthaliana* 26(1/2) 1992: 158–92.

—, Evert P. Kwaardgras, et al., eds. *The Return of Looted Collections (1946–1946). An Unfinished Chapter: Proceedings of an International Symposium to Mark the 50th Anniversary of the Return of Dutch Book Collections from Germany*. Amsterdam, 1997.
(Hereafter: *Return of Looted Collections*)

Hryb, Tomash. "Belaruski zahranichny arkhiŭ u Praze." *Kalos'se: Belaruski litaraturna-navukovy chasapis* (Vilnius) 1 (1935).

Hrynchenko, Olena. "Chy potribne nam zoloto skifiv?" *Den'* 119 (25 June 1997): 7.

Hyrych, Ihor. "Arkhiv-Muzei Perekhodovoï doby pro ruinatsiiu kyïvs'kykh pam'iatok u 1918–1942 rokakh." *Starozhytnosti* 1992 (1): 5.

Iakovlieva, Larysa. "Praz'ki fondy v Kyievi." *Pam'iatky Ukraïny* 1994 (3–6[26]): 120–22.

Isaievych, Iaroslav. "Ukrainian Studies—Exceptional or Merely Exemplary?" *Slavic Review* 54(3) Fall 1995: 702–708.

Isnard, Jacques, and Michel Tatu. "Moscou accepte de restituer 20 tonnes de documents des Deuxièmes bureaux." *Le Monde* 14 November 1992.

Ivanov, Ievhenii Mykhailovych. "Ukraïns'ki fondy, perevezeni z Moskvy." *Arkhivna sprava* 4 (1927): 44–65.

Iziumov, Aleksandr Filaretovich. *Otdel dokumentov. Russkii zagranichnyi istoricheskii arkhiv v Prage (1923–1932 gg.).* Prague, 1932. [Microfiche ed.=IDC-R-11,232.]

—. "Zapiska o Russkom Istoricheskom Arkhive." In Sergei Porfir′evich Postnikov, *Politika, ideologiia, byt i uchenye trudy russkoi èmigratsii: 1918–1945: Bibliografiia. Iz kataloga biblioteki RZI arkhiva.* Ed. Sergei Blinov. 2 vols. New York: Norman Ross Publishing, 1993, vol. 2, pp. 400–416.

Jacob, Louis. *La clause de livraison des archives publiques dans les traités d'annexion.* Paris: Giard et Bière, 1915.

Jarvinen, Markkü. "Convention of The Hague of 1954: Convention for the Protection of Cultural Property in the Event of Armed Conflict." In *CITRA 1993–1995*, pp. 147–54.

Jeltsch, Karin. "Der Raub des Neptunbrunnens aus Schloss Peterhof." In *"Betr: Sicherstellung,"* pp. 67–74.

Joachim, Erich, and Walter Hubatsch, eds. *Regesta historico-diplomatica Ordinis S. Mariae Theutonicorum, 1198–1525.* 5 vols. Göttingen: Vandenhoeck and Ruprecht, 1948–1973.

Kahn, Joseph P. "A Bach Score: Accident and Adventure Lead to a Collection Long Thought Lost." *Boston Globe* 30 September 1999: E1, E7.

Kania, ks. Janusz. "Katalog mikrofilmów Ośrodka Archiwów, Bibliotek i Muzeów Kościelnych przy Katolickim Uniwersytecie Lubelskim." No. 5. Lublin, 1985. [=*Archiwa, Biblioteki i Muzea Kościelne* 51 (1985): [5]–115.]

Kappeler, Andreas. "Ukrainian History from a German Perspective." *Slavic Review* 54(3) Fall 1995: 691–701.

Kapran, Mikhail Ia. "Mezhdunarodnoe sotrudnichestvo sovetskikh arkhivistov." *Sovetskie arkhivy* 1968 (3): 32–39.

Karwasińska, Jadwiga (Hedvige). "La remise des archives dans les traités de l'Est européen." In *VIIIè Congrès International des Sciences Historiques, Zurich 1938; Communications Présentées,* vol. 1. Paris, n.d., pp. 52–53.

Kasinec, Edward, and Richard J. Kneeley. "The Slovanská knihovna in Prague and its RZIA Collection." *Slavic Review* 51(1) Spring 1992: 122–30.
  See also their introduction to the microfiche edition of the RZIA catalog, listed above under Slovanská knihovna [Slavonic Library] in Prague, for which this article serves as the basis.

Kecskeméti, Charles. "The Action by Unesco and ICA since 1976, Part 2." In *CITRA 1993–1995*, pp. 79–85.

—. *Archival Claims: Preliminary Study on the Principles and Criteria to be Applied in Negotiations.* Paris: UNESCO, 1977. (PGI-77/WS/1) French original: *Les contentieux archivistiques. Étude préliminaire sur les principes et les critères à retenir lors des négociations.* Paris: UNESCO, 1977 (PGI-77/WS/1) dated 30 June 1977. Condensed edition: *Actes de la 17ème CITRA*, pp. 108–30.

—. "Contested Records: The Legal Status of National Archives." *The Unesco Courier* February 1985: 9–11.

—. "Displaced European Archives: Is it Time for a Post-War Settlement?" *American Archivist* 55 (Winter 1992): 132–40.

—, and Evert Van Haar. *Model Bilateral and Multilateral Agreements and Conventions Concerning Transfer of Archives.* Paris, 1981. (PGI-81/WS/3) Arabic, French, Russian, and Spanish editions are also available from UNESCO.

Kent, George O. "The German Foreign Ministry's Archives at Whaddon Hall, 1948–58." *American Archivist* 24 (January 1961): 43–54.

—, comp. and ed. *A Catalogue of Files and Microfilms of the German Foreign Ministry Archives, 1867–1920.* Washington, 1959.

Kappeler, Andreas. "Ukrainian History from a German Perspective." *Slavic Review* 54(3) Fall 1995: 691–701.

Ketelaar, Eric. "Archivists in War." In *CITRA 1993–1995*, pp. 159–63.

—. "Understanding Archives of the People, by the People, and for the People." In *Washington Conference, 1998,* pp. 749–61.

Kline, Thomas R. "The Russian Bill to Nationalize Trophy Art: An American Perspective." *Spoils of War: International Newsletter* 4 (August 1997): 31–35.

Kloosterman, Jaap. "Rossika za rubezhom: Arkhivy Mezhdunarodnogo instituta sotsial'noi istorii." *Problemy zarubezhnoi arkhivnoi Rossiki,* pp. 121–23.

Knyshevskii, Pavel. *Dobycha: Tainy germanskikh reparatsii.* Moscow: Soratnik, 1994. See also the review and summary article by Mark Deich, "Podpisano Stalinym: 'Dobycha tainy germanskikh reparatsii.'" *Stolitsa* 29 (1994) 191: 18.

German edition: [P. N. Knyševskij]. *Moskaus Beute: Wie Vermögen, Kulturgüter und Intelligenz nach 1945 aus Deutschland geraubt wurden.* Munich: Olzog, 1995.

—. "Dobycha—V adres komiteta po delam iskusstv postupilo iz pobezhdennoi Germanii svyshe 1 milliona 208 tysiach muzeinykh tsennostei." *Moskovskie novosti* 50 (23–30 October 1994): 18.

Kolasa, Ingo. "Sag mir wo die Bücher sind…: Ein Beitrag zu 'Beutekulturgütern' und 'Trophäenkommissionen.'" *Zeitschrift für Bibliothekswesen und Bibliographie* 42(4) July/August 1995: 350–52.

—. "Preface." In Ingo Kolasa and Klaus-Dieter Lehmann, eds. *Die Trophäenkommissionen,* pp. 11–20.

—, and Klaus-Dieter Lehmann, eds. *Die Trophäenkommissionen der Roten Armee: Eine Dokumentensammlung zur Verschleppung von Büchern aus deutschen Bibliotheken.* Frankfurt-am-Main: Vittorio Klostermann, 1996. [=*Zeitschrift für Bibliothekswesen und Bibliographie,* Sonderheft 64.]
(Hereafter: *Die Trophäenkommissionen*)

Kopteltsev, Valentin. "The General Goals of the Conference and the Looted Art Problem." In *Washington Conference, 1998,* pp. 319–20.

Kopyleva, Ol´ga N. "K probleme sokhrannosti GAF SSSR v gody Velikoi Otechestvennoi voiny." *Sovetskie arkhivy* 1990 (5): 37–44.

—. "Tsentral´nye gosudarstvennye arkhivy SSSR v gody Velikoi Otechestvennoi voiny, 1941–1945 gg." Candidate dissertation. Moscow: RGGU, 1991.

Korkmasova, Evgenia [A.]. "Review of the Russian Press for 1997 on the Question of the Restitution of Cultural Valu[abl]es (Part 1)" *Spoils of War: International Newsletter* 4 (August 1997): 48–51; "Part 2," ibid., no. 5 (June 1998): 41–43; and "Part 3," ibid, no. 6 (February 1999): 22–24.

—, and A. L. Ponomarev, comps. *Katalog der Drucke des XVI.Jahrhunderts aus den Beständen des VGBIL/ Katalog nemetskoiazychnykh izdanii XVI veka v fondakh VGBIL/Catalogus librorum sedecimi saeculi qui in totius Rossiae Reipublicae literarum externarum Bibliotheca asservantur.* Ed. N. V. Kotrelev. Moscow: "VGBIL," 1992, 1996. [Preface and introduction in German and Russian; annotations in German. Added Latin title page: *Catalogus librorum sedecimi saeculi qui in totius Rossiae Reipublicae literarum externarum Bibliotheca asservantur.*]

—, E. V. Zhuravleva, and N. N. Zubrov, comps. *Trofeinye knigi iz biblioteki Sharoshpatakskogo reformatskogo kolledzha (Vengriia) v fondakh Nizhegorodskoi gosudarstvennoi oblastnoi universal'noi nauchnoi biblioteki: Katalog.* Moscow: "Rudomino," 1997.
Added English title page: *Displaced books from Sárospatak Calvinist College Library (Hungary) in the collections of Nizhny Novgorod Regional Research Library.*
Also available electronically at the VGBIL website.

Kostiuk, Stepan, and Vita Susak. "L'vivs'ka kolektsiia rysunkiv Al'brekhta Diurera." *Halyts'ka brama* 12(36) (December 1998): 11.

Kot, Serhii I. "Iak povertalysia nashi kleinody: Z istoriï pravovoho vrehuliuvannia problemy ukraïns'kykh kul'turnykh tsinnostei v Rosiï." *Khronika 2000* 27–28 (Kyiv 1998): 603–25.

—. "Malovidomyi dokument z istoriï ruinuvannia pam'iatok Kyievo-Pechers'koï Lavry pid chas Druhoï svitovoï viiny." In *Ukraïns'kyi arkheohrafichnyi shchorichnyk,* n.s. 3–4 (1999): 575–92.

—. "Povernuty kul'turni nadbannia mozhna, bula b dobra volia." *Viche* n.s. 5(50) May 1996: 129–44.

—. "Restytutsiia chy konfiskatsiia?: Rosiis'kyi zakon pro peremishcheni pid chas Druhoï svitovoï viiny kul'turni tsinnosti ta Ukraïna." *Polityka i chas* 1998 (8): 27–35.

—. "The Ukraine and the Russian Law on Removed Cultural Valu[abl]es." *Spoils of War: International Newsletter* 5 (June 1998): 9.

—. *Ukraïns'ki kul'turni tsinnosti v Rosiï: Problema povernennia v konteksti istoriï ta prava.* Kyiv: Soborna Ukraïna, 1996. [=*Povernennia kul'turnoho nadbannia Ukraïny: Dokumenty svidchat',* 1.]

—. "Zahybel' Uspens'koho soboru: Versiï…" *Khronika 2000* 17–18 (1997): 348–64.
"Pisliaslovo." Photographs with remarks by Hryhorii Poloiushko, pp. 365–67.

—, and Iurii Koreniuk. "Mykhailivs'ki pam'iatky v rosiis'kykh muzeiakh." *Pam'iatky Ukrainy* 1999 (1[122]): 63–82 + XXVI–XXVIII.

—. "Rosiia povynna povernut' Ukraïni tsinnosti z Mykhailivs'koho Zolotoverkhoho soboru v Kyievi." *Stolytsia* 11(36) 1997: 6, 9.

—, and Oleksii Nestulia. *Ukraïns'ki kul'turni tsinnosti v Rosiï: Persha sproba povernennia, 1917–1918.* Kyiv: Soborna Ukraïna, 1996. [=*Povernennia kul'turnoho nadbannia Ukraïny: Dokumenty svidchat',* 1.]

Kotrelev, Nikolai V. "Plach o pogibeli russkoi biblioteki." In *Redkie knigi i rukopisi: Izuchenie i opisanie (Materialy Vsesoiuznogo nauchno-metodicheskogo soveshchaniia zaveduiushchikh otdelami redkikh knig i rukopisei bibliotek vuzov. Leningrad, 24–26 ianvaria 1989 g.).* Leningrad: Izd-vo Leningradskogo universiteta, 1991, pp. 107–109. English edition: "Lamentation on the Ruin of the Russian Library." *Kul'turologiia: The Petersburg Journal of Cultural Studies* I(3) 1993: 147–50.

Kovalenko, Iurii. "Skandal, ne dostoinyi Rossii." *Izvestiia* 172 (8 September 1994): 5.

Kovalevskaia, Tat'iana. "Gel'mut Kol' vidit luchshee budushchee Ukrainy." *Rabochaia gazeta Ukrainy* 132 (5 September 1996): 1.

Koval's'kyi, Mykola [Nikolai Pavlovich Koval'skii]. *Istochniki po istorii Ukrainy XVI–XVII vv. v Litovskoi metrike i fondakh prikazov TsGADA: Uchebnoe posobie.* Dnipropetrovsk: DGU, 1979.

—. *Istochnikovedenie istorii ukrainsko-russkikh sviazei (XVI–pervaia polovina XVII v.): Uchebnoe posobie.* Dnipropetrovsk: DGU, 1979.

—, V. V. Strashko, and G. V. Boriak, comp. *Metodicheskie rekomendatsii po ispol'zovaniiu dokumentov Litovskoi metriki XVI v. v kurse istochnikovedeniia otechestvennoi istorii (regesty dokumentov aktovykh knig Litovskoi metriki 191–195).* Dnipropetrovsk: DGU, 1987.

Kowalski, Wojciech. *Art Treasures and War: A Study on the Restitution of Looted Cultural Property, Pursuant to Public International Law.* London: Institute of Art and Law, 1998.

—. *Likwidacja skutków wojny w dziedzinie kultury.* 2nd ed. Warsaw: Instytut Kultury, 1994. 1st edition: [Warsaw]: Instytut Kultury, 1990. English edition: *Liquidation of the Effects of World War II in the Area of Culture.* Warsaw: Institute of Culture, 1994. The English edition has fewer appended documents.

—. "Repatriatsiia kul'turnykh tsennostei v situatsii ustupok territorii i raspada mnogonatsional'nykh gosudarstv." In *Restytutsyia kul'turnykh kashtoŭnastsei,* pp. 21–52.

—. *Restytucja dziel sztuki w prawie międzynarodowym.* Katowice: Uniwersytet Śląski, 1989. Prace Naukowe Uniwersytetu Śląskiego w Katowicach, no. 1091.

—. "Russian Law: The Polish Perspective." *Spoils of War: International Newsletter* 4 (August 1997): 36–38.

Kozlov, Vladimir Petrovich. "Printsipy 'Osnovy zakonodatel'stva Rossiiskoi Federatsii ob Arkhivnom fonde Rossiiskoi Federatsii i arkhivakh.'" *Novaia i noveishaia istoriia* 1993 (6): 12–5

—. "Vyiavlenie i vozvrashchenie zarubezhnoi arkhivnoi Rossiki: Opyt i perspektivy." *Vestnik arkhivista* 1993 (6[18]): 11–23.

—. "Zarubezhnaia arkhivnaia rossika: Problemy i napravleniia raboty." *Novaia i noveishaia istoriia* 1994 (3) May–June: 13–23.

—, ed. *Problemy zarubezhnoi arkhivnoi Rossiki: Sbornik statei.* Moscow: "Russkii mir," 1997.

—, and Patricia Kennedy Grimsted, eds. *Arkhivy Rossii: Moskva i Sankt-Peterburg. Spravochnik-obozrenie i bibliograficheskii ukazatel'.* Moscow: "Arkheograficheskii tsentr," 1997.

Krushel'nyts'ka, Larysa. "The Case of the Ossolineum Collection." *Spoils of War: International Newsletter* 5 (1998): 25.

—. "Pravdyvo pro Ossolineum." *Pam'iatky Ukraïny* 1994 (3–6[26]): 85–86.

—. "Zbirky Ossolineumu restytutsiï ne uliahaiut'." *Universum* 3–4 (1997): 42–45.
Summary edition: *Halyts'ka brama* 12(36) December 1997: 6–7.

—, ed. *L'vivs'ka naukova biblioteka im. V. Stefanyka NAN Ukraïny: Dokumenty, fakty, komentari.* Lviv: LNB, 1996.

Kryciński, Stanisław. "Svidchennia Stanislava Krytsins'koho pro obstavyny vyiavlennia arkhivu Naukovoho tovarystva im. Shevchenka v budynku Natsional'noï biblioteky u Varshavi." In *Slidamy pam'iati: Litopysnyi kalendar.* Warsaw: Vyd-vo Ukraïns'kyi arkhiv, 1996, pp. 112–13.

Kryvadubskaia, Nataliia. "Materyialy pa historyi ŭ Belaruskai bibliiatetsy i muzei imia Frantsishka Skaryny ŭ Londane." In *Restitutsyia kul'turnykh kashtoŭnastsei,* pp. 169–75.

Kuhn, Petra. "Comment on the Soviet Returns of Cultural Treasures Moved because of the War to the GDR." *Spoils of War: International Newsletter* 2 (July 1996): 45–47.

Kuleshov, S. V., Iu. P. Sviridenko, O. V. Agafonov, and T. S. Kabochkina. *Natsional'nye otnosheniia v SSSR i sovetologiia: Tsentry, arkhivy, kontseptsii.* Moscow: MGIAI, 1988.

Kulishov, Valerii. "The History of the Soviet Repositories and Their Contents." In *The Spoils of War: WWII and Aftermath*, pp. 171–74.

Kuntze, Edward. "Sprawy rewindykacyjne. Prace Delegacji Polskiej w Moskwie i ich metoda." In *Pamiętnik IV Powszechnego Zjazdu Historyków Polskich w Poznaniu, 6–8 grudnia 1925*, vol. 1, section VIB. Lviv, 1925.

Kupchyns'kyi, Oleh Antonovych. "Vtracheni perhamentni hramoty mist i sil Halychyny XIV–pershoï polovyny XIX st." In *Bibliotekoznavstvo ta bibliohrafiia: Mizhvidomchyi respublikans'kyi zbirnyk statei* (Kyiv) 1982: 72–95.

Kurtz, Michael J. "The End of the War and the Occupation of Germany, 1944–1952: Laws and Conventions Enacted to Counter German Appropriations, the Allied Control Council." In *The Spoils of War: WWII and Aftermath*, pp. 112–16.

—. *Nazi Contraband: American Policy on the Return of European Cultural Treasures, 1945–1955*. New York: Garland Press, 1985.

Kuz'min, Evgenii. "Netrofeinaia istoriia." *Literaturnaia gazeta* 1990 (41): 10.
English edition: *The Literary Gazette International*, 1990 (17): 6.

—. "Neizvestnye stranitsy istorii nemetskikh bibliotechnykh kollektsii v gody Vtoroi mirovoi voiny." In *Restitutsiia bibliotechnykh sobranii*, pp. 17–24.

—. "Taina tserkvi v Uzkom." *Literaturnaia gazeta* 1990 (38) 18 September: 10.
English edition: "The Mystery of the Church in Uzkoye." *The Literary Gazette International* 16(2) October 1990: 20.

—. "Vyvesti…unichtozhit'…spriatat'…Sud'by trofeinykh arkhivov." (Interview with Patricia Kennedy Grimsted.) *Literaturnaia gazeta* 39 (2 October 1991): 13.

Lanskii, L. R., and V. A. Putintsev. "Rukopisi proizvedenii Gertsena v 'Prazhskoi' i 'Sofiiskoi' kollektsiiakh: Opisanie." *Literaturnoe nasledstvo* 63 (1956): 725–52.

Laskarzewska, Hanna. "Biblioteka króla Stanisława Augusta Poniatowskiego przechowywana w Kijowie." *Cenne, bezcenne/utracone—Valuable, priceless/lost* 1997 (4): 10–11.
Reprinted from *Dziennik Kijowski*, 1996, nos. 7, 8, 10, 12, and 14.
Ukrainian edition: forthcoming in *Bibliotechnyi visnyk*, 1999.

—. "Księgozbiór króla Stanisława Augusta Poniatowskiego w Kijowie: Historia, stan obecny, rejestracja." *Biuletyn Informacyjny Biblioteki Narodowej* 1996 (2[137]): 7–12.

Lazorenko, Iuliia. "Dolia bibliotek pid chas Druhoï svitovoï viiny." *Bibliotechnyi visnyk* 1995 (6): 8–10.

Lemmermeier, Doris. "Germany." *Spoils of War: International Newsletter* 2 (July 1996): 25–26.

—. "Germany." *Spoils of War: International Newsletter* 4 (1997): 78.

Lenz, Wilhelm. "Die Verlagerung des Revaler Stadtarchivs im Rahmen des 'Archivschutzes' während des Zweiten Weltkrieges." In *Reval: Handel und Wandel vom 13. bis zum 20. Jahrhundert*. Ed. Norbert Angermann and Wilhelm Lenz. Lüneburg: Institut Norddeutsches Kulturwerk, 1997, pp. 397–443. [=*Schriften der Baltischen Historischen Kommission*, 8.]

"Les archives secrètes du 2e Bureau sont demandées une nouvelle fois à la Russie par Paris." *Le Monde* 13 February 1992.

Leszczyński, Mariusz. "Archiwum Archidiecezji w Lubaczowie." *Archiwa, Biblioteki i Muzea Kościelne* 53 (1986): 57–66.

Lewick, Laura. "Return Art Stolen during Wars, Now." *Wall Street Journal* 16 February 1995: A12.

Lewis, Nigel. *Paperchase: Mozart, Beethoven, Bach. The Search for Their Lost Music*. London: Hamish Hamilton, 1981.

Losiievs'kyi, I. Ia., et al., comps. *Bibliotechni fondy Kharkova v roky Druhoï svitovoï viiny: Dokumenty*. Ed. I. O. Blokhina et al. Kyiv, 1997. [= *Dolia kul'turnykh skarbiv Ukraïny pid chas Druhoï svitovoï viiny: Arkhivy, biblioteky, muzeï*, 2.]

Lozenko, Liudmyla I. "Arkhivni vtraty Ukraïny: Vyvezene do Rosiï." *Pam'iatky Ukraïny* 1994 (3–6[26]): 87–91.

—. "O. Ohloblyn pro arkhiv Chornomors'koho flotu." *Pam'iatky Ukraïny* 1994 (3–6[26]): 116–19.

—. "Praz'kyi ukraïns'kyi arkhiv: Istoriia i s'ohodennia." *Arkhivy Ukraïny* 1994 (1–6): 18–30.

—. "Ukraïns'ki viis'kovi arkhivy—vidibrana spadshchyna." *Pam'iatky Ukraïny* 1994 (3–6[26]): 109–15.

—. "Z istorii Praz'koho ukraïns'koho arkhivu." In *Mizhnarodni zv'iazky Ukraïny: Naukovi poshuky i znakhidky*. Kyiv, 1997, pp. 85–94.

—, and Pavlo Sokhan'. "Povernuty pysemni skarby." *Kyïvs'ka starovyna* 1993 (2): 2–9.

—. "Vtrachene z arkhiviv. Chy nazavzhdy?..." *Literaturna Ukraïna* 1993 (3) 21 January (4516): 6.

Lozyts'kyi, Volodymyr S. *Istoriia mizhnarodnoho arkhivnoho spivrobitnytstva (1898–1998 rr.).* Kyiv, 1999.

—. "Pravovi zasady mizhnarodnoho spivrobitnytstva v haluzi restytutsiï arkhivnykh fondiv i dokumentiv: Istoriia, problemy, perspektyvy." In *"Pravovi aspekty restytutsiï,"* pp. 54–62.
Republished in *Arkhivy Ukraïny* 1997 (1–6): 15–22.

Machatková, Raisa [Makhatkova], comp. *Inventáře a katalogy fondů Státního ústředního archivu v Praze—Ukrajinské muzeum v Praze, UM, (1659) 1925–1948: Inventář/Inventari i katalohy fondiv Derzhavnoho tsentral'noho arkhivu v Prazi—Ukraïns'kyi muzei v Prazi, UM, (1659) 1925–1948: Opys fondu.* Kyiv and Prague: IUAD, 1996. [=Naukovo-dovidkovi vydannia z istoriï Ukraïny, 41.]

Magerovskii, Lev. *Bibliografiia gazetnykh sobranii Russkogo istoricheskogo arkhiva za gody 1917–1921.* Prague, 1939. [="Inventari Arkhiva Ministerstva vnutrennikh del v Prage," Ser. B, "Inventari RIA," 1]
Reprint edition: (with intro. by Richard Kneeley.) New York: Norman Ross Publishing, 1994.

Mahieu, Bernard. "Tableau historique des accords portant sur des transferts d'archives." In *Actes de la 17ème CITRA*, pp. 39–69.
Originally appended to Christian Gut, "Constitution et reconstitution."

Makarov, Vladimir. "Involuntary Journey of Books from Paris to Minsk." *Spoils of War: International Newsletter* 6 (February 99): 25–27.

Makashin, S. A. "'Sofiiskaia' kollektsiia rukopisei iz arkhiva Gertsena i Ogareva." *Izvestiia Akademii nauk SSSR. Otdelenie literatury i iazyka* 13 (1954) 5: 456–63.

Maksakova, Lidiia V. *Spasenie kul'turnykh tsennostei v gody Velikoi Otechestvennoi voiny.* Moscow, 1990.

Maksimova, Ella. "Arkhivnyi detektiv." *Izvestiia* 177 (25 June 1989): 4.

—. "Arkhivy frantsuzskoi razvedki skryvali na Leningradskom shosse." *Izvestiia* 240 (3 November 1991): 8.

—. "Arkhivy KPSS i KGB perekhodiat v sobstvennost' naroda." *Izvestiia* 205 (28/29 August, 1991): 3.

—. Comments in "Skandal, ne dostoinyi Rossii." *Izvestiia* 172 (8 September 1994): 5.

—. "Piat' dnei v osobom arkhive." *Izvestiia* 49–53 (17–21 February 1990).

—. "Sokrovishcha Rossii rasseiany po miru—Kak ikh vernut'?" *Izvestiia* 30 (16 February 1994): 7.

Maksimychev, Igor' F. "'Peremeshchennoe,' ne znachit 'nich'e': Nanesti ushcherb natsional'nym interesam mozhno i iz samykh blagorodnykh pobuzhdenii." *Nezavisimaia gazeta* 26 July 1996: 2.

Mal'dzis, Adam. "Byelorussia." *Spoils of War: International Newsletter* 5 (June 1998): 74.

—. "The Tragic Fate of Belarusan Museum and Library Collections during the Second World War." In *The Spoils of War: WWII and Aftermath*, pp. 77–80.

Mańkowski, Tadeusz. "Ossolineum pod rządami sowieckimi." *Czasopisma Zakładu Narodowego im. Ossolińskich* 1 (1992): 135–55.

Markina, Tat'iana. "Mozaiki Mikhailovskogo sobora mogut vernut'sia na Ukrainu." *Kommersant Daily* 119 (4 July 1998): 7.
  Includes short statements by Lidiia Iovleva, Deputy Director for Science, State Tret'iakov Gallery, "Togda schitali, chto…obmen ravnotsennyi"; Mikhail Piotrovskii, Director, State Hermitage, "Eksponaty mogut byt' vozvrashcheny"; Nikolai Grinev, of the Novgorod State Consolidated Museum-Preserve, "Takie voprosy dolzhny reshat'sia na urovne pravitel'stva"; and Protoierei Viktor Petliuchenko, Deputy Head of the Division of Foreign Church Relations, Moscow Patriarchate, "Freski i mozaiki dolzhny byt' vozvrashcheny tserkvi."

Mashchenko, Elena. "Ukrainskie arkhivy vozvrashchaiutsia na rodinu." *Zerkalo nedeli* 48 (29 November 1997) 165: 15.

Masterov, Valerii. "Reshenie o rasstrele prinimalos' v TsK." *Moskovskie novosti* 43 (25 October 1992): 9.

Materialy do rozrobky kontseptsiï diial'nosti Instytutu ukraïns'koï arkheohrafiï. Do Vseukraïns'koï narady "Ukraïns'ka arkheohrafiia s'ohodni: Problemy i perspektyvy." Kyïv, 16–18 hrudnia 1992 r. Kyiv, 1992. [="Problemy edytsiinoï ta kameral'noï arkheohrafii: Istoriia, teoriia, metodyka," 11.]

Matthäus, Jürgen. "'Weltanschauliche Forschung und Auswertung': Aus den Akten des Amtes VII im Reichssicherheitshauptamt." *Jahrbuch für Antisemitismus-Forschung* 5 (1997): 287–96.

Matveeva, Irina G. "Deiatel'nost' Tsentral'nogo khranilishcha muzeinykh fondov i primernye svedeniia o postupleniiakh knizhnykh fondov iz chisla vozvrashchennykh v Rossiiu." *Informatsionnyi biulleten' Rossiiskoi bibliotechnoi assotsiatsii* 11 (St. Petersburg, 1998): 174–88.

—. "Diial'nist' Tsentral'noho skhovyshcha muzeinykh fondiv po rozshuku vtrachenykh kul'turnykh tsinnostei u pershi povoienni roky." In *Materialy natsional'noho seminaru, Chernihiv, 1994*, pp. 243–46.

—. "Problemy vozvrashcheniia knizhnykh fondov." In *Lesy Belaruskikh materyial'nykh*, pp. 21–22.

Matwijów, Maciej. "Ewakuacja zbiorów polskich ze Lwowa w 1944 r." *Rocznik Lwowski* 1995/1996: 31–46.

—. "Mieczysław Gębarowicz (1893–1984), ostatni dyrektor lwowskiego Ossolineum." *Czasopismo Zakładu Narodowego im. Ossolińskich* 2 (1993): 9–71.

—. "Lwowskie Ossolineum w listach Mieczysława Gębarowicza z lat 1943–1946." *Czasopismo Zakładu Narodowego im. Ossolińskich* 1 (1992): 159–62.

—. *Walka o lwowskie dobra kultury w latach 1945–1948.* Wrocław: Towarzystwo Przyjaciół Ossolineum, 1996.

—. "Zbiory rękopiśmienne Zakładu Narodowego im. Ossolińskich we Lwowie w latach 1939–1946." *Czasopismo Zakładu Narodowego im. Ossolińskich* 10 (1999): 211–41.

—, et al. "Wniosek rewindykacyjny zbiorów Zakładu Narodowego im. Ossolińskich—Rękopisy." In *Wnioski rewindykacyjne*, pp. 36–47.

Mazur, Zygmunt, OP. "Dominikanie we Lwowie (1939–1946)." *Tygodnik Powszechny* 1990 (38).

Mazuritskii, Aleksandr M. *Ocherki istorii bibliotechnogo dela perioda Velikoi Otechestvennoi voiny, 1941–1945 gg.* Moscow: RGB–Moskovskii gosudarstvennyi universitet kul'tury, 1995.

—. "Restitutsiia knizhnykh sobranii." *Knizhnoe obozrenie* 1993 (3): 54–56.

Mękarski, S., and K. Remerowa. "Księgozbiór z Honfleur ks. Witolda Kazimierza Czartoryskiego w lwowskiej Bibliotece Uniwersyteckiej." Lviv, 1928.

Meshkov, Dmytro. *Dnipropetrovs'ki arkhivy, muzeï ta biblioteky v roky Druhoï svitovoï viiny: Anotovanyi perelik dokumentiv i materialiv.* Kyiv, 2000. [=Dolia kul'turnykh skarbiv Ukraïny pid chas Druhoï svitovoï viiny: Arkhivy, biblioteky, muzeï, 3; Problemy edytsiinoï ta kameral'noï arkheohrafiï: Istoriia, teoriia, metodyka, 24.]

—. "Dnipropetrovs'ki arkhivy pid chas Druhoï svitovoï viiny." *Materialy natsional'noho seminaru, Chernihiv, 1994*, pp. 188–93.

Meyer, Karl E. "Russia's Hidden Attic: Returning the Spoils of World War II." *New York Times* 1 February 1995: A20.

Meyer-Landrut, Joachim. "Die Behandlung von staatlichen Archiven und Registraturen nach Völkerrecht." *Archivalische Zeitschrift* 48 (1953): 45–120.

Mikhal'chanka, A. M., and T. A. Varab'iova, eds. *Dakumenty pa historyi Belarusi, iakiia zberahaiutstsa ŭ tsentral'nykh dziarzhaŭnykh arkhivakh SSSR.* Minsk: BSE im. P. Brouki, 1990.

Miler, Jacek. "Zbiory lwowskie (II): Księgozbiór z Honfleur." *Cenne, bezcenne/utracone—Valuable, priceless/lost* 4(16) August 1999: 23.

Misiło, Eugeniusz [Ievhen Misylo]. *Akcja "Wisła": Dokumenty.* Warsaw: Archiwum Ukraińskie, 1993.
Ukrainian edition: *Aktsiia "Visla": Dokumenty.* Trans. Ivan Svarnyk. Lviv and New York: NTSh, 1997. [=Ukraïnoznavcha biblioteka NTSh, 8].

—. "Etnotsyd: Etap I. Pereselennia ukraïntsiv z Pol'shchi v URSR 1944–1946." *Slidamy pam'iati: Litopysnyi kalendar* 1 (Warsaw, 1996): 31–108.

—. "Ukraïns'ki tsinnosti u varshavs'komu skhovyshchi." In *Slidamy pam'iati: Litopysnyi kalendar* 1 (Warsaw, 1996): 109–12.

—, ed. *Repatriacja czy deportacja: Przesiedlenie Ukraińców z Polski do USRR 1944–1946.* 2 vols. Warsaw: Archiwum Ukraińskie, 1996–1999.

Mosiakin, A. "Prodazha." *Ogonek* 6 (4–11 February 1989): 18–22; 7 (11–18 February 1989): 16–21; 8 (4–11 March 1989): 26–29.

Mozzati, Marco. "La battaglia degli archivi." In *La modernizzazione in Asia e Africa: Problemi di storia e problemi di metodo. Studi offerti a Giorgio Borsa.* Pavia: Ed. Viscontea, 1989, pp. 213–44.

Müller, Hartmut. "'...for safekeeping': Bremer Archivschutzmassnahmen im Zweiten Weltkrieg und ihre Folgen." In *Bremisches Jahrbuch* 66 (1988): 409–22. [=*Festschrift für Wilhelm Lührs und Klaus Schwarz.*]

Mushynka, Mykola. "Muzei vyzvol′noï borot′by Ukraïny u Prazi ta ioho ostannii dyrektor Symon Narizhnyi." In *"Russkaia, ukrainskaia i belorusskaia èmigratsiia,"* 1995, vol. 1, pp. 806–815.

—. *Muzei vyzvol′noï borot′by Ukraïny ta dolia ioho fondiv.* Melbourne: Monash University, Slavic Section, 1996.

Musial, Torsten. *Staatsarchive im Dritten Reich: Zur Geschichte des staatlichen Archivwesens in Deutschland, 1933–1945.* Potsdam: Verl. für Berlin-Brandenburg, 1996. [=Potsdamer Studien 2.]

Muzychuk, O. V. "Nove nadkhodzhennia TsDIAK Ukraïny." *Arkhivy Ukraïny* 1995 (1–3): 77–78.

Mykhal′chuk, Vasyl′. *Ukraïns′ka biblioteka im. Symona Petliury v Paryzhi: Zasnuvannia, rozvytok, diial′nist′ (1926–1998).* Kyiv: Vyd-vo im. Oleny Telihy, 1999.

Myronets′, N. "Dokumenty fonda Nikity Shapovala kak istochnik dlia izucheniia ukrainskoi èmigratsii v Chekhoslovakii (Tsentral′nyi gosudarstvennyi arkhiv vysshikh organov vlasti i upravleniia Ukrainy, g. Kiev)." In *"Russkaia, ukrainskaia i belorusskaia èmigratsiia,"* 1995, vol. 2, pp. 565–71.

"Nachinaem restituirovat′, no Germanii ne dadim nichego." *Kommersant* 127 (21 July 1999): 10.

Naumov, Oleg. "O mezhdunarodnom proekte komp′iuterizatsii Arkhiva Kominterna." *Nauchno-informatsionnyi biulleten′ RTsKhDNI* 10 (1998): 5–27.

Nicholas, Lynn. *The Rape of Europa: The Fate of Europe's Treasures in the Third Reich and the Second World War.* New York: Alfred A. Knopf, 1994.
German edition: *Der Raub der Europa.* Munich: Kindler Verlag, 1995.
Additional editions have appeared in Dutch, French, Japanese, Spanish, Polish, and Portuguese (in Brazil), among other languages.

Nikandrov, Nikolai. "Problemy vyiavleniia kul′turnykh tsennostei prinadlezhashchikh odnoi strane i peremeshchennykh na territoriiu drugoi strany v gody Vtoroi mirovoi voiny." In *Restytutsyia kul′turnykh kashtoŭnastsei,* pp. 58–67.

—. "Russia." *Spoils of War: International Newsletter* 6 (February 1999): 50–52.

—. "The Transfer of the Contents of German Repositories into the Custody of the USSR." In *The Spoils of War: WWII and Aftermath,* pp. 117–20.

Nikolayenko, Olena. "Mystery of Bach Archive Solved." *Kyiv Post* 32 (12 August 1999): 5.

Novikova, Elena E. "Nauchno-prakticheskaia konferentsiia 'Problemy zarubezhnoi arkhivnoi Rossiki.'" *Otechestvennye arkhivy* 1994 (2): 121–22.

Oldenhage, Klaus. "Bilateral and Multilateral Cooperation for the Reconstitution of the Archival Heritage." In *CITRA 1993–1995,* pp. 129–33.

Omel'chenko, Vasyl'. "Oleksander Ohloblyn (zhyttia i diial'nist')." In *Zbirnyk na poshanu prof. d-ra Oleksandra Ohloblyna/Collected Essays in Honor of Professor Alexander Ohloblyn.* New York, 1977, pp. 57–63. [=Ukraïns'ka Vil'na Akademiia Nauk u SShA, *Naukovyi zbirnyk* 3].

Paczkowski, Józef (Joseph). "La remise des actes en connexion avec les changements de frontières entre les États." In *La Pologne au V-e Congrès International des Sciences Historiques, Bruxelles 1923.* Warsaw, 1924, pp. 199–211.

Paszkiewicz, Urszula. *Inwentarze i katalogi bibliotek z ziem wschodnich Rzeczypospolitej (spis za lata 1553–1939).* Warsaw: Wyd-wo DiG, 1998. [=Polskie dziedzictwo kulturalne, Seria B: Wspólne Dziedzictwo.]

—. *Rękopiśmienne inwentarze i katalogi bibliotek z ziem wschodnich Rzeczypospolitej (spis za lata 1553–1939).* Warsaw: Wyd-wo DiG, 1996. [=Polskie dziedzictwo kulturalne, Seria B: Wspólne Dziedzictwo.]

Pavlova, Germaine. "The Fate of the Russian Imperial Libraries." *Bulletin of Research in the Humanities* 87(4) 1986–1987: 358–403.

—. "Prodazha Sovetskim Soiuzom knig iz bibliotek imperatorskoi familii, 1920–1930 gg." In *Books, Libraries and Information in Slavic and East European Studies: Proceedings of the Second International Conference of Slavic Librarians and Information Specialists.* Ed. Marianna Tax Choldin. New York: Russica Publishers, 1986, pp. 111–28.

Pavlova, Tat'iana F. "A. F. Iziumov i RZIA." *Otechestvennye arkhivy* 1996 (4): 28–37.

—. *Metodicheskie rekomendatsii po sostavleniiu mezharkhivnogo spravochnika po fondam byvshego Russkogo zagranichnogo istoricheskogo arkhiva v Prage (b. RZIA).* Moscow: TsGAOR SSSR, 1991.

—. "Russkii zagranichnyi istoricheskii arkhiv v Prage." *Voprosy istorii* 1990 (11): 19–30.

—, et al., eds. *Fondy Russkogo zagranichnogo istoricheskogo arkhiva v Prage: Arkhivnyi putevoditel'.* Comp. Ol'ga N. Kopyleva et al. Moscow: ROSSPEN, 1999.
    Publication subsidy was provided by a consortium of European research institutions—IISH (Amsterdam), BDIC (Paris-Nanterre), and the Feltrinelli Foundation (Milan). The guide appeared just as this study was going to press, but archivists at GA RF had discussed the production with me from the outset and kindly showed me copies of proof copies of appropriate chapters.

"Peredacha dokumentov Natsional'nomu arkhivu Frantsii." *Voprosy arkhivovedeniia* 1960 (6).

Pešák, V. "Zpráva o činnosti Ruského historického archivu, Ukrajinského historického kabinetu a Běloruského archivu v létech 1939–1946." *Ročenka slovanského ústavu v Praze*, vol. 12, *Za léta 1939–1946.* Prague, 1947, pp. 211–21.

Petropoulos, Jonathan. *Art as Politics in the Third Reich: The Collecting Policies of the Nazi Elite.* Chapel Hill: University of North Carolina Press, 1996.

Petrov, Ihor. "Nimets'ki foto vykryvaiut' zlochyny NKVS." *Chas* 27 February–5 March 1997: 71.

Petrov, Nikita. "Politika rukovodstva KGB v otnoshenii arkhivnogo dela byla prestupnoi…" *Karta: Nezavisimyi istoricheskii zhurnal* (Riazan) 1 (1993): 4–5.
    With documentary appendix: "Reshenie ob arkhivakh KGB" (signed by D. A. Volkogonov), pp. 6–7.

Petrusheva, Lidiia I. "Dokumenty prazhskoi kollektsii v nauchno-spravochnom apparate Gosudarstvennogo arkhiva Rossiiskoi Federatsii." In *"Russkaia, ukrainskaia i belorusskaia èmigratsiia,"* 1995, vol. 1, pp. 91–97.

Phillips, Geraldine N. "Duplication before Restitution: Costs and Benefits—the US Experience." In *CITRA 1993–1995*, pp. 167–71.

Pieyns, Jean. *Feasibility Study of a Data Base on National Historical Sources in Foreign Repositories.* Paris: UNESCO, 1981. (PGI-81/WS/25)
    Arabic, French, Russian, and Spanish editions are also available from UNESCO.

Piiuk, Boris. "Ty mne—Ia tebe." *Itogi* 16(49) 22 April 1997: 13–14.

Pijaj, Stanisław, comp. *Archiwa rodzinno-majątkowe w zbiorach
państwowych we Lwowie.* Warsaw: Ministerstwo Kultury i Sztuki, 1995.
[=Polskie dziedzictwo kulturalne, Seria B: Wspólne Dziedzictwo.]

Pikhoia, Rudol'f G. "Sotrudnichestvu s zarubezhnymi partnerami—ravnopravnuiu osnovu." (Interview by A. V. Shavrov.) *Otechestvennye
arkhivy* 1992 (2): 15–16.

Plokhy, Serhii M. "The History of a 'Non-Historical' Nation: Notes on the
Nature and Current Problems of Ukrainian Historiography." *Slavic
Review* 54(3) Fall 1995: 709–16.

Podaný, Václav, and Hana Barvíková, et al. *Russkaia i ukrainskaia
èmigratsiia v Chekhoslovatskoi respublike, 1918–1938: Putevoditel' po
arkhivnym fondam i sobraniiam v Cheshskoi respublike.* Trans. L'ubov
Beloševská and Marina Luptáková. Prague: Euroslavica, 1995. [="Trudy
po istorii Cheshskoi Akademii nauk/Studia Historiae Academiae
Scientiarum Bohemicae"; Sponsors: Arkhiv Akademii nauk Cheshskoi
respubliki; Literaturnyi arkhiv Muzeia natsional'noi literatury; and
Slavianskii institut AN ChR.]
A Czech edition was issued simultaneously.

Polian, Pavel. *Zhertvy dvukh diktatur: Ostarbaitery i voennoplennye v
Tret'em reikhe i ikh repatriatsiia.* Moscow: "Vash vybor TsIRZ," 1996.

Poloiushko, Hryhorii. "Pisliaslovo." In *Khronika 2000* 17–18 (1997):
365–67.
Photographs (with commentary) regarding the destruction of the Uspens'kyi
sobor, as a postscript to the article by Serhii Kot, "Zahybel' Uspens'koho soboru:
Versiï…" *Khronika 2000* 17–18 (1997): 348–64.

Pomrenze, Seymour J. "Offenbach Reminiscences and the Restitutions to the
Netherlands." In *Return of Looted Collections*, pp. 10–18.

—. "Policies and Procedures for the Protection, Use, and Return of Captured
German Records." In *Captured German Records*, pp. 5–30.

Popov, Andrei V. *Russkoe zarubezh'e i arkhivy: Dokumenty rossiiskoi
èmigratsii v arkhivakh Moskvy: Problemy vyiavleniia, komplektovaniia,
opisaniia, ispol'zovaniia.* Moscow: IAI RGGU, 1998. [=Materialy k
istorii russkoi politicheskoi èmigratsii, 4.]

Posner, Ernst. *Archives and the Public Interest: Selected Essays.* Ed. Ken
Munden. Washington, DC: Public Affairs Press, 1967.

—. "The Effect of Changes of Sovereignty on Archives." *American Archivist* 5(3) July 1942: 141–55.
Republished in his *Archives and the Public Interest,* pp. 168–81.

Poste, Leslie I. "Books Go Home from the Wars." *Library Journal* 73 (1 December 1948): 1699–1704.

—. *The Development of U.S. Protection of Libraries and Archives in Europe during World War II.* Fort Gordon, GA: U.S. Army Civil Affairs School, 1964.
Revised from a doctoral dissertation prepared at the University of Chicago, 1958.

Postnikov, Sergei Porfir´evich. *Politika, ideologiia, byt i uchenye trudy russkoi èmigratsii: 1918–1945: Bibliografiia. Iz kataloga biblioteki RZI arkhiva.* Ed. Sergei Blinov. 2 vols. Intro. by Edward Kasinec and Robert H. Davis, Jr. New York: Norman Ross Publishing, 1993.

Poświęcony profesorowi Mieczysławowi Gębarowiczowi w setną rocznicą urodzin. Wrocław, 1994. [= *Czasopismo Zakładu Narodowego im. Ossolińskich* 4 (1994).]

"Predlozheniia gruppy ekspertov gosudarstv-uchastnikov SNG dlia resheniia voprosov, sviazannykh s pravopreemstvom v otnoshenii gosudarst-vennykh arkhivov" Minsk, 23 April 1992. *Vestnik arkhivista* 1992 (3[9]): 10–11.

Prokopenko, Anatolii S. "Arkhivy frantsuzskoi razvedki skryvali na Leningradskom shosse." *Izvestiia* 240 (3 November 1991).

—. "Dom osobogo naznacheniia. (Otkrytie arkhivov.)" *Rodina* 1992 (3): 50–51.

Prott, Lyndel V. *Commentary on the UNIDROIT Convention on Stolen and Illegally Exported Cultural Objects, 1995.* Leicester: Institute of Art and Law, 1997.

—. "Principles for the Resolutions of Disputes Concerning Cultural Heritage Displaced during the Second World War." In *The Spoils of War: WWII and Aftermath,* pp. 225–30.

—. "The Role of UNESCO 'International Committee for Promoting the Return of Cultural Property' in the Resolution of Disputes Concerning Cultural Property Removed in Consequence of the Second World War." *Spoils of War: International Newsletter* 5 (June 1998): 59–61.

—, and P. J. O'Keefe. *Law and the Cultural Heritage.* Vol. 1: *Discovery and Excavation.* Professional Books Limited, 1984. Vol. 3: *Movement.*

London and Edinburgh: Butterworths, 1990.
When completed, this multivolume study should include a most definitive study
of many broader problems that will likewise affect archival migration and
restitution. The bibliography included is also of significance in bringing together
legal instruments from different countries and international organizations, as well
as the voluminous secondary literature on the subject. As announced in a recent
advertising brochure, the series published by Butterworths & Co Ltd., London,
the fifth volume is planned to cover legal principles and special regulations to
protect the cultural heritage.

—. *Handbook of National Regulations Concerning the Export of Cultural
Property/Manuel des réglementations nationales relatives à l'expor-
tation des biens culturels.* Paris, 1988. (CC–88/WS/27 Rev)
French edition: *Manuel des réglementations nationales relatives à
l'exportation des biens culturels.* Paris: UNESCO, 1988. (CC–88/WS/27
Rev)

—. *National Legal Control of Illicit Traffic in Cultural Property.* Paris, 1983.
(CLT–83/WS/16)
French edition: *Mesures législatives et réglementaires nationales visant
à lutter contre le trafic illicite de biens culturels.* Paris: UNESCO, 1983.
(CLT–83/WS/16)

Pruszyński, Jan. "Wniosek rewindykacyjny księgozbioru Witolda K.
Czartoryskiego z Oddziału Rzadkiej Książki Biblioteki Uniwersytetu im.
Iwana Franki." In *Wnioski rewindykacyjne,* pp. 103–106.

—, ed. *Wnioski rewindykacyjne księgozbioru Ossolineum oraz Dziel sztuki i
zabytków ze zbiorów lwowskich.* Warsaw: Ministerstwo Kultury i Sztuki,
1998, pp. 36–47. [=Polskie dziedzictwo kulturalne, Seria C: Materiały i
Dokumenty.]

Pshenichnyi, A. P. "Arkhivy na okkupirovannoi territorii v gody Velikoi
Otechestvennoi voiny." *Otechestvennye arkhivy* 1992 (4).

—. "Repressii arkhivistov v 1930-kh godakh." *Sovetskie arkhivy* 1988 (6):
44–48.

Pyrih, Ruslan [Ruslan Pirog]. "Arkhivy Kompartii Ukrainy: Problemy
intergratsii v sistemu gosudarstvennoi arkhivnoi sluzhby." In *Arkhivy
byvshikh KP,* pp. 64–66.

—. "'Ukraïns'kyi arkhiv' Mykyty Khrushchova: Problemy vidnovlennia ta
vykorystannia." In *Materialy natsional'noho seminaru, Chernihiv, 1994,*
pp. 182–87.

—. "Vylucheni dokumenty Mykyty Khrushchova." *Pam'iatky Ukraïny* 1994 (3–6[26]): 129–31.

"Return Bach to Germany." *Kyiv Post* 32 (12 August 1999).

Richards, Pamela Spence. "Scientific Communication in the Cold War: Margarita Rudomino and the Library of Foreign Literatures during the Last Years of Stalin." *Libraries and Culture* 31(1) Winter 1996: 235–46.

Rill, Gerhard, Elisabeth Springer, and Christiane Thomas. "60 Jahre österreichisch-jugoslawisches Archivübereinkommen. Eine Zwischenbilanz." *Mitteilungen des Österreichischen Staatsarchivs* 35 (1982): 288–331.

Rudomino, Adrian. "Knigi voiny." *Nashe nasledie* 49 (1999): 79–96.

—. "Polveka v plenu." *Nashe nasledie* 32 (1994): 92–96.

Rychkov, P. A. "Dzherela Rosiis′koho derzhavnoho voienno-istorychnoho arkhivu do istoriï mistobuduvannia u Pravoberezhnii Ukraïni." *Arkhivy Ukraïny* 1992 (5–6): 52–61.

Savitskii, P. N. *Razrushaiushchie svoiu rodinu (snos pamiatnikov iskusstva i rasprodazha muzeev SSSR).* Berlin: Izd. Evraziitsev, 1936.

Schädler, Patrik. "Fürstliches Hausarchiv und Sokolov-Archiv. Gestern begann der Austausch: Fürst Hans-Adam 'kauft' sein Eigentum zurück." *Liechtensteiner Vaterland* 172 (31 July 1997): 1.

Schieche, Emil. "Tyska Ordens arkiv, dess nuvarande ode och dess oppnande for vetenskaplig forskning." *Historisk tidskrift* 13(3) 1950: 185–97.

Schmidt, Wolfram "Übernahme von Archivgut aus der UdSSR." *Archiv-mitteilungen* 39(5) 1989: 179–80.

Schmitt, Jean-Marie. "UNESCO: Attacks on Cultural Property Criminalised. A New Protocol Allows for Prosecution of Organisations and Individuals, Putting Pressure on Art Market Professionals." *The Art Newspaper* 93 (June 1999): 6.

Schöbel, Gunter. "Eine kleine Geste an die Ukraine: Rückgabe von verschleppten Büchern." In *Displaced Books: Bücherrückgabe,* pp. 68–74.
Earlier published in *Der Rotarier* (Hamburg) 10 (October 1998): 22–27.

Schulze, Dorothee. *Die Restitution von Kunstwerken zur völkerrechtlichen Dimension der Restitutionsresolutionen der Generalversammlung der Vereinten Nationen.* Bremen: Übersee-Museum Bremen, 1983.

A doctoral dissertation that emphasizes works of art rather than archives, but
brings together a significant bibliography.

"Scripta Manent." *Bulletin of Central and East-European Activities* (IISH) 2
(August 1992): 3–4.

Sebta, Tet′iana [Tat′iana] M. "Kolektsiia dokumentiv Shtazi iak dzherelo
doslidzhennia doli ukraïns′kykh kul′turnykh tsinnostei pid chas Druhoï
svitovoï viiny." *Arkhivy Ukraïny* 1995 (1–3): 69–76.

—. "Kyïvs′ka chastyna materialiv Ainzatsshtabu reikhsliaitera Rozenberga."
Arkhivy Ukraïny 1997 (1–6): 53–73

Sedel′nikov, Valerii. "Arkhiv, o kotorom dolgo molchali." (Interview with
Natal′ia Davydova.) *Moskovskie novosti* 15 (15 March 1990): 16.

Selavinskii, Mikhail. In *Kul′tura* 15 (17 April 1997): 1.

"Semper Manent." *Bulletin of Central and East-European Activities* (IISH) 3
(September 1992): 4.

Sevast′ianov, Aleksandr. "Bol′she, chem trofei—Polemika…s Igorem
Maksimychevym." *Nezavisimaia gazeta* 14 September 1996: 6.

Shepelev, Valerii N. "Novye fakty o sud′be dokumentov 'Smolenskogo
arkhiva' (po materialam RTsKhIDNI)." In *Problemy zarubezhnoi
arkhivnoi Rossiki*, pp. 124–33.

—, ed. "Sud′ba 'Smolenskogo arkhiva.'" *Izvestiia TsK KPSS* 1991 (5):
135–38.

Shvydkoi, Mykhail E. In *Kul′tura* 15 (17 April 1997): 1.

Sibille, Claire. "Les Archives du Ministère de la Guerre recupérées de
Russie." *Gazette des Archives* 176 (1997): 64–77.

Sidorov, Evgenii. "Foreword." In *Five Centuries of European Drawings: The
Former Collection of Franz Koenigs: Exhibition Catalogue,
2.10.1995–21.01.1996.* Milan: Leonardo Arte, 1995, p. [5]. [Sponsors:
Ministry of Culture of the Russian Federation; Pushkin State Museum of
Fine Arts.]

—. "U Zolota Shlimana ne mozhet byt′ 'khoziaina,' Ne politicheskie
spekulianty, a zakon i zdravyi smysl dolzhny reshit′ sud′bu
peremeshchennykh tsennostei." *Izvestiia* 159 (25 August 1995): 9.

Siehr, Kurt. "Comment on the Russian Federal Law of 1997 on Cultural
Valu[abl]es." *Spoils of War: International Newsletter* 4 (August 1997):
38–39.

Siemieński, Józef (Joseph). "Respect des fonds. Application internationale." In *VIIIè Congrès International des Sciences Historiques, Zurich 1938. Communications Présentées*, vol. 1. Paris, n.d., pp. 63–65.

—. "Rewindykacja Archiwów Koronnych." *Archeion* 1 (1927): 33–60.

Simpson, Elizabeth, ed. *The Spoils of War: World War II and Its Aftermath. The Loss, Reappearance, and Recovery of Cultural Property*. New York: Harry N. Abrams, 1997.

Slezkine, Yuri. "Can We Have Our Nation-State and Eat It Too?" *Slavic Review* 54(3) Fall 1995: 717–19.

Snyder, Timothy. "'To Resolve the Ukrainian Question Once and For All': The Ethnic Cleansing of Ukrainians in Poland, 1943–1947." *Journal of Cold War Studies* 1(2) 1999: 86–120.

—. *The Reconstruction of Nations: Poles, Ukrainians, Lithuanians, Belarusians, 1569–1999*. New Haven: Yale University Press, 2001.

Sokhan', Pavlo. "Stan i perspektyvy rozvytku ukraïns'koï arkheohrafiï." *Ukraïns'kyi arkheohrafichnyi shchorichnyk*, n.s. 1 (1992): 9–18. [=Ukraïns'kyi arkheohrafichnyi zbirnyk, 4.]

—, and Vasyl' Danylenko. "Perspektyvy diial'nosti viddilu vyvchennia ta publikatsiï zarubizhnykh dzherel z istoriï Ukraïny." *Ukraïns'kyi arkheohrafichnyi shchorichnyk*, n.s. 1 (1992): 42–45. [=Ukraïns'kyi arkheohrafichnyi zbirnyk, 4.]

—, and Liudmyla Lozenko. "Povernuty pysemni skarby." *Kyïvs'ka starovyna* 1993 (2): 2–9.

—. "Vtrachene z arkhiviv. Chy nazavzhdy?..." *Literaturna Ukraïna* 1993 (3) 21 January 1993 (4516): 6.

Sokolov, Nikolai A. *Ubiistvo Tsarskoi sem'i*. Berlin: Slovo, 1925.
  An account of the assassination of the imperial family in 1918 by an investigator in the Okhrana, with related documentation.

"Spoils of War." *The Economist* 15 April 1995: 80.

"Spravedlivoe reshenie v nespravedlivykh obstoiatel'stvakh." *Kul'tura* 27 (29 July–4 August 1999): 1.

"Sprawozdanie z wyjazdu do Przemyśla w dn. 23.X.–1.XI.46 r. (4.II.1946)." In *Slidamy pam'iati: Litopysnyi kalendar* (Warsaw) 1 (1996): 134–35.

Starostin, Evgenii Vasil'evich. "Professor Starostin o zatronutoi probleme." *Otechestvennye arkhivy* 1992 (4): 26–27.

Stepanskii, Aleksandr D. "Arkheografiia: Termin, ob″ekt, predmet." *Otechestvennye arkhivy* 1996 (3): 16–25.

—. "K 225-letiiu russkoi arkheografii." *Otechestvennye arkhivy* 1992 (6): 16–24.

Stępniak, Władysław. "Klauzule archiwalne Konwencji Wiedeńskiej z 8 IV 1983 roku." *Archeion* 79 (1985): 5–38.

—. *Sukcesja państw dotycząca archiwaliów.* Warsaw: PWN, 1989.

Stroev, Evgenii. "Pora poniat′: My nikomu nichego ne dolzhny." *Rossiiskaia gazeta* 4 August 1994: 7.

Stuzhynskaia, Nina. "Materyialy pa historyi Belarusi u Ruskim zamezhnym histarychnym arkhive." In *Restytutsyia kul′turnykh kashtoŭnastsei*, pp. 188–92.

Suchodolski, W. "Wykonanie art. XI traktatu ryskiego w zakresie archiwów państwowych." *Archeion* 1 (1927): 66–78.

Sukhova, Svetlana. "Iskusstvo dolzhno prinadlezhat′ . . . " *Segodnia* 54 (19 March 1997): 3.

Surmach, Hanna (A.) "Belorusskii zagranichnyi arkhiv." In *"Russkaia, ukrainskaia i belorusskaia èmigratsiia," 1995*, vol. 1, pp. 85–90.

—. "Poshuki strachanykh arkhivaŭ pa historyi belaruskai dziarzhaŭnastsi (Praha, Maskva, Paryzh)." In *Restytutsyia kul′turnykh kashtoŭnastsei*, pp. 185–88.

Svarnyk, Halyna. "Arkhiv Dmytra Dontsova." *Pam'iatky Ukraïny* 1994 (3–6[26]): 122–28.

—. "Arkhiv Naukovoho tovarystva im. Shevchenka v Natsional′nii bibliotetsi u Varshavi." In *Z istoriï Naukovoho tovarystva imeni Shevchenka.* Lviv: NTSh, 1998. [=*Pratsi sesii, konferentsii, sympoziumiv, kruhlykh stoliv*, 10.]

—. "Arkhiv Naukovoho tovarystva im. Shevchenka zi L′vova v Natsional′nii bibliotetsi u Varshavi." In *Slidamy pam'iati: Litopysnyi kalendar* 1 (Warsaw, 1996): 114–23.

—. "L′vivs′ki zbirky u Varshavi (Arkhiv Naukovoho tovarystva im. Shevchenka v Natsional′nii bibliotetsi u Varshavi)." *Halyts′ka brama* 12(36) December 1997: 12.

—, comp. "Spysok materialiv z arkhivu Naukovoho tovarystva im. Shevchenka u L′vovi, iaki teper zberihaiut′sia u Viddili rukopysiv

Natsional'noï biblioteky u Varshavi." In *Slidamy pam'iati: Litopysnyi kalendar* 1 (Warsaw, 1996): 124–27.

"Swap of Archives." *China Daily* 5 September 1996.

"Taina 'Gotskoi biblioteki.'" *Pravda* 11 May 1994: 1, 3.

Tarasov, Igor' N., and Tat'iana N. Viktorova. "Novye aspekty sotrudnichestva Rosarkhiva s ministerstvami i vedomstvami." *Otechestvennye arkhivy* 1995 (2): 15–19.

Tarasov, Vladimir P. "The Return of Archival Documents Moved to the USSR as a Result of World War II." *Spoils of War: International Newsletter* 6 (February 1999): 53–55.

—. "Soglashenie arkhivnykh sluzhb Rossii i Pol'shi." *Otechestvennye arkhivy* 1992 (4): 120–21.

Teteriatnikov, Vladimir M. "'Kholodnaia voina' za muzeinymi shtorami—Kak rossiiskie iskusstvovedy sdaiut v plen shedevry, okazavshiesia v SSSR posle pobedy nad Germaniei v 1945 godu." *Pravda* 29 March 1995: 4.

—. "Ograbiat li vnov' russkii narod? Tragicheskaia sud'ba kul'turnykh tsennostei, peremeshchennykh v rezul'tate Vtoroi mirovoi voiny." *Pravda* 73 (22 May 1996): 4.

—. *Problema kul'turnykh tsennostei peremeshchennykh v rezul'tate Vtoroi mirovoi voiny: Dokazatel'stvo rossiiskikh prav na "kollektsiiu Kenigsa."* Moscow and Tver: Obozrevatel', 1996. [=*Obozrevatel'/Observer: Informatsionno-analiticheskii zhurnal,* special issue.]

Tikhvinskii, Sergei L. "Pomoshch' Sovetskogo Soiuza drugim gosudarstvam v vossozdanii natsional'nogo arkhivnogo dostoianiia." *Sovetskie arkhivy* 1979 (2): 11–16.

Tolz, Vera. "New Situation for CPSU and KGB Archives." in RFE/RL *Report on the USSR* 3(38) 20 September 1991: 1–4.

—. "The Katyn Documents and the CPSU Hearings." *RFE/RL Research Report* 1(44) 6 November 1992: 27–33.

Tsaplin, Vsevolod Vasil'evich. "Arkhivy, voina i okkupatsiia (1941–1945 gody)." Moscow, 1968. Typescript with hand corrections by the author, signed and dated 20 January 1969.
    The author kindly made a copy of his typescript available to me in 1991. It has since been deposited with his personal papers in RGAE, 777/1/11.

—. "O prave sobstvennosti na arkhivnye dokumenty v diplomaticheskikh aktakh dorevoliutsionnoi i sovetskoi Rossii." *Otechestvennye arkhivy* 1992 (4): 20–25.

—. "O rozyske dokumentov, pokhishchennykh v gody voiny iz arkhivo-khranilishch SSSR." *Otechestvennye arkhivy* 1997 (5): 7–25; and (6): 12–28.

—. "Spravka o dokumental'nykh materialakh, peredannykh pravitel'stvam inostrannykh gosudarstv." Typescript with handwritten corrections added and signed by V. V. Tsaplin (3 February 1969).

Tumarkin, Nina. "The Great Patriotic War as Myth and Memory." *The Atlantic* 1991 (6) June (267): 26–44.

—. *The Living and the Dead. The Rise and Fall of the Cult of World War II in Russia.* New York: Basic Books, 1994.

—. "The War of Remembrance." In *Culture and Entertainment in Wartime Russia.* Ed. Richard Stites. Bloomington: Indiana University Press, 1995, pp. 194–207.

Tyszkowski, Kazimierz. "Rewindykowane rękopisy Biblioteki Publicznej w Petersburgu." *Pamiętnik IV Powszechnego Zjazdu Historyków Polskich w Poznaniu, 6–8 grudnia 1925.* Vol. 2: *Protokoły,* pt. 2, *Dodatki.* Lviv, 1925, pp. 230–36.

"Ukrainskie tsennosti ostalis' v Rossii." *Kommersant Daily* 119 (4 July 1998): 7.
    Reprinted in *Kievskie vedomosti* 1 August 1998: 10.

Ul'ianovs'kyi, Vasyl'. "Do kontseptsiï naukovo-doslidnoï ta vydavnychoï diial'nosti naukovo-informatsiinoho viddilu." *Ukraïns'kyi arkheo-hrafichnyi shchorichnyk,* n.s. 1 (1992): 47–53.

Vdovina, Natal'ia. "Prizraki trofeinogo arkhiva: Kniaz' fon Likhtenshtein, shtabs-kapitan Sokolov i deputaty Gosdumy RF." *Rossiiskie vesti* 186 (2 October 1996): 1–2.

Verlagert—Verschollen—Vernichtet: Das Schicksal der im 2. Weltkrieg aus-gelagerten Bestände der Preußischen Staatsbibliothek. Berlin: Staats-bibliothek zu Berlin-Preußischer Kulturbesitz, 1995.

V'ialets', Adriana. "Svit maie pochuty," with the appended "Spysok predmetiv iz muzeïv Ukraïny: U zbirkakh muzeïv ta inshykh skhovyshch Rosiï." *Pam'iatky Ukraïny* 1994 (1–2[25]): 84–91.
    Reprinted as document no. 208 in *Ukraïna v mizhnarodno-pravovykh vidnosynakh,* book 2, pp. 768–79.

Visti Muzeiu vyzvol'noï borot'by Ukraïny. Prague, 1925–1944. [Microfiche ed.: IDC-R-14,894.]
Edited by D. V. Antonovych. Only the first 22 issues (Prague, 1925–1938) were included in the microfiche edition, as copies of the others were not available at the time it was prepared.

Voigt, Gudrun. *Die kriegsbedingte Auslagerung von Beständen der Preußischen Staatsbibliothek und ihre Rückführung*. Hannover: Laurentius Verlag Raimund Dehmlow, 1995. [=Kleine historische Reihe, 8.]

Von Hagen, Mark. "Does Ukraine Have a History?" *Slavic Review* 54(3) Fall 1995: 658–73.

von Jena, Kai, and Wilhelm Lenz. "Die deutschen Bestände im Sonderarchiv in Moskau." *Der Archivar* 45(3) 1992: 457–67.

"Vozvrashchenie ganzeiskikh arkhivov." *Sovetskie arkhivy* 1991 (1): 111.

de Vries, Willem. *Sonderstab Musik: Music Confiscations by the Einsatzstab Reichsleiter Rosenberg under the Nazi Occupation of Western Europe*. Amsterdam: Amsterdam University Press, 1996.
German edition: *'Sonderstab Musik'—Organisierte Plünderungen in Westeuropa 1940–45*. Foreword by Fred K. Prieberg. Köln: Dittrich Verlag, 1998.

Vrublevskaia, Valentina, and Sergei Kot. "Cultural Property of the Ukraine Lost as a Result of World War II—Problems of Research and Restitution." In *Cultural Treasures 1994*, pp. 120–21.

Walichnowski, Tadeusz. *Przynależność terytorialna archiwaliów w stosunkach międzynarodowych*. Warsaw: PWN, 1977.

Walter, Bernhard. *Rückführung von Kulturgut im internationalen Recht*. Bremen, 1988. [=Veröffentlichung aus dem Übersee-Museum Bremen," Reihe D, Band 14(15).]
Surveys different international legal ramifications of claims for cultural restitution, although the emphasis is on general cultural property (a chapter deals with the Elgin Marbles).

Wegner, Bernd. "Deutsche Aktenbestände im moskauer Zentralen Staatsarchiv. Ein Erfahrungsbericht." *Vierteljahrshefte für Zeitgeschichte* 40(2) 1992: 311–19.

Welter, Friedrich. "Die Musikbibliothek der Sing-Akademie zu Berlin." In *Sing-Akademie zu Berlin: Festschrift zum 175 jährigen Bestehen*. Ed. Werner Bollert. Berlin: Rembrandt Verlag, 1966, pp. 33–47.

Whitehead, P. J. P. "The Lost Berlin Manuscripts." *Notes* 33(1) September 1976: 7–15.

Williams, Robert C. *Russian Art and American Money, 1900–1940.* Cambridge, MA: Harvard University Press, 1980.

Wolfe, Robert, ed. *Captured German and Related Records: A National Archives Conference.* Athens, OH: Ohio University Press, 1974. [=National Archives Conferences, vol. 3.]

—. "Sharing Records of Mutual Archival Concern to the Federal Republic of Germany and the United States of America." In *Proceedings of the Xth Congress of the International Council on Archives.* Bonn, 1984, pp. 292–302. [=*Archivum*, 32.]

Wolfgang, Ulrich. "The Material Losses of the German Freemasons." *Spoils of War: International Newsletter* 3 (1996): 18–21.

Wolff, Christoph. "From Berlin to Łódź: The Spitta Collection Resurfaces." *Notes* (December 1989): 311–27.

Wolton, Thierry. "L'histoire de France dormait à Moscou." (Interview with Anatolii Prokopenko.) *L'Express* 21 November 1991.

Wooley, Leonard. *A Record of the Work Done by the Military Authorities for the Protection of the Treasures of Art and History in War Areas.* London: HMSO, 1946.

Wróbel-Lipowa, Krystyna. *Rewindykacja archiwaliów polskich z ZSRR w latach 1945–1964.* Habilitation diss., Uniwersytet Marii Curie-Skłodowskiej (Lublin), 1982. [=Rozprawy Wydziału Humanistycznego, Rozprawy hablitacyjne, 26.]

Wyczawski, Hieronim Eugeniusz, OFM. *Przygotowanie do studiów w archiwach kościelnych.* s.l.: Wyd-wo "Calvarianum," 1989[1990].

Zaiets', Vasyl'. "Svoia maty naidorozhcha." *Kul'tura i zhyttia* 11 (September 1996): 1.

Zapevalov, Valentin. "Igra v ambitsii: Na konu bol'shie kul'turnye tsennosti." *Literaturnaia gazeta* 32 (7 August 1996): 9.

Zielińska, Teresa. "Zbiór archiwalny Aleksandra Czołowskiego w zasobie Archiwum Głównego Akt Dawnych." *Archeion* 89 (1991): 38–60.

Zhitomirskaia, Sara V., L. V. Gapochko, and B. A. Shlikhter. "Arkhiv V. D. Bonch-Bruevicha." *Zapiski Otdela rukopisei* 25 (1962): 7–79.

Zhukov, Iurii N. *Operatsiia Èrmitazh: Opyt istoriko-arkhivnogo rassledovaniia.* Moscow: Moskvitianin, 1993.

Zhukov, Maksim, et al. "Nachinaem restituirovat', no Germanii ne dadim nichego." *Kommersant* 127 (21 July 1999): 10.
Includes interviews and statements about the Constitutional Court decision regarding the law on cultural treasures by Minister of Culture Vladimir Egorov, Mikhail Piotrovskii, and others.

Zhurba, Oleh I. *Kyïvs'ka Arkheohrafichna komisiia, 1843–1921. Narys istoriï i diial'nosti.* Kyiv, 1993.
Based on the author's candidate dissertation defended in 1989 in Dnipropetrovsk.

—. "Problemy ta perspektyvy doslidzhennia diial'nosti Kyïvs'koï Arkheohrafichnoï komisiï." In *Materialy iuvileinoï konferentsiï, prysviachenoï 150-richchiu Kyïvs'koï Arkheohrafichnoï komisiï (Kyïv, Sedniv, 18–21 zhovtnia 1993 r.)* Ed. Pavlo Sokhan' and Hennadii Boriak. Kyiv, 1997, pp. 34–50. [="Problemy edytsiinoï ta kameral'noï arkheohrafiï: Istoriia, teoriia, metodyka," 30.]

Zh[ylets'kyi], H. P. "Peredacha arkhivnykh materialov Ukrainy." *Arkhivnoe delo* 1926 (8–9): 117–23.

Zhyvotko, Arkadii. *Desiat' rokiv Ukraïns'koho istorychnoho kabinetu (1930–1940).* Prague, 1940. [=Inventari Arkhivu Ministerstva vnutrishnikh sprav, series S, 1; Microfiche (1988): IDC-R-14,920.]
Reprint edition: Norman Ross Publishing, New York, 1994.
Drafts and proofs remain in TsDAVO, 3866/1/21 and 22, and also an untitled and undated copy as 3866/3/3.

Bibliographies of Note for Secondary Literature

Berkhoff, Karel C. "Ukraine under Nazi Rule (1941–1944): Sources and Finding Aids." *Jahrbücher für Geschichte Osteuropas* 45(1) (1997): 85–103; 45(2) (1997): 273–309.

Brun, Peter. *"Beutekunst" : Materialien zu einer Bibliographie des neueren Schrifttums über das Schicksal des im Zweiten Weltkrieg von der Roten Armee in Deutschland erbeuteten Kulturgutes (Musems-, Archiv- und Bibliotheksbestände).* Berlin: Staatsbibliothek zu Berlin-Preußicher Kulturbesitz, 1997. [=Literaturnachweise zu aktuellen Russland-Themen, 1; Staatsbibliothek zu Berlin–Preußicher Kulturbesitz, Veröffentlichungen der Osteuropa–Abteilung, vol. 21.]

Rossika. Vyiavlenie i vozvrashchenie zarubezhnykh arkhivnykh dokumentov: Teoriia, praktika, opyt: Operativnyi vypusk.

No. 1: *Bibliograficheskii ukazatel' otechestvennoi literatury.* Moscow, 1993.

No. 2: *Bibliograficheskii ukazatel' zarubezhnoi literatury.* Moscow, 1993.

Zarubezhnaia arkhivnaia Rossika: Part 1: *Ukazatel' opublikovannykh materialov v fondakh NBFA.* Moscow, 1993. Part 2: *Knigi na inostrannykh iazykakh.* Moscow, 1993– .

Internet Resources[*]

"ArcheoBiblioBase" (Ukraine) website: <http://www.huri.harvard.edu/ abbukr/index.html>.
> With updated information on Ukrainian archives, now maintained by the Harvard Ukrainian Research Institute website at Harvard University.

"Archives of Russia" ArcheoBiblioBase website: <http://www.iisg.nl/~abb>.
> With updated information on Russian archives, now maintained by IISH, can be accessed through the IISH/IISG website out of Amsterdam.

Russian version: <http://www.openweb.ru/rusarch>

"Archives of Ukraine." Official website of the State Committee on Archives of Ukraine (DKAU; site in Ukrainian): <http://www.scarch.kiev.ua>.

International Council on Archives website: <http://www.ica.org>.

"Project for Documentation of Wartime Cultural Losses" website: <http://docproj.loyola.edu>.
> Provides the text of the Russian law and English translation: "Federal Law on Cultural Valuables Displaced to the U.S.S.R. as a Result of World War II and Located in the Territory of the Russian Federation"—an authoritative English-language translation by Konstantin Akinsha and Lynn Visson, together with the original Russian text. Also provides a succinct summary of the major provisions of the law and advice for prospective claimants.

Rosarkhiv website: <http://www.rusarchives.ru>

Spoils of War website: <http://www.beutekunst.de> and <http://www.lostart.de>
Russian versions: <http://www.Spoils.libfl.ru/>; <http://www.libfl.ru/restitution>

---

[*]   These selected websites listed below have been verified as of May 2001.

UNESCO website: <http://www.unesco.org/>.
  cultural property: <http://www.unesco.org/culture/legalprotection/>.
  bibliography: <http://unesdoc.unesco.org/ulis/unesbib.html>.

United Nations website: <http://www.un.org/>.
  Treaty collection: <http://untreaty.un.org/>.

United States. Department of State website: <http://www.state.gov/>.
  Webpage on Holocaust Issues:
  <http://www.state.gov/www/regions/eur/holocausthp.html>.
  Webpage for Washington Conference on Holocaust-Era Assets:
  <http://www.state.gov/www/regions/eur/holocaust/heac.html>.
  Also provides access to the downloadable conference proceedings.

United States Holocaust Memorial Museum website:
  <http://www.ushmm.org>.
  Provides inventories of Holocaust-related archival materials held on microfilm by
  the Holocaust Museum and links to other Holocaust-era assets sites.

United States. National Archives and Records Administration. Website on
  Holocaust Assets:
  <http://www.nara.gov/research/assets/>.

VGBIL website: <http://www.libfl.ru/restitution>
  Provides full texts of Russian 1998 law on World War II cultural property,
  amendments made in 2000, and related documents. Presents conference reports,
  bibliography, and Russian translations of *Spoils of War: International Newsletter.*

Index

A
Abramchyk, Mikola, 337
Academy of Architecture of the UkrSSR,
    trophy books, 265
Academy of Music, National (*earlier*,
    Kyiv Conservatory), trophy
    musicalia, 273, 275–76, 464
Academy of Sciences, All-Ukrainian
    (VUAN)
    Institute of Jewish Proletarian Culture,
        Kyiv, 230, 242–43, 481
    Museum of Art, 169
Academy of Sciences, Russian Imperial
    archeographic expeditions in Ukrainian
        lands, 64, 151
Academy of Sciences of the UkrSSR
    (AN UkrSSR)
    and Ossolineum, 430 (*See also*
        Ossolineum)
        Ossolineum Commission (1989), 435
    post-World War II reparations, 251
    trophy books, 264
    See also individual institutes and
        libraries
Academy of Sciences of the USSR (AN
    SSSR)
    archeographic expeditions in the
        UkrSSR, 64
    and RZIA transfer from Prague, 364,
        366–67, 374
    See also individual institutes and
        libraries
Academy of Sciences of Ukraine,
    National (NAN). *See individual*
    institutes and libraries
access, archival
    ICA recommendations, 90, 487
    mutual Russian-Ukrainian, and 1995
        agreement, 492
    Ossolineum collection in Lviv, 427
    post-1991 Ukraine
        émigré materials, 382–85
        and reference needs, 383–87, 493
        and spoils of war, 466
    Russian, post-1991 restrictions, 35,
        110, 249, 255, 384–85, 419–22,
        477–78
    in Russian law, post-1991, 29–31

Soviet-period restrictions, 3, 45, 427
    for Ukrainians in Germany, 462
    See also declassification, archival; *and*
        reference facilities and finding aids,
        archival
Adler, Friederich, papers, 292, 305
AGAD (Archiwum Główne Akt
    Dawnych), 292n34, 588
    Baworowski Collection, 446
    Czołowski Collection, 441–42
Agitprop (Agitation and Propaganda
    Division), CPSU. *See* Communist
    Party of the Soviet Union (CPSU)
Agricultural Academy, Ukrainian,
    Poděbrady, 343, 344, 348–49
Akinsha, Konstantin, xlvi, 248, 250n5,
    252, 254, 255, 477
Aksel′rod, Pavel, papers, 292
Akulenko, Viktor, 405–406
Aleksandrov, Grigorii, 282
Aleksandrova, Olena, 229, 267n53
Alford, Kenneth D., 237
All-Russian (*earlier*, All-Union)
        Scientific-Research Institute for
        Documentation and Archival
        Affairs (VNIIDAD), 43, 79, 81
Allied Control Council (Germany, 1945–
        1949), records, 469, 477
Amber Chamber at Tsarskoe Selo
    (Pushkin), plundered by Künsberg
    Commandos, 182
Amsterdam
    International Institute of Social History
        (IISH/IISG)
        and ArchioBiblioBase Project,
            xxxvii–xxxviii, 692
        plundered records from, 292, 304–
            305
        and rescue of displaced archives, 107,
            412
        return of looted books from Russia,
            394
    symposium on restitution of WWII
        displaced cultural treasures (1996),
        472–73
    University of Amsterdam
        library restitution from Russia, 258–
            59, 394

Rosenberg, Alfred, 200, 315, 343. *See also* ERR
Roskomarkhiv. *See* Rosarkhiv
Rossica, archival
  barter with trophy archives for retrieval, 411–17
  defining, xxxv, 22, 92, 155, 332, 333, 412
  Moscow conference on (1993), xxxviii, 22, 412–13
  trophy Rossica in Moscow, 374–77
  and Ucrainica, xxxv, xxxviii, 16, 21–22, 46–47, 155, 491
  and typology of, 21–22, 137–74
  See also RZIA; *and* Ucrainica
Rothschild banks, looted records, 290
royal families, European, plundered files, 290, 304
RSFSR. *See* Russian Soviet Federated Socialist Republic (RSFSR)
RSHA (Reichssicherheitshauptamt; Reich Security Main Office)
  Amt IV (Gestapo)
    files in Kyiv, 324
    plundered French archives, 296–301
    Soviet-seized files from Kherson, 291
  Amt VII (Ideological Research and Analysis), plundered archives, 201, 288–96, 305, 309, 321, 359, 494
  records (captured) of
    in Germany, 585, 586
    in Moscow, 288, 292–95, 359, 392n11
    in Warsaw, 295–96, 585, 615
RTsKhIDNI (Russian Center for Preservation and Study of Documents on Modern History). *See* RGASPI
Rudomino, Adrian, 262
Rudomino, Margarita, 226–28, 258–259, 261–62, 263–66
Rudychiv, Ivan, papers, 358
RUP. *See* Revolutionary Ukrainian Party (RUP), archives
Rus´, 32–33. *See also* "Kyivan Rus´"; *and* Ruthenia, local records from
Russian Art, Kyiv Museum of, 59, 316
Russian Center for Preservation and Study of Documents on Modern History (RTsKhIDNI, *earlier,* TsPA, *now* RGASPI). *See* RGASPI
Russian Cultural-Historical Museum (Prague), archives, 365, 368, 373

Russian Empire, 31, 32, 33, 375, 490, 492
  Archive of Foreign Policy of (AVPRI), 65
  Imperial Academy of Sciences, 64
  post-World War I breakup of, 84, 490
  State Archive of (pre-1917, St. Petersburg), 24, 65
  succession of States, and archival devolution, 23, 38–41, 85–87, 490
  post-WWI to Poland, 86–87
  Ukrainian territories, 2, 3, 47, 155–56
Russian Federation
  archival agreement with United Kingdom, 417
  Archival Fond of (*See* Archival Fond of the Russian Federation)
  archival law, "Basic Legislation" (1993), 29–37, 110, 111, 113, 173, 398
  Central Cartographic-Geodesic Fond, 36, 147
  Central State Fond of Standards and Technical Conditions, 36, 147
  Commission on Restitution, 180
  cultural agreement with Ukraine (1994), 492–93
  cultural treasures nationalization law (1998), xlvii, 18, 253, 295, 390–91, 395–97, 398–406, 411, 422, 476–77, 489–91
    Constitutional Court decision on, 410–11, 484–85
    international criticism, 390–91, 405–10, 476–79
    passage of, 80, 82, 390, 395–97, 398–405, 422
    Ukrainian reaction, 405–407
  Duma, 411, 413–16 (*See also above* cultural treasures nationalization law; *and below* Parliament)
  Federal Archival Service (*See* Rosarkhiv)
  Federal Security Service (FSB), archives, 34–35
  Foreign Intelligence Service (SVR), archives, 34, 35
  Ministry of Atomic Energy, archives, 34
  Ministry of Culture, and restitution, 184, 219, 221–23, 400, 470, 477, 478
  Ministry of Defense, archives, 34
  Ministry of Internal Affairs, archives, 34, 35

 **Ukrainian Research Institute
Harvard University**
Selected Publications

A Prayer for the Government: Ukrainians and Jews in Revolutionary Times, 1917–1920. Henry Abramson. Hardcover, ISBN 0-916458-88-1; Softcover, ISBN 0-916458-87-3.

Cultures and Nations of Central and Eastern Europe: Essays in Honor of Roman Szporluk. Ed. Zvi Gitelman et al. Softcover, ISBN 0-916458-93-8.

The Great Soviet Peasant War. Bolsheviks and Peasants, 1917–1933. Andrea Graziosi. Softcover, ISBN 0-916458-83-0.

Ukraine in the World: Studies in the International Relations and Security Structure of a Newly Independent State. Ed. Lubomyr A. Hajda. Softcover, ISBN 0-916458-83-0.

Kistiakovsky: The Struggle for National and Constitutional Rights in the Last Years of Tsarism. Susan Heuman. Hardcover, ISBN 0-916458-61-X.

The Military Tradition in Ukrainian History: Its Role in the Construction of Ukraine's Armed Forces. Kostiantyn P. Morozov, et al. Softcover, ISBN 0-916458-73-3.

Above and Beyond: From Soviet General to Ukrainian State Builder. Kostiantyn Morozov. Hardcover, ISBN 0-916458-77-6.

Carpatho-Ukraine in the Twentieth Century: A Political and Legal History. Vincent Shandor. Hardcover, ISBN 0-916458-86-5.

The Strategic Role of Ukraine: Diplomatic Addresses and Essays (1994–1997). Yuri Shcherbak. Softcover, ISBN 0-916458-85-7.

To receive a free catalog of all Harvard Ukrainian Research Institute publications (including the journal *Harvard Ukrainian Studies*) please write, fax, or call to:

HURI Publications
1583 Massachusetts Avenue
Cambridge, MA 02138 USA
tel. 617-495-4053 *fax.* 617-495-8097
e-mail: huri@fas.harvard.edu
on-line catalog for HURI Publications: www.huri.harvard.edu

HURI Publications are distributed by Harvard University Press:
1-800-448-2242 (U.S. and Canada) 1-617-495-2242 (others)
e-mail: hup@harvard.edu
on-line catalog for HUP: www.hup.harvard.edu